Running Microsoft BackOffice Small Business Server

**SHARON CRAWFORD AND
CHARLIE RUSSEL**

PUBLISHED BY
Microsoft Press
A Division of Microsoft Corporation
One Microsoft Way
Redmond, Washington 98052-6399

Copyright © 1998 by Sharon Crawford and Charlie Russel

All rights reserved. No part of the contents of this book may be reproduced or transmitted in any form or by any means without the written permission of the publisher.

Library of Congress Cataloging-in-Publication Data
Crawford, Sharon.
    Running Microsoft BackOffice Small Business Server / Sharon Crawford, Charlie Russel.
       p.   cm.
    Includes index.
    ISBN 1-57231-688-8
    1. Microsoft BackOffice.   2. Client/server computing.
3. Microsoft Windows NT Server.   I. Russel, Charlie.   II. Title.
QA76.9.C55C73   1998
005.7'1376--dc21   98-9358
                                                                             CIP

Printed and bound in the United States of America.

2 3 4 5 6 7 8 9   QMQM   3 2 1 0 9

Distributed in Canada by ITP Nelson, a division of Thomson Canada Limited.

A CIP catalogue record for this book is available from the British Library.

Microsoft Press books are available through booksellers and distributors worldwide. For further information about international editions, contact your local Microsoft Corporation office or contact Microsoft Press International directly at fax (425) 936-7329. Visit our Web site at mspress.microsoft.com.

Macintosh is a registered trademark of Apple Computer, Inc. ActiveX, BackOffice, FrontPage, Microsoft, Microsoft Press, Windows, and Windows NT are registered trademarks of Microsoft Corporation. Other product and company names mentioned herein may be the trademarks of their respective owners.

Acquisitions Editor: David Clark
Project Editor: Victoria Thulman
Manuscript Editor: Ina Chang
Technical Editor: Dail Magee, Jr.

For Harold A. Turner, a generous coworker and compassionate friend. Remembering his warm heart and good deeds is a comfort to everyone who knew him.

xvii   *Preface*
xxi   *Acknowledgments*

Contents

▲▲▲ 1 PART ONE
PREPARATION AND PLANNING

■ 3   **Chapter 1**
       Looking at the Big Picture
  4   What's in Small Business Server?
  7   A Single Domain
  7   A Single Server
  8   Two Clients
  8   Licensing
  9   Administration of Small Business Server
  9   Who Is Small Business Server For?
  10   How to Use This Book
  11   Points to Remember
  11   What's Next

■ 13   **Chapter 2**
       Networks and Windows NT Server 4
  14   How Does a Network Work?
  16   Network Operating Systems
  16   Differences Between Servers and Clients
  17   Features of the Windows NT Operating System
  17   Domains vs. Workgroups
  21   Points to Remember
  21   What's Next

v

	23	**Chapter 3** **Selecting Hardware**
	24	The Hardware Compatibility List
	25	Server Hardware
	31	The Clients
	32	Points to Remember
	33	What's Next
■	35	**Chapter 4** **Before You Install**
	36	Planning for Security
	39	Choosing a File System
	40	Naming Conventions
	41	System Requirements: The Server Computer
	42	System Requirements: The Client Computer
	43	Points to Remember
	43	What's Next
▲▲▲	45	**PART TWO** **INSTALLATION AND SETUP**
■	47	**Chapter 5** **Installing Small Business Server**
	48	A Preinstallation Checklist
	51	Starting the Setup
	53	The Setup Program: Step by Step
	61	Points to Remember
	61	What's Next?
■	63	**Chapter 6** **Postinstallation**
	64	The To Do List
	82	Other Common Postinstallation Tasks
	90	More Typical Postinstallation Tasks
	90	Points to Remember
	91	What's Next?

93 Chapter 7
Configuring and Managing Disks

- 94 The Search for Disaster Protection
- 94 Defining Our Terms
- 96 Managing Disks
- 97 Using Disk Administrator
- 99 Making Partitions
- 103 Using Volume Sets
- 107 Using Mirror Sets
- 112 Creating an Emergency Repair Disk
- 113 Points to Remember
- 113 What's Next

115 PART THREE
PERFORMING BASIC TASKS

117 Chapter 8
Maintaining User Information

- 118 Adding a New User
- 119 Removing a User Account
- 120 Reviewing or Changing User Information
- 121 Changing a User's Password
- 122 Managing User Access
- 124 User Manager for Domains
- 128 Managing User Rights
- 130 Using System Policy to Manage User Environments
- 131 Using System Policy Editor
- 136 Points to Remember
- 136 What's Next?

■	137	**Chapter 9** **Managing Printers**
	138	Printer Terminology
	139	Planning Network Printing
	140	Managing Printers
	163	Points to Remember
	163	What's Next
■	165	**Chapter 10** **Sharing Information on the Network**
	166	Managing Shared Folders
	172	Managing Folder Size
	174	Shares vs. Share Permissions
	175	Share Permissions
	177	Folder and File Permissions
	179	Who Can Share Folders
	179	Points to Remember
	180	What's Next
■	181	**Chapter 11** **Managing Computers on the Network**
	183	Setting Up a Computer
	185	Adding a User to an Existing Computer
	186	Logging On to a Client Locally
	187	Removing a Computer from the Network
	187	Reinstating a Removed Computer
	188	Closing Open Files
	188	Disconnecting Users
	189	Adding SBS Components to the Server
	190	Adding SBS Components to a Client Computer
	191	Installing or Removing an Application on the Server
	193	Adding or Removing Components of Microsoft Windows NT Server
	194	Points to Remember
	194	What's Next

- **195 Chapter 12
Using the Control Panel**
  - 196 Accessibility Options
  - 198 Add/Remove Programs
  - 198 Console
  - 201 Date/Time
  - 202 Devices
  - 203 Dial-Up Monitor
  - 204 Display
  - 205 Fax Client and Fax Server
  - 206 Fonts
  - 209 Internet
  - 210 Keyboard
  - 212 Licensing
  - 213 Mail
  - 213 Modem Sharing Server
  - 214 Modems
  - 218 Mouse
  - 222 MS DTC
  - 223 Multimedia
  - 225 Network
  - 225 ODBC
  - 225 PC Card (PCMCIA)
  - 226 Ports
  - 226 Printers
  - 226 Regional Settings
  - 227 SCSI Adapters
  - 227 Server
  - 229 Services
  - 229 Sounds
  - 231 System
  - 234 Tape Devices

234	Telephony
235	UPS
236	WSP Client
237	Points to Remember
237	What's Next

239	**Chapter 13**
	Backing Up and Restoring Data
240	Backup Terminology
240	Backups *Are* Mission Critical
243	Configuring a Backup Device
245	Removing a Backup Device
246	Backing Up Your Data
252	Restoring Data
256	Verifying a Backup
256	Scheduling a Backup
260	Backing Up a Client
261	Alternative Backup Programs
261	Points to Remember
261	What's Next

| 263 | **Part Four** |
| | **Organizing Communications** |

265	**Chapter 14**
	Managing E-Mail
266	Basic E-Mail Handling
267	Managing E-Mail Distribution Lists
271	Managing Users and Their Mail Boxes
272	Managing the E-Mail Connection
274	E-Mail Reports
280	Solving E-Mail Problems
286	Points to Remember
286	What's Next

■	**287**	**Chapter 15**
		Sending and Receiving Faxes
	289	Installing Fax Modems
	290	Configuring Fax Services
	292	Adding and Removing Fax Printers
	294	Controlling User Access to Fax Printers
	295	Changing How Faxes Are Received
	297	Managing Fax Jobs
	297	Generating Fax Reports
	298	Managing Fax Cover Pages
	299	Fax Troubleshooting
	300	Fax Client Options
	300	Points to Remember
	300	What's Next
■	**301**	**Chapter 16**
		Managing Modem Pools
	303	Creating a Modem Pool
	304	Adding a Modem to a Pool
	307	Configuring a Client to Use a Modem Pool
	308	Checking the Status of a Modem Pool
	308	Points to Remember
	308	What's Next
■	**309**	**Chapter 17**
		Managing Internet Access
	310	Getting Connected
	317	Connecting to an Existing ISP Account
	324	Getting Your Own Internet Domain Name
	330	Controlling User Access to the Internet
	331	Points to Remember
	332	What's Next

- **333** **Chapter 18**
  Managing Connectivity
  - 334 TCP/IP
  - 343 Name Resolution
  - 346 IPng (IPv6)
  - 347 Using Windows NT Server Administration Tools for TCP/IP
  - 351 Points to Remember
  - 352 What's Next

- **353** **Chapter 19**
  Administering Remote Access
  - 354 Setting Up a User for Remote Access
  - 354 Setting Up a Client Computer for Remote Access
  - 362 Using Remote Access Admin
  - 365 Points to Remember
  - 365 What's Next

▲▲▲ **367** **PART FIVE**
ADMINISTERING SERVER COMPONENTS

- **369** **Chapter 20**
  Creating a Web Site with FrontPage
  - 370 What Is the World Wide Web?
  - 371 Understanding Web Pages
  - 371 Planning a Web Site
  - 372 Organizing a Web Site
  - 372 Installing FrontPage
  - 373 Creating a Web Site
  - 374 How FrontPage Works
  - 374 Using FrontPage Explorer
  - 376 Using FrontPage Editor
  - 382 Creating Special Effects with FrontPage
  - 386 Publishing Your Web Site
  - 386 Creating an Intranet
  - 387 Points to Remember
  - 387 What's Next

Chapter 21
Managing an Intranet Web Server — 389

- 390 — WWW Service
- 391 — FTP Service
- 391 — Configuring Services
- 395 — Intranet Resources
- 396 — Points to Remember
- 396 — What's Next

Chapter 22
Microsoft Proxy Server — 397

- 398 — What Is a Proxy Server?
- 398 — Installing and Configuring Proxy Server
- 406 — Upgrading to Proxy Server 2
- 411 — Points to Remember
- 411 — What's Next

Chapter 23
Using Crystal Reports — 413

- 414 — The Sample Reports
- 416 — Creating a Report from a Sample
- 418 — Distributing Reports
- 420 — Points to Remember
- 420 — What's Next

Chapter 24
Understanding SQL Server — 421

- 422 — What Is a Relational Database?
- 423 — Structured Query Language
- 427 — Rules of Database Design
- 430 — Using SQL Server
- 441 — Administrative Tasks
- 445 — Other SQL Server Tools
- 448 — User Interface
- 448 — Points to Remember
- 448 — What's Next

449 PART SIX
FINE-TUNING AND TROUBLESHOOTING

451 Chapter 25
Monitoring and Fine-Tuning the Network

452	Windows NT Diagnostics
454	Performance Monitor
458	Event Viewer
462	Filtering Event Logs
463	Configuring Event Logs
464	Auditing Files, Folders, and Printers
467	Points to Remember
468	What's Next

469 Chapter 26
Introducing the Microsoft Windows NT Registry

471	How the Registry Is Structured
472	The HKEY_LOCAL_MACHINE Hive
473	The HKEY_USERS Hive
475	The HKEY_CLASSES_ROOT Hive
475	The HKEY_CURRENT_USER Hive
475	The HKEY_CURRENT_CONFIG Hive
475	Data Types Used in the Registry
477	Files in the Registry
479	Backing Up and Restoring the Registry
484	Editing Keys and Values
492	Before You Install New Software
494	Points to Remember
494	What's Next

■	495	**Chapter 27** **Troubleshooting**
	496	Standard Operating Procedures
	497	Printers and Printing
	499	E-Mail
	499	Managing Users
	500	Backups
	500	Files and Folders
	501	Internet Access
	501	Modems
	502	Remote Access Service
	503	Faxes
	503	Security
	504	Setting Up Computers
	504	Disks
	505	Tips and Tricks from the Experts
	508	Points to Remember
	508	What's Next
■	509	**Chapter 28** **Disaster Recovery:** **When All Else Fails**
	510	Creating a Recovery Plan
	511	The Server Won't Boot—Now What?
	512	The Last Known Good Configuration Menu
	513	Emergency Repair Disks
	516	The Emergency Boot Disk
	518	Mirrored Boot Partitions
	519	Restoring a Failed Server
	521	Points to Remember
■	523	**Appendix** **Keyboard Shortcuts**
	527	*Glossary*
	539	*Index*

PREFACE

Microsoft BackOffice Small Business Server (SBS) is, first and foremost, a sensational bargain. At a terrific price, you can acquire Microsoft Windows NT Server, Microsoft Exchange Server, Microsoft SQL Server, Microsoft Proxy Server, and a host of other components that many small businesses need but that have been prohibitively expensive to buy separately. In addition, all of these components have been optimized to work together with the absolute minimum of administration.

However—and you knew there'd be a however, didn't you?—Small Business Server is not without its blemishes. Many of these are the unavoidable result of quilting together so many elements into one package. Combining multiple components can create considerable complexity—a fact that keeps thousands of computer consultants busy—but the aim of Small Business Server is to eliminate or at least hide that complexity. It largely succeeds, but you must handle the product with care in some areas. For example, you must pay precise attention to hardware requirements and carry out the installation "just so." In addition, the new network faxing and modem sharing services are afflicted with a few version 1.0 eccentricities.

In this book, we aim to provide the information you need to install and configure Small Business Server successfully and painlessly. We've been using Small Business Server for some time and have been in touch with numerous other users in several countries. As a group, we've found solutions to many problems as well as ways to prevent those problems in the first place.

What's in the Book

We've divided *Running Microsoft BackOffice Small Business Server* into six parts, roughly corresponding to each stage in the development of a Small Business Server network.

- ♦ **Part One: Preparation and Planning** Perhaps you've heard the famous quote by Thomas Edison: "Genius is one percent inspiration and ninety-nine percent perspiration." Modify that slightly and you have a good motto for network building: "A good network is one percent implementation and ninety-nine percent preparation." That's why this book begins with four chapters of planning advice. The first chapter is an overview of Small Business Server, its components, features, and licensing. It is followed by a chapter on networking, one on the necessary hardware, and one with security advice and issues for you to consider before you install.

- **Part Two: Installation and Setup** This part takes you through the process of installing Small Business Server and configuring your hardware. Also included is a chapter on setting up fault-tolerant hard drive storage to protect your data.

- **Part Three: Performing Basic Tasks** The six chapters in this part cover the day-to-day tasks of running a network: setting up user accounts, arranging information sharing among users, adding and removing computers and printers, and backing up and restoring data.

- **Part Four: Organizing Communications** This part covers the various types of communication that Small Business Server makes possible. The chapters discuss e-mail, fax services, modem sharing, connecting to the Internet, and remote access.

- **Part Five: Administering Server Components** In this part, we cover additional components that you might use as a part of your Small Business Server network. Consult these chapters to learn how to construct a web site; use an intranet; and employ SQL Server, Proxy Server, or Crystal Reports.

- **Part Six: Fine-tuning and Troubleshooting** The last part covers important material on network health. One chapter covers the monitoring tools included with Windows NT Server, and another tells you how to solve common problems. Also included is a chapter on the Registry—the brains of Windows NT Server—and some advice to mull over if you're contemplating doing brain surgery. And if, despite your best efforts, the network falters, you can consult the last chapter, which explains how to recover from a disaster.

At the end of the book are an appendix of keyboard shortcuts and a glossary.

NOTE

Most chapters include notes that explain alternative ways to perform a task or that provide additional important information.

> **Tip**
>
> Tip boxes show you ways to perform tasks more quickly or in a not-obvious manner.

> **Special Information**
>
> Additional topics and background information are set off in sidebars.

Talk Back! We're Listening

We have done our best to make this book as accurate and complete as a single-volume reference can be. However, since Small Business Server is so large and complex, we're sure that alert readers will find omissions and even errors. If you have suggestions, corrections, or tips, please let us know at *sbsbook@scribes.com*.

We really do appreciate hearing from you.

Acknowledgments

Our first and greatest thanks is to David J. Clark, acquisitions editor at Microsoft Press. Not only is he a fine human, he's also a great editor—supplying appropriate doses of support and encouragement and playing the Dutch uncle whenever necessary.

We are immensely grateful to the wonderful editorial team put together for this book. If ever there was a Dream Team, this was it.

Project editors are assigned the duty of pulling all the disparate parts of a project together—sometimes a messy process. To us, project editor Victoria Thulman was all calm competence. Surely things couldn't have gone as smoothly as they appeared to, but she fit all the pieces together without a single seam showing. Our copy editor, Ina Chang, was also splendid. She made many improvements to the text, making suggestions that were both perceptive and kind.

We particularly appreciate Dail Magee, Jr., who is the perfect technical editor—careful without being censorious. He found our mistakes and fixed them with great good humor. Being corrected can be painful; working with Dail was fun at every step.

Other wonderful contributors at Microsoft Press include desktop publishers Elizabeth Hansford and Paula Gorelick, proofreader Patricia Masserman, and electronic artist Travis Beaven.

We owe a lot to the extremely bright and generous participants in the Small Business Server newsgroup (*microsoft.public.backoffice.smallbiz*), especially Grey Lancaster and Birk Binnard. If what goes around does indeed come around, both gentlemen are in for many blessings. Others who went boldly into Small Business Server where none had gone before and came out with gems of information—which they kindly shared—include Reynald Valliere, Jerrold Pace, John Nelson, Larry Buchanan, Doug Swallow, Andy Dunda, and Paul Fitzgerald.

Thanks to Dianne Lennox at Hewlett Packard, who provided a suitable server and support. We liked the NetServer E40 so much that we went out and bought a second one just like it.

And as always, thanks to Dianne King and Dr. Rudolph S. Langer, who first set us on this road.

Part One
Preparation and Planning

If there's one dominant theme in this book, it's that careful preparation and planning are necessary for the launching of a successful network. Part One covers the groundwork you'll have to do and the decisions you'll need to make before installing Small Business Server.

Chapter 1

Looking at the Big Picture

4	**What's in Small Business Server?**
	Shared Files and Printers — 5
	Electronic Mail and Scheduling — 5
	Modem Sharing — 5
	Network Faxing — 5
	Internet Connectivity — 5
	Server Components — 6
7	**A Single Domain**
7	**A Single Server**
8	**Two Clients**
8	**Licensing**
9	**Administration of Small Business Server**
9	**Who Is Small Business Server For?**
10	**How to Use This Book**
11	**Points to Remember**
11	**What's Next**

Chapter 1
Looking at the Big Picture

Small businesses are the heart and soul of most national economies. In early America, the blacksmith, general store, and feedlot operation were indispensable. Today, the auto repair shop, grocery store, and lumberyard are part of everyday life. For every General Motors, there are dozens of smaller companies (some of them making the parts and equipment that keep General Motors going), all of them playing an important role in the community.

In the past, small businesses were pretty humble operations. They couldn't hope to achieve the economies of scale available to large companies, which made growth and competition difficult. Today, smaller businesses have access to the same tools and technology available to the Big Boys. Link your computers with electronic mail, a dynamic web site, and a set of appropriate computer applications, and your 5-person advertising agency or your 15-person engineering firm can compete with anyone.

This has been true for some years, yet most small businesses aren't fully engaged, technically speaking. A primary problem has been the high price tag associated with setting up a network. Unless you just happen to have a network administrator on staff (or failing that, money to burn), a full network is expensive to install and even more expensive to maintain.

Microsoft solves that conundrum with BackOffice Small Business Server. Now it's possible to put together what amounts to a *turnkey* network for smaller operations—a network that's easy to install and even easier to maintain. Small Business Server is largely successful at providing that network, although a few speed bumps remain. Our aim in writing this book is to guide you around those bumps so that you can get the most out of Small Business Server with a minimum of difficulty.

What's in Small Business Server?

Small Business Server supplies a network in a single package—a suite of Microsoft server applications integrated with Microsoft Windows NT Server 4. This allows users to share resources; to use fax, e-mail, and other modem-based communications; and to gain access to the Internet.

A complete solution for organizations with 25 or fewer workstations, Small Business Server provides all the software you need, an easy upgrade path for when you outgrow any of the components, and self-administering tools that you don't have to be a network guru to use. In fact, you can perform virtually all network-type chores using the built-in wizards that guide you through every step.

When you set up Small Business Server, you'll have a fully operational Windows NT network that allows sharing of resources such as modems and printers and provides e-mail, faxing, and Internet access. The Small Business Server environment is optimized for small companies. It's not a departmental server or a "branch" server—it's a single package with all the networking pieces necessary to run a small business.

Shared Files and Printers

Networking began as a way to share files and printers. Users on a network can access the same files, databases, and sometimes applications. Windows NT Server provides these services to all network users wherever they're physically located—in the office or on the road.

Electronic Mail and Scheduling

Small Business Server includes Microsoft Exchange Server 5 to allow e-mail communication between users and with people on the Internet. You can also schedule meetings and other events and coordinate them through your network.

Modem Sharing

Small Business Server adds a function that's been long sought by businesses—the ability to share modems and to pool modems on the server. You can connect as many as four modems to the server, and they can be shared as a pool. If one modem is busy, a user will automatically be routed to the first available one in the pool. Users can access the Internet and send and receive e-mail without needing their own individual modem and phone line.

Network Faxing

Users can also share a single fax device attached to the server. Incoming faxes can be printed or routed to a local mail box. When users send a fax from their computers, it goes through the fax server software on the server computer.

Internet Connectivity

With Small Business Server, connecting to the Internet has never been easier, even if you have never done it before. A built-in wizard guides you through the steps of selecting an Internet service provider (ISP) and setting up an account. All the tools for publishing a web site, exchanging e-mail, and browsing the World Wide Web are included.

Server Components

All the applications in Small Business Server are integrated with Windows NT Server and are installed on one computer on the network (the server). This computer in turn supplies files and other services to the computers (clients) on the network. You'll find an introduction to Windows NT Server in Chapter 2.

The server applications that make up Small Business Server are shown in Table 1.01.

Table 1.01
Server Components Included with Small Business Server

Application	Description
Microsoft NT Server 4 with Service Pack 3	The basic operating system for the network, which provides support for file and printer sharing, application service, remote access service (RAS), user accounts, TCP/IP, and security. Includes (but does not install) IPX and NetBEUI protocols.
Microsoft Exchange Server 5	Provides for sending and receiving of e-mail over the network and on the Internet. Also includes scheduling functions.
Microsoft Fax Server 1	Lets users on the network send faxes from their computers. Also enables routing of inbound faxes to a shared folder or a printer.
Microsoft Proxy Server 1	Improves performance for groups of users accessing the Internet. Also can be part of a security system to protect the network from unauthorized intruders.
Microsoft Modem Sharing Server 1	Enables users to access modems installed on the server and manages the sharing of a modem pool on the server.
Internet Information Server (IIS) 3	Manages a web server (Internet or intranet).
SQL Server 6.5	Manages databases for Windows NT Server–based systems. Includes data replication, management tools, and Internet integration. In Small Business Server, all user databases (including log files) are limited to a total size of 1 GB.
Microsoft Index Server 1.1	A search engine that provides full-text indexing and querying of documents in Hypertext Markup Language (HTML), text, and other formats. Enables users to find specific information on Internet or intranet web sites.
Crystal Reports 4.5	Uses data from server applications such as IIS and Exchange Server to generate reports on such things as e-mail volume or web site visits.
Microsoft Active Server Pages 1	An application environment that combines HTML pages, scripts, and Microsoft ActiveX server components to create Web-based business solutions.

A Single Domain

Small Business Server is a single *security domain* network. A security domain is a logical grouping of computers that share common security and user account information; it is administered as a single unit. Small Business Server can't be an additional domain on an existing network and does not support trust relationships.

A Single Server

In a Small Business Server network, the server is the *primary domain controller* (PDC). A PDC maintains a directory database that contains the security and account information for the domain. The PDC uses this database to validate user accounts when users log on to the domain. In a Small Business Server network, only the server is configured as the PDC because a domain can have only one PDC.

To add another computer running Windows NT Server to a Small Business Server network, the computer must be installed as a *backup domain controller* (BDC) or as a member server. A BDC contains a copy of the PDC's directory database and can also validate user accounts. A member server is often called an *applications server* because it is typically used for storing and running user applications. A member server does not validate user accounts.

NOTE

The BDC or the applications server must be installed with the full Windows NT Server. The server in Small Business Server works only as a PDC, and only one copy of Small Business Server can be installed on a network.

All of the various server components that come with Small Business Server have to be installed on the PDC. They can't be offloaded onto another server. So if you conclude that the PDC has to be a computer with lots of RAM, a fast CPU, and major amounts of hard drive space, you're right.

For More Information

You'll find more on servers and clients and domain controllers in Chapter 2, where the Windows NT Server 4 operating system gets more attention.

Two Clients

You can run Small Business Server with one of two types of client machines:

- **Computers running Windows NT Workstation 4** These are ideal clients. They're completely compatible and very robust. However, they must use version 4; earlier versions of Windows NT Workstation can't be used as clients.

- **Computers running Microsoft Windows 95** By the time Microsoft Windows 98 is released, you'll undoubtedly be able to turn Windows 98 computers into clients, but such a fix doesn't exist yet.

In keeping with Microsoft's goal of simplicity and ease of administration, Small Business Server includes no provisions for connecting Macintosh, UNIX, or other operating systems except with limited file and print services. Such machines might or might not be able to use Proxy Server, and use of other server components is seriously limited. If you have needs that absolutely can't be met by Windows NT or Windows 95 machines, you should upgrade to the full BackOffice package.

Licensing

The definition of small business usually depends on who's doing the defining, but in the case of Small Business Server, it's any business with 25 or fewer computers. Small Business Server is licensed "by machine," so your business can have more than 25 employees and still fit the definition.

When you buy Small Business Server, you purchase a certain number of licenses. The basic package comes with five, and you can buy packets of five licenses up to a total of 25. The key thing to remember is that each license represents one concurrent connection to the server. So if you have five licenses, you can have five computers connected to the server. They can be local computers or remote ones.

NOTE

Twenty-five is currently the upper limit for licenses. To connect more computers, you have to upgrade to BackOffice.

Having five licenses doesn't mean you're limited to five users. You can have as many users as you want—but no more than five computers connected to the server at one time. To add a sixth computer, you have to purchase a packet of five additional licenses.

The license count does not include the administrator's connection. Even if you have maxed out the number of licensed connections, an administrator can still connect to the server for maintenance or troubleshooting.

Administration of Small Business Server

Small Business Server has not reached that nirvana known as "zero administration," but it's at least manageable by a nonexpert. All administration tasks are centralized in what's called a *management console.* (See Figure 1.01.) You can click on any of the icons to open an additional page with clear, graphical steps to follow.

FIGURE 1.01

Common tasks are easy to perform using the management console.

It's even easy to add icons to the console for tasks that are specific to your network. Underneath, you're still dealing with Windows NT Server 4, so if you're ambitious or an experienced Windows NT user, all the usual administrative tools are just a menu click away.

Who Is Small Business Server For?

No sooner is a product released than people start looking for ways to make it do things it wasn't meant to do. This is true for Small Business Server as well. The thing to remember is that Small Business Server has absolute limitations built into it and also some relative limitations. A relative limitation is something that can be worked around—more or less—but such workarounds can sometimes be more trouble than they're worth.

As we mentioned earlier, Small Business Server is absolutely limited to 25 concurrent connections to the server. Print servers or other computers that don't require a logon don't count as part of the total. Another absolute limitation is 1 GB for all SQL Server databases.

As a practical matter, however, Small Business Server is best for a company or an organization with the following characteristics:

- **A single location** This can be with or without remote users—that is, people who connect to the network from home or while traveling.

- **An existing or planned dial-up connection for e-mail and the Internet** ISDN and dedicated lines can be configured, but you'll need outside help.

- **A staff person who will learn about all aspects of Small Business Server** You should have a person on staff who is willing to use this book to customize the setup, troubleshoot any problems, and handle upgrades as the need arises.

The best thing about Small Business Server (other than all the goodies you get for a relatively modest price) is that it provides a high-tech set of solutions without the usual high-tech cost. Buying a network is often like buying a house—or, heaven forbid, a boat—in that the initial cost is just the beginning of an ongoing and continuous outflow of resources.

However, with Small Business Server, a reasonably savvy person can set up and maintain a network with only a modest amount of help. You can turn to a consultant or to your brother-in-law for assistance, but that will only guarantee that the outflow will continue. Or you can use this book—not only to get you started but also to see you through times of trouble.

How to Use This Book

This book is divided into six sections, grouped around various types of tasks necessary to install and maintain a Small Business Server network. Part One, which includes this chapter plus three more, gives you the background information necessary for a successful installation.

Part Two takes you through the installation step by step. The installation process is streamlined, but it is important that you do everything correctly because it's always easier to do things right the first time than to make fixes later. (Corrections are, of course, possible, but our aim is to make Small Business Server even easier to use, not to introduce complications.)

Part Three deals with setting up the basic elements of your Small Business Server network—user profiles, sharing information, configuring printers, and so forth. Part Four is all about communications—setting up your users to connect to each other and to the outside world. Here you'll find chapters on faxing, modem sharing, e-mail, and Internet access. This part also provides information on setting up remote access if you have users who need to connect to Small Business Server from home or while traveling.

Part Five covers additional server components. Here you'll learn how to make and manage your own Internet or intranet web site using tools included with Small Business Server. This part also includes chapters on Proxy Server, SQL Server, the use of Crystal Reports, and configuring the Small Business Server administrative interface to be even more useful. Finally, Part Six shows you how to fine-tune your network and troubleshoot any problems that arise.

For best results, start here and continue straight through Part Three. Consult the chapters in Parts Four and Five as you need them. Go to Part Six only when you're looking to improve your existing performance or solve a problem.

In general, touch typists prefer the keyboard to the mouse, so we've included an appendix of keyboard shortcuts. There's also a glossary of networking terms in the back of the book.

POINTS TO REMEMBER

- Microsoft Small Business Server supplies a complete network in a single package in the form of a suite of Microsoft server applications integrated with Windows NT Server 4.
- Small Business Server operates only as a single domain—there is no support for domain trust relationships.
- All of the server components reside on the Small Business Server primary domain controller even if you have a backup domain controller.
- Supported clients are Windows NT Workstation 4 and Windows 95.

WHAT'S NEXT

In Chapter 2, you'll find a review of Windows NT Server 4, the foundation on which Small Business Server is built. Although you don't need in-depth knowledge of Windows NT Server to install and use Small Business Server, the more you know, the better off you'll be.

Chapter 2

14	**How Does a Network Work?**	
	What Are the Components of a Network?	15
16	**Network Operating Systems**	
16	**Differences Between Servers and Clients**	
	Servers Use Network Operating Systems	16
	Clients Use Workstation Operating Systems	17
17	**Features of the Windows NT Operating System**	
17	**Domains vs. Workgroups**	
	Do Workgroups Work?	17
	Defining Domains	18
	Domain Components	20
21	**Points to Remember**	
21	**What's Next**	

Networks and Windows NT Server 4

Chapter 2

Networks and Windows NT Server 4

As we discussed in the first chapter, the operating system underlying Microsoft BackOffice Small Business Server is Microsoft Windows NT Server 4, the latest version of Microsoft's mission-critical enterprise operating system. It's an appropriate choice as the underlying operating system for a small business suite of server products. After all, your business is certainly "mission critical" to you and your employees!

In this chapter, we'll give you all the background you need on servers, clients, and networks without confusing you with unnecessary details and acronyms.

How Does a Network Work?

If you've ever made a phone call or used a bank ATM, you've already used a network. A network, after all, is simply a collection of computers and peripheral devices that can share files and other resources. The connection can be a cable, a telephone line, or even a wireless channel.

Your bank's ATM consists of hardware and software connected to central computers that know, among other things, how much money is in your account. When you call across town or across the country, telephone company software makes the connection from your phone through multiple switching devices to the phone you're calling. It happens every day without our awareness of the complicated processes behind the scenes.

Both the telephone and ATM networks are maintained by technicians and engineers who plan, set up, and maintain all the software and hardware. With Small Business Server, no one has to be dedicated to maintaining the network and its operating system full time because Microsoft has included a variety of tools and a special interface to make network maintenance easier. The tools are limited to those that make the most sense in a small business environment, so you don't have to choose from a dizzying array of options just to add a new user or perform some other simple task. The result is a much simpler interface.

What Are the Components of a Network?

A traditional network includes a variety of hardware pieces (media): the computers themselves, hardware to physically connect them, and any miscellaneous devices (such as printers) that reside on the network. The computers are either servers or clients (workstations). The physical connection is made with pieces of wire that connect to a central hub or perhaps daisy-chain from computer to computer, or the connection can be an infrared signal, a radio wave, or even fiber optic cable.

Servers Provide Services

Servers are machines that provide services. Seems simple enough, doesn't it? Essentially, it is. The problem comes when people confuse the physical box that's providing the service with the service itself. Any computer or device on a network can be a server for a particular service. The server doesn't even have to be a computer in the traditional sense. For example, you might have a "print server" that is simply a device connected to the network on one side and to a printer on the other. The device has a tiny brain with just enough intelligence to understand when a particular network packet is intended for it and to translate the packet into something the printer can understand.

Small Business Server uses a single computer as the physical server box, but that box provides a variety of services to the network beyond the usual file and print services. These include faxing, modem sharing, database services, e-mail, security, and web publishing.

Clients Use Services

A client is anything on the network that uses a server's services. Clients are usually the other computers on the network. The client machines avail themselves of printers on the network, databases on a server, and other services that aren't available on their local hard drives. Usually clients are not as powerful as servers, but they're perfectly capable computers on their own.

Media Connect Servers and Clients

The actual network media that connect the various servers and clients of your network include the network cards that are part of the server or client, the physical wire between them, and various other components such as hubs, routers, and switches. When all are working as they should, we pretty much forget about them and take them for granted; but when one portion of the network media fails, troubleshooting and repair can be frustrating and expensive. This is a good reason to buy high-quality network components from vendors and dealers who support their products.

Network Operating Systems

On an ordinary PC, the operating system's job is to manage the file system, handle the running of applications, manage the computer's memory, and control the input from and output to attached devices such as modems and printers. A network operating system (NOS) expands that role to include the following:

- Managing remote file systems
- Running shared applications
- Managing input from and output to shared network devices
- CPU scheduling of networked processes

When the NOS is distributed among all the connected computers, the result is a peer-to-peer network. Microsoft Windows 95 and Microsoft Windows for Workgroups, operating on their own, have this kind of network.

Small Business Server uses a *client-server* network, which has a single, centralized server and multiple clients running Windows 95 or Microsoft Windows NT Workstation. The central computer on which most of the network operating system runs is the server; the computers that make use of the resources managed by the server are the clients.

Differences Between Servers and Clients

Even though servers and clients in a Small Business Server network use similar hardware, they have very different roles, which are reflected in the operating systems they run.

Servers Use Network Operating Systems

Because Small Business Server supplies services to as many as 25 users and because you depend on it to run your business, a high-powered, robust operating system is essential. When your users rely on a server to get their work done and to keep the business running, not only do you want to avoid frequent failures, but also you don't want to have to reboot!

In addition to supplying print, file, or other services, the NOS must provide network security. The security must be configurable from minor to very stringent because different businesses and organizations have varying needs—although all of them need some level of security to protect their data.

Clients Use Workstation Operating Systems

Like other computers, client machines on a network need an operating system. However, a workstation operating system doesn't have to be as sturdy as the operating system running on a server. Rebooting a workstation can be a pain for the user, but it doesn't usually disrupt anyone else's work.

Nor does a client machine require a built-in security system, because security is provided by the NOS and is managed by the server. However, the more advanced the client operating system is, the better it is at cooperating with the NOS in areas of security and sharing over the network.

On a Small Business Server network, you are limited to using client machines running Windows 95 and Windows NT Workstation as your supported operating systems.

Features of the Windows NT Operating System

Windows NT Server 4 is a proven, reliable, and robust operating system with the features necessary to run a business of virtually any size. Within Small Business Server, Windows NT Server has been specially tuned for optimum support of 5 to 25 users and the specialized needs of a small business environment. Some of the features that make Windows NT Server ideal as a small business server include:

- Easy installation (almost fully automated in Small Business Server)
- A robust yet easy-to-administer security model
- The NTFS file system that fully supports long filenames, dynamic error recovery, and security
- Support for a broad range of hardware and software

Domains vs. Workgroups

Microsoft provides two different networking models in its operating systems—domains and workgroups. Small Business Server supports only the domain model of Microsoft networking, but it's worthwhile to go over why this decision makes sense, even in a very small business.

Do Workgroups Work?

Microsoft introduced the concept of the *workgroup* with Windows for Workgroups. The workgroup is a logical grouping of several computers whose users are connected and who want to share resources. Usually, all the computers in a workgroup are equal, which is why such setups are referred to as *peer-to-peer* networks. Although resources can be concentrated in a single computer, there are no advantages to doing so.

Workgroup networks are appealing because they're easy to set up and maintain. Individual users manage the sharing of their resources by determining what will be shared and who will have access. A user can allow other users to share a printer, a CD-ROM drive, a hard drive, or only certain files. The difficulty arises when it's necessary to distinguish between users to set different levels of access. Passwords can be used for this purpose, but as the network gets larger, passwords proliferate and the situation becomes increasingly complicated. Users who are required to have numerous passwords start using the same one over and over or choose passwords that are easy to remember—and therefore easy to guess. If you have dial-up connections and an employee leaves the company to work for your biggest competitor, passwords have to be changed and everyone in the workgroup has to be notified of the new passwords. Security, such as it is, falls apart.

Another problem that occurs when a workgroup becomes too large is that with so many resources, users can have trouble locating the ones they need. The informal nature of workgroups also means that there's no centralized administration or control. Everything has to be configured computer by computer. This lack of central administration and control, along with limited security, makes the workgroup model a bad choice for all but the smallest businesses.

Defining Domains

To provide centralized management and a secure environment to protect your small business, Small Business Server was created as a full domain networking environment. This means you don't have to maintain each workstation individually, since they are all managed from the primary server. There are, however, three important networking differences between Small Business Server and regular Windows NT Server 4:

- Small Business Server can be run only as a single domain. It does not support multiple domains and trust relationships.

- Normally, no backup domain controller (BDC) is present on the network. You can add one, however, by installing the full Windows NT Server 4 on a machine and defining its role as a BDC.

- The Small Business Server server must be a primary domain controller (PDC).

The domain is really just a type of workgroup that includes a server. It is a logical grouping of users who are connected by more than the cables between their computers. The goal is still to let users share resources within the group and to make it easier for the group to work. The key difference is the existence of a server for the group. This provides a single point of administration and control.

> **NOTE**
>
> *The Microsoft networking domain isn't the same as domains on TCP/IP networks (the domain concept used on the Internet). In this book, we'll use domain only in the Microsoft networking sense of the word, and if we talk about an Internet domain name, we'll make that clear.*

Additional Users

When adding a new user to the domain, you don't have to go around to each computer and enter all the information. As the administrator, you can simply log on to any Windows or Windows NT machine in the domain and add the new user. During that single session, you can specify what resources the new user will be able to access. The change will be immediately recognized across the entire domain.

All users, including the newest, can get at their resources, no matter which machine is being used. Permission to access resources is granted to individual users or to a group of users, not to individual computers. And when you need to restrict access to a sensitive document or directory, you can simply log on to a single workstation and make the change across the entire domain. You can grant or restrict access by individual user or by groups of users easily and quickly.

Access Control

In a workgroup, you are limited as to which of your machine's resources you can make available to the rest of the workgroup. At the simplest level, you can either share the resource or not. To go beyond that, you can put a password on the level of access to the resource. This offers some control over access to the resource. But you have virtually no control if your machine is physically accessible to anyone else.

Small Business Server provides what's called *discretionary access control*. Some users can create a document or make changes to an existing one, while other users can only read the document. And still other users can't even *see* it. You can set access for an individual file, for files within a directory, or for the entire directory. Small Business Server lets you set the *granularity* of the security as needed—fine granularity for a more specific level of security or coarse for a lower, broader level of security. This makes security administration easy.

Domain Components

These are the basic components of the Small Business Server network:

- A PDC
- Possibly a BDC
- Workstations running Windows 95 or Windows NT Workstation 4

Let's look at each of these components to get a better idea of how they function.

Primary Domain Controller

The PDC enforces the security policies for the domain and is the main repository for the accounts database. It might not be the primary holder of the shared resources of the domain, but even without that, it's still the most important machine in the domain. In a typical Small Business Server network, the resources of the domain will most likely be primarily or exclusively on this computer.

When you want to change the user account database, you can do it only on the PDC. Regardless of where you are logged in when you make the change, the actual change occurs on the PDC. Changes you make are automatically propagated to any BDCs.

Backup Domain Controller

The traditional wisdom says that a Windows NT Server domain can, and in most cases should, have one or more BDCs. These controllers each contain a copy of the accounts database and can validate user logons and access to resources. If a catastrophic failure of the PDC occurs, one of the BDCs can be promoted to a PDC and the network will continue to function normally (except for access to resources that were physically on the failed server). However, in most small businesses with single domain environments such as a Small Business Server network, chances are you won't have a BDC. Frankly, most small businesses simply aren't willing to spend the money to buy two full-blown servers. And even if you turn one of your plain old desktop machines into a BDC, you still have the additional cost for the extra Windows NT Server license.

In a small domain with a limited number of users, a BDC isn't absolutely required, but it does provide some real advantages. When there's only one PDC on the network, the entire network will be disabled if that server isn't available. When there's a BDC and the PDC is down-and-out, users can continue to log on and use any of the local resources on the network. This makes it fairly easy to provide for redundancy of critical shared resources in the event of a failure. But the design of Small Business Server means that if a server crashes, you won't have access to the Internet, Microsoft Exchange, your fax server, or any other resources residing on the server. So you're actually better off making sure you have good backups and a sound disaster recovery plan for your primary server rather than depending on a secondary server that won't give you the features you depend on.

Workstations

To reap all the benefits of Small Business Server, your workstations must be running Windows 95 or Windows NT Workstation 4. In this book, we generally assume that your client is running Windows 95 to connect to your Small Business Server because it's the most likely scenario. The overhead and hardware requirements are substantially less than for Windows NT Workstation. However, we won't ignore Windows NT Workstation, and we'll always point out any differences.

POINTS TO REMEMBER

- Small Business Server is a Windows NT–based client-server network with the Small Business Server server providing the services, clients using the services, and media connecting them all.

- A network operating system handles remote file systems, the running of shared applications, input and output to shared network devices, and CPU scheduling of networked processes.

- A BDC will allow your users to log on if the server crashes, but because all the server components are on Small Business Server, they won't have access to e-mail, faxing, or any other resources residing on the server. This makes backups and disaster recovery planning essential.

WHAT'S NEXT

In the next chapter, we'll move on to a brief survey of how to plan and place your hardware. Having the right hardware—and placing it in locations where it doesn't have to be moved about—can simplify everything about having a network.

Chapter 3

Selecting Hardware

- 24 **The Hardware Compatibility List**
- 25 **Server Hardware**
  - Designing the System — 25
  - Selecting Processors — 26
  - How Much Memory? — 26
  - Hard Drives — 27
  - Backup Devices — 29
  - Resource Locations — 30
  - Initial Size vs. Expected Growth — 31
- 31 **The Clients**
  - How Much Memory? — 32
  - Selecting Processors — 32
  - Hard Drives — 32
- 32 **Points to Remember**
- 33 **What's Next**

CHAPTER 3
Selecting Hardware

Microsoft Small Business Server uses the same basic Hardware Compatibility List (HCL) as Microsoft Windows NT does, with some important exceptions. However, even more than with Microsoft Windows NT Server 4, on which it's based, you must be sure that your hardware matches that list. This is especially true for modems. If you expect your modems to work correctly, you must use a modem that's on the HCL, and if you're going to pool modems, they must all be the same model and have the same version of firmware. Even the slightest difference will prevent them from working correctly.

The Hardware Compatibility List

The hardware that works with Small Business Server is on the Microsoft BackOffice Small Business Server HCL Supplement and on the Windows NT Server HCL. Copies of these lists are included in the box with Small Business Server, but they are also available on the Web. The general rule is that if a product is included on the Windows NT Server HCL, it is compatible with Small Business Server, unless it is one of the following:

- A network adapter card
- A fax modem
- A multiport serial adapter board

In these three categories, only a subset of the Windows NT Server hardware has been thoroughly tested and is assured of working. Especially for modems, it is unlikely that any item not on the short supported list will fully work for both dial-up networking and fax. Stick to the following modems:

- Diamond SupraSonic 336V+
- Diamond Supra FAX Modem 288 external
- Hayes Accura External 288 V.FC+FAX (Model 5205AM)
- Hayes Optima External 288 V.34/V.FC+fax+Voice*

- US Robotics Courier v.Everything external
- US Robotics Courier v.Everything internal
- US Robotics Sportster 33600 external
- US Robotics Sportster 33600 internal

The list of supported hardware is updated regularly, but the list of fully tested modems probably won't change much until the next release of Small Business Server. You can find the most current list of supported hardware at Microsoft's web site: *www.microsoft.com/backoffice/backofficesmallbiz/showcase/hcl.asp*. From there, you can link to the Windows NT Server HCL.

We don't want to belabor the point, but with Small Business Server, it is crucial that you or your vendor clearly understand and follow the HCL. Much of the installation of Small Business Server is automated, and it makes certain assumptions about the users and use of the system. For these reasons, you're much more likely than with Windows NT Server to run into installation problems if you don't follow the list. And if you have installation problems, you'll have a tough time fixing them all because the installation doesn't offer many opportunities to backtrack and fix things that didn't go right.

Let's take a few moments to look at the overall system requirements and what they mean. The HCL is essential information, but it doesn't help you plan or design your system for optimum performance.

Server Hardware

The server is the core of your Small Business Server system. On this one machine rests your hopes and fears, along with all the hardware resources that, at a large corporation, are usually locked away in a secure server room controlled by the IS department. But while the server need not require a huge investment, you should take some time to think about your business needs and how best to match those needs with a server.

Designing the System

When you design the core server for your Small Business Server network, you must take into account a variety of factors about your business to ensure that the server meets your current needs and can reasonably grow to meet your needs if your business expands. Some of these factors are listed on the following page.

- The number (and type) of employees
- The type of business
- How you intend to use your Small Business Server network to enhance your business
- What applications you want to run
- What your internal support resources are
- How critical the data you'll be collecting with this network will be to your business

Once you answer some of these questions, you'll be in a better position to decide what server to get. And while we won't make specific brand suggestions, we do recommend that you go with a supplier and a brand that understand Small Business Server and are prepared to support it fully.

Selecting Processors

The first and most important question to ask is what *type* of processor you want for your server. Small Business Server supports both Intel x86 and DEC Alpha processors. Both have their adherents, and both have their strengths, but we think that an Intel x86 processor (or one of the AMD or Cyrix processors that are fully compatible with the Intel) is probably the safest choice. An exception to this might be when your particular application is extremely processor intensive and you know that the software is fully supported on the Alpha.

The HCL says that any Pentium processor running at 100 MHz or faster is sufficient, but in reality this will be a very busy machine, and a 100 MHz Pentium will be hard pressed to handle all the work. We suggest a 166 MHz Pentium as a better starting point. Any Pentium Pro or Pentium II machine should be sufficient, and any Alpha-based system will have sufficient processing power for most situations.

How Much Memory?

The minimum requirement for Small Business Server is listed as 64 MB of RAM, and we think this is a reasonable starting point for businesses at the lower end of the supported spectrum. But as you grow, you'll find that more RAM will provide a definite improvement.

The requirements for RAM will vary significantly depending on the services you use. Microsoft Exchange is a big RAM user, although it has been optimized to use less in Small Business Server. (The same is true of SQL Server.) Simple file and print services don't necessarily require large amounts of RAM, even though they are certainly happier with more. However, each user you add increases the RAM requirements. A reasonable starting point is 64 MB of RAM for the base system and an additional 32 MB for each additional five users. However, if your business runs an application that relies heavily on a database, you might need to double these numbers.

Another concern is the type of RAM. In the old days, RAM came in only one form, "parity RAM." This RAM uses an extra bit to enable the processor to test the accuracy of the eight bits of a given byte to make sure that they are what they're supposed to be. However, with RAM prices shooting through the roof several years ago, a movement began to use non-parity RAM. The argument was that RAM almost never failed and self-diagnosis wasn't really very important anyway. This essentially fallacious argument has become even less compelling as the price of RAM has dropped to the point where it is no longer the limiting cost factor in performance. And on a server, especially, we think it is a good idea to use either parity RAM or ECC RAM. It might be acceptable to use non-parity EDO RAM on a laptop, where space, energy requirements, and cost are all compelling factors, but do yourself and your business a favor and pay the slight extra cost to make sure your server's RAM can at least detect when it has a problem.

The one sure thing we've seen is that you'll never have too much RAM. Small Business Server provides excellent tools for determining the current performance bottleneck, and you should certainly use them before simply throwing RAM at a problem. However, when you initially specify your system, make sure you leave room to add more RAM than you currently need, and make sure you won't have to remove any of the current RAM to do it. Nothing is more frustrating than finding that your server *can* hold 256 MB of RAM but that when the system was set up someone decided to save a few pennies and bought 16 MB SIMMs, which used up all the slots, so you have to remove some or all of the existing RAM to get the memory you need.

Hard Drives

The minimum hard drive requirement for Small Business Server is a 2-GB hard drive. And like most minimums, it's likely to be woefully inadequate. Depending on what applications you'll be using and how heavy your database requirements are, you'll probably need at least twice that amount of hard drive space. But more important than the actual size of the hard drives is the type and arrangement of the hard drives.

IDE vs. SCSI

For the typical client or home PC, an IDE hard drive is probably adequate. However, on a server you definitely don't want to use IDE hard drives. They simply don't work well when multiple users and applications are making demands on them. Stick to SCSI. Newer technologies are on the way, such as FibreChannel, but these are still in their early (read: *expensive*) days.

SCSI has, unfortunately, a certain amount of mystery about it. It's generally considered "difficult" to set up and configure, and many people get nervous about it. This reaction is largely left over from the early days when standards were lacking and you could easily find yourself with two SCSI devices that couldn't work together. But those days are pretty much over, and a careful system builder should have no problem setting up and configuring your SCSI subsystem.

One important consideration that is especially true of SCSI: You generally get what you pay for. If you buy the cheapest cable and SCSI card, you're setting yourself up for problems and will end up frustrated. Stick to a name-brand SCSI card, and don't go for the bottom end of the product line. In addition, buy only the best cables you can find. Cables are *not* the place to get "economical," because you'll end up paying more later when the cheap cables fail.

To RAID or not

RAID is short for Redundant Array of Inexpensive Disks and is a method of building protection against hard drive failure into your system. We'll talk about RAID in detail in Chapter 7, but it's worth spending a moment on it here. Microsoft provides a very limited kind of RAID called disk mirroring or RAID Level 1 in Small Business Server, but you might want to consider alternative solutions if your business will depend on your server being available 100 percent of the time.

A number of third-party, hardware-based RAID solutions will work with any version of Microsoft NT Server, including Small Business Server. We suggest that you first find out whether your system vendor offers a server that either includes RAID by default or has it as an add-on option. This will offer the advantage of a single point of contact for support in case of problems, and the RAID will be more directly integrated into the system. Most of the major vendors have RAID options available, even on their small, business-class servers.

RAID offers both a high degree of protection from failure and potentially faster access to your hard drives, depending on the type of RAID. However, this doesn't come without significant costs. The overall hardware cost for RAID tends to be two to four times more than for an equivalent amount of hard drive space using standard drives and controllers, and you can double that again if you need to have hot-swappable drives. But if you really, really can't afford to have your system down because of a hard drive failure, a hot-swappable RAID array is definitely the way to go.

If your server will be primarily a file and print server that shares files and applications over the network, you should probably go with RAID Level 5. This uses the concept of parity to store sufficient information to recover everything if a single drive fails and spreads that parity information across all the drives in the array. With applications in which read access to the hard drives is the primary concern (loading an application, opening a file, serving up predominantly static web pages, or accessing the information stored in a database), RAID 5 provides excellent speed and protection against failure.

If your server use will mostly require write access to the hard drive, however, you should use RAID Level 1 (mirroring) or RAID Level 0+1 (mirroring plus stripping). Examples of write-intensive hard drive access are adding records to a database, installing new software, creating new files and documents, and serving up dynamic web pages. The catch with RAID 1 and 0+1 is that they are more expensive to implement, since you lose 50 percent of your hard drive space for the mirror. The good part, however, is that they provide unequaled protection against failure—you have a complete copy of the information—and the reduction in performance during a drive failure is not nearly as significant as with RAID 5.

Backup Devices

Backing up: Everyone tells you to do it, and few people do it as well or as consistently as they should. This is, in no small part, because the means of backing up are expensive and often difficult to use. But when you have a catastrophic failure—and we mean *when*, not *if*—you'll be awfully glad that you have a current backup. And you'll be awfully glad that you know how to restore it. We'll go into the mechanics of creating and restoring backups in Chapter 14 and we'll explain the hows and whys of a disaster recovery plan in Chapter 31, but both require that you first have a backup device. In general, a backup device is a tape drive, although alternatives certainly exist.

Tape drives are *boring*. Yup. No question about it—it's hard to work up any excitement about buying and installing a new tape drive. So get it out of the way at the very beginning and make sure a good one is included with your system. The questions you need to ask about it are pretty straightforward:

- Is it supported in Windows NT?
- Will a single tape hold everything on all your hard drives?
- Is it SCSI?
- How fast is it?

The first question, of course, is crucial. If Windows NT Server doesn't support the tape drive, there's no point in getting it. But you might also want to know if it requires special drivers from the manufacturer or if it runs with the default drivers included with Windows NT.

The second question is also extremely important. You *can* use a tape drive that requires you to do a backup across multiple tapes; the backup program included with Small Business Server supports tape spanning. But we're all human—if the backup requires someone to be present and to manually change tapes, it's much less likely to happen than if you simply have to change the tape on your way out the door at night. The chances of a single-tape backup being done on a regular basis are 10 times greater than for a multiple-tape backup. Thus your chance of significant data loss in the event of a catastrophic failure are 10 times less. Figure that into your cost estimates, and you'll quickly decide on a tape device or library that will handle a full backup of your entire system without requiring human intervention.

The third and fourth questions are less crucial but still worth asking. Since all your hard drives are on SCSI, you might find that an IDE-based tape drive is perfectly adequate, but we're of the school that prefers to stick with SCSI for our backups. And under no circumstances should you trust your business to one of those tape drives that uses a floppy controller.

The speed of backup is an issue mostly for businesses that run beyond normal business hours. Good backups should be made when the least work is being done on the system, because fewer files will be open. So if your business is essentially shut down for 8 to 10 hours every night, making an overnight backup is not likely to be a problem. In this situation, the only reason to be concerned about the speed of the backup device is for recovery. The slower the backup device, the longer it will take to get up and running if you have a catastrophic failure.

Resource Locations

Small Business Server is designed around a single, central server. This server provides virtually all the services on the network—which in most small offices is not an issue. But if you're spread out across several offices, you should consider where to locate resources such as printers. Probably the best bet is to use a network printer or a print server. Printers designed to sit directly on the network are quite common, and the incremental cost over that of a printer that supports only a parallel interface is not much. Or you can go with a standalone network print server such as the Hewlett-Packard JetDirectEX, which lets you connect a printer (or printers) to a simple network device and then manage it entirely from your SBS server. To the client machines, the printer looks like it's directly attached to the server, but it's actually connected to the network, and you can physically locate it near the users who need to use it.

Don't figure on using someone's Windows 95 workstation as a local print server. You'll have an unhappy user, and maintaining and configuring the printer will be significantly more trouble. Plus, every time the user has to reboot that computer, someone else's print job might get screwed up. Recycle an old 486 as a print server or buy a network print server. You'll have much happier users in the long run, and the incremental cost won't be that much.

Initial Size vs. Expected Growth

We've already talked a bit about how to size your server for expected growth, but a few more words won't hurt. Few problems are more expensive and disruptive to your business than having your computer system suddenly run out of capacity and need to be replaced or upgraded. But you also can't afford to spend large amounts of money on a system simply to provide for growth to twice your current size if you don't expect to grow to that size any time soon. So it's always a balancing act—trading off cost now against time and disruption later.

Probably the easiest thing to add to support additional users in a crunch is RAM—*if* you've planned ahead and your server still has available memory slots. You can bring the server down, take the cover off, and pop in a couple more SIMMs of RAM in a few minutes, but only if you left yourself some room.

Adding additional hard drive space is almost never as simple. Unless you have one of those expensive RAID towers with hot-swappable drives and a RAID controller that supports dynamic configuration of hard drives, you're talking about several hours of work, at least, to add additional hard drives and configure them into your system. So think about how much hard drive space you'll need, and then double it—at least. Hard drives are relatively inexpensive, and it's a false economy to skimp on them at the beginning.

If your motherboard supports multiple processors, you can easily add an additional processor and double your processing power. But this can be tricky, since Windows NT requires a different kernel to support the second processor and upgrading is not for the faint of heart. Given the cost of processors, we suggest that if you're likely to need a second processor for your Small Business Server server in less than a year, go ahead and buy it now. The disruption is likely to be significantly less than if you need to do it later. But few small businesses will actually require a dual-processor machine. They will mostly be those that do large amounts of database work.

The Clients

The server is, of course, only one part of the hardware configuration. You also need to think about hardware on the client side—the PCs that your users work on every day. Users don't care about the server as long as it does its job. But they do care about the PCs they have in front of them.

How Much Memory?

In all our years in this business, we've never heard a user complain that his or her PC has too much RAM. And we probably never will. But you still need to be realistic about the costs of the PCs you use in your business. Even though RAM prices have come down, they're still a significant portion of the cost of a business PC.

For most users of office suite applications, a Windows 95 machine with 16 MB of RAM is minimally sufficient. Most users, however, will be much happier with 32 MB, and if they are running Windows NT Workstation, you will almost certainly want to go with 32 MB. If a user's real RAM needs go beyond 64 MB, they should be running Windows NT Workstation, not Windows 95. And unless you have a bunch of database modelers or graphic designers working for you, you probably won't have to worry about this.

Selecting Processors

Virtually any PC that can run Windows 95 or Windows NT Workstation 4 can be an effective client on your Small Business Server system. But these days, you'll want at least a Pentium-class computer. If you have older 486 PCs with sufficient hard drive space, however, they can be effective for occasional use or as spares in case of failure.

Hard Drives

For client workstations, we're not as adamant about the need for SCSI. For most users, IDE is perfectly sufficient and significantly cheaper. But don't bother with a hard drive smaller than 1 GB unless it's one of those recycled 486s that will get only occasional use. The cost of hard drive space has come way down, and nothing makes a Windows 95 machine run more slowly than a lack of hard drive space.

If you have power users who run multiple applications simultaneously while surfing the Internet or who run high-end programs that hit the disk a lot, spend the extra money for SCSI. The incremental cost isn't that much, and your users will be happier in the long run. And more productive. But make the investment only if their computing actually requires it.

POINTS TO REMEMBER

- You must select hardware from the Hardware Compatibility List, paying particular attention to network cards, fax modems, and multiport serial adapter boards.

- Use of hardware that doesn't conform to the HCL will eventually lead to problems and might cause the installation to fail.
- The minimum requirements are just that—the bare minimum. In particular, the server should be as powerful as you can reasonably afford.
- Plan hardware with your current needs in mind but also with an eye to the future.

WHAT'S NEXT

The planning for your Small Business Server network is almost complete. In the next chapter, we'll go over some final preinstallation issues such as security and the specific system requirements for both the server and clients.

Chapter 4

Before You Install

36	**Planning for Security**
	Physical Security — 37
	User Security — 37
	File Security — 38
	Security from Intruders — 39
39	**Choosing a File System**
40	**Naming Conventions**
41	**System Requirements: The Server Computer**
42	**System Requirements: The Client Computer**
43	**Points to Remember**
43	**What's Next**

Chapter 4
Before You Install

Yes, here we are at Chapter 4 and we're still talking about planning. We can almost hear the cry of "But this is all supposed to be *easy!*" Well, it is, but it's also much like painting a room, where 90 percent of the job is preparation—washing, patching, masking—not simply rolling paint onto a surface. Skimp on the preparation and you'll waste a lot of time and energy (not to mention paint). Likewise, every hour that you invest in planning your Small Business Server installation will save you many hours later.

In this chapter, we'll go over some additional elements that you need to consider, such as security, the file system to choose, and how to name your computers. We'll then review the specific system requirements for the server and for client computers.

Planning for Security

Most people believe, at least in the abstract, that security is a Good Thing—that is, until they forget a password, are denied access to documents they want, have to walk down the hall for print output because they can't print to the nearest printer, or can't download the latest, coolest bit of software from the Internet. At that point, security becomes a roadblock to doing their jobs. On the flip side, users will complain bitterly about "lax security" when it's their stuff that someone else has accessed and maybe changed or even destroyed. Ideally, you want to make your security so thorough that no one can access anything without specific permission, while making the enforcement of that security so transparent that no one notices it.

The four basic areas of security are:

- Physical security
- User security
- File security
- Security from intruders

No matter how large or small your network, you need to be aware of all of these, although the emphasis on one or another will change as the size of your network changes.

Physical Security

Any computer, whether it's a network server, a desktop workstation, a portable notebook, or a public access terminal in a shopping mall kiosk, needs to be physically secure. Unless your computer case has a self-destruct mechanism (and we've never seen this except in spy movies), if someone can walk away with your computer, he or she can access your data.

This doesn't mean you have to bolt down all of your computers or lock your server in a vault. A workstation sitting in an open area of your office can actually be more secure than one in a closet—because people can see what's happening to it. As long as the office is locked during hours when no one's around, this is relatively safe. The location of the network server, however, deserves a little more thought. You'll want quick access to it during the business day, protection from accidental power-downs and reboots, and a means of locking it away during off hours.

◆ Can the Server Be a Workstation Too?

A server that can handle the demands of Small Business Server is a pretty big investment for most small businesses, so the question naturally arises whether the server can also be used as a workstation. In general, it's probably OK. The person using the server as a workstation *might* sometimes feel that the machine is a little slow. If so, that can usually be solved by adding more RAM to the server—far cheaper than buying a whole new machine.

You do want to be sure that anyone using the server knows that he or she cannot reboot at random or turn the computer off without notifying the entire network in advance. As long as that is understood, using the server as a workstation is not only safe but also a good use of resources.

User Security

User security has two aspects: facilitating users' access to the resources they need for their jobs and keeping from them—even hiding from them—resources that they don't need. The latter aspect includes your company's most confidential information as well as other users' personal property.

In general, you want users to have to remember only one password, which they have to enter only once, to gain access to the network and its resources. You can also require a second password to access highly sensitive resources. Do this sparingly, however. People can remember two or three passwords fairly easily, but beyond that they either start writing their passwords down and taping them to the computer monitor or start choosing similar or related passwords—easy to remember but also easy to guess.

◆ Rules for Good Passwords

A good password has the following characteristics: It is not a rotation of the characters in a logon name (how many brain cells would it take to figure that one out?), it contains at least two alphabetic and one nonalphabetic character, and it is at least six characters long. Furthermore, you should avoid using your name or initials, those of your significant other or your children, or even any of these items combined with other easily available personal data such as your birthdate or phone number.

Among the best passwords are alphanumeric acronyms of phrases that have some deeper meaning to the user but are meaningless to anyone else. For example, we have a family joke based on the rather rude expression "Go sit on a fruitcake!" For a while, we used the password *Gsoaf2*. (The *2* represents *twice*.) It's almost an ideal password. After all, what are the odds of someone unknown to us actually guessing it?

It pays to educate your users about passwords and password privacy, but most of all, it pays to heed your own advice: Be sure that the password you select for administration is a good password, and be sure to change the password fairly frequently.

For More Information

See Chapter 8 for more information on setting password policies.

File Security

There are also two aspects to file security—controlling access to the file and protecting the integrity of the file. Small Business Server has an easy and direct method for controlling who has access to which files. (See the section titled "Managing Shared Folders" in Chapter 6 for details.) In most circumstances, this is quite adequate. However, the Microsoft Windows NT operating system allows for even greater file security. If you need to get granular—that is, to get very specific about who can see what, right down to the level of individual files—you can do so. This is not where you should start, however. You should add file restrictions only when necessary because it's all too easy to get bogged down in a net of conflicting and overlapping permissions.

For More Information

For more information on how to set additional permissions and shares, see Chapter 10.

Security from Intruders

Keeping out the bad guys is what usually comes to mind when the topic of security is raised. But in real life, far more damage is done by those inside the company—inadvertently, for the most part—than those outside. Nevertheless, there are a few steps you should take to minimize the risk of intrusion.

All your users should be required to change their passwords periodically. Previously used passwords should not be immediately reusable. Accounts should be set to lock out when invalid passwords are entered. (Three attempts should be permitted, to allow for typographical errors.)

If your users will be dialing into your network from home or other remote sites, you might want to include more security than domain-level password authorization. You can configure your Remote Access Server to call back a predetermined number when a user dials in. As long as the user always calls from the same place, this works well. You can also place a third-party security device between the remote client and the Remote Access Server. An example of such a device is a so-called "smart card" that can be inserted in a card reader on the remote machine and authenticated by a security device on the host network. Only if this authorization succeeds is the remote user allowed to access the network.

> **Tip**
>
> *Administrators should have two accounts on the system—one administrative account and one "normal user" account. Because of the privileges associated with administrative accounts, such accounts are a prime target for intruders. Don't make your normal user account a member of the administrator's group (because it will thereby acquire administrative privileges and will no longer be a normal user account). Use the administrator account only while performing administrative tasks; for all other work, switch to the normal user account.*

Choosing a File System

You can install Small Business Server on a partition formatted as FAT (File Allocation Table) or NTFS (NT File System). While FAT has lower overhead than NTFS, it lacks the security and recoverability features built into NTFS. FAT is *not* an appropriate choice for a server. Here are some of the features of NTFS that make it preferable:

- Permissions can be assigned to directories or even individual files. Files can retain their permissions even when they are moved.

- No one can gain unauthorized access to an NTFS system by booting from a floppy.

- Because transactions are logged before they're carried through, the system can recover in the event of a failure. Disk repair utilities aren't needed.

- NTFS constantly monitors its disk areas; if it finds damage, it takes the bad area out of service and moves the data in that area to another area. This is called a *hot fix*, and it's invisible to any running application.

- Fragmentation is less of a problem on an NTFS partition because the system always attempts to locate a contiguous block of hard drive space large enough to hold the file being stored.

Although only computers running Windows NT can directly use NTFS files, network users can access files on NTFS partitions without difficulty even if they're using MS-DOS, OS/2, UNIX, or any flavor of Microsoft Windows (Windows 3.1, Windows for Workgroups, or Windows 95).

Aside from its lack of security, a major downside to FAT is that its cluster sizes are very large on the sort of large disks needed on a server. This means enormous quantities of disk space are wasted. Admittedly, hard drives are cheap, but there's no need to be profligate.

Naming Conventions

Each computer on the network must have a unique name up to 15 characters long. The installation routine offers you a name for the server based on the name of your organization. By default, this name will be as long as possible, all the way up to that 15-character limit. A name this long can be a nuisance—to remember and to type in—so you might want to shorten it. (This option is available during installation.)

The server name can't be changed without completely reinstalling Small Business Server—something you obviously want to avoid. So think carefully before assigning a name. It should be something that clearly identifies the machine as being the server, isn't too long, and isn't too cute. (What's cute today is sure to be annoying tomorrow.)

The names of client machines *can* be changed later, but it's not something you want to do often. Once the network is set up, individuals might use files or folders on other client machines. A name change will require remapping, which isn't difficult but is bound to cause confusion; the idea is to keep administration time to a minimum.

A client computer can be named for its function, location, or user. Of course, any of these can change over time, but you can probably predict which is likely to be the most stable in your organization.

It can be tempting to give names that are more abstract. Resist this temptation unless you have five or fewer client machines and expect no growth. Users will find it challenging to memorize more than a few computers named after Norse gods or cartoon superheroes.

For More Information

Deciding on a user name standard is covered in Chapter 6.

System Requirements: The Server Computer

If you've ever installed Windows NT Server, you know that planning and preparation are the bulk of the job. The installation of Small Business Server is even more dependent on advance planning because the setup program attempts to automate many operations that would ordinarily require your input. Computers and the state of programming being what they are, automated steps are not very intelligent, so as the system administrator, you must offer only choices that the setup program understands.

Here are the basic requirements for the server as defined by Microsoft:

- Intel and compatible systems: 100 MHz Pentium or higher processor (166 MHz Pentium or higher recommended)
- RISC-based systems: Alpha processor
- 64 MB of RAM
- One 3.5-inch high-density disk drive
- 2 GB of hard disk space
- CD-ROM drive
- Super VGA or other video graphics adapter (800 × 600 × 64K colors)
- Network adapter card (see Small Business Server Hardware Requirements)
- One or more modems for using Modem Sharing Service, Fax Service, Dial-Up Networking, and Internet access software; all modems must

be the same brand and model and must appear in the Hardware Compatibility List Supplement

- Multiport board listed in the Hardware Compatibility List Supplement (for multiple modems)
- Microsoft Mouse or compatible pointing device
- Tape backup device (not required, but highly recommended)

NOTE

In general, most hardware that is compatible with Windows NT Server 4 is compatible with Small Business Server. The exceptions are noted in the Hardware Compatibility List Supplement that comes with your software. The Supplement can also be found on the Web at www.microsoft.com/backoffice/backofficesmallbiz/showcase/hcl.asp.

Actual requirements will vary depending on what you decide to install and how active your server will be, but in general, you can consider this the absolute minimum configuration. A 166 MHz Pentium processor is very much at the low end of what most servers need. Additional RAM will also help performance.

Microsoft also recommends adding as many of the following items as your budget will allow:

- Additional hard disks for file storage or disk mirroring (a dynamically updated duplicate of your computer's information)
- Additional phone lines dedicated to faxing and Dial-Up Networking
- An uninterruptable power supply (UPS)

System Requirements: The Client Computer

Small Business Server lets you integrate a variety of client computers into your network. If these computers are using Windows 95 or Windows NT Workstation 4, your users can access all the features of Small Business Server. With some additional configuration, users of Microsoft Windows for Workgroups (Windows 3.11) can also have access to the features of Small Business Server. And finally, with some additional configuration, the following client computers can use the Small Business Server file and print services: Windows NT Workstation 3.x, Windows 3.x, MS-DOS, the Apple Macintosh operating system, and various versions of UNIX.

Here are the hardware requirements for a Small Business Server client computer:

- PC with a 386DX processor or higher (486DX or higher recommended)
- 16 MB or more of RAM
- One 3.5-inch high-density disk drive
- 60 MB of free hard disk space recommended
- Super VGA video graphics adapter (800 × 600 × 256K colors)
- A network adapter card from the Hardware Compatibility List Supplement

Again, the processor, RAM, and hard drive space requirements are the minimum you can get by with. If you don't use faster processors and more RAM in particular, you might find performance to be unacceptable.

POINTS TO REMEMBER

- Networks should be physically secure. If you can't watch it, lock it up.
- Require passwords but limit the number of passwords per user. Otherwise, it becomes difficult for users to remember them.
- Add an extra layer of security for remote access users.
- NTFS is the file system of choice for a secure Small Business Server network.
- Think carefully about the names you want to use for your server and client computers.
- Microsoft's minimum system requirements are just that—minimums. For better performance, use faster processors and more RAM.

WHAT'S NEXT

These first four chapters have introduced you to many of the concepts and features of Small Business Server while preparing you for the actual installation. In the next chapter, we'll step you through a final checklist and the actual installation on the server.

Part Two

Installation and Setup

Part Two provides step-by-step instructions for installing BackOffice Small Business Server and walks you through the initial tasks of setting up users and hardware. We also look at methods of protecting data on the server, because you should deal with security issues early in the life of your SBS network.

Chapter 5

Installing Small Business Server

48	**A Preinstallation Checklist**
	1. Verify Hardware Compatibility — 48
	2. Review the System Requirements — 49
	3. Review the Disk Partitions — 49
	4. Decide on a File System — 49
	5. Decide on Server and Domain Names — 50
	6. Connect the Hardware and the Cables — 50
	7. Gather Company Information — 50
	8. Choose the Administrator Password — 51
	9. Format Some Floppies — 51
51	**Starting the Setup**
53	**The Setup Program: Step by Step**
61	**Points to Remember**
61	**What's Next?**

Chapter 5

Installing Small Business Server

At this point, you should be pretty well prepared to start installing Microsoft BackOffice Small Business Server. But before you actually insert the first CD in the drive, let's go over one last checklist to make sure everything will go smoothly.

A Preinstallation Checklist

The installation of Small Business Server is as foolproof as it can be, but it is not without its perils. You must follow Microsoft's plan and instructions, or you can get quite far into the installation process only to discover that your system is suddenly hanging and you've absolutely no clue why. The following sections explain what you need to do to increase your chances of success.

1. Verify Hardware Compatibility

Make sure that all of your hardware—especially your network adapter card, fax modem, and/or multiport serial adapter board—is on the list of approved models on the Microsoft Windows NT Hardware Compatibility List (HCL) and the Small Business Server Hardware Compatibility List Supplement. This is essential because hardware on a server that "almost" works will inevitably raise your blood pressure and shorten your life span. Not worth it.

> **NOTE**
>
> *Most hardware that's compatible with Microsoft Windows NT Server is compatible with Small Business Server. The exceptions are noted in the Hardware Compatibility List Supplement that comes with the software. For the latest version of that list, visit the Microsoft web site at www.microsoft.com/backoffice/backofficesmallbiz/showcase/hcl.asp.*

To get good use from the fax server and from modem sharing, you should install at least two fax modems. These fax modems must be listed in the Hardware Compatibility List Supplement, and they must also be identical to one another or they will not work as a pool. Identical means the same model from the same manufacturer, each using the same version of firmware.

Generally, if you buy the modems at the same time from the same dealer, you can be confident that they're identical. But even then, make sure you can return any modems that don't conform to the standard.

2. Review the System Requirements

Review the system requirements for server and client computers, and verify that your hardware components meet those minimum requirements. The requirements for both are detailed in Chapters 3 and 4.

3. Review the Disk Partitions

To install Small Business Server, you must have at least 2 GB of free disk space on the hard disk on which you want to install the system files. You have three partition options during setup, each corresponding to a different initial system configuration, so select the one that most closely corresponds to the situation on your server-to-be:

- If you have no operating system installed or if you want to reformat (or repartition and reformat) your hard disk, make sure the first partition is a primary partition that is set to active, has been formatted, and has at least 2 GB of free space.

- If your first partition is too small, you'll see a screen that shows your partition and file system information. Select the partition on which you want to install Small Business Server, and continue. If you select a FAT-formatted partition, the file system will be converted to NTFS during setup. This is most common on computers that have Alpha processors.

- If you are running Microsoft Windows 95 or Windows NT, you can run sbssetup.exe from the root of disc 1. However, you still need a hard disk with 2 GB of free space.

4. Decide on a File System

Small Business Server's file system of choice is NTFS, not FAT. In fact, if you install Small Business Server on an unpartitioned hard disk, you will be presented with the option of selecting your file system. In this situation, select NTFS, not FAT, because Windows NT Server cannot secure local files and folders on a FAT partition, so FAT presents a network security risk that you probably want to avoid. If asked during setup, you can choose either to retain an already-existing NTFS-formatted partition or to format the partition as either FAT or NTFS. Again, we beg you to select NTFS since it's by far the superior choice in terms of network security. It's OK if you reformat an existing NTFS partition, but remember that you'll eliminate any preexisting files by doing so.

WARNING!

You cannot install Small Business Server on a FAT32 partition.

For More Information

For more details about FAT and NTFS, see "Choosing a File System" in Chapter 4.

5. Decide on Server and Domain Names

During installation, you'll be prompted for a name for the server machine you're setting up as well as a name for the entire domain. Small Business Server volunteers to generate names based on the name of your company or organization, but you might find these names ungainly. Once you accept a name or provide your own, you can't change it without a complete reinstallation of Small Business Server. This is obviously undesirable in the extreme, so give it a little thought because you'll be living with these names for quite a while.

The server name, which is used to identify this Small Business Server computer on your network, can contain up to 15 characters. The domain name, which is the name of your network, can contain up to 12 characters. Users will see this name when they browse for resources using Network Neighborhood. Keep the names as short as possible. Your client computers will also have names, so you'll have to decide how to identify them as well. Remember that names based on function or location are better than names based on who uses the machine.

6. Connect the Hardware and the Cables

Connect all the hardware and the cables to your server machine, and turn on any external devices. The setup program is smart enough to prompt you to turn on an external modem if it doesn't find an internal one. (At least one modem is required for server setup.) However, it can't detect many other kinds of hardware (network hubs, for example) unless they're turned on, so if they're turned off at this point, your installation might fail without explanation.

7. Gather Company Information

Small Business Server requires three pieces of company information for setup: the name of the person to whom Small Business Server is registered (usually the same person who will manage the server), a company name or an organization name, and a business fax number. Optional items include the following, which you can enter during setup: address, city, state or province, ZIP or postal code, country, and phone number with area code. It's generally easiest to enter all of this information during setup since Small Business Server saves it and will recall it whenever appropriate.

8. Choose the Administrator Password

Before you get to the relevant screen during the installation process, it's smart to have a password in mind for the Administrator account. Ideally, the Administrator password should:

- Be mixed uppercase and lowercase
- Contain both alphabetic and nonalphabetic (numeric) characters
- Be six to eight characters long
- Be easy to type
- Be difficult to guess

Don't use your name, your spouse's name, your dog's name, your birth date, your address, or any other easily guessed word. You need something that you can remember easily but that has meaning only for you. Be sure to guard the Administrator password closely, sharing it with no more than one trusted associate (or possibly two), because anyone who knows it can access (and potentially change) your server.

> **For More Information**
>
> See the sidebar titled "Rules for Good Passwords" in Chapter 4.

9. Format Some Floppies

Before embarking on the installation process, have on hand some formatted high-density disks for creating an Emergency Repair Disk (ERD) and disks for the Small Business Server client installation. You'll need one disk for the ERD and one for each client computer you'll be setting up, so do the math based on the projected size of your network.

Starting the Setup

Now that you've got what you need to install Small Business Server, it's time to get down to it. If you've done your homework and have followed the advice we've given you, the installation should be relatively painless. Here are the steps:

1. Make sure all external system devices (including your external modem and/or network hub) are properly installed and turned on.
2. Insert the Small Business Server Compact Disc 1 into your CD-ROM drive.

3. Insert the Microsoft Small Business Server Setup Disk 1 into drive A.

4. Turn on your computer if it is off, or reboot it if it is already on.

5. Insert Setup Disk 2 when prompted and press Enter; the setup program will copy files to your hard drive.

6. Insert Setup Disk 3 when prompted and press Enter; the setup program will copy more files to your hard drive and check to see which file system is in place on the hard drive. There are three possible situations:

    - If your hard disk has an NTFS partition and you want to remove existing files and install Small Business Server on a clean FAT partition (something we don't recommend doing), select the Format The Partition Using The FAT File System option. Note, however, that Windows NT Server cannot secure local files and folders on a FAT partition, which is precisely why FAT isn't a good choice. If you select this option, you must press F to confirm that you want to format the hard disk.

    - If your hard disk has an NTFS partition and you want to install Small Business Server on a clean NTFS partition, select the Format The Partition Using The NTFS File System option. Be aware, however, that this will destroy all data on the disk. If you select this option, you must press F to confirm that you want to format the hard disk.

    - If you want to keep your current file system and preserve existing files, select the Leave The Current File System Intact (No Changes) option, and then press Enter.

7. When the setup program begins copying files to your hard drive, remove the floppy disk from drive A.

8. After the files are copied, your computer should restart.

NOTE

Remote installation of Small Business Server is not supported, so you cannot install Small Business Server over a network from a network share or from a shared CD-ROM drive. You can run the setup program only from the CD-ROM drive in the computer that is designated as your SBS server.

The Setup Program: Step by Step

And now for the actual setup of your Small Business Server. Be sure to follow all the steps described below because we've included some tips that will help you avoid some common installation problems.

1. The first screen you'll see is the License Agreement page, which contains all sorts of tedious legal language. Read all the text, pressing the PgUp key to scroll up or pressing PgDn to scroll down. When you get to the bottom of the agreement, you'll have exactly two choices—to accept the Microsoft agreement or not. We advise you to accept the agreement, because if you don't, you've reached the end of the line; if you click No, you'll see an error message indicating that you have elected not to accept the Small Business Server licensing agreement. Setup will then abort. If, however, you click I Agree, you'll be able to continue with the Small Business Server setup.

2. In the Name And Organization dialog box, type the name of the person who will manage the server and the name of your company or organization. Notice that this automatically generates computer and domain names based on the information you enter. The computer name, which can contain up to 15 characters, will identify this Small Business Server computer on your network. Users will use this name to connect to resources on the server. The domain name, which can contain up to 12 characters, is the name of your network. Users will see this name when they browse for resources using Network Neighborhood.

   If you want to accept these default computer and domain names, you don't need to do anything else here; if you want to change these names, however, this is an excellent time to do so. Once the setup is complete, you can't change these names without reinstalling Small Business Server from scratch. Click Next to continue.

WARNING!

Once Small Business Server is installed on your server, you cannot change the computer name for the server or the domain name you've chosen, so think carefully about these names before you commit yourself.

3. In the Registration text box, enter the CD key. This is the 10-digit number labeled *CD Key* on the jewel case that contains the Small Business Server CD. To continue the setup, you must specify the CD key number. Click Next to continue.

4. Next you should see the Windows NT Setup dialog box. Click Next to begin the Windows NT Server setup.

5. Setup will begin the process of detecting your hardware, copying files to your system, and installing the Windows NT operating system. The first hardware that the setup program searches for is the network adapter. If it can't find your network adapter or if setup identifies it incorrectly, be sure to correct this information manually after the Windows NT Server installation is complete and before you begin the Small Business Server setup. It's not impossible to change this information once Small Business Server is installed, but it's considerably more difficult than getting it right at the start. Now is also a good time to check yet again that your network adapter is of a make and model specified on the Small Business Server Hardware Compatibility List Supplement.

NOTE

If the setup program cannot detect your network adapter card, it will install a Microsoft Loopback adapter, which will allow the installation to continue. If this happens, you must manually configure your network adapter card after the Windows NT Server installation is complete. Be sure to do this, and then restart your computer before starting the Small Business Server setup process. If you're absolutely certain that you have a network adapter card in your computer and that it's one of the "approved" ones, make sure it's installed properly. If you're still having problems, consider installing the network adapter card in another computer to make sure it's working properly.

6. The next piece of hardware that the setup program searches for is the modem. Verify that the port and drivers are correct and that your modem is of a make and model specified on the Small Business Server Hardware Compatibility List Supplement. Click Next to continue.

NOTE

If the Install New Modem dialog box appears during the setup process, be sure to indicate the manufacturer and model of your modem. If Standard Modem is selected and this does not reflect the modem you actually have, click Change to configure your modem manually, select the manufacturer and model of your modem, and then click OK.

7. When you see the Date/Time Properties dialog box (Figure 5.01), click the arrow to select the correct time zone for your location from the list.

If your time zone observes daylight saving time, select the Automatically Adjust Clock For Daylight Saving Changes check box. Click on the Date & Time tab to set the correct date and time, and then click Close to continue the setup process.

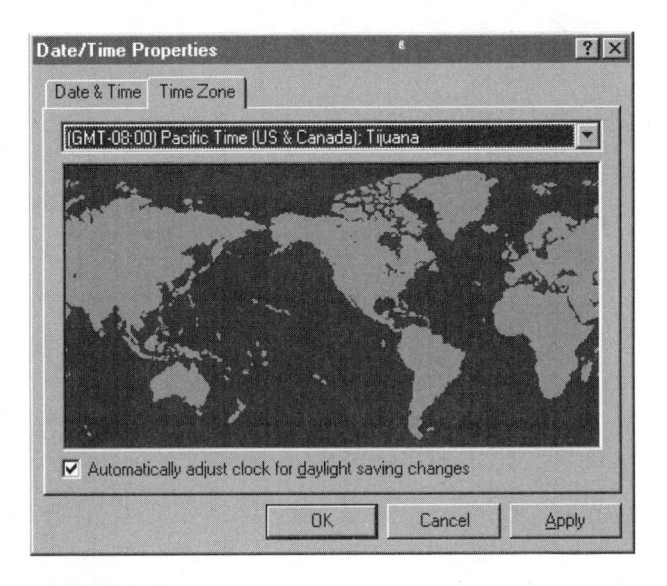

FIGURE 5.01

The Date/Time Properties dialog box.

> **Tip**
>
> *Setup cannot detect your system's time zone. Instead, it defaults to Greenwich mean time (GMT). To display the correct time on your system, you must select the correct time zone from the drop-down list.*

8. At this point, the setup program will restart your system one or more times. When it finishes rebooting, you should see the first page of the Microsoft Small Business Server Setup Wizard, shown in Figure 5.02 on the following page.

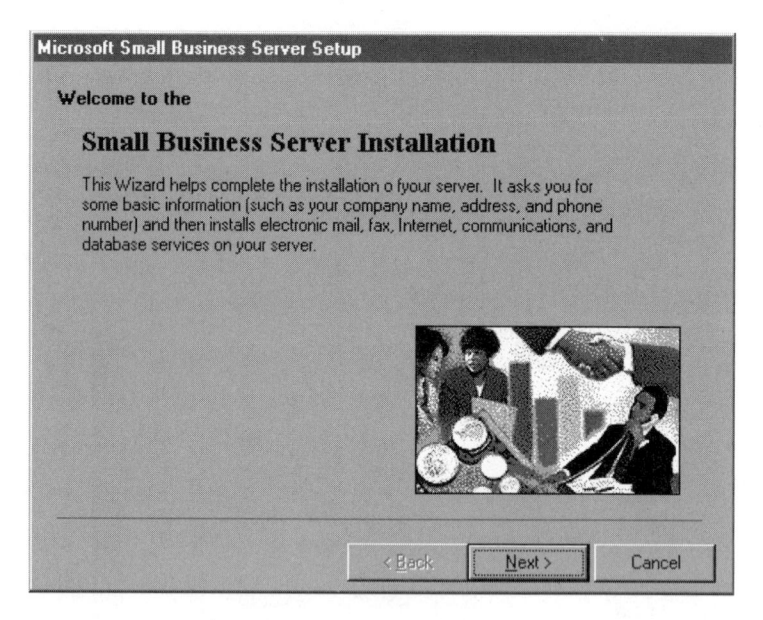

FIGURE 5.02

The Microsoft Small Business Server Setup Wizard.

> ◆ **Tip**
>
> *As your system starts up, you might see the OS Loader starting, followed by a list of operating systems to select from. Most people will see two items on the list: BackOffice Small Business Server and BackOffice Small Business Server (VGA mode). If, however, you're installing Small Business Server on a system that already has another operating system installed on it, you might see other items on the list.*

9. Now that you're under the guidance of the Microsoft Small Business Server Setup Wizard, all you have to do is fill in the requested information and use the Back button or the Next button to move between pages. You can change information entered on previous screens if you discover that the information you entered was either incorrect or inappropriate. On the first page of the wizard, click Next to continue.

10. On the second page of the wizard (Figure 5.03), enter information about your business. The information you can provide includes the name of the person who will be managing your server (which you entered during setup); a company name or an organization name (which you also entered during setup); a street address, city, state or province,

ZIP or postal code, and country; a phone number; and a fax number. When you're satisfied that you've entered enough information to identify your company or organization, click Next to continue.

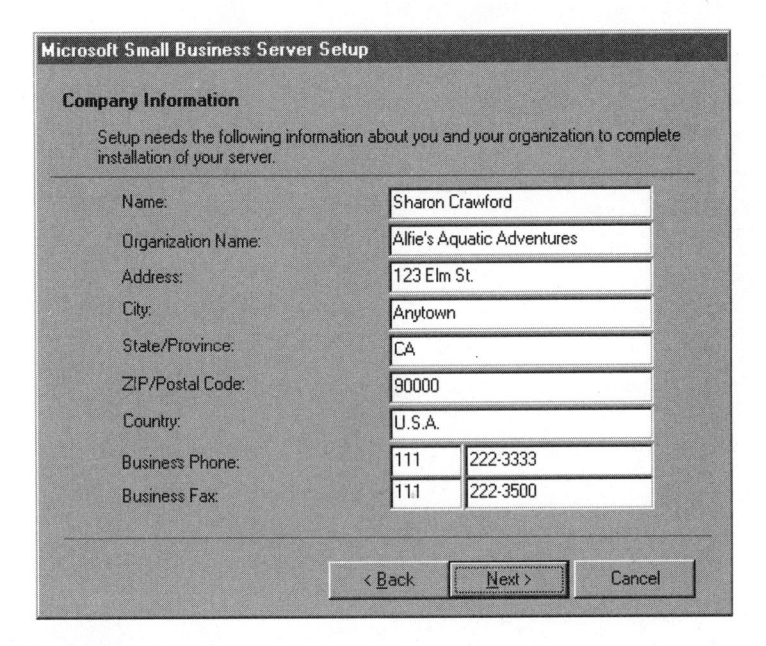

FIGURE 5.03

The second page of the wizard, in which you enter information about your business.

Tip

Take the time to enter your company information during setup because Small Business Server saves it and uses it later. For example, the User Account Wizard displays this information when you add a new user. If you don't provide this information during installation, you must reenter it each time you add a new user.

NOTE

A fax number is required to move to the next screen. If your business does not have a fax number, enter zeroes so you can continue. This value can be modified later if your company adds a fax number.

11. The third page (Figure 5.04) lets you specify Complete Installation or Custom Installation of Small Business Server. Microsoft recommends the Complete Installation, which installs everything you need to use all the features of Small Business Server. The Custom Installation lets you select specific components to install. If you select this option, you must click Next, and then, on the Custom Installation page, select the components you want to install. After you specify the kind of installation you want, click Next to continue.

NOTE

The Microsoft Internet Connection Wizard, Microsoft Active Server Pages, Microsoft Internet Explorer, and Microsoft Small Business Server are required components.

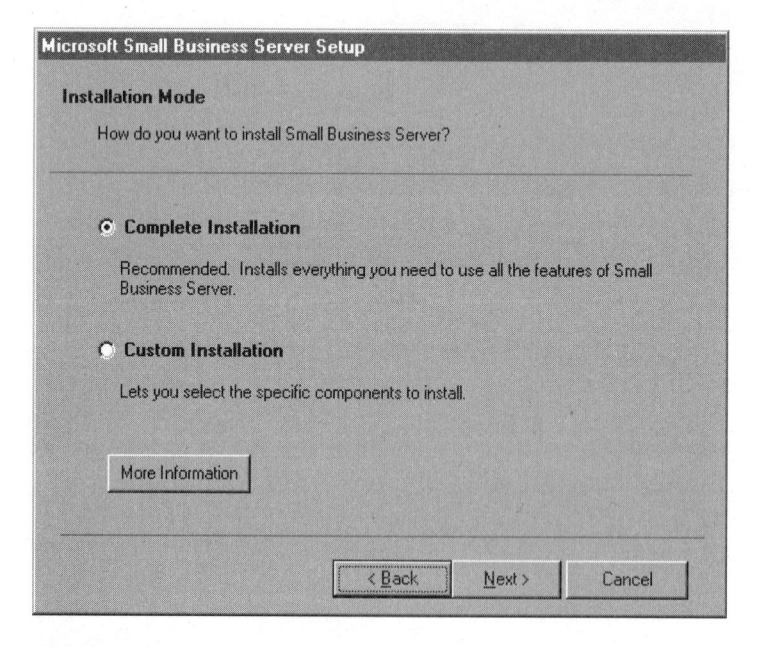

FIGURE 5.04

The third page of the wizard, on which you specify the type of installation.

12. On the fourth page, shown in Figure 5.05, you select a password for the Administrator account. (The account has been created by the setup program.) Type your password in the first text box, and then type the

58 INSTALLATION AND SETUP

same password in the second text box to confirm your choice. When you're satisfied with your Administrator password, click Next to continue to the next page of the wizard.

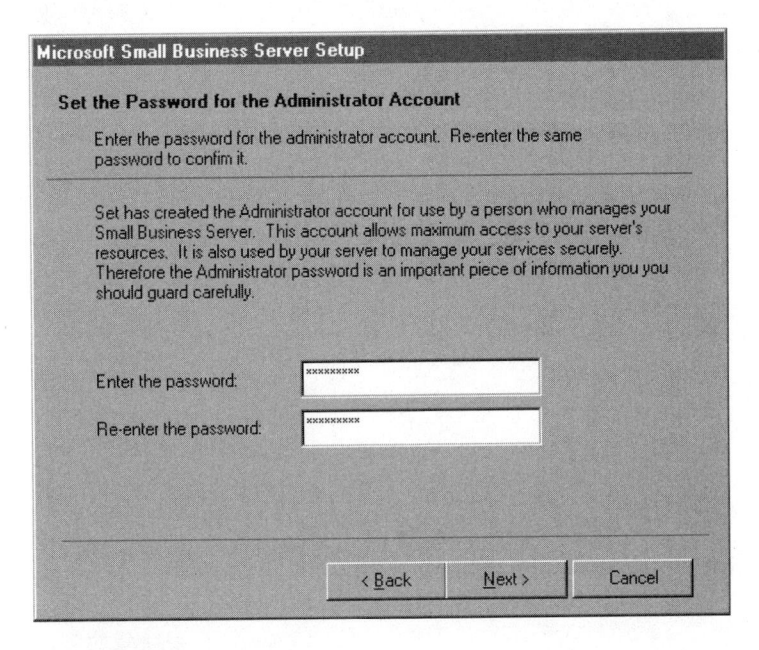

FIGURE 5.05

The fourth page of the wizard, on which you select a password for the Administrator account.

WARNING!

The Administrator account allows maximum access to your server's resources. Your server also uses it to manage your services securely. Therefore, the password for this account is a very important piece of information. Be sure to remember it, be sure to change it often, and don't share it with more than one other trusted individual.

13. The fifth page, shown in Figure 5.06 on the following page, might seem to indicate that you're almost done. But whether this is actually so depends on the speed of your equipment and the number of Small Business Server components you've opted to install. If you have a relatively slow hard disk or CD-ROM drive and you're performing a

complete installation, the process of copying files and installing Small Business Server can take well over an hour. If your equipment is new and fast or you've opted for a custom installation with fewer components, the process might take less time. Either way, you should prepare to spend some time twiddling your thumbs as the setup program finishes its work.

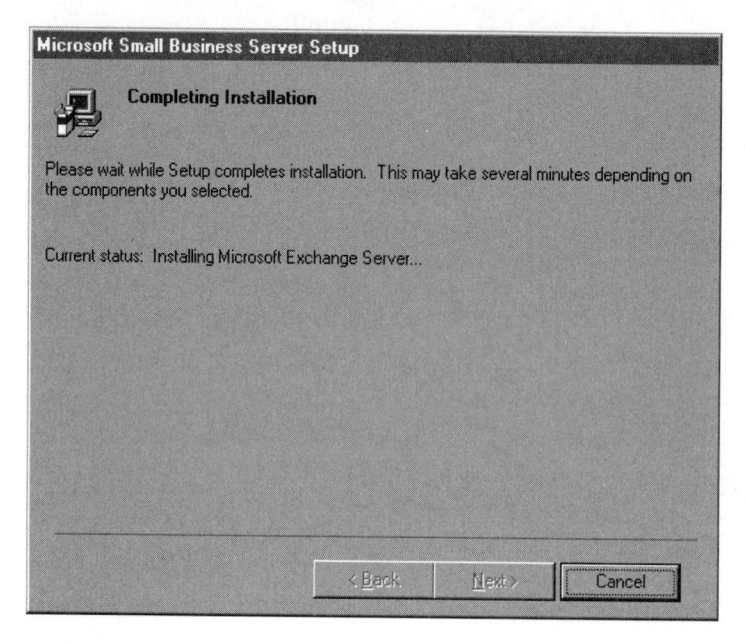

FIGURE 5.06

The fifth page of the wizard.

14. When prompted, insert Disc 2 and click OK. A message will inform you that copying client application files to your computer will take 5 to 10 minutes. This might be a generous understatement; in many cases, it takes longer.

15. Now you're really almost through. You can click Finish and then Yes to restart your computer and log on automatically as Administrator. This will let you complete the installation of Small Business Server.

Time to take a breath. You've successfully installed Small Business Server. You still need to perform a number of tasks before your system configuration is complete, but the hardest part of the job is behind you.

POINTS TO REMEMBER

- Be sure to read the installation instructions in this chapter carefully before you begin the setup process.

- Check each and every hardware component to make sure that it's on the Windows NT Hardware Compatibility List or the Small Business Server Hardware Compatibility List Supplement.

- If you encounter any problems during installation, see Appendix A in the Small Business Server *Start Here* manual.

WHAT'S NEXT?

Now that the basic installation is complete, in the next chapter we'll guide you through the configuration tasks for your specific network. From here on, most of the tasks are simple; you just have to decide which ones you need to perform right away and which ones to skip for now.

Chapter 6

Postinstallation

64 The To Do List
- Adding a Printer — 65
- Adding Users — 67
- Setting User Resources — 72
- Setting Up a Client Computer — 75
- Signing Up with an Internet Service Provider — 79
- Adding User Licenses — 81
- Creating an Emergency Repair Disk — 81

82 Other Common Postinstallation Tasks
- Configuring Additional Hardware — 82
- Letting Your Employees Use the Network — 87
- Connecting to the Internet — 88
- Remote Access Service and Dial-Up Networking — 89
- Microsoft Fax Server — 90

90 More Typical Postinstallation Tasks

90 Points to Remember

91 What's Next?

Chapter 6
Postinstallation

Even though you've successfully installed Microsoft Small Business Server on the computer designated as your server, you're not quite ready to use your network yet. Before you and your users can start reaping the benefits of your new system, you must complete a few remaining tasks.

The To Do List

After the setup program finishes doing its thing and restarts your computer, you'll be presented with the To Do List (Figure 6.01). Here you can complete and customize your Small Business Server installation by adding new printers or users, setting up a computer, signing up with an Internet service provider, adding user licenses, or creating an Emergency Repair Disk. All the work is handled by wizards, so once again, all you have to do is type in the requested information or select the appropriate option.

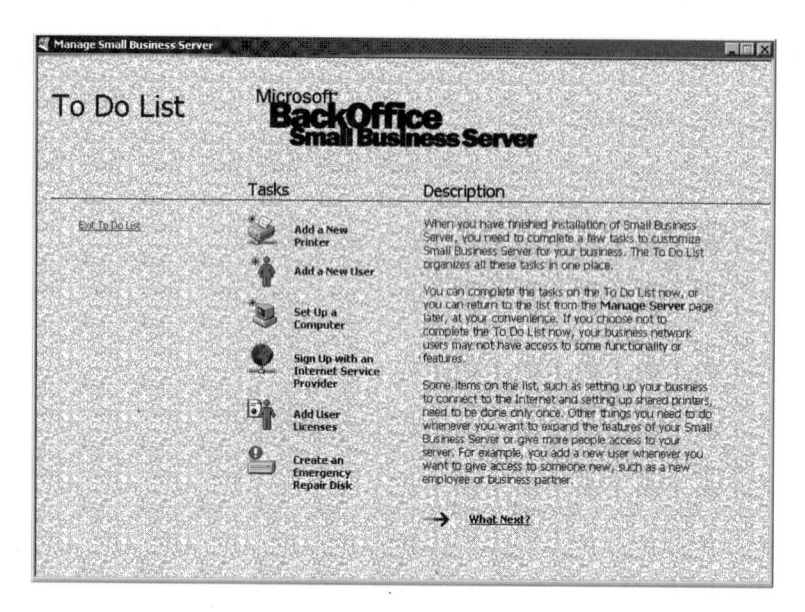

FIGURE 6.01
The To Do List.

To start configuring your server, select an item on the To Do List by clicking on its icon. To exit to the main page of the Small Business Server console, click on the Exit To Do List link. The following sections describe the items on the To Do List.

> **Tip**
>
> *The To Do List is also available at any time from the Small Business Server console. Choose the Manage Server command from the Start menu, and then click on the Return To To Do List link.*

Adding a Printer

Once you physically connect a printer to the server, you have to add it to the server by following these steps:

1. Click the Add A New Printer icon on the To Do List. This will start the Add Printer Wizard. This is a good time to check again that your printer is connected to the server and turned on.

2. On the first page of the wizard, shown in Figure 6.02, specify which computer will manage this printer—the server (My Computer) or a network printer server. If your network is small and your server isn't overly burdened with other tasks, it's probably OK to connect a printer or printers to the server directly. If your network handles a lot of printing, you might want another computer to handle the printing requests. After you select an option, click Next.

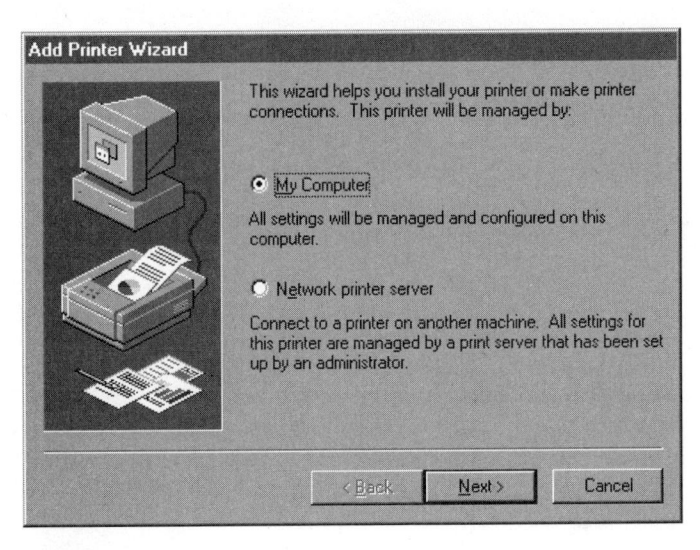

FIGURE 6.02
The first page of the Add Printer Wizard.

3. The next page, shown in Figure 6.03, lets you specify the port to which the printer is connected. Select the check box that corresponds to the port to which your printer is connected, or click the Add Port button if you don't see the port listed. If you need to configure the port, click the Configure Port button and use the buttons in the Ports dialog box to change any settings. To take advantage of printer pooling, you can select the Enable Printer Pooling check box and then select the ports to which the identical print devices are attached. Note that all print devices in a pool must use the same printer driver.

   Click Next to continue.

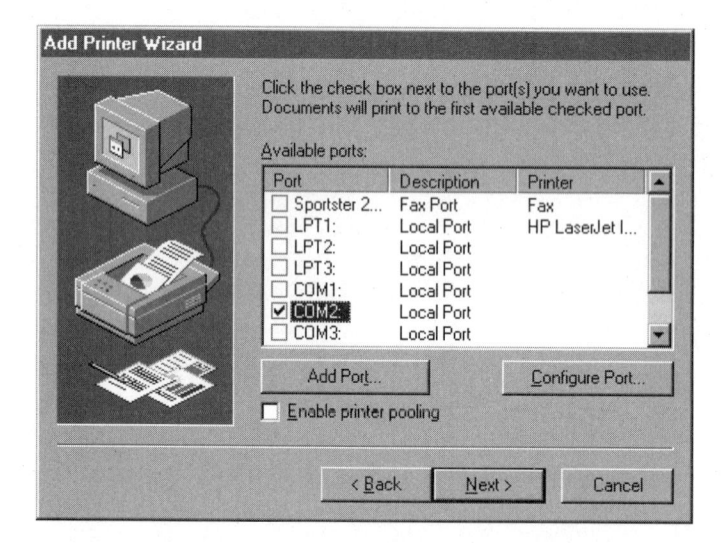

FIGURE 6.03

The page that lets you specify, add, and configure ports.

4. The next page lets you specify the manufacturer and model of the printer you're adding. Be aware that you might need to click the Have Disk button and insert the printer manufacturer's driver disk in order to copy the appropriate drivers to your system. When you're satisfied that your printer information is correct, click Next.

5. On the next page, you can name your new printer. You can accept the default name suggested by the wizard, or you can type a different name. Here you can also specify whether you would like Microsoft Windows–based programs to use this printer as the default printer. Make your selections, and then click Next.

6. The next page, shown in Figure 6.04, lets you indicate whether the printer will be shared by other network users. Normally, the printer is shared unless you have some overriding need to restrict access. You can accept the default share name suggested by the wizard, or you can type a different name. After you give the printer a share name, specify all operating systems used on computers that will print to this printer by selecting their names in the selection box. Click Next to continue.

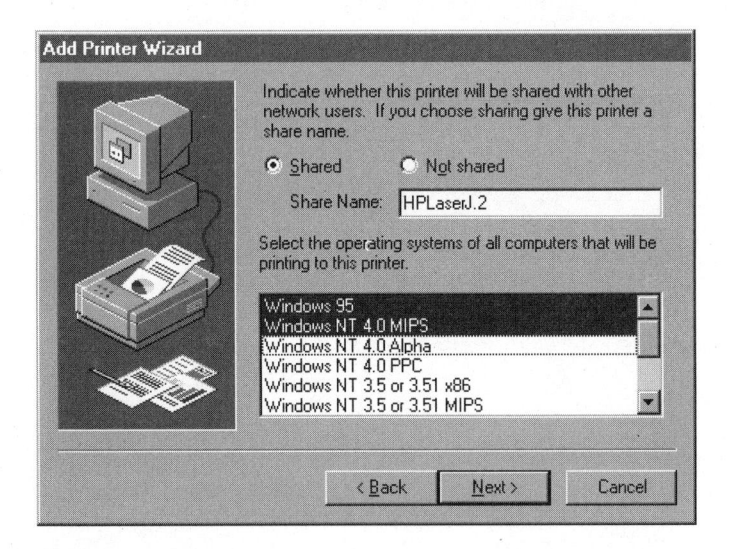

FIGURE 6.04

The page that lets you indicate whether the printer will be shared with others on the network.

7. The next page asks whether you'd like to print a test page. It's advisable to do so, just to make sure that everything is set up correctly. Click Finish, and you'll be returned to the To Do List.

Adding Users

To add a user, click on the Add A New User icon on the To Do List. This will start the User Account Wizard and open the page shown in Figure 6.05 on the following page.

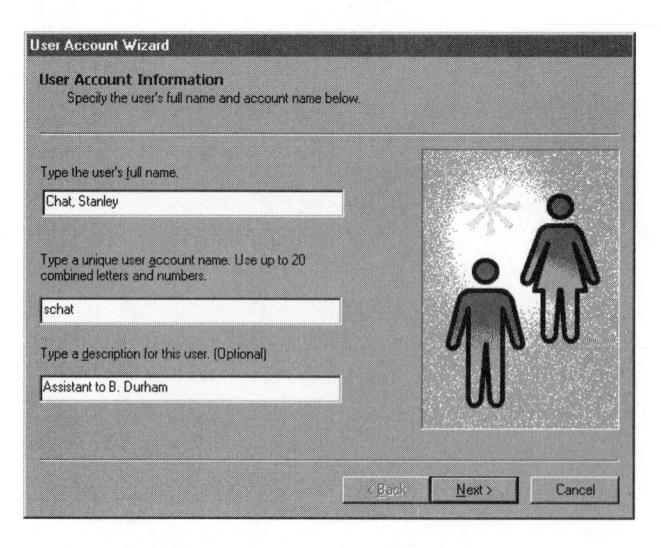

FIGURE 6.05

The wizard's User Account Information page.

NOTE

You can have as many user accounts as you want—no matter how many licenses you own. So make a user account for everyone who uses the network. Not only is it more convenient for everyone to have an individual account but also it's more practical. A user's problem can be a lot easier to troubleshoot if he or she is not signing on under a series of "borrowed" names.

A user account in Small Business Server contains a great deal of information, starting with the user's name, the account name, and an optional description.

The Full Name field identifies the user by his or her full (real-life) name. For convenience, you might want to adopt the practice of showing the Full Name as last name first, followed by the first name. So instead of showing Bernard C. Durham, the Full Name box would show Durham, Bernard C. In a very small network, first names work just as well.

The Account Name field specifies the user's user name. A user name must be unique and can have up to 20 characters, including uppercase and lowercase letters and numbers.

◆ **A User Name Standard**

You should decide on a policy for user names even before you create the first user account. You should think about your current, as well as future, users' needs. But even with only a few users, don't make user names at or even near the 20-character limit because if you do, too much typing will be required for a simple logon.

Here are some options for user names that you can adapt to your own situation:

- First name plus last initial—for example, MichaelG and SusanM. In the case of duplicate first names, you can add numbers (MichaelG1 and MichaelG2) or enough letters to provide identification (SusanMat and SusanMur).

- First name plus a number—for example, Dave112 and Dave113. This approach is a pain for all concerned. It's hard to remember your own user name and even harder to identify other user names.

- First initial plus last name—for example, Lsmith. If you have both a Linda Smith and a Louise Smith, you could use LiSmith and LoSmith, or Lsmith1 and Lsmith2.

- Last name plus an initial. This is useful in a large network. When you have multiple users with the same last name, you can add a few letters, as in SmithLi or SmithLo.

No matter which approach you use, not only must you accommodate the existing users on your network, but you must also be able to integrate future users. So even if the company's next hire is U Ti or Cholmondely Pepperell-Glossup, your user name convention will still be able to handle it.

The Description field is optional. It's sometimes used to identify the user's job title, department, or both since the company information that you'll enter shortly doesn't appear everywhere you might want it to.

After you type the necessary information on the page, click Next to move to the Create A Password page.

You can opt to have the wizard generate a password for the user (the default option), or you can specify the user's password yourself. The advantage of the former is that it doesn't require you to think; the advantage of the latter is that you can specify a password that the user has a fighting chance of remembering. After you make your selection, click Next.

If you decided to let the wizard generate a password for the user, you should see a page that looks like the one in Figure 6.06. Be sure to copy the password from the screen so that you can tell the user what it is. On this page, you must also specify whether the user can change this password. The default choice—allowing the user to change it—is a good idea because you want the user to have a password that he or she is comfortable with.

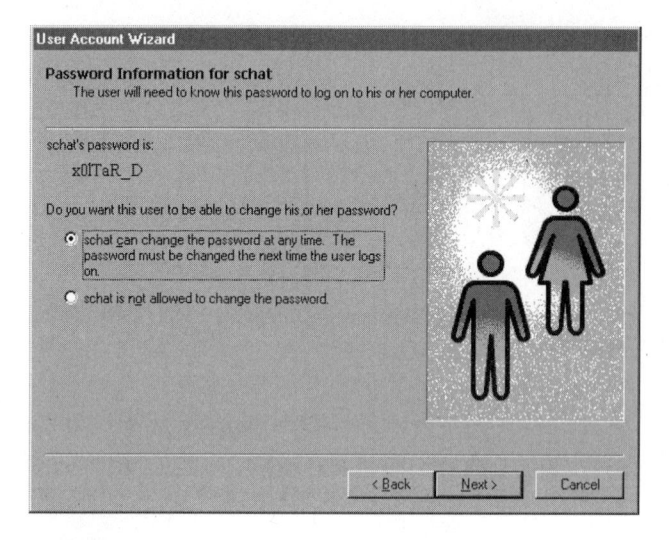

FIGURE 6.06

The Password Information page with a wizard-generated password.

If you opted to specify a password for the user, you should see a page that looks like the one in Figure 6.07. For starters, type a password in the Password text box. Regardless of what you type, you'll see only asterisks on the screen. To confirm your choice, type the same password in the Confirm Password text box. At the bottom of this page, you must specify whether the user can change this password. Click Next to continue.

The Company Information page is the first of a series of three pages that let you provide other users with useful information about who this user is and how to contact him or her. Here you can enter the new user's job title, company name (this field should already display the company name entered during the Small Business Server setup), department, office, assistant (if applicable), and phone number. Type any information you want, and then click Next.

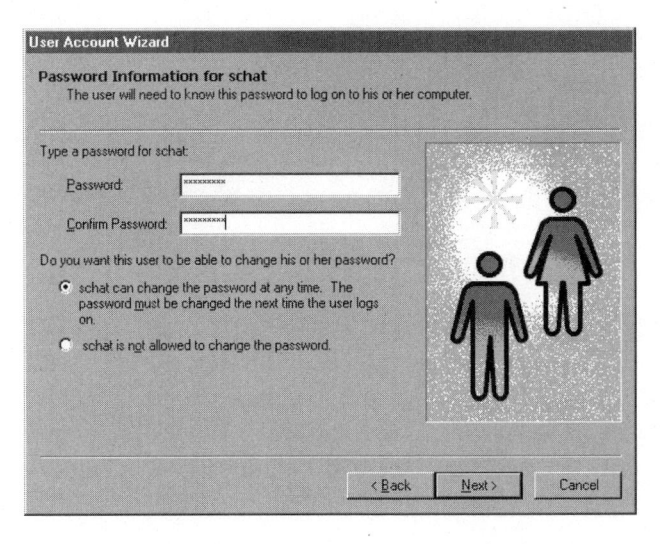

FIGURE 6.07

The Password Information page for specifying a password.

On the Address Information page, type the user's street address, city, state, zip code, and country if these differ from the address information entered during the setup process (that is, if you'd like other users to know how to reach this person live or via "snail mail").

Click Next, and you'll see the Communication Information page, where you can type numbers for the user's business and home telephones (including alternative numbers, if applicable), fax, mobile phone, assistant, and pager. When you're through telling the world how to communicate with this new user, click Next.

Next you'll see the Select The E-Mail Distribution Lists page, shown in Figure 6.08 on the following page. The left side of the screen displays a list of all existing e-mail distribution lists on your SBS server. The right side shows the e-mail distribution lists to which this new user currently belongs. To add the user to a distribution list, select the list in question on the left side of the page and click the Add button; to remove the user from a list, select the list on the right side of the page and click Remove. When you finish, click Next.

For More Information

On a new network, you won't have existing e-mail distribution lists. See Chapter 14 for information on how to build them.

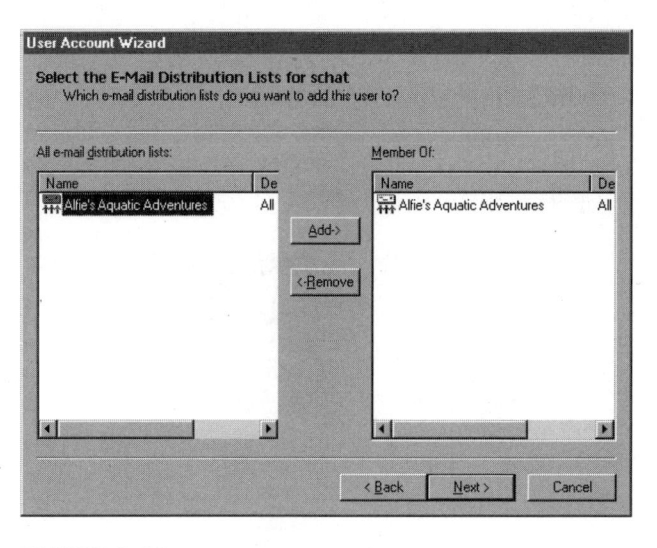

FIGURE 6.08

The Select The E-Mail Distribution Lists page.

You should see the Create User Account page. To create the account, click Finish; you can click Back to change any or all of the settings you specified in the wizard. After the User Account Wizard finishes creating an account for the user, you should see a dialog box that indicates this and confirms the new user's account name. If you click OK, the User Resource Wizard will start.

Setting User Resources

The User Resource Wizard lets you specify which system resources a user has access to. Once the wizard is invoked, which happens automatically if you follow the steps described in the previous section, you should see the page shown in Figure 6.09.

> **For More Information**
>
> *If you just installed Small Business Server, the shared folders will be only those that were created by Small Business Server and are automatically shared. For information on how to share existing folders, see Chapter 10.*

The left side of the Select The Shared Folders page shows a list of all shared folders on your SBS server. The right side shows two things: the folders for which this user has read-edit-delete privileges and the folders for which the user has read-only privileges. Read-edit-delete privileges allow a user to examine, change, or remove any file in a shared folder. Read-only privileges allow a user to examine any file in a shared folder, but nothing else; this is the "look but don't touch" option. To grant the user permission to share a particular folder, select the folder on the left side of the page and click the Add button. Be sure to review the kind of access this user has to each shared folder. Click Next to continue.

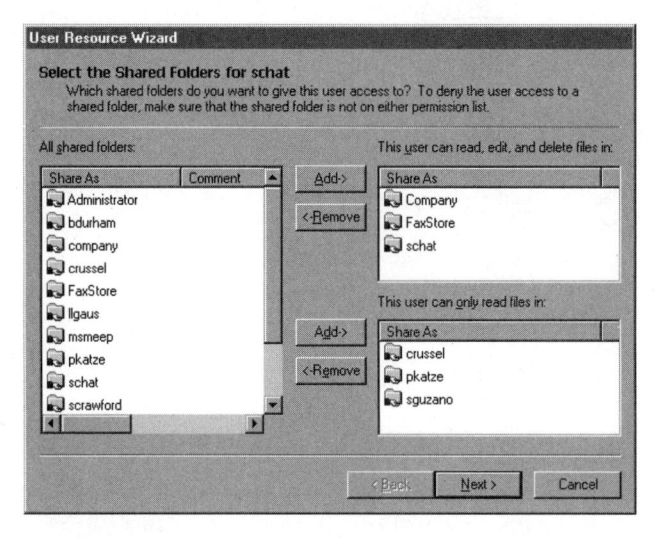

FIGURE 6.09

The Select The Shared Folders page.

NOTE

As you'll learn in Chapter 10, it pays not to hand out read-edit-delete privileges too freely. On the other hand, being too restrictive can make more work for you. Except in the case of very sensitive material, assume trustworthiness (but keep good backups).

On the next page, the Select The Shared Printers page, the left side displays a list of all shared printers on the network and the right side shows the printers this user has access to. To change the user's access to a particular printer, select that printer and click the Add or Remove button to perform the desired action. When you finish granting this user rights to printers, click Next.

On the Select The Shared Fax Printers page, you can grant the user access to the fax devices connected to your network. These are referred to as *fax printers*, even though they are actually fax modems. To change the user's access to a particular fax printer, select that fax device and click the Add or Remove button to perform the desired action. When you're done, click Next.

On the next page, the Select Additional Access Rights page, you have to decide whether to grant this user one, both, or neither of two additional rights—the right to access the Internet and the right to connect to the server via a modem. In most cases, it makes sense to grant your users access to the Internet so that they can send e-mail and surf the World Wide Web. (However, if for any reason you don't want this user to be able to do these things, here's your chance to put your foot down.) To grant this user Internet access, select the Access The Internet check box.

Dial-up access via a modem can be a big advantage for users who work from home or are often on the road since it lets them check e-mail and perform other everyday operations while logged in remotely. If this new user is likely to need this kind of access, select the Use A Modem To Access The Server Computer check box. When you finish granting the user additional rights, click Next.

NOTE

The Access The Internet check box will be grayed out if you haven't configured your Internet connection. To come back later and add any of these permissions, choose Manage Users on the Small Business Server console's Tasks page.

On the next page, you can indicate whether to grant the user administrative privileges. The default choice is No since most users don't need this kind of power. But at least two people should have administrative privileges—if only to cover for each other in case of illness and during vacations.

After you make your choice, click Next to move to the Update Resource Permissions page, which asks you whether you're ready to update the user's resource permissions.

To update the user's resource permissions, click Finish, or click Back to change any or all of the above settings. Once the User Resource Wizard finishes updating resource permissions for this new user, you should see a dialog box confirming this fact. When you click OK, you'll be asked whether you want to run the Set Up Computer Wizard to configure a client computer for this user.

If you choose No, you're done, and you'll end up right back where you started—at the To Do List.

NOTE

To set up a client computer later, choose Manage Computers on the Small Business Server console's More Tasks page.

Setting Up a Client Computer

If, upon completing the tasks in the User Resource Wizard, you choose Yes in the confirmation dialog box, the Set Up Computer Wizard will start working its magic. This wizard creates a setup disk that a user can use to enable his or her computer to "talk" to your SBS server.

> **Tip**
>
> *You can also start the Set Up Computer Wizard by clicking on the Set Up A Computer icon on the To Do List.*

When you see the Welcome To The Set Up Computer Wizard page, click Next. This will take you to the Set Up The Computer page, shown in Figure 6.10.

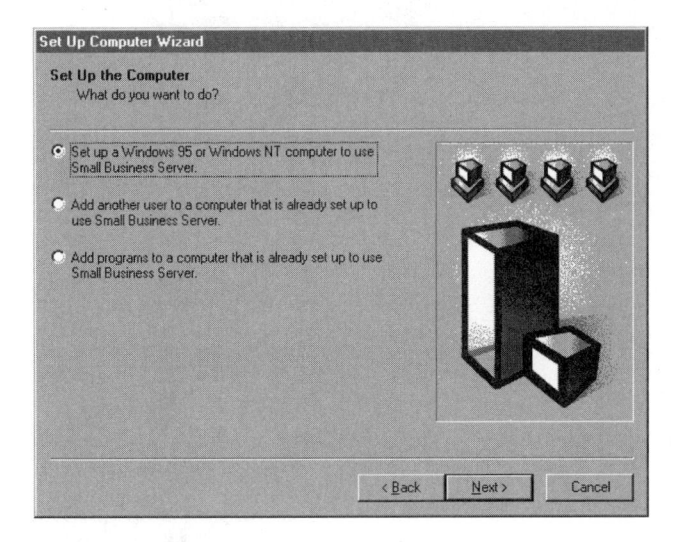

FIGURE 6.10

The Set Up The Computer page.

As you can see, this page gives you three options: You can set up a Microsoft Windows 95 or a Microsoft Windows NT computer to use Small Business Server, add another user to a computer already set up to use Small Business Server, or add programs to a computer already set up to use Small Business Server. Select the option that corresponds to the task you'd like to perform, and then click Next to continue. The following section describes these tasks.

Setting up a Windows 95 or Windows NT computer

If you've chosen to set up a Windows 95 or Windows NT computer to use Small Business Server, the Specify The Computer Name page (Figure 6.11) is the first step in the process. Here you can either accept the suggested name for the user's computer or type a different name.

If you haven't had the foresight to devise a naming scheme for your network, accept the suggested name because this will ensure that the computer names on your network adhere to some kind of logic. When you're done naming this computer, click Next.

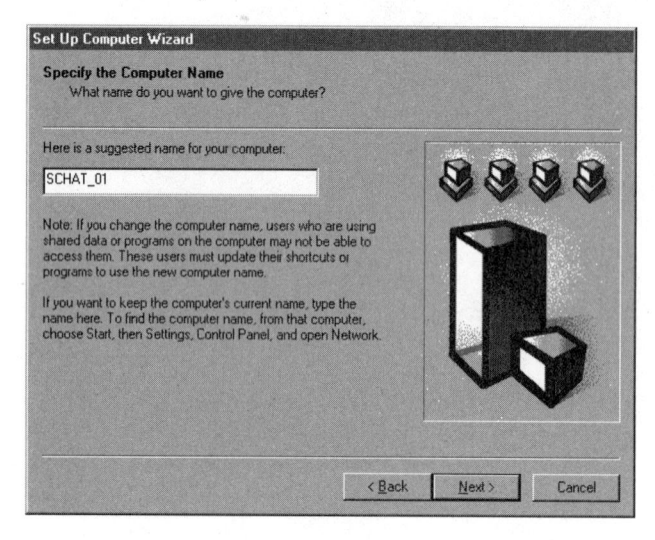

FIGURE 6.11

The Specify The Computer Name page.

On the Operating System page, specify which operating system is installed on the computer you're setting up, Windows 95 or Windows NT 4. Click Next to continue.

On the Select The Programs To Install page (Figure 6.12), you indicate whether to install Small Business Server client programs on the computer you're setting up. To proceed without installing any client programs, select the I Do Not Wish To Install Any Programs At This Time option, and then click Next.

To install some or all of the client programs listed, select the Install The Programs Checked In The List Below option and then use the check boxes to select or deselect individual programs. The components you can choose to install here include Microsoft Internet Explorer 3.02 (the Internet browser), a modem sharing client, a Microsoft Outlook e-mail client, a proxy client, and a Windows 95 fax client. When you're satisfied, click Next to continue.

> **Tip**
>
> *The total disk space required to install just these five programs is 57 MB, so make sure that there's enough free space on the hard disk of the computer you're setting up before you order up the whole package.*

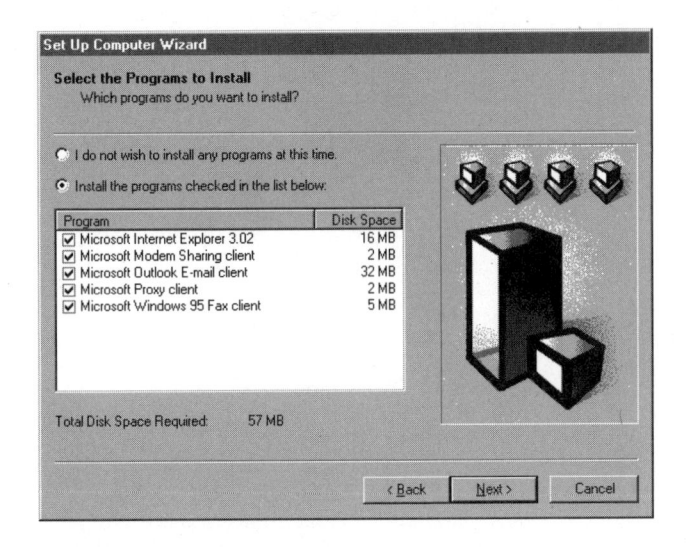

FIGURE 6.12

The Select The Programs To Install page.

The next page prompts you to create a setup disk. Label a 1.44 MB disk, and insert it into the floppy disk drive. After you take these steps, click Next and let the wizard do the job. It will format the disk (if necessary) and then copy the appropriate files to it. Before you click Finish to complete this process, review the instructions for setting up the new client computer. While you're at it, fill in the new user on the details; in theory, anyway, setting up a client computer is simple enough that anyone should be able to do it.

Adding another user to a client computer

If you've chosen to add another user to an existing Small Business Server client computer, you should see the Specify The Computer Name page, shown in Figure 6.13 on the following page. Notice that the left side of the page shows a list of the computers already on your network. To add a user to one of these computers, select the name of the computer in the list, and then click Next.

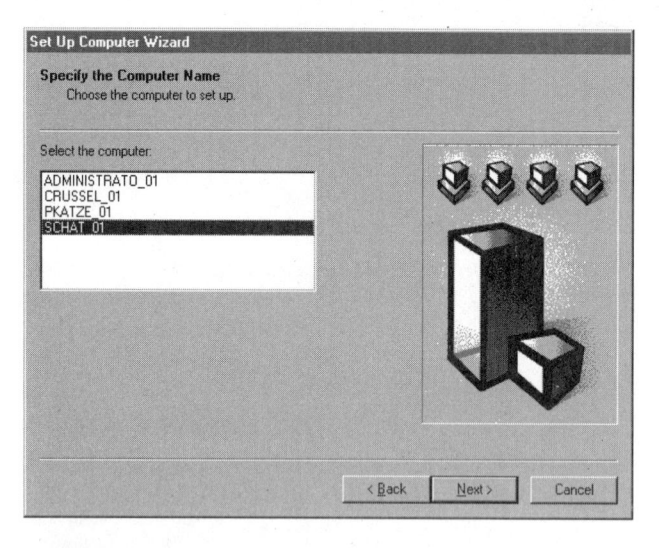

FIGURE 6.13

The Specify The Computer Name page.

Next the Select The Programs To Install page (shown in Figure 6.12) lets you indicate whether to install Small Business Server client programs on the computer to which you're adding a user. To proceed without installing any client programs, select the first option button and then click Next. To install some or all of the client programs listed, select the second option button and then use the check boxes to select or deselect individual programs. Click Next to continue.

When you arrive at the Create The Setup Files page, you're almost done adding your new user. If you click Next, the wizard will copy the new user's setup files to the appropriate location. There's no need for a floppy disk here because the setup files are copied to a directory on your SBS server. When the wizard is done copying files, click Finish and you're all set.

Adding programs to a client computer

If you've chosen to add programs to an existing Small Business Server client computer, you should see the Specify The Computer Name page (Figure 6.13). The left side of the page shows a list of the computers already on your network. To add programs to one of these computers, select the name of the computer in the list and then click Next.

Now you should see the Select The Programs To Install page. This page strongly resembles the one shown in Figure 6.12, but with one difference: Here the second option button has been selected for you. Use the check boxes to specify which program or programs to install, and be sure to keep track of how much hard disk space you'll need on the client computer. When you're done, click Next.

When you see the Create The Setup Files page, you're almost done adding your new programs. If you click Next, the wizard will copy the necessary setup files to the appropriate location. There's no need for a floppy disk here because the setup files are copied to a directory on your SBS server. When the wizard is done copying files, click Finish, and you're all set.

Signing Up with an Internet Service Provider

To sign up with an Internet service provider (ISP), click on the Sign Up With An Internet Service Provider icon on the To Do List. This will bring up a series of informational screens touting the advantages of having your business connected to the Internet. To start the Internet Connection Wizard, locate the text that says "Click here to connect your business to the Internet" on the left side of the screen, and click on the word *here*.

When you see the Begin Automatic Setup page (Figure 6.14), read the advice that the screen offers you. Click Next, and the wizard will check and update any necessary network and modem settings and display the Location Information page (Figure 6.15).

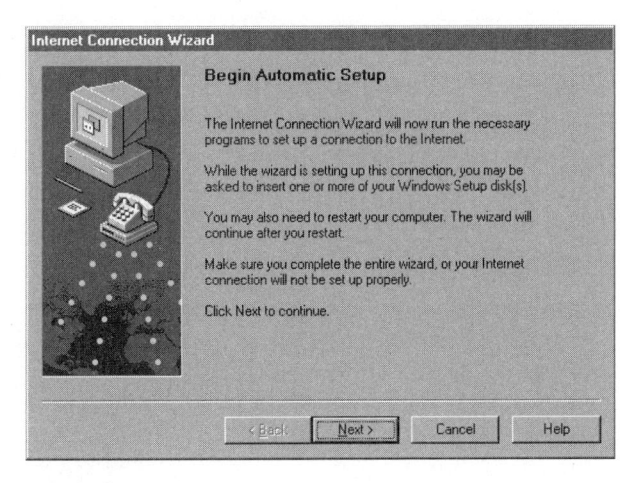

FIGURE 6.14
The Begin Automatic Setup page.

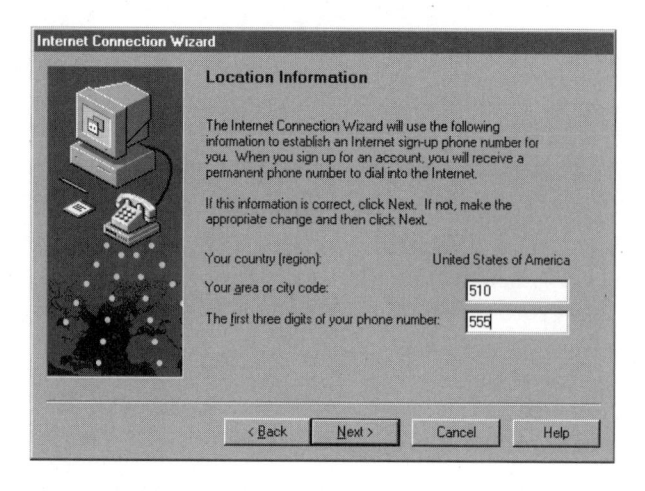

FIGURE 6.15

The Location Information page.

On the Location Information page, type your area code and the first three digits of your phone number. Click Next, and you should be connected automatically to Microsoft's Internet Referral Server, which will retrieve a list of ISPs for your location, language, and operating system.

When the list of ISPs has been downloaded to your computer, select a provider from the list by clicking on the appropriate check mark icon under Sign Me Up. To see more providers, click on the question mark and scroll up or down the list. If you'd prefer to do your own research into ISPs in your area (always a good idea, particularly if you can locate an ISP that someone else you know is happy with), click Cancel to halt the Internet Connection Wizard. You'll return to the wizard's first informational screen; to return to the To Do List, click the close box (the one with the × in it) in the upper right corner.

If you opt to sign up with one of the providers listed and you click on the appropriate check mark icon under Sign Me Up, you should see the Connecting dialog box while the Internet Connection Wizard dials the ISP you selected. Once you're connected, follow the ISP's registration instructions, completing all information and recording any user names or passwords. After you register with the ISP, you'll see the Internet Connection Wizard's Congratulations page, indicating that you're ready to connect to the Internet.

If you don't want to register your domain name immediately, click No when asked if you'd like to run the Set Up An Internet Domain Name Wizard. If, on the other hand, you'd like to go whole hog and register your domain name now, click Yes and follow the sure guidance of the wizard.

Adding User Licenses

To activate additional user licenses for Small Business Server, click on the Add User Licenses icon on the To Do List. This will bring up an informational screen about adding user licenses. Here you can see how many user licenses your business or organization currently has, and you'll learn that in order to add more licenses, you must purchase a Small Business Server Client Add Pack. If you've already purchased a Client Add Pack, proceed as follows to activate your additional user licenses. Otherwise, to return to the To Do List, click the close box in the upper right corner of the screen.

Before you add licenses, have your Client Add Pack disk(s) at hand. We strongly recommend that you carefully read and take the precautions on the Add User Licenses informational screen; this is your best hedge against disaster. To activate the additional licenses, insert Client Add Pack Disk 1 into your floppy drive and click on the Click Here To Start Setup link. Follow the screen's instructions on restarting your system, and the licenses will be added to your system. Once your system finishes rebooting, click the close box in the upper right corner to return to the To Do List.

Creating an Emergency Repair Disk

To create an Emergency Repair Disk (ERD) to use on your server in case of difficulty, click on the Create An Emergency Repair Disk icon on the To Do List. This will bring up the Create An Emergency Repair Disk screen with some instructions on it. Read the instructions, and then locate the text that says "Click here to start the Repair Disk Utility" and click on the word *here*. Be sure to have a blank high-density floppy disk handy since you'll need to insert one when the time is right. Once the system finishes saving the necessary configuration files, insert the floppy disk in the drive when prompted so that the configuration files can be copied to it. When the utility completes its task, be sure to label the ERD and store it in a safe place; after all, you never know when you might need it.

NOTE

An ERD is easy to create, so make a habit of creating a new one every time you make changes to the hardware or software setup on your server. Having a current ERD on hand is good insurance in case of a disastrous failure. For more on disaster recovery, see Chapter 28.

Once you complete the tasks on the To Do List, you're almost ready to go. However, there are still a few other things you might want to do before proclaiming your network ready, so keep reading.

Other Common Postinstallation Tasks

So you've added a printer and at least one user to your network, set up that user's computer, signed up with an ISP, added user licenses, and created an ERD. "What else is there to do?" you might ask. Good question. You still might want to configure additional hardware; actually give your users access to the network; connect to the Internet; and set up Remote Access Service, Dial-Up Networking, and Microsoft Fax Server. Here, in that order, is how to accomplish these feats.

Configuring Additional Hardware

You probably noticed while installing Small Business Server that hardware configuration is not always as automatic as it might be. Windows NT has made considerable progress in this area, but it still can't touch the plug-and-play ease of Windows 95. Although the setup program detected your network adapter card and modem (perhaps with a little help) during the Small Business Server installation, you might want to take advantage of other hardware components. Items that might not have been detected during the setup process include a sound card, a tape backup device, additional network cards, a multiport serial board, and additional printers. Configuring these devices is simple if you follow the steps outlined in the sections below.

Configuring a sound card

To configure additional hardware, you must be logged on using an account with administrative privileges. Open the Small Business Server Online Guide by choosing Manage Server from the Start menu and then clicking on the Online Guide tab. From here, single-click the plus sign next to Getting Started and then click Complete Setup For Non-Detected Hardware.

Click on Activate A Sound Card. This will invoke a utility that leads you through the entire process. On the first screen of the sound card utility, click on the link to open the Control Panel, and then follow these steps:

1. Double-click on the Multimedia icon to open the Multimedia Properties dialog box.

2. Click on the Devices tab (Figure 6.16). Select Audio Devices, and then click the Add button.

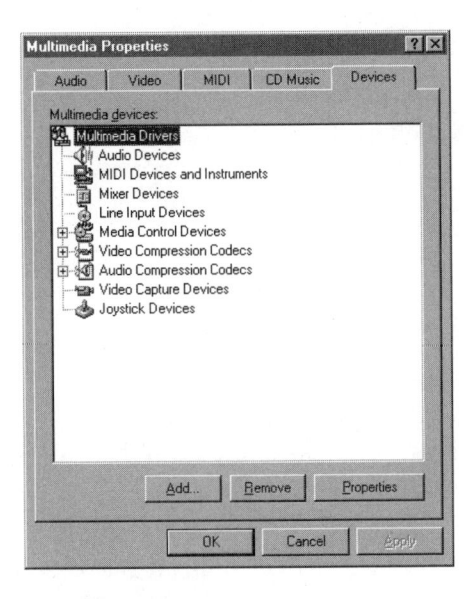

FIGURE 6.16

The Devices tab of the Multimedia Properties dialog box.

3. In the Add dialog box (Figure 6.17), double-click on the make and model of sound card installed in your computer. If your sound card is not listed, select Unlisted Or Updated Driver in the list, click OK, and then specify the location of the files in question.

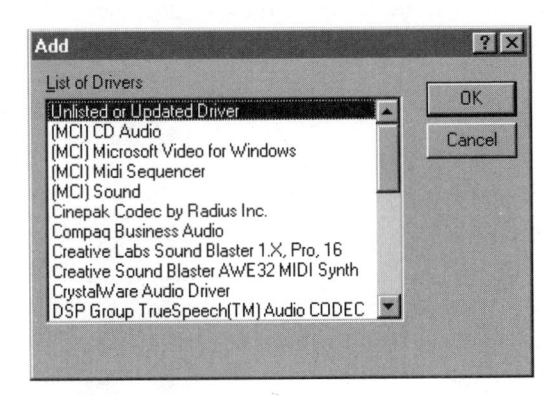

FIGURE 6.17

The Add dialog box.

CHAPTER 6 *Postinstallation* **83**

4. When prompted, insert the appropriate disk (either the manufacturer's disk or Small Business Server Disc 1) into the floppy drive or CD-ROM drive and follow the instructions on the screen to copy and install the appropriate driver for your sound card.

NOTE

It's sometimes tricky to get sound cards to work properly, so don't be surprised if you need to experiment a little before your sound card is configured correctly.

Configuring a tape backup device

To configure a tape backup device, be sure that you are logged on using an account with administrative privileges. Choose Manage Server from the Start menu, and then click on the Online Guide tab. From here, single-click the plus sign next to Getting Started, and then click on Complete Setup For Non-Detected Hardware.

Click Install A Tape Backup Device. This will invoke a utility that leads you through the entire process. First the tape backup device utility kindly reminds you that before you can install a tape backup device, you must purchase one. It also reminds you of the importance of using a tape backup device listed on the Windows NT Hardware Compatibility List or the Small Business Server Hardware Compatibility List Supplement. Do pay attention to this advice; devices that are not on the list are likely to cause you more trouble than they're worth, and they might not work at all.

Once you purchase, install, and turn on your tape backup device, click on Click Here in the second item of the tape backup device utility screen. This will begin the hardware detection process. Insert Small Business Server Disc 1 into your CD-ROM drive when prompted; the appropriate files will be copied to your computer. That's all there is to it.

Configuring additional network cards

To configure an additional network card, make sure you're logged on using an account with administrative privileges. Choose Manage Server from the Start menu, and then click on the Online Guide tab. From here, single-click the plus sign next to Getting Started, and then click on Complete Setup For Non-Detected Hardware.

Click on Install Additional Network Cards, and follow these steps:

1. Click on the Click Here link on the first page of the configure network card utility to open the Network dialog box.

2. Click on the Adapters tab (Figure 6.18). Click the Add button and follow the instructions on the screen to configure your additional network cards.

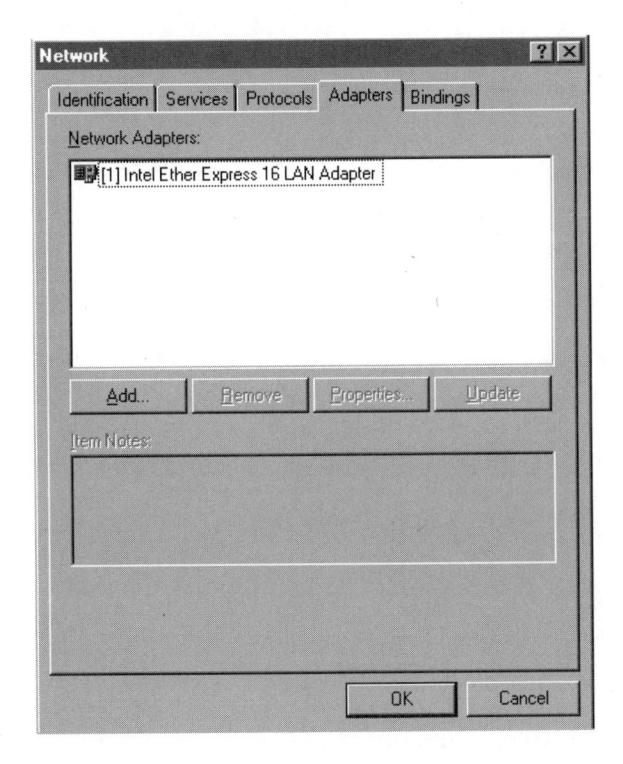

FIGURE 6.18

The Adapters tab of the Network dialog box.

Configuring a multiport serial board

To configure a multiport serial board, you must be logged on using an account with administrative privileges. Install the board in the server, choose Manage Server from the Start menu, and then click on the Online Guide tab. From here, single-click the plus sign next to Getting Started, and then click on Complete Setup For Non-Detected Hardware.

Click on the Install A Multiport Serial Board link, and then follow these steps:

1. Click on the Click Here link in the first item in the configure multiport serial board utility to open the Network dialog box.

2. Click on the Adapters tab (shown in Figure 6.18); click the Add button.

3. Select the appropriate device in the list, and then click OK. This will open the Port Configuration dialog box, which allows you to set the appropriate I/O and memory address range for your multiport serial board. Check the documentation that came with your device for information on what these settings should be.

4. When you're satisfied with the settings, click OK to close the Port Configuration dialog box, and then click OK to close the Network dialog box.

5. Click Yes to restart your computer.

Before you can use your multiport serial board, you must install each of the modems you want to use with the Install New Modem Wizard and add them to the modem pool. To invoke the Install New Modem Wizard now, use the link near the bottom of the Install A Multiport Serial Board Utility screen. If you'd like to read the procedure for adding a modem to the modem pool, there's a link for that too.

For More Information

If you want to change settings in your Remote Access Service phone book, you must modify the relevant phone book entry. See Chapter 19 for details, or read the instructions at the bottom of the Install A Multiport Serial Board Utility screen.

Configuring additional printers

To add a printer, you must be logged on using an account with administrative privileges. Make sure that the printer in question is connected to the network and turned on. Choose Manage Server from the Start menu, and then click on the Online Guide tab. From here, single-click the plus sign next to Getting Started, and then click on Complete Setup For Non-Detected Hardware and follow these steps:

1. Click on Add Printers To Your Network to open an informational screen with a Click Here link. Click on the link to start the Add Printer Wizard.

2. The wizard will first ask whether the printer will be managed by the server or attached to another machine. This is a good time to check again that your printer is connected and turned on.

3. Select the relevant option and click Next to open the Port And Port Configuration page.

4. Specify the appropriate printer port, and configure that port (if necessary). Select the check box that corresponds to the port to which your printer is connected, or click the Add A Port button if you don't see the port listed. If you need to configure the port, click the Configure Port button and use the buttons in the Ports dialog box to change settings. If you want to take advantage of printer pooling, click in the box next to Enable Printer Pooling and then select the ports to which the identical print devices are attached. Note that all print devices in a pool must use the same printer driver.

5. Click Next to open the Manufacturer And Model page.

6. Specify the manufacturer and model of the printer you're adding. You might need to click the Have Disk button and insert the printer manufacturer's driver disk in order to copy the appropriate driver to your system.

7. When you're satisfied with your printer information, click Next. You'll see a page on which you can name your new printer. You can accept the default name suggested by the wizard or type a different name. Here you can also specify whether you'd like Windows-based programs to use this printer as the default printer.

8. Make your selections, and then click Next to move to the Printer Sharing page.

9. Normally, the printer is shared unless you have some overriding need to restrict access. You can accept the default share name suggested by the wizard, or you can type a different name. After you give the printer a share name, specify all operating systems used on computers that will print to this printer by selecting their names in the list at the bottom of the page. Click Next to continue.

10. The next page will ask if you'd like to print a test page. It's advisable to do so, just to ensure that everything is set up correctly. Click Finish to complete the process.

Letting Your Employees Use the Network

Letting your employees use the network is actually a three-step process: You add users, you add their computers, and then you might need to review your user license situation. Here's what to do before you can let your employees use the network.

Adding users

Actually, we've already told you how to add users to your system; see the section titled "Adding Users." Repeat this process as many times as necessary to add all your employees to your system, and then you're set. For detailed information about managing users and maintaining user information, see Chapter 8.

Adding client computers

This is something else you already know how to do; to add client computers to your system, see the section titled "Setting Up a Client Computer." Repeat this process as many times as necessary to ensure that each employee has access to a client computer. That's all there is to it. For detailed information about managing computers, see Chapter 18.

Reviewing your user license situation

As you learned in Chapter 1, Small Business Server will support up to 25 concurrent connections. Depending on the size of your business, you might be entirely satisfied with the licenses that come with the basic Small Business Server package. As your business grows, however, you might need more licenses. If this is the case, contact the vendor that sold you Small Business Server and buy as many Client Add Packs as you think you'll need. Each Client Add Pack gives you five additional user licenses. To add user licenses, follow the instructions in the section titled "Adding User Licenses," and your network should be ready to support your new users.

Connecting to the Internet

If you'd like to use your Small Business Server network to connect to the Internet, you must sign up with an ISP. You might also want to register your company or organization's domain name if your ISP doesn't do this for you or if you want to register a different domain name. Earlier in this chapter, in the section titled "Signing Up with an Internet Service Provider," we covered the basic procedure for connecting with an ISP.

Registering your domain name

If you opted not to register your domain name when you invoked the Internet Connection Wizard and signed up with an ISP, it's not too late. By using one of Small Business Server's many console options, you can still register your domain name more or less automatically.

To invoke the Set Up An Internet Domain Name Wizard, first be sure you're logged on using an account with administrative privileges. Choose Manage Server from the Start menu, click on the More Tasks tab, and then click the Manage Internet Access button on the More Tasks page. This will open the Manage Internet Access page. Click on the Set Up An Internet Domain Name link, and you're off and running; be sure to follow the wizard's instructions carefully to ensure that your domain name will be registered promptly and correctly.

NOTE

After you register a domain name using the wizard, it takes approximately 24 hours for the domain name to be fully replicated on the Internet. In the meantime, e-mail sent to you that uses your newly registered domain name might not be delivered to you and might be returned to the sender. To bypass this problem, for the first 24 hours you should have Internet users send e-mail to the address that you received from your ISP when you signed up for Internet access. This 24-hour propagation period does not affect your ability to send e-mail.

Remote Access Service and Dial-Up Networking

Remote Access Service (RAS) is a networking service that was installed on your SBS server during setup if you selected the Complete Installation option. RAS allows your server to answer incoming calls from remote users, who are able to dial in and connect to your server via a modem. Remote users can send and receive e-mail and faxes and copy files from your network if they have the proper permissions. RAS is only half the picture, however; to connect to the server, remote users must have Dial-Up Networking installed and configured on their client computers. See Chapter 19 for complete details on how to install and configure Dial-Up Networking.

If you're keen on establishing remote connections to your server right away, be sure to meet the following requirements:

- RAS is installed and running on your server.

- Dial-Up Networking is installed and configured on the remote users' client computers.

- Any remote users' accounts have been granted the right to log on remotely. You use the User Resource Wizard to make this so—see Chapter 8 for complete details.

Once you meet these requirements, two things need to happen:

- The remote users' client computers must define a Dial-Up Networking connection.

- The remote users' client computers must make the connection and be logged on by the server.

Once these things happen, your remote users should be able to dial into your server without further delay.

Microsoft Fax Server

Like RAS, Microsoft Fax Server was installed on your server during setup if you selected the Complete Installation option. You're not quite ready to begin faxing the world yet, however; you must first create fax printers and make sure your users have the appropriate client software installed on their client computers. Complete details on all aspects of faxing can be found in Chapter 15, so we won't repeat ourselves here.

And with that, you're ready to loose your employees on your brand-new Small Business Server network. As you'll see below, you might still want to do a few more things before too much time goes by, but at this point your network should be fully functional.

More Typical Postinstallation Tasks

Last but not least, we'd like to suggest some other postinstallation tasks that make sense now that your network is up and running. Here are our ideas for your consideration, along with cross-references to the chapters that explain how to do what needs to be done.

- Add shared folders for company information (Chapter 10).
- Set up e-mail distribution lists (Chapter 14).
- Create a company Internet site (Chapter 20).
- Create an internal company intranet site (Chapter 21).

Of course, you can always do these things later on, but the first two items are better done sooner rather than later because they're necessary for everyday work.

POINTS TO REMEMBER

- The To Do List should be your first stop after installing Small Business Server. It's a good starting point for performing the tasks that must be accomplished before your network is ready to go.

- Other common postinstallation tasks include configuring additional hardware; connecting your employees to the network; connecting to the Internet; and setting up RAS, Dial-Up Networking, and Microsoft

Fax Server. Depending on your situation, you might want to do some or all of the things we described in the previous section.

♦ Some other typical postinstallation tasks—including adding shared folders, setting up e-mail distribution lists, and creating company intranet and/or Internet sites—aren't quite as pressing, but you might find them beneficial to your company or organization.

WHAT'S NEXT?

In this chapter, you learned how to complete and customize your Small Business Server installation. Next we'll tell you about disk configuration and setting up hard disks for maximum safety and security.

Chapter 7

Configuring and Managing Disks

94	**The Search for Disaster Protection**
94	**Defining Our Terms**
96	**Managing Disks**
97	**Using Disk Administrator**
99	**Making Partitions**
	Creating a Primary Partition — 99
	Creating an Extended Partition — 102
	Creating Logical Drives — 103
103	**Using Volume Sets**
	Creating a Volume Set — 104
	Extending a Volume Set — 105
	Deleting an Existing Volume Set — 107
107	**Using Mirror Sets**
	Creating a Mirror Set — 108
	Breaking a Mirror Set — 109
112	**Creating an Emergency Repair Disk**
113	**Points to Remember**
113	**What's Next**

Chapter 7
Configuring and Managing Disks

What does a server really provide on a network? Probably its most important services are giving users the ability to store files (sometimes very big ones) and providing those files when they're asked for. Most of the critical files you need to run your business are stored on the server, and you can't afford to lose them.

The Search for Disaster Protection

Traditionally, large businesses used a variety of techniques to ensure that files stored on a server were both secure and safe. These solutions tended to be expensive, but when spread across all of the supported workstations and buried in a large MIS budget, they were feasible. The same solutions would *not* be feasible or acceptable in most small businesses, but that doesn't change the very real need of those small businesses to protect themselves from disaster.

Solutions have been available for small businesses to provide redundancy and disaster protection of the disk subsystems, but these solutions have generally been hardware based and thus substantially more expensive than many businesses can afford. With Microsoft Small Business Server, you have an excellent software solution that provides full data redundancy and disaster recovery without a huge cost.

The underlying Microsoft Windows NT Server 4 operating system in Small Business Server uses the Disk Administrator application to provide both disk mirroring and volume sets. Mirroring creates a complete copy of your hard drive partitions on a completely separate hard drive of equivalent or greater size. If either of these fails, you still have full access to your data while you replace the failed drive.

Volume sets let you extend the size of your existing hard drives without having to add a drive letter. So if your database is running out of room, you can add a hard drive and then create a volume set that spans the old hard drive with the new one, creating a single partition that is the size of the two added together.

Defining Our Terms

Before we go through the details of how to use Disk Administrator, we should go over some definitions to make sure we're all using the same words to mean the same things.

- Physical drive—the actual hard drive itself, including case, electronics, platters, and all that stuff. Not terribly important to Disk Administrator.

- Partition—a portion of the hard drive that acts as a single unit. In many cases, this is the entire hard drive space, but it needn't be.

- Primary partition—a portion of the hard drive that's been marked as a potentially bootable unit by an operating system. MS-DOS can support only a single primary partition, but Windows NT can support multiple ones. There can be only four primary partitions on any hard drive.

- Extended partition—a nonbootable portion of the hard drive that can be subdivided into logical drives. Each hard drive can have only a single extended partition, but the partition can be divided into multiple logical drives.

- Logical drive—a section, or partition, of a hard drive that acts as a single unit. An extended partition might, for example, be divided into multiple logical drives.

- Volume set—a collection of portions of hard drives used as a single unit. A volume set is formatted like a single drive and can have a drive letter assigned to it, but it spans multiple physical drives. A volume set provides no fault tolerance and actually increases your exposure to failure, but it does permit you to make more efficient use of the available hard drive space.

- RAID (Redundant Array of Inexpensive Drives)—the use of multiple hard drives in an array to provide for larger volume size, fault tolerance, and increased performance. RAID comes in different levels, such as RAID 0, RAID 1, RAID 5, and so forth. Higher numbers don't indicate greater performance or fault tolerance, just different methods of doing the job. Small Business Server only supports RAID 1 (mirroring) with Disk Administrator.

- Stripe set—a collection of multiple hard drive portions serving as a single entity. Unlike a volume set, though, it uses special formatting to write to each of the portions equally in a stripe to provide increased throughput. Like a volume set, a stripe set doesn't provide any fault tolerance and actually increases your exposure to failure. A stripe set is often referred to as RAID 0, although this is a misnomer because plain striping includes no redundancy. Striping is supported in Small Business Server, but we don't recommend it because it provides no redundancy (use a mirror set for that) and doesn't get you out of a space crunch (use volume sets for that).

- Mirror set—a pair of hard drive partitions that contain exactly the same data and appear to the world as a single entity. Disk mirroring can use two drives on the same hard drive controller or it can use separate controllers, in which case it is sometimes referred to as *duplexing*. In the event of failure of either of the hard drives, the other hard drive can be split off from it and continue to provide complete access to the data stored on the drive, providing a high degree of fault tolerance. This technique is called RAID 1.

- SLED (Single Large Expensive Disk)—used less often than RAID, this is the opposite strategy. Rather than using several cheap hard drives and using redundancy to provide fault tolerance, you buy the best hard drive you can and bet your entire network on it. If this doesn't sound like a good idea to you, you're right. It's not.

Managing Disks

Your entry into managing your disk resources in Small Business Server is the Manage Disks page of the Small Business Server console, as shown in Figure 7.01.

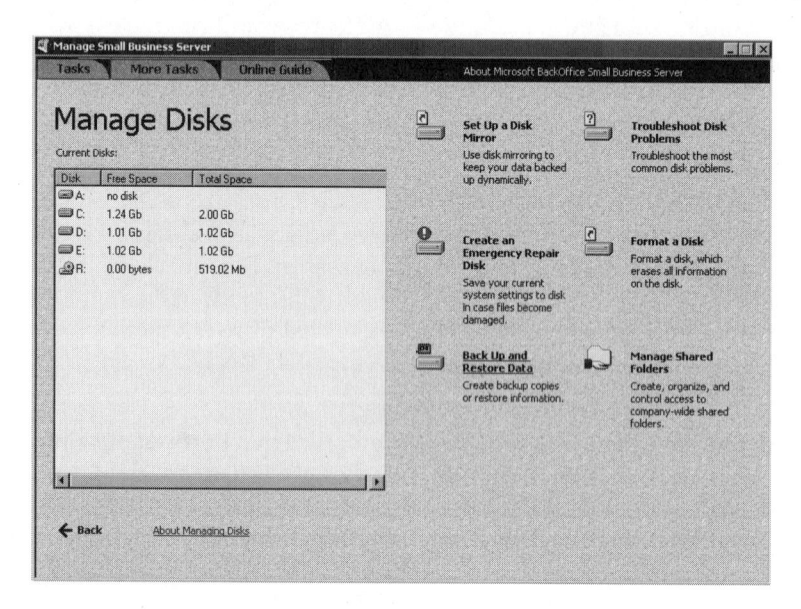

FIGURE 7.01

The Manage Disks page of the Small Business Server console lets you control and manage your disk resources.

From here, you might be taken to Disk Administrator, the Backup application, or the Manage Shared Folders page. Or you might simply get instructions on how to do a task using another set of tools. Since most of what we're concerned with in this chapter is the Disk Administrator functions, let's go there first. Clicking on the Set Up A Disk Mirror icon opens a help screen, shown in Figure 7.02, that guides you through the process of creating a mirror and also gives you a link to open Disk Administrator. Or you can open Disk Administrator directly by going to the Start menu and choosing Programs, Administrative Tools (Common), and then Disk Administrator.

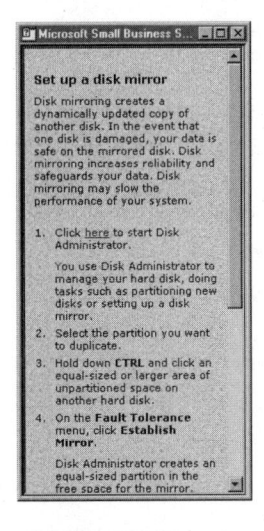

FIGURE 7.02

The instructions for setting up a disk mirror provide a link to Disk Administrator.

Using Disk Administrator

Disk Administrator is your tool for managing the hard disk subsystem, including removable drives such as Bernoulli, Zip, and SyQuest drives. The main screen is shown in Figure 7.03 on the following page. You can use Disk Administrator to create, modify, or remove partitions and format drives and to assign hard drive letters to specific volumes, as well as to create mirror sets to protect you from drive failure.

FIGURE 7.03

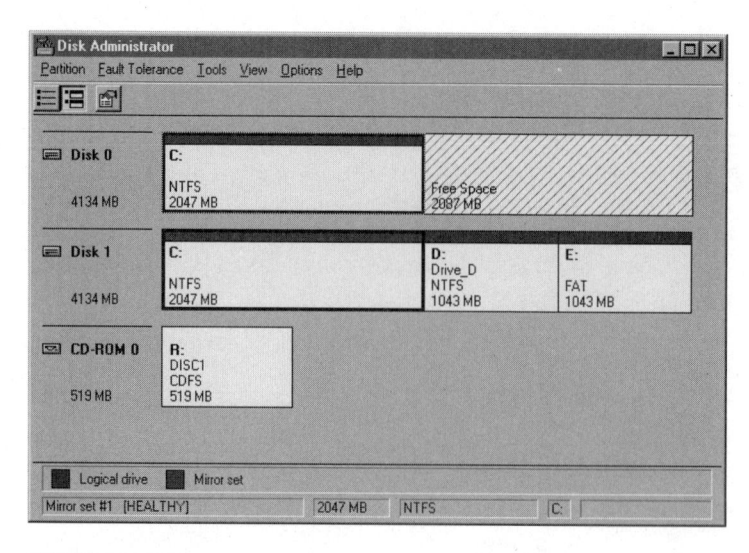

The Disk Administrator screen.

If your Disk Administrator screen doesn't look like the one in Figure 7.03, choose Disk Configuration from the View menu.

At any time when you're in Disk Administrator, you can point at a portion of a disk and click with the right mouse button to open a popup menu. For an existing partition, you'll see this menu:

When you right-click on an area of free space, you'll see this one:

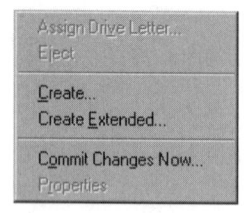

Both provide shortcuts to many of the functions described later in this chapter.

98 INSTALLATION AND SETUP

Making Partitions

A physical hard drive can be divided into as many as four partitions, of which one can be an extended partition. However, if you attempt to use Disk Administrator to create more than a single primary partition, you'll get a warning message like that shown in Figure 7.04, telling you that what you're about to do isn't supported in MS-DOS. This is pretty much irrelevant information, since you're not likely to be running MS-DOS much on your Small Business Server system. Furthermore, with Small Business Server, you should be using all NTFS partitions, so you wouldn't be able to see them from MS-DOS anyway.

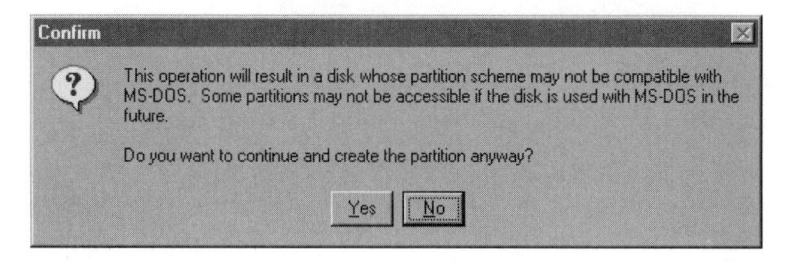

FIGURE 7.04

Disk Administrator will warn you before letting you do something that isn't supported by MS-DOS.

You can, however, create an extended partition in addition to the primary partition for the drive without Disk Administrator complaining. An extended partition lets you divide a drive into multiple drive letters for logical grouping. This can be useful for organizing your available drive space into different functions, but in the long run the more drive letters you have, the more administration will be required. You should weigh this potential increase in administrative work against the problems of having a single, humongous drive with everything on it; finding anything on one big drive is difficult. Your particular situation will dictate what the best balance is.

Creating a Primary Partition

To create a primary partition with Disk Administrator, follow these steps:

1. Select the free space that will contain the partition, and choose Create from the Partition menu. This will bring up the Create Primary Partition dialog box, shown in Figure 7.05 on the following page.

FIGURE 7.05

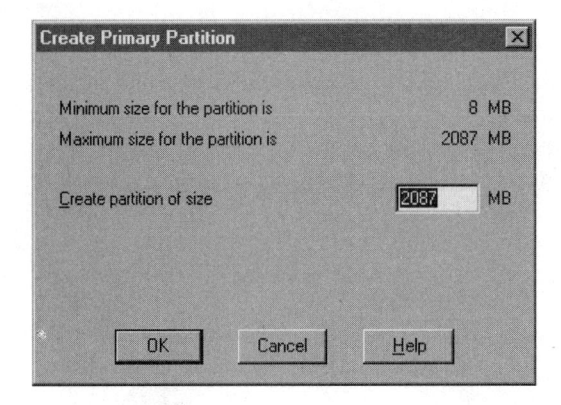

Disk Administrator's Create Primary Partition dialog box.

2. Once you create a new primary partition, Disk Administrator will immediately assign a drive letter to it, and your new display will look like Figure 7.06. This new drive letter, however, doesn't really mean anything and doesn't actually exist until you commit to the change you just made. So you can't, for example, select the new partition and format it—Disk Administrator won't let you.

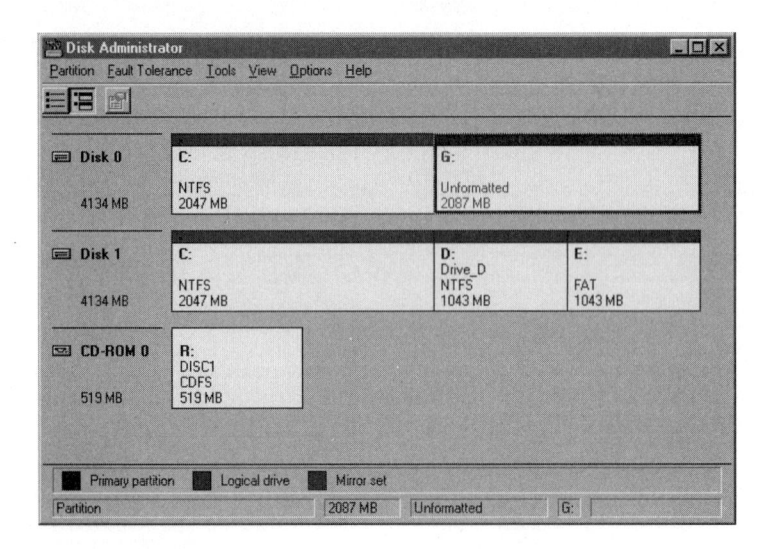

FIGURE 7.06

Disk Administrator automatically assigns a drive letter to the new primary partition.

100 INSTALLATION AND SETUP

3. Choose Commit Changes Now from the Partition menu, and you'll get one last chance to back out before your new partition is permanent, as shown in Figure 7.07.

4. Once you commit to the changes, you'll see an acknowledgment and some sage advice, as shown in Figure 7.08. Disk Administrator will suggest that you update your Emergency Repair Disk with the new partition information. As we'll see in Chapter 28, this is good advice that will make it easier to recover in case of a catastrophic failure.

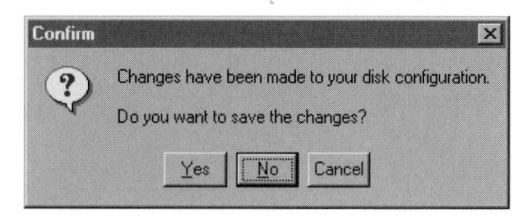

FIGURE 7.07

Disk Administrator gives you a chance to back out before it makes the new partition permanent.

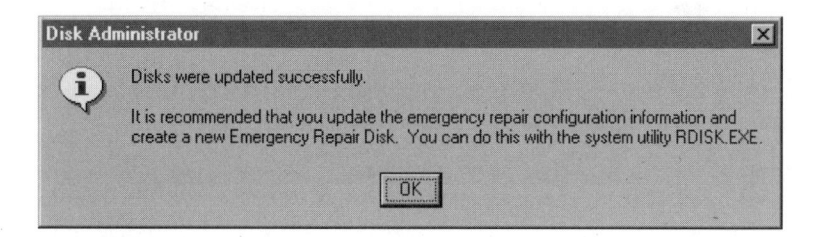

FIGURE 7.08

Whenever you make changes to your disk configuration, you should update your repair disk.

5. Now the Format command is enabled on the Tools menu. Choose it, and you'll see the dialog box shown in Figure 7.09 on the following page. Type a volume label, if you wish, for the new drive and specify either FAT or NTFS formatting. Click OK and you'll get a last-minute warning that any data on the volume will be overwritten.

FIGURE 7.09

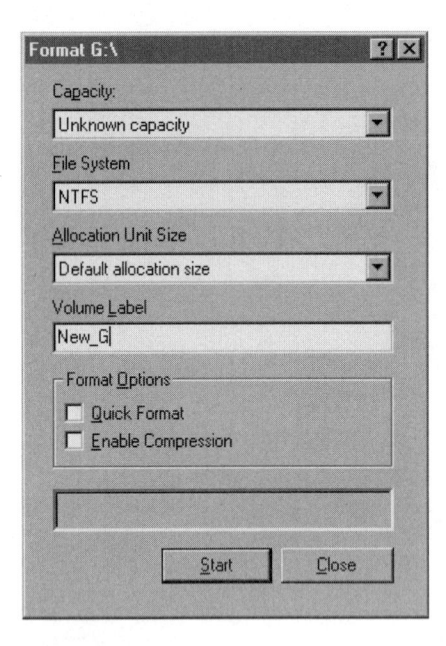

In the Format dialog box, you can format a drive as either NTFS or FAT and add a label to the volume.

6. Click OK again and the formatting will begin. While the formatting is going on, the dialog box will update you using a progress bar.

7. When the formatting is complete, you'll get a message saying so. Click OK, and then click Close to close the Format dialog box.

> **Tip**
>
> *If you have Microsoft Windows Explorer (or any other application) open to display the contents of any partition, Disk Administrator will not let you modify that partition—you'll be told it's "locked," or something similar.*

Creating an Extended Partition

You can create a single, extended partition on a hard drive, ranging in size from 1 MB to all the free space available. If you do create an extended partition, the maximum number of primary partitions on the drive is reduced to three.

The steps to create an extended partition are much like the ones in the preceding section for creating a primary partition:

1. Open Disk Administrator, and select an area shown as Free Space on the hard drive.
2. Choose Create Extended from the Partition menu.
3. In the dialog box that opens, select the size you want (you don't have to use all the available free space) and click OK.

Creating Logical Drives

Once you create the extended partition, you can create one or more logical drives:

1. Click on the extended partition to select it, and then choose Create from the Partition menu.
2. In the Create Logical Drive dialog box, enter the size of the logical drive you want to create.
3. Click OK, and the drive will be set up.

When you exit Disk Administrator, you'll be asked if you want to save the changes you made to your disk configuration. This is your last chance to backtrack. Click No and the changes will not be made permanent. Click Yes and the changes will be made. Depending on what changes you made to the disk configuration, this might result in the system rebooting. For this reason, as well as common sense, it's a good idea to schedule your disk maintenance tasks for a time when no one else is using the system or might be inconvenienced by an unexpected reboot. Unfortunately, Disk Administrator will not let you finish your disk changes and then schedule a reboot for some later time, holding the changes in abeyance until that point. For reasons known only to Microsoft, this is not supported.

Using Volume Sets

Volume sets do not provide increased protection against data loss, but they can be a useful tool for taking two or more smaller partitions and creating a single larger partition that can get you out of a bind if you're running out of space in a critical file system. Volume sets were more crucial in the past, when you wanted to be able to use every last scrap of expensive and scarce hard drive space. As hard drives have gotten larger and cheaper, the need for volume sets has declined. Nevertheless, if you have some old, smaller hard drives hanging around that don't provide enough space on their own to be useful, you can easily create a volume set out of them. Or, if you find your users suddenly running out of space and you don't want to do major rearrangement of drive letters to install a new, larger hard drive, you can simply extend the current partition onto that new hard drive.

A volume set combines the unused space on one or more drives (up to 32 drives) into a single entity that is larger and thus more useful.

Creating a Volume Set

To create a volume set or to extend an existing partition or a volume set, follow these steps:

1. Open Disk Administrator, and select the first area that you want to include in the volume set. Hold down the Ctrl key, and click on any pieces of free space that you want to include in the volume set.

2. After you select all the pieces, choose Create Volume Set or Extend Volume Set from the Partition menu, and you'll see the dialog box shown in Figure 7.10. You can use the maximum size shown or enter a smaller size. Click OK.

NOTE

You'll see the Create Volume Set command if you're starting out with no existing partition in the new volume set, and you'll see the Extend Volume Set command if you're extending an existing partition.

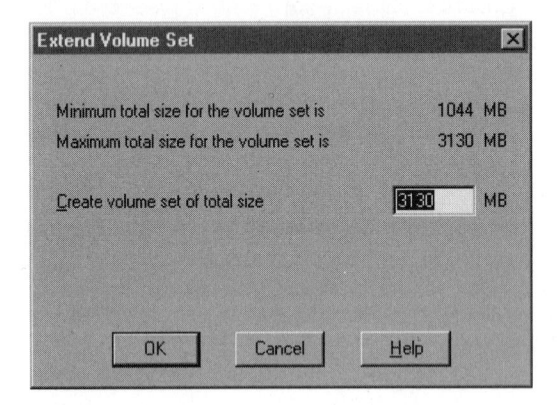

FIGURE 7.10

You can extend a partition to another drive to create a single, larger drive.

3. Disk Administrator will highlight in bright yellow the pieces that make up the volume set. Before you can use the volume set, you'll need to format it, but you can't do that until you commit to the change. Choose Commit Changes Now from the Partition menu, which will bring up the Confirm dialog box, shown earlier in Figure 7.07.

4. To accept the changes, click OK. You'll get a valuable reminder to update the Emergency Repair Disk. Click OK again.

WARNING!

When you click OK in the Confirm dialog box, Disk Administrator might warn you that this change requires a reboot of your system. If it does, you're pretty much stuck. When you click OK, Windows NT will start the shutdown procedure, so be sure you're really in a position to shut down your server. And be prepared to wait—it might take a while for the reboot to complete because the formatting might take place during the reboot.

After you restart Small Business Server (if that was required, and it usually is), you might have at least one task left before you can use the new volume set. Start Disk Administrator again, and select the volume set you just created. It'll be highlighted in yellow (unless you've changed the default colors for Disk Administrator, of course) and might have either Unknown or Unformatted as the format type if you created your volume set entirely out of unused, unpartitioned space. If you're simply extending an existing NTFS partition, it will be formatted exactly as the original piece was.

Choose Format from the Tools menu, and add a label if you want. You can even format the volume set with a FAT partition, but it makes no sense because you won't have access to it from MS-DOS or Microsoft Windows 95 anyway. Also, FAT partitions, including volume sets, cannot be extended. Only NTFS partitions and volume sets can be extended. Once you confirm that you really want to format the volume set, Disk Administrator will finally format it and assign the next available drive letter to it. This is fine for most situations, but if you need the drive to have a specific drive letter, simply set the drive letter by choosing Drive Letter from the Tools menu and changing the drive letter.

Once you format the volume set, it will be immediately available without further administration. To your applications, it will appear as a drive letter no different from any other. And it will be treated in the same way for sharing to the network.

NOTE

There is one other important thing you need to keep in mind about volume sets. If any drive of the volume set fails, the entire volume set becomes unavailable. So rather than being more reliable than a standard drive, a volume set is actually less reliable, since the failure of any portion of the volume set will cause the entire volume set to fail.

Extending a Volume Set

Once you create a volume set, you can easily extend it to add additional drives or portions of drives. This is one of the most important benefits of using volume sets, since you can quickly provide additional drive space to your users without having to worry about changes to drive letter assignments or other such problems. You simply add the additional disk and then extend the volume set to include the new disk.

The process takes one or two reboots of the system, however, so plan accordingly. The first time, you'll need to shut the system down to physically add the new drive. Of course, if you're merely using additional free space from existing drives, you'll be spared this shutdown, but a reboot is required later in the process.

To extend an existing volume set, you follow essentially the same steps that you do when creating a new volume set from scratch:

1. Open Disk Administrator, and select the volume set to be extended.

2. Hold down the Ctrl key, and select the free space you want to add to the volume set. A black border will appear around the selected areas.

3. Right-click on the selected free space, and choose Extend Volume Set from the popup menu.

4. In the dialog box that opens, enter the *total* amount of space the volume set will contain or accept the default of all available space. The dialog box shows a minimum amount (the current volume set plus 1 MB per selected area) and a maximum amount (the current volume set plus *all* the available free space you selected). Click OK.

5. Right-click on the new volume set, and choose Commit Changes Now from the popup menu.

NOTE

You can also use the popup menu to change the volume set's drive letter from the default one.

6. Respond to the various dialog boxes, including the last one, to reboot the server.

This reboot will take a bit longer than usual. The new piece of the volume set must be formatted, which can take a while. And since this is all done before the login prompt, it can be a bit unnerving. But don't worry, the additional piece will be automatically formatted and appended to the existing volume set without disturbing the existing data.

NOTE

Even though Disk Administrator should be able to extend a volume set without losing any data on the existing set, always make sure you have at least one verified backup, and preferably two, before doing any disk reconfiguration. Never forget Murphy's Law!

Deleting an Existing Volume Set

To delete an existing volume set, select the volume set by clicking on any portion and then choose Delete from the Partition menu. This will bring up the dialog box shown in Figure 7.11, warning you that all data in the volume set will be lost.

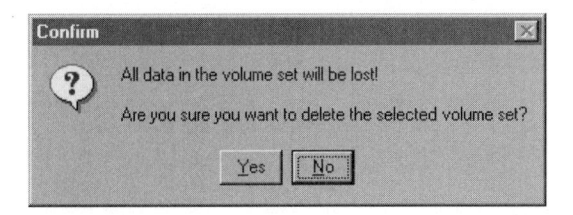

FIGURE 7.11

Disk Administrator warns you that deleting a volume set will delete all data within it.

Click Yes and the volume set will be deleted. But you'll still be asked if you want to commit to the changes before this action becomes final.

You can make a volume set larger without having to delete it first and without losing any data. But you can't make it smaller without drastic action. You have to completely delete the volume set and recreate it, thus losing any data on it. Our wish list includes more dynamic resizing of partitions without requiring a reboot of the server.

Using Mirror Sets

The primary method of providing data integrity and redundancy in Small Business Server is RAID 1, or mirroring. (Microsoft literature refers to this configuration as a *mirror set*.) Actually, in the case of Small Business Server, this can be *disk mirroring*, which is two disks with identical information written to them at the same time and running off the same controller, or it can be *disk duplexing*, which uses a separate controller for each disk, eliminating the single point of failure in the controller. This is the only fault-tolerant array supported by Small Business Server, although, as we mentioned earlier, you can also use third-party hardware RAID controllers. In full Windows NT Server 4, you also have the option of running RAID 5 in software, but we think that RAID 5 is best left for hardware solutions.

A mirrored drive can be read in substantially less time than a standalone hard drive, since both halves of the mirror can be given independent instructions to read data at the same time. The speed of a mirror set is virtually as fast as that of the individual standalone drives, since both drives can be written to independently. This is especially true if you are duplexing instead of simply mirroring.

Creating a Mirror Set

To create a mirror set, first select the partition that will be the master of the mirror and then select a piece of free space on another disk that is at least as large as the partition you will be mirroring. In our example, shown in Figure 7.12, we'll mirror the D partition of disk 2 onto the open space on disk 0.

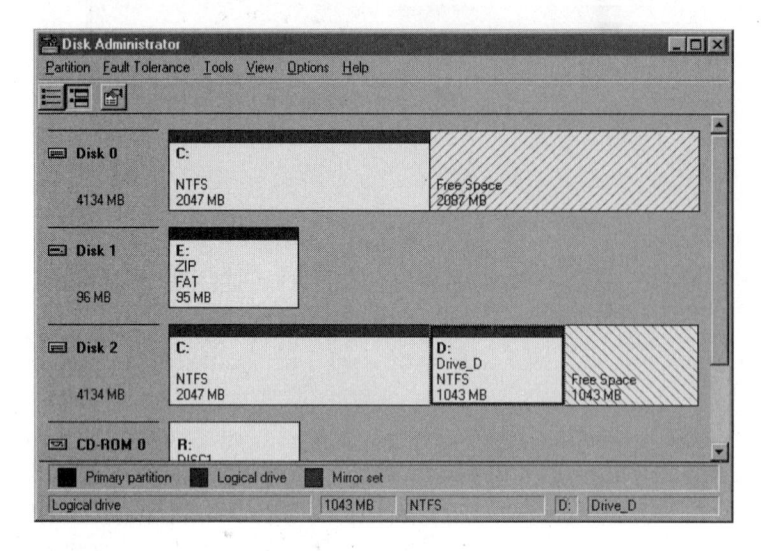

FIGURE 7.12

We're about to mirror drive D of disk 2 onto disk 0.

1. Click on the partition that will be the *master* of the mirror (Drive_D in the figure).

2. Hold down the Ctrl key while clicking on the free space that will be converted into a mirror of the original. Both will be outlined in black.

3. Choose Establish Mirror from the Fault Tolerance menu, and the display will immediately change to show the mirror set, as shown in Figure 7.13. However, like almost everything else you do in Disk Administrator, nothing really happens until you commit to the changes.

4. Right-click on one of the mirrors, choose Commit Changes Now from the popup menu, and confirm that you really mean it.

FIGURE 7.13

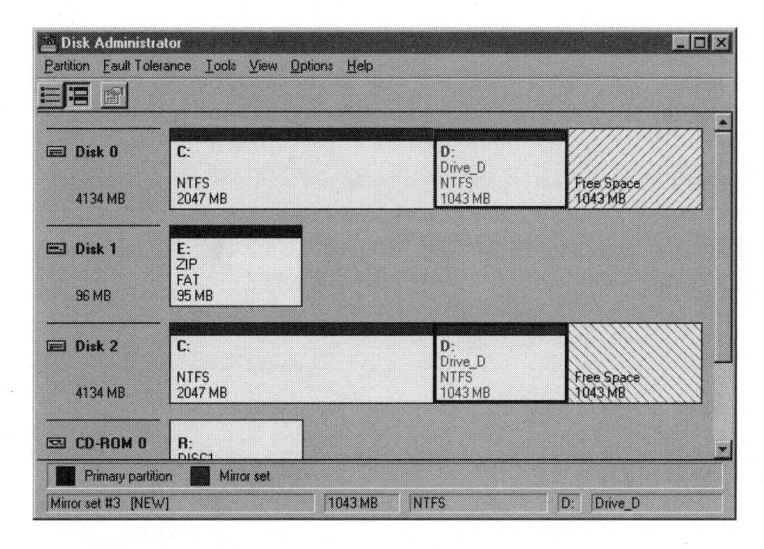

Disk Administrator immediately identifies the mirror set, but it won't duplicate the data until you commit to the changes.

You'll get a warning about updating your Emergency Repair Disk to show the new information, and you'll have to acknowledge that advice. Finally, Disk Administrator will actually make the changes and your hard drive will start grinding away. If you get tired of the constant commit-confirm-advise cycle, just remember that it's for your own good.

Disk Administrator's status bar will change to show that the new mirror is initializing. Your original disk will continue to be available while this goes on, which is nice, but your overall disk performance will suffer a bit while the data is being copied.

When the mirror is fully initialized and the status line in the Disk Administrator has changed to HEALTHY, the process is complete. Now when there's a change to the data stored on the drive, the change will be written simultaneously to both disks. Any data that needs to be read from the drive can be read from either half of the mirror, and thus the overall read access time will be substantially less than with a single disk partition.

Breaking a Mirror Set

If there's a hardware failure in one portion of the mirror set, you must break the mirror set to recover from the failure. You'll continue to have access to your data during the process, however.

In fact, your first clue to the failure might appear when you start Disk Administrator and see the error message shown in Figure 7.14. Event Viewer will also have recorded the problem.

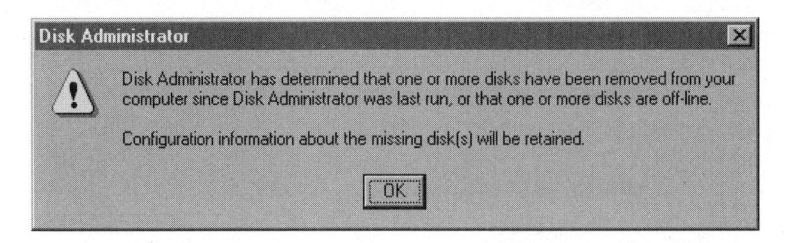

FIGURE 7.14

Disk Administrator will notify you that a disk is missing and will save the configuration of the disk.

After you acknowledge this warning, Disk Administrator will start and you'll see the half of the mirror set that still exists—it will still show as a mirror set—but now the status bar will show BROKEN next to the mirror description. You can continue to use your disk, but you will have no redundancy until the failed hardware is replaced.

To replace the hardware, you should first break the mirror and then shut down the system. To break the mirror, right-click on the portion that remains and choose Break Mirror from the popup menu. This will bring up a warning message. Click Yes to confirm that you really do want to break the mirror. The Disk Administrator display will change to show only a single partition where the mirror was. But the actual break won't occur until you commit to the changes. If Disk Administrator can't lock the disk because a process is using some portion of the disk, you'll get an error message like that in Figure 7.15.

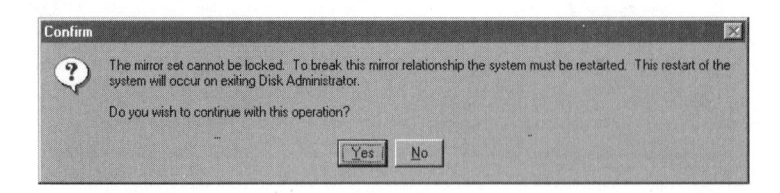

FIGURE 7.15

Disk Administrator must be able to lock the mirrored drive in order to break the mirror. In some cases, a reboot might be required.

At this point, you have two choices: You can figure out which process has an open file on the drive, shut it down, and then try again; or you can simply acknowledge that Disk Administrator is the boss and let it reboot the server. Your choice will depend on the particular situation. Let's face it, you'll have to bring the system down soon, anyway, to replace the failed drive. But if you're not ready to do that yet, click No and Disk Administrator will back out. You can leave the mirrored drive alone until you're ready to actually replace the hardware.

Once you replace the failed hardware of your mirror set, simply follow the steps above to reestablish the mirror just as if it were new. If the failure was caused by a bad controller or a loose cable on a duplexed drive—or some other circumstance in which the actual drive was unaffected—the system still won't be able to reestablish the mirror without it being broken first. So if you postpone breaking the mirror set until after you replace the hardware, when you restart the system and then open Disk Administrator, you'll see the mirror set in place but the status bar will show the mirror set as broken. This means it won't actually be functioning as a mirror set until you reestablish the mirror—and you can't reestablish the mirror set unless you break it first. (Hey, we don't make up these rules, you know.)

Go ahead and break the mirror by right-clicking on the existing partition and choosing Break Mirror from the popup menu. After the mirror is broken, you'll see two individual partitions, like the ones shown in Figure 7.16.

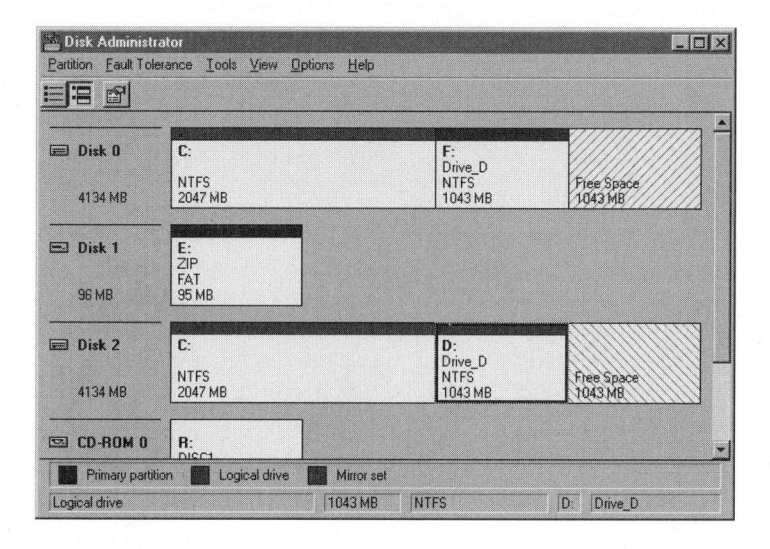

FIGURE 7.16

Once you break the mirror, you might see both original partitions, but you must be sure to remember which one was unbroken.

CHAPTER 7 *Configuring and Managing Disks* **111**

Even if you're dealing with a situation in which the drives themselves were never damaged, the data probably won't be the same on the two partitions (which is why you should break the mirror before you replace the failed hardware). If you get in this situation, you *must* remember which was the failed portion. You'll need to delete that partition to create unused space and then reestablish the mirror. If you accidentally delete the partition that was good, you'll end up with potential data loss all the way back to when the mirror was *originally* broken. Not at all what you want.

NOTE

> *Mirrored partitions of the boot partition require special handling in the event of a failure and are covered in Chapter 28, where we talk about disaster recovery. Mirrored boot partitions do provide full recoverability, as you would hope and expect, but recovery requires a special boot disk and somewhat different procedures depending on what kind of hardware you're running, Intel x86 or RISC.*

Creating an Emergency Repair Disk

Whenever you make changes to your disk configuration, you should make a new version of your Emergency Repair Disk (ERD). The ERD is the one tool that makes recovering from a disaster more likely to be successful, since it contains a wide variety of information about your system, including how your hard drives are configured. Without the ERD, your chances of recovery in case of a catastrophic failure are materially less than they are with it. So please keep your ERD up to date.

You can create an ERD on the Manage Disks page of the Small Business Server console (shown earlier in Figure 7.01). When you click on Create An Emergency Repair Disk, Windows NT will automatically save current information onto the hard drive and then prompt you to insert a floppy disk.

When you insert a floppy disk into the A drive and click OK, the disk will be formatted and the current configuration information will be saved onto it. When the process is done, you'll be warned that the disk contains sensitive security information and you'll be prompted to store it in a secure location. This is good advice, but we think the security issue is likely to be less important than making sure the disk is stored where you can find it when you need it.

POINTS TO REMEMBER

- Disk Administrator is your tool for managing the hard disk subsystem, including removable drives such as Jaz, Zip, and SyQuest.
- Mirroring is the only fault-tolerant array supported by Small Business Server, but you can use a third-party hardware RAID controller to provide other kinds of RAID, such as RAID 5 and RAID 0+1.
- Volume sets and stripe sets (RAID 0) provide no fault tolerance and actually increase your exposure to drive failure. We don't recommend stripe sets for Small Business Server.
- You can use volume sets to get out of a space crunch fairly quickly without having to completely rearrange drive letters, move files around, change shortcuts, and so forth.
- Volume sets can be extended only if they are formatted with NTFS.
- Disk pieces for stripe sets and mirror sets should all be of essentially equal size and characteristics.
- You must break a failed mirror set before you can rebuild it.
- Always, always, always update your Emergency Repair Disk whenever you make changes to your disks.

WHAT'S NEXT

In this chapter, we covered the tasks of managing your disks, including how to create mirror sets to protect your data in the event of a catastrophic hard drive failure and how to use volume sets to extend an existing partition when it gets low on space. In the next chapter, we'll cover how to manage the users on your Small Business Server system, including adding new users, assigning them privileges, and changing their passwords.

Part Three
Performing Basic Tasks

The third part of this book provides details about ongoing administrative tasks: setting up and maintaining user accounts, setting shares and permissions, adding client computers, and managing networked printers. This part also includes a chapter on the critical task of backing up your data.

Chapter 8

Maintaining User Information

118	Adding a New User
119	Removing a User Account
120	Reviewing or Changing User Information
121	Changing a User's Password
122	Managing User Access
124	User Manager for Domains
	Setting Logon Hours 124
	Setting Password Rules 125
128	Managing User Rights
	User Rights Policy 128
130	Using System Policy to Manage User Environments
131	Using System Policy Editor
	Templates 131
	Creating a New Default System Policy 133
	Connecting to the Registry Remotely 136
136	Points to Remember
136	What's Next?

Chapter 8
Maintaining User Information

Network administrators everywhere agree that running a network would be great fun were it not for those pesky users. This is such a well-worn joke that it's worthwhile to pause and consider whether there's any truth to it. While it's accurate to say that some users show amazing resourcefulness in their ability to screw things up, it's also true that a lot of user problems are not the fault of the users themselves. Often, it's the way accounts are set up and permissions are granted that sets the stage for trouble.

In this chapter, you'll find all the necessary information on setting up accounts for your users and configuring those accounts to make them suitable for your network. Microsoft Small Business Server provides a single interface for managing just about every aspect of user accounts. We'll explain how to add and remove users from the network as well as how to adjust information in user accounts.

Adding a New User

Since Small Business Server licenses limit only the number of simultaneous connections to the server, you can have as many user accounts as you need. So create a user account for *every person* who uses the network. Not only is this more convenient for users, but also it provides a practical advantage to the administrator. Problems can be a lot easier to troubleshoot if users are not signing on under a series of "borrowed" names. It's not unusual for one person to have more than one account or for two or three people to share a single computer. Whatever the reason, the number of user accounts might well exceed the number of licenses you have.

To add a new user account to Small Business Server, follow these steps:

1. From the Start menu, choose Manage Server.

2. On the Tasks page of the Small Business Server console, click on Manage Users. This will open the page shown in Figure 8.01.

3. Click on the Add A New User icon to start the New Account Wizard.

4. Fill in the various pages of the wizard just as you did when creating an account in Chapter 6.

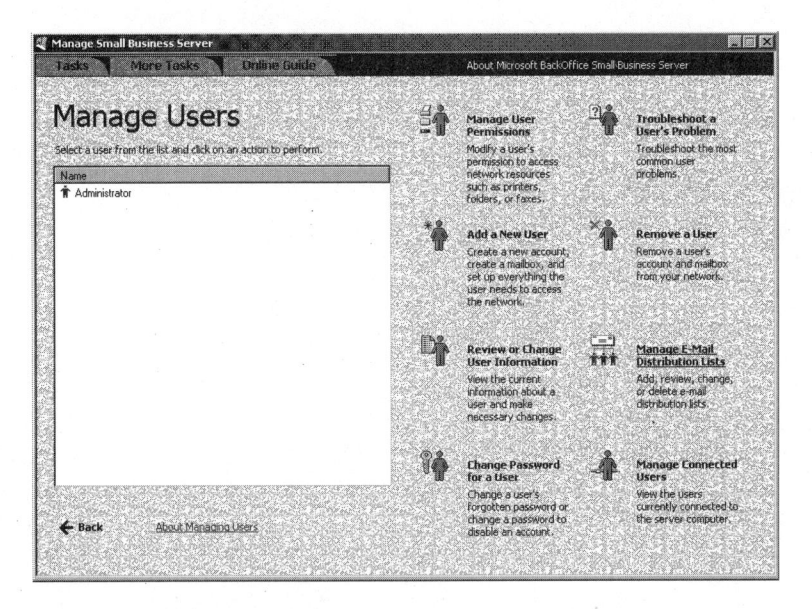

FIGURE 8.01

On this page, you can carry out most tasks relating to user accounts.

5. Click the Finish button on the last page.

6. You'll be asked whether you want to set up a client computer for this user. If you do, click Yes and follow the procedure described in the section titled "Setting Up a Client Computer" in Chapter 6.

When you're all done, you'll be returned to the Manage Users page with the new user added to the list on the left side of the page.

NOTE

To access the Manage Users page, you must be logged on to the server using an account with administrative privileges.

Removing a User Account

When you delete a user account, the user's electronic mail box is also removed. However, any personal folders associated with the account must be deleted manually. To remove a user from your network, take the following steps.

1. Choose Manage Server from the Start menu.
2. On the Tasks page, click on Manage Users.
3. Select the name of the user account you want to delete, and then click on the Remove A User icon. This will open the Delete User Account page of the User Account Wizard. (See Figure 8.02.)
4. To delete this user's account, click Finish; otherwise, click Cancel to abort the operation.

FIGURE 8.02

The Delete User Account page.

Reviewing or Changing User Information

To review or change user information, select a user's name on the left side of the Manage Users page and then click on the Review Or Change User Information icon. This will open the User Account Information page of the User Account Wizard. (See Figure 8.03.) The only difference between creating a new user account and reviewing or changing account information is that a user's account name cannot be changed once an account is created; as you can see, the account name option is grayed out. If it's precisely this information that you want to change, you must delete the user account and create a new one with a different user name.

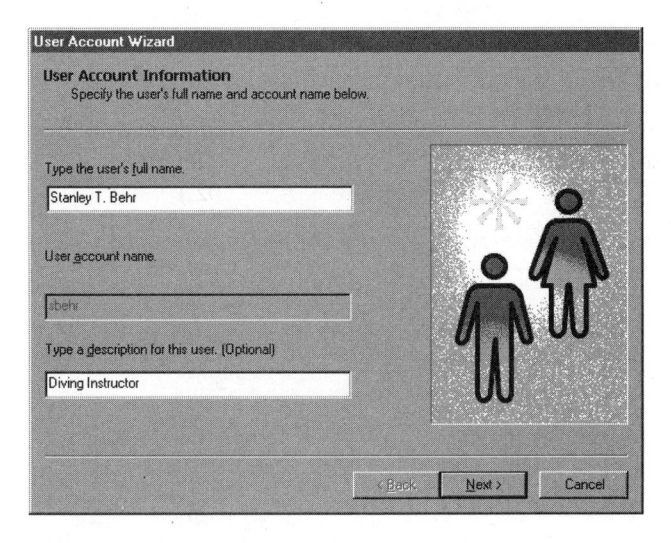

FIGURE 8.03

The User Account Information page with the account name option disabled.

NOTE

When you delete a user account and set up a new one, you must supply the new account with all the shares and permissions. This is true even if the new account is set up with information identical to that of the deleted account, including the account name. Each account is unique.

Changing a User's Password

All too often, users forget passwords. If a password is lost, there's no way to look it up and tell the user what it is. The only solution is for the administrator to change the password. The user can then change it again to something that he or she can (one hopes) remember. To change an existing password, follow these steps:

1. Select the user's name in the list on the left side of the Manage Users page, and then click on the Change Password For A User icon. This starts the Change Password Wizard, which will guide you through all the necessary steps.

2. On the Create A Password page, you can have the wizard generate a password (the default option) or you can specify a password yourself. After you make a selection, click Next.

3. If you opted to let the wizard generate a password, you should see a page that looks like the one in Figure 8.04. Be sure to copy the password from the screen so that you can tell the user what it is. At the bottom of the page, you must specify whether the user can change this password.

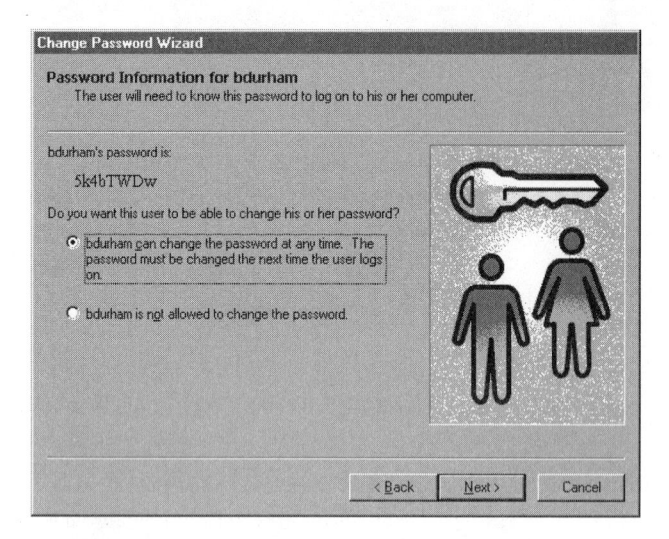

FIGURE 8.04

The Password Information page.

4. If you opted to specify a password, type a password in the Password text box. Regardless of what you type, you'll see asterisks on the screen. To confirm your choice, type the same password in the Confirm Password text box. At the bottom of the page, you must specify whether the user can change this password.

5. The Change Password For User page informs you that this user's password is about to be changed and gives you one last chance to change your mind. Click Finish to complete the operation, or click Back to review or change password information.

Managing User Access

Under most circumstances, the creation of shared folders is all you need in the way of file security. If a folder on the server isn't shared, users can't even see it. To manage a user's access to shared system resources, select his or her name on the left side of the Manage Users page, and then click on the Manage User Permissions icon. This starts the User Resource Wizard (Figure 8.05), which lets you specify what system resources a user has access to.

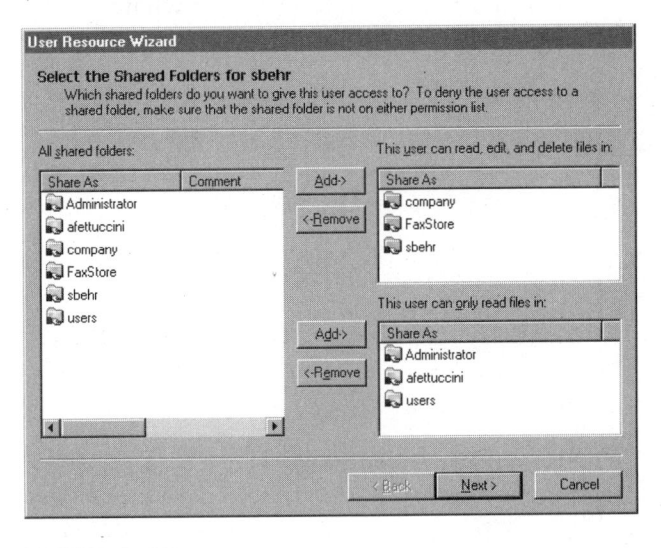

FIGURE 8.05

The Shared Folders page of the User Resource Wizard.

NOTE

If you just installed Small Business Server, the shared folders will be only those created by Small Business Server and automatically shared. For information on how to share existing folders, see Chapter 10.

◆ Troubleshooting a User's Problem

If a user is experiencing difficulties with access or error messages, click on the Troubleshoot A User's Problem icon on the Manage Users page. This starts the online troubleshooting user manual, which displays a list of topics. Select the relevant topic, and follow the instructions. A great many problems can be easily solved with just one or two steps here.

For more help with troubleshooting, see Chapter 27.

CHAPTER 8 *Maintaining User Information* **123**

User Manager for Domains

As we've mentioned before, underneath all the graphics and wizards of Small Business Server, the tools of Microsoft Windows NT Server are still available. Many are quite easy to use and can save you time—especially once you feel comfortable with regular administrative tasks. For example, changing a password can be done in fewer steps and just as simply with User Manager for Domains.

In the following sections, we'll go over some of the settings that only User Manager for Domains can handle. Whether you *need* to make these settings is a decision only you can make.

Setting Logon Hours

When a new user account is created, the user is granted, by default, permission to log on at any time. If you want to restrict someone's logon time to particular hours or particular days, here's how to do it:

1. From the Start menu, choose Programs, Administrative Tools (Common), and then User Manager For Domains.

2. Select the user account you want to change. Choose Properties from the User menu to open the User Properties dialog box, shown in Figure 8.06.

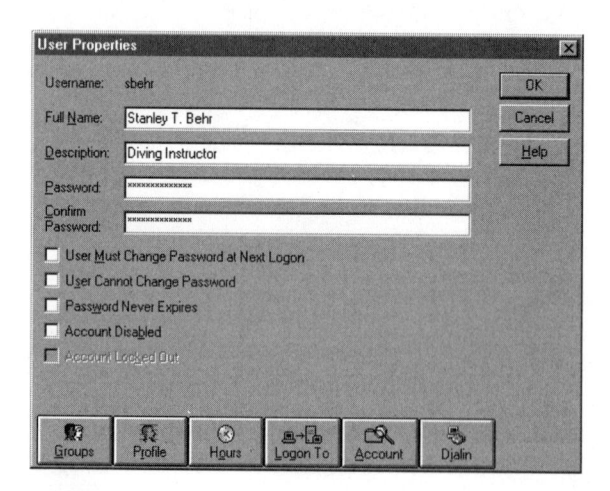

FIGURE 8.06

The User Properties dialog box.

3. Click the Hours button to open the Logon Hours dialog box.

4. To disallow an entire day, click the button for that day and then click Disallow.

5. To disallow certain hours, select the hours and click Disallow. Then click OK.

Figure 8.07 shows the setup for a user who is allowed to log on only between 9 A.M. and 6 P.M., Monday through Friday. If he attempts to log on at any other time, he'll get an error message.

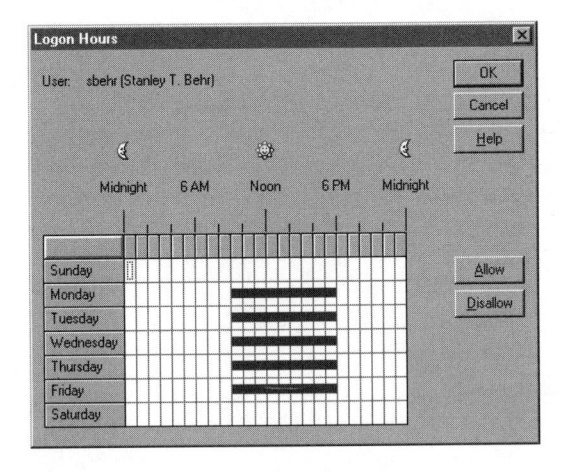

FIGURE 8.07

This user can log on only during business hours.

If this user is still logged on at 6 P.M., when his official hours expire, he'll receive a warning message but will be allowed to continue working; however, he will not be allowed to make any new connections to the server. That means he can work on files he already has open, but he can't fax, check for new e-mail, or do any other procedure that requires a new connection to the server. Once he logs off, he can't log on again until the next business day at 9 A.M.

NOTE

It's possible—though probably not advisable—to forcibly disconnect any user who has exceeded his or her logon hours. See page 127 for details.

Setting Password Rules

In general, users want to have an easy-to-remember password that they don't have to change. Ever. As we explained in Chapter 4, this is a poor idea. But even when the administrator lectures and hectors about changing passwords, users will resist—if only by doing nothing. Luckily, the administrator can force a degree of compliance by setting password rules for all users. To do so, open User Manager for Domains and choose Account from the Policies menu. This will open the dialog box shown in Figure 8.08.

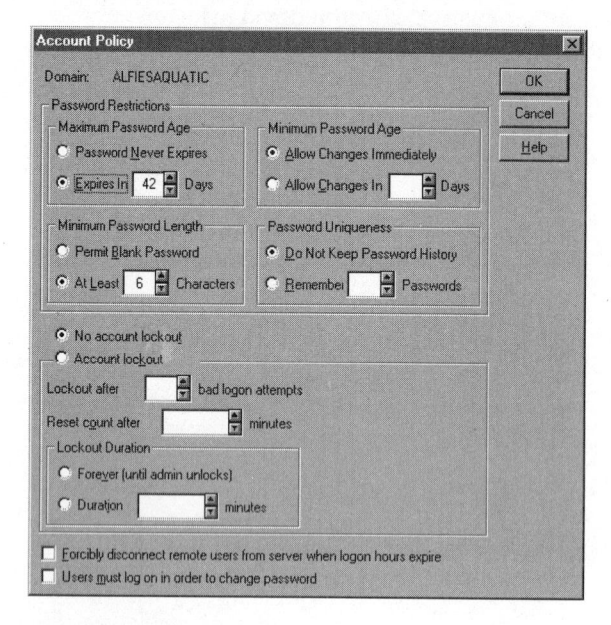

FIGURE 8.08

The Account Policy dialog box.

Setting password restrictions

As you can see, there are plenty of options under Password Restrictions for setting password rules that stick:

- Maximum Password Age—sets the amount of time a password can be in effect before the system requires the user to choose a new one.

- Minimum Password Age—determines how long a password must be used before a new one can be chosen. This protects against users who, when required to enter a new password, do so and then immediately switch back to their old favorite.

- Minimum Password Length—sets a minimum number of characters. Short passwords are easier to guess, so it's best to require a password of at least 6 to 8 characters.

- Password Uniqueness—sets the number of new passwords that a user must employ before reusing that old favorite. If you set a value here, you must specify a password age under Minimum Password Age.

Account lockout

Farther down in the dialog box is a section called Account Lockout. If you fill in this section (in other words, select anything other than No Account Lockout), the provisions will apply to every user account in the domain.

NOTE

Stricter security is called for if your network employs dial-up connections. The easier it is for an outsider to get at your logon screen, the more precautions you should take.

Given enough time and tries, most passwords can be guessed. To prevent this, you can set the number of times or length of time that someone can try to log on before being locked out of the system:

- Lockout After—sets the number of times a user can try to log on before being locked out. You can probably assume that anyone who can't log on after five tries has either forgotten the password or is an intruder.

- Reset Count After—sets the number of minutes the system will wait after a set of bad logon attempts before a logon can be attempted again. A high number here will ensure that the user will contact the administrator about the problem. (You can decide how you feel about that.)

- Lockout Duration—Sets the length of time that an account will be locked out. But if you're going to use lockout at all, you should use the Forever option. That way, no one can attempt to break in to the network without you learning of it. For example, if you specify only a limited period, it can expire before the legitimate user returns to the workstation. This legitimate user can then log on as usual and neither you nor the user will know that anything untoward has happened.

At the bottom of the Account Policy dialog box are two check boxes. The first check box is for the forcible disconnect discussed earlier in this chapter in the section titled "Setting Logon Hours." If time restrictions have been set for a user, selecting this check box will disconnect users who overstay their time limit. Note that this option has no effect on computers running operating systems other than Windows NT.

The second check box, when selected, requires a logon before a password can be changed. This means that a user with an expired password cannot log on to change to a new password. If this box is deselected, a user can log on to change an expired password without having to engage the help of an administrator.

Managing User Rights

On any network, legitimate users must be able to log on and then get to the resources they need, while unauthorized users must be kept out. The challenge for the administrator is to make the network as secure as it needs to be, and no more.

What a user can and can't do depends on the rights and permissions he or she has been granted. Rights and permissions are not exactly the same. *Rights* are particular tasks that a user (or group) can perform and are defined using User Manager for Domains. The ability to back up files or log on to a server, for example, is a right that the administrator giveth or taketh away. *Permissions* specify the access a user (or group) has to specific objects such as files, directories, and printers. Chapter 10 explains how additional permissions are set.

User Rights Policy

Windows NT Server has two built-in categories of user rights: regular and advanced. Whole sets of user rights are included in each category. Because the built-in groups are designed very cleverly (this *is* Microsoft, after all) it's rarely necessary to change the assignments.

By default, Small Business Server assigns all users to the Domain Users group. User accounts with administrative privileges are also members of the Domain Administrators group. On a small network, it's rarely necessary to add more groups or to change the default rights, but of course you can if you need to.

To view or change the rights assigned to a user or a group, open User Manager for Domains and choose User Rights from the Policies menu. You'll see the User Rights Policy dialog box, shown in Figure 8.09

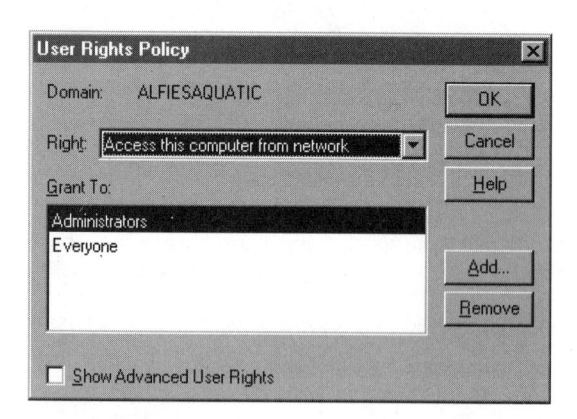

FIGURE 8.09
The User Rights Policy dialog box.

Regular rights

At the top of the dialog box is the name of the domain for which you're defining user rights. To see the entire list of user rights, click the down arrow next to the displayed user right. In the Grant To box are the names of the individuals and groups who have the displayed right in this domain. Use the Add and Remove buttons to add or remove groups or individuals.

Table 8.01 lists the regular rights in Windows NT Server, what each right means, and which groups have that right by default.

Table 8.01
Regular User Rights in Windows NT Server

Right	Definition	Groups
Access this computer from network	The right to log on to this computer through the network	Administrators Everyone
Add workstations to domain	The right to create computer accounts	None by default. But Administrators and Server Operators can add computers without being specifically granted this right.
Back up files and directories	The right to back up all files on the computer	Administrators Backup Operators Server Operators
Change the system time	The right to set the computer's internal clock	Administrators Server Operators
Force shutdown from a remote system	Not implemented	
Load and unload device drivers on the network	The right to install and uninstall drivers for devices	Administrators
Log on locally	The right to log on to a Windows NT Server computer	Account Operators Administrators Backup Operators Domain Users Print Operators Server Operators
Manage auditing and security log	The right to manage the auditing of files, directories, and other resources	Administrators
Restore files and directories	The right to restore files and folders; supersedes any permission restrictions	Administrators Backup Operators Server Operators

(continued)

Table 8.01 *continued*

Right	Definition	Groups
Shut down the system	The right to shut down Windows NT	Account Operators Administrators Backup Operators Print Operators Server Operators
Take ownership of files or other objects	The right to take ownership of files, folders, and other objects that are owned by other users	Administrators

Advanced rights

If you select the Show Advanced User Rights check box, the list in the User Rights Policy dialog box will grow considerably longer. Programmers writing Windows NT applications are usually the only people who use the advanced rights. There's only one that you might use: Bypass Traverse Checking. This allows a user to go through directory trees (folder structures) even if he or she doesn't have permission to access the directories being passed through. This doesn't give the user any right to change or read the folders being traversed, just the ability to pass through.

Using System Policy to Manage User Environments

In Windows NT Server, the look, feel, and configuration of the user's desktop are stored as part of his or her profile in the registry. As system administrator, you can manage user profiles by enforcing mandatory profiles or you can use the system policy to manage the configuration of user accounts.

The system policy lets you control what users can do from the desktop, but it doesn't give you absolute control of mandatory profiles. However, it has the distinct advantage of allowing you to grant users control of some aspects of their environment without letting them even see (let alone change) certain other areas. Perhaps you want to enforce a mandatory screen saver that kicks in after two minutes of inactivity and requires the user's password to gain access to the machine after the screen saver kicks in. This is a reasonable security precaution in some environments and is quite easy to implement using system policy.

System policy also lets you control logon and network access for specific computers in the domain or for all computers. You can set things such as whether the Shutdown button is available from the logon screen or whether remote access users can use anonymous ftp to log on to the machine.

With System Policy Editor (Figure 8.10), you can change the system policy for all users and machines or for individual users or machines, making it easy to customize your settings for special situations. To open System Policy Editor, choose Programs, Administrative Tools, and then System Policy Editor from the Start menu.

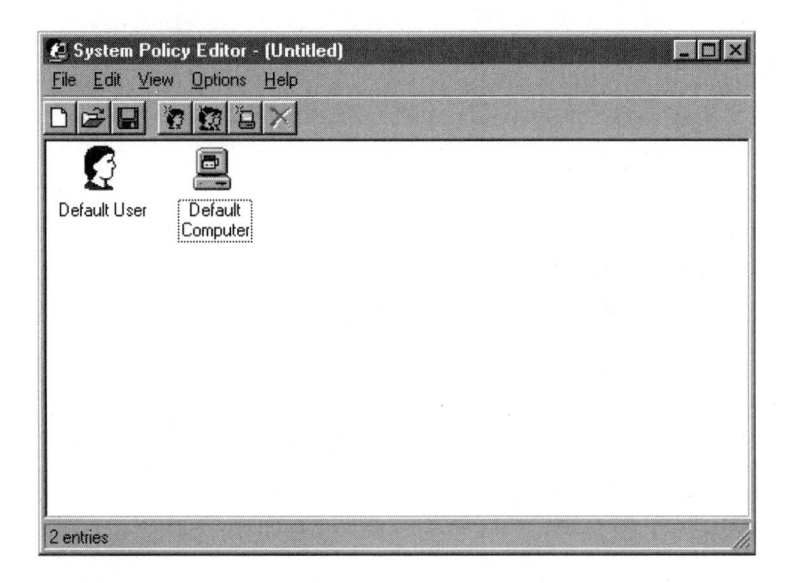

FIGURE 8.10

System Policy Editor lets you change the system policy for users and computers in the domain.

Using System Policy Editor

You can use System Policy Editor to create default settings for computers and users in the domain or for individual users, groups of users, or specific machines in the domain. You can even use System Policy Editor to set policy for Microsoft Windows 95 machines in your domain if user profiles are enabled on the Windows 95 machines.

Templates

Windows NT Server includes a set of system policy templates that provide a starting place to edit the registry settings for Windows NT Server, Microsoft Windows NT Workstation, and Windows 95 machines on your network. When System Policy Editor is installed, it copies three template files to your %SystemRoot%\inf subfolder.

- COMMON.ADM—contains a template for settings common to both Windows NT and Windows 95
- WINDOWS.ADM—contains a template for settings specific to Windows 95
- WINNT.ADM—contains a template for settings specific to Windows NT

When you start System Policy Editor, it automatically loads the templates for Windows NT machines. You can add the Windows 95 template, or any other template provided by a software manufacturer, by copying the .ADM file to the same subfolder.

Adding templates to System Policy Editor

You can add a template to System Policy Editor so that you can change the settings for additional items:

1. Close any open policy files.
2. Copy the template file to the %SystemRoot%\inf subfolder.
3. On the Options menu, choose Policy Template to bring up the Policy Template Options dialog box, shown in Figure 8.11.

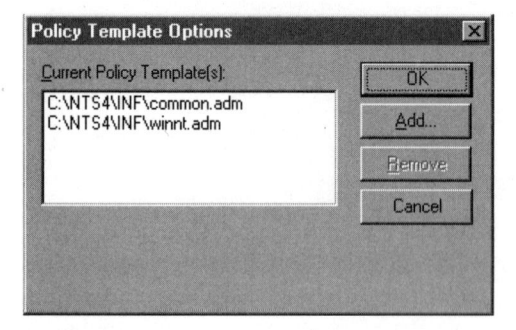

FIGURE 8.11

In the Policy Template Options dialog box, you can add or remove templates from System Policy Editor.

4. Click Add, and then select the template file you want to add.
5. After you finish adding all the template files you want to add, click OK. System Policy Editor will load the additional template files. These templates will remain loaded until you remove them and will be available for any policies you create.

Removing templates from System Policy Editor

You can remove a template from System Policy Editor by taking these steps:

1. Close any open policy files.
2. From the Options menu, choose Policy Template to bring up the Policy Template Options dialog box, shown earlier in Figure 8.11.
3. Select the template you want to remove.
4. Click Remove, and then select the template file you want to remove.
5. After you remove all the template files you want to remove, click OK, and System Policy Editor will unload the unwanted template files.

Creating a New Default System Policy

To create a new system policy and make it active, you must first create the policy and then move or copy it into the NETLOGON directory of the Primary Domain Controller for the domain. Then you must give it a special name: NTconfig.pol.

> ◆ **Managing System Policy Changes**
>
> Before you make any system policy changes, we suggest that you make a copy of the current system policy and put it in a safe place so that you have a fallback point. Every good system administrator has a technique for handling changes that affect system stability. We keep fallback versions of the registry, system policies, and so forth in a "changes" folder using filenames that clearly identify the change by date and by nature. (What's the point of having long filenames if you can't take advantage of them sometimes?)
>
> Whatever method you use, be consistent and conscientious about it. It's all too easy to make a change that doesn't work. If you make changes in an incremental and clearly documented way, however, and have safe versions to fall back on, it's a *lot* easier and faster to recover.

Computer policy

To create a new default computer policy that will be used by all computers on the network, take the following steps:

1. Start System Policy Editor.
2. Choose New Policy from the File menu.
3. Double-click on the Default Computer icon to bring up the Default Computer Properties dialog box, shown in Figure 8.12.

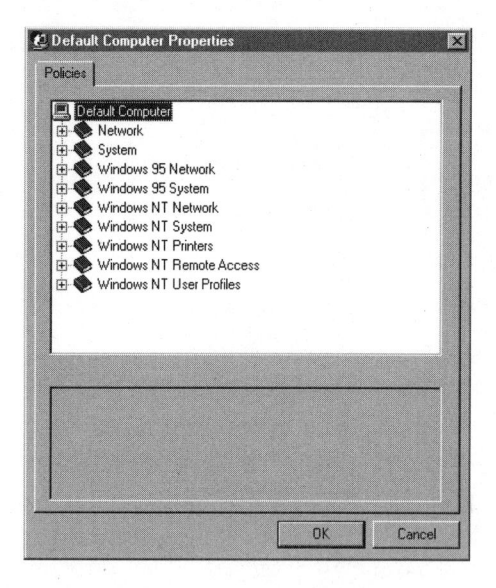

FIGURE 8.12

In the Default Computer Properties dialog box, you can change the default system policies for all the computers in your domain.

4. Each book represents an area of the registry that you can modify. Double-click on the book for the policy that you want to modify. For example, to remove from all the computers in your network the ability to shut down from the logon dialog box, you open the Windows NT System and Logon books, as shown in Figure 8.13. Deselect the Enable Shutdown From Authentication Dialog Box check box.

NOTE

The check boxes in System Policy Editor have three states: cleared (to disable the policy), checked (to enable the policy), and gray (to not change the policy from its current state). Be sure not to click on check boxes you don't want to change.

5. After you make your changes, click OK to return to the main System Policy Editor window.

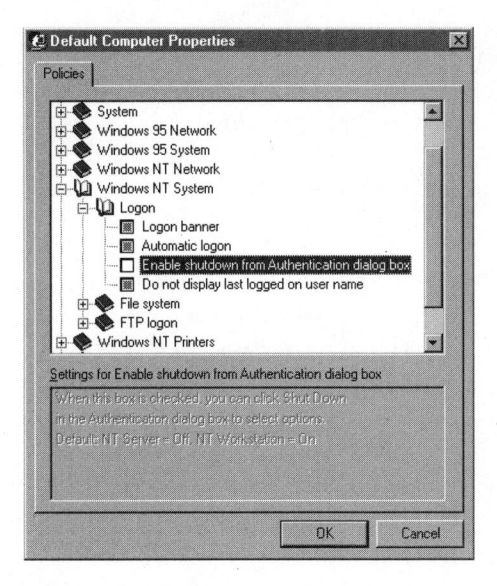

FIGURE 8.13

In this example, we're changing the shutdown policy for the network.

User policy

To make changes to the default user policy, take the following steps:

1. Double-click on the Default User icon to bring up the Default User Properties dialog box, where you can change how users can configure their desktops and use the Control Panel, or you can apply a variety of restrictions to various aspects of the user interface.

2. Click OK to return to the main System Policy Editor window.

Saving and implementing the new policy

To save and implement your new default system policy for both computers and users, follow these steps:

1. Choose Save As from the File menu.

2. Type the default configuration policy filename and location: *PDCName*\NETLOGON\NTConfig.Pol.

3. Click Save, and the new policy will be in effect for all future logons.

NOTE

We like to first save any policy changes to a separate subfolder under a more descriptive name and then copy the data to the default configuration file. This makes it much easier to recover to a known condition if the change you made was not as well thought out as you might have hoped. Plus, it gives you a useful audit trail.

Connecting to the Registry Remotely

You can also use System Policy Editor to connect to the registry on a remote computer and to modify the settings for that computer and the current user. From the main System Policy Editor window, choose Connect from the File menu. Type the computer name of the computer whose registry you want to modify, and then select from the list of available user profiles to edit. This is almost the same as before, but now you're no longer showing icons for the Default Computer or Default User.

Once you're connected to the computer you want to modify, you can change the same settings as above, but now you're changing them for only the particular user and machine you're connected to. The check boxes are now regular, binary check boxes because you're directly editing the value.

POINTS TO REMEMBER

- You can have as many user accounts as you need, so create a user account for each person who uses the network.

- When you delete a user account, the user's electronic mail box is also removed, but any personal folders associated with the account must be deleted manually.

- Use System Policy Editor to control particular aspects of a user's environment.

WHAT'S NEXT?

In this chapter, we covered adding and changing user information on your Small Business Server network. In Chapter 9, you'll learn about managing network printers.

Chapter 9

Managing Printers

- 138 **Printer Terminology**
- 139 **Planning Network Printing**
- 140 **Managing Printers**
  - Controlling User Access — 141
  - Adding a New Printer — 142
  - Changing Printer Settings — 148
  - Managing Printer Jobs — 159
  - Troubleshooting Printers — 160
  - Removing a Printer — 161
  - Managing the Logical Printer — 161
- 163 **Points to Remember**
- 163 **What's Next**

Chapter 9

Managing Printers

An investment in hardware pays off only to the extent that the equipment is used. One of the great advantages of a network—although far from the only one—is the ability to share many kinds of hardware. Investing in a top-of-the-line printer makes sense if it's actually printing for more than a few minutes here and there during the day. Without a network, everyone who needs a printer has to have his or her own machine—not a sensible approach even if we're talking about inexpensive dot matrix or ink-jet printers. But put just one high-end printer on the network, and you can spread the cost across all of your users while improving the quality of all your print jobs.

Printer Terminology

In general, Microsoft Small Business Server makes things pretty clear when it comes to printers. However, the underlying operating system, Microsoft Windows NT, uses some special and sometimes confusing terms when referring to printers. First, it's important to differentiate between a *print device,* which is the actual machine that does the printing, and a *printer,* which in Microsoft terminology is the software interface between the application and the actual print device. Therefore, a printer in Microsoft terminology is actually a logical entity.

In this chapter, and in fact the entire book, we'll refer to the print device simply as the "printer." We'll refer to the software interface as the "logical printer." The Novell NetWare and IBM OS/2 networking environments use the term *print queue* (meaning the logical printer) instead of *printer,* but the net effect is the same. Small Business Server supports any printer that works with Windows NT—in other words, virtually any printer.

You can have one logical printer associated with a single printer, which is the arrangement shown in Figure 9.01. Here, a print job in Small Business Server goes to a logical printer, which in turn sends it to the printer.

You can also have several logical printers associated with a single printer. In this arrangement, you can configure logical printers at different priority levels so that one is for normal printing and the others are for jobs that can wait to be printed later. For a printer that uses both Postscript and PCL, having two logical printers allows users to choose either type of printing.

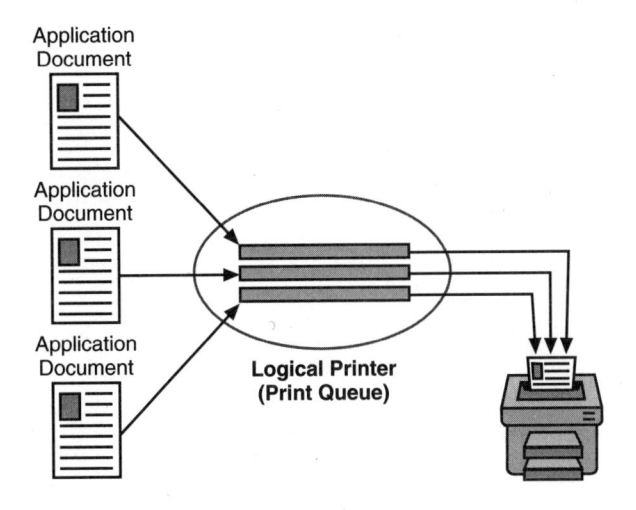

FIGURE 9.01

Example of jobs routing through a logical printer to a printer.

You can also have a single logical printer associated with multiple printers. If all of the printers use the same printer driver—an arrangement called a *printer pool*—a single logical printer will send jobs to the first available printer. The advantage of a printer pool is that the administrator can add or remove printers without affecting user configurations because the printers are interchangeable. The disadvantage of a printer pool is that there's no way to predict which printer will receive which job. So don't pool printers when they're physically far apart because you'll have people running hither and yon trying to figure out where their print job ended up.

Planning Network Printing

One of the advantages of Small Business Server is that it gives you one central point of administration—the server. You can configure and control everything from that one machine. If you want to keep printer control on the server, you have only two ways to set up printers. One method is to attach them directly to the server. This works well if you have only one printer; you just plug it into the server's parallel port and you're ready to go.

However, if your printer is very busy, the server has to dedicate a fair amount of CPU time to servicing that parallel port—CPU time that won't be available to take care of all the other chores a server on a Small Business Server network needs to do. In that case, a printer with a network interface card is a better solution. Most business-standard printers come with a network connection or offer the connection as an option. You can control a printer connected directly to the network in this way from the server without using any of the server's resources.

Managing Printers

Managing printers is not about the printers themselves but about how they are connected to and managed as part of your Small Business Server network. You have to decide which printers should be shared, who has access to which printer, and more.

The Manage Printers page of the Small Business Server console is your headquarters for managing all printer functions. To access the Manage Printers page, make sure you're logged on using an account with administrative privileges. From the Start menu, choose Manage Server and then click on the Manage Printers icon on the Tasks page. This will open the Manage Printers page shown in Figure 9.02.

> ◆ **Using a Dedicated Printer Server**
>
> You also have the option of setting up a dedicated printer server on a Small Business Server network. There are definite advantages to this approach, especially if you already own printers and have an older computer available to play the printer server role. Consider the following possibilities:
>
> - ◆ A dedicated printer server can be almost any older computer. If it can run Microsoft Windows 95, it can be a printer server.
> - ◆ Two printers can be connected—one to a parallel port, one to a serial port—on an old computer without modification.
> - ◆ If you add a multiport serial card, you can drive even more printers.
> - ◆ When tallying up licenses, you don't have to count the printer server as a connection because it doesn't connect to the server.
>
> The disadvantage to this approach is that it removes printer control from the server. Permissions and restrictions must be set on the printer server itself, so you have to go to that machine to make any changes or to troubleshoot a printing problem. Printer security is minimal in this setup, but then printer security isn't a big issue in most small businesses. Realistically speaking, if someone's using the high-end color printer to produce garage sale leaflets, it's a management problem, not a computer problem.

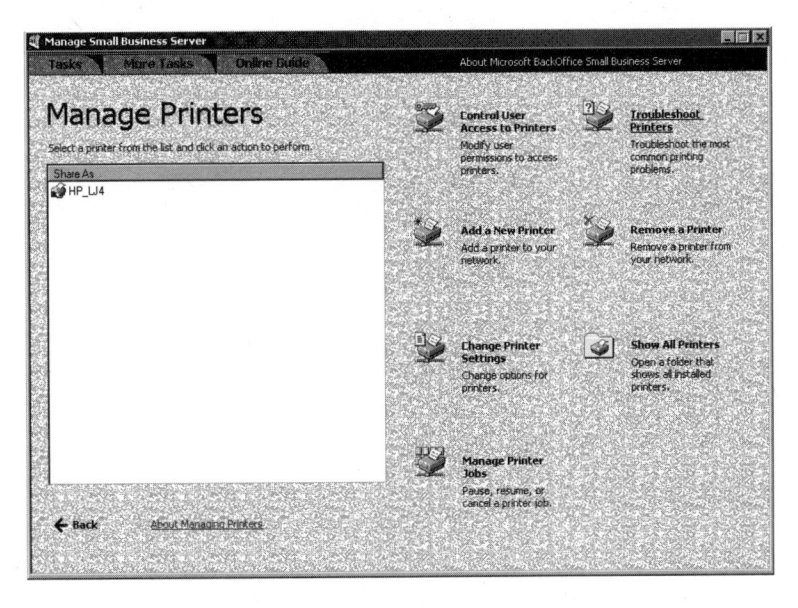

FIGURE 9.02

The Manage Printers page of the Small Business Server console.

On the left side of the page is a list of the shared printers connected to your Small Business Server network. On the right side is a series of icons for carrying out essential printer management tasks. The function of each icon is described in the following sections.

Controlling User Access

To determine which users have access to a particular printer, select the printer whose access you want to control by clicking on its entry in the list, and then click on the Control User Access To Printers icon. This will invoke the Printer Access Wizard and bring up the page shown in Figure 9.03 on the following page.

The left side of the page lists all the users on your network, and the right side shows the users who can print to the printer you've selected. To grant or revoke a user's right to print on this printer, select the user's name and then click the Add or Remove button to carry out the desired modification.

Next you should see the Update Permissions page. Click the Back button to make additional modifications, or click Finish to update the permissions for the printer you selected. When you see a message box confirming that this printer's permissions have been updated, click OK and you'll be returned to the Manage Printers page.

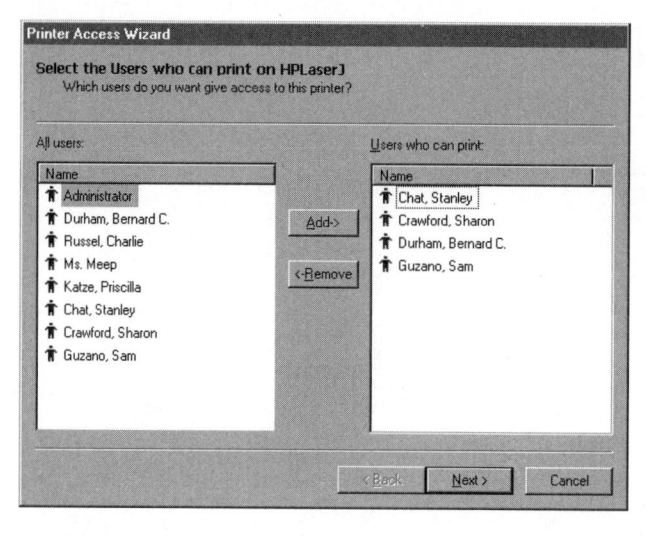

FIGURE 9.03

The wizard's Select The Users Who Can Print page.

Adding a New Printer

Once you physically connect a printer, the Add Printer Wizard will walk you through the process of configuring and sharing your printer. The procedure varies slightly depending on whether you're adding a printer to a print server or adding it to the server.

Adding a printer to be controlled by the server

The server controls printers that are connected to it directly or connected to it by way of a printer's network interface card. Follow these steps to set up such a printer:

1. From the Start menu, choose Manage Server and then click on the Manage Printers icon on the Tasks page.

2. On the Manage Printers page, click on the Add A New Printer icon to start the Add Printer Wizard. This will bring up the page shown in Figure 9.04. Check again to see that your printer is connected and turned on.

3. Specify that the server is controlling the printer by selecting the My Computer option. Click Next to continue.

4. On the next page of the wizard (Figure 9.05), you specify the appropriate printer port. If the port to which the printer is physically attached is in the Available Ports list, select its check box. If you want to take advantage of printer pooling, select the Enable Printer Pooling check box and then select the ports to which the identical print devices are attached.

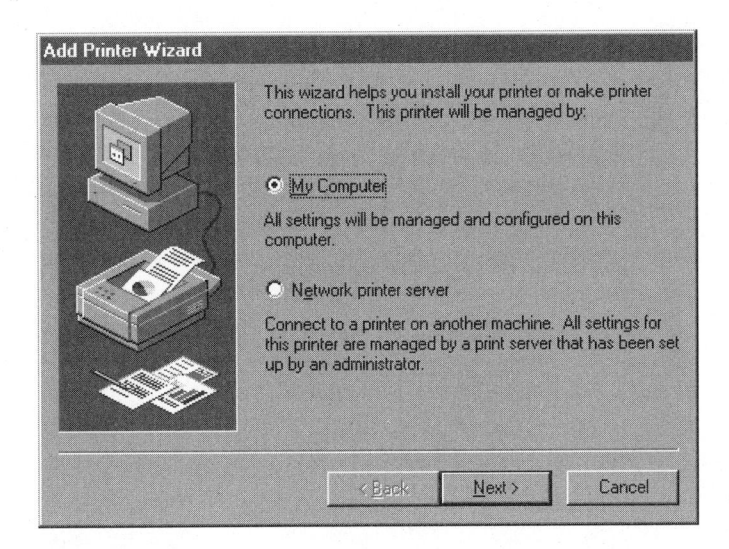

FIGURE 9.04
The first page of the Add Printer Wizard.

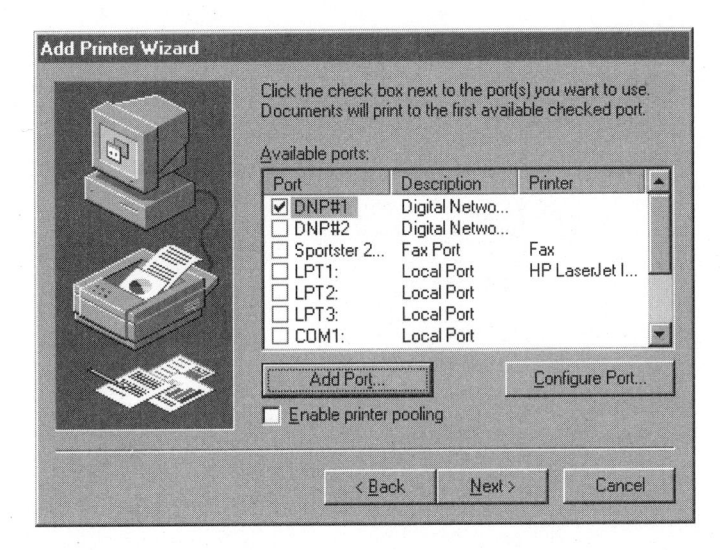

FIGURE 9.05
The page for specifying a printer port.

NOTE

For printer pooling, all print devices in the pool must use the same printer driver.

5. If the port to which the printer is physically attached is not in the list shown, click Add Port to bring up the Printer Ports dialog box, shown in Figure 9.06.

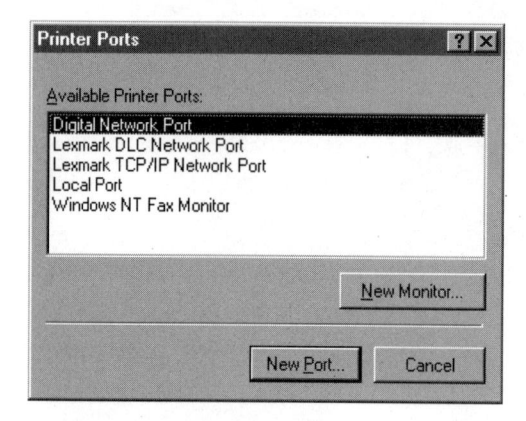

FIGURE 9.06

The Printer Ports dialog box.

6. If you're adding a new port, select the kind of port you want to add and click New Port. This will bring up the Add Port dialog box. (See Figure 9.07.)

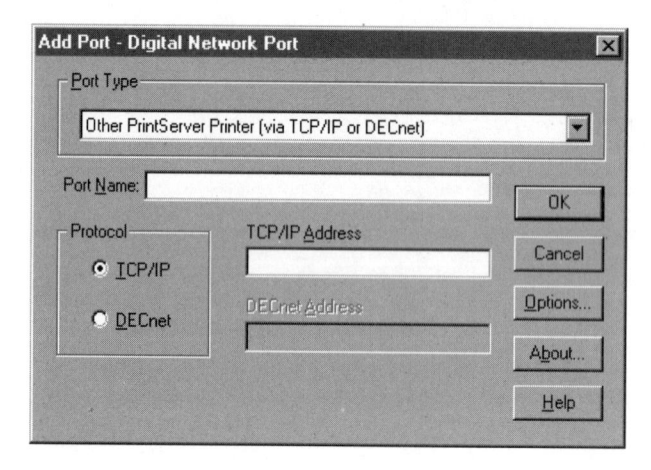

FIGURE 9.07

The Add Port dialog box.

7. When specifying a name for the new port, be sure to choose one that describes the printer or the printer port clearly because you won't be able to change it later. Enter the requested information about the kind of port you've chosen, and click OK. Click OK to add the new port, and you should find yourself back at the screen where you specified the printer port (Figure 9.05), with the check box next to your new port selected. Click Next to continue.

8. Next you'll see a page for specifying the manufacturer and model, shown in Figure 9.08. Specify the manufacturer and model of the printer you're adding by selecting the appropriate items in the Manufacturers and Printers lists. Be aware that you might need to click the Have Disk button and insert the printer manufacturer's driver disk in order to copy the appropriate driver to your system. When you're satisfied that your printer information is correct, click Next.

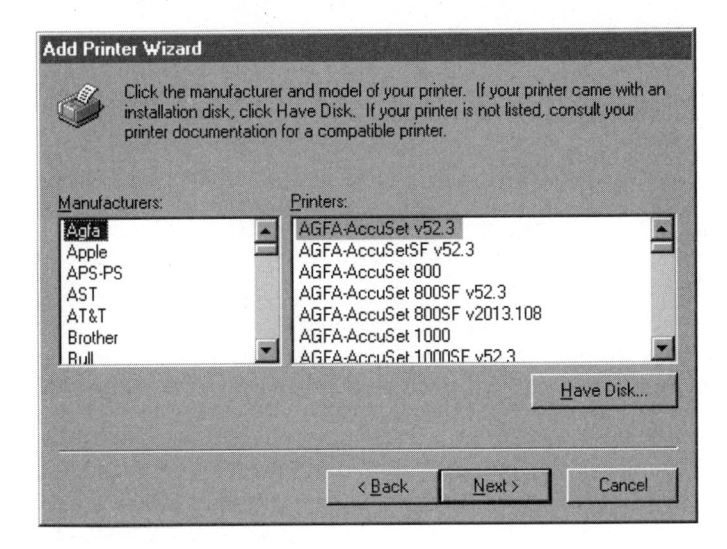

FIGURE 9.08

The page for specifying the manufacturer and model of the printer.

9. You'll see a page on which you specify a printer name. (See Figure 9.09 on the next page.) You can either accept the default name suggested by the wizard or enter a different name. If you enter a name of your own, however, be sure that the name clearly describes the printer's function or location. Here you can also specify whether you'd like Windows-based programs to use this printer as the default printer. Click Next to continue.

CHAPTER 9   *Managing Printers*   **145**

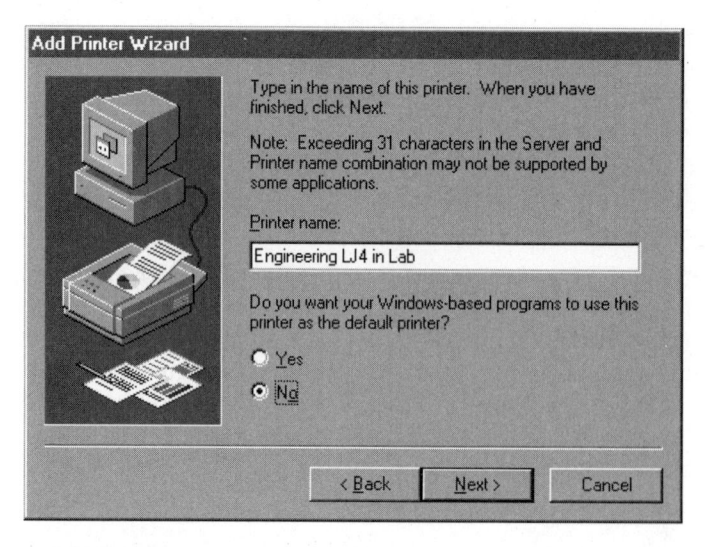

[Screenshot of Add Printer Wizard dialog showing printer name field with "Engineering LJ4 in Lab" entered, and Yes/No radio buttons for default printer selection with No selected.]

FIGURE 9.09

The page for specifying a printer name.

10. Next you'll see the page shown in Figure 9.10, in which you specify whether the printer will be shared. Normally, the printer will be shared unless you have some overriding need to restrict access. You can either accept the default share name suggested by the wizard or enter a different name. Again, be sure that the name clearly describes the printer's function or location. After you give the printer its share name, specify all operating systems used on computers that will print to this printer by selecting them in the list. Click Next to continue.

11. You'll now see a page asking whether you'd like to print a test page. It's always a good idea to print a test page on your new printer, so select Yes. If the Files Needed screen appears, prompting you for the location of a file, insert Small Business Server Disc 1 into your CD-ROM drive. Under Copy Files From, type *x:\i386*, where *x* is the drive letter of your CD-ROM drive, and then click OK. Click Finish, and you're almost done adding a new printer.

12. When it finishes printing the test page, Small Business Server will give you a chance to confirm that everything went as expected. If the test page printed correctly, click Yes and you're done. If it did not print correctly, click No to start up the Small Business Server Help system. The

Help application will walk you through the steps to troubleshoot and fix your printer.

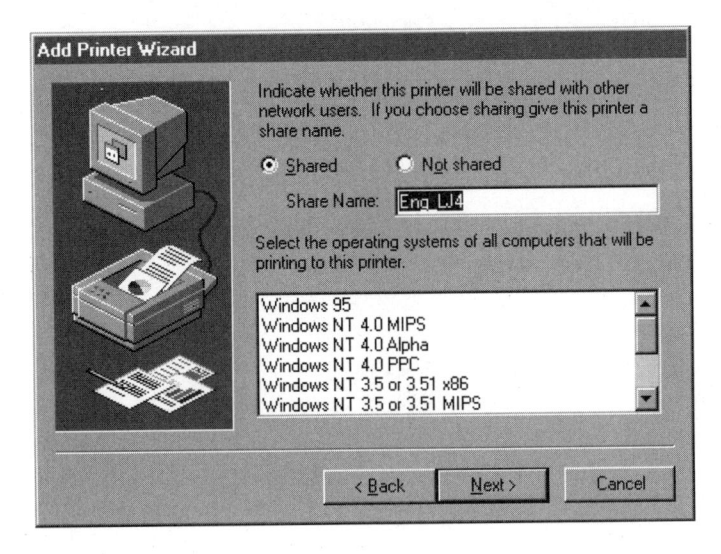

FIGURE 9.10

The page for specifying printer sharing.

You've now added a new printer to your system. You should find yourself right back where you started—that is, on the Manage Printers page.

Adding a printer to be controlled by a printer server

If you're connecting a new printer to a printer server or to a client machine, follow these steps:

1. From the Start menu, choose Manage Server and then click on the Manage Printers icon on the Tasks page.

2. On the Manage Printers page, click on the Add A New Printer icon to start the Add Printer Wizard. (The first wizard screen was shown earlier in Figure 9.04.) Check again that your printer is connected and turned on.

3. Select the Network Printer Server option, and then click Next to open the Connect To Printer dialog box, shown in Figure 9.11 on the following page.

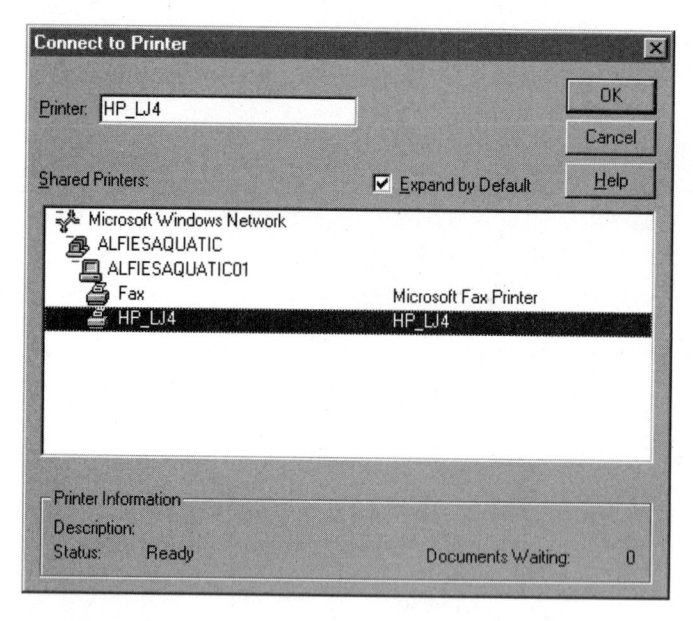

FIGURE 9.11
The Connect To Printer dialog box.

4. Double-click on the computer name and then select the printer. Click OK.

NOTE

The printer you're adding must already be installed on the client machine or on the machine that you're using as a printer server.

Changing Printer Settings

In Small Business Server, "printer settings" include a host of options that range from the most basic to the most advanced. The Change Printer Settings icon on the Manage Printers page gives you direct access to the Printer Properties page, where you can change any or all of a printer's settings.

To change a printer's settings, from the Start menu choose Manage Server and then click on the Manage Printers icon on the Tasks page. On the Manage Printers page, click on the Change Printer Settings icon. This will start the Review Or Change Printer Properties utility, shown in Figure 9.12. Click the Here link in item 1.

FIGURE 9.12

The Review Or Change Printer Properties utility.

This opens the Printers folder. (See Figure 9.13.) Right-click on the printer whose settings you want to change, and choose Properties from the popup menu. This opens the printer's Properties dialog box (shown in Figure 9.14 on the following page) with the General tab displayed.

FIGURE 9.13

The Printers folder.

CHAPTER 9 *Managing Printers* **149**

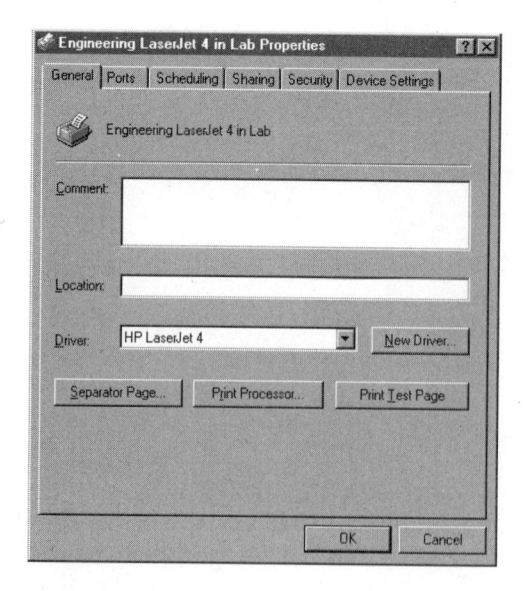

FIGURE 9.14

The General tab of the printer's Properties dialog box.

> **Tip**
>
> *If you find it more convenient, you can access the Properties dialog box for any printer from the Start menu by choosing Settings-Printers and then right-clicking on the printer and choosing Properties from the popup menu. This is also a quick way to pause printing or to purge jobs from a particular printer.*

Changing general printer properties

On the General tab of the Properties dialog box, you can add a comment pertaining to this printer, add text identifying its location, change the printer driver or add a new driver, add a separator page between documents, change the print processor, or print a test page.

Adding a comment or location information To add a comment about this printer, enter it in the Comment text box. A comment might be an identifying name such as *HP LaserJet* or *Lexmark Color*. To identify the location of this printer, type a location description in the Location text box.

Changing or adding a printer driver There might come a time when you want to change a printer driver because the manufacturer has come up with a new one that solves some problem or other that you're having. The Driver drop-down list box lists the printer drivers installed on your system. To add a new driver, click New Driver and you'll be prompted for the location of the driver. Place the manufacturer's driver disk or Small Business Server Disc 1 into the appropriate drive, and then specify where the driver files are located. When the files have been copied to your system, you're all set.

Adding a separator page   A separator page between documents can be useful if the printers on your network tend to be busy and documents stack up quickly. To add a separator page, click the Separator Page button to bring up the Separator Page dialog box. Here you can specify the location of the file you want to use for this purpose. Click Browse to search for a file. When you're done, click OK. That's all there is to it.

> **Tip**
>
> *To create a separator page, open WordPad or another word processor. Using a large typeface, type Separator or Job Break or some other phrase that makes sense to you. Save the file. Specify this file when filling out the Separator Page dialog box.*

Adding, deleting, and configuring ports

The Ports tab (Figure 9.15) of the printer's Properties dialog box lets you add, delete, and change the configuration of printer ports on your system.

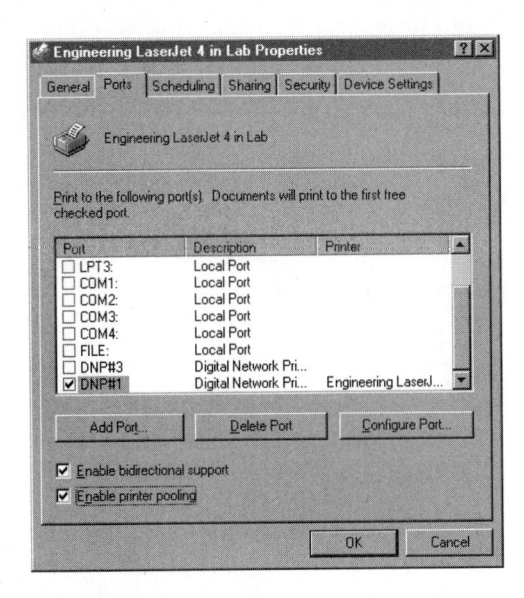

FIGURE 9.15

The Ports tab of the printer's Properties dialog box.

Adding a port   To add a port, follow these steps:

1. Click Add Port on the Ports tab of the printer's Properties dialog box, and you should see the Printer Ports dialog box (shown earlier in Figure 9.06). Select the kind of port you'd like to add, and then click New Port.

2. In the Add Port dialog box, shown earlier in Figure 9.07, specify the port type, protocol, and address. Give the port a name that clearly identifies the printer or the printer port; you won't be able to change the name later without deleting the port and adding it in again. Click OK, and you should see the Printer Ports dialog box once again.

3. Click Close, and you'll be returned to the Ports tab of the Properties dialog box.

Deleting a port   Deleting a port couldn't be simpler. On the Ports tab, select the name of the port you'd like to delete and then click Delete Port. You'll see a confirmation dialog box asking whether you'd really like to delete this port from your system. If so, click Yes and the deed will be done. Otherwise, click No and the port will remain untouched.

Changing port settings   To configure a port, click Configure Port on the Ports tab, and you should see the Configure Port dialog box (practically identical to Figure 9.07), which contains information about the port type, protocol, and address. Change the value of any items you wish, and then click OK. You'll be returned to the Ports tab of the Properties dialog box.

Setting printer availability

You can make some fine-tuning adjustments to the printer using the Scheduling tab of the printer's Properties dialog box. (See Figure 9.16.) In general, the default settings work well, and you probably shouldn't change them unless you have a good reason to do so. However, you might want to make one or more printers available only during certain hours. To do this, follow these steps:

1. From the Start menu, choose Settings-Printers.

2. Right-click on the printer whose settings you want to change, and choose Properties from the popup menu.

3. Click on the Scheduling tab of the Properties dialog box.

4. Select the From option button, and specify beginning and ending times for printer availability. Click OK when you finish.

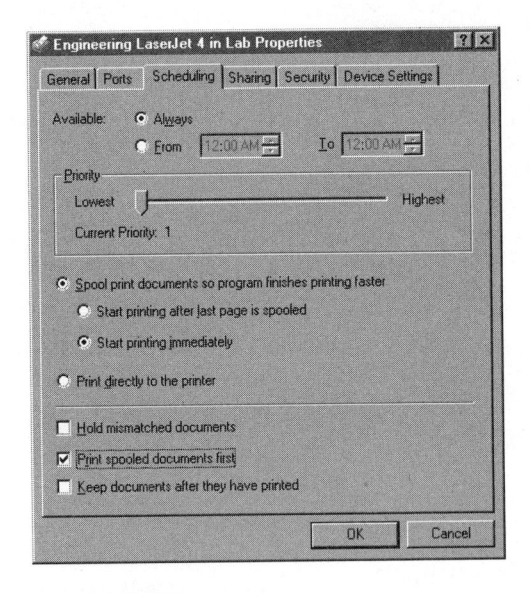

FIGURE 9.16

The Scheduling tab of the printer's Properties dialog box.

Sharing printers

As you've already seen, the normal printer installation process allows you to specify printer sharing. But you can also start or stop sharing as a separate step. The Sharing tab of the Properties dialog box (shown in Figure 9.17 on the following page) lets you do just that. Perhaps you want to experiment with the printer locally before making it available to the network, or perhaps something about the printer has changed and you want to change the share name. Whatever your reasons, here are the steps to follow:

1. To share a printer that was not previously shared, select the Shared option and give the printer a name.

2. If your printer will be used by operating systems other than the ones you specified during installation, you can choose to have the printer drivers for these systems loaded on the server, which will further reduce the overhead to the clients. Select the drivers you want to support in the Alternate Drivers list box, and you're done.

CHAPTER 9 *Managing Printers* **153**

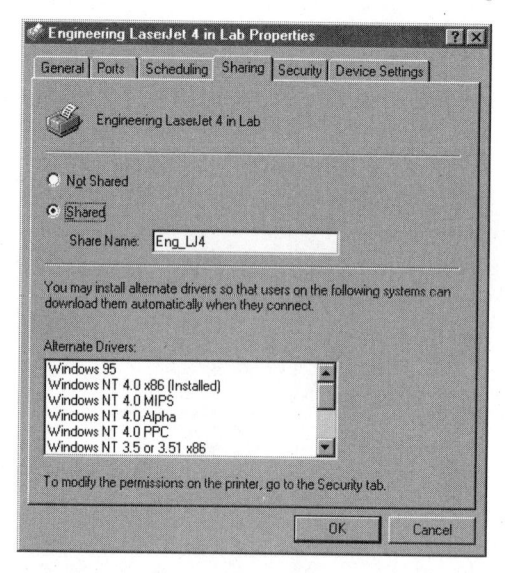

FIGURE 9.17

The Sharing tab of the printer's Properties dialog box.

Configuring printer security

The Security tab of the Properties dialog box (Figure 9.18) is the gateway to three categories of information: permissions, auditing, and ownership.

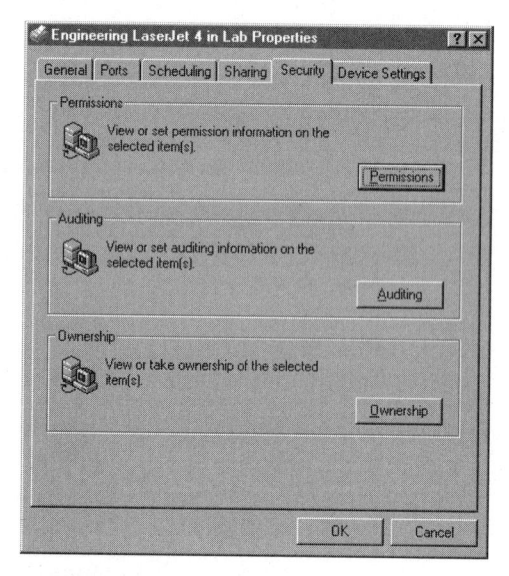

FIGURE 9.18

The Security tab of the printer's Properties dialog box.

154 PERFORMING BASIC TASKS

Permissions   To view or modify user permissions for this printer, follow the steps below:

1. Click the Permissions button to open the Printer Permissions dialog box. (See Figure 9.19.)

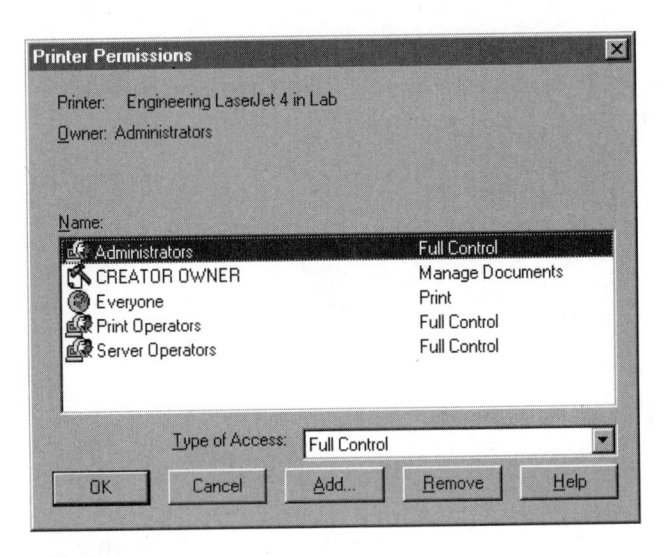

FIGURE 9.19

The Printer Permissions dialog box.

2. To change printer access permission for one of the users or the groups listed, select the user or the group, and then select the type of access from the Type Of Access drop-down list box. Click OK, and the user or group access will be changed.

3. To add a new user or a group to the set of permissions, click Add. This will bring up the Add Users And Groups dialog box (shown in Figure 9.20 on the following page), which lets you assign to specific users and groups a permission level for an object. Select the user or the group you want to add. (Click Show Users to include individual users in the list.) Click Add in the Add Users And Groups dialog box. When you finish adding users or groups, select the type of access you want to grant them and then click OK.

NOTE

You can add only one type of permission at a time in the Add Users And Groups dialog box, but you can easily change individual permissions back in the Printer Permissions dialog box.

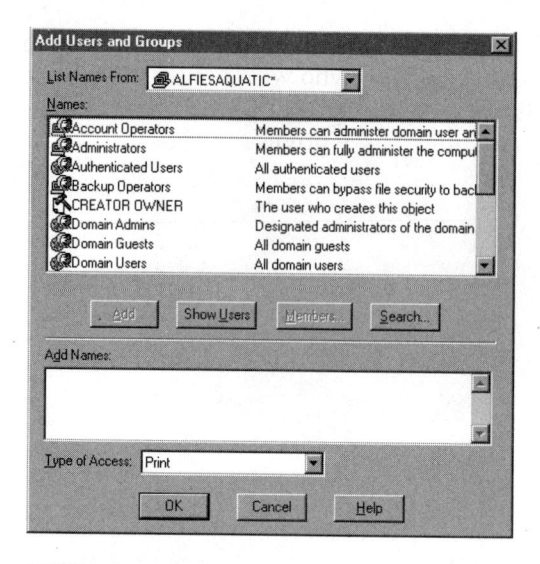

FIGURE 9.20

The Add Users And Groups dialog box.

4. To delete the permissions setting for a user or a group, select the user or the group and click Remove in the Printer Permissions dialog box.

5. When you finish viewing or modifying the permissions for the printer, click OK in the Printer Permissions dialog box.

Auditing   Another important aspect of printer security and administration is being able to see who has been using and, even more to the point, abusing the system. Printer auditing allows you to keep track of whether a user or a group is successfully using a particular printer option.

Do you want to make sure you'll always know if your boss is having difficulty using the printer? No problem: Set up an audit log to record any failures from his account. Do printing logjams beset your network? Set up an audit log to track what's happening so that you can take steps to clear the mess away.

In the Printer Auditing dialog box, you can keep track of the success or failure (or both) of the following "events":

- **Print** Changes to print status, priority, and so forth.
- **Full Control** Changes to print spooler status, priority, and so forth.
- **Delete** Deletions of print jobs.
- **Change Permissions** Changes to permissions.

- **Take Ownership** Changes to ownership of the printer. By default, the printer is "owned" by the person who was logged on when the printer was installed. Only the owner can set rights and permissions for a printer. Someone with administrative privileges can take ownership.

WARNING!

Event logs can get very large, very quickly on a busy system. Use printer auditing sparingly. It increases the overhead on any actions being audited because it requires that the events be written to the event log, and the logs can grow rapidly.

To view or change the auditing on a print queue, follow these steps:

1. Click Auditing on the Security tab of the printer's Properties dialog box to open the Printer Auditing dialog box. If auditing is enabled, the window will look like the one in Figure 9.21. (The default setting for printer auditing is disabled. To enable auditing, start User Manager, choose Audit from the Policies menu, select Audit These Events, and click OK.)

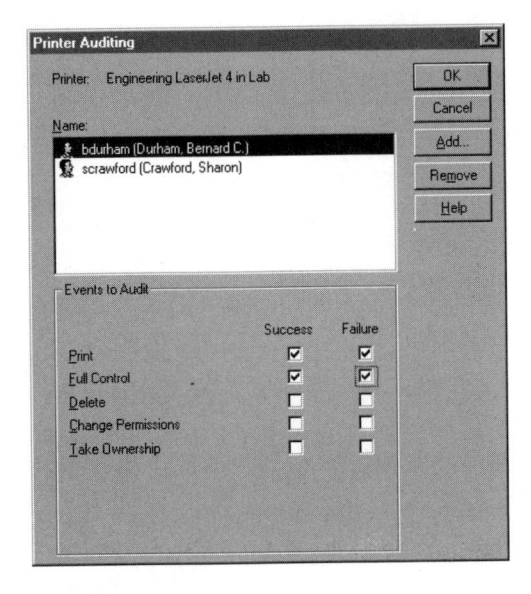

FIGURE 9.21

The Printer Auditing dialog box with auditing enabled.

2. To audit an event for a user or a group, click Add to bring up the standard Add Users And Groups dialog box (shown earlier in Figure 9.20).

In the Add Names text box, enter the names of the users or the groups whose use of the printer you want to monitor. Click OK to return to the Printer Auditing dialog box. The dialog box will now display the users or the groups you have chosen to audit, along with the kinds of printing events you can audit.

3. Select the user name or the group name, and then select the check boxes for the events you want to audit for that user or group. You can choose to audit both the success and the failure of any event. If you decide to stop auditing a particular user or a group, select the user name or the group name and click Remove.

When you're finished viewing or modifying the events being audited for this printer, click OK. Then click OK again to exit the Properties dialog box.

Ownership   To view current ownership or take ownership of a printer, click Ownership on the Security tab of the printer's Properties dialog box. This will bring up the Owner dialog box. (See Figure 9.22.) If you have the proper permissions, you can take ownership of this printer by clicking Take Ownership. Otherwise, click Close to return to the Security tab.

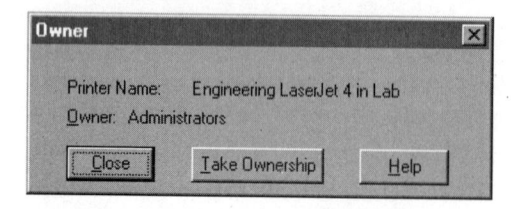

FIGURE 9.22

The Owner dialog box.

Changing device settings

Each printer has its own device-specific settings, which you can modify to match your needs. Click on the Device Settings tab of the printer's Properties dialog box to see something resembling Figure 9.23, which displays the list of settings for a Hewlett Packard LaserJet 4 printer.

If you have anything other than the default amount of memory installed on the printer, the value for Installed Memory (Kilobyte) might be incorrect. Change this if you've added extra memory. If you've added print cartridges to the printer since the device settings were last updated, add them here as well.

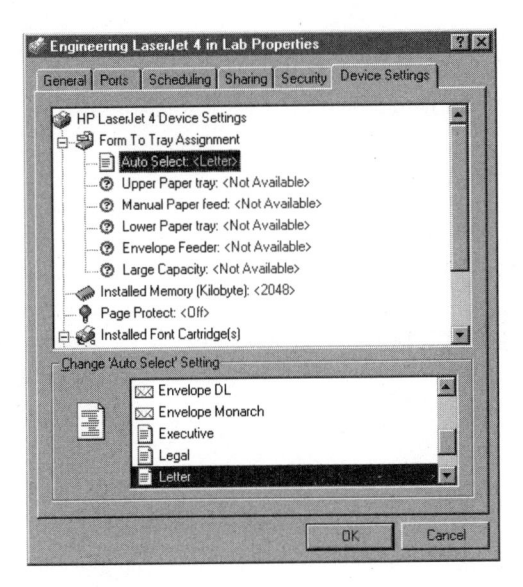

FIGURE 9.23

The Device Settings tab of the printer's Properties dialog box.

NOTE

You can also access a printer's device settings from the Start menu by choosing Settings-Printers and then right-clicking on the icon for the printer in question and choosing Properties from the popup menu.

Managing Printer Jobs

Sooner or later, you'll have to pause or delete a job that "gets stuck" in the process of printing. To begin, open the Manage Printers page of the Small Business Server console, select the printer whose jobs you'd like to manage, and then click on the Manage Printer Jobs icon. This will open the Manage Printer Jobs page.

On the left side of the page is a list of print jobs that have been sent to this printer. On the right side are links that perform the following functions:

- To pause a print job, select the job in the list and click on the Pause A Print Job icon. This will cause the job to stop printing temporarily.

- To cancel a print job, select the job in the list and click on the Cancel A Print Job icon. This will delete the job from the print queue.

- To resume a print job, select the job in the list and click on the Resume A Print Job icon. This is the antidote to the Pause A Print Job icon and will cause a paused print job to resume printing.

- To return to the Manage Printers page, simply click on the Return To Manage Printers icon.

Troubleshooting Printers

Small Business Server includes a very handy troubleshooting utility for printers, which can handle almost any printer problem that might arise. First click on the Troubleshoot Printers icon on the Manage Printers page to invoke the Troubleshooting Printers utility, shown in Figure 9.24.

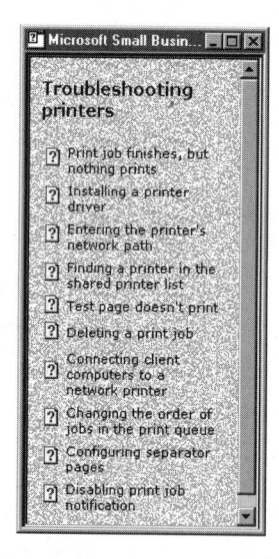

FIGURE 9.24

The Troubleshooting Printers utility.

Locate a description of the problem you're having. If you can't find an exact match, select the closest topic you can find. Click on the question mark icon corresponding to the topic, and then follow the instructions on the screen. This utility covers a surprisingly broad range of printer problems—certainly most, if not all, that are likely to occur on a small network.

Removing a Printer

Small Business Server makes removing a printer from your system about as easy as it can be. Just select the printer in the list on the Manage Printers page, and then click on the Remove A Printer icon. You'll be asked to confirm whether you want to remove this printer. If you're sure you do, click Yes; otherwise, click No and the printer status will remain unchanged.

Managing the Logical Printer

Clicking on the Show All Printers icon on the Manage Printers page opens the Printers folder (shown earlier in Figure 9.13), where you can right-click on a particular printer and manage print jobs on the fly. On the popup menu, Pause Printing and Set As Default are toggles that do exactly what their names suggest. Document Defaults lets you set or change paper size, orientation, and resolution (among other things); and Purge Print Jobs quickly deletes all print jobs in the queue.

Choose Open after right-clicking on a printer, and you'll see the documents waiting in line to be printed. Figure 9.25 shows the dialog box for a paused printer with two documents waiting in the print queue.

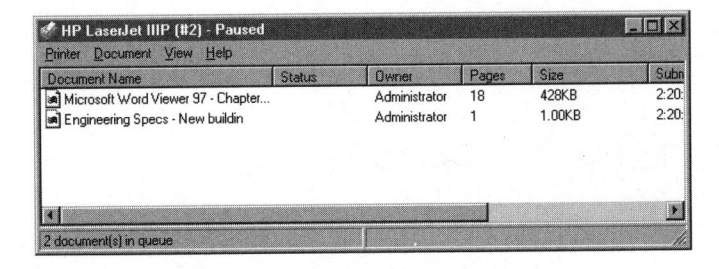

FIGURE 9.25

The dialog box for a paused printer showing documents in the print queue.

Right-click on a document to bring up the menu shown here:

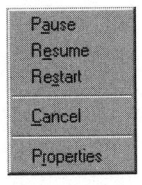

From this menu, you can pause the printing of a document in the queue, resume printing a document that is paused in the queue, restart a document from the beginning, or delete a document from the queue entirely. Pause is a useful command when you have a problem with a printer and you need to stop any jobs that are being sent to it while you fix the problem.

You can also use this menu to change the properties of a print job on the fly. Perhaps you just realized that your 400-page document is going to tie up the printer for a while and your boss really needs that shopping list printed out before he goes home. Or you want to notify the administrative assistant that you've printed out a stack of new hardware requisitions, which now need to be entered into the system. No problem. Right-click on the document, and choose Properties. You'll see the dialog box shown in Figure 9.26.

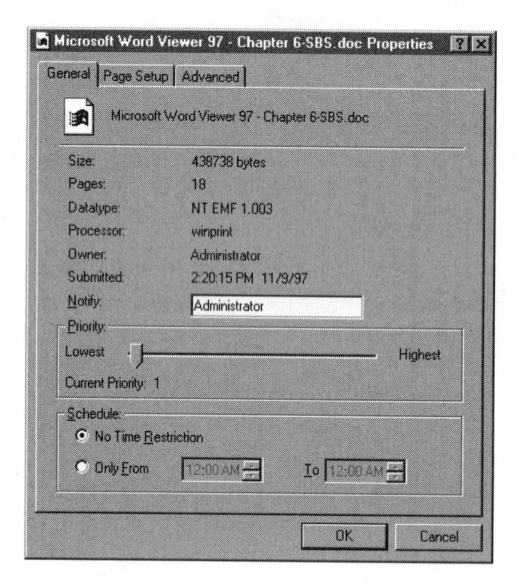

FIGURE 9.26

Example of a document's Properties dialog box.

In the Properties dialog box, you can change or view the properties of a document in the print queue. For example, you can make sure that a specific document is the next one printed by giving it the highest priority of the documents in the queue. You can also change the time when the document is scheduled to print and who will be notified when the document is printed. So you can take that 400-page document and schedule it to print after everyone has gone home. You can change the Notify field so that the system notifies the administrative assistant when the requisitions are finished. All you have left to do is crank up the priority on your boss's shopping list. You look like a genius. We wish that all administrative tasks were that easy.

POINTS TO REMEMBER

- Always plan network printing before randomly adding (and naming) printers; this will help minimize all kinds of frustration.
- The physical printer and the logical printer are managed separately.
- The Manage Printers page is your headquarters for all essential printer functions.
- You can also get at printer settings from the Start menu by choosing Settings-Printers.
- For printers to be pooled, they must all be using the identical printer driver.

WHAT'S NEXT

In this chapter, you learned all about managing printers. In Chapter 10, we'll tell you how to take advantage of another major benefit of networked computers: sharing information. You'll learn how to share folders, control access to shared folders, and much more.

Chapter 10

Sharing Information on the Network

166	**Managing Shared Folders**	
	Sharing a Folder	167
	Unsharing a Folder	171
	Controlling User Access to Shared Folders	171
172	**Managing Folder Size**	
	Compressing a Folder	173
	Uncompressing a Folder	173
	Moving a Shared Folder	173
	Moving a Folder That Isn't Shared	174
174	**Shares vs. Share Permissions**	
175	**Share Permissions**	
	Assigning Share Permissions	175
177	**Folder and File Permissions**	
	Viewing Permissions for Folders	177
	Assigning Permissions for Files	177
179	**Who Can Share Folders**	
179	**Points to Remember**	
180	**What's Next**	

Chapter 10
Sharing Information on the Network

The whole point of having a network is to share resources among users. However, sharing of network resources requires an extension of the security features that begin with user accounts and passwords. In other words, you must make sure that all users have access to the resources they need without compromising the security of files and other resources.

When considering how best to share information across your network, you have to be concerned with the two types of capabilities on which Microsoft Small Business Server security rests: shares and permissions. These are defined roughly as follows: *Shares* are folders (directories) that are made available to users over the network, and *permissions* are file system capabilities that are granted to users. For the most part, you'll manage all your security with shares. You'll allow users convenient access to the files they need while restricting access to files they don't. Only occasionally will you need to restrict access using permissions, which we'll discuss later in this chapter.

NOTE

This chapter addresses file and folder access only. For information about permissions for other kinds of resources, see "Managing User Rights" in Chapter 8.

In this chapter, we'll begin with a discussion of the two pages of the Small Business Server console that are relevant to managing file and folder permissions. Then we'll explain shares and permissions in more detail so that you'll understand how best to apply them to your network situation.

Managing Shared Folders

The Manage Shared Folders page of the Small Business Server console is your headquarters for sharing folders across the network. From here, you can share and unshare folders, control user access to shared folders, manage folder size, move a folder, and more.

Sharing a Folder

Shared folders are a great convenience if several people need access to the same files. To share a folder on your Small Business Server network, follow these steps:

1. Make sure you're logged on using an account with administrative privileges. From the Start menu, choose Manage Server; on the Tasks page, choose Manage Shared Folders. This will open the page shown in Figure 10.01.

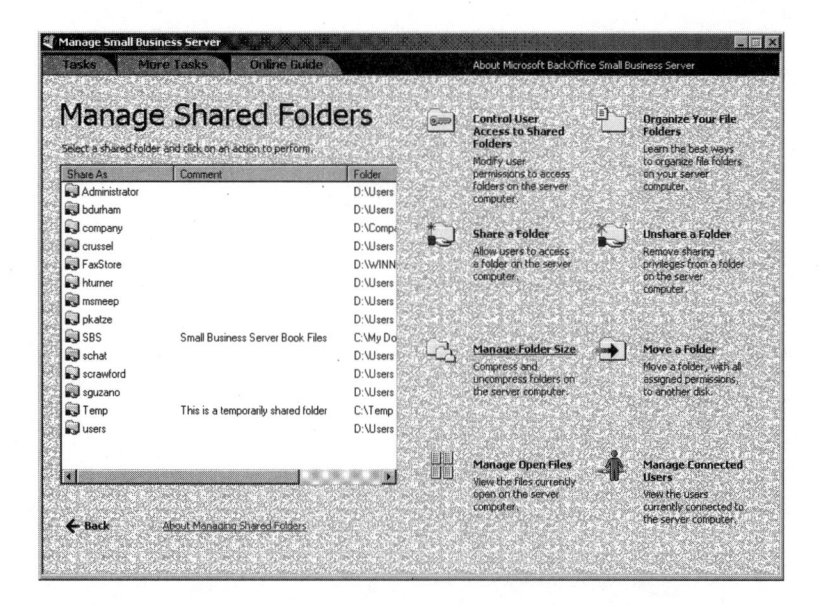

FIGURE 10.01

The Manage Shared Folders page.

2. Click on the Share A Folder icon. This will bring up the Share A Folder Wizard, whose first page is shown in Figure 10.02 on the following page.

3. Select the folder to be shared. As you can see, this page lists all the drives on your network. To expand the view of a drive's contents, click the plus sign next to the drive letter of the folder you'd like to share, and then click on the folder to be shared. You can also type the path and name of the folder in the text box at the bottom of the screen or type a new name to create a new folder. Click Next to continue.

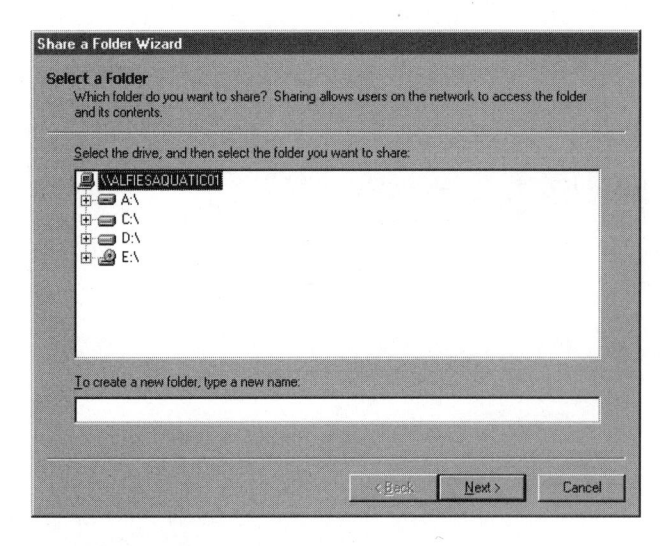

FIGURE 10.02

The first page of the Share A Folder Wizard.

4. On the second page of the wizard (Figure 10.03), type a name for the shared folder in the first text box and a description of the shared folder (if desired) in the second. Click Next to continue.

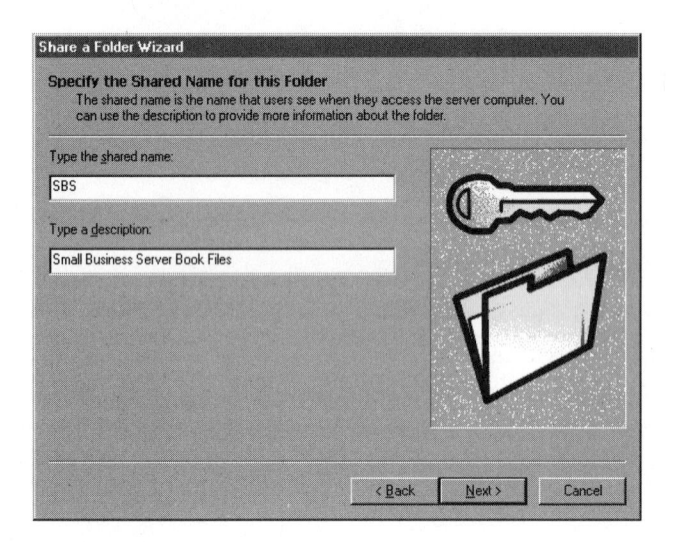

FIGURE 10.03

The wizard's second page.

168 PERFORMING BASIC TASKS

5. On the third page of the wizard (Figure 10.04), the left side lists all users on your Small Business Server network. On the right side are two other lists of users: The users listed in the top box (by default, all users on your system) will have read-write-edit permission for the contents of this shared folder, and users listed in the bottom box will have read-only permission. That is, the users in the top box can open, change, and save changes to a file in this folder, while the users in the bottom box can do nothing more than open and examine a file. To grant or revoke read-write-edit or read-only permissions for a specific user, select the name of the user to add or remove in one of the lists, and use the Add or Remove buttons to make the change.

NOTE

To deny a user access to a shared folder, make sure that his or her name does not appear in either of the boxes on the right side of the Select The Users Who Can Access page.

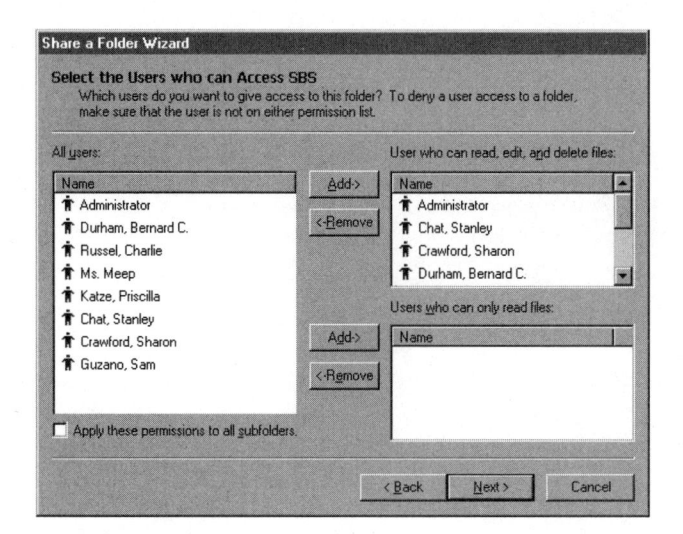

FIGURE 10.04

The wizard's Select The Users Who Can Access page.

6. If you want to apply these same permissions to any folder(s) within this shared folder, select the Apply These Permissions To All Subfolders check box. Click Next to continue.

7. The last page gives you a chance to either rethink your settings or put them into effect. Click Back to change any or all settings, or click Finish to share this folder.

8. Click OK in the confirmation dialog box and you should find yourself back on the Manage Shared Folders page.

With that, you've successfully shared a folder on your Small Business Server system.

NOTE

Two shared folders are created during the Small Business Server installation: the Company folder and the Users folder. The Company folder is for documents used by many people in your organization, such as a template for a legal contract or a billing invoice. The Users folder, which has the same name as a logged-in user, is for documents created by an individual user. On Microsoft Windows 95 and Microsoft Windows NT clients, shortcuts to these shared folders are automatically created on the clients' desktops.

WARNING!

Never move the folder named Users Shared Folders, and don't be tempted to move the folder by moving the Manage Server console. Doing so will cause all your user information to disappear from Small Business Server. Even if you move the Users Shared Folders folder to another location and then move it back to its original location, you won't be able to recover the loss. You will have to add all users again or, in the worst case scenario, reinstall Small Business Server.

◆ Sharing Folders on FAT and NTFS Drives

Shared folder access is somewhat trickier on FAT-formatted drives than on NTFS drives. For example, you must be careful if you use the Share A Folder icon to share a folder on a FAT drive and then try to restrict access to just one or two users. Unless you subsequently set the share permissions for this folder (see the sidebar titled "A Warning About Shared Folders on FAT Partitions" later in this chapter), other users will still have read-only access to this folder and the files in it. That is, they'll still be able to look at (but not touch) the files stored there. If you have sensitive files that you don't want anyone else to see, we recommend keeping them on floppy disks (thus avoiding potential network security glitches altogether) or ensuring that they're stored on an NTFS drive, where security is easier to achieve.

Unsharing a Folder

This procedure is the antidote to sharing a folder. If you unshare a folder, it becomes invisible (and thus unavailable) to users on the network. If you want to stop sharing a folder with a particular user or users, skip ahead to the next section, "Controlling User Access to Shared Folders." Otherwise, to stop sharing a folder across the network, follow these steps:

1. Make sure you're logged on using an account with administrative privileges. From the Start menu, choose Manage Server; on the Tasks page, choose Manage Shared Folders.

2. On the Manage Shared Folders page, select the folder you want to stop sharing, and then click on the Unshare A Folder icon. This will bring up a dialog box asking you to confirm whether you'd really like to stop sharing this folder.

3. If you click Yes, the folder will no longer be shared. Its entry will be removed from the shared folders list. If you click No, the folder will remain shared and will remain in the list.

Controlling User Access to Shared Folders

At some point, you'll undoubtedly want to change a user's permissions to access shared folders—when you change your mind about who you want accessing the contents of a shared folder or when you decide that it is safer to grant users read-only access to a particular folder. To make the changes, follow these steps:

1. Make sure you're logged on using an account with administrative privileges. From the Start menu, choose Manage Server; on the Tasks page, choose Manage Shared Folders.

2. On the Manage Shared Folders page, select a folder from the list and click on the Control User Access To Shared Folders icon. This will bring up the Shared Folder Access Wizard, whose first page is all but identical to the one shown in Figure 10.04 on page 169.

3. Use the Add and Remove buttons to adjust the lists of users in the read-edit-delete (top right) or the read-only (bottom right) privileges list. When you finish adjusting user permissions, click Next.

NOTE

To deny a user any access to a shared folder, make sure that his or her name does not appear in either of the lists on the right side of the wizard's Select The Users Who Can Access page.

4. Now you should see the Update Permissions page, which indicates that your changes are about to be applied. Click Back to change any settings, or click Finish to update this shared folder's permissions on your system.

Judicious management of user access to shared folders keeps sensitive files away from those who don't need to see them and, more important, prevents careless changes to vital documents.

Managing Folder Size

When a number of users share the same folders, hard disk space on your server can become scarce. In that case, you might want to use the Manage Folder Size icon on the Manage Shared Folders page to compress or uncompress a shared folder or to move a shared folder to a new location. Compressed folders are slower to access, so you'll probably want to compress folders only as a temporary measure.

From the Start menu, choose Manage Server; on the Tasks page, choose Manage Shared Folders. On the Manage Shared Folders page, select the folder in question from the list and click on the Manage Folder Size icon. This will bring up the Manage Folder Size page. (See Figure 10.05.)

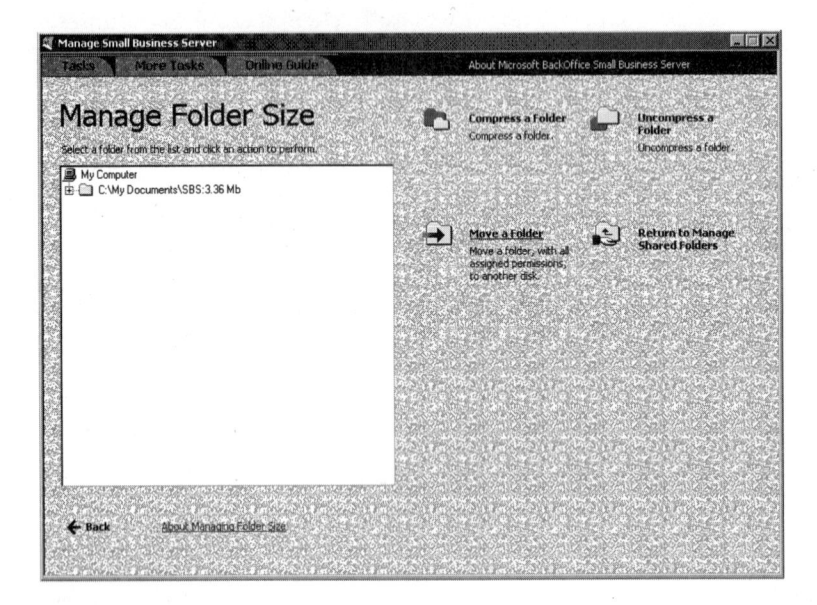

FIGURE 10.05

The Manage Folder Size page.

Compressing a Folder

To compress a folder, select it from the list on the Manage Folder Size page and then click on the Compress A Folder icon. The folder will be compressed, and you'll see a message to that effect.

NOTE

The Compress A Folder icon works only with NTFS folders.

Uncompressing a Folder

To uncompress a folder, select it from the list on the Manage Folder Size page and then click on the Uncompress A Folder icon. If the operation was successful, you'll see a message box confirming this. Click OK, and you'll find yourself back on the Manage Folder Size page. If something went wrong, you'll see an error message informing you why the folder you selected couldn't be uncompressed.

NOTE

The Uncompress A Folder icon works only with NTFS folders.

Moving a Shared Folder

The easiest way to move a shared folder in Small Business Server is to use the Manage Server interface. From the Start menu, choose Manage Server; on the Tasks page, choose Manage Shared Folders. On the Manage Shared Folders page, select the folder in question from the list and then click on the Move A Folder icon. This will start the Move Folder Wizard, whose first page is shown in Figure 10.06.

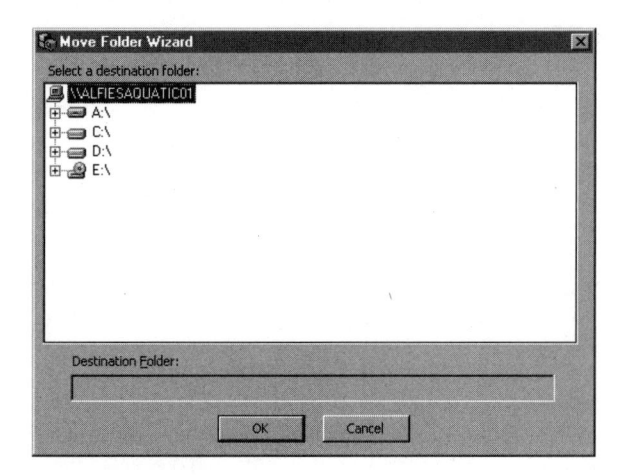

FIGURE 10.06
The opening page of the Move Folder Wizard.

CHAPTER 10   *Sharing Information on the Network*   **173**

On this page, select the destination drive and folder for the folder you'd like to move and then click OK. If all goes well, you'll see a message box confirming that the folder has been moved. Click OK, and you'll find yourself back on the Manage Folder Size page. If, on the other hand, all doesn't go well, you'll see an error message informing you why the folder you selected couldn't be moved.

NOTE

The Move A Folder icon works only with NTFS folders.

Moving a Folder That Isn't Shared

You're likely to have some folders on the server that aren't shared with users. To move a folder that isn't shared, follow these steps:

1. From the Start menu, choose Programs and then Windows NT Explorer.
2. Find the folder you want to move. Using the right mouse button, click on the folder and drag it to the new location.
3. When you release the mouse button, a pop-up menu will ask whether you want to move the item, copy it, or make a shortcut.
4. Choose Move, and the folder will appear in the new location.

You can open a second instance of Windows NT Explorer so that you can drag the folder directly from one location to another. Or you can move the folder to the desktop. Open the new location in Windows NT Explorer, and drag the folder there.

Shares vs. Share Permissions

Shares and share permissions, which sound very much alike, are not at all the same. Shares apply to folders only. Until a folder is shared, no one on the network can see it or gain access to it. When you share a folder in Small Business Server, you can specify who has access to it (and the files it contains) by adding users to or removing users from the lists on the Select The Users Who Can Access page (shown in Figure 10.04 on page 169).

On a FAT volume, you can share a folder and then add restrictions in the form of *share permissions*. However, the restrictions are only at the folder level, not at the file level. You can assign a user Full Control, Read, Change, or No Access permission. We'll explain exactly what each type of permission means in just a moment.

On an NTFS volume, folders have the same share permissions as those on a FAT volume but another layer of permission beyond that is available. Each folder has a Security properties page that allows more precise restrictions. Each file also has this Security properties page, so access can also be restricted or granted for individual files. These *folder permissions* and *file permissions* can further restrict access. For example, you can share a folder and grant access to it to a particular user or users and then use the Security properties page to set more restrictive permissions for the folder as a whole or file-by-file within the folder.

As a rule, it's best to leave share permissions at their default settings. Then, if need be, you can use the folder and file permissions for security control. The ability to apply restrictions to practically the microscopic level in Microsoft Windows NT Server can quickly produce complexities you do not want to deal with on "live" files. Start with the fewest restrictions on your users, and add to them only as necessary. Keep it simple.

Share Permissions

A share permission establishes the maximum level of access for the folder being shared. The permissions assigned on the Security properties page for shared folders (or for the files within shared folders on NTFS drives) can be more restrictive than the share permissions but can't expand permission. For example, a user who has Read permission for a folder won't be able to change or delete a file even if he or she has Change permission for the share. Microsoft Windows NT 4 share permissions, from most restrictive to least restrictive, are described in Table 10.01.

Table 10.01
Windows NT 4 Share Permissions

Type of Share Permission	Type of Access Allowed
No Access	Prevents all access to the folder (including its files and subfolders).
Read	Allows viewing of the file and subfolder names, viewing and copying of the data in files, and running applications.
Change	Allows Read access. Also allows adding files and subfolders to the shared folder, changing data in the files, and deleting files and subfolders.
Full Control	Allows Change access. Also allows changing permissions (NTFS volumes only) and taking ownership (NTFS volumes only).

Assigning Share Permissions

To assign a share permission, right-click on the folder and choose Properties from the pop-up menu. Click on the Sharing tab, and then click Permissions to open the dialog box shown in Figure 10.07 on the following page. Select the type of access you want to assign from the drop-down list at the bottom of the dialog box. Use the Add and Remove buttons to add or remove users from the list of users who have this type of access.

[Screenshot of the Access Through Share Permissions dialog box, showing Access Through Share: Temp, with a Name list containing: Administrator (Administrator) — Full Control; CREATOR OWNER — Read; crussel (Russel, Charlie) — Full Control; Guest — Read; INTERACTIVE — Read; IUSR_ALFIESAQUATIC01 (Internet Guest Ac — Read; scrawford (Crawford, Sharon) — Full Control. Type of Access: Full Control. Buttons: OK, Cancel, Add..., Remove, Help.]

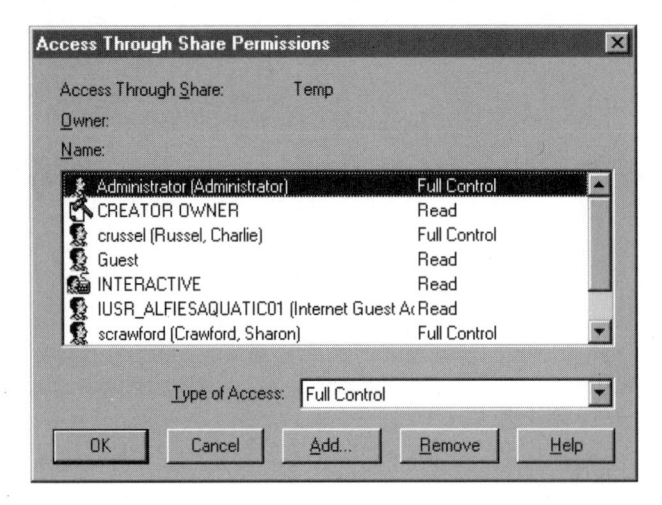

FIGURE 10.07

The Access Through Share Permissions dialog box.

◆ A Warning About Shared Folders on FAT Partitions

If you've shared a folder on a FAT-formatted drive that contains files that you want only certain users to see, beware! To deny read-only access to this folder across the network (access that all users have unless you intentionally do something about it), follow these steps:

1. Right-click on the folder in Windows NT Explorer, and choose Properties from the pop-up menu. Click on the Sharing tab, and then click Permissions to open the Access Through Share Permissions dialog box (shown above).

2. Scroll down the Name list until you see an entry for NETWORK. Select this entry, and then click Remove. Only the users you specified when you shared this folder (whose names should appear as individual entries on the Name list) will be able to view the files in this folder. If you want to prevent users with Interactive privileges from gaining read-only access to the files in this folder, select the entry for INTERACTIVE and then click Remove. Click OK to return to the Properties dialog box for this folder, and then click OK to update its share permissions.

Note that it's not necessary to perform these steps on an NTFS-formatted drive because that file format has built-in security features that the FAT format lacks.

Folder and File Permissions

On an NTFS volume, you can set permissions all the way down to the file level, which means you can give one user read-only access, another user full control, and everyone else no access to the same file. We repeat, you *can* do this—but in this approach lies madness for all but the most meticulous of control freaks (who are, arguably, already mad).

Always try to operate your system with the simplest possible set of permissions. Assign as few restrictions as possible, and assign them to groups, not to individuals. Don't assign file-by-file permissions unless it is truly unavoidable. Managing the minutiae of permissions can quickly soak up all of your time and much of your life's blood as well.

Viewing Permissions for Folders

Sharing a folder on an NTFS volume is best done using the Share A Folder icon on the Manage Shared Folders page, but it pays to remember that when you assign folder permissions, you are also assigning permissions for all of the files and subfolders in the folder. To check your work and view the permissions for a shared folder, follow these steps:

1. Right-click on the folder, and choose Properties from the pop-up menu.
2. Click on the Security tab, and then click Permissions.
3. If you want to add a user to or remove a user from the Name list, the best way is to use the Control User Access To Shared Folders icon on the Manage Shared Folders page. See the earlier section titled "Controlling User Access to Shared Folders" for complete instructions on how to do this.

Assigning Permissions for Files

It's certainly possible to take advantage of NTFS security features by assigning permissions for individual files, but we urge you to think carefully before doing so because you could end up spending a lot of time resetting file permissions. If you're sure that you want to set permissions on a particular file, here's how:

1. Right-click on the file, and choose Properties from the pop-up menu.
2. Click on the Security tab, and then click Permissions to open the File Permissions dialog box. (See Figure 10.08 on the following page.)

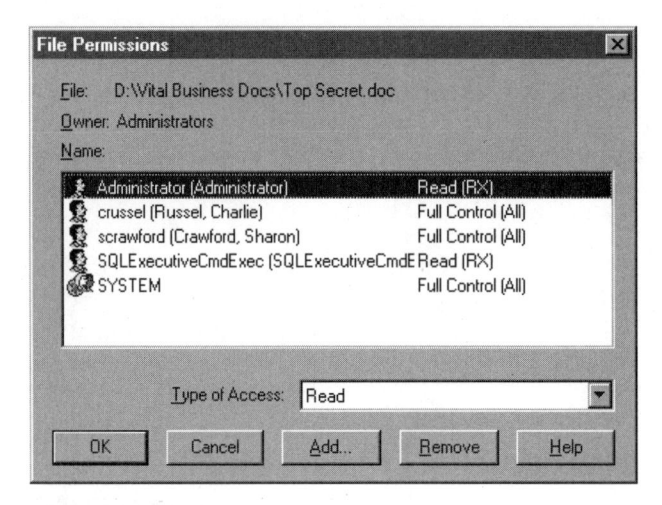

FIGURE 10.08

The File Permissions dialog box.

3. To remove a user from the list of users with file permissions, select the name and click Remove.

4. To add a user to the list of users with file permissions, click Add. This will open the Add Users And Groups dialog box. (See Figure 10.09.)

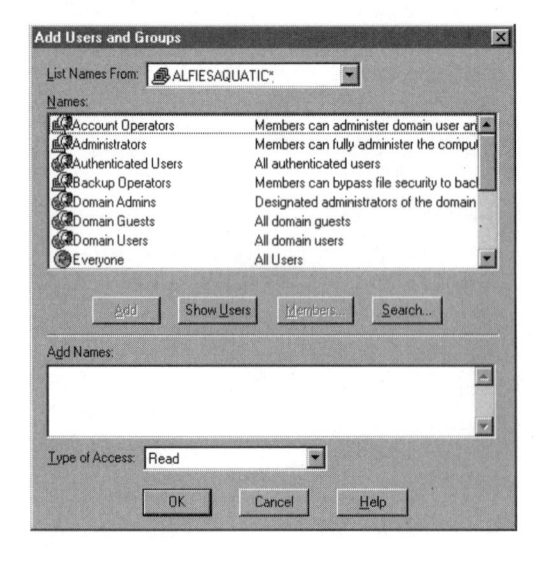

FIGURE 10.09

The Add Users And Groups dialog box.

178 PERFORMING BASIC TASKS

5. Although this dialog box offers you a huge array of options, we think it's safest to stick to the basics. Click Show Users to add a list of the users on your network to the Names list, and then scroll down the list until you find the user you want to add.

6. Select the user's name and click Add, set the type of access using the drop-down list, and click OK. Now the user should appear in the Name list.

7. Click OK to return to the Properties dialog box for this file, and then click OK to update its permissions.

After you complete these steps, you might want to reopen the file's Properties dialog box to determine whether the permissions for this file are set the way you want them to be.

Who Can Share Folders

As the above sections imply, the answer to the question "Who can share folders?" depends on a number of factors:

- Whether a folder has been shared across the network
- Whether the volume on which the folder is located is FAT-formatted or NTFS-formatted
- How share permissions (FAT volumes) and folder and file permissions (NTFS volumes) are set

In theory, it's possible to share every folder on the network with every user, but you probably won't ever want to do this. A more likely scenario is that you have a series of folders to which everyone needs access and that are shared with all users, and you have a smaller number of folders to which only certain people need access and that are shared with just those users.

POINTS TO REMEMBER

- Until a folder is shared, no one has access to it over the network.
- Share permissions are the only restrictions available for folders on FAT partitions.

- Share permissions establish the maximum level of access available to resources shared on the network. Other permissions assigned to a folder or a file (on an NTFS volume) can be more restrictive, but they can't be less restrictive than share permissions.

- Permissions are additive, except for the No Access permission, which can override all other permissions.

- Keep share and permission assignments as simple as possible. It's very, very easy to weave a tangled web—and very, very hard to extricate yourself from it later.

WHAT'S NEXT

Chapter 11 will guide you through the complexities of managing the computers on your Small Business Server network.

Chapter 11

Managing Computers on the Network

183	Setting Up a Computer	
	At the Server	183
	At the Client Computer	184
185	Adding a User to an Existing Computer	
186	Logging On to a Client Locally	
187	Removing a Computer from the Network	
187	Reinstating a Removed Computer	
188	Closing Open Files	
188	Disconnecting Users	
189	Adding SBS Components to the Server	
190	Adding SBS Components to a Client Computer	
191	Installing or Removing an Application on the Server	
193	Adding or Removing Components of Microsoft Windows NT Server	
194	Points to Remember	
194	What's Next	

CHAPTER 11

Managing Computers on the Network

After you add users and set up shared folders and permissions, only a few basic chores remain. In this chapter, we'll cover some of the tasks that administrators have to do often—add computers to the network, add users to existing client computers, install Microsoft BackOffice Small Business Server components, and install software on the server. In addition, we'll cover a few chores that are less common but still essential—closing open files, disconnecting users, and removing computers from the network.

To manage the computers on your network, make sure you're logged on using an account with administrative privileges. From the Start menu, choose Manage Server. When you see the first page of the Small Business Server console (the Tasks page), click on the More Tasks tab and then click on the Manage Computers icon. This will bring up the Manage Computers page, shown in Figure 11.01.

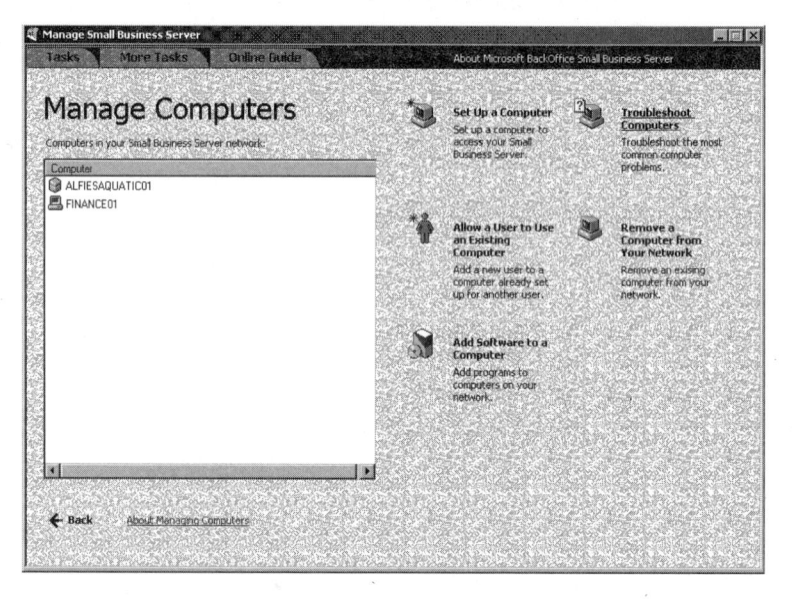

FIGURE 11.01

The Manage Computers page.

On the left side of the page is a list of the computers on your Small Business Server network. On the right side are five icons for carrying out essential computer management tasks. The function of each icon is described in the following sections.

Setting Up a Computer

Adding a new computer to your network involves two steps. One step is performed at the server, the other at the new client computer.

At the Server

First you need to run the Set Up Computer Wizard on the server to tell the server about the new computer and what you want installed on it. The wizard creates a setup disk that the user can take to the new computer to complete the setup process. Here are the steps to follow:

1. From the Start menu, choose Manage Server. Click on the More Tasks tab, and then choose Manage Computers.

2. Click on the Set Up A Computer icon. On the Select A User page that opens, select the name of the person who'll be using this new computer. Click Next.

3. On the Specify The Computer Name page (Figure 11.02), you can accept the suggested name for the user's computer or type a different name. Click Next.

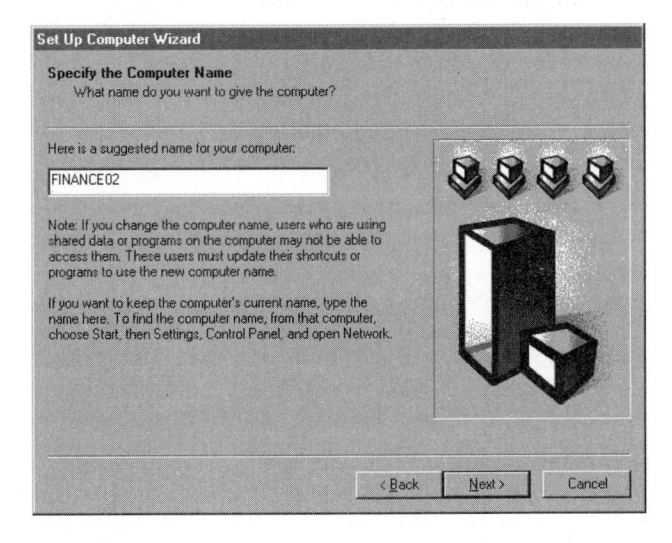

FIGURE 11.02

The Specify The Computer Name page.

4. On the Operating System page, specify which operating system is installed on the computer you're setting up. Click Next.

5. On the Select The Programs To Install page, select the programs you want to install. To proceed without installing any client programs, click the option button labeled I Do Not Wish To Install Any Programs At This Time and then click Next.

6. When you arrive at the Create The Setup Disk page, label a disk and insert it in the server's floppy disk drive. Click Next, and let the Set Up Computer Wizard do the rest. It will format the disk (if necessary) and then copy the appropriate files to it.

At the Client Computer

Take the setup disk (created in the previous section) to the new computer, and follow these steps:

1. Start the computer you want to set up. Make sure all the network cables are connected.

2. Log on to the computer using an account that has administrative privileges.

3. Insert the setup disk in the floppy drive.

4. From the Start menu, choose Run.

5. Type *a:\setup.exe* in the Open text box.

6. An automated program will run; it will require little input from the user. After the setup process is complete, the client computer will reboot and the user can log on.

NOTE

If you're installing Microsoft Windows NT Workstation or Microsoft Windows 95 on a new computer in order to add it to a Small Business Server network, don't install networking on the client. The setup disk created by the server will painlessly install all necessary networking components.

7. The Client Installation Wizard will install the software that was specified in step 5 of the previous procedure. This might take a few minutes, particularly if you're installing all the available client programs.

8. Click Finish when the installation is done. You'll need to reboot to apply all the new settings.

Adding a User to an Existing Computer

Once you set up a computer for a particular user, you can add another user to the existing setup. Of course, any user can log on from any client and even access shared folders; but to use e-mail, have access to modems on the server, and so forth, the user must be formally added to that computer.

To add a user for this purpose, do the following:

1. From the Start menu, choose Manage Server. Click on the More Tasks tab, and then choose Manage Computers.
2. Click on the Allow A User To Use An Existing Computer icon.
3. Select the name of the user you want to add to the client. Click Next.
4. Select the computer, and click Next again.
5. Select the programs you want installed for this user on the client computer. Click Next twice.
6. The setup files are prepared for the user. Click Finish.

Next, go to the client computer and log on using an account with administrative privileges. On the client, follow these steps:

1. Click OK to complete the installation of the client software.
2. From the Start menu, choose Programs, Administrative Tools, and then User Manager.
3. Double-click on Administrators in the Groups list box.
4. In the Local Group Properties dialog box (Figure 11.03), click the Add button.

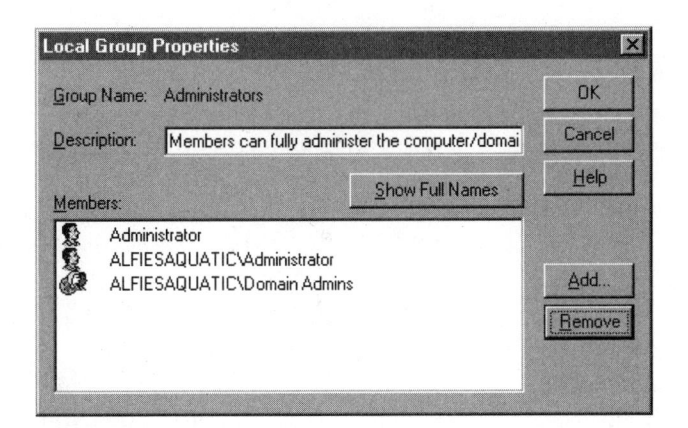

FIGURE 11.03

Adding the user to the local Administrators group.

5. In the Add Users And Groups dialog box (Figure 11.04), select the user in the Names list and then click Add.

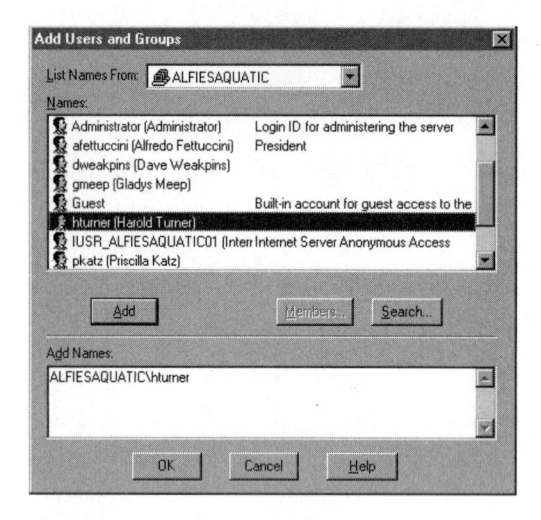

FIGURE 11.04

Selecting the domain user hturner to be a local administrator.

Back in the Local Group Properties dialog box, the user has been added to the local Administrators group. Click OK.

A user who is also a local administrator can make modifications, install software, and configure the client machine. The user doesn't have to log on locally; he or she can log on as a member of the Small Business Server domain. However, the user's rights and privileges on the server will remain unchanged.

Logging On to a Client Locally

What does it mean to log on locally? And why would anyone want to do it? A user with a user account on the client can log on to that computer (as opposed to the Small Business Server domain) and install software on the client and configure it pretty much in any way. But then, so can someone who's been added to the Administrators group using the method described in the previous section. In addition, the locally logged on user won't have access to the server components such as the shared modems or the fax services and won't be able to access the Internet. So why do it?

The ability to log on locally is important if the machine is frequently disconnected from the network, as in the case of a laptop that travels with a user. And it's handy if the server is not available—if it's down for maintenance or whatever. The local user can still log on and get at the files stored on the client computer.

Giving someone the ability to log on locally to a client requires several steps, but none is complicated. Log on to the client using a client account with administrative privileges (an administrative account is always created when Microsoft Windows NT is installed), and then follow these steps:

1. From the Start menu, choose Programs, Administrative Tools, and then User Manager.

2. Choose New User from the User menu.

3. Provide the user name, full name, and a password. Click the Groups button.

4. Unless you want to limit the user's ability to change the computer setup, make the user a member of the Administrators group for this machine.

5. Click OK. In the New User dialog box, click Add.

Now, even when the server is off line or when the client is disconnected from the network, the user can still log on to the client.

NOTE

None of this applies to Windows 95 clients because a user can always log on locally. Only Windows NT Workstation clients have sufficient security to require the steps detailed above.

Removing a Computer from the Network

Small Business Server makes removing a client computer from your network about as easy as it can be. Just select the computer in the list on the Manage Computers page, and then click on the Remove A Computer From Your Network icon. You'll see a message box asking you to confirm whether you want to remove this computer. If you're sure you do, click Yes. You might have to reboot the server to delete the computer from the list.

Reinstating a Removed Computer

If you remove a computer from the network and later decide to reconnect it, the procedure is just like the one described in the section titled "Setting Up a Computer" earlier in this chapter. You have to create a setup disk on the server and then take the disk to the computer you want to reinstate.

> **Tip**
>
> *If you reinstate the client with the same user name and computer name it had before, other users on the network might not have to update their shortcuts to this machine.*

Closing Open Files

If you're getting ready to do a backup or need to reboot the server, any open files will be disrupted and data can be lost. Be sure that no files are open before you do anything that could cause a problem. Of course, you could just announce to everybody, "Hey, I'm going to reboot the server! Close everything down!" This would probably even work. But there are times when a poorly behaved application creates files that won't shut down willingly. Then you need a method of forcing the matter.

Fortunately, Small Business Server provides a quick path to open files. From the Start menu, choose Manage Server and then click on the Manage Shared Folders icon. Select the folder you want to check, and then click on the Manage Open Files icon. On the Manage Open Files page, you'll see a list of the files that are open in that folder.

To close a file, select it and then click on the Close File icon. Click on the Close All Files icon if (you guessed it) you want to close all the open files in the folder.

Disconnecting Users

For even more direct action, you can forcibly disconnect users. This is advisable only when no other reasonable alternative is available because it can cause a certain amount of hard feeling if you cut people off willy-nilly. From the Start menu, choose Manage Server, Tasks, and Manage Shared Folders, and then click on the Manage Connected Users icon. On the Manage Connected Users page, you should see a list of connected users on the left side and four icons on the right.

To disconnect a user from the network, select the user's name in the list and then click on the Disconnect User icon. You'll be prompted to confirm the disconnection. To disconnect everyone from the server, click on the Disconnect All Users icon, and it shall be so.

Adding SBS Components to the Server

If you didn't install some of the server components at the time of installation, you can add them at any time. In general, adding components requires a reboot of the server to update the new settings, so it's best to perform this kind of maintenance when a reboot will cause the least disruption. Follow these steps:

1. Put the Small Business Server CD in the server's CD-ROM drive.

2. Double-click on the My Computer icon on the desktop, and then double-click on the CD-ROM drive icon.

3. Double-click on the icon for sbssetup.exe to open the Small Business Server startup screen (Figure 11.05).

FIGURE 11.05

The startup screen is the place to begin for adding and removing server components.

4. Click the Add/Remove Software button. Click on the Install/Uninstall tab of the Add/Remove Programs Properties dialog box. (See Figure 11.06 on the following page.)

5. Select Microsoft Small Business Server in the software list, and then click the Add/Remove button.

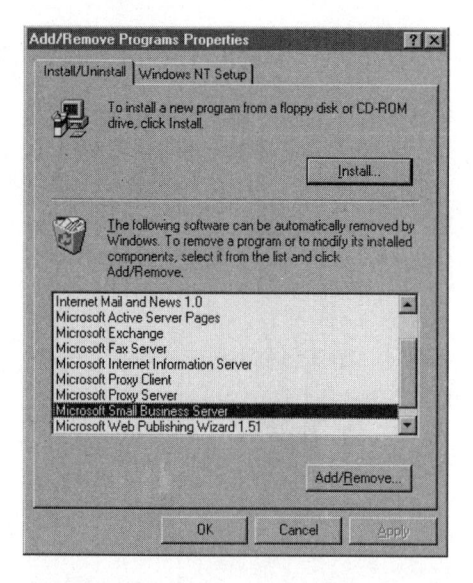

FIGURE 11.06

Select Microsoft Small Business Server to add or remove components.

6. Click Next to bypass the company information page.

7. On the next page, you can view a list of components. Those with selected check boxes are already installed. If you select a check box, the corresponding item will be installed. If you deselect a check box, the corresponding item will be removed. Select the component you want to install and click Next.

8. The installation will proceed. You'll be prompted to restart the computer in order to update the settings.

Adding SBS Components to a Client Computer

Most of the server components have a server part and a client part. If you add or update some part of Small Business Server, you must install the client portion as well as the server portion. Follow these steps:

1. From the Start menu, choose Manage Server. Click on the More Tasks tab, and then choose Manage Computers.

2. Click on the Add Software To A Computer icon. This will start the Set Up Computer Wizard.

3. On the Select A User page, select the user of the computer to which you want to add software, and then click Next.

4. Select the computer in the list, and then click Next. This will bring up the Select The Programs To Install page, shown in Figure 11.07.

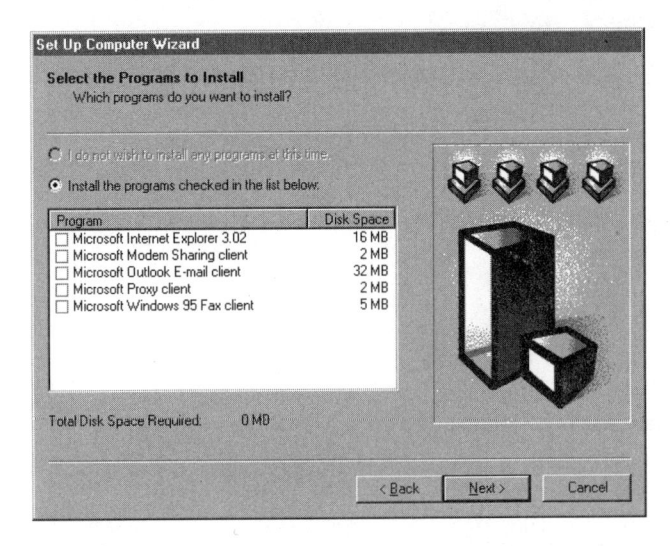

FIGURE 11.07

On this page, you select the programs to install on the client.

5. Note that on this page, the second option is selected for you. Use the check boxes to specify which program or programs you want to install, and be sure to keep track of how much hard disk space you'll need on the client computer. When you're done, click Next.

6. On the Create The Setup Disk page, click Next. The wizard will copy the necessary files to the client.

When the user next logs on to the client, the installation will be complete.

Installing or Removing an Application on the Server

Any software manufacturer who wants the right to put a Windows NT logo on a product is supposed to make sure the program can uninstall itself. This is meant to correct a problem in previous versions of Windows NT that made it very difficult to completely remove a program and all of its associated files.

Programs written for versions of Windows NT before version 4 don't have this uninstall capability. And some programs written specifically for Microsoft Windows NT 4 leave bits of themselves cluttering your hard disk even after they are uninstalled. This situation will probably improve over time. How the major programs written for Windows NT 4 handle the Add/Remove feature varies widely. Some uninstall themselves without a fuss; others give you the option of removing all or parts of the program. You have to select the program and click Remove to see. *Nothing* will be uninstalled without your OK.

Although the Remove behavior of the Add/Remove feature isn't always predictable, Add/Remove is an easy-to-use tool for installing new programs. Just follow these steps:

1. Make sure that the Install/Uninstall tab of the Add/Remove Programs Properties dialog box (shown on page 190) is open.

2. Click Install. This will start the Install Program From Floppy Disk Or CD-ROM Wizard (Figure 11.08), which will do the job for you.

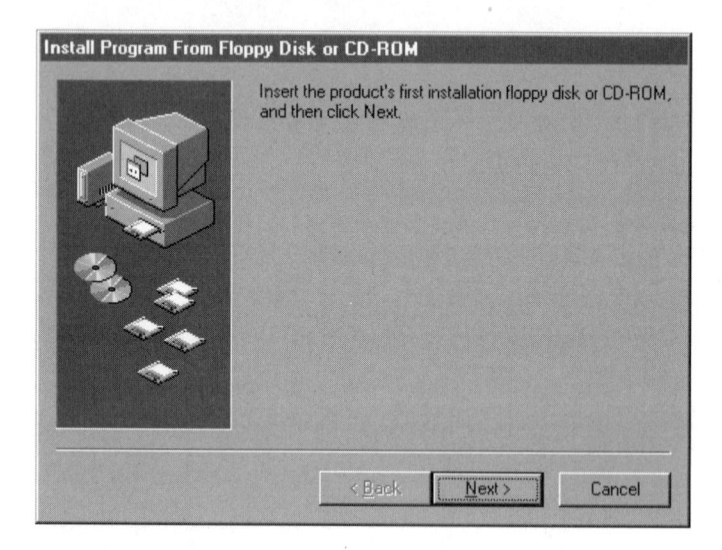

FIGURE 11.08

The first page of the Install Program From Floppy Disk Or CD-ROM Wizard.

3. Insert the floppy disk or CD containing the application's setup or installation program into the appropriate drive; click Next. The program will search for an installation program first in drive A, then in drive B, and finally in the CD-ROM drive. Click Finish to continue.

4. The installation program of the application will take over, so follow the instructions on the screen to finish installing your application.

5. Click OK once or twice until you end up back on the More Tasks page, and you're done.

NOTE

Administrative privileges are necessary to install software on a client as well as on the server.

Adding or Removing Components of Microsoft Windows NT Server

Windows NT Server also has components that can be added to or removed from the server. To change what's installed as part of the Windows NT operating system, follow these steps:

1. From the Start menu, choose Settings and then Control Panel. In the Control Panel, double-click on the Add/Remove Programs icon.

2. Click on the Windows NT Setup tab of the Add/Remove Programs Properties dialog box (Figure 11.09). Select any group, and click Details to see the individual components.

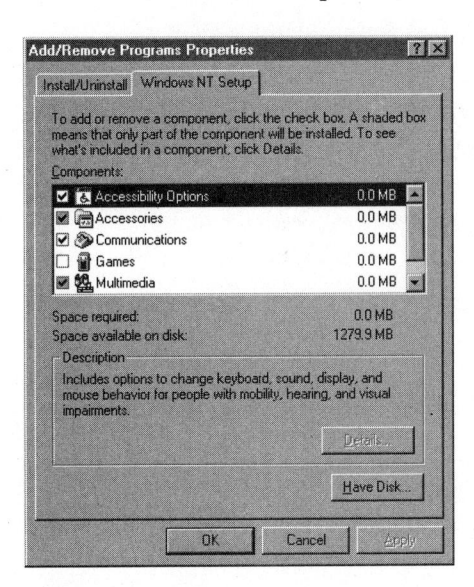

FIGURE 11.09

The Windows NT Setup tab of the Add/Remove Programs Properties dialog box.

CHAPTER 11 *Managing Computers on the Network* **193**

3. As you click on each item in a group, a description of the item's function will appear at the bottom of the page. The rules are simple:

- If an item is checked, it's installed. Deselect the check box, and it'll be removed.
- If an item is not checked, it's not installed on your system. Select its check box, and it'll be installed.
- If the check box is gray, part of the component is selected for installation. Click the Details button to specify which parts you want to install or remove.

4. Click OK once or twice until the window closes. If prompted, return the Small Business Server CD to the CD-ROM drive.

For More Information

To troubleshoot problems with the server or network, see Chapter 27.

POINTS TO REMEMBER

- For a user to log on locally to a computer, he or she must have a user account on that local machine—not just a network user account.
- Adding and removing software from the server might require a reboot, so schedule this maintenance during off-hours if possible.
- The servers that are part of Small Business Server have both a server component and a client component. When you install or update the servers, both components must be installed for the program to work.

WHAT'S NEXT

In this chapter, you learned how to manage the client computers on your Small Business Server system. In the next chapter, we'll move on to the Control Panel, the "nerve center" for your server.

Chapter 12

Using the Control Panel

- 196 Accessibility Options
- 198 Add/Remove Programs
- 198 Console
- 201 Date/Time
- 202 Devices
- 203 Dial-Up Monitor
- 204 Display
- 205 Fax Client and Fax Server
- 206 Fonts
- 209 Internet
- 210 Keyboard
- 212 Licensing
- 213 Mail
- 213 Modem Sharing Server
- 214 Modems
- 218 Mouse
- 222 MS DTC
- 223 Multimedia
- 225 Network
- 225 ODBC
- 225 PC Card (PCMCIA)
- 226 Ports
- 226 Printers
- 226 Regional Settings
- 227 SCSI Adapters
- 227 Server
- 229 Services
- 229 Sounds
- 231 System
- 234 Tape Devices
- 234 Telephony
- 235 UPS
- 236 WSP Client
- 237 Points to Remember
- 237 What's Next

CHAPTER 12
Using the Control Panel

If you've fiddled around with the Control Panel at all, you know that it's an operations center for Microsoft Windows NT Server, with additional functions for Microsoft BackOffice Small Business Server. Most of the settings specific to Small Business Server are better reached using the Small Business Server console, but a good many of the Windows NT Server settings are reachable only through the Control Panel.

This chapter includes a section on each of the icons in the Control Panel, in alphabetic order. If the settings reached via an icon are detailed elsewhere in this book, you'll be pointed to the correct location.

To open the Control Panel, choose Settings, Control Panel from the Start menu. You can also reach the Control Panel by clicking on its icon on the More Tasks page of the Small Business Server console.

Accessibility Options

The accessibility options are installed automatically in Small Business Server, but they're turned off by default. To turn on any of the options, double-click on the Accessibility Options icon to open the Accessibility Properties dialog box (Figure 12.01). Here you'll find options for adding sound to the usual visual cues, adding visual cues to the sound cues, and making the keyboard and mouse easier to use for those of us with dexterity problems.

FIGURE 12.01

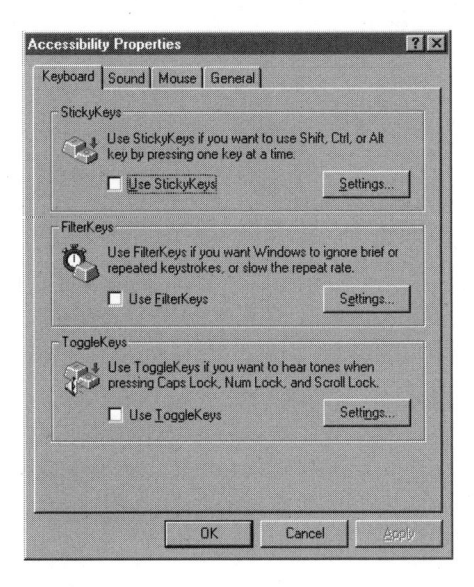

The Accessibility Properties dialog box.

Not all of the settings are obvious, so when you come across one that you can't identify, click on the question mark in the upper right corner of the dialog box and then click on the text for more information.

After you select your settings, don't leave until you click on the General tab and check the Automatic Reset section. Select the Turn Off Accessibility Features After Idle check box if you want the options turned off when the computer hasn't been used for the period specified in the Minutes box. Deselect the check box if you want to make the selection of options permanent.

> **Tip**
>
> *The ToggleKeys option on the Keyboard tab is of great help if you often hit the Caps Lock key inadvertently and look up to find your text looking like cALL mS. gAUS-gROSS iN tRINIDAD-tOBAGO. With the Use ToggleKeys check box selected, you'll hear a quiet but distinct warning beep when Caps Lock is switched on.*

Add/Remove Programs

Chapter 11 has sections devoted to adding and removing programs as well as the various components of Small Business Server, so check there for details on how the Add/Remove Programs icon works.

Console

The Console window, sometimes referred to as the DOS window, is your command line interface to Windows NT. You can customize the default console window by double-clicking on the Console icon to bring up the Console Windows Properties dialog box, shown in Figure 12.02.

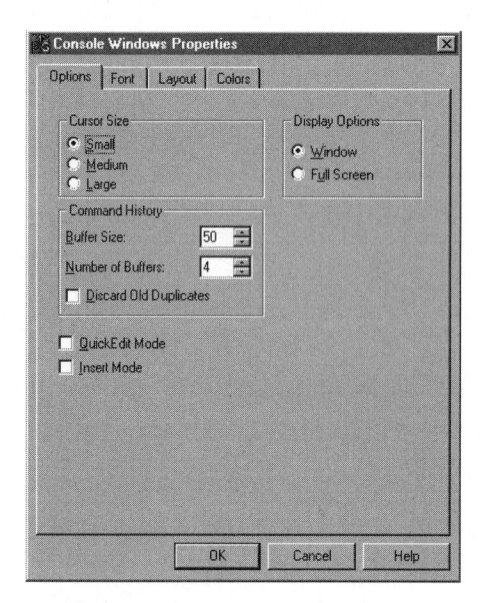

FIGURE 12.02

The Console Windows Properties dialog box.

Before you get carried away customizing your Console window, it's useful to know that the tabs of the Console Windows Properties dialog box overlap with the DOS Properties sheet for a given program. Changes you make here become the default for all windows. But changes to a particular program's DOS Properties sheet are seen only by that program.

Options Tab

The Options tab of the Console Windows Properties dialog box, shown in Figure 12.02, gives you control over a number of things. Here's an overview of what the settings mean:

- **Cursor Size** You can specify that the cursor be small (the default), medium, or large, depending on how often you plan to use the command prompt and how good your eyes are.

- **Display Options** If you're running a graphical program, you'll probably want to have it use the full screen, but most text-based programs run better in a window, so make your display selection based on the kinds of programs you'll be running most often.

- **Command History** By default, you're given a buffer large enough to "remember" the last 50 commands you executed, which should be enough for even the nerdiest among us. And you've got four buffers, so that makes for 200 commands altogether—which should be enough for most purposes. If you're really into having squeaky-clean buffers, select the Discard Old Duplicates check box; any duplicate commands will magically disappear.

- **QuickEdit Mode** This option allows you to use your mouse to select text for cut-and-copy operations. If this check box is deselected, you must use the Mark command on the program's Edit menu to mark text.

- **Insert Mode** Select this check box if you want text to be inserted at the cursor. If insert mode is not enabled, text typed at the cursor replaces the existing text (overtypes).

Font Tab

The Font tab of the Console Windows Properties dialog box lets you select a font style and size for your Console window. There's even a Window Preview feature so that you can see how your selection will look.

To select a font size, scroll through the Size list until you see a size you like. Select it, and that's all there is to it. To select a typeface, select one from the Font list. Before you OK your way out, check the Window Preview box to make sure you're pleased with the results.

Layout Tab

The Layout tab of the Console Windows Properties dialog box lets you select a screen buffer size, a window size, and a window position. Frankly, you'll probably never need to change these settings, but in case you're curious, here's what they are:

- **Screen Buffer Size** This setting determines the width and height of the Console window. The width setting determines the number of characters in each line, and the height setting determines how many lines are stored in memory. If the current window size is smaller than the screen buffer size settings, scroll bars are displayed so that you can scroll back through the information.

- **Window Size** Here you can specify the visible width and height, in characters, of the Console window.

- **Window Position** This setting specifies the left and top position of the Console window. If you'd like the system to position the window (this is usually the best thing to do), select the Let System Position Window check box.

Colors Tab

The Colors tab of the Console Windows Properties dialog box (Figure 12.03) is where you can really display your individualistic (and perhaps artistic) tendencies. Some people prefer the plain old black background with grayish text, while others prefer to perform command prompt functions in living color. Suit yourself. Here's what you need to know about the settings on the Colors tab:

- **Screen Text** Select this option to change the color of the screen text in a Console window.

- **Screen Background** This option lets you change the color of the screen background in a Console window.

- **Popup Text** Select this option to change the color of the text in a pop-up window.

- **Popup Background** This option lets you change the color of the background in a pop-up window.

- **Selected Color Values** You can use these boxes to increase or decrease the amount of primary color used in a color. The valid range is from 0 to 255 in the Red, Green, and Blue boxes.

- **Palette (color boxes)** This row of 16 squares displays the colors available for your text and backgrounds. Click one to change the color of the currently selected text or background. Use the Selected Color Values boxes to change the color that appears in a color box.

FIGURE 12.03

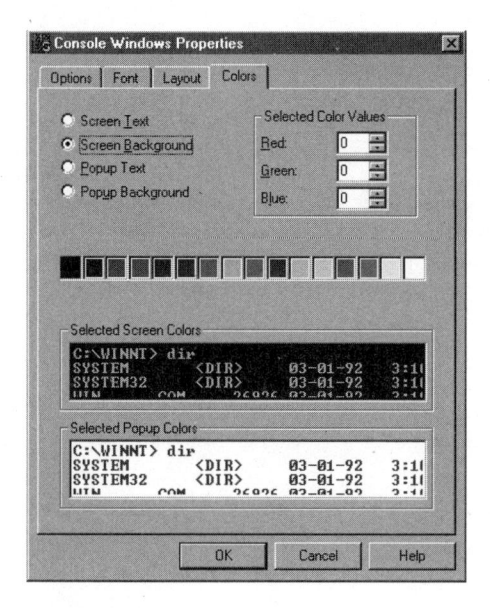

The Colors tab of the Console Windows Properties dialog box.

◆ **Selected Screen Colors** This little window gives you a preview of your selected screen colors. Be sure that you like your selections before you click OK.

◆ **Selected Popup Colors** This window, like the Selected Screen Colors window, is for preview purposes. If you've monkeyed with the pop-up text or the background settings, it's probably a good idea to make sure your new settings will be legible.

Date/Time

Double-click on the Date/Time icon in the Control Panel, and you'll see the Date/Time Properties dialog box (Figure 12.04 on the following page). If you're logged on using an account with administrative privileges, you can use this dialog box to adjust your system's date and time settings.

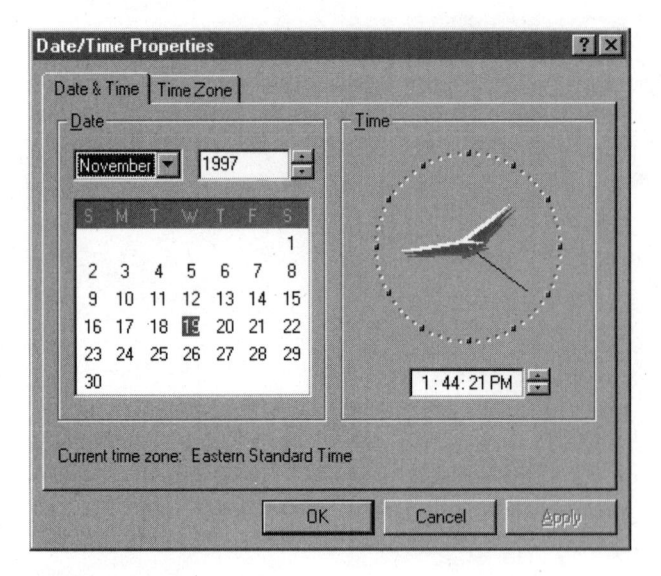

FIGURE 12.04
The Date/Time Properties dialog box.

On the Date & Time tab, select the appropriate month, year, day, and time. Use the Time Zone tab to specify which time zone you're in and whether the system should automatically adjust the clock for daylight saving changes.

NOTE

If you failed to specify the appropriate time zone during installation, Small Business Server puts you in Greenwich Mean Time (GMT). Use the Date/Time element of the Control Panel to correct this oversight.

Devices

Double-click on the Devices icon in the Control Panel, and you'll see a mysterious-looking list of items. (See Figure 12.05.) This is actually an inventory of devices on your system, including basic items such as your keyboards, ports, and mouse and more complicated items such as hardware and software drivers.

FIGURE 12.05

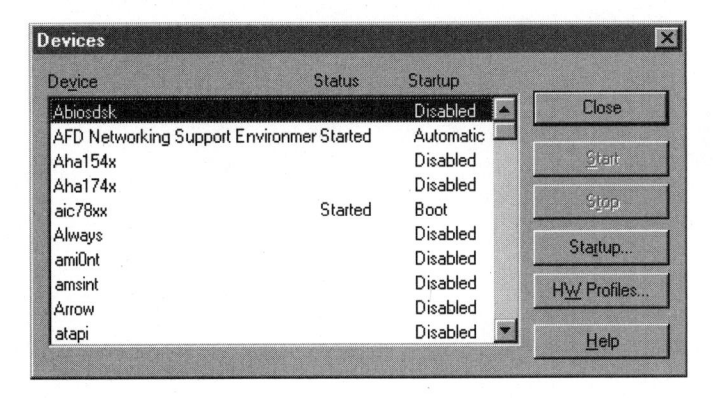

The Devices dialog box.

Unless you're absolutely sure that you know what you're doing, we advise leaving these settings alone. In most cases, the default settings are the appropriate ones, and if you inadvertently change a device setting, you might have a hard time figuring out what's wrong with your system.

Dial-Up Monitor

If you have Dial-Up Networking or Remote Access Service installed, you'll have an icon for the Dial-Up Networking Monitor, which lets you keep tabs on your modem network connection.

For Your Information

Remote Access Service is covered in Chapter 19, where you'll learn all the details about connecting to the outside world.

Display

The Display icon lets you control all the settings that affect your screen display, including colors, screen savers, typefaces in windows and dialog boxes, and resolutions. If you double-click on the Display icon, you'll see something that resembles Figure 12.06.

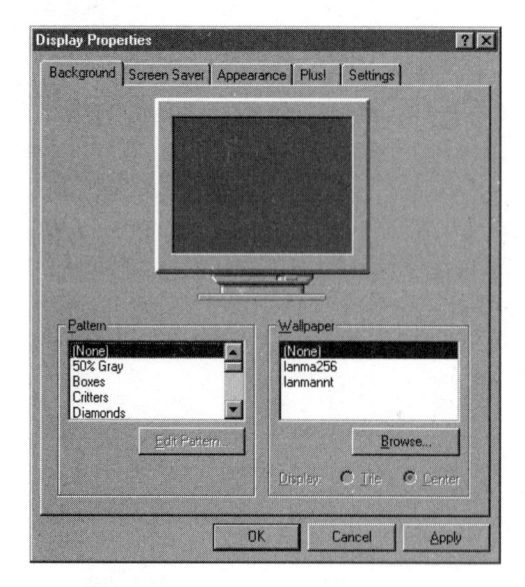

FIGURE 12.06

The Display Properties dialog box.

Here's a brief overview of what you can do on each tab of the Display Properties dialog box:

- ◆ **Background** Select the pattern of the background or the wallpaper that will be displayed in your main Small Business Server window.

- ◆ **Screen Saver** Specify whether you'd like to use a screen saver, set screen saver settings, preview a screen saver, indicate whether your screen saver should be password protected, and determine the interval that Small Business Server should wait before starting the screen saver.

- **Appearance** Select a color scheme for various screen elements in Small Business Server, including the inactive and active windows, selected menu options, window text, message box, message text, and more. Experiment with changing colors if you like, but be sure that whatever combination you select is legible.

- **Plus!** Change icons and alter some of the visual settings on your computer. Use the buttons and check boxes to tailor the appearance of Small Business Server to suit your taste.

- **Settings** Change the number of colors in your palette, the resolution of the desktop area, font size, refresh frequency, video modes, and display type. Also, a handy button allows you to test your display settings. Be sure to use it if you alter something major such as the desktop resolution. Otherwise, you might find that everything on your screen has become impossibly tiny and therefore illegible.

NOTE

Proper display settings for your equipment should have been detected during Small Business Server installation. If not, or if you change your mind about the desktop resolution or swap one monitor for another, for example, the Display element of the Control Panel will help you keep your system up to date.

Fax Client and Fax Server

Fax Client

Fax Server

This book has a whole chapter devoted to managing fax services on your Small Business Server system. See Chapter 15 for complete details.

Fonts

TrueType fonts are managed in Small Business Server in a clear and understandable way. To see the list of fonts on your computer, double-click on the Fonts icon.

Selecting and Viewing Fonts

The Fonts folder is a little different from the usual folders in that the menus show some new items. On the View menu, shown in Figure 12.07, you'll find, in addition to the choices for viewing icons and lists, a command called List Fonts By Similarity.

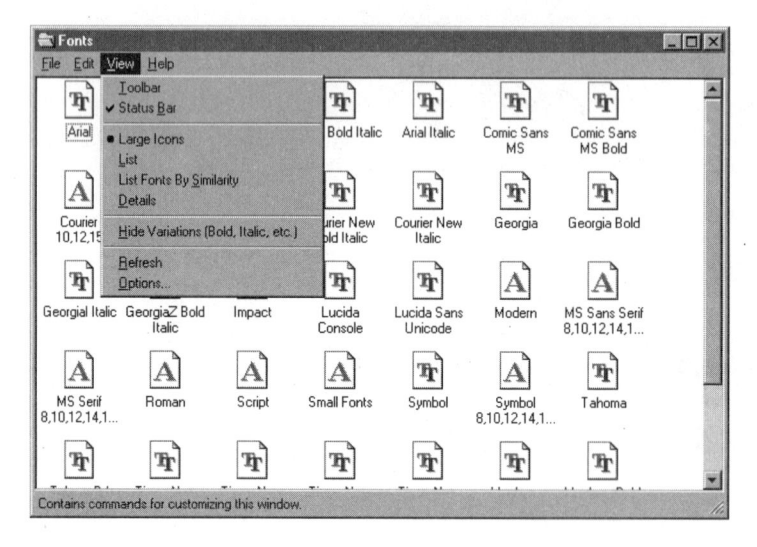

FIGURE 12.07

The View menu is a little different in the Fonts folder.

> **Tip**
>
> *If your font list is long and unwieldy, select the Hide Variations option on the View menu. That will conceal font variations such as italic and bold and make the list easier to look through.*

If you choose List Fonts By Similarity, the Fonts folder will change to resemble Figure 12.08. Select a font in the drop-down list at the top of the window; the other fonts will line up in terms of their degree of similarity. Before you make a commitment, you can double-click on a font. A window will open with a complete view of the font.

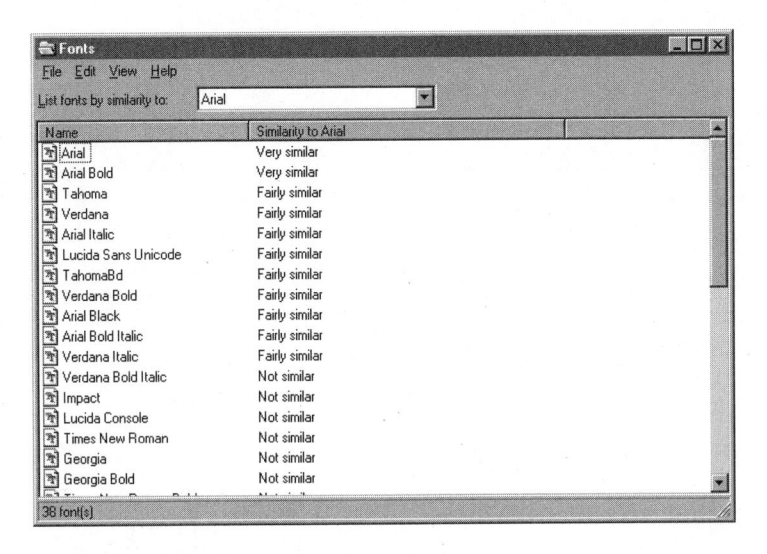

FIGURE 12.08

You can view the fonts listed in the order of their resemblance to a specific font.

TrueType fonts that you have located elsewhere can be moved to this folder, but fonts don't have to be physically located in the Fonts folder to be recognized by Small Business Server. You can make a shortcut to a font in another folder and put the shortcut in the Fonts folder. The shortcut is all you need for the font to be installed.

Fonts that are identified with an icon like the one below are not TrueType fonts. They're not scalable, which means that at large point sizes they tend to look crummy. (See Figure 12.09 on the following page.) Many of these fonts can be used only in limited point sizes.

FIGURE 12.09

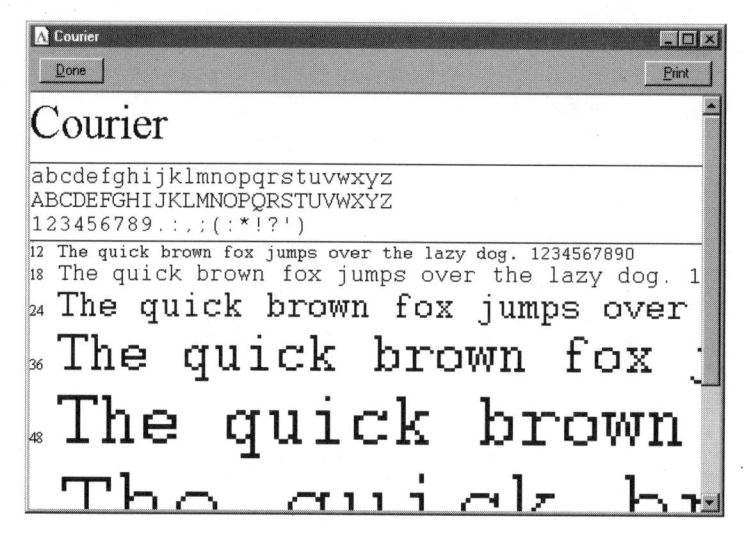

Non–True Type fonts are not much to look at in larger sizes.

Installing New Fonts

Installing new fonts is a pretty easy project. Just click on the Fonts icon in the Control Panel and choose Install New Font from the File menu. In the Add Fonts dialog box (Figure 12.10), you can specify the drive and the directory where the fonts reside. If there are one or more TrueType fonts at the location you specify, they'll show up in the List Of Fonts list box.

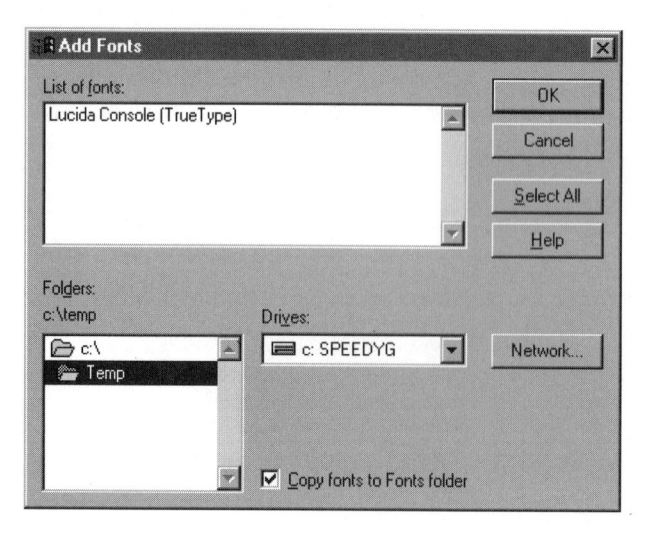

FIGURE 12.10

The Add Fonts dialog box.

Select the font or fonts you want installed, and then click OK. Some font packages might have to be installed like other programs. Use the Add/Remove Programs icon, as described in Chapter 11.

NOTE

Other types of fonts, such as those installed by Adobe Type Manager, will reside elsewhere on your hard drive, depending on the location you selected. You can't put them in the Fonts folder or view them by double-clicking. However, numerous applications are able to display fonts, and most font installation programs have their own viewers.

Internet

Internet

If your Small Business Server computer is connected to the Internet, you can double-click on the Internet icon in the Control Panel to configure your Internet connection. Here's an overview of what you can do on the tabs of the Internet dialog box:

- **General** Change how web pages are displayed on your computer, what your default home page will be, how much disk space to dedicate to temporary Internet files, and how much history to maintain. You can also set a variety of cosmetic options, such as colors and fonts.

- **Security** Set security by zone, including defining trusted sites that don't require high security settings.

- **Content** Enable content ratings so that you can control which sites can be seen as well as maintain security certificates and set your personal information.

- **Connection** Specify how you're connected to the Internet, specify whether to use a proxy server (required with Small Business Server), and set the options for the proxy server. For more on proxy servers, see Chapter 22.

- **Programs** Specify the programs used for reading e-mail and news and the viewers for different file types, as well as your default calendar and contact list programs.

- **Advanced** Set options for the use of Microsoft Internet Explorer. For the most part, the default options are preferable. However, if you want to make specific changes to the security or viewing settings, this is the tab to use.

> **Tip**
>
> *If you're unsure about the effect of a change, make careful notes on the original setting and make only one change at a time.*

Keyboard

Keyboard

During installation, Small Business Server finds the keyboard plugged into your computer and recognizes it, so you normally don't have to fuss with the keyboard settings. But if you need to change keyboards, adjust the keyboard's speed, or install a keyboard designed for another language, double-click on the Keyboard icon in the Control Panel to see the Keyboard Properties dialog box (Figure 12.11).

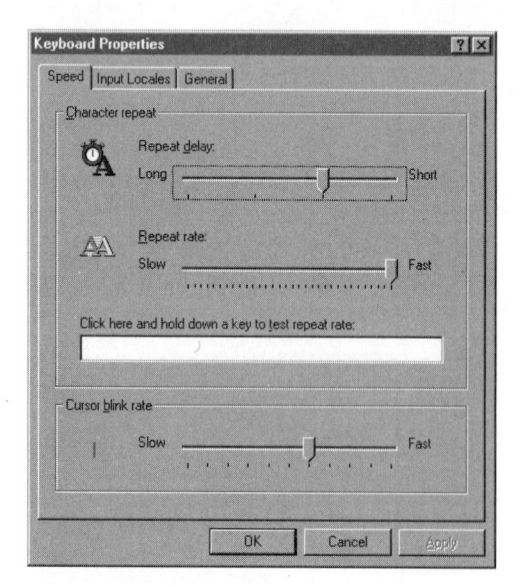

FIGURE 12.11
The Keyboard Properties dialog box.

Changing Your Keyboard

If you're changing keyboards or if Small Business Server recognizes one type of keyboard when in fact you have a different kind, go directly to the General tab. The Keyboard Type text box shows what Small Business Server thinks is your keyboard. If that's wrong, click the Change button and follow these steps:

1. In the Select Device dialog box, click Show All Devices.
2. Select the correct keyboard from the list. If you have special installation software, click Have Disk.
3. Click OK, and Small Business Server will install the correct keyboard either from your disk or from its own set.

You might have to reboot your computer before the keyboard is completely recognized by Small Business Server.

Keyboard Speed

Click on the Speed tab of the Keyboard Properties dialog box (shown in Figure 12.11) to adjust keyboard rates. Here are the available settings:

- **Repeat Delay** Determines how long a key must be held down before it starts repeating. The difference between the Long and Short settings is only about a second.

- **Repeat Rate** Determines how fast a key repeats. Fast means that if you hold down a key you almost instantly get a vvvvvvvvvvvery long stream of letters. (Click in the practice area and press a key to test this setting.)

- **Cursor Blink Rate** Makes the cursor blink faster or slower. The blinking cursor on the left demonstrates the setting.

Keyboard Languages

If you need multiple language support for your keyboard, click on the Input Locales tab of the Keyboard Properties dialog box. (See Figure 12.12 on the following page.) Click the Add button to select languages from Afrikaans to Swedish—including 15 varieties of Spanish. If you have more than one language selected, the settings on the Input Locales tab let you choose a keyboard combination to switch between languages.

FIGURE 12.12

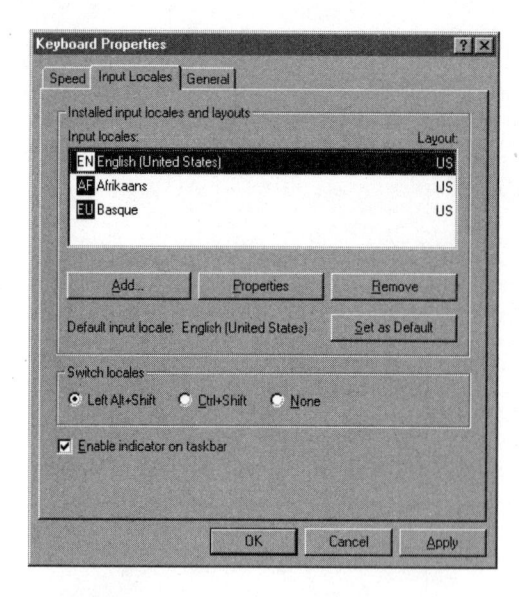

The Input Locales tab of the Keyboard Properties dialog box.

Select the language you want as the default (the one that's enabled when you start your computer), and click the Set As Default button. Select Enable Indicator On Taskbar, and an icon will appear on your Taskbar. Right-click on it and you can instantly switch between languages.

Licensing

The Licensing icon is disabled because the licensing for Small Business Server is different from the licensing of Windows NT Server alone. To check your license status (or to add new user licenses), choose Manage Server from the Start menu. Click on the Online Guide tab of the Small Business Server console. On the Contents page, click the plus sign next to Server and then click the plus sign next to Managing User Licenses. (See Figure 12.13.)

```
□ 🖳 Server
    📄 Keeping Your Server Running
  ⊞ 🔧 Adding or Removing Hardware
  ⊞ 🔧 Adding or Removing Software
  ⊞ 🖳 Changing Computer Settings
  □ 📘 Managing User Licenses
      📄 Overview
      📄 Add user licenses
```

FIGURE 12.13

On the Contents page of the Small Business Server console's Online Guide tab, you can check your license status.

Click Overview to review your current license status and the restrictions on the Client Add Pack, which is used to add more licenses. Click Add User Licenses for instructions on how to run the Client Add Pack.

Mail

Mail

The Mail icon will appear in the Control Panel if you opted to install mail services when you installed Small Business Server. Chapter 14 discusses mail services in detail.

Modem Sharing Server

Modem Sharing

Chapter 16 is all about administering modem pools. Check there for information on the settings for the Modem Sharing icon.

Modems

Modems

Double-click on the Modems icon in the Control Panel, and you'll see the Modems Properties dialog box. Here you can add or remove a modem, examine or change a modem's properties, and modify your dialing properties (settings that tell the modem where you're dialing from, whether to dial a number for an outside line, and so forth). If your modem was properly detected during the Small Business Server installation, you should see an entry for it here.

Adding a Modem

To add a modem to your Small Business Server system, follow these steps:

1. In the Modems Properties dialog box, click Add to see the first page of the Install New Modem Wizard. (See Figure 12.14.)

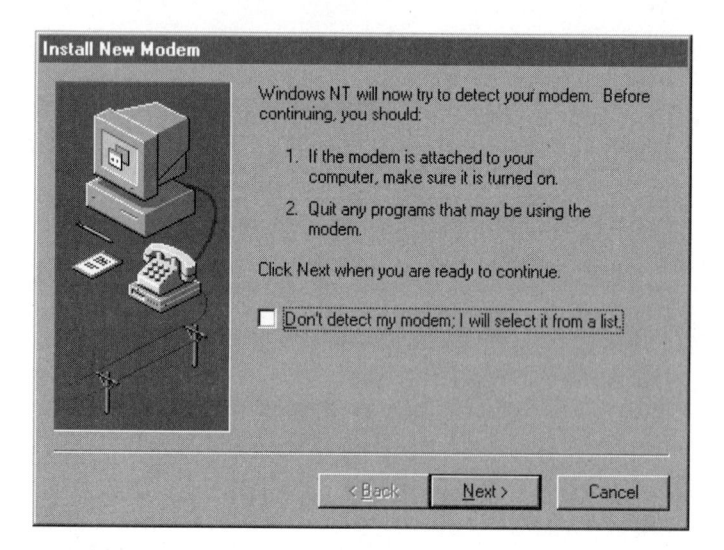

FIGURE 12.14

The first page of the Install New Modem Wizard.

2. Before you begin installing a new modem, make sure the modem is attached to your computer and turned on and quit any programs that

might be using the modem. Click Next to continue to let Small Business Server detect your modem; skip to step 5. If you'd rather select your modem from a list, select the Don't Detect My Modem check box and then click Next.

3. If you're selecting your modem from the list, specify the modem's manufacturer (left pane) and model (right pane) on the wizard's next page. Click Have Disk and insert the appropriate floppy disk or CD if you need to install drivers that came with your modem.

4. On the next page (Figure 12.15), specify the port on which the modem should be installed. Select the option button for the port the modem is attached to, and click Next. If Next is grayed out (as shown in the figure), select the All Ports option button, select the appropriate port, and then click Next. Now skip to step 7.

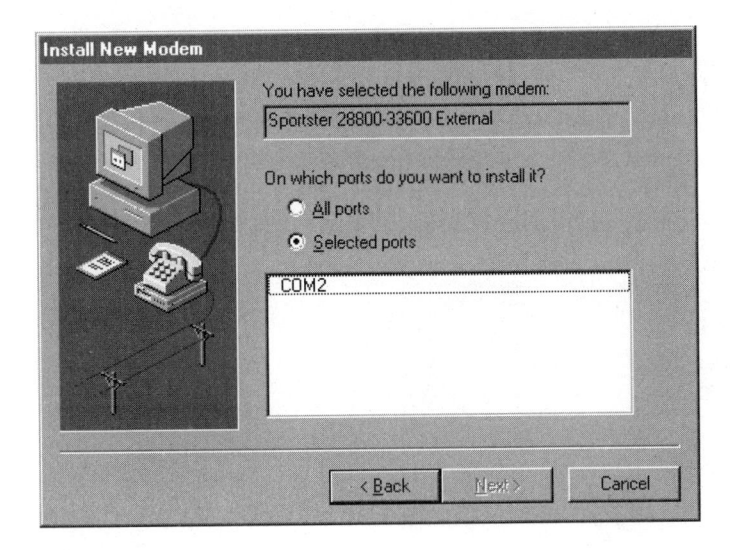

FIGURE 12.15

The port-selection page of the Install New Modem Wizard.

5. While Small Business Server is attempting to detect your modem, you'll see an informational page.

6. If Small Business Server detects a standard modem and this does not reflect the kind of modem you have, click Change and specify the modem's manufacturer and model. Click Have Disk and insert the appropriate floppy disk or CD if you need to install drivers that came with your modem.

7. Small Business Server will now install your modem. When it's done, you'll see a screen telling you this. Click Finish, and your modem will be ready to go.

Removing a Modem

Removing a modem is simple; just select the modem in the Modems Properties dialog box, and click Remove. You should see a message box asking you whether you really want to remove the modem. If you do, click Yes and the modem will be removed. If you don't, click No and the modem will be left as is.

NOTE

If you remove a modem from your system, you might need to restart Small Business Server before the change is recognized.

Viewing or Changing Modem Properties

To view or change a modem's properties, follow these steps:

1. In the Modems Properties dialog box, select the modem whose properties you'd like to see, and click Properties. This will open the modem's Properties dialog box. (See Figure 12.16.)

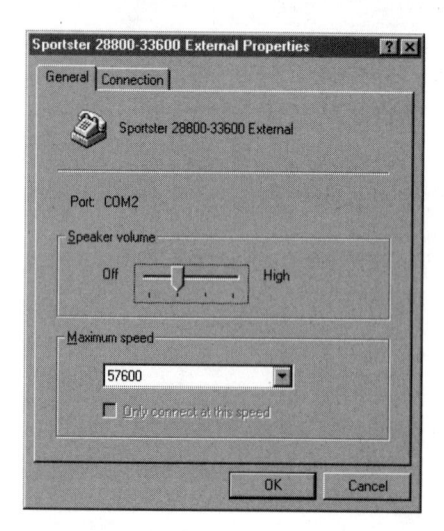

FIGURE 12.16

The Properties dialog box for an "approved" Small Business Server modem.

2. On the General tab, you can set the speaker volume and maximum connection speed for the modem.

3. On the Connection tab (Figure 12.17), you can change the connection and call preferences for the modem. The figure shows some typical settings for a modem on the Small Business Server Hardware Compatibility List Supplement.

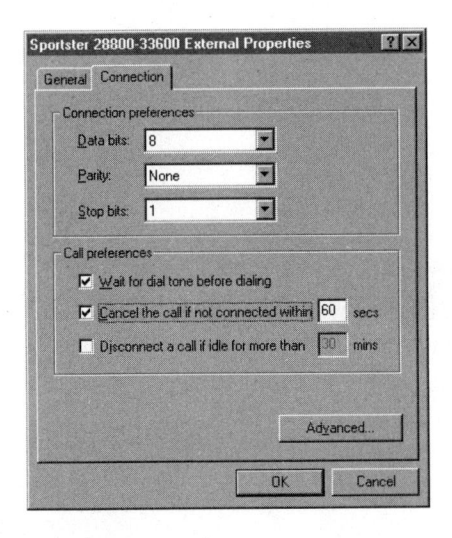

FIGURE 12.17

Typical connection settings for an "approved" modem.

4. Click OK when you finish viewing or changing the modem's properties. You should find yourself back in the Modems Properties dialog box.

Dialing Properties

The Dialing Properties dialog box (Figure 12.18 on the following page) lets you tell your modem which location you're dialing from, whether you need to dial a number to get an outside line, and more. Select a dialing location from the drop-down list, and fill in any other information required for calling from your current location. Click OK when you're done, and you'll return to the Modems Properties dialog box.

FIGURE 12.18

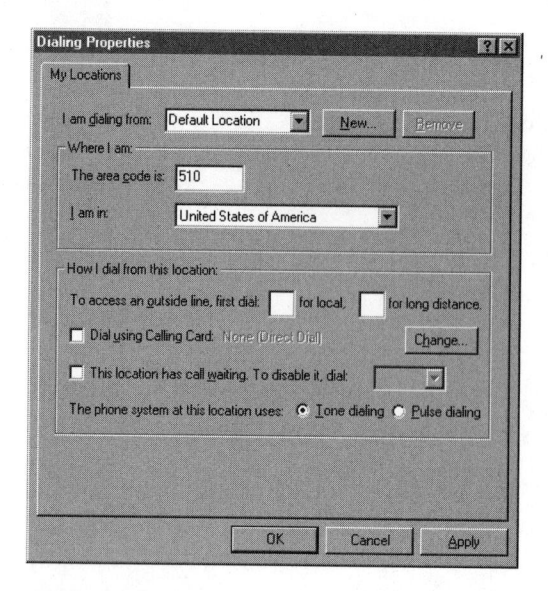

The Dialing Properties dialog box.

When you're finished examining your modem properties or making changes, click Close to return to the Control Panel.

Mouse

Because the mouse is used so much in Small Business Server, it's important that you set it up so that it's comfortable to use. To change how your mouse operates, double-click on the Mouse icon in the Control Panel. This will bring up the Mouse Properties dialog box. (See Figure 12.19.) The following sections describe the settings you can change on the tabs of this dialog box.

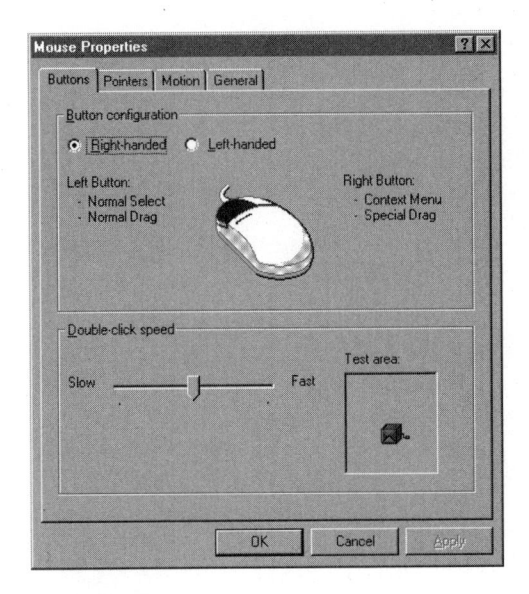

FIGURE 12.19

The Mouse Properties dialog box.

Buttons Tab

The Buttons tab (shown above) lets you swap your left and right mouse buttons (the two outside ones on a three-button mouse) and change the double-click speed (the amount of time allowed between two mouse clicks for them to be counted as a double-click). Use the two option buttons at the top of this tab to swap the mouse buttons, and use the slider at the bottom to change the double-click speed. If you move the double-click slider one notch to the left or right, click Apply to try out your new settings. Keep changing the double-click speed until you find a speed that you like.

Pointers Tab

Small Business Server comes with an assortment of new mouse pointers, so you can select ones that you like. You'll probably find them a big improvement over the default pointers. A few of the pointers included with Small Business Server are animated, and animated cursors are also on their way to becoming the kind of cottage industry that icons were with earlier versions of Microsoft Windows and Windows NT. Animated cursors can be downloaded from many online services and are also distributed as shareware.

> **NOTE**
>
> *Your display must be set to at least 256 colors for the animated cursors to work. To check your settings, double-click on the Display icon in the Control Panel and click on the Settings tab. The color palette must be set for 256 colors, High Color, or True Color.*

The Pointers tab of the Mouse Properties dialog box (Figure 12.20) displays the default pointers that come with Windows NT Server.

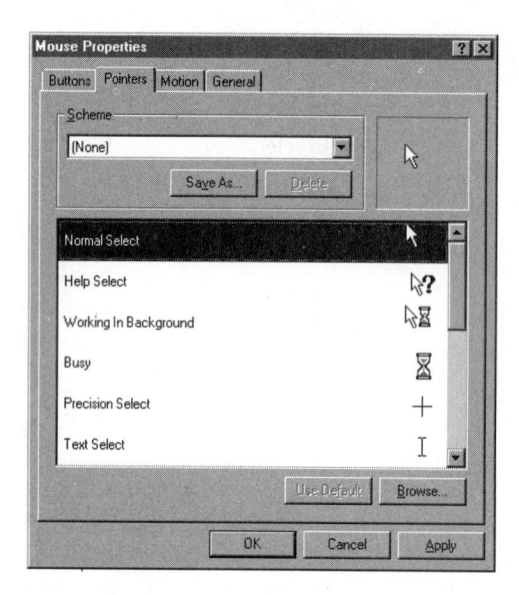

FIGURE 12.20

The Pointers tab of the Mouse Properties dialog box.

Once you understand what each pointer represents, you'll be better able to select appropriate substitutes. Table 12.01 describes what each pointer does.

To change a pointer, follow these steps:

1. On the Pointers tab, select the pointer you want to change and click Browse.
2. The Browse dialog box will open. Click on a selection to display it in the Preview box. (Files with an .ani extension are animated cursors.)
3. After you select the one you want, click Open. If you accumulate a large number of animated cursors, you might want to gather them in a folder within the Cursors folder.

Table 12.01
Small Business Server's Pointers and Their Functions

Pointer	Description/Meaning
Normal Select	The normal pointer for selecting items.
Help Select	Click the ? button, and then click on the area you want information about.
Working In Background	Something is going on in the background. (You can often move to another area and do something else, however.)
Busy	Just hang in there. Small Business Server or an application is doing something and can't be disturbed.
Precision Select	Cross-hairs for very careful selection.
Text Select	The I-beam that's used to select text.
Handwriting	When you're using a handwriting input device.
Unavailable	Sorry, you can't drag a file to this location because either the area is unacceptable or the application won't accept drag and drop.
Resizing (includes Vertical Resize, Horizontal Resize, Diagonal Resize 1, and Diagonal Resize 2)	Cursors that appear when you can move a window border.
Move	When you choose Move from the System menu or a right-click menu, you'll see this cursor, which allows you to move the window using the arrow keys.
Alternate Select	Used in the FreeCell card game. Probably other uses to come.

To save a selection of pointers, click Save As and enter a name for the scheme. After you save the set, it will appear in the Scheme drop-down list and you can select it at any time.

Motion Tab

On the Motion tab of the Mouse Properties dialog box, you can change the pointer speed. Move the slider under Pointer Speed one notch to the left or to the right, and then click Apply to try the new setting. If you'd like the mouse to snap to the default button in dialog boxes, make sure the appropriate check box is selected.

General Tab

On the General tab of the Mouse Properties dialog box, you can change the type of mouse or pointing device you're using. To do so, follow these steps:

1. Connect the new mouse or pointing device to your computer.

2. On the General tab, click Change. You should see a list of devices compatible with your hardware.

3. Select a pointing device, and then click OK. Small Business Server will copy the driver files to your computer. If prompted, insert Small Business Server Disc 1 into your CD-ROM drive. If you'd rather use driver files supplied by the manufacturer of your pointing device, click Have Disk and insert the appropriate floppy disk or CD.

4. Click OK to return to the General tab.

MS DTC

Double-click on the MS DTC icon to open the MS DTC Client Configuration dialog box (Figure 12.21), where you can select a computer to use as the default distributed transaction coordinator for your network. The choice will be grayed out if you do not have an application on your network performing distributed transactions.

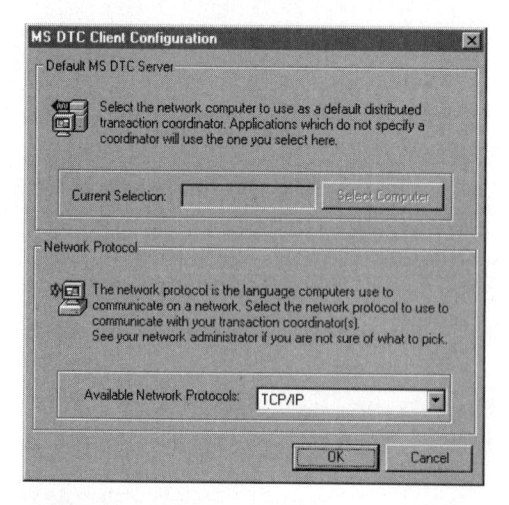

FIGURE 12.21

The MS DTC Client Configuration dialog box.

The MS DTC icon is installed when Microsoft SQL Server is installed.

Multimedia

Multimedia

Double-click on the Multimedia icon to open the Multimedia Properties dialog box. The tabs available will depend on the hardware and software installed.

- **Audio** On this tab, you can set audio playback and recording options. Use the Preferred Device drop-down list in the Playback section to specify a playback device, and use the Volume slider to adjust playback volume. Use the Preferred Device drop-down list in the Recording section to specify a recording device, and use the Volume slider to adjust recording volume. Select the recording quality from the Preferred Quality drop-down list. Use the Customize options only if you're a real audio whiz. If you want to use only preferred devices for recording and playback, select the appropriate check box at the bottom of this tab.

- **Video** Here you can select settings for video clips in a window or on the full screen and specify the size for video viewing. The larger the window, the poorer the quality, unless you have very high-end video equipment.

- **MIDI** On this tab, you can configure MIDI devices and sound schemes.

- **CD Music** Here you can select a CD-ROM drive for audio playback and regulate headphone volume.

- **Devices** On this tab, you can add, remove, view, or change the properties of the multimedia devices attached to your computer.

Adding a Multimedia Device

To add a multimedia device to your system, follow these steps:

1. On the Devices tab of the Multimedia Properties dialog box, click Add. This will bring up the Add dialog box shown in Figure 12.22 on the following page, which contains a list of drivers for devices recognized by Windows NT Server.

FIGURE 12.22

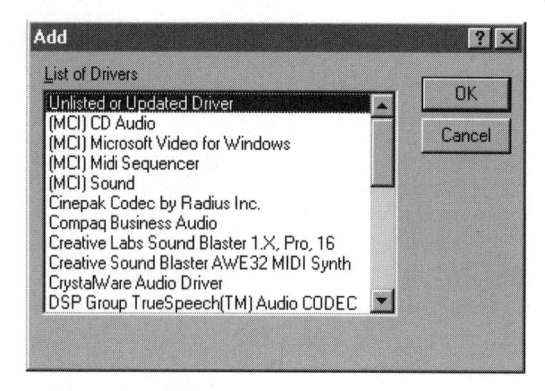

The Add dialog box lists available drivers for multimedia devices.

2. Select the driver you want to install, and click OK.

3. Depending on the device you've selected, you'll see a series of dialog boxes requesting I/O, interrupt, DMA channel, and other types of reasonably technical information. Consult the instructions supplied by the manufacturer of your device if you're unsure what the settings should be.

4. If at first you don't succeed, try, try again. To coax your multimedia devices into doing what they should, you might need to experiment a bit. The best advice we can offer is to consult a friend or a colleague who's a multimedia expert—sometimes that's the only way to make your equipment work properly.

Removing a Multimedia Device

Removing a multimedia device is easy; you just select the device from the list in the Multimedia Properties dialog box and click Remove. You'll see a message box asking you to confirm that you really want to remove this device. If you do, click Yes and it's gone. If you don't, click No and the device will be left as is.

Viewing or Changing the Properties of a Multimedia Device

To view or change the properties of a multimedia device, select the device from the list in the Multimedia Properties dialog box and click Properties. You'll see a box that provides information about the device and, for some devices, a Settings button that you can use to change any relevant settings.

Network

Network

If you're logged on using an account with administrative privileges and you double-click on the Network icon, you'll see the Network dialog box, whose tabs let you configure network hardware and software.

ODBC

ODBC

The ODBC icon in the Control Panel helps you to maintain ODBC (Open Database Connectivity) data sources and drivers. It's only useful if you have database applications installed that provide ODBC drivers, so don't be surprised if the result of double-clicking on this icon is a blank-looking box.

PC Card (PCMCIA)

PC Card (PCMCIA)

The PC Card (PCMCIA) icon in the Control Panel enables PCMCIA sockets and allows you to change PCMCIA settings. On the Socket Status tab of the PC Card (PCMCIA) Devices dialog box, you can click Stop to end a PC Card's connection prior to removing it. The Global Settings tab lets you manually configure memory (rarely done) and provides a check box for disabling a PC Card's sound effects (which is useful when you tire of the disagreeable sound of a modem connection).

Ports

Ports

Double-clicking on the Ports icon brings up the Ports dialog box, which displays the ports currently installed in your computer. Click the Add button to configure an additional port. If you add a serial adapter board for modem pooling (see Chapter 16), you might have to use the Ports icon to get everything set up properly.

Printers

Printers

Chapter 9 explains how to install and remove printers and change printer settings.

Regional Settings

Regional Settings

If you're using a program that supports international symbols, changing the Regional Settings can affect how the program displays currency, time, and numbers. To change these settings, double-click on the Regional Settings icon.

First select the geographic area on the Regional Settings tab, and then confirm or change the individual settings. Your system will have to be rebooted for the settings to take effect.

SCSI Adapters

SCSI Adapters

This icon lets you add or remove a SCSI adapter and view the properties of all SCSI adapters installed in your system. Double-click on the SCSI Adapters icon, and in the SCSI Adapters dialog box, select the adapter whose properties you want to view, and then click the Properties button. The important information in the Properties dialog box is the message on the CardInfo tab that says, "The device is working properly." If you notice that the buttons on the Driver tab are grayed out, don't panic—this is so you can't accidentally modify the device driver for your SCSI adapter. Chances are, you'll never need to reconfigure the device driver if your SCSI adapter was detected properly during Small Business Server installation.

Adding or Deleting a Driver

If you ever need to add or remove a driver for a SCSI adapter, you can use the buttons on the Drivers tab. To add a driver, click Add and specify the manufacturer and model of your SCSI adapter in the Install Driver dialog box. Click Have Disk if you want to install a driver supplied by the manufacturer of your SCSI adapter.

To delete a driver, select the driver and click Remove. In the confirmation box, click Yes to remove the driver or click No to leave it as is.

Server

Server

Double-click on the Server icon in the Control Panel to open the Server dialog box (Figure 12.23 on the following page), which displays and manages local server properties.

FIGURE 12.23

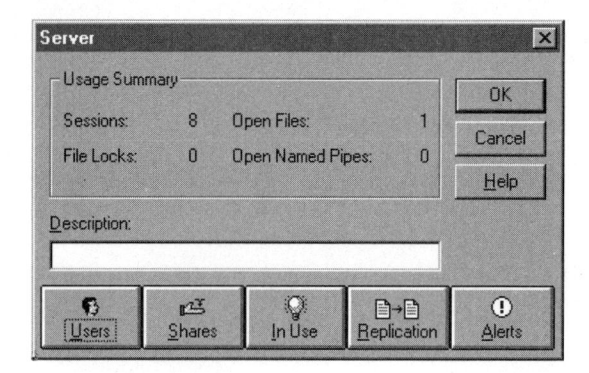

The Server dialog box.

Click the Users button to open the User Sessions dialog box, which shows connected users and the resources being used.

Click the Shares button to see the Shared Resources dialog box (Figure 12.24). This dialog box provides a complete list of shares on your system and lets you see who's accessing which share. You can also disconnect a user or all users from a share if necessary.

When clicked, the In Use button gives you a handy way to see which resources are currently in use; you can close a single resource or all resources if you want.

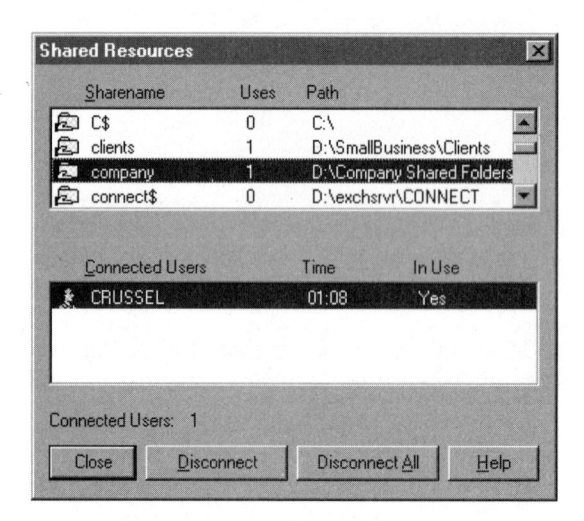

FIGURE 12.24

The Shared Resources dialog box.

Services

Services

The Services icon opens the Services dialog box, where you can start and stop various Windows NT services and control the startup parameters of the services. Changing these settings blindly can get you into really serious trouble, so our advice is: *don't*. About the only exception is starting and stopping Microsoft Exchange services to ensure a valid backup. The details are covered in Chapter 13.

Sounds

Sounds

Double-click on the Sounds icon in the Control Panel to open the Sounds Properties dialog box (Figure 12.25), where you can set and change sound schemes.

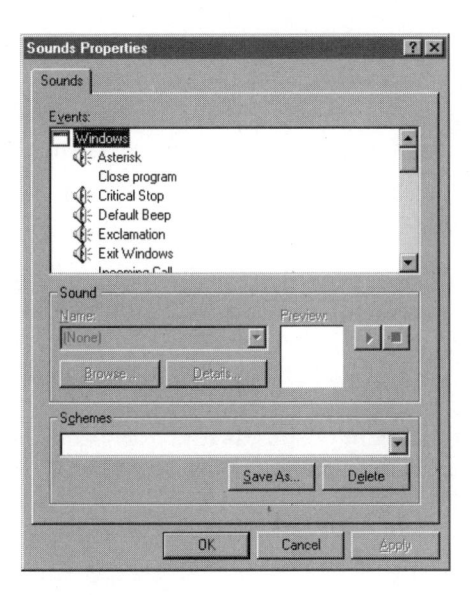

FIGURE 12.25

The Sounds Properties dialog box.

NOTE

To play the sounds that come with Windows NT Server, you need a sound card and speakers (or you have to wear headphones all the time).

The Events list shows everything on your system that can be associated with a sound. Most are Windows NT Server events. For example, opening a program can cause a sound, as can maximizing or minimizing a window and many other actions.

Many new applications include sound capabilities. Their sounds might not end up in the list because they're configured in the program.

If there's a Speaker icon next to the event, a sound is associated with it. Select the event—the name of the sound file will appear in the Name text box—and click the button next to the Preview window to hear the sound.

Sound schemes are included with Windows NT Server; you can select one of them from the drop-down list.

NOTE

If sound schemes don't appear in the Schemes drop-down list, you must install them. Double-click on the Add/Remove Programs icon in the Control Panel. On the Windows NT Setup tab, select Multimedia, click the Details button, and select the sound schemes you want. Click OK, and then follow the instructions.

Customizing a Sound Scheme

The default sound scheme that comes with Windows NT Server is probably not ideal for your use. Fortunately, there's a way to make as many customized sound schemes as you like. Here's how:

1. In the Sounds Properties dialog box, select an item from the Events list.

2. Select a file from the Name drop-down list. To make sure it's the one you want, click the Preview button to hear it. Select (None) in the Name list for an event that you want to keep silent.

3. Repeat steps 1 and 2 until you complete the list.

4. Click Save As to save this assortment of sounds under a specific name. (The new scheme will appear in the Schemes drop-down list.)

> **Tip**
>
> *Windows NT Server stores all its sound files in the Media folder. You'll probably want to move any additional sound files you acquire to that folder because using a single location makes setting up and changing sound schemes much easier.*

System

The System Properties dialog box that opens when you double-click on the System icon in the Control Panel can also be accessed by right-clicking on My Computer and choosing Properties from the pop-up menu. You won't use most of the settings if your computer is working properly. It's only when things go awry that you have to change anything here.

Environment Tab

The Environment tab of the System Properties dialog box (Figure 12.26) displays information about system and user variables.

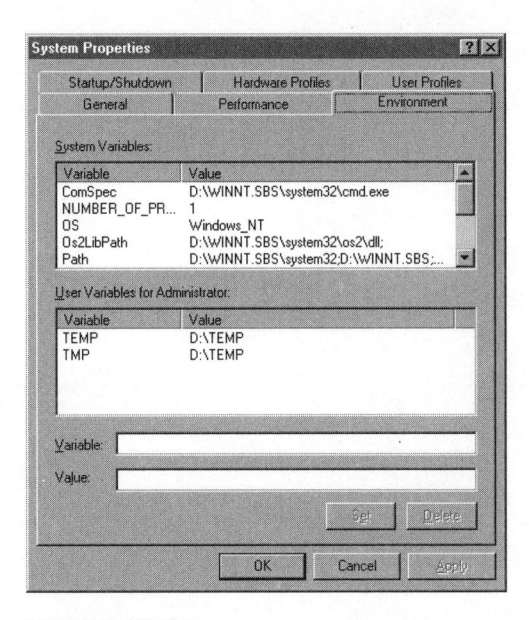

FIGURE 12.26

The Environment tab of the System Properties dialog box.

If you need to establish a variable, enter it in the text boxes at the bottom of the tab, and then click Set. To delete a variable, select it and click the Delete button. In general, the environment variables are rarely changed.

General Tab

The General tab tells you which version of Windows NT Server you're using, the registered owner, and a little bit about the type of computer.

Hardware Profiles Tab

The Hardware Profiles tab shows the available hardware profiles on your system. If you're using a portable computer with a docking station, hardware profiles are sometimes used to enable or disable certain drivers, depending on whether you are docked or undocked. Most newer laptops and docking stations are sophisticated enough to detect this without the use of profiles. On a regular server such as Small Business Server, however, you should almost certainly leave this alone.

Performance Tab

The Performance tab (shown in Figure 12.27) has two sections. The first is for setting the priority for the application running in the foreground. You might want to change this on a workstation, but not on a server. If you boost the performance of the foreground application, other functions working in the background are bound to slow down.

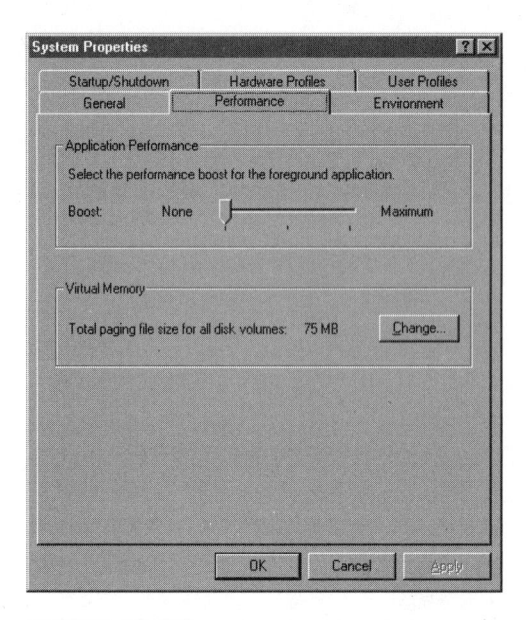

FIGURE 12.27

The Performance tab of the System Properties dialog box.

The second section is for setting virtual memory. Click the Change button to view the settings for Virtual Memory. You can also increase the maximum size for the Registry in the Virtual Memory dialog box.

In general, the default settings should not be changed unless you have an application that specifically requires a larger paging file.

For Your Information

For more on the Registry, see Chapter 26.

Startup/Shutdown Tab

The Startup/Shutdown tab (Figure 12.28) allows you to specify startup and shutdown options, such as which operating system should be the default when you boot up your computer and what the system should do in case of a STOP error. One useful change you can make here is to reduce the time that Windows NT sits and waits at the startup menu before actually booting up. The default is 30 seconds, a ridiculously long time. We like to set this to 5–10 seconds.

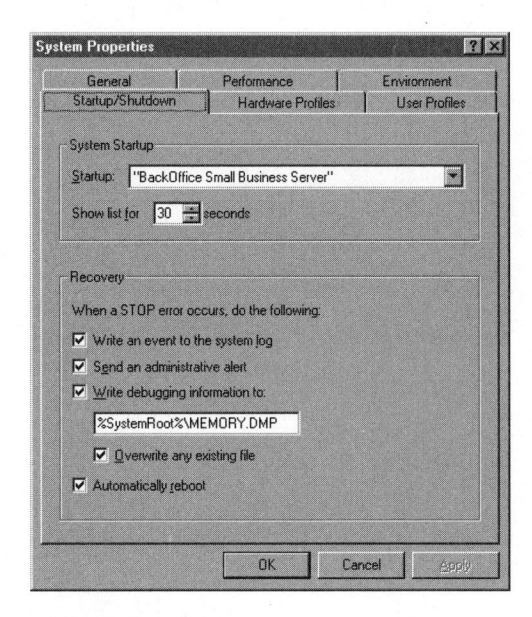

FIGURE 12.28

The Startup/Shutdown tab of the System Properties dialog box.

User Profiles Tab

The User Profiles tab enables switching between two types of user profiles, which are files that contain desktop settings and other information related to the Windows NT Server logon. In case you're wondering, a user profile is created when a user logs on for the first time. If you often use different computers, a different (local) user profile can be created on each computer you use or you can set up what's called a *roaming user profile* that is the same on every computer you use. By default, a user profile is a local profile. To try using a roaming profile, consult the Small Business Server Online Guide for information about how to arrange this.

Tape Devices

Tape Devices

The Tape Devices icon on the Control Panel opens the Tape Devices dialog box, which displays information about tape devices installed on your system and the drivers that run them. Click the Properties button to view the properties of a tape device, or click the Detect button to detect a previously undetected tape device.

Use the Add button on the Drivers tab to install and configure a tape device.

> **For Your Information**
>
> *For complete details on installing and configuring a tape device, see the section titled "Configuring a Backup Device" in Chapter 13.*

Telephony

Telephony

Double-clicking on the Telephony icon on the Control Panel leads you to the Dialing Properties dialog box, whose contents relate to your modem's dialing properties and the drivers the modem uses to communicate with other computers.

Dialing Properties

On the My Locations tab of the Dialing Properties dialog box (Figure 12.29), you can fill out the information for your location. Click the New button to supply additional locations for a laptop.

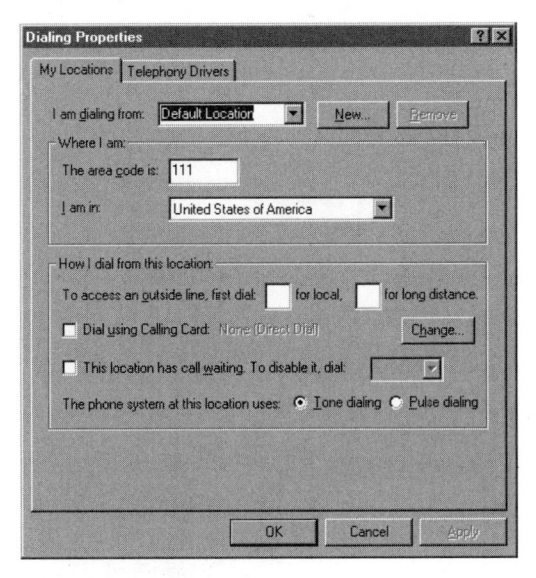

FIGURE 12.29
The My Locations tab of the Dialing Properties dialog box.

Telephony Drivers

On the Telephony Drivers tab of the Dialing Properties dialog box, you can install and configure telephony drivers—the software that your modem uses to "talk" to other computers. In most situations, the Windows NT Server default, TAPI Kernel-Mode Service Provider, will work just fine.

UPS

Double-click on the UPS icon in the Control Panel to install an uninterruptible power supply (UPS). In the UPS dialog box (Figure 12.30), select the Uninterruptible Power Supply Is Installed check box and specify which port the device is attached to. Use the check boxes in the UPS Configuration section to set options for the UPS, and use the check boxes in the UPS Characteristics section to describe the device you're installing. If you're unsure about some of these settings, consult the instructions that came with your UPS. When you're satisfied that your UPS is properly installed, click OK to return to the Control Panel.

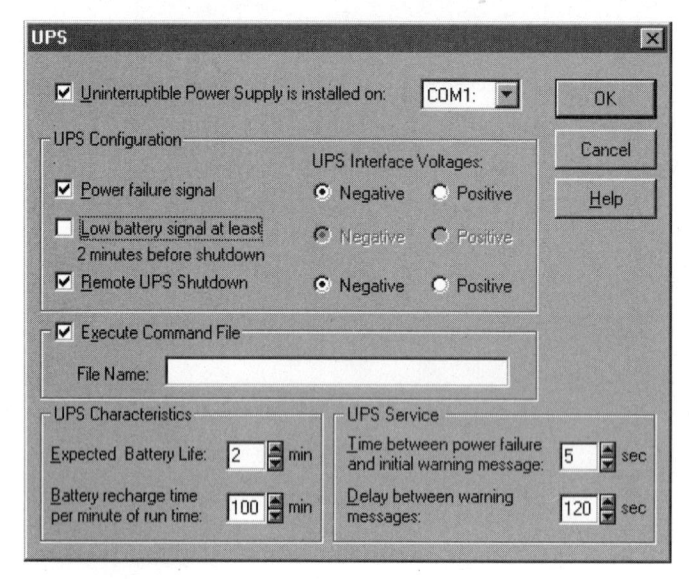

FIGURE 12.30

The UPS dialog box.

WSP Client

The WSP Client icon on the Control Panel lets you enable or disable the WinSock Proxy client. In the Microsoft WinSock Proxy Client dialog box (Figure 12.31 on the following page), click the Update Now button to specify where the relevant files are located. In most cases, the default settings are correct.

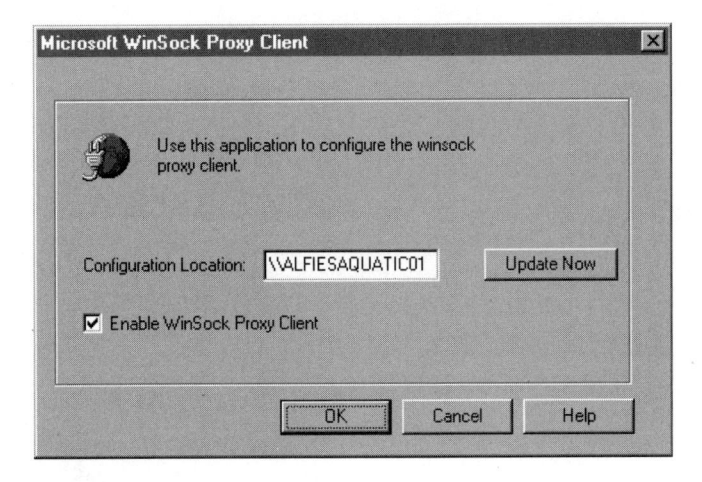

FIGURE 12.31

The Microsoft WinSock Proxy Client dialog box.

POINTS TO REMEMBER

- ◆ The Control Panel is the operations center for Windows NT Server.
- ◆ The Small Business Server console provides the easiest access to many of the Control Panel functions, especially those particular to Small Business Server.
- ◆ When using the Control Panel, be careful when making changes.

WHAT'S NEXT

In this chapter, you learned about the icons on the Control Panel. Chapter 13 will cover a topic that's absolutely essential but that nobody ever wants to hear about: how to back up and restore data on your network.

Backing Up and Restoring Data

Chapter 13

- 240 **Backup Terminology**
- 240 **Backups *Are* Mission Critical**
  - Backup Hardware — 241
  - Designing Your Strategy — 241
  - Incremental vs. Differential Backups — 242
- 243 **Configuring a Backup Device**
- 245 **Removing a Backup Device**
- 246 **Backing Up Your Data**
  - Handling Exchange Server — 249
- 252 **Restoring Data**
- 256 **Verifying a Backup**
- 256 **Scheduling a Backup**
  - Enabling the Schedule Service — 257
  - Running *ntbackup* with a Batch File — 258
  - Running the Batch File Automatically with the *at* Command — 260
- 260 **Backing Up a Client**
- 261 **Alternative Backup Programs**
- 261 **Points to Remember**
- 261 **What's Next**

Chapter 13
Backing Up and Restoring Data

Microsoft BackOffice Small Business Server includes the same Backup application that is included with Microsoft Windows NT Server. While it's not quite adequate for managing the backup needs of a large enterprise network, it's actually a pretty good program that might well meet all the backup needs of a smaller business. And you *do* have backup needs.

Backup Terminology

You'll need to understand a number of terms when dealing with backups. Here's a short list of the most important ones:

- Backup device—the hardware device that backups are saved on.
- Backup media—the tape, disk, or CD on which the backup is stored.
- Full backup—just what it says. This backup includes all files in a given selection set.
- Incremental backup—all the files in a given selection set that have changed since the last backup. To restore, you need the last full backup and all the incremental backups since that one.
- Differential backup—all the files in a given selection set that have changed since the last full backup. To restore, you need the last full backup and the latest differential backup.

Backups *Are* Mission Critical

In large businesses with complex networks, one of the most important jobs of the system administrator is to manage and maintain the backups. It's also one of the most thankless tasks—you almost never get awards for doing good backups, but if you fail to provide a backup when someone needs to recover a critical file, you find out how quickly you can get in trouble.

The typical small business doesn't have a dedicated system administrator, but that doesn't mean there's no need for dependable backups to protect sensitive or critical documents. The good news is that the task is substantially easier with Small Business Server, since there's typically only a single server to back up, and it *should* have a tape drive installed in it. If your server doesn't have a tape drive, now's the time to run out and get one.

Backup Hardware

The core of any backup procedure is the actual device that's used to hold the backups. Among the possible solutions are writeable CDs, removable hard drives, and magneto-optic drives, but the most common and generally the most cost-effective and satisfactory option is that old dependable—a tape drive. Since this is the only backup device that is supported natively by Small Business Server, we'll focus on tape drives. For any other type of backup device, you'll need different software (which might be included with the backup device itself). Many third-party backup solutions support a variety of devices.

Even limiting yourself to tape drives leaves a pretty broad range to choose from. To make the choice simpler, consider two factors. First is the actual capacity of an individual tape. You'll want to buy a tape drive that will hold your entire hard drive on a single tape, preferably without relying on compression. The reason for this requirement is simple: If your entire system can fit on a single tape, you won't have to come up with any complicated strategies to make sure you have a good backup. All you have to do is make sure someone is assigned to change the tapes every day and back up the machine every night. This is both the easiest strategy and the one most likely to be carried out.

The second criterion for the tape drive should be the interface. We make no secret that we're partial to SCSI for any server, and we think it's still the best choice for connecting to your tape drive. But you can finally get good IDE tape drives, and they might make perfectly good sense for many small businesses. But on no account should you go with a tape drive that uses the floppy controller, the parallel port, or a special, proprietary interface card. These are simply not up to the task of providing an absolutely reliable backup solution that you can bet your business on.

Designing Your Strategy

When deciding on a backup strategy, weigh these factors: the capacity of the backup device, the technical sophistication of your staff, the importance of the data, and the amount of time available to do the backup. All of these enter into the equation of how often you should do what kind of backup and how many tapes you'll end up using.

The simplest solution is to back up everything onto a single tape, every single workday. We think this is the best possible strategy because it has the fewest ways in which it can go wrong. And it offers the easiest way to restore your backups after a disaster. When you're trying to recover after a disaster, you want simple and easy—you'll have enough other things to worry about without having to figure out which files are on which tape.

If you go with this simple backup strategy, the only other question to deal with is how many tapes to use and how to rotate them. Here again, we recommend the simplest solution—use one tape for every workday in the week, and then take the last tape of the week and store it somewhere that's not in the same building as your server. Replace the tape you take offsite with a fresh tape every week. You can pay lots of dollars to a special service that will pick up your tapes every week, keep them in a special vault, and deliver them to you whenever you want them. Or you can simply stick that last tape in your pocket every Friday night and take it home with you and keep it there—assuming that you don't live in the same building as your business, of course.

If your hard drive space grows to the point where you can no longer fit all your files on one tape, you'll have to come up with an alternative strategy. The goal is still to keep it as simple as possible—our experience shows that only simple backup plans actually get carried out. One possible alternative is to do a full backup of a different drive letter every day, and an incremental backup of all the other drives. Unfortunately, this means that you never have a baseline to go back to without some complicated figuring. Another alternative is to do a two-tape (or more) backup less often and then do an incremental or a differential backup every day.

Incremental vs. Differential Backups

If your backup strategy or hardware dictates that you can't do a full, complete backup every time, you'll need to use either a differential or an incremental backup method in between full backups. Which should you choose? Usually, you should use the differential backup for your mid-cycle backups. Since each differential backup contains all the files that have changed since the last full backup, you need only two tapes to recover completely—the last full backup and the most recent differential backup. Plus, if there is a problem with the latest differential backup, you can restore the one before, and at most you'll lose only the work you did in between the two.

With incremental backups, you must have all the tapes since the last full backup, and they must be restored in order. If there are problems with any of the tapes, you might well miss a critical file. Restoring will also take longer. So why would anyone choose an incremental backup strategy? Mostly because of time. Since you only have to save files that have changed since the last time you ran a backup, there are fewer files to save, which cuts down on the time you need to set aside for the backup to run.

Configuring a Backup Device

Before you can run the Backup program, you must tell Small Business Server about your backup device. (For reasons that must have made sense to someone at the time, Windows NT does not automatically install the driver for your tape drive, even though the installation routine detects the tape drive's presence.) On the Tasks page of the Small Business Server console, click on the Back Up And Restore Data icon to bring up the page shown in Figure 13.01.

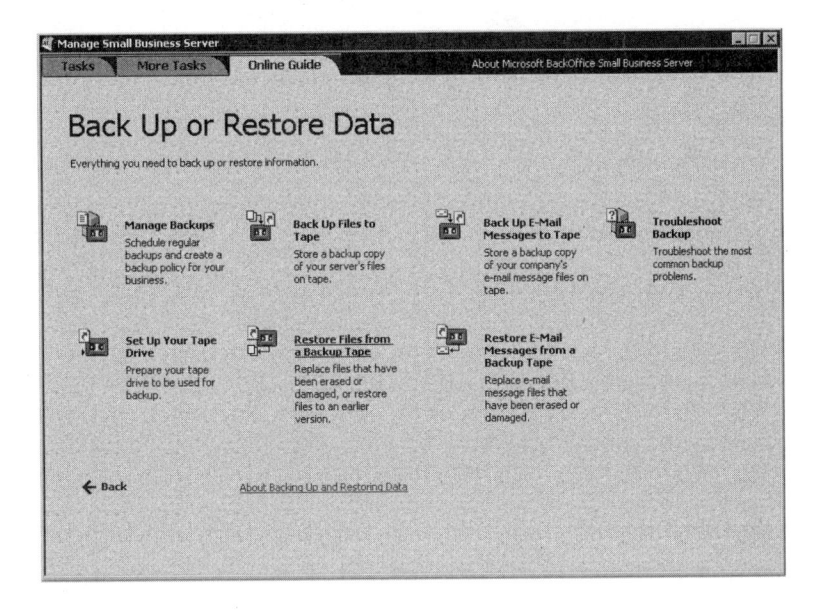

FIGURE 13.01

The Small Business Server console provides a task-oriented front end to the backup process.

From here, click on the Set Up Your Tape Drive icon to bring up the instructional page shown in Figure 13.02 on the following page. This page contains a link to the Tape Devices dialog box. When you click on this link the first time, Windows NT Server will automatically detect any supported tape devices on the server and you'll see a message box like the one shown in Figure 13.03, also on the following page.

FIGURE 13.02

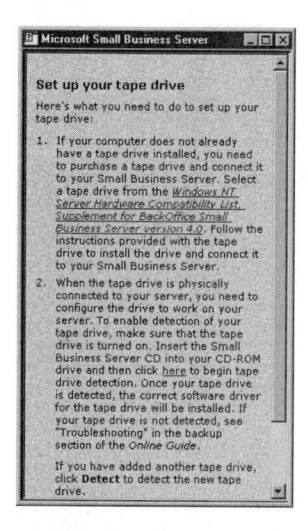

The Small Business Server console gives you detailed instructions for setting up a tape drive.

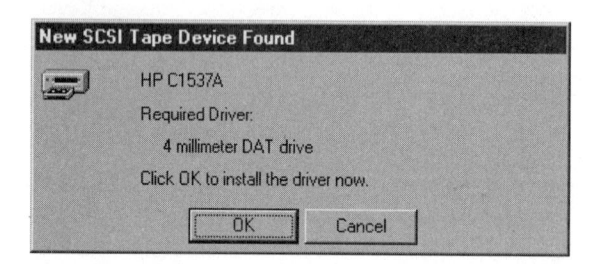

FIGURE 13.03

Windows NT Server detects your tape devices and installs their drivers.

Click OK to install the drivers for your tape drive. You'll need to have Disc 1 of Small Business Server on hand. Windows NT will automatically load the files from the CD, and you'll get confirmation in the Tape Devices dialog box (Figure 13.04) that the driver has been loaded. Click OK, and your tape drive will be ready to use the Backup application.

FIGURE 13.04

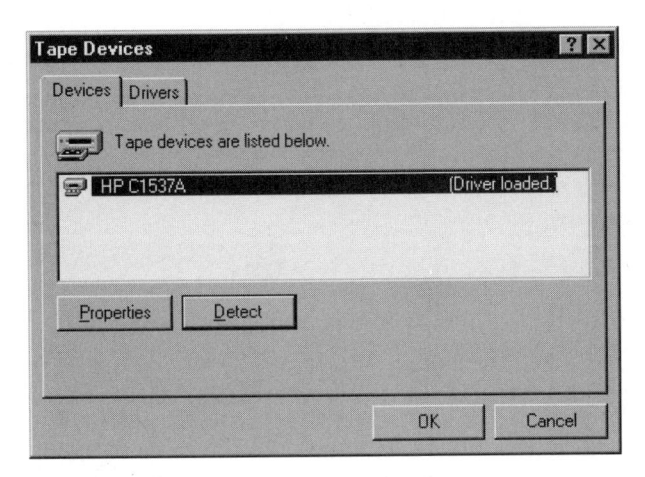

Windows NT Server loads and enables the drivers for your tape drive.

Removing a Backup Device

If you change the type of tape drive, you must tell Windows NT about the change. The first time you reboot after the hardware has been changed, you'll probably see the ever-popular Windows NT message about a device or a service that failed to start, as shown in Figure 13.05. That's OK, since you know why you've gotten the message—the tape drive has changed.

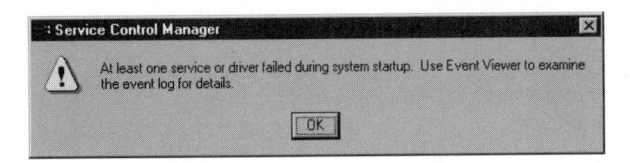

FIGURE 13.05

Whenever Windows NT can't start a service or initialize a driver, you'll see this error message when you first boot up.

Follow the process in the previous section to add a tape drive, but this time remove the old one at the same time. When you're done, you must reboot again, of course. After the server reboots, you should be able to use your new tape drive.

> **Tip**
>
> If you know what driver your new hardware will need, you can save yourself a reboot (and the error message) by loading the new driver and removing the old one before you actually change the hardware.

CHAPTER 13 Backing Up and Restoring Data **245**

Backing Up Your Data

Having your tape drive recognized and available for Small Business Server is nice, but it's hardly useful unless you actually do something with it. The first thing you need to do is perform an actual backup of your server. Since this is our first backup, you'll do a full backup of all of the drives on the server. We want to get a good, verified backup before we do anything else.

To do a full backup of the server, follow these steps:

1. On the Tasks page of the Small Business Server console, click on the Backup And Restore Data icon.

2. Click on the Back Up Files To Tape icon to bring up the window shown in Figure 13.06.

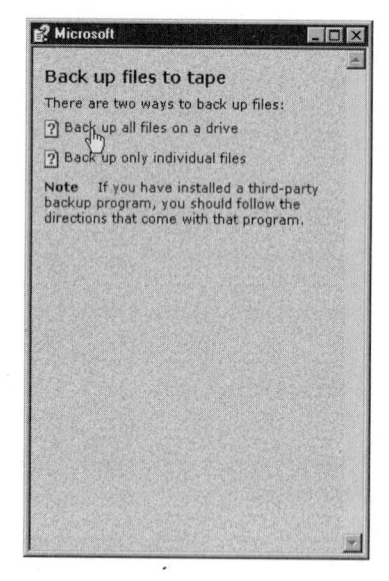

FIGURE 13.06

The Small Business Server console walks you through the backup process.

3. Click on the line that reads "Back up all files on a drive" to open the set of instructions shown in Figure 13.07.

FIGURE 13.07

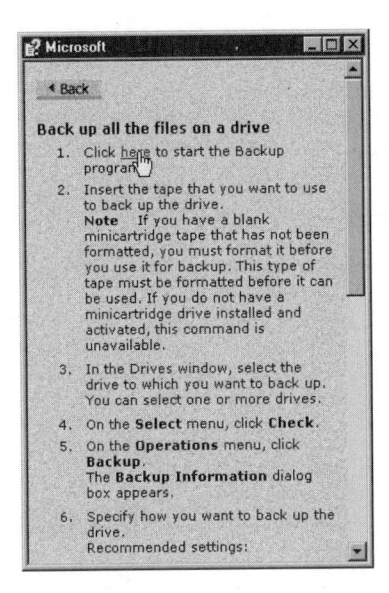

Small Business Server provides instructions to guide you through the backup process.

4. Click on the link in item 1 to open the Backup application (shown in Figure 13.08). Select the check box next to the drive icon for each drive you want to back up. This will select all the files on the selected drive.

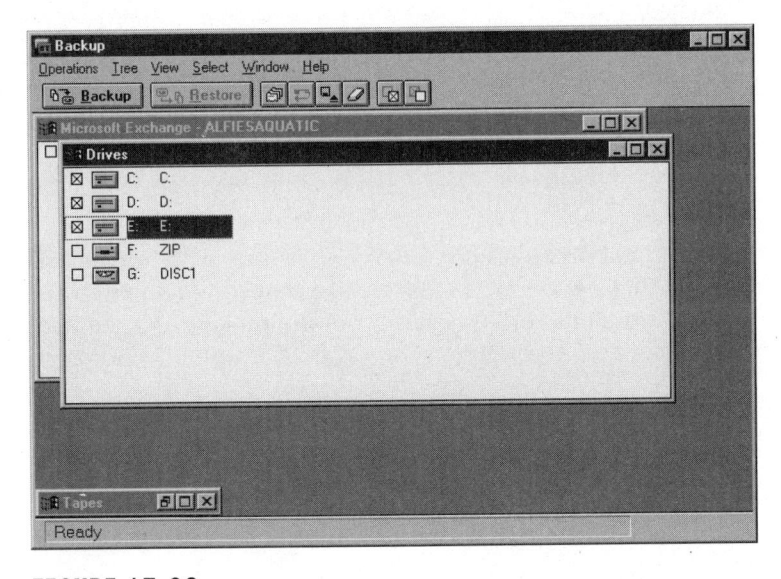

FIGURE 13.08

The Backup application lets you save multiple drives to a single tape.

CHAPTER 13 *Backing Up and Restoring Data* **247**

5. Make sure there's a fresh tape in the drive, and click the Backup button to bring up the dialog box shown in Figure 13.09. Three sets of backups are shown (you have to use the scroll bar to see them). You'll have one set for each drive letter that you selected in the Backup window.

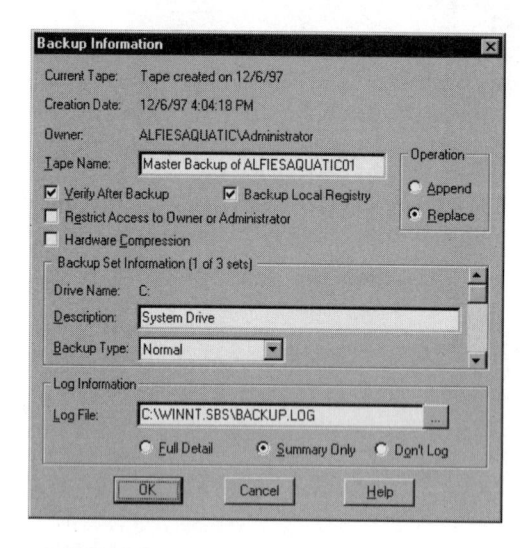

FIGURE 13.09

The Backup application provides numerous backup options.

6. Since this is a master backup, and our first one, select the Backup Local Registry and Verify After Backup check boxes. Type a more meaningful name for the tape, and if you're backing up more than one drive, we suggest that you type a description for each drive. Use the scroll bar on the side of the Backup Set Information section to get to the other sets on the backup. Finally, make sure that Backup Type is set to Normal, as shown, and click OK to start the backups.

7. If the tape in the drive has already been used for a Windows NT backup, you'll get a warning message like that shown in Figure 13.10. If you have any doubts at all, back out of the process and put in a fresh tape; go ahead and overwrite the tape if you're sure it's OK to do so.

FIGURE 13.10

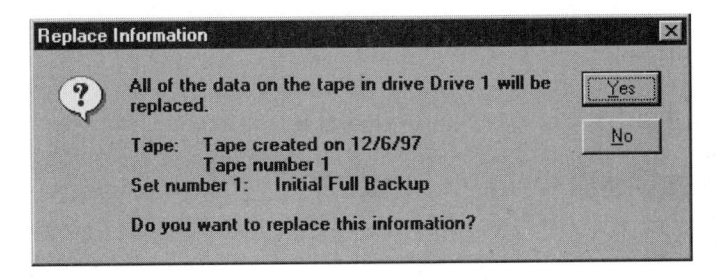

The Backup application will warn you before it lets you overwrite one of its tapes.

8. The Backup application will keep you informed of its status and will list any files that it can't back up, as shown in Figure 13.11. You'll likely see an error here if Microsoft Exchange Server was running at the time of the backup. We'll discuss how to handle that situation next.

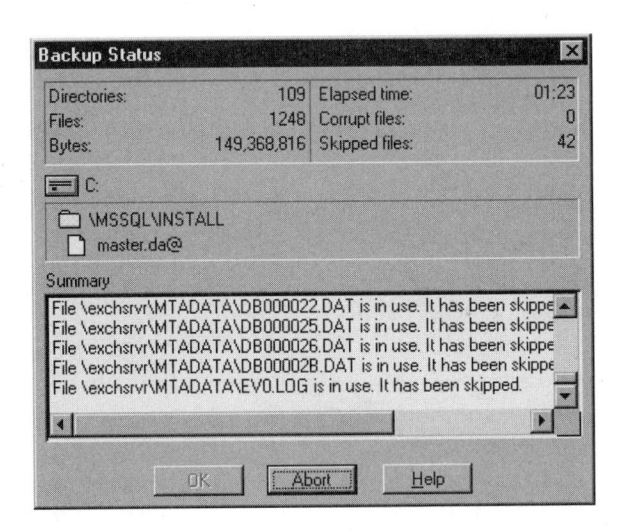

FIGURE 13.11

The Backup application lets you know exactly what it is (and isn't) doing.

Handling Exchange Server

There are two basic ways to deal with Exchange Server and its files during a backup. One way uses the Backup application's purported ability to back up an Exchange Server database live, and the other requires you to shut down Exchange first so that the Backup application can get exclusive access to the files. Both ways have their proponents. The "official" Small Business Server method has you back up the database without shutting it down. Our preference is to do what is known as a "cold" backup by first shutting down Exchange and then running the backup with the files not busy. Only when the backup is complete do we start up the database.

Doing a cold backup of Exchange

Normally, the Backup application can't back up files that are open, a category that usually includes the Exchange database. To do a cold backup, you must first shut down Exchange. Follow these steps:

1. In the Control Panel, double-click on the Services icon to open the Services dialog box.

For More Information

For more information on the Control Panel and its applications, see Chapter 12.

2. Select Microsoft Exchange System Attendant, and then click the Stop button. This will also stop all the other, dependent services after first letting you confirm that this is what you really want to do.

3. Follow the steps outlined on page 246 under "Backing Up Your Data" to back up the drive or drives on which Exchange and its files reside.

4. Once you complete the back-up-and-verify cycle, remove the tape from the drive, slide the Write Protect tab to protect the tape, and then restart each service that belongs to Exchange.

Doing a hot backup of Exchange

The alternative to doing a cold backup is to back up the Exchange database while Exchange is still running. Small Business Server includes a special add-on to the Backup application that is supposed to make this work. To use it, follow these steps:

1. On the Tasks page of the Small Business Server console, click on the Backup And Restore Data icon.

2. Click on the Back Up E-Mail Messages To Tape icon to bring up the window shown in Figure 13.12.

3. Click on the link in item 1 to open the Backup application, shown in Figure 13.13. Select any of the check boxes in the left-hand pane, and all three will be selected, as shown in the figure.

FIGURE 13.12

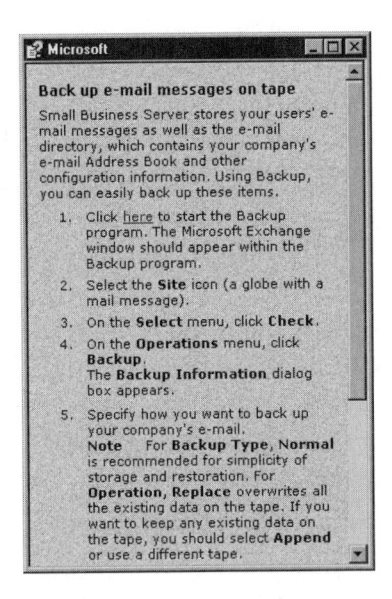

The Small Business Server console makes Exchange backups simple.

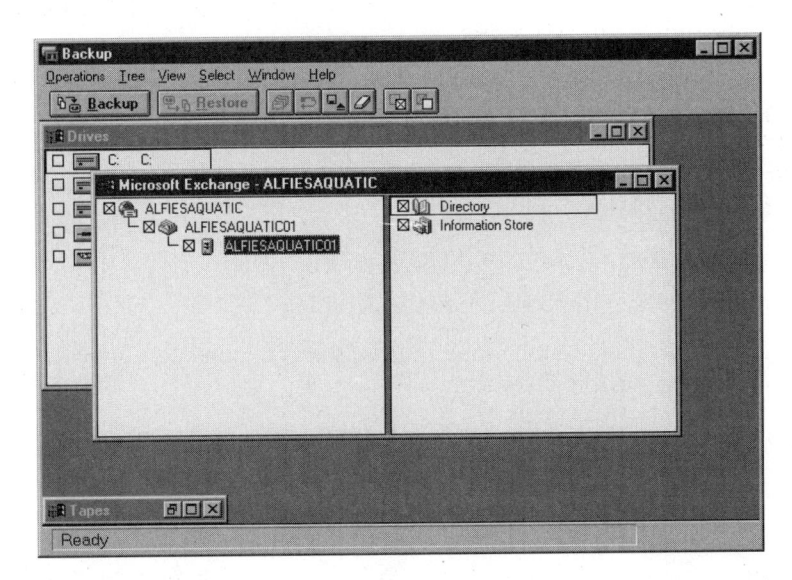

FIGURE 13.13

The Backup application lets you save your Exchange database without having to shut down Exchange completely.

4. Make sure there's a fresh tape in the drive, and click the Backup button to bring up the dialog box shown in Figure 13.09 on page 248.

5. Select the Verify After Backup check box. No backup can be considered any good if it hasn't been verified. Type a more meaningful name for the tape. Finally, make sure that Backup Type is set to Normal, as shown in Figure 13.09, and click OK to start the backups.

6. If the tape in the drive has already been used for a Windows NT backup, you'll get a warning message like that shown in Figure 13.10 on page 249. If you have any doubts, back out of the process and put in a fresh tape; go ahead and overwrite the tape if you're sure it's OK to do so.

7. The Backup application will keep you informed of its progress and will store the information in a log file for later examination.

Restoring Data

Creating a backup is the necessary first step of the backup process, and one has to sincerely hope that the second step—restoring files that have been previously backed up—is never, ever required. If you need to do a restore operation, it generally means that someone or something has failed and the best you can hope for is that you lost only a little data since your last backup.

Even if you never have to restore a backup because of data loss or hardware failure, you should test your backups by doing a sample restore operation. Nothing is more frustrating than learning that the backups you've been depending on are not restorable when you really need them. We suggest that you do periodic spot checks of your backups. Just in case.

To restore data from a backup, follow these steps:

1. Insert the backup tape into the tape drive.

2. On the Tasks page of the Small Business Server console, click on the Backup And Restore Data icon.

3. Click on the Restore Files From A Backup Tape icon to bring up the window shown in Figure 13.14.

4. Click on the line that reads "Restore only individual files" to open the set of instructions shown in Figure 13.15. (If you're in the midst of a serious disaster and you need to restore an entire backup set, click on the line that reads "Restore all files in a backup set." The general instructions are the same. But we strongly suggest that you try the restore process with a few files as a test *before* you need to recover from a disaster.)

FIGURE 13.14

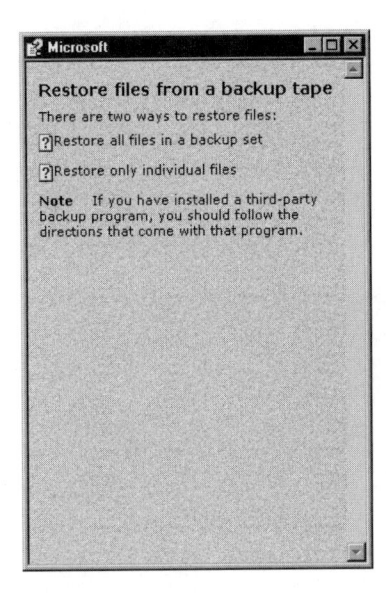

Restoring your files from a backup is a straightforward process.

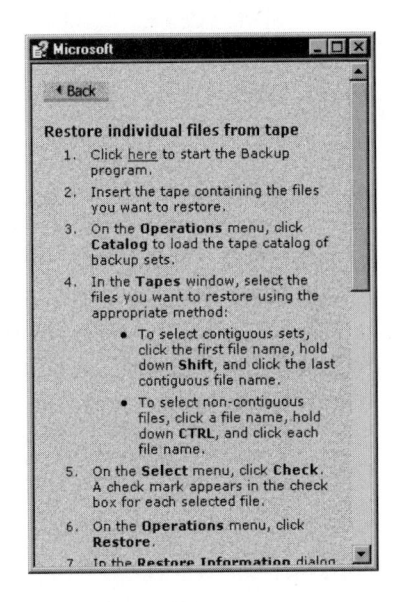

FIGURE 13.15

Small Business Server provides instructions to guide you through the restoration process.

CHAPTER 13 *Backing Up and Restoring Data* **253**

5. Click on the link in item 1 to open the Backup application, shown in Figure 13.08 on page 247.

6. Choose Catalog from the Operations menu to read the contents of the tape. When the catalog is complete, you can select the individual files to restore by double-clicking on the drive letter of the drive where the files you need are stored. This will open another window that shows the directory tree that was backed up. (See Figure 13.16.)

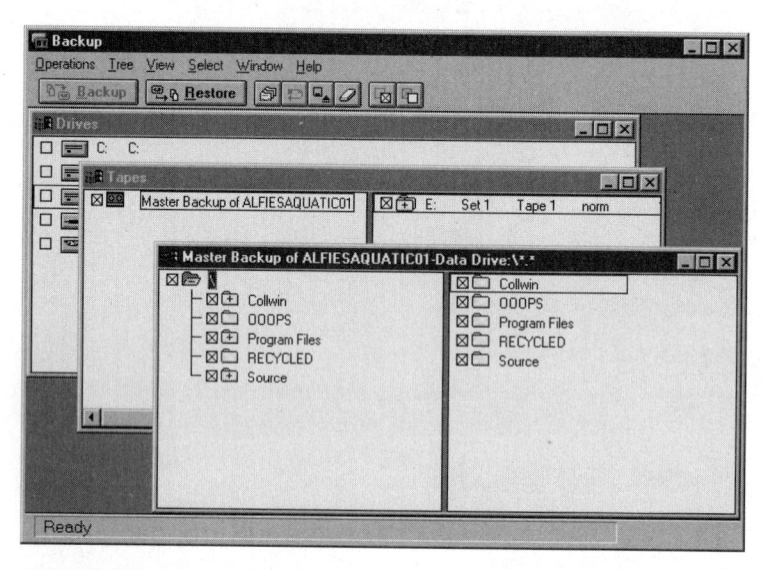

FIGURE 13.16

You can select one or more files to restore, or you can restore the entire set.

7. After you select the files you want to restore, click the Restore button to bring up the dialog box shown in Figure 13.17.

8. We strongly suggest that you get in the habit of overriding the default and restoring files to a different drive or path. This gives you much more flexibility and prevents you from inadvertently overwriting a file. To do this, select a different drive or type a different directory. Our preference is to have a directory called *Restore* on each drive that becomes the top of the restoration path. If this directory doesn't exist, the Backup application will create it during the restore process.

9. Select the Restore File Permissions check box and the Verify After Restore check box. Select the Restore Local Registry check box only if you are actually trying to restore the registry.

FIGURE 13.17

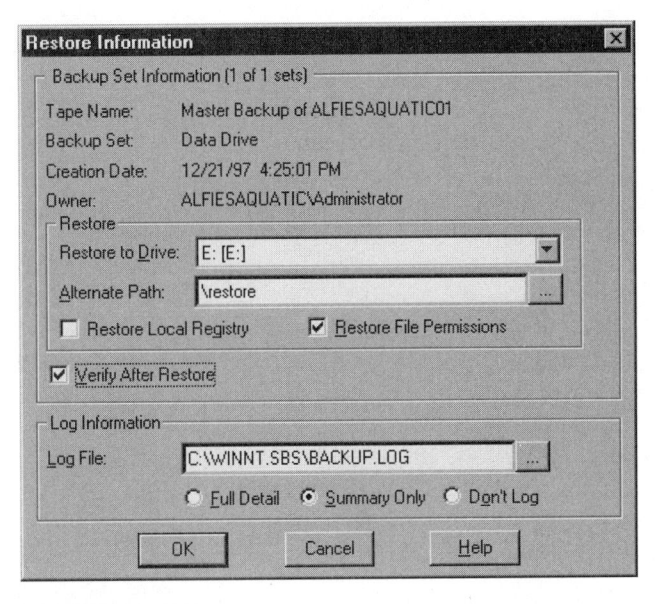

You can restore files to their original location (the default) or to a different location.

10. The Backup application will keep you informed of its status and will list any files that it can't restore in the Verify Status dialog box, as shown in Figure 13.18. If all goes well, you'll see that comforting line at the bottom: "The operation was successfully completed."

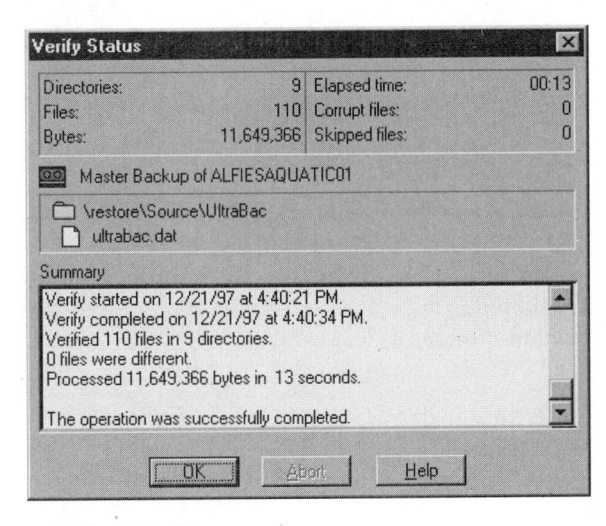

FIGURE 13.18

Files that can't be restored by the Backup application are listed in the Summary section of this dialog box.

CHAPTER 13 Backing Up and Restoring Data **255**

11. Now you can complete the process by moving the files from the Restore directory to their original locations. Of course, if you restored the files back to their original locations, this step isn't necessary.

Verifying a Backup

There's really only one way to verify a backup, and that's to attempt to restore files from it. And while we strongly recommend that you periodically check the validity of your backups in this way, you should also verify them while you're actually backing up. To do this, simply select the Verify After Backup check box in the Backup Information dialog box (Figure 13.09 on page 248) and the Backup application will check the validity of each file in the backup set after the backup is completed. However, this verification is significantly less valid than an actual restore operation, so we strongly suggest that you periodically check your backups by restoring them.

Third-party backup products usually include a separate verification operation that lets you manually verify the individual files on the tape. This approach is generally more reliable than the automatic verification that Backup performs, since in the best cases it does a bit-by-bit verification of the data stored on the tape and compares it against the actual file on disk.

Scheduling a Backup

Backups are nice and backups are necessary, but backups don't get done if someone has to remember to fire them off before going home every night. Third-party backup programs generally include some sort of automatic scheduler application that starts a predefined backup. Sadly, Microsoft doesn't include anything like this in Small Business Server. But it does include two command-line utilities that can be combined to automatically schedule a backup: the *at* and *ntbackup* commands.

The *at* command is a simple way to tell Windows NT to fire off a command or a process automatically at a set time. The command can be run only by someone with administrative privileges, and it's dependent on the Schedule service being started, which is *not* the default for Windows NT. We could write a whole chapter on the deficiencies of the scheduler, but we'll settle for simply showing you how to create a simple, automatic backup. If you need more details, we suggest that you use this as a starting point and create your own template.

Here are the three steps for doing automated backups on your SBS server:

1. Set up the Schedule service to start automatically.
2. Create a batch file to run the backup from the command line.
3. Set the batch file to run automatically, using the *at* utility.

Let's go over each step in detail. Remember, we're creating only a basic starting configuration here. Your needs might dictate a far more involved backup strategy. Also, keep in mind that batch files must be pure ASCII files, so always use Microsoft Notepad to create and edit them. Never use Microsoft Word or even Microsoft WordPad to edit them—it's too easy to make a mistake and end up with an unusable file.

Enabling the Schedule Service

To enable the Schedule service and to set it up to start automatically, follow these steps:

1. In the Control Panel, open the Services application. Select the Schedule service, as shown in Figure 13.19.

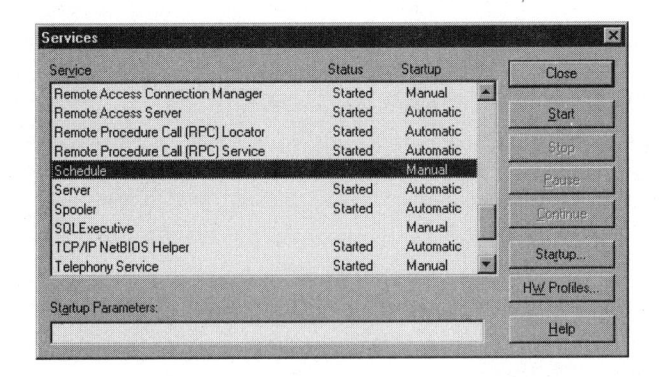

FIGURE 13.19

The Schedule service is turned off by default.

2. Click the Startup button, and in the Service dialog box, change the Startup Type to Automatic, as shown in Figure 13.20 on the following page. Click OK.

FIGURE 13.20

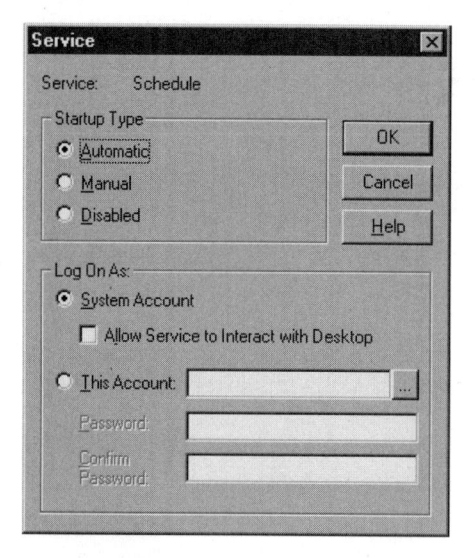

Set the Schedule service to automatically start when Windows NT starts.

3. Start the Schedule service by clicking the Start button. Once the service starts, you can close the Services application and the Control Panel.

Running *ntbackup* with a Batch File

To be able to automate the backup process, you must first create a batch file with the necessary commands in it. We'll show you a typical batch file that will shut down the Exchange services, if they're running, and then do a full backup of drives C, D, and E. You have to restart the Exchange services separately, however, with another *at* command. Windows NT batch files aren't smart enough to know when to restart the services, so you have to figure out the standard time needed to complete the backup and then create the necessary *at* commands to restart them at some point after the backup has finished.

To create the batch file, follow these steps:

1. Open Notepad and create a file with the following two lines in it, as shown in Figure 13.21:

   ```
   net stop "Microsoft Exchange System Attendant"
   ntbackup backup c: d: e: /v /b /d "Automatic Full Backup" /t normal
   ```

258 PERFORMING BASIC TASKS

```
fullback - Notepad
File Edit Search Help
net stop "Microsoft Exchange System Attendant"
ntbackup backup c: d: e: /v /b /d "Automatic Full Backup" /t normal
```

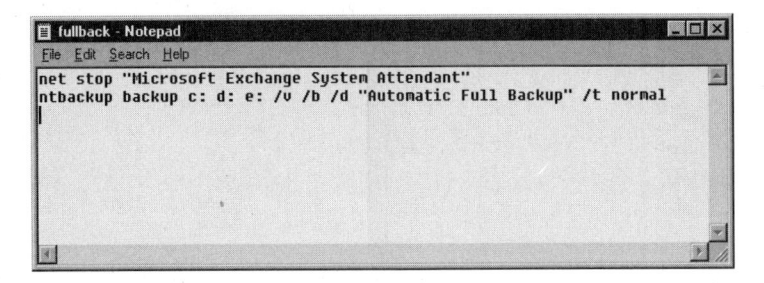

FIGURE 13.21

Use Notepad to create a backup command (batch) file.

2. Save the file as *fullback.cmd* in your Windows NT directory (C:\WINT.SBS by default).

That's all there is to it. But let's take a moment to look at the command lines we created to see what they mean. The first line stops the Microsoft Exchange System Attendant, which in turn stops all the other Exchange services, since they're all dependent on it.

The second line contains the commands to do the actual backup. Working across from the left:

- *ntbackup*—the name of the command.
- *backup*—the operation to be performed. The options are backup or eject.
- *c: d: e:*—the paths to be backed up. You can specify individual directories but not individual files.
- */v*—verify the tape once the backup is complete.
- */b*—back up the registry as well.
- */d "Automatic Full Backup"*—the description that will be written to the backup tape.
- */t normal*—what kind of backup will be performed. The options are normal, copy, incremental, differential, and daily.

There are other options as well, but these are the most useful. You can see the other options by typing *ntbackup /?* on the command line.

> **NOTE**
>
> You'll also need to create a batch file to restart the Exchange services using the net start syntax. Schedule this job after your backup has had time to complete. The two command lines you'll need in the batch file are as follows:
>
> ```
> net start "Microsoft Exchange Information Store"
> net start "Microsoft Exchange Internet Mail Service"
> ```

Running the Batch File Automatically with the *at* Command

Now that we have started the Schedule service and created the batch file, we need to submit the batch file to the scheduler. The command line for this is:

```
at 23:00 /every:M,T,W,Th,Fr cmd /c fullback.cmd
```

Let's take a moment to look at that command line. From the left, we have:

- *at*—the actual command that parses the rest of the line to submit the job to the scheduler.
- *23:00*—the time of day the job will run. A 24-hour clock is used.
- */every:M,T,W,Th,Fr*—the days the job will run. Other options are S, Su, or a number for the day of the month. Days are separated by commas; no spaces are allowed.
- *cmd /c*—the command that loads a command processor so that we can run a batch file. If we were running an executable file, we wouldn't need to do this.
- *fullback.cmd*—the batch file to run.

To run the batch file only once, we could use */next:* followed by a day or a date instead of using the */every:* option. But we're unlikely to want to run a backup program only once—we'd probably just do it manually instead.

Backing Up a Client

The Backup application doesn't provide any direct method to back up client computers. What you can do is create a shared drive on the client computer, and then mount that shared drive on the server and back up the drive letter. We think this is a particularly weak approach, but in a Small Business Server environment you can tolerate it because the system is designed to store all critical files on the server, where they can be backed up automatically. You'll probably want users who store important files on their local machines to get in the habit of either saving their work periodically to the server or backing up their files to floppies every night.

Alternative Backup Programs

You can find a variety of alternative backup programs on the market. The best known is probably Seagate Backup Exec (*www.seagatesoftware.com/bewinnt*), which is written by the same people who wrote the Backup application in Small Business Server. A less cute but faster (and for some, more desirable) option is BEI UltraBac (*www.ultrabac.com*). Finally, there's the seriously cute (too cute for us)—Cheyenne's ARCserve (*www.cheyenne.com*).

All three of the backup programs just mentioned have a lot more features than Small Business Server's built-in Backup application. All have their pluses and minuses. But you don't actually *need* any of them. You might find, however, that they are worth the extra price because they allow you to schedule and manage your backups much more easily and they can back up client workstations automatically—a definite plus.

POINTS TO REMEMBER

- Small Business Server supports only tape drives for backup.
- No backup should be considered reliable until you test it by restoring data from it.
- Small Business Server can schedule backups from the command line only.
- You can back up Exchange Server without shutting it down, but not automatically.

WHAT'S NEXT

Now that you've got your system backed up and protected from disaster, we'll show you how to configure and set up your Exchange Server to handle all your e-mail and messaging needs.

Part Four

Organizing Communications

This part of the book is all about communications. You'll learn how to set up electronic mail, send and receive faxes, configure remote access so that employees outside of the office can use the network, and connect to the Internet.

Chapter 14

Managing E-Mail

- 266 Basic E-Mail Handling
- 267 Managing E-Mail Distribution Lists
  - Creating a Distribution List — 268
  - Modifying a Distribution List — 270
  - Deleting a Distribution List — 270
- 271 Managing Users and Their Mail Boxes
  - Managing Mail Box Size — 271
- 272 Managing the E-Mail Connection
  - Changing the Dial-Up Interval — 272
  - Forcing an Immediate Send and Receive Cycle — 273
- 274 E-Mail Reports
  - Enabling Message Tracking — 274
  - Server Summary Report — 277
  - Top N Message Receivers Report — 277
  - Top N Message Senders Report — 278
  - Daily Message Traffic Report — 279
- 280 Solving E-Mail Problems
  - Troubleshooting E-Mail — 280
  - Troubleshooting E-Mail Distribution Lists — 284
- 286 Points to Remember
- 286 What's Next

Chapter 14

Managing E-Mail

A basic service that users on a network expect and need is electronic mail, or, as it is more commonly known, e-mail. If you think about it, this is a revolutionary change from the earlier days of desktop PCs, when the primary form of communication was "sneakernet" and electronic mail meant writing your memo on the computer, printing it, and then putting the printed memo into interoffice mail.

Today users expect to be able to handle the vast majority of their office correspondence electronically. And they expect to be able to use the e-mail system 100 percent of the time—not 90 percent or even 98.7 percent of the time, but 100 percent of the time. They expect to use it to work collaboratively on projects and to connect to the outside world. If you really want to increase your user noise level, mess up the e-mail.

Microsoft BackOffice Small Business Server includes the full Microsoft Exchange Server and client, as well as Microsoft Outlook 97. Exchange Server is a full-featured, powerful, yet easy-to-use electronic messaging system that gives you not only internal company e-mail but also full Internet e-mail to let you connect to current and potential customers and suppliers. The full Exchange Server and client are part of the default Small Business Server installation on the server; workstations get both the standard Exchange client and the full Outlook 97 client.

Basic E-Mail Handling

To keep your e-mail operations running smoothly, you must perform a variety of ongoing maintenance tasks, including system backups (see Chapter 13 for complete details on how to schedule and perform backups); creating, modifying, and removing e-mail distribution lists; and monitoring the space occupied by users' mail boxes. Fortunately, most of these tasks can be handled right from the Small Business Server console. A few operations, however, might require you to use Microsoft Exchange Administrator.

In the following sections, you'll learn the basics of handling e-mail with Small Business Server, including:

- How to manage e-mail distribution lists
- How to manage users and their mail boxes
- How to send e-mail
- How to fix common e-mail problems

As you'll see, e-mail distribution lists are a great convenience because they allow you to send a single message to many people at once without taking up a lot of precious disk space on your server. Knowing how to use distribution lists effectively will increase your productivity and reduce the chances that your e-mail system will become sluggish.

Users' mail boxes are a potential trouble spot on a network, since users who send a lot of e-mail, especially messages with attachments, can end up eating up disk space more quickly than you might suspect. By using Exchange Administrator, you can avert user mail box trouble before it happens.

Finally, it's important to know how to set up your system to send e-mail at regular intervals and, should the need arise, how to send e-mail immediately. We'll show you how to accomplish these tasks quickly and easily.

Managing E-Mail Distribution Lists

An e-mail distribution list is a group of recipients created to expedite mass mailing of messages and other information. But what does this mean in practice? One obvious use is a distribution list that includes just managers or heads of departments. In a small business, you might not have too many department heads, but you can create distribution lists of only two or three people—the sales department plus marketing, or the shipping department and everyone involved in finance. These lists can be in addition to a distribution list that includes everyone so that you can send messages to the entire organization.

Thanks to a handy icon on the Small Business Server console, managing e-mail distribution lists is easy. To manage these lists on your Small Business Server network, make sure you're logged in using an account with administrative privileges. On the More Tasks page of the Small Business Server console, click on the Manage E-Mail Distribution Lists icon. This will bring up the Manage E-Mail Distribution Lists page shown in Figure 14.01 on the following page. From here, you can create, remove, or modify a distribution list.

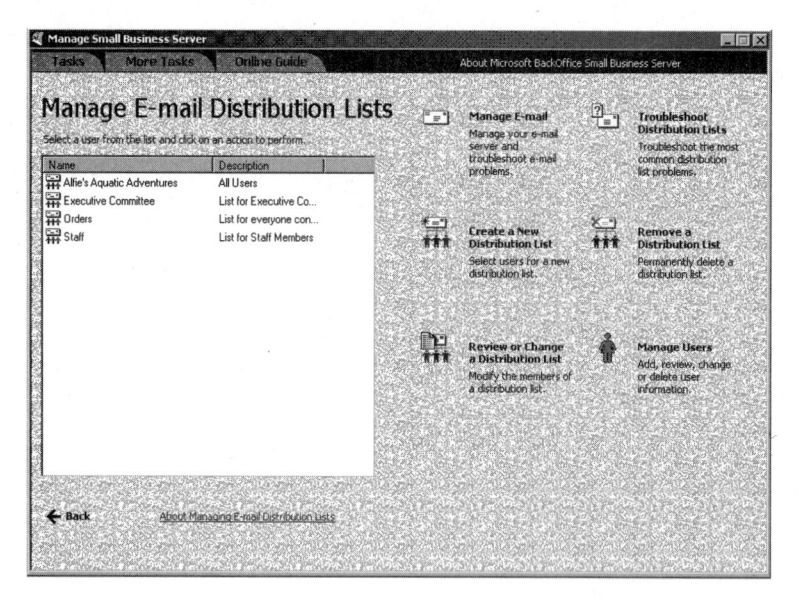

FIGURE 14.01

The Small Business Server console's Manage E-Mail Distribution Lists page.

Creating a Distribution List

To create a new distribution list, take the following steps:

1. On the Manage E-Mail Distribution Lists page, click on the Create A New Distribution List icon to start the E-Mail Distribution List Wizard, whose first page is shown in Figure 14.02.

2. Type a display name for the new e-mail distribution list and a mail box to use for it. (The wizard will create a mail box with this name if it doesn't already exist.) You can also enter an optional description of the list in the appropriate box. Click Next to continue.

3. On the next page of the wizard, shown in Figure 14.03, select the users or distribution lists that you want in the new list and click Add. If you change your mind about any of them, select it on the Members side and click Remove. Click Next.

4. On the Create page, you have one last chance to go back and change the distribution list by clicking the Back button. Otherwise, click Finish to create the distribution list, and then click OK when you get confirmation that it has been created.

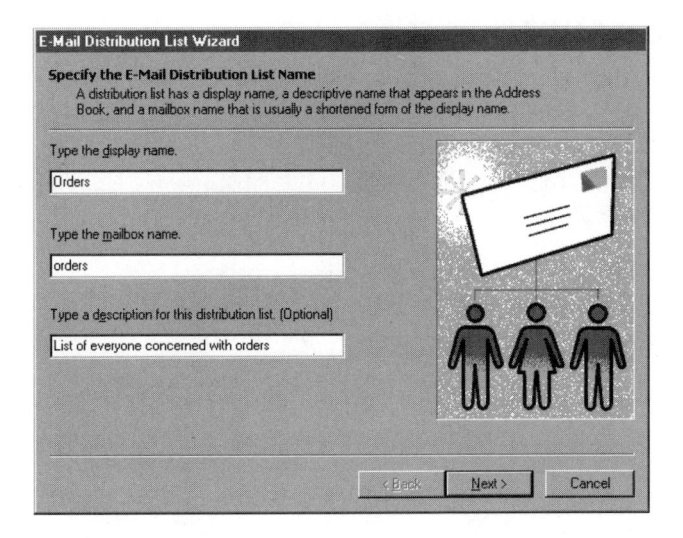

FIGURE 14.02

The first page of the E-Mail Distribution List Wizard.

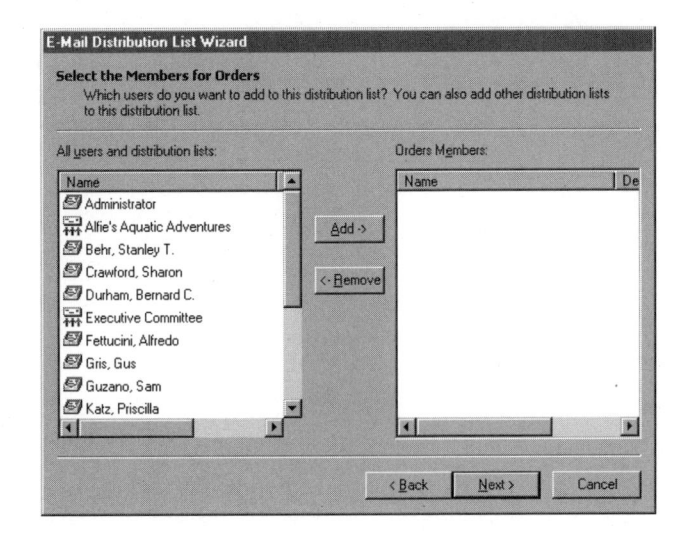

FIGURE 14.03

The wizard's Select The Members page.

CHAPTER 14 *Managing E-Mail* **269**

Modifying a Distribution List

To modify any of the properties of an existing distribution list, follow these steps:

1. On the Manage E-Mail Distribution Lists page, select the list you want to change, and then click on the Review Or Change A Distribution List icon. You'll see the first page of the E-Mail Distribution List Wizard, shown in Figure 14.04.

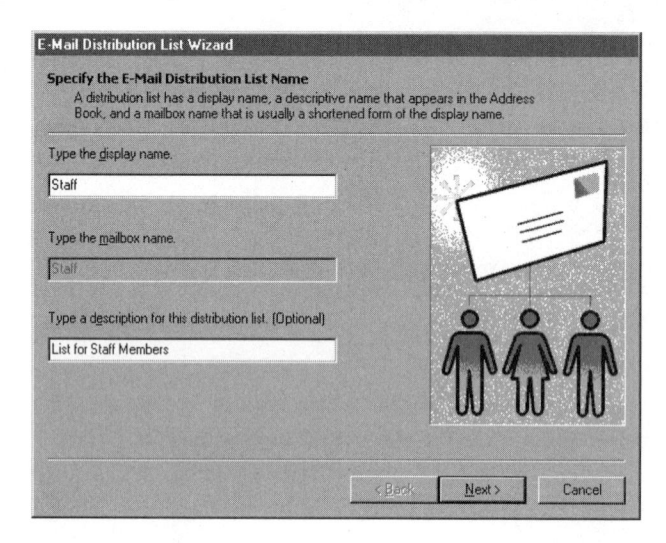

FIGURE 14.04

The wizard's first page.

2. Edit the display name and description of this distribution list by typing your changes in the appropriate text boxes. Note that the text box for the mail box name is grayed out; you cannot change this name because once a distribution list is created, the mail box associated with it can't be changed. Click Next to continue.

3. On the Select The Members page, select the users you want to add to or remove from this e-mail distribution list by selecting their names one at a time and clicking Add or Remove. Click Next to continue, and then click Finish to confirm the changes. You'll get a final confirmation message when the change is made.

Deleting a Distribution List

To delete a distribution list, select its name on the Manage E-Mail Distribution Lists page and click on the Remove A Distribution List icon. You'll see a page of the E-Mail Distribution List Wizard asking you to confirm the removal. Click Finish, and the distribution list will be removed. If you change your mind, simply click Cancel.

Managing Users and Their Mail Boxes

E-mail is a useful and valuable tool, but many users are a lot like pack rats—they want to keep their e-mail forever, so their mail boxes keep growing. This can put quite a strain on your server resources, so you might need to impose a limit on the size of individual mail boxes. This will encourage users to save their important messages to local personal folders, thus relieving the load on the server.

Managing Mail Box Size

Follow these steps to manage the size of your users' mail boxes:

1. From the Start menu, choose Programs, then Microsoft Exchange (Common), and finally Microsoft Exchange Administrator.

2. If this is the first time you're running Exchange Administrator, you'll see the Connect To Server dialog box. Type your server name in the text box, and click OK. If you've run Exchange Administrator before, double-click on your server name.

3. Double-click on Configuration, then Servers, and finally your server name.

4. Select Private Information Store, and click the Properties button on the menu bar (the button that shows a hand pointing to a piece of paper—the leftmost button in the third group of buttons). This will open the Private Information Store Properties dialog box, shown in Figure 14.05.

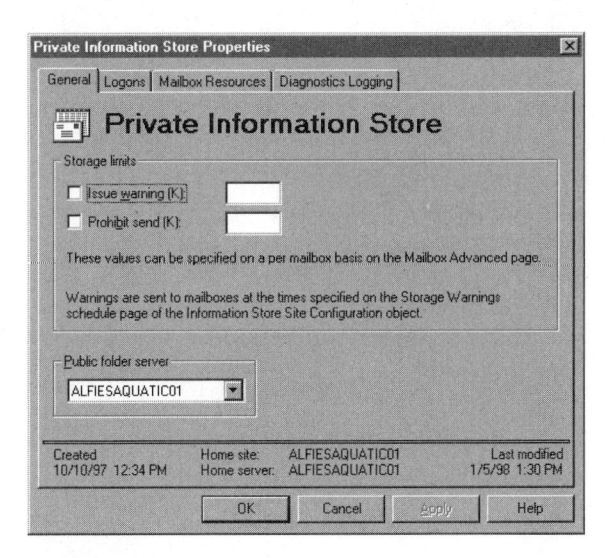

FIGURE 14.05

The Private Information Store Properties dialog box.

CHAPTER 14 *Managing E-Mail* **271**

5. Select the Issue Warning check box, and enter the mail box size that will trigger a warning message. To enforce an upper limit on mail box size, select the Prohibit Send check box and enter a value. This value will be the maximum size of a mail box in kilobytes; a user who exceeds the limit will be unable to send any e-mail until he or she does some clean-up. Incoming messages will not be affected.

6. Click OK to close the dialog box, and then exit Exchange Administrator.

Your users will receive an e-mail message whenever their mail boxes threaten to exceed the specified limit. They'll learn to store their messages in local folders rather than let them pile up on the server.

Managing the E-Mail Connection

Once you've signed up with an Internet service provider (ISP), Small Business Server will dial your ISP once an hour throughout the day to check for and deliver new e-mail. Outgoing messages will be stored on the server until it can connect to your ISP. Depending on your business, you might find this interval a good fit or totally inappropriate. Not to worry—you can easily change the interval, and you can always force an immediate send and receive cycle.

Changing the Dial-Up Interval

To have Small Business Server check for and deliver e-mail at an interval other than once an hour, follow these steps:

1. From the Start menu, choose Programs, then Microsoft Exchange (Common), and finally Microsoft Exchange Administrator.

2. If this is the first time you're running Exchange Administrator, you'll see the Connect To Server dialog box. Type your server name or use the Browse button. Since you need to worry only about a single Exchange Server, select the Set As default check box and then click OK. You won't be asked this question a second time.

3. Under Configuration, double-click on Connections and then double-click on Internet Mail Service in the right pane. This will open the Properties dialog box for your Internet e-mail connection.

4. Click on the Dial-Up Connections tab to see the page where you can set the dial-up interval and conditions shown in Figure 14.06 on the following page.

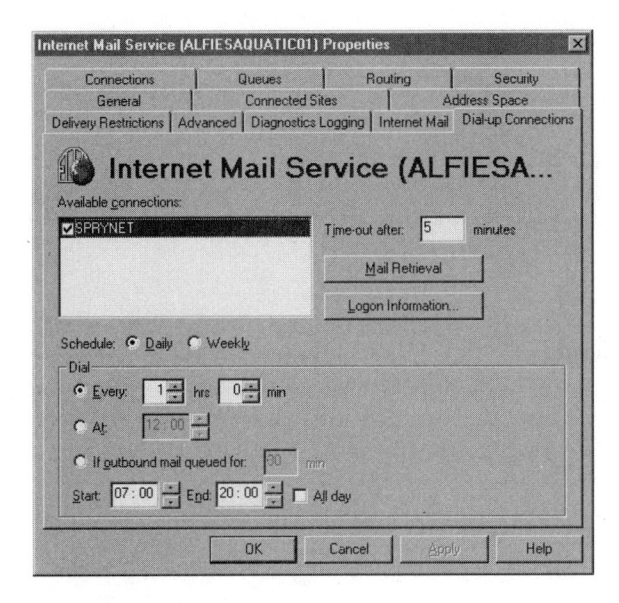

FIGURE 14.06

The Dial-Up Connections tab of the Properties dialog box.

5. Change the dial-up connection conditions as needed. For example, to have Small Business Server check for and deliver new e-mail every half-hour on a daily basis, seven days a week, select the Daily option button and then the Every option button. Change the interval to 30 minutes. You can set the hours of operation as well.

6. When you're done changing the dial-up schedule, click Apply and you'll get a warning that your changes haven't yet taken effect. Changes to the Internet Mail Service require you to stop and restart the Microsoft Exchange Internet Mail Service from the Services applet of the Control Panel. (This will also happen automatically when you reboot your server.)

7. From the File menu, choose Exit to close Exchange Administrator.

Forcing an Immediate Send and Receive Cycle

If you want the e-mail messages waiting in your system's queue to be sent immediately or if you want to check for incoming messages, click on the Send And Receive Mail Now icon on the Manage E-Mail page. Small Business Server will connect to the Internet and send any waiting outgoing messages and collect any messages that your ISP is holding for you.

E-Mail Reports

Over time, you might want to know more about the e-mail traffic on your Small Business Server network. With Small Business Server's built-in version of Crystal Reports, you can get reports that show who's been sending and receiving e-mail, how many messages have been sent, the size of the messages, and much more. Here's how to generate four different kinds of reports about the state of your e-mail system:

1. From the Start menu, choose Manage Server and then click on the Manage Electronic Mail icon.

2. Click on the Generate E-Mail Reports icon, and you'll see the Electronic Mail Reports page, shown in Figure 14.07. This page lists the kinds of reports available and offers icons that automatically generate each type of report, provided that you've enabled message tracking. (See the next section for instructions.)

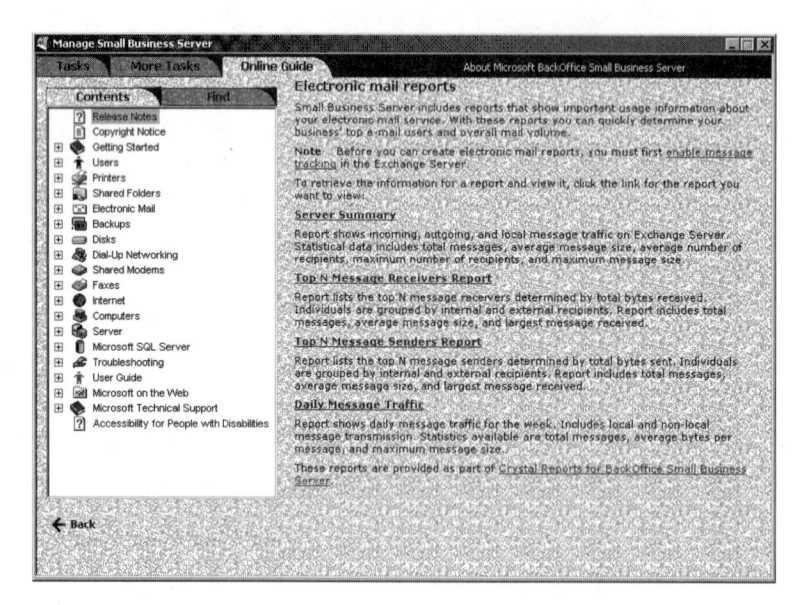

FIGURE 14.07

The Electronic Mail Reports page.

Enabling Message Tracking

Before you can create all these nifty e-mail reports, you must first enable message tracking in the Exchange Server. Just follow these steps:

1. From the Start menu, choose Programs, then Microsoft Exchange (Common), and finally Microsoft Exchange Administrator.

2. If this is the first time you're running Exchange Administrator, you'll see the Connect To Server dialog box. Type your server name or use the Browse button. Since you need to worry only about a single Exchange Server, select the Set As Default check box and then click OK. You won't be asked this question a second time.

3. Double-click on your server name, on Configuration, and then on Information Store Site Configuration in the right pane. This will open the Information Store Site Configuration Properties dialog box, shown in Figure 14.08.

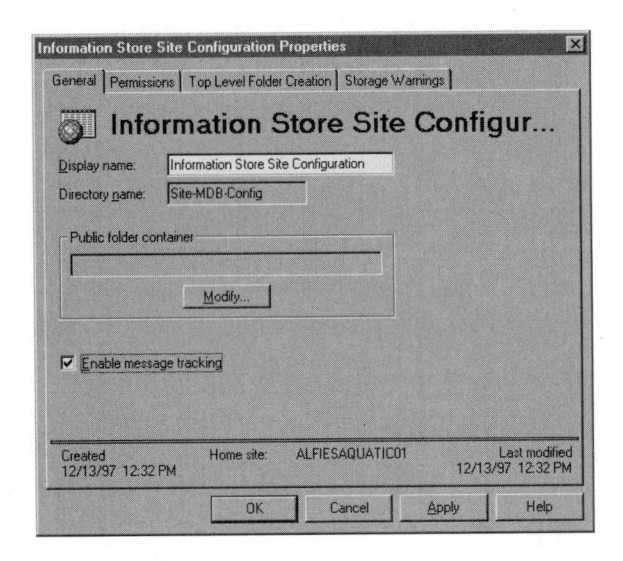

FIGURE 14.08

The Information Store Site Configuration Properties dialog box.

4. Make sure that Enable Message Tracking is selected, and then click OK.

5. Click Connections in the left pane, and then double-click on Internet Mail Service in the right pane. This will open the Internet Mail Service Properties dialog box. Click on the Internet Mail tab, shown in Figure 14.09.

6. Make sure that Enable Message Tracking is selected, and then click Apply. You'll see a message warning you that your changes haven't yet taken effect. Most changes to the Internet Mail Service require you to stop and restart the Exchange Internet Mail Service from the Services control panel. (This will also happen automatically when you reboot your server.) Click OK to acknowledge the warning, and then click OK again to exit the Internet Mail Service Properties dialog box.

CHAPTER 14 *Managing E-Mail* **275**

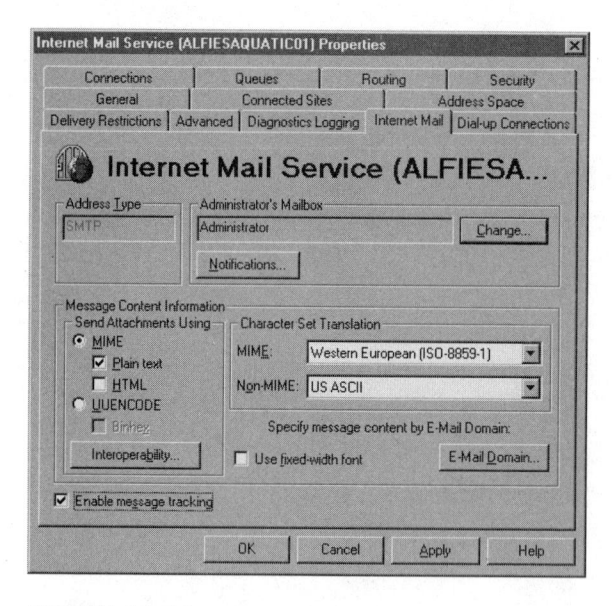

FIGURE 14.09

The Internet Mail tab of the Internet Mail Service Properties dialog box.

7. To close Exchange Administrator, choose Exit from the File menu.

8. Open the Control Panel, and double-click on the Services icon. In the Services dialog box, select Microsoft Exchange Internet Mail Service, as shown in Figure 14.10, and then click Stop. When the service stops, click the Start button to restart it, and then click Close. Your changes have now been enabled.

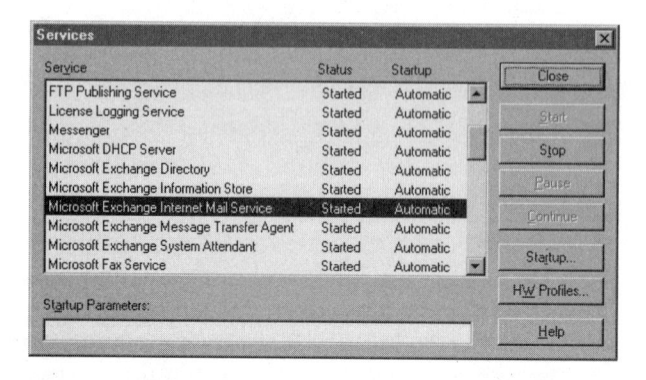

FIGURE 14.10

You must start and stop the Exchange Internet Mail Service for most changes to take effect.

276 ORGANIZING COMMUNICATIONS

Server Summary Report

A Server Summary is a report containing information about incoming, outgoing, and local message traffic. In this report, you can see the number of messages sent, the average message size, the average number of recipients per message, and the maximum number of recipients of a message. This report is especially useful if your e-mail system has become sluggish and you're not sure why. It gives you a quick overview of the message traffic. Both the total number of messages and their average size are key indicators of the server load.

To see a Server Summary report, from the Start menu choose Manage Server, then Manage Electronic Mail, and finally Generate E-Mail Reports. Click on the Server Summary icon to get a report that looks like Figure 14.11.

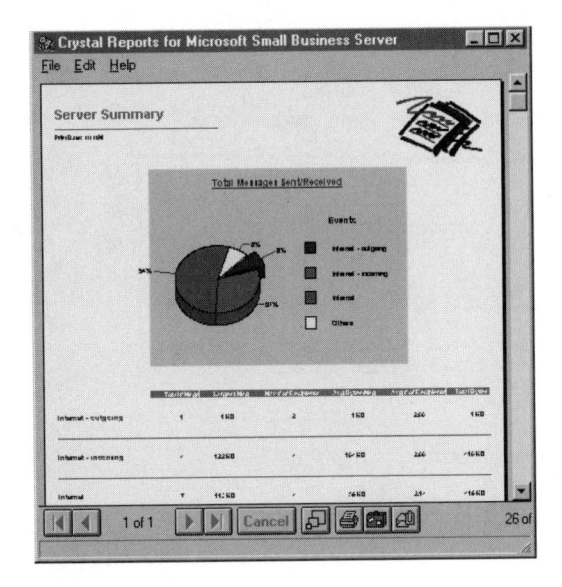

FIGURE 14.11

A Server Summary report.

Top N Message Receivers Report

The Top N Message Receivers report gives you details about who in your organization receives the most mail. The report shows you statistics on mail received from internal sources and from external sources. The information includes total messages received, average message size, and largest message received. This report is useful if you're considering adjusting users' mail box limits individually. Some jobs—customer service, for example—can require a large volume of e-mail. You might want to allow more disk space for message storage for people in those sorts of jobs.

To see a Top N Message Receivers report, from the Start menu choose Manage Server, then Manage Electronic Mail, and finally Generate E-Mail Reports. Click on the Top N Message Receivers icon to produce a report like the one shown in Figure 14.12.

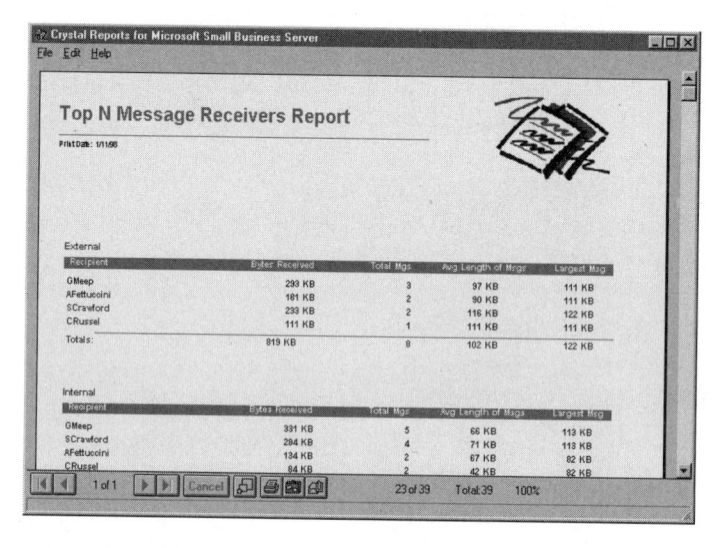

FIGURE 14.12

A Top N Message Receivers report.

Top N Message Senders Report

The Top N Message Senders report provides details about mail being sent and to whom. It shows statistics on mail sent to internal sources and to external sources so that you can see at a glance who's using e-mail the most. Information includes total messages sent, average message size, and largest message sent. This report is useful if you're concerned about overall server performance and where your e-mail load is located. If the load is distributed fairly equally across all users and the server is being taxed, you'll have to make adjustments to improve performance across the board.

To see a Top N Message Senders report, from the Start menu choose Manage Server, then Manage Electronic Mail, and finally Generate E-Mail Reports. Click on the Top N Message Senders icon to see a report like the one shown in Figure 14.13.

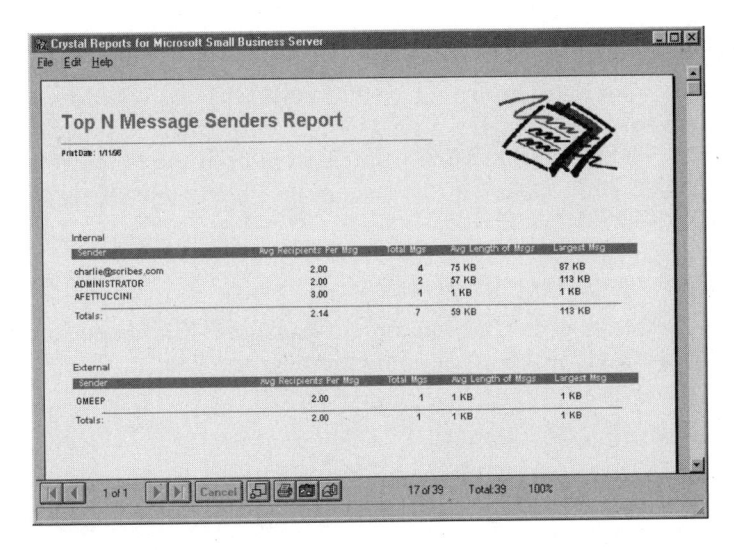

FIGURE 14.13

A Top N Message Senders Report.

Daily Message Traffic Report

The Daily Message Traffic report gives you daily local and Internet message transmission figures for the past week. Statistics include total messages transmitted, average bytes per message, and largest message received. This report is useful for monitoring how your server is performing given the e-mail demands that are being made on it, especially when used in combination with the Server Summary report. It can also help you to balance your load by pointing out days that are particularly busy or particularly light. If you have any standard reports or e-mail correspondence that are sent out weekly or monthly, you might want to change the day of the week that these messages are sent in order to balance the load.

To see a Daily Message Traffic report, from the Start menu choose Manage Server, then Manage Electronic Mail, and finally Generate E-Mail Reports. Click on the Daily Message Traffic icon to see the report.

For More Information

Crystal Reports produces the messaging reports described previously. You'll find more information on Crystal Reports and how it can help you track your network in Chapter 23.

Solving E-Mail Problems

Because e-mail is such an important part of networks, it's nice to know how to troubleshoot when something goes wrong. Fortunately, Small Business Server offers you access to handy troubleshooting utilities from both the Manage E-Mail page and the Manage E-Mail Distribution Lists page. Here's a brief rundown of the problems that these utilities cover.

Troubleshooting E-Mail

Click on the Troubleshoot E-Mail icon on the Manage E-Mail page, and you'll see a list of possible e-mail problems, as shown in Figure 14.14.

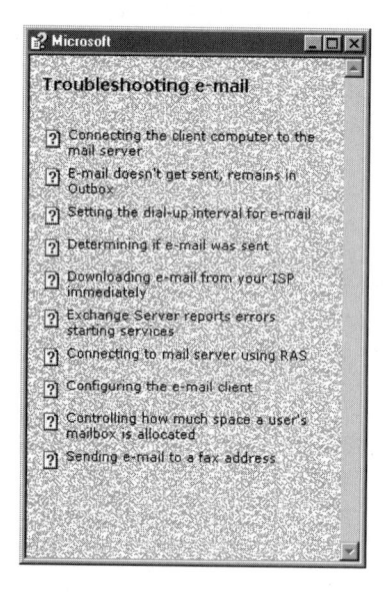

FIGURE 14.14

The e-mail troubleshooting utility.

Although we won't give you complete details of the solutions to these problems, here are some basic strategies for dealing with problems similar to ones that the troubleshooting utility describes.

You have trouble connecting the client computer to the mail server

If you're using a client computer and are having trouble connecting to the mail server, the utility suggests that you consider three possibilities: there's something wrong with the client e-mail profile, the client can't connect to the server at all, and

Exchange services aren't available. If the problem turns out to be with the client e-mail profile, you must start Outlook and follow the troubleshooting utility's instructions for configuring the profile properly.

To test whether the client can connect to the server, try accessing a shared folder on the server; if you can't do this, chances are that the server is down or there's a physical problem of some kind (a loose or disconnected cable, for example). Check the server and the cabling, and then try again to access a shared folder on the server.

If you suspect that Exchange services are not available, you must open the Services control panel to verify that these services (particularly the Internet Mail Service) are up and running. Sometimes it's helpful to stop and then restart these services in case everything didn't go quite right at startup.

E-mail remains in the Outbox

If you have this problem, the troubleshooting utility asks you three questions:

- Are there errors in your server log files?
- Are Exchange services up and running?
- Can you connect to your ISP?

If there are errors in your system or application log files, you have a system problem. Follow the utility's instructions for checking the log files, and then, if you're still experiencing problems, see Chapter 25 of this book.

To see whether Exchange services are up and running, open the Services control panel. If necessary, stop and then restart Exchange services (in particular, the Internet Mail Service).

If you can't connect to your ISP, there are two possible sources of the problem: you or your ISP. To rule out a problem on your end, try using your browser to connect to the Internet. If that doesn't work, check your modem and network cabling—something might have come loose or unplugged. If you suspect that the problem is on the ISP's end, you probably have to contact its technical support staff to find out what's going on.

You want to change the dial-up interval

This item on the troubleshooting utility's list is intended for those who aren't happy with Small Business Server's default setting, which instructs your server to dial your ISP once an hour to check for and send e-mail. For complete instructions on how to change the dial-up interval, see the section titled "Changing the Dial-Up Interval" earlier in this chapter.

You can't tell whether e-mail was sent

Determining whether e-mail has been sent is easy; you just open the Manage E-Mail page of the Small Business Server console and look at the mail queue figures on the left side of the page. This shows you at a glance whether any e-mail is waiting to be sent and if so, how many messages are in the queue. If you already have this page open and you want to make sure that it shows current information, right-click in an empty spot and choose Refresh from the pop-up menu.

You want to download e-mail immediately

To download mail from your ISP immediately, click on the Send And Receive Mail Now icon on the Manage E-Mail page. See the earlier section titled "Forcing an Immediate Send and Receive Cycle" for instructions on how to make this happen.

Exchange Server reports errors in starting its services

The troubleshooting utility suggests three avenues of inquiry if you see messages stating that Exchange Server services are not working properly. They are listed here in order of what you might try first, second, and third.

1. Check to see whether you have enough memory.
2. Check to see whether you have enough hard disk space.
3. Make sure that your TCP/IP domain name is found during initialization.

As a temporary fix to increase the available memory, open the System control panel and change the virtual memory setting. This will make Windows NT think that it has more memory. This will help until you can install more memory in your server, which you should do quickly because of the performance hit you'll take when operating without enough RAM. Limited memory is the single most common cause of slowdowns on the server.

To initialize the Exchange directory and information store, you must have at least 20 MB of free hard disk space. If you don't have this much free space, Exchange won't run properly, so clear some disk space and start the services again. You'd better plan to get more hard drive space because Exchange files tend to grow and grow. You should also consider running Exchange Optimizer, a utility that examines your hard drives, RAM, and user configurations and makes recommendations on where to put the Exchange files and set the necessary tuning parameters. If you decide to move some of the files based on Exchange Optimizer's recommendations, it will automatically move the files for you.

TCP/IP domain name problems are a bit more complex than memory or hard disk problems, so consult the troubleshooting utility for complete details on how to ensure that your domain name is found during initialization.

You want to connect to the mail server using RAS

As the troubleshooting utility will tell you, there are three requirements for setting up a computer to connect to the mail server using Remote Access Server (RAS):

1. A modem and Dial-Up Networking must be installed on the computer.
2. The administrator or someone else with administrative privileges must grant remote access permission to the user.
3. The user must have an Exchange profile that allows him or her to download e-mail from a remote location.

> **For More Information**
>
> For details on how to install Dial-Up Networking, see Chapter 19.

You need to configure the e-mail client

When you use the Set Up Computer Wizard to configure a client computer that already has an e-mail client installed, the setup program will not configure settings for sending and receiving mail from Small Business Server. This might surprise you; however, it's to your benefit because it allows you to decide when and how to update your e-mail software. The Configuring The E-Mail Client icon on the troubleshooting utility's list provides details on how to configure e-mail settings manually; once you're ready to make a switch, follow the instructions and you'll be all set.

You want to limit the space allocated to a user's mail box

As we discussed earlier, overly large user mail boxes can impede the performance of your e-mail system. For complete details, see the section titled "Managing Mail Box Size" earlier in this chapter.

You want to send e-mail to a fax address

Although this is listed in the troubleshooting utility, it's hardly a problem. But the utility provides instructions on how to send e-mail to a fax address. (It arrives as a fax.)

For More Information

You can learn more about using the fax client and server in Chapter 15.

Troubleshooting E-Mail Distribution Lists

If you're having problems with an e-mail distribution list, you can get troubleshooting help by choosing Manage Server from the Start menu. On the Tasks page, click on Manage Electronic Mail and then Manage E-Mail Distribution Lists. Click on the Troubleshoot E-Mail Distribution Lists icon, and you'll see a listing of distribution list pitfalls, as shown in Figure 14.15.

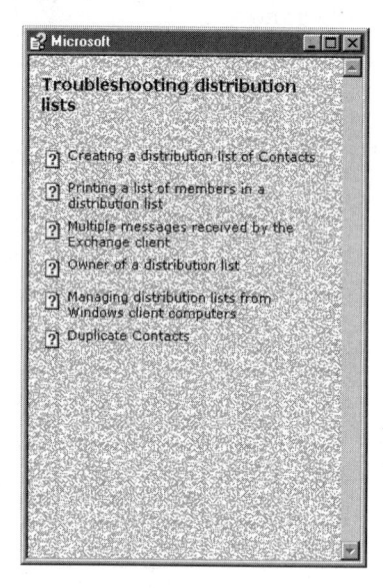

FIGURE 14.15

The e-mail distribution lists troubleshooting utility.

Actually, most of the items on this list offer instructions on how to perform additional distribution list management tasks rather than solutions to problems; in any case, here's an introduction to the topics in this troubleshooting utility.

Creating a distribution list of contacts

There are three steps to creating a distribution list of contacts: assigning contacts to a common category, grouping contacts by category, and creating a new e-mail message to send to your new distribution list. If this is what you want to do, simply carry out the steps described by the utility.

Printing a list of members in a distribution list

This item provides details on how to print a list of members in a distribution list, which can be particularly helpful if you want to review the membership of a large list in preparation for some judicious pruning.

Multiple messages received by the Exchange client

This item is more an explanation of why the Exchange client sometimes receives multiple messages rather than a fix for the problem; if you read all the way to the bottom of the information provided, you'll see another application of the programmers' "it's a feature, not a flaw" argument.

Owner of a distribution list

At the moment, it's not terribly important who the owner of a distribution list is because, as this item informs you, the owner field is currently used for informational purposes only. If you read the information, however, you'll learn about some possible uses for the owner field, just in case future releases of Small Business Server make it more functional than it is now.

Managing distribution lists from Windows client computers

Here you'll learn how to manage distribution lists from Windows client computers: First you grant permissions to a list manager, and then the list manager can go ahead and do his or her thing. Allowing someone to manage a distribution list from a client computer can be a great convenience. It means that you don't have to give that person permission to log onto the server directly, which is always a potential security problem. It also means that if you're working on the server, you don't have to get off to let the other person fix a list problem.

Duplicate contacts

This item is the only one on the list that actually provides the solution to a problem. In some situations, you can end up with a bunch of duplicate contacts in Outlook if you import a Personal Address Book that has personal distribution lists defined. If you do have trouble with this, simply follow the instructions to solve the problem.

POINTS TO REMEMBER

- The Manage E-Mail page is your headquarters for performing basic e-mail management tasks.
- Use e-mail distribution lists to organize communication within your company or organization.
- Monitor mail box sizes and set a limit if they threaten to overwhelm the server's resources.
- E-mail reports can help you track usage and spot potential problems.

WHAT'S NEXT

In this chapter, you learned how to manage the sophisticated mail messaging system built into Small Business Server. In the next chapter, we'll cover the use of the fax server and client.

Chapter 15

Sending and Receiving Faxes

- 289 **Installing Fax Modems**
- 290 **Configuring Fax Services**
  - Sending Faxes — 291
  - Receiving Faxes — 291
  - Sending Faxes to an Exchange Mail box — 292
- 292 **Adding and Removing Fax Printers**
  - Adding a Fax Printer — 293
  - Removing a Fax Printer — 294
- 294 **Controlling User Access to Fax Printers**
- 295 **Changing How Faxes Are Received**
- 297 **Managing Fax Jobs**
- 297 **Generating Fax Reports**
- 298 **Managing Fax Cover Pages**
  - Editing an Existing Cover Page — 298
  - Creating a New Cover Page — 299
- 299 **Fax Troubleshooting**
- 300 **Fax Client Options**
- 300 **Points to Remember**
- 300 **What's Next**

Chapter 15

Sending and Receiving Faxes

The built-in fax server and client in Microsoft BackOffice Small Business Server are unique to Small Business Server. At this point, even the Enterprise edition of BackOffice doesn't include them. The fax server and client are more than enough to handle the load in a typical office.

In conjunction with modem pooling (see Chapter 16), Microsoft Fax Service can save you a substantial amount of money in both hardware and software. Fax modems attached to the server can be used to send faxes by anyone on the network. Faxes received via fax modems can be automatically printed or sent to a mail box. There's no need for special faxing software or for a fax modem on every desktop.

◆ Faxes, Modems, and Remote Access

Fax modems can be used on a Small Business Server network for faxing, for connecting to the Internet, and for remote access when employees are at home or on the road. If you add multiport boards to your server, the server can support up to 12 modems, with up to 4 assigned to the fax server, up to 4 assigned to each modem pool, and up to 4 assigned to remote access. Keep these numbers in mind as you set up combinations of modem functions.

In general, you want incoming or outgoing faxes to roll over to an available fax device if the first one is busy. For that to happen, your fax modems must be in a modem pool (of up to four fax modems). Similarly, incoming remote access calls should roll over to the first free remote access line. This also requires a modem pool.

If you require four or fewer modems altogether, the problem is solved—you assign them all to the same modem pool. For more than four modems, you have to think through the pool assignments and configure each modem as described in this chapter and in Chapters 16 and 19.

Installing Fax Modems

The easiest way to install fax modems is to have them plugged in and ready to go when you install Small Business Server. The setup program will detect and install them with little or no input from you.

WARNING!

You must reboot the server in order for new modem settings to take effect, so you should add and remove modems—like any other hardware—at a time when shutting down the server will cause the least disruption to the network.

To install a fax modem after Small Business Server has been installed, plug the modem into the server, turn on the modem, and then follow these steps:

1. From the Start menu, choose Settings and then Control Panel. Double-click on the Modems icon.

2. In the Modems Properties dialog box, click the Add button. This will start the Install New Modem Wizard.

3. You can let the wizard detect the new modem, or you can supply information about the manufacturer and model yourself.

4. After the modem is installed, you'll see a message box saying that dial-up networking must be configured (Figure 15.01). Click Yes.

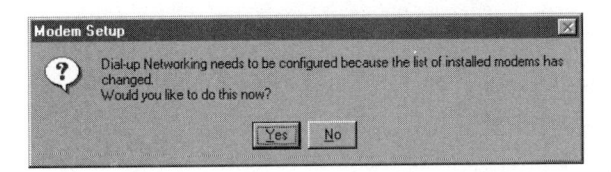

FIGURE 15.01

When the list of modems changes, dial-up networking must be reconfigured.

5. In the Remote Access Setup dialog box, click the Add button. The Add RAS Device dialog box (Figure 15.02 on the following page) will open, showing the modem you just installed. Click OK.

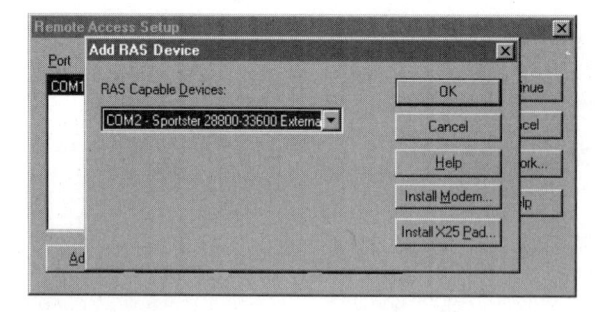

FIGURE 15.02

Adding the modem to the list of RAS devices.

6. In the Remote Access Setup dialog box, select the newly installed modem and click the Configure button.

7. In the Configure Port Usage dialog box, specify the function for this modem, as shown in Figure 15.03. It can dial out only, receive calls only, or dial out and receive calls. Click OK, and then click Continue.

You must shut down and restart the server before the new settings take effect.

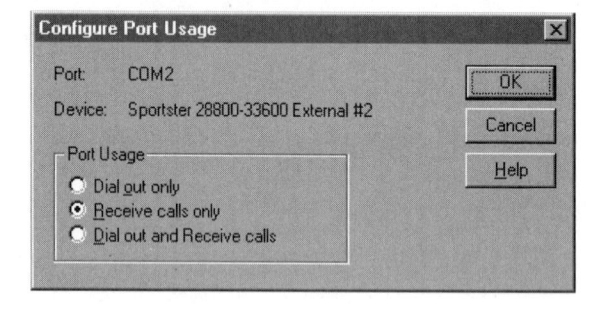

FIGURE 15.03

Setting send and receive options for the modem.

To remove a fax modem from the server, double-click on Modems in the Control Panel, select the modem you want to delete, and click the Remove button. You must reboot after a removal as well.

Configuring Fax Services

After you add a fax modem, double-click on Fax Server in the Control Panel to configure the fax settings. From there, you can set up all the fax options, including send and receive options.

Sending Faxes

On the Send tab of the Fax Server Properties dialog box (Figure 15.04), make sure that there are check marks next to all the devices. We configured both fax devices to show the same Transmitting Station ID (TSID) so that recipients see only one fax number no matter which device transmitted the fax.

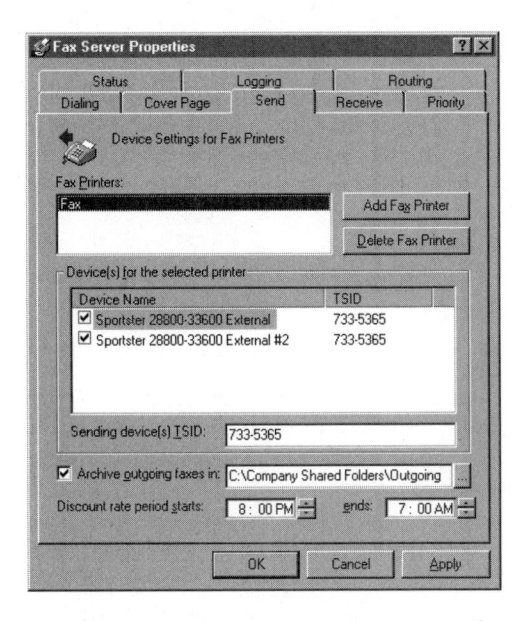

FIGURE 15.04

The Send tab of the Fax Server Properties dialog box.

Outgoing faxes aren't tracked unless you supply a destination in the Archive Outgoing Faxes text box. We created a folder named Outgoing Faxes and put it in the Company Shared Folders folder, where everyone can read it. You can archive faxes in a nonshared folder as well; you simply supply the path to it in the text box.

Receiving Faxes

On the Receive tab of the Fax Properties dialog box, put check marks next to the devices that are to receive faxes. You can have the faxes automatically printed out, saved in a folder on the network, sent to a local inbox, or a combination of these three choices. However, you must have at least one destination selected.

> **Tip**
>
> *If you're saving incoming and outgoing faxes in a folder on the server, be sure to clear out the folders periodically. The faxes are received as TIFF graphics, and a single page will average about 50 KB. If you send and receive many faxes, this can add up quickly.*

Sending Faxes to an Exchange Mail Box

The fax server allows faxes to be printed, delivered to a folder on the network, or delivered to a "profile." If you'd like to deliver faxes to an Exchange mail box other than Administrator, you first need to configure the appropriate profile on the server and then tell the fax server to deliver faxes to that profile. To deliver faxes to a profile, follow these steps:

1. From the Start menu, choose Settings and then Control Panel. Double-click on the Mail icon.

2. In the Mail Properties dialog box, click the Show Profiles button.

3. Click the Add button, and supply the information for the new profile. Be sure to give the profile a sensible name (perhaps the name of the user), enter the server's machine name, and select the mail box you prefer.

4. After you create the profile, double-click on Fax Server in the Control Panel and then click on the Receive tab.

5. For each modem, click Send To Local Inbox and select the profile you just created. Faxes will show up in the mail box of the user you specified in the profile no matter where that user is logged on.

NOTE

Microsoft Outlook doesn't "see" faxes in the same way it "sees" e-mail, so the delivery of a fax won't produce a warning beep or display an icon on the Taskbar.

Adding and Removing Fax Printers

When Small Business Server installs Microsoft Fax Service, it creates a single fax printer for sending faxes. You can add additional fax printers if traffic increases and you need to distribute the burden of fax printing across the network. For example, if you have different discount billing rate periods for domestic and long-distance calling, you can create one fax printer with the discount rate period set for international use and another for domestic use. You can also create printers for different people or groups in your organization. Each printer can be configured to use its own cover pages, archive sent faxes in a particular location, and use a different pool of devices.

Adding a Fax Printer

Follow these steps to add a fax printer to your Small Business Server network:

1. Make sure you're logged on using an account with administrative privileges. From the Start menu, choose Manage Server. Click on the More Tasks tab, and then choose Manage Faxes.

2. On the Manage Faxes page, click on the Add Or Remove Fax Printers link, and you'll see the first page of the Add Or Remove Fax Printer utility.

3. Click on the arrow icon next to Add A Fax Printer.

4. Click on the link that opens the Send tab of the Fax Server Properties dialog box, and you'll see instructions for adding a fax printer to your network.

5. Click Add Fax Printer, and you'll see the Add Fax Printer dialog box, as shown in Figure 15.05.

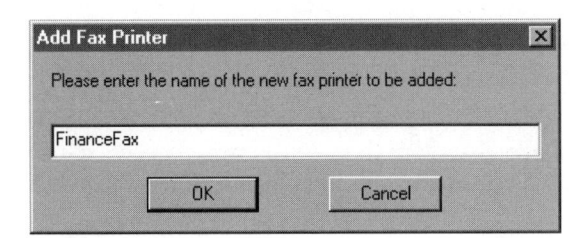

FIGURE 15.05

The Add Fax Printer dialog box.

6. Type a name for the new fax printer, and click OK. The new fax printer will be added to your network.

7. At this point, you might want to select the new fax printer and either examine the tabs of its Properties sheet or use the links on the Manage Faxes page to ensure that the settings for this fax printer meet your needs.

Removing a Fax Printer

To remove a fax printer from your network, follow these steps:

1. Make sure you're logged on using an account with administrative privileges. From the Start menu, choose Manage Server. Click on the More Tasks tab, and then choose Manage Faxes.

2. On the Manage Faxes page, click on the Add Or Remove Fax Printers link, and you'll see the first page of the Add Or Remove Fax Printer utility.

3. Click on the arrow icon next to Remove A Fax Printer.

4. Click on the link that opens the Send tab of the Fax Server Properties box.

5. Select the fax printer you want to remove, and click Delete Fax Printer. Confirm the deletion.

> **WARNING!**
>
> *If you delete the default fax printer (named simply* Fax*), you'll have serious trouble getting the Fax Service to work again. In fact, we had to delete the Fax Service and reinstall it to regain the ability to fax.*

Controlling User Access to Fax Printers

If fax usage isn't evenly distributed across your network, you might want to make adjustments in user access. For example, a heavy user might need exclusive or near-exclusive use of a fax printer, while someone who prints out only an occasional fax can share a fax printer with other users.

Take these steps to control the flow of fax printer traffic on your network:

1. Make sure you're logged on using an account with administrative privileges. From the Start menu, choose Manage Server. Click on the More Tasks tab, and then choose Manage Faxes.

2. On the Manage Faxes page, select the fax printer whose access you want to control, and then click Control User Access To Fax Printers. This will start the Printer Access Wizard, whose first page is shown in Figure 15.06.

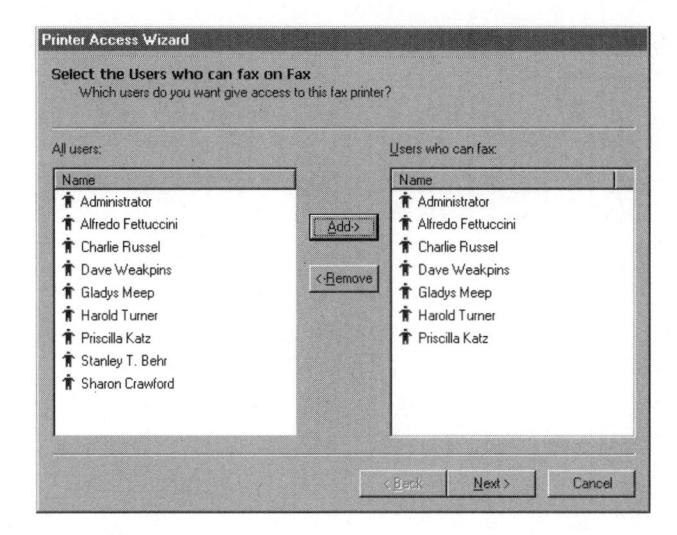

FIGURE 15.06
The first page of the Printer Access Wizard.

3. This page lists all users on the network on the left and the users who have permission to use this fax printer on the right. To grant a user permission to use this fax printer, select his or her name on the left and click Add. To remove a user from the list, select his or her name on the right and click Remove. Click Next to continue, and then click Finish to update the permissions.

> **Tip**
>
> *If your correctly installed fax modem refuses to answer a call, check the Ports (Control Panel) settings and make sure they match the settings you see in the Modems Properties dialog box. We once had the Flow Control for our US Robotics Sportster modems mysteriously reset from Hardware (which works) to None (which doesn't).*

Changing How Faxes Are Received

Once installed, the Fax Service automatically answers incoming fax calls. Small Business Server gives you three options for how faxes are handled after they have been received. You can print them as they are received, you can save them in a folder anywhere on your network, or you can deliver them to a local profile on the server—or any combination of the three. The Change How Faxes Are Received link on the Manage Faxes page allows you to specify the options you prefer. Just follow these steps:

1. Make sure you're logged on using an account with administrative privileges. From the Start menu, choose Manage Server. Click on the More Tasks tab, and then choose Manage Faxes.

2. On the Manage Faxes page, click on the Change How Faxes Are Received link.

3. Read the information on the next page, and then click on the link to open the Receive tab of the Fax Server Properties dialog box (Figure 15.07).

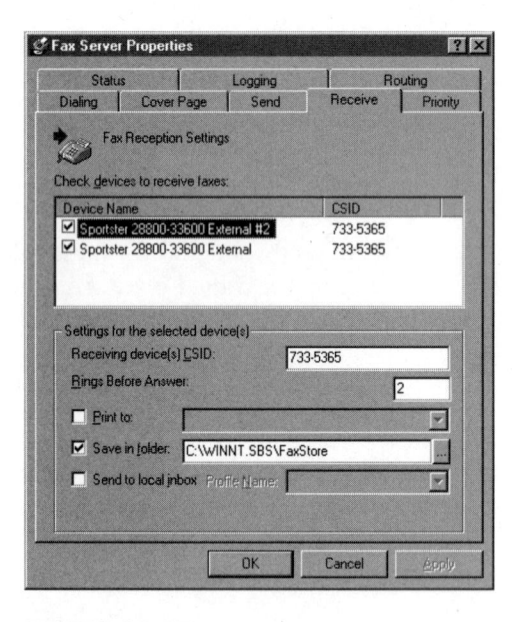

FIGURE 15.07

The Receive tab of the Fax Server Properties dialog box.

4. Select the fax device in question, and select the check box that corresponds to how you want incoming faxes handled. To print faxes as they are received, select the Print To check box and use the drop-down list to specify a printer. To save faxes to a folder on your network (the default setting), select the Save In Folder check box and specify a folder for this purpose. To send faxes to a local inbox, select the Send To Local Inbox check box and use the drop-down list to select the appropriate profile name.

5. After you make your selections, click OK; your faxes will be handled in the manner you specified.

> **Tip**
>
> *To change the send and receive options more readily the next time, from the Start menu choose Setting and then Control Panel. Double-click on the Fax Server icon.*

Managing Fax Jobs

When more than one person is faxing on your network, you might need to step in at times to manage fax activity. Jobs get "stuck," modems hang, a user with a lengthy fax to Lima, Ohio, accidentally starts to send it to Lima, Peru—you know, the usual things. To get at the list of queued-up outgoing fax jobs, follow these steps:

1. From the Start menu, choose Manage Server; click on the More Tasks tab, and choose Manage Faxes.

2. On the Manage Faxes page, select a fax printer and then click on the Manage Fax Jobs link.

3. The next page lists current fax jobs on your system on the left; on the right are links labeled Cancel A Fax Job, Restart A Fax Job, and Return To Manage Faxes. Select the fax job you want to cancel or restart, and click on the appropriate link, or click on Return To Manage Faxes.

WARNING!

Do not go into the Printers folder to cancel fax jobs. Always perform fax management using the Small Business Server console.

Generating Fax Reports

If you're curious about who's been sending and receiving all those faxes on your network and where they've been going to or coming from, the Generate Fax Reports link on the Manage Faxes page will help satisfy your curiosity. Here's how to access the information you crave:

1. Make sure you're logged on using an account with administrative privileges. From the Start menu, choose Manage Server; click on the More Tasks tab, and choose Manage Faxes.

2. On the Manage Faxes page, click on the Generate Fax Report link, and you'll see the first page of the Fax Reports utility.

3. Click on the link corresponding to the type of report you want. You can generate reports on received and sent faxes, top telephone numbers from which faxes were received, and top telephone numbers to which faxes were sent.

Managing Fax Cover Pages

The installation of the Microsoft Fax Service creates four default cover pages that users can send with faxes. You can also edit the cover pages and create new ones.

Editing an Existing Cover Page

To customize an existing cover page, make sure you're logged on using an account with administrative privileges. From the Start menu, choose Settings and then Control Panel; double-click on the Fax Server icon.

Click on the Cover Page tab of the Fax Server Properties dialog box, select the cover sheet file you want to edit, and click Open. Figure 15.08 shows the "confidential" sheet open in the Fax Cover Page Editor.

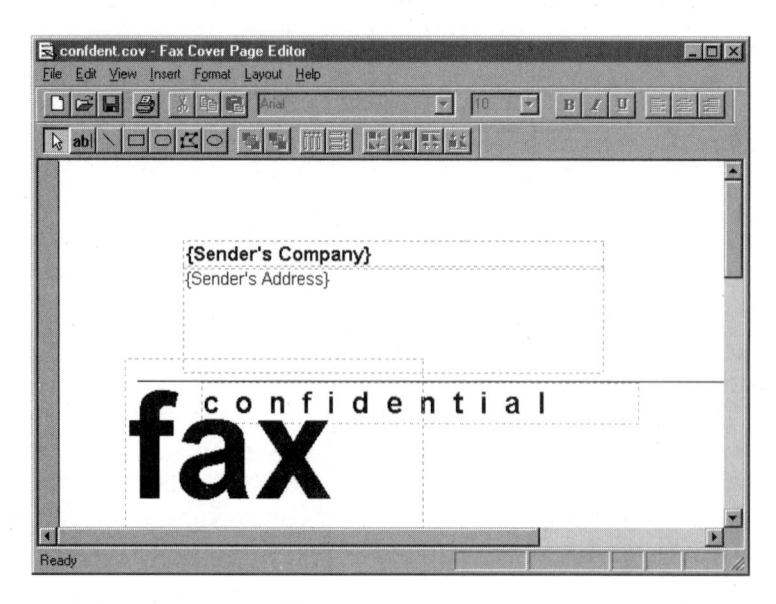

FIGURE 15.08

Editing an existing cover page.

> **Tip**
>
> *The sender information on the cover page comes from the data you provided when you set up the fax client. To change this information, from the Start menu choose Programs, Fax, and then Fax Configuration.*

On existing pages, you can delete fields and move them around. However, if you want to do a lot of formatting—inserting graphics and so forth—it's much easier to create a new cover page.

Creating a New Cover Page

If none of the default cover pages is to your taste, here's how to create a new one:

1. Make sure you're logged on using an account with administrative privileges. From the Start menu, choose Manage Server; click on the More Tasks tab, and choose Manage Faxes.

2. On the Manage Faxes page, click on the Create A Cover Page link; this will start the Create And Manage Cover Pages utility.

3. Read the information, and then click on the link to open the Cover Page tab of the Fax Server Properties dialog box.

4. Click New, and you'll open the Fax Cover Page Editor with a blank cover page file.

5. Create and save your cover page, and you're all set. Your new cover page will appear in the list on the Cover Page tab of the Fax Server Properties dialog box.

> **Tip**
>
> *To restrict users to the cover pages listed, select the Clients Must Use These Cover Pages check box at the bottom of the Cover Page tab of the Fax Server Properties dialog box. This prevents users from creating their own personal fax cover pages.*

Fax Troubleshooting

The fax server software in Small Business Server borders on the temperamental. Once you have it set up—which isn't difficult—we strongly advise you to avoid changes. It's quite easy to make alterations that render the whole fax setup inoperable.

Eventual improvements to the software are bound to help the situation, but in the meantime, fixes are available for the easier problems.

The most common difficulties are addressed in the Fax Troubleshooter, which you can access from the Manage Faxes page. If your problem isn't addressed there, go to Chapter 27. First consult the section titled "Faxes," and then try the sections titled "Modems" and "Remote Access Service."

Fax Client Options

Most of the properties for sending and receiving faxes, creating and sharing fax printers, and configuring fax devices are set on the server. Clients can determine scheduling, choice of fax printer (when more than one is available), the information on cover pages, and the choice of cover page. (Installation of the client software is covered in Chapter 6.)

To access client fax options on a client computer, from the Start menu choose Programs, Fax (Common), and then Fax Configuration. To review or change the client options for faxing from the server, choose Settings, Control Panel, and then Fax Client.

POINTS TO REMEMBER

- ♦ If you want incoming and outgoing faxes to be automatically rolled over to the first available fax modem, all the fax devices must be identical.

- ♦ With multiport boards added, your server can support up to 12 modems—but no more than 4 modems each can be assigned to the fax server, to each modem pool, and to remote access.

- ♦ Fax printers are not printers. Don't attempt to manage them from the Printers folder. Always make changes in the Fax Server Properties dialog box.

WHAT'S NEXT

Modem sharing makes the pooling of fax resources possible. In the next chapter, we'll cover the basics of setting up and managing a modem pool.

Chapter 16

Managing Modem Pools

- 303 Creating a Modem Pool
- 304 Adding a Modem to a Pool
- 307 Configuring a Client to Use a Modem Pool
- 308 Checking the Status of a Modem Pool
- 308 Points to Remember
- 308 What's Next

Chapter 16
Managing Modem Pools

Modem pooling is a function that network users have wanted for quite some time. Until now, your only choices were to buy a modem for each user (and pay for individual phone lines) or to buy one or more expensive (and hard-to-configure) "network modems." With modem pooling, a few inexpensive modems attached to the server can handle the needs of all your users.

The most important thing to understand about modem pooling is that *all* the modems in a pool must be of the same make and model. Because any user can access any modem, the pooling software requires that the modems be identical. Only modems on the Microsoft BackOffice Small Business Server Hardware Compatibility List can answer both fax and remote access calls. If you want to use other types of modems, they will work, but they will not receive both types of calls.

If you install Small Business Server with four or fewer modems, all four will, by default, be configured for faxing, remote access, and regular modem use. They'll also be in the same modem pool. This means that the modems will be used on a first come, first served basis. If you want to be sure that there's always a modem available for remote access, for example, you must create a separate modem pool for remote access.

> **Tip**
>
> *If you must add modems after the installation of Small Business Server, do it when the rest of the network is not in use. Installation and configuration require you to reboot the server several times, even if you get everything right.*

You can set most modem pool functions using the Small Business Server console. (Click on the More Tasks tab, and then click on the Manage Modem Pools icon.) But the instructions in this chapter will bypass the console because we think it adds an unnecessary layer of complexity to an already complex topic.

Creating a Modem Pool

If you want to create a modem pool that includes modems that are already installed, you must first delete those modems and then reinstall them after the new modem pool is created.

If additional ports are needed, install the multiport serial board (be sure to use one from the Hardware Compatibility List) according to the manufacturer's instructions. Double-click on the Ports icon in the Control Panel to verify that all the ports are available and configured properly.

To create the modem pool, follow these steps:

1. Double-click on the Modem Sharing icon in the Control Panel.
2. On the General tab of the Modem Sharing Admin dialog box, click the Stop button to stop the modem sharing service.
3. Click on the Configuration tab. (See Figure 16.01.) You'll see the current list of modem pools, the ports that are available, and the ports that are assigned to each pool.

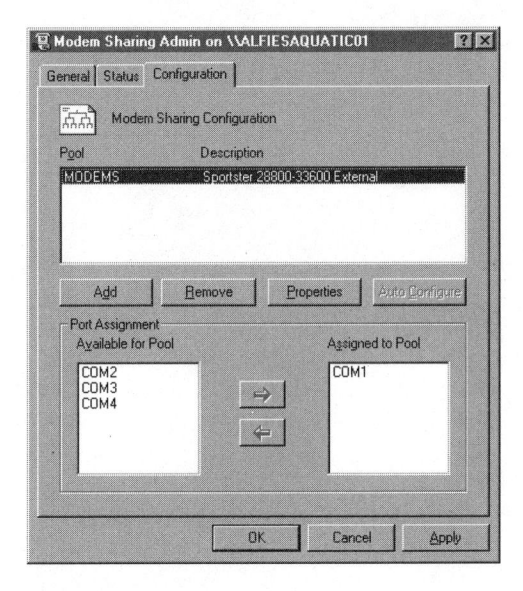

FIGURE 16.01

The currently available modem pools.

4. Click the Add button. Provide a descriptive name for the new modem pool, and then click OK.

5. With the new modem pool selected, select a port to assign to the pool and then click the right-pointing arrow. Repeat this until you've assigned all the ports as you want them.

6. Go back to the General tab, and start the modem sharing service again. Click OK.

Adding a Modem to a Pool

To add a modem to a pool, the pool must first exist. Create the modem pool as described previously. Next install the modem. Make sure the modem is plugged in, turned on, and connected to the correct port on the server, and then follow these steps:

1. Double-click on the Modems icon in the Control Panel.

2. In the Modem Properties dialog box, click the Add button. The Install New Modem Wizard will start. Click Next to let the wizard detect the modem. (See Figure 16.02.)

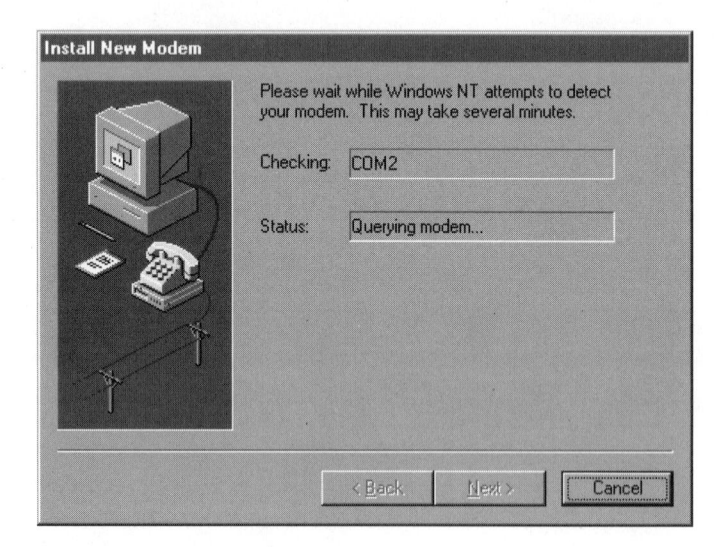

FIGURE 16.02

The Install New Modem Wizard will detect a new modem.

3. The wizard will report on what it finds, as shown in Figure 16.03. If the report isn't correct, click the Change button, and then supply the right information.

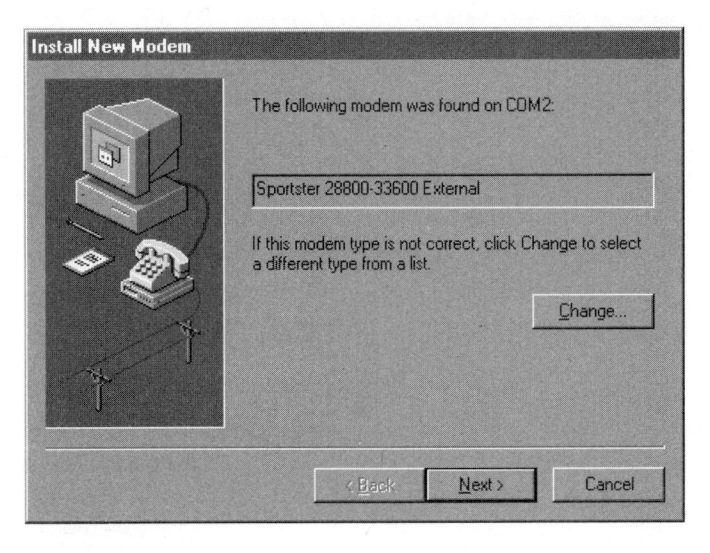

FIGURE 16.03

The wizard reports on what it has detected.

4. Continue stepping through the wizard. When installation is finished, you'll be advised that a reboot is necessary before you can use the new modem.

> **Tip**
>
> *If you have more than one modem to install, repeat the previous steps until all are installed and then reboot just once.*

5. Next you have to configure dial-up networking. In the message box, click No if you have additional modems to install. Click Yes if you're done adding modems.

6. In the Remote Access Setup dialog box, click the Add button. Select the device to add, and then click OK. (If the device you want isn't listed, click Install Modem and run the Modem Setup Wizard.) Repeat this until all the modems you added are listed in the Remote Access Setup dialog box.

7. Select each modem in turn, and click Configure. Verify that the Port Usage setting matches how the modem will be used. For example, in Figure 16.04 on the following page, the Dial Out Only option is selected because the modem on COM2 will be dedicated to Internet access. Click OK.

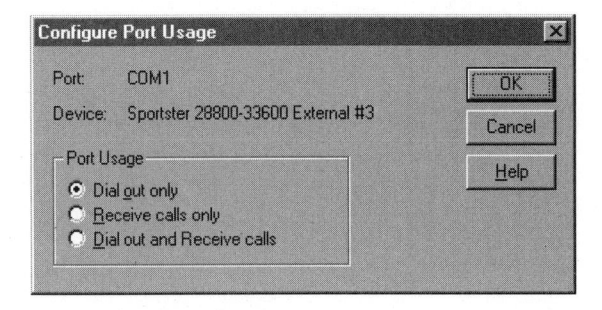

FIGURE 16.04

Setting up a modem that will be used only to dial out.

8. For each modem, click Network. In the Network Configuration dialog box (Figure 16.05), look at the Dial Out Protocols options. TCP/IP should be selected. For Internet access, no other protocol is needed. (If the modem's port is set for Receive Calls Only, this section will be grayed out.)

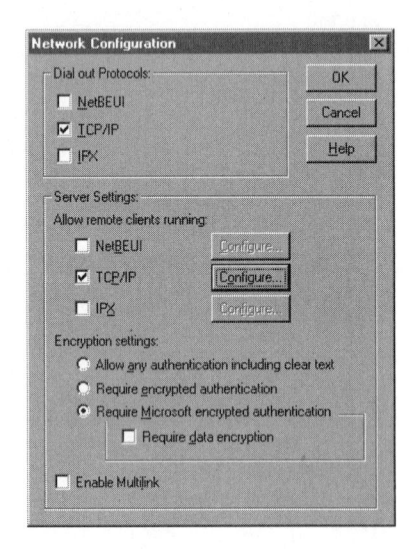

FIGURE 16.05

Setting protocols for dialing out and for remote access.

9. If the modem will be used for remote access, select TCP/IP in the Server Settings section and click the Configure button. In the TCP/IP Configuration dialog box, specify whether clients can access the entire network or just the server. The default setting to use DHCP to assign remote TCP/IP addresses should be left as is. Click OK.

> **For More Information**
>
> *For more on administering remote access, see Chapter 19.*

10. When all of the new modems are configured for remote access, click Continue in the Remote Access Setup dialog box. You'll be prompted to reboot; this is necessary for all the settings to take effect.

> ◆ **Multilinking, or Getting More Bandwidth**
>
> Not everyone can afford a connectivity pipeline larger than a regular phone line. However, you can combine multiple phone lines to create considerably more bandwidth. This process is called *multilinking*. With multilinking, the combined channels can send and receive more data more quickly. Unfortunately, multilinking for the Internet depends on finding an Internet service provider (ISP) that supports it—and this is still relatively rare. (Multilinking for remote access is covered in Chapter 19.)

Configuring a Client to Use a Modem Pool

When the Small Business Server client software is installed, a modem sharing port is also installed. This port is connected to the modem pool on the server. To use this port, follow these steps:

1. Log on to the client machine using an account with administrative privileges. From the Start menu, choose Settings and then Control Panel. Double-click on the Modems icon.

2. In the Modem Properties dialog box, click the Add button and let the Install New Modem Wizard search for the modem port. After querying the available ports, it will report that it has found a "Standard Modem."

3. Click Change, and select the modem type that corresponds to the modems in the server's modem pool. Click Finish.

After the modem is installed, it will appear in the Modems Properties dialog box (Figure 16.06 on the following page) on the client machine. The client machine will now connect through the first modem found of the type installed.

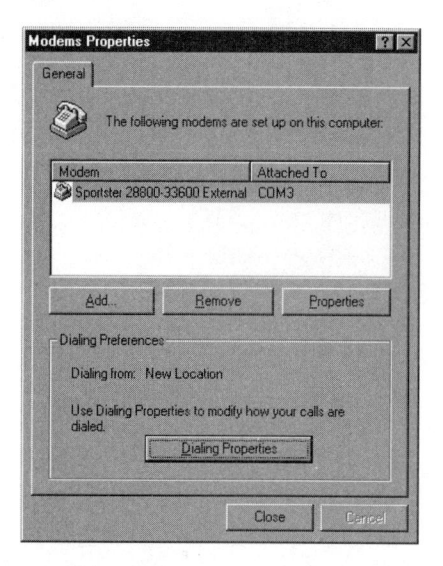

FIGURE 16.06

The newly installed modem on the client computer.

Checking the Status of a Modem Pool

To check on the status of a modem pool, double-click on the Modem Sharing icon in the Control Panel. Click on the Status tab, and select the modem pool in question from the drop-down list. In the window, you'll see activity information on the modems in that pool.

POINTS TO REMEMBER

- All of the modems in a pool must be identical.
- Only modems on the SBS Hardware Compatibility List can answer both fax and remote access calls.
- To use modems on the server, each client must have a modem installed to the modem sharing port.

WHAT'S NEXT

Once modems are installed on both the server and the clients, you can establish an Internet connection. The next chapter explains how to set up an account with an ISP, as well as how to connect to an existing account.

Chapter 17

Managing Internet Access

- **310** Getting Connected
  - Signing Up with an Internet Service Provider — 310
  - Configuring Workstations — 317
- **317** Connecting to an Existing ISP Account
  - Configuring for Dial-Up Accounts — 318
  - Configuring for a Full-Time Connection — 321
  - Configuring for a Second-Level Domain Name — 321
- **324** Getting Your Own Internet Domain Name
  - Signing Up for Your Own Domain Name — 325
- **330** Controlling User Access to the Internet
- **331** Points to Remember
- **332** What's Next

Chapter 17
Managing Internet Access

For many small businesses, the most difficult task associated with using the Internet is getting the network connected and then setting up individual workstations to use it effectively. With Microsoft BackOffice Small Business Server, that task is made remarkably easy. In this chapter, we'll step you through the process of connecting your network to the Internet, whether you have an existing account with an Internet service provider (ISP) or need to set one up. We'll also describe how to get your own Internet domain name and how to manage the Internet connection.

Getting Connected

The Internet is simply the world's largest network. But like all large networks, it imposes some specific requirements that you must meet before you can connect to it. In theory, anyone can connect to the Internet, but in reality virtually no one (except some very, very large businesses) connects to it directly. Instead, most of us connect to an ISP, which manages the connection and all the details of how the network (or workstation) integrates into the larger Internet network.

In this chapter, we'll make a connection for Alfie's Aquatic Adventures and acquire a useful domain name. Fortunately, Small Business Server makes this a straightforward process, from finding an ISP to signing up with it and configuring all the details for the network. If you already have an account with an ISP, the section titled "Connecting to an Existing ISP Account" will help you set up Small Business Server to use the account.

Signing Up with an Internet Service Provider

The first step in getting connected is to locate and sign up with an ISP. Microsoft has arranged with a number of different ISPs in various locations to provide special sign-up procedures that work with Small Business Server to automate the process. Locating one of these ISPs is straightforward when you use the Microsoft Internet Referral Service and the Small Business Server wizards.

Finding an ISP

To find an ISP near you, take these steps:

1. On the More Tasks page of the Small Business Server console, click on the Sign Up With An Internet Service Provider link to start the Internet Connection Wizard, whose first page is shown in Figure 17.01.

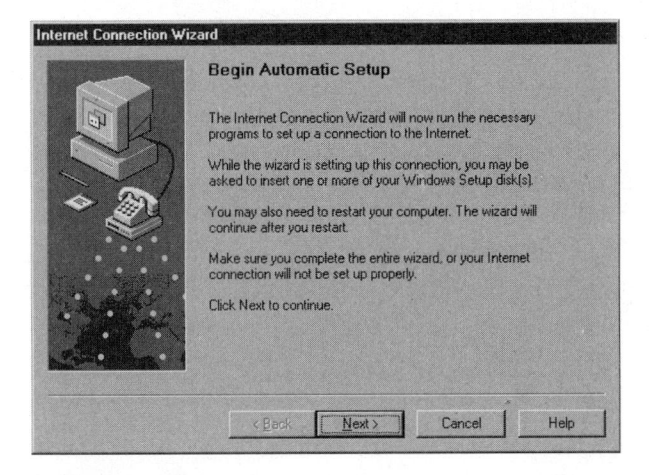

FIGURE 17.01

The Internet Connection Wizard walks you through the steps to connect to the Internet.

2. Click Next, and you'll be asked to select a modem to use. Select the one you want to use, and then click OK.

3. Next you have to answer questions about your area code and phone exchange, as shown in Figure 17.02 on the following page, so that the wizard can find a local phone number for the Microsoft Internet Referral Service.

4. Click Next, and the wizard will connect you to the Internet Referral Service and list the supported ISPs in your area, as shown in Figure 17.03 on the following page.

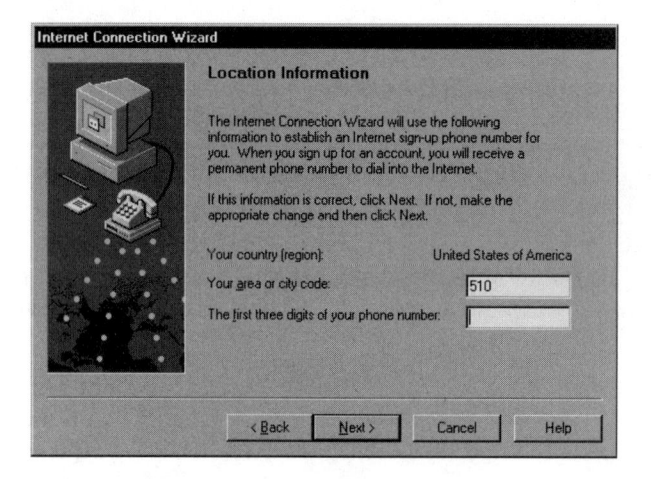

FIGURE 17.02

The wizard needs your phone information in order to find a local phone number for you to call.

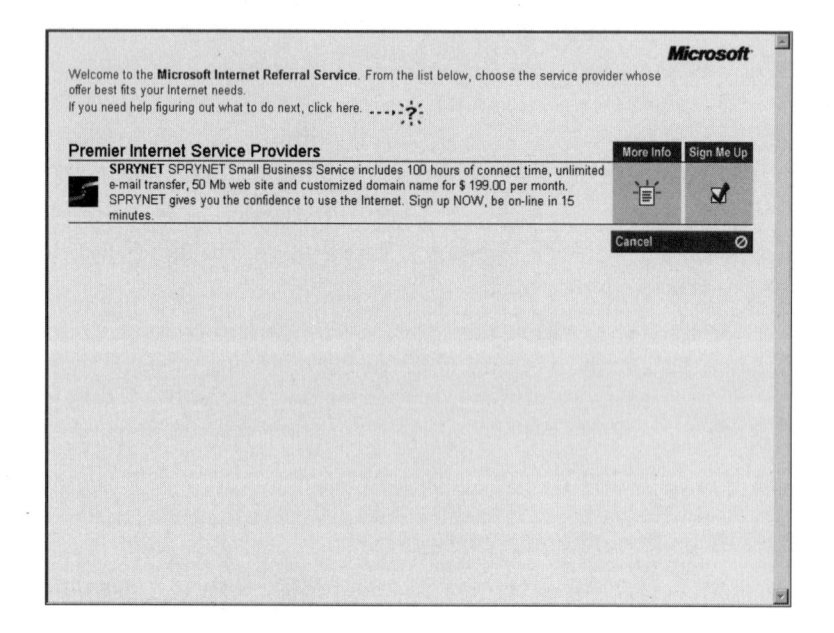

FIGURE 17.03

The Microsoft Internet Referral Service shows you the supported ISPs in your area.

5. Your list of ISPs is likely to be different from that shown in the figure. You should carefully consider the options offered by the various ISPs and select the ISP that best fits your needs and your budget. After you make a decision, click on the Sign Me Up icon, and the wizard will walk you through the rest of the sign-up process.

The sign-up process

For each ISP, you'll likely see a somewhat different series of wizard pages and questions. We'll follow the entire process for one ISP—Sprynet—to give you an idea of the questions and the steps involved.

1. On the Microsoft Internet Referral Service screen, click on the Sign Me Up icon. Small Business Server will dial the local connection number (Point of Presence, or POP) for the ISP. Once connected, you'll see a welcoming screen, as shown in Figure 17.04.

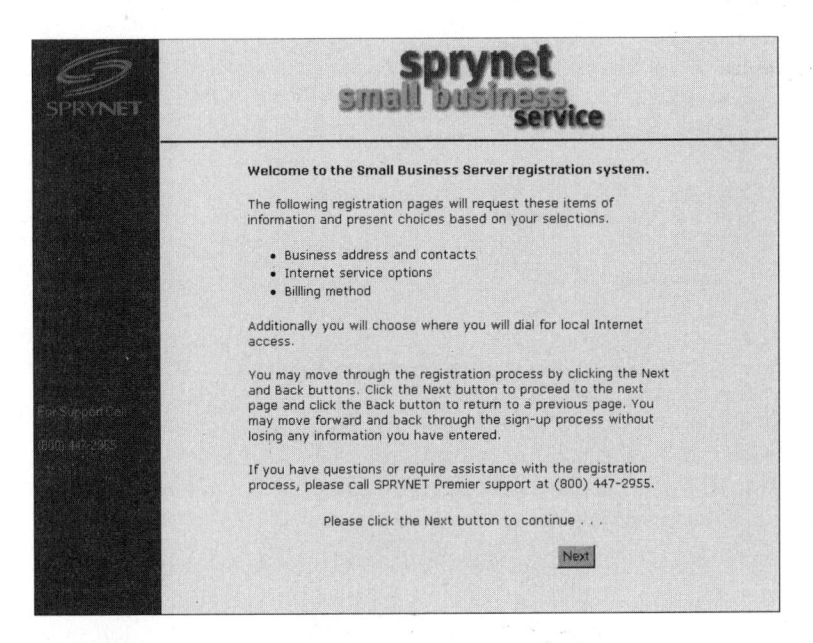

FIGURE 17.04

The welcoming screen for the Sprynet Small Business Service registration system.

CHAPTER 17 *Managing Internet Access* **313**

2. Click Next at the bottom of the screen, and you'll see the screen shown in Figure 17.05, where you have to enter some basic information about your company. We've filled it in with details about our fictitious Alfie's Aquatic Adventures. Fields labeled with bold type are required. The others are optional.

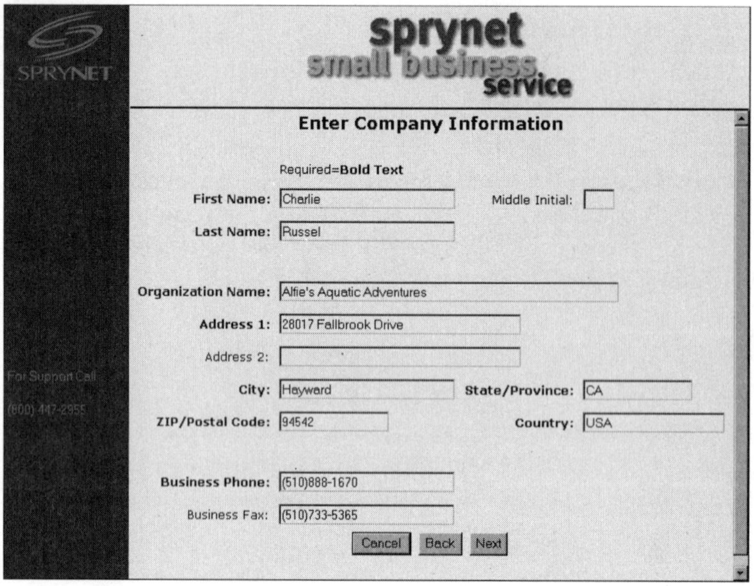

FIGURE 17.05

You must fill in basic information about your company.

3. Click Next to move to the next screen, where you select the state in which you live. At any point in this process, you can back up to a previous screen by clicking the Back button or you can cancel out of the process entirely using the Cancel button.

4. Click Next again to see a list of cities and local access numbers. Select the phone number closest to your location. Remember that you want to avoid any long-distance charges if possible. Scroll to the bottom of the screen, and click Next again.

5. Now you have to enter a password for this account and decide on a domain name, as shown in Figure 17.06. (We strongly suggest that you follow the rules for good passwords that we presented in Chapter 4.) Sprynet lets you choose a third-level domain; it will add *ioffice.com* to the end of the domain name you specify. If the name has been taken, you'll have to select a different one. Click Next when you finish.

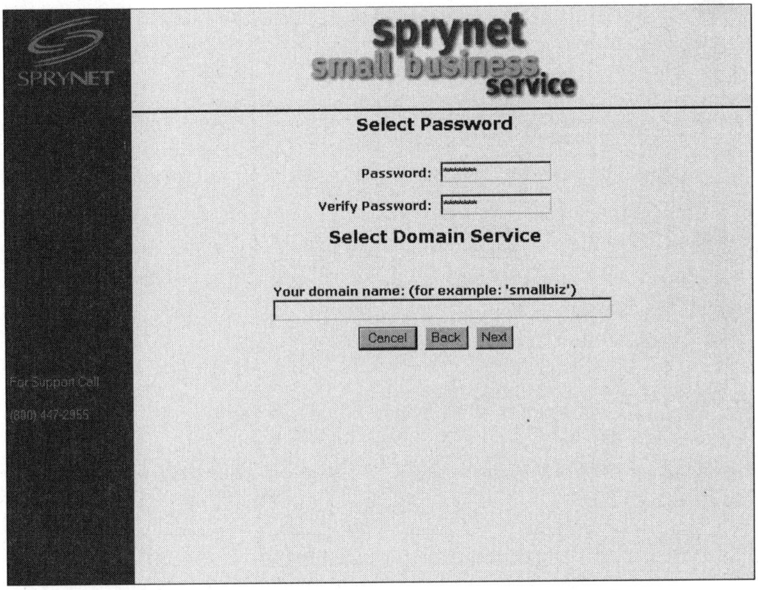

FIGURE 17.06

Specify a password and a domain name for your Internet account.

6. Now you can begin the fun part—filling in the credit card information. A credit card is the only method of payment for Sprynet's service—direct billing is not an option.

7. Finally, Sprynet will configure your server for automatic connection to Sprynet. When the configuration is complete, you'll see a confirmation screen like that shown in Figure 17.07 on the following page—including the actual account name used by Sprynet and the account name to use for your web page. We strongly suggest that you print this screen and store it in a safe place.

FIGURE 17.07

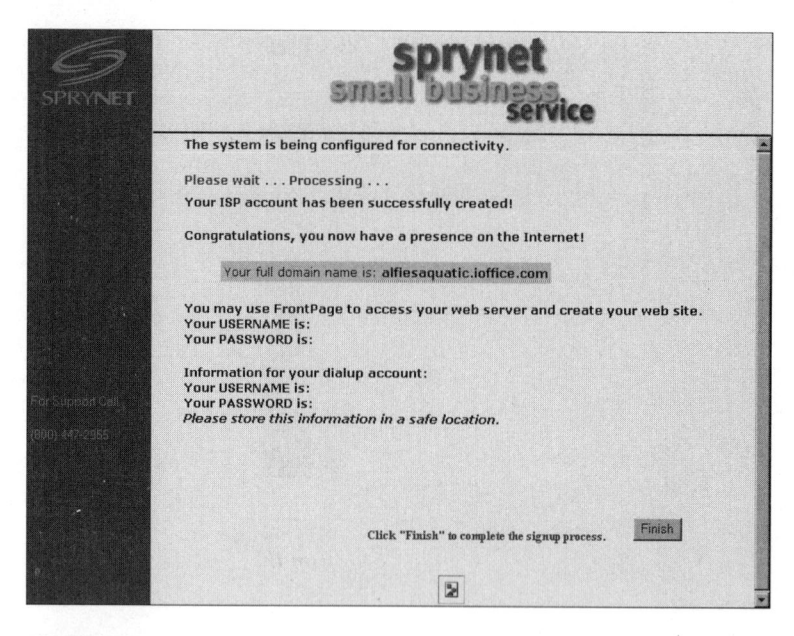

When your server is configured for connecting to an ISP, you'll see a confirmation screen that provides details about your dial-up and web server accounts.

8. After you print the information, click Finish. The connection will be closed, and you'll be back in the Internet Connection Wizard, as shown in Figure 17.08. The wizard will confirm that the setup is complete and that your network is configured to automatically connect to the Internet. In the process, your Exchange server will also have been set up to handle your Internet mail and the Internet Mail Service will have been started.

> **Tip**
>
> *In general, Internet access brings great benefits to a company—although at first you might feel like the new kid on a huge, completely unfamiliar college campus. Expect to spend a certain amount of time getting your bearings and learning how to find what you're looking for. Despite what you might hear in the media, this is not mindless "surfing" unless you make it so.*

FIGURE 17.08

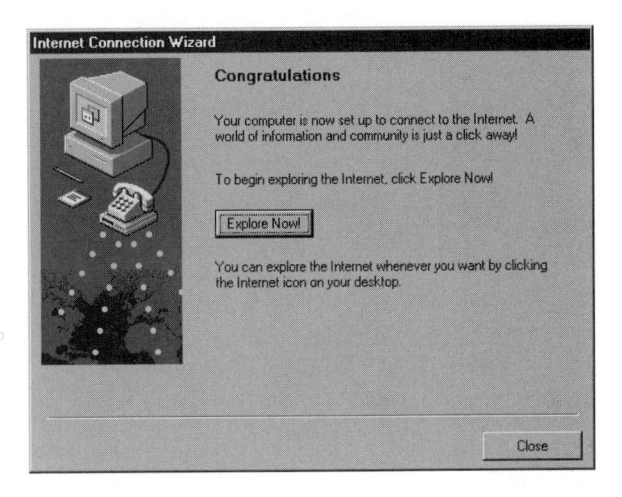

The Internet Connection Wizard will confirm that you're ready to connect to the Internet.

Configuring Workstations

You don't have to do anything special to configure the workstations on your network. When you use the Manage Computers page of the Small Business Server console to set up a computer, a variety of options will be set for that computer that allow it to connect to the Internet through the server. So once the server is set, the workstations will come along for the ride. The proxy server application that runs on the server provides the connection mechanism. The workstations' Microsoft Internet Explorer options are set to automatically use the proxy server as their gateway to the Internet; this means you don't need to change anything on the individual workstations.

Connecting to an Existing ISP Account

Many small businesses already have an account with an ISP. If you have one, you don't have to cancel it or change all your Internet information—as long as your ISP supports Small Business Server and you're willing to do a little manual configuration.

There are two kinds of accounts that you have to worry about. One is an account that uses a modem to connect to the Internet only as needed, called a *dial-up account*, which allows mail to be transferred intermittently. The other is an account that uses a modem to establish a full-time connection to the ISP. In both cases, you have to configure the web hosting services, the proxy server, and Microsoft Exchange Server to support the existing connection.

Configuring for Dial-Up Accounts

There are two basic kinds of dial-up accounts—those with large services such as CompuServe, MSN, and AOL, and those with companies whose sole business is providing Internet access. In either case, you are likely to have an individual mail box account for each user (probably an account known as a POP3 account). Although these accounts provide Internet e-mail, they lack the full features, flexibility, and centralized storage that you get by using Exchange Server as your own e-mail server. Also, each user must have his or her own Internet account.

With Small Business Server, all you need is a single account for the entire company. All Internet mail is delivered to Exchange Server. Individual accounts are maintained by Exchange, and Internet e-mail messages are simply a part of the full-featured e-mail of Exchange.

If your ISP doesn't support Small Business Server, you might want to switch to one that does—or convince your current ISP to provide the support. If you're with one of the large services, you'll probably have to change, but many smaller ISPs already support Small Business Server, and more will soon.

Web hosting services

If your existing ISP supports posting to your web site via ftp, you can continue to use the ISP for this service even if it doesn't provide full support for Small Business Server. To make the Web Post Wizard work correctly, you must edit the registry using Registry Editor to add or modify the necessary registry key. This is not for the faint of heart, and you should make a backup of the existing registry first. The following keys must be added (or modified, if they already exist); you must substitute the correct values for the portions in italics.

```
HKEY_LOCAL_MACHINE\SOFTWARE\Microsoft\SmallBusiness\Internet\WEB_INFO
FTP_Path "ftp://yourftppublishingroot"
InternetSite "http://yourinternetsitename"
Name "your publishing account name"
Password "your publishing account password"
```

> **For More Information**
>
> For details on backing up your Registry and using the Registry Editors, see Chapter 26.

Exchange Mail

If your current ISP supports the intermittent connection of an SMTP server, you can use Exchange Server with that connection. You must tell your ISP what you'll be doing, and then configure Exchange to receive mail from the ISP, as follows:

1. Start Microsoft Exchange Administrator. (From the Start menu, choose Programs, Microsoft Exchange [Common], and then Microsoft Exchange Administrator.)

2. If this is the first time you're running Exchange Administrator, you'll see the Connect To Server dialog box, as shown in Figure 17.09. Type the name of your server, and select the Set As Default check box so that you won't see this dialog box again. Click OK.

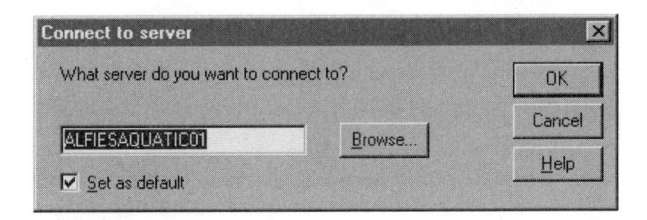

FIGURE 17.09

The first time you run Exchange Administrator, you must specify what server to connect to.

3. Choose New Other from the File menu, and then choose Internet Mail Service. You'll likely get a message saying that a new Internet Mail Service can't be created in the current parent container and offering to switch to the appropriate container. Click OK to accept this and start the Internet Mail Wizard, whose first page is shown in Figure 17.10 on the following page.

4. The wizard will walk you through the process of creating the connection and starting up the service. You have to provide details of your ISP account and set it up for a dial-up connection.

FIGURE 17.10

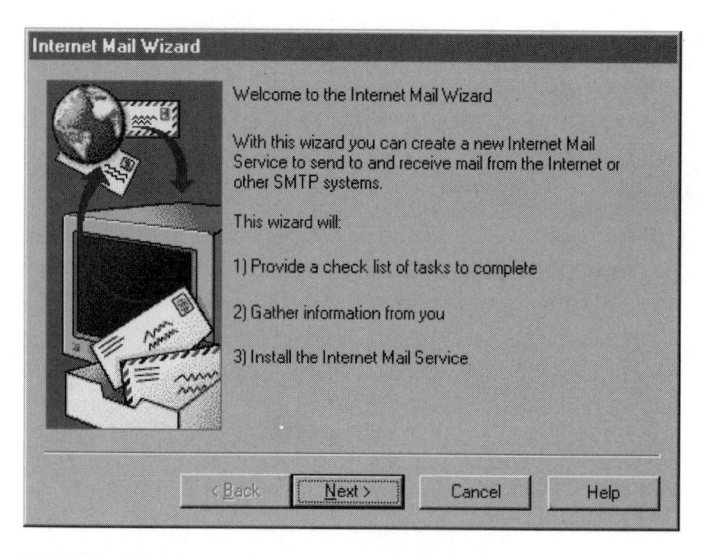

The Internet Mail Wizard walks you through the steps to create a new Internet Mail Service.

Configuring the proxy server

The final component you have to configure with your ISP is Microsoft Proxy Server. The proxy server acts as a "gateway" between your network and the Internet, helping to protect your internal network, and also provides a robust and easy way to connect to the Internet without a full-time connection or a large number of dedicated IP addresses.

To configure the proxy server, take these steps:

1. Double-click on My Computer, and then double-click on the Dial-Up Networking icon to create a new Remote Access Service (RAS) phone book entry for your ISP. Fill in the information needed to connect to your current ISP.

2. From the Start menu, choose Programs, Microsoft Proxy Server, and then Auto Dial Configuration to open the dialog box shown in Figure 17.11. Make sure the Enable Dial On Demand check box is selected. If you want to limit the hours of operation, do so here.

3. Click on the Credentials tab, and select the Remote Access Service phone book entry you created in step 1. Fill in the rest of the entries as instructed by your ISP.

4. Click OK, and you're all set.

FIGURE 17.11

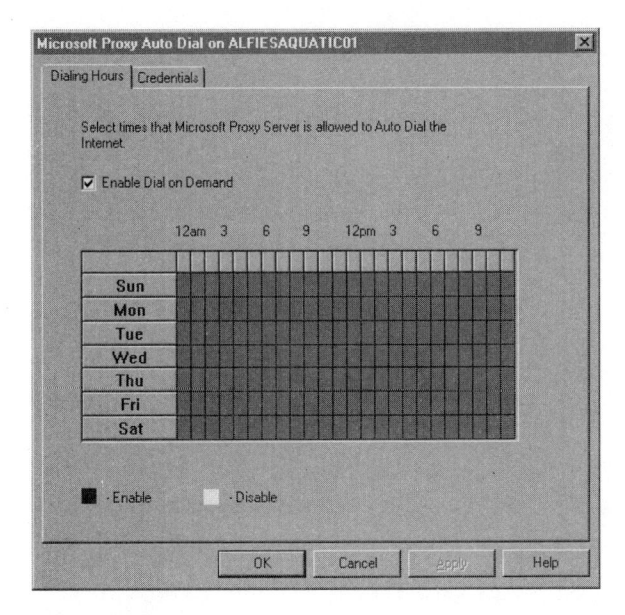

For an intermittent dial-up connection, you must enable Proxy Server to automatically dial up your ISP.

Configuring for a Full-Time Connection

To configure your server for a full-time modem connection to your ISP, you follow the same basic steps described previously for an intermittent dial-up connection. However, for a full-time connection, you must deselect the Enable Dial On Demand check box; this will set Proxy Server to not automatically dial up your ISP.

Configuring for a Second-Level Domain Name

By default, most ISPs will give you a third-level domain name (*alfiesaquatic.ioffice.com*, for example). If your ISP has given you this kind of domain name and you want your own second-level domain name (such as *alfiesaquatic.com*) instead, follow the steps in the section titled "Getting Your Own Internet Domain Name" later in this chapter. If you already have the rights to your own second-level domain name, you must make some adjustments to Exchange so that it will work correctly; your ISP must also make some changes.

What your ISP has to do

Your ISP must create the necessary DNS record to map your second-level domain name to the existing third-level domain name. Then it must change that third-level domain name to your new third-level domain name. All of this must occur at the ISP level because the ISP is responsible for maintaining your DNS records.

◆ Using an ISDN Router or Other High-Speed Connection

Unfortunately, Microsoft supports only modem connections to the Internet in the initial version of Small Business Server. While this is probably adequate for a small business that doesn't depend on the Internet for much more than e-mail and a web site, it certainly isn't a big enough "pipe" for a company with additional needs—especially if it's near the 25-user limit. You *can* make Small Business Server work with an ISDN router or other high speed connection, but this requires a fair amount of configuration. The basic steps are as follows:

1. Install Small Business Server, and connect to the Internet using a supported modem or modems. You'll also need two network cards installed—one physically connected to the internal network and the other physically connected to the router.

2. Install the ISDN line and router; work with your local telephone company and ISP to configure them. The ISP will give you the IP address for the router. The router will have no physical connection to the internal network, only to the second network card on the server.

3. Configure the second network card to the IP address provided by your ISP. This network card will be physically connected to the router, but not to the rest of the network, and it will have *only* TCP/IP on it, with all extraneous bindings disabled.

4. Configure Proxy Server to use the second network card rather than the dial-up connection.

5. Configure the Exchange Server Internet Mail Connector to use a network connection rather than the dial-up connection.

If all this sounds too daunting, get help from a consultant or a value-added provider who understands the issues.

What you have to change in Exchange

Your ISP has to change the Internet records that point to your new domain, but you have to change how Exchange thinks your domain should be addressed. Otherwise, if the two are out of synch, things definitely won't work as expected. To make the changes in Exchange:

1. Start Exchange Administrator. (From the Start menu, choose Programs, Microsoft Exchange [Common], and then Microsoft Exchange Administrator.)

2. If this is the first time you're running Exchange Administrator, you'll see the Connect To Server dialog box (shown in Figure 17.09 on page 319). Type the name of your server, and be sure to select the Set As Default check box so that you won't see this dialog box again. Click OK.

3. In the left pane of Exchange Administrator, open the Site object (if it isn't already open) by clicking on the plus sign. The name will be identical to the name of your server.

4. Open the Configuration object in the left pane, and double-click on Site Addressing in the right pane to open the Site Addressing Properties dialog box (Figure 17.12). Click on the Site Addressing tab.

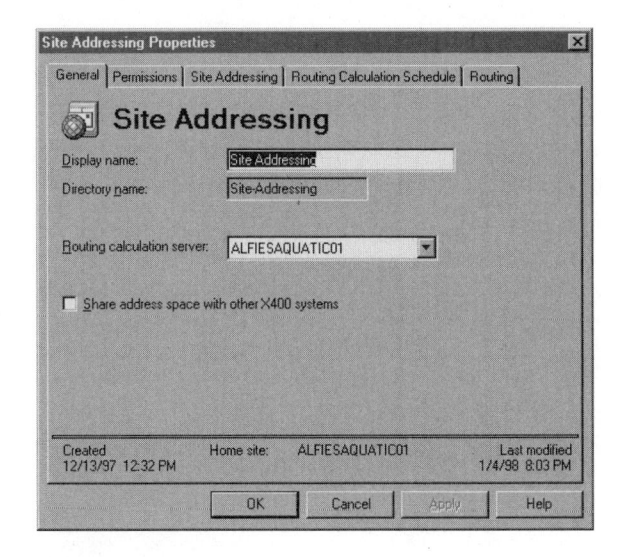

FIGURE 17.12

The Site Addressing Properties dialog box lets you change the Internet addresses used by Exchange.

5. Select the SMTP address line, and then click Edit. In the SMTP Properties dialog box, change the address to reflect your second-level domain (for example, *@alfiesaquatic.com*), as shown in Figure 17.13.

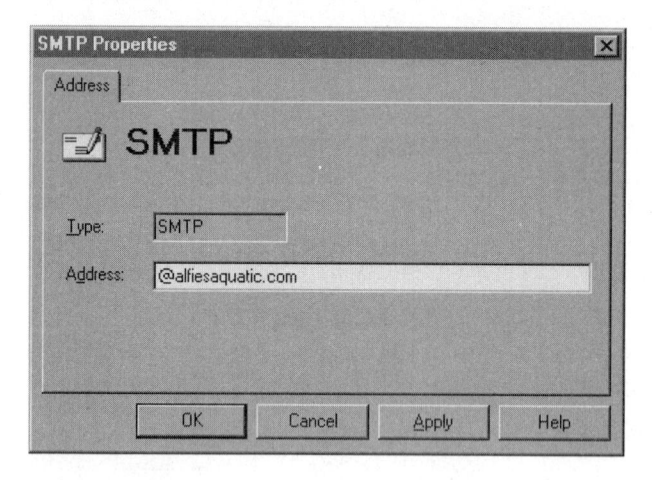

FIGURE 17.13
Your SMTP address must accurately reflect your domain name.

6. Click OK enough times to close all the dialog boxes, and then click Yes when you are asked whether all the e-mail addresses should be updated.

7. That's it. Once you stop and restart the Internet Mail Service, the changes you've made will take effect.

For More Information

For more on the Internet Mail Service and Exchange in general, see Chapter 14.

Getting Your Own Internet Domain Name

If your business depends on customers and potential customers being able to reach you via the Internet, you need an Internet domain name that is both easy to remember and clearly belongs to your business. Since the default connection through your

ISP will give you a third-level domain name (such as *alfiesaquatic.ioffice.com*), you might want to get your own second-level domain name (such as *alfiesaquatic.com*). This will be easier for your customers to find, since they can search with a variety of techniques to find you, and the name will be easier to remember as well.

There are a couple of catches. For one, it might be difficult to get the exact domain name you want—the explosive growth of the Internet has caused serious problems with domain registrations and has resulted in a whole new set of first-level domains being created just to handle it. The other catch is the $70 it will cost you to register the name, and then the $35 a year every subsequent year to keep it.

If your business doesn't depend on the Internet to find new customers and to maintain a current customer base and if your primary reason for connecting is to be able to do research and send e-mail, you should probably spare yourself the expense of getting and maintaining a second-level domain name. The name you get when you sign up with an ISP will be perfectly adequate.

However, second-level names won't be any easier to get in the future, so if you expect to grow and possibly do business on the Internet, there's no time like the present.

Signing Up for Your Own Domain Name

Like the initial sign-up with an ISP, the process of acquiring your own domain name is scripted and works with little input from you. Small Business Server even handles the reconfiguration from your original third-level domain name to your new second-level domain name. Here are the steps:

1. On the More Tasks page of the Small Business Server console, click on the Manage Internet Access icon.

2. On the Manage Internet Access page, click on the Set Up An Internet Domain Name icon. This will start the Domain Registration Wizard, whose first page is shown in Figure 17.14 on the following page. This page provides some background information on Network Solutions, Inc., the entity that manages the registration of domain names, and it warns you that there is a fee for the service.

[Screenshot of Domain Registration Wizard Welcome screen]

FIGURE 17.14

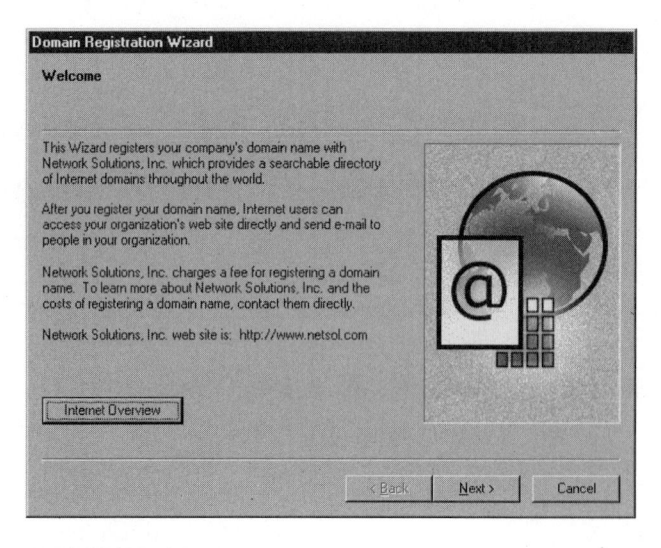

The Domain Registration Wizard walks you through the steps to register your domain name.

3. Click the Internet Overview button for additional information on the Internet, or click Next to begin the process of registering your domain name.

> **Tip**
>
> *You should have several possible names ready because your first choice might be taken. If* alfiesaquatic.com *had not been available, we could have tried* alfie.com, alfies-aquatic.com, *or* alfiesaqua.com—*all of which would have worked quite nicely.*

4. On the page shown in Figure 17.15, enter the domain name you want and click Next. The wizard will automatically dial up the Internet to check whether that name has been taken. If it hasn't, it will be registered in the commercial domain, which means it will automatically get *.com* added after the name.

FIGURE 17.15

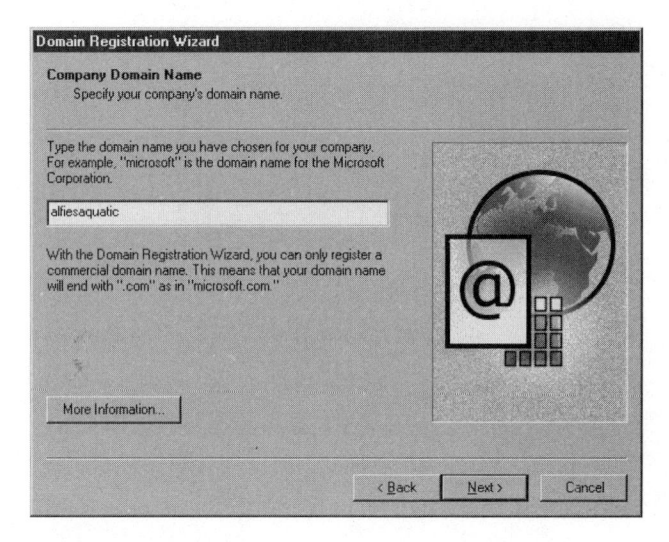

Enter the domain name you want.

5. If the domain name you specified has already been taken, you'll get a message like that shown in Figure 17.16. Click OK, and try again.

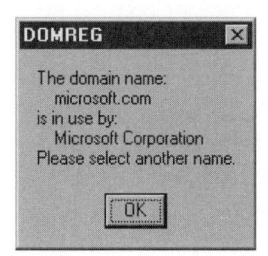

FIGURE 17.16

This domain name has already been taken.

If the name is found to be unique, however, the wizard will ask you to fill out all the necessary information for registration, as shown in Figure 17.17 on the following page. Enter the information, and then click Next.

FIGURE 17.17

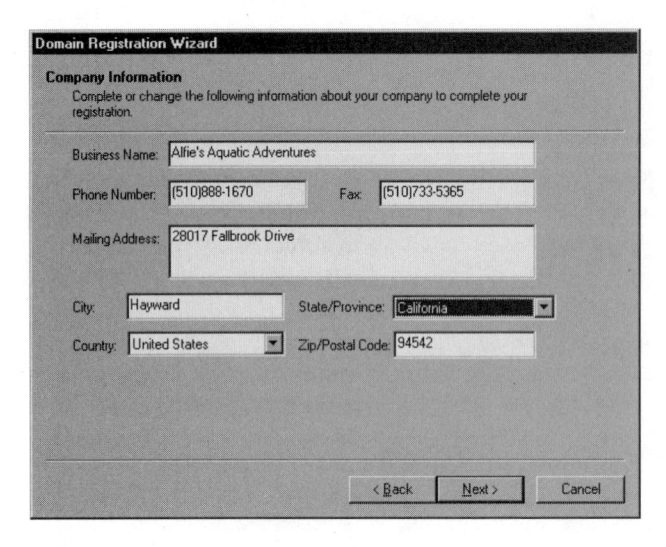

You must fill in the information about your company for the registration process.

6. On the next page, you must enter contact information, as shown in Figure 17.18. The contact person should be the individual responsible for the network, the company's chief financial officer, or some other company officer. Click Next to continue.

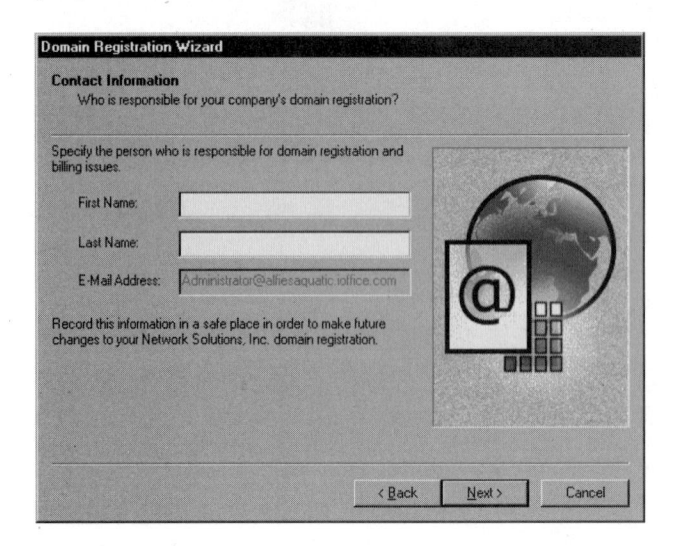

FIGURE 17.18

Your registration contact person will get all the bills and be notified of any changes in your domain name registration information.

7. On the Password Information page, specify a password that you will be able to remember but that is *different* from your normal network password. You'll probably want to write this one down and store it in a safe place, since you'll need it rarely—if ever. Click Next.

8. On the final page before the actual registration begins, you have one last chance to back out. If you want to rethink any of your answers, you can back up using the Back button or you can cancel out completely. If you click Next, the wizard will connect to the Internet and complete the registration process—and you'll be committed to paying the $100 registration fee. Your registration information will be sent to Network Solutions, Inc., and your Internet account and your server will be reconfigured for the new domain name, as described on the next page of the wizard (Figure 17.19).

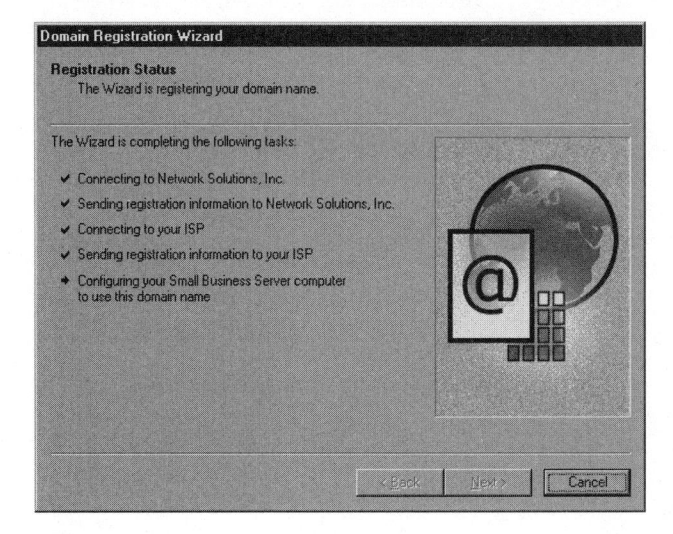

FIGURE 17.19

The wizard handles all the reconfiguration and registration details automatically.

WARNING!

Although the Domain Registration Wizard offers a Cancel button during the online registration, we strongly recommend that you not use it. Your server could easily be left in an intermediate state and be unable to connect properly to the Internet.

9. When the registration process is complete, the wizard will confirm your new domain name and will confirm that your system has been reconfigured.

It normally takes about 24 hours for the name change to propagate across the entire Internet, so you should wait that long before giving out your new e-mail address. But even after the new e-mail address is in place, your old one (with the third-level domain name originally assigned by your ISP) will continue to work.

Controlling User Access to the Internet

You can allow a user access to the Internet or not. In Small Business Server, there's no built-in way to restrict a user to only certain sites or certain times of the day (a limitation that we suspect will soon be corrected by an SBS service pack).

When a user account is set up for the first time, the user is granted or denied the right to access the Internet. To change this setting, follow these steps:

1. On the More Tasks page of the Small Business Server console, click on the Manage Internet Access link to bring up the Manage Internet Access page, as shown in Figure 17.20.

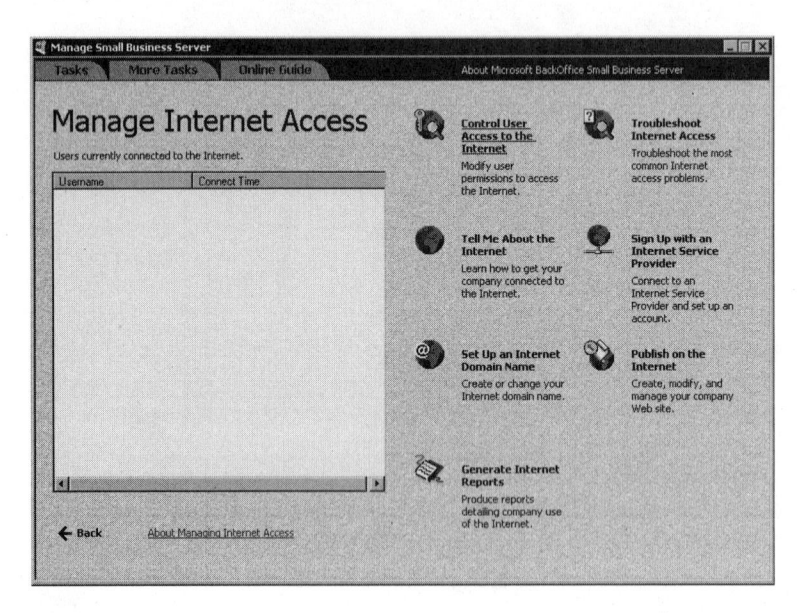

FIGURE 17.20

The Manage Internet Access page is a gateway to a variety of Internet-related functions.

2. Click on the Control User Access To The Internet link, and you'll see the opening page of the Internet Access Wizard, as shown in Figure 17.21. From here you can add or remove users from the list of those allowed to access the Internet. Make your changes, and then click Next.

FIGURE 17.21

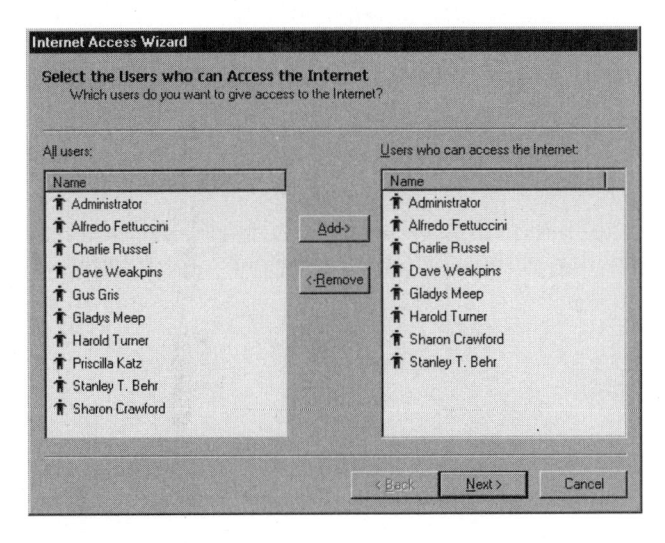

You can control which users have access to the Internet.

3. On the next page, click Finish or click Cancel to cancel out and not change anything.

That's all there is to managing which users have access to the Internet. It's pretty much a binary operation—you can either grant a user full access or deny access.

> **Tip**
>
> *You can install software on workstations that restricts access to certain types of web sites or newsgroups. This, however, is akin to sending out a memo declaring your lack of confidence in your employees. Besides, an employee who needs to be monitored is a big problem—one that can't be solved by simply cutting off Internet access.*

POINTS TO REMEMBER

- Before you can access the Internet, you must sign up with an ISP.
- Your ISP will probably give you a third-level domain name, but you can get your own second-level domain name using the Domain Registration Wizard.

- If you already have an ISP, you can still use Small Business Server to connect to it, although you have to do some manual configuration to make it work.
- You can manually configure Small Business Server to use an existing second-level domain name.
- Only users with permission are allowed to access the Internet; you can take away that permission at any time using the Internet Access Wizard.

WHAT'S NEXT

Now that we've got your network connected to the Internet and your domain name registered, the next chapter will cover TCP/IP, the underlying networking protocol of the Internet, and explain how to manage it in a Microsoft Windows NT environment.

Managing Connectivity

CHAPTER 18

334	**TCP/IP**	
	TCP, UDP, IP—I'm So Confused...	334
	IP Addresses and What They Mean	337
	Routing and Subnets	340
343	**Name Resolution**	
	Domain Name System	343
	Windows Internet Name Service	346
346	**IPng (IPv6)**	
	Why	346
	Where and When	347
347	**Using Windows NT Server Administration Tools for TCP/IP**	
	WINS Manager	347
	DHCP Manager	349
351	**Points to Remember**	
352	**What's Next**	

Chapter 18
Managing Connectivity

The underlying method, or *protocol*, connecting workstations to your Microsoft Windows NT Server is TCP/IP; it's the only protocol that Microsoft BackOffice Small Business Server installs by default. There's a myth that TCP/IP is impossibly difficult to understand, but it really isn't. In this chapter, we'll cover some of the underlying concepts—not enough to make you a TCP/IP guru, but enough for you to keep your network functioning.

TCP/IP

Whole books have been written about TCP/IP and its many aspects, most of which we don't have to worry about here. But while you don't need to know about the intricacies of programming a TCP connection or what to expect as a return value from a *gethostbyname()* call, you *do* need to understand what the protocol does and how to configure it.

The most important thing to remember about TCP/IP is that it isn't a single entity. TCP/IP is short for Transmission Control Protocol/Internet Protocol. These are just two of the many protocols included in the TCP/IP suite of protocols. Each protocol has its own specialized use.

Two other crucial facts about TCP/IP are that it's everywhere and it isn't controlled by any single company or vendor. Both IPX/SPX and NetBEUI are proprietary protocols, each developed and ultimately controlled by an individual vendor. TCP/IP, on the other hand, is an open standard controlled by the Internet Engineering Task Force (IETF) and by the users of the Internet in the form of RFCs (Requests for Comment). Anyone can submit an RFC for consideration and inclusion in the written definitions of the protocols and policies of the Internet and TCP/IP.

TCP, UDP, IP—I'm So Confused...

Unfortunately, TCP/IP is chock-full of those MLAs (multiple-letter abbreviations) that computer nerds just love—and that the rest of the world finds totally confusing and threatening, which is probably why computer nerds love them so much. In a perfect world, we might be able to get rid of them all, but for the moment we're stuck with them. And when you think about it, Transmission Control Protocol/Internet Protocol *is* a bit of a mouthful. So let's look at the pieces that make up the TCP/IP suite of protocols, what their differences are, and some of the ways that they are used as part of the overall suite.

TCP

Transmission Control Protocol (TCP) is designed to be, in the words of RFC 793 (the defining RFC for the protocol), "a connection-oriented, end-to-end reliable protocol designed to fit into a layered hierarchy of protocols which support multi-network applications."

Let's take a closer look at those words:

- Connection-oriented—TCP provides for transmission of packets (datagrams) between two points and connects them, sending the packet from one computer or device to another.

- End-to-end—TCP packets have specific endpoints designated, and the packets are passed along the wire and ignored by all devices except the endpoint of the packet and any device that needs to direct it.

- Reliable—This is the key point of TCP. When a program such as ftp uses TCP for its protocol, the TCP/IP suite takes responsibility for the reliability of the communications. The protocol provides interprocess communication to ensure that the packets not only get to their destinations but also get there in the order that they were sent. If a packet is missed, the protocol will communicate that information back to the sending device so that the packet is resent.

Because TCP has to create a reliable connection between two devices or processes, substantially more overhead is involved with each packet than with other, less reliable protocols within the suite. But by the same token, the programmer writing the application that uses TCP doesn't have to include a lot of error checking and handshaking in the application itself.

UDP

User Datagram Protocol (UDP) is a connectionless, transaction-oriented protocol that sends packets with a minimum of protocol overhead. It provides no guarantee that the packet will be received by its intended recipient or that packets will be received in the order that they were sent. UDP is frequently used in broadcast messages (bootp and DHCP requests, for example), for which there is no specific recipient. It can also be used by applications that are willing to spend the extra internal overhead to ensure reliable delivery and decrease the overall overhead of the underlying protocol. UDP is defined in RFC 768.

IP

Internet Protocol (IP) is the core protocol of the TCP/IP suite. To quote from RFC 791: "The Internet Protocol is designed for use in interconnected systems of packet-switched computer communication networks." It does not provide any additional services beyond its primary function—to deliver a packet of bits (a datagram) from point A to point B over any network "wire" it happens to encounter along the way.

NOTE

We use the term wire *very loosely in this book to indicate the physical network connection between two points. In fact, that wire could just as easily be a piece of optical fiber or even a radio wave or an infrared wave. But in all cases, it functions as the transmission "pipe" through which the packets travel.*

IP itself doesn't know anything about the information in the packet it carries, nor does it have any provision beyond a simple checksum to insure that the data is intact or that it has reached its destination. That is left to the other pieces of the TCP/IP suite.

Microsoft Windows Sockets

Windows Sockets is a standard way of allowing applications to communicate with a TCP/IP stack without having to worry about the underlying variations in the TCP/IP stack implementation.

In the past, there were many vendors of TCP/IP protocol and applications suites that ran on MS-DOS–based computers, and each was slightly different. This made it extremely difficult to write an application that required TCP/IP and that would still work with all of the possible TCP/IP implementations. The Windows Sockets interface was designed to get around this problem by providing a set of Application Programming Interface (API) calls that would be uniform regardless of the underlying differences in the actual implementation of TCP/IP.

Windows Sockets version 1 had a fair amount of difficulties and soon gave way to version 1.1. The current version of Windows Sockets supported by Windows NT Server is version 2, which provides full backward compatibility with earlier versions while providing expandability, improved functionality, and support for additional features.

RFCs

RFCs come in many different flavors, but all have the same intent and a somewhat similar format. They allow a diverse group of people—the users of the Internet—to communicate and agree on the architecture and functionality of the Internet. Some RFCs are official documents of the IETF that define the standards of TCP/IP and the Internet, while others are simply proposals for standards. Still others fall somewhere in between. Some are tutorial in nature; some are quite technical. But all provide a way to organize an essentially anarchic entity, the Internet.

We won't attempt to list all of the RFCs, nor do we expect that you will want or need to read and understand them all. But you should certainly know where to find them and what some of the most important ones are. You can find listings of RFCs in a number of places, but our favorite site is *www.cis.ohio-state.edu/hypertext/information/rfc.html*. The RFCs are organized and linked to make it easy to find information. This site, however, isn't nearly as current or up to date as the official RFC site, at *ds.internic.net/ds/dspg01.html*. If you want to be absolutely sure that you've got the most accurate and up-to-date information, you should visit the latter site.

Table 18.01 lists some of the most important RFCs and their subject matter.

Table 18.01
Some Key RFCs and Their Subject Matter

RFC	Subject
RFC 791	Internet Protocol (IP)
RFC 792	Internet Control Message Protocol (ICMP)
RFC 793	Transmission Control Protocol (TCP)
RFC 768	User Datagram Protocol (UDP)
RFC 854	Telnet Protocol
RFC 959	File Transfer Protocol (FTP)
RFC 821	Simple Mail Transfer Protocol (SMTP)
RFC 822	Standard for the format of ARPA Internet text messages
RFC 1117	Internet numbers
RFC 991	Official ARPA Internet protocols
RFC 1034	DNS—concepts and facilities
RFC 1035	DNS—implementation and specification

IP Addresses and What They Mean

To the Internet and the computers on your local network, your IP address is much like your street address is to your mail carrier. It identifies your computer uniquely using a simple, 32-bit addressing scheme. This scheme, which originated in the late 1960s and early 1970s, uses four octets separated by dots, in the form *w.x.y.z*, to describe a combination of the network address and the local machine address on that network.

Networks are of class A, B, or C. These classes describe networks (sometimes referred to as *licenses*) of very different sizes and degrees of complexity. The licenses to use a range of IP addresses are controlled by the InterNIC (Internet Network

Information Center), which used to be managed and controlled by the U.S. government but is now handled by a separate, commercial organization.

Class A networks

A class A network has an address that begins with a number from 0 through 127 for the first portion (w) of the address to describe the network itself. The remainder of the address is the local device's address on that network. The class A address 127, however, has a special meaning and isn't available for use. (See the sidebar below.) Thus, there are 127 possible class A addresses in the world, and each one of those class A networks can contain more than 16 million unique network devices. Obviously, this would be a pretty large network, and there aren't many of them. All of the class A addresses were taken a long time ago and belong to such entities as the U.S. Department of Defense, Stanford University, and Hewlett-Packard.

> ### ◆ 127: The Loopback Address
>
> All IP addresses that begin with the network number 127 are very special. They are interpreted by your network card as a "loopback" address. Any packet sent to an address beginning with 127 is treated as if it has reached its intended address, and that address is the local device. Packets addressed to 127.0.0.1 are thus treated the same as packets addressed to 127.37.90.17—both addresses are actually your current machine, as are all the other 16 million addresses in the 127 class A network. You, too, can have your very own class A network. Of course, you can only talk to yourself, but who cares when such prestige is involved?

Class B networks

A class B network has an address that begins with a number from 128 through 191 for the first portion (w) of the address to describe the network itself. The remainder of the address is the local device's address on that network. There are approximately 16,000 class B networks, each of which can have more than 64,000 unique addresses on it. That's still a pretty large network, and most of the class B networks were assigned long ago to large organizations or companies such as Rutgers University and Toyota Motor Corporation.

Many of the addresses in the class B address space have been broken up into smaller groups of addresses and reassigned. Large Internet service providers (ISPs), for example, use this technique to more efficiently use the available address space.

Class C networks

A class C network has an address that begins with a number from 192 through 223 for the first portion (w) of the address to describe the network itself. The remainder of the address is the local device's address on that network. This makes for a total of roughly 2 million class C networks, each of which can have up to 254 devices. This is enough for a small business or a department but hardly enough for a major corporation.

Class D and Class E addresses

An IP address with a number from 224 through 239 for the first portion (w) of the address is known as a class D address. Class D addresses are used for multicast addresses. The IP address space from 240 through 247 for the initial portion is a class E address. This space is reserved for future use.

> ### ◆ IP Addresses for Networks That Will Never, Ever Be Connected to the Internet
>
> Suppose you know that your internal, private network will never be directly connected to the Internet? Not unreasonable, but should you use any old numbers, then? Well, no, you shouldn't. A special set of network addresses is reserved for just such use. These are defined in RFC 1918, and by using them you can comfortably use a substantially larger address space than you would otherwise be able to.
>
> This also protects the integrity of the Internet. In some cases, networks have connected to the Internet using addresses already assigned to other organizations. This has caused substantial problems. Since the special network addresses are officially only for private networks, they are automatically filtered at routers, thereby protecting the Internet.
>
> Small Business Server uses these special addresses for its special networking, and it protects the Internet by hiding any and all addresses on its internal network from being seen by other Internet machines through the use of the built-in proxy server that comes with Small Business Server.
>
> The special addresses are:
>
> - 10.0.0.0 through 10.255.255.255—a single Class A network
> - 172.16.0.0 through 172.31.255.255—16 contiguous Class B networks
> - 192.168.0.0 through 192.168.255.255—256 contiguous Class C networks
>
> If you need to create a test network, for example (or, if for some other reason, you won't ever connect to the Internet except by means of a proxy server or other method of masking and converting addresses), but you need or want to use TCP/IP for your network protocol, you should use one of these ranges of addresses.

Small Business Server uses Microsoft Proxy Server to get around the network address shortages by using the proxy server to hide your network from the world. It uses the private, reserved set of class A addresses (10.0.0.0 through 10.255.255.255) for the server and the workstations on your network and lets the proxy server hide those addresses from the Internet. It's a slick trick, and one that makes life much easier for you, since you don't need to worry about getting a big block of addresses from either the InterNIC or your ISP.

Routing and Subnets

While most small business networks are small enough that they can be set up as a single, flat network, their servers still need to understand and deal with gateways to connect the network to the Internet. With Small Business Server, your server is also your gateway to the world, and this should be set automatically by the installation program. But a little background information never hurts, especially since it can make life easier if you run into problems and need to do some basic troubleshooting.

If every single computer on the Internet had to know where every single other computer on the Internet was and how to get there, the overhead would be enormous. And if every time you printed a document to the printer next door every other computer on the Internet would see those packets, the entire Internet would come to a crashing, screeching halt. Obviously, there must be a way to filter and route the packets so that you can easily print to your network printer without disrupting other networks but still reach any other IP address on the Internet without having to know a whole lot about how to get there. Enter subnets, routers, and gateways.

Subnets

A subnet is simply a portion of the network that operates as a separate network without having to worry about what happens outside that portion—and without events on that portion disrupting the rest of the network. This is usually a separate physical piece of "wire" that has only a single point of contact with other areas of the network through a router or a bridge.

In order for this portion of the network to see and communicate directly only with other computers in this portion, we use something called a *subnet mask*. This is an address, again in the *w.x.y.z* form, that masks or blocks areas outside this portion of the network. A typical mask for a class C network is 255.255.255.0. OK, that's nice, but what does it mean? Well, without going into a long treatise on binary numbering, it means that if your IP address is something like 10.0.0.2, the address at 10.0.100.135 (for example) is hidden from you, and you can send a packet to that address only by first passing that packet to a gateway or a router that knows where you are and either knows where the other network is or knows who to ask about where it is. If, on the other hand, you want to send a packet to the printer at 10.0.0.135, that's no problem—you can see that address, so the packet goes straight to the printer.

◆ Binary Masks

A subnet works by letting you "see" only those portions of the IP address space that aren't masked by a 1. If we have a typical C class address of 192.168.222.17, for example, and our subnet mask is 255.255.255.0, we can see addresses only in that last portion of the address beyond the last dot.

The important point is that you can see any portion of the address that has a 0 for the subnet mask, but no portion of the address that has a 255 in it. Remember that this is all actually done in binary, and if you understand how that works you can figure out the mask you need or what the one you have is actually doing. If you're not comfortable with binary numbers, now's a good time to start getting comfortable.

All the subnet masks on a single portion of your network must be the same. If they aren't, you'll have all sorts of weird problems. One machine might be able to send a packet to another, but the other won't be able to send the packet back.

Gateways

A gateway can be several different things on a network, but for the moment we'll talk about it only from the perspective of subnets and routing. Remember, we said that if you've got a subnet mask of 255.255.255.0, if the y portion of your IP address is 222, you can't see an IP address on a portion of the network with a y portion of 223.

The solution is a gateway. A gateway is a physical device—usually a router, but sometimes simply another computer with more than one network card in it—that is physically connected to both portions of the network. The gateway takes your packets from the 222 portion and sends them over to the 223 portion. It thus acts as a gatekeeper between the two portions of the network, keeping the traffic in the 222 portion on the 222 segment and letting that traffic through to the 223 segment only if it recognizes that the packet really belongs there.

Routers

A router is a device that connects to more than one physical segment of the network and sends packets between those segments as required. If it doesn't know where the packet goes, it knows who to ask for directions—another router. It constantly updates its routing tables with information from other routers about the best way to get to various parts of the network. If your network is part of the Internet, that router must be able to handle a huge number of possible routes between locations and decide instantaneously on the best way to get from point to point.

◆ Routing Flaps

As the Internet has grown exponentially, the technology for resolving addresses has been stressed to the limit—sometimes past the limit. When a major router on the Internet goes down, even momentarily, all the other routers on the Internet have to tell each other about it and recalculate the best way to get to various places that used that router as part of the path. This results in large numbers of packets passing back and forth just to maintain and update the information about the available routes. Even worse, everyone's trying to do it at the same time. The traffic can get so heavy that the updates can't occur properly, since they can't get the information through the traffic. The whole Internet, or a large portion of it, then comes to a virtual halt.

So far, this hasn't happened very often, but it is becoming more of a problem. Plus, current router technology is reaching its limit in being able to calculate the best route when major changes occur due to the failure of a key router. The doomsayers would have us believe that the Internet will fail in the near future. We doubt it, but we are concerned nonetheless. The next generation of TCP/IP (known as IPng or IPv6) will help, as will new algorithms for the calculations. And you can bet that a whole lot of money and energy is being spent to come up with the best possible algorithm for handling the problem.

Routing protocols

The finer details about how routing protocols work and the algorithms involved in routing and address resolution are beyond the scope of this book. But you'll find it useful to know what some of the protocols are, if only so you don't get concerned when someone throws out yet another abbreviation. You can at least nod knowingly. The most common TCP/IP address resolution protocols are as follows:

- ◆ Address Resolution Protocol (ARP)—maps the IP address to its physical hardware address (MAC address), allowing you to send something to an IP address without having to know what physical device it is.

- ◆ Reverse Address Resolution Protocol (RARP)—maps the physical hardware address (MAC address) to the IP address, allowing you to determine the IP address when you know only the physical hardware address.

- ◆ Proxy Address Resolution Protocol (Proxy ARP)—a method for implementing subnets on older versions of TCP/IP that don't understand subnetting. Described in RFC 1027.

Name Resolution

Well, all that stuff about addresses, numbers, and whatnot is nice, but few of us really want to deal with the numbers of all the sites we worry about. For one thing, numbers can easily change. Companies are continually upgrading the server equipment used to run their web sites, especially for popular locations. Reconfiguring an entire machine to a different address is, at best, a royal pain, depending on the operating system. But it's easy enough to buy a new machine, give it a number on your network, build and test your web page on an internal network, and then, when you're ready to go, simply put the new machine in place and change a line in your DNS entry. When it propagates to the rest of the Internet, you're in business. And you don't need to worry about any downtime because the original machine will be in place until after the new one is up and fully recognized.

So that's *why* it's better to deal with easy-to-remember names. Now we'll take a look at *how* names are handled in the TCP/IP and Internet world.

Domain Name System

The Domain Name System (DNS) was designed in the early 1980s, and in 1984 it became the official method for mapping IP addresses to names. Since then, modifications have been made to the overall structure of the DNS database and some of the ways that it works, but the overall result is still remarkably like the original design. Microsoft doesn't use DNS for handling the names of computers on your internal Small Business Server network—that's the job of WINS—but it *does* use DNS for all the connections it makes to the Internet and for resolving names there.

> **For More Information**
>
> *See RFC 1591 for an overview of DNS. See RFC 1034 and RFC 1035 for the actual specification.*

The domain name space

The term *domain name space* is sometimes used to describe the tree-shaped structure of all the domains from the root ("." or "dot") domain to the outermost leaf of the structure. This hierarchical structure separates each portion of the domain name space with a dot, which means you always know where you are in the tree.

Before the Internet moved to DNS, a single master file (hosts.txt) had to be sent by ftp to everyone who needed to convert from numbers to names. This obviously created enormous overhead even when the Internet was still relatively small, and it would have become totally unworkable very quickly. But DNS is a distributed database that is extensible—additional information can be added as needed—and it permits local administration of local names while maintaining overall integrity and conformance to standards.

Root domains

Root domains are the first level of the tree below the root. They describe the kinds of networks within them using two or three letters. So we have *.com* for commercial networks, *.edu* for educational ones, *.au* for Australian ones, and so forth. As you can see, there are geographical root domains as well as functional root domains.

The original root domains had a decidedly U.S.-centric flavor and were functionally based—not surprising, given that most of them were originally set up and administered by the U.S. Department of Defense. But as the Internet grew, this approach made little sense, especially with a distributed database like DNS in place that allowed for local administration and control. So the geographical root domains were added.

Where domain names come from and how to get one

Seems like everyone who runs a business wants to have a separate domain. So, if you want to have your own domain name, how do you go about it? Who decides whether you get the name, and who tells you whether someone else already has it? The InterNIC, of course. The process for getting a domain name is pretty simple:

1. Decide what name you'd like to have. Also come up with several alternatives and variants—you'll probably need them.
2. Research existing names to find out if yours is already in use, and try the variants as well until you find one that isn't taken.
3. Create the necessary DNS records on your DNS server (or have your ISP do it).
4. Register the name with the InterNIC.
5. Pay US$70 when the InterNIC sends you the bill, or you'll lose the domain name. The fee is good for two years; after that, you'll be billed $35 per year.

How do you do the research? Well, the simplest and best way is to go to the InterNIC's registration home page and use the Whois link to see if someone already has the name you want. The address is *rs.internic.net/rs-internic.html*.

When you're ready to actually register the name, you use the same address. But if you're connecting to the Internet through an ISP and they'll be maintaining your

DNS records, by all means let them do the dirty work and set everything up. You'll still want to do research first, of course.

> **For More Information**
>
> *For more information about ISPs, see Chapter 17.*

Finally, a word of warning. Domain names used to be free and forever, but those days are gone. If you don't pay your bill from the InterNIC, you'll lose your domain name, and by the time you try to reregister it, chances are someone else will have grabbed it. The available short names are disappearing at a rapid rate, and many people are finding that they need to think up longer alternatives to find something that isn't taken. And don't even *think* of trying to get a really slick name with *net* or *internet* in it—they're long gone.

With Small Business Server, you're spared the need to have your own domain name because the signup process for connecting to the Internet creates one for you. Alfie's Aquatic Adventures, for example, ended up with the domain name *alfiesaquatic.ioffice.com*, which is a perfectly good name. But for someone to find this business on the Internet, it might be a lot easier if the name were simply *alfiesaquatic.com*. With Small Business Server, you can set yourself up this way using wizards to guide you through the registration process.

How names are resolved into addresses

When you click on a link to *www.microsoft.com* and Microsoft Internet Explorer tries to go there, what actually happens? How does it find *www.microsoft.com*? The short answer is that it asks the primary DNS server listed in the TCP/IP properties page on the workstation you're on. OK, but how does that DNS server know?

When a TCP/IP application wants to communicate with or connect to another location, it needs the address of that location. But it usually starts out knowing only what name it's looking for, so it first has to resolve that name into an IP address. The first place it looks is in the locally cached names and IP addresses that it has resolved recently. After all, if you asked about *www.microsoft.com* 15 minutes ago, why should it go through all the trouble of looking it up again? Chances are that the IP address hasn't changed in that span of time.

But suppose you haven't been surfing the Net in the last couple of days and your DNS server doesn't have any recent information about *www.microsoft.com*. Well, if it doesn't know, it asks around to see if anyone else knows. It sends out a special UDP packet on the network (in this case, the network is the Internet) and asks whether anyone recognizes the name. Ultimately, the query will be resolved by one of the other DNS servers—up to the authoritative DNS server for the root domain.

> **For More Information**
>
> *For more on DNS and how it works and is configured, see* Microsoft Windows NT Server 4.0 Resource Kit *(Microsoft Press) or* DNS and BIND *by Albitz and Liu (O'Reilly).*

DHCP

One problem with setting up computers to use the Internet, whether via a direct connection or via a proxy server, is setting all the options for TCP/IP on each and every computer in the organization (especially if some are only intermittently connected). The answer for Small Business Server is the Dynamic Host Configuration Protocol (DHCP).

During the initial installation of Small Business Server, all the options for TCP/IP are set up automatically on the server. Using DHCP, all the necessary configuration details for the client computers are set without the client or its user having to know anything about the details of TCP/IP. And because all the work has been taken out of this configuration nightmare, the whole process is painless *and* virtually foolproof.

Windows Internet Name Service

The Windows Internet Name Service (WINS) is a way to map IP addresses to NetBIOS names. While DNS provides all the information that most traditional TCP/IP applications need to know about a computer's name, it actually provides too much information. Windows NT generally needs only the NetBIOS name. DNS works off the *fully qualified domain name—server1.mycompany.com* or some such—but for Windows Networking, all we care about is the NetBIOS name, which is usually something like SERVER1. WINS maps the IP address to a NetBIOS name. The Small Business Server installation program automatically sets up your WINS configuration on the server, so you are unlikely to ever have to muck around with it.

IPng (IPv6)

Another buzzword you'll hear thrown around, especially by those who are concerned with Internet connectivity, is IPng—or IPv6, as it is now called. This is the next generation of Internet Protocol (IP), which is designed to get around the very limited IP address space of the current IP version.

Why

As we pointed out earlier, there simply aren't enough addresses to connect all the devices and computers that people want to connect, and this is going to be a serious problem very quickly.

Where and When

To find a solution to the limitations of the 32-bit address space and the routing protocols in the current structure of TCP/IP, the IETF and others began working on solutions several years ago. While different solutions were originally proposed from several working groups, over time these have sorted themselves out into a consensus on the next generation of IP, known as IPng or IPv6 (Internet Protocol version 6). This was formally accepted by the IETF in December 1994 and is documented in RFC 1752.

IPv6 defines a 128-bit IP address space that is compatible with the current implementation of TCP/IP (version 4, or IPv4) but provides a greatly increased address space (3×10^{38}) along with the inclusion of additional information in the packets to provide improved routing and handling of mobile devices.

The important thing to understand about IPv6 is that it is evolutionary, not revolutionary. We don't have to worry about waking up one morning and finding that we have to reconfigure every machine we're responsible for. We can make the transition gradually because the protocol should be able to coexist in most situations with IPv4 implementations.

Using Windows NT Server Administration Tools for TCP/IP

In the unlikely event that you need to change the settings for DHCP or WINS, Microsoft includes the native Windows NT tools for configuring these two services. We don't think you'll ever have to use these, but if you do, here are the necessary details.

WINS Manager

WINS Manager allows you to easily set up and manage a WINS server to resolve IP addresses into the NetBIOS names you'll need for browsing your network. If you've installed the WINS server, you'll have a choice on the Start menu's Administrative Tools (Common) menu for WINS Manager.

Adding a server

You can add a WINS server to those managed by WINS Manager by choosing Add WINS Server from the Server menu. If you're running a second Windows NT Server on the network, you might want to do this. But we think it's pretty unlikely. You can add the server either by name or by IP address. By default, you'll see the local server in the left pane of the WINS Manager window, as shown in Figure 18.01 on the following page. The right pane of the WINS Manager window shows the current statistics for the selected WINS server.

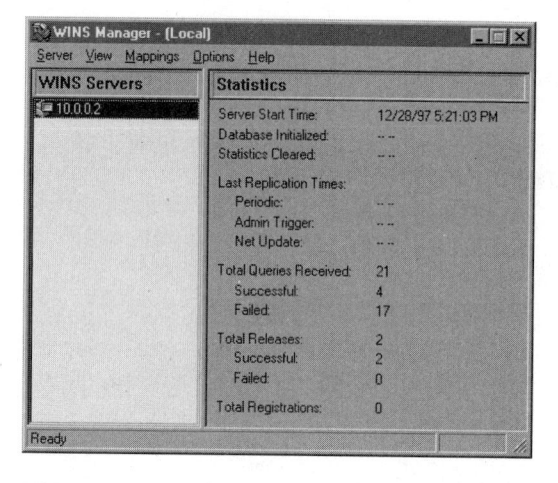

FIGURE 18.01

WINS Manager.

WINS Manager functions

WINS Manager lets you manage all the functionality of the Windows Internet Naming Service in a single application, even in the unlikely event that you're running multiple WINS servers. The supported functions are:

- Add WINS Server—lets you add additional WINS servers to manage

- Delete WINS Server—removes the selected WINS server from local management

- Detailed Information—displays detailed statistics about the selected WINS server

- Configuration—lets you modify server configuration information, including expiration times, replication parameters, and logging

- Replication Partners—lets you add or delete replication partners and set options for the replication

- Show Database—shows the full WINS database, including static mappings, as shown in Figure 18.02

- Initiate Scavenging—purges the WINS database and does general cleanup on it

- Static Mappings—lets you add assign names to fixed IP addresses manually

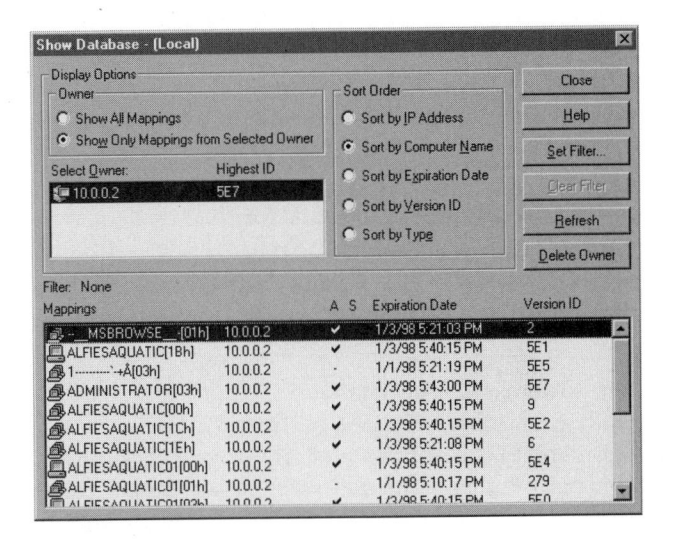

FIGURE 18.02

The WINS database contains all the NetBIOS name-to-IP address mappings of the WINS server.

> **For More Information**
>
> For more details on WINS, see Microsoft Windows NT Server 4.0 Resource Kit (Microsoft Press).

DHCP Manager

DHCP Manager, like WINS Manager, lets you manage the DHCP options from a single application, even in the unlikely event that you have multiple DHCP servers on your network. DHCP Manager lets you administer all of the properties and functionality of your DHCP servers, including the following:

- Add—adds a DHCP server to the list of managed servers
- Remove—removes the selected server from the list of managed servers
- Create Scope—creates a new scope for the selected subnet
- Scope Properties—edits the properties for the selected subnet
- Deactivate or Delete the Scope—temporarily deactivates and reactivates a scope on the server or permanently deletes it

CHAPTER 18 *Managing Connectivity* **349**

- Add Reservations—adds reserved addresses to the scope for particular clients
- Active Leases—shows active client leases, including reserved addresses
- DHCP Options:
  - Scope—edits the configuration options for the selected scope
  - Global—edits the global client configuration options
  - Default—edits the default client configuration options

The DHCP server lets you preconfigure many of the options that would normally have to be set manually for a standard, fixed-address TCP/IP device. With DHCP Manager, you can set many of the options globally or you can set them individually for each scope. Individual clients can override these default settings, of course, but with Small Business Server this is neither necessary nor desirable if the installation has set up your DHCP options correctly.

The options you can configure on a per-scope, global, or default basis are:

- Time Offset
- Router
- Timer Servers
- Name Servers
- DNS Servers
- Log Servers
- Cookie Servers
- LPR Servers
- Impress Servers
- Resource Location Servers
- Host Name
- Boot File Size
- Merit Dump File
- Swap Server
- Root Path
- Extensions Path
- IP Layer Forwarding
- Non-Local Source Routing
- Policy Filter Masks
- Maximum DG Reassembly Size
- Default Time-to-Live
- Path MTU Aging Timeout
- Path MTU Plateau Table
- MTU Option
- All Subnets are local (for MTU)
- Broadcast Address
- Perform Mask Discovery
- Mask Supplier Option
- Perform Router Discovery
- Router Solicitation Address

- Static Route
- Trailer Encapsulation
- ARP Cache Timeout
- Ethernet Encapsulation
- Default Time-to-Live
- Keepalive Interval
- Keepalive Garbage
- NIS Domain Name
- NIS Servers
- NTP Servers
- Vendor-specific Info
- WINS/NBNS Servers
- WINS/NBT Node Type
- NetBIOS Scope ID
- X Window System Font
- X Window System Display
- NIS+ Domain Name
- NIS+ Servers
- Bootfile Name
- Mobile IP Home Agents

Whew! As you can see, you have a long list of potential options to set with DHCP. For Small Business Server, you generally won't need to set any of them. The installation program should get them all correct.

For More Information

For details about the various DHCP options, see Microsoft Windows NT Server 4.0 Resource Kit *or* Running Microsoft Windows NT Server 4.0 *(both from Microsoft Press).*

POINTS TO REMEMBER

- TCP/IP is not a single protocol but a suite of protocols and applications.

- TCP/IP standards are set by the IETF.

- TCP/IP standards and proposed changes are published in the form of Requests for Comment (RFCs).

- Windows NT Server provides tools for administering WINS and DHCP servers.

- Small Business Server uses DHCP for all of the client computers on its network.

- IPv6 (IPng) is compatible with IPv4 and will be implemented gradually over the next several years.

WHAT'S NEXT

In this chapter, we covered the intricacies of TCP/IP. In the next chapter, we'll cover setting up and maintaining Remote Access Service so that your users can work remotely just as if they were locally connected to the network.

Chapter 19

Administering Remote Access

- 354 **Setting Up a User for Remote Access**
- 354 **Setting Up a Client Computer for Remote Access**
  - Preparing a Windows NT Workstation Client for Remote Access — 355
  - Configuring the Dial-Up Connection — 356
  - Connecting Remotely Using Windows NT Workstation — 358
  - Connecting Remotely Using Windows 95 — 358
  - Starting the Outlook Client — 360
- 362 **Using Remote Access Admin**
  - Starting and Stopping RAS — 362
  - Checking Communication Ports — 362
  - Disconnecting RAS Users — 363
  - Sending Messages to Connected Users — 363
  - Checking User Information — 364
- 365 **Points to Remember**
- 365 **What's Next**

Chapter 19
Administering Remote Access

Remote access simply means the ability to connect to a network from a distant location. The only difference between a remote computer and a workstation connected directly to the network is slower data transfer speeds for the remote user. For people who do some or all of their work from home or while on the road, remote access is a useful, if somewhat slow, way to access files and check messages.

Remote access is configured when you install Microsoft BackOffice Small Business Server and again when you make changes to the installed modems.

Setting Up a User for Remote Access

When you add a new user (see Chapter 8), you can grant that user the right to remotely access the server. Changing that setting is easy; just follow these steps:

1. On the Tasks page of the Small Business Server console, click Manage Users.
2. Select the name of the user, and click Manage User Permissions.
3. Click Next three times to bypass the Shared Folders, Shared Printers, and Shared Fax Printers pages.
4. On the Select Additional Access Rights page, select the Use A Modem To Access The Server Computer check box to grant remote access; deselect it to disallow access. Click Next twice more, and then click Finish.

Setting Up a Client Computer for Remote Access

A user with remote access can dial in and connect to the server. The user can then use any shared folders on the server just as if he or she had connected from a client machine at work. By far the easiest way to set up a laptop for remote access is to plug it into the network, configure it as a client (including e-mail and dial-up networking), and then disconnect it. When the user makes a connection to the server with this laptop from a remote location, he or she can open Microsoft Outlook to collect and send e-mail.

The following sections explain how to remotely connect a Microsoft Windows NT Workstation client and a Microsoft Windows 95 client.

Preparing a Windows NT Workstation Client for Remote Access

Follow the steps described in Chapter 11 to add the client computer to your Small Business Server network and set it up for the user who'll be dialing in remotely. If the client is plugged into the network, this will be all the easier to do.

WARNING!

The modem sharing service installed on the server (which allows clients to use shared modems) cannot coexist with Dial-Up Networking (which is needed to connect to the server from a remote location). If a computer will be used as a remote client, configure it to use only its own modem and remove modem sharing if it's installed.

Next make sure that the client's modem is installed and plugged in. Using an account with administrative privileges, open My Computer and double-click on Dial-Up Networking.

You'll be advised that the phone book is empty and you'll be prompted to create a new entry. Click OK, and the Phonebook Entry Wizard will guide you through the process. On the wizard's Server page (Figure 19.01), the check boxes do not apply to a Small Business Server connection, so leave them deselected and click Next.

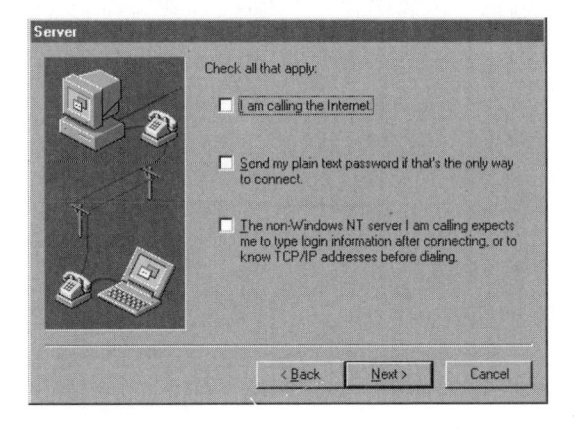

FIGURE 19.01

Leave these check boxes deselected for a connection to Small Business Server.

On the next page of the wizard, enter the phone number that the client must dial in order to connect to the server. Click Alternates to provide additional numbers. Click Next, and then click Finish.

Configuring the Dial-Up Connection

In the Dial-Up Networking window (Figure 19.02), click the More button to specify these additional settings:

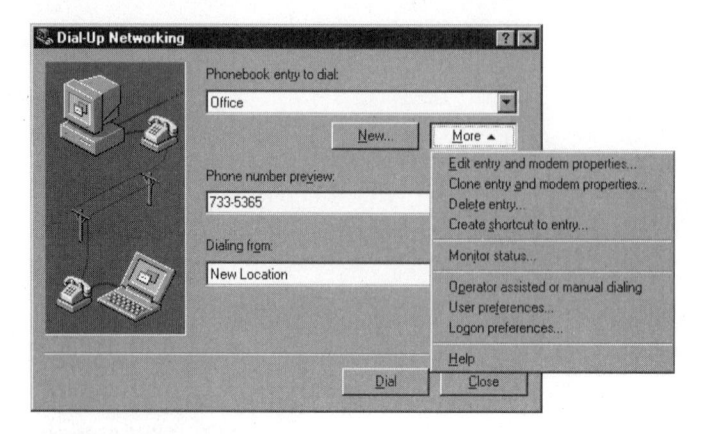

FIGURE 19.02

Specifying additional dial-up settings.

- **Edit Entry And Modem Properties** Opens the Edit Phonebook Entry so that you can change the phone number to be dialed or the modem to be used, change the protocol or the type of connection, or specify a script.

- **Clone Entry And Modem Properties** Allows the reproduction of a complicated connection that might include scripts or particular TCP/IP addresses. Rather than type all that information a second time—which could introduce errors—you can use this to make a copy of a connection and change elements as needed.

- **Delete Entry** Self-explanatory.

- **Create Shortcut To Entry** Instead of opening My Computer and Dial-Up Networking to make a frequently used connection, choose this entry to create a desktop shortcut.

- **Monitor Status** Opens the Dial-Up Networking Monitor. (See Figure 19.03.)

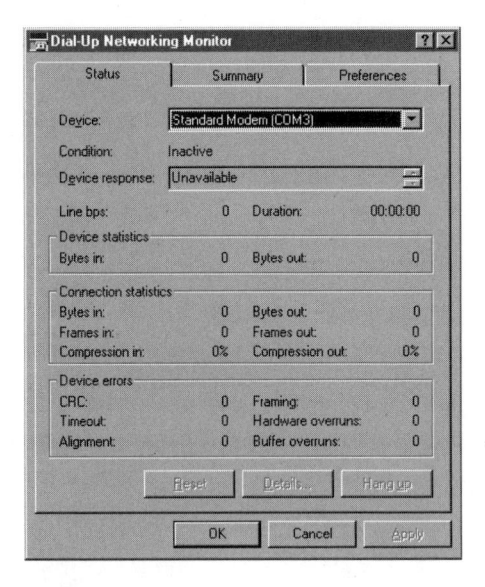

FIGURE 19.03

The Dial-Up Networking Monitor reveals lots of statistics—some of them useful.

- **Operator Assisted Or Manual Dialing** This is a toggle setting. Choose it to turn it on. (A check mark will appear in the menu.) Choose it a second time to turn it off. When it's on, you can pick up a phone connected to the modem and dial a number manually to make a connection.

- **User Preferences** Provides more options for the connection.

NOTE

For a user with administrative privileges, an additional item called Logon Preferences is available. This offers options to the person using Logon Using Dial-Up Networking at the initial logon to the system.

Connecting Remotely Using Windows NT Workstation

Making the dial-up connection to Small Business Server is now a simple matter. The modem must be connected to the computer and to a telephone line. Open My Computer, double-click on Dial-Up Networking, and choose the location to dial (if you have more than one). Click the Dial button.

The modem will connect to Small Business Server, your name and password will be verified, and the connection will be made.

NOTE

If you log on to the client computer locally, you must provide the name of the Small Business Server domain in the same dialog box with your name and password.

Now you can open Network Neighborhood and access shared folders. Create desktop shortcuts for the ones you use most often. Or right-click on a shared folder and choose Map Network Drive.

Connecting Remotely Using Windows 95

Connecting from a Microsoft Windows 95 machine is slightly different. To set up Dial-Up Networking, follow these steps:

1. Open My Computer. Double-click on Dial-Up Networking, and then on Make New Connection.

2. In the Make New Connection dialog box, type a name for the connection and verify that the correct modem is selected. Click Next.

3. Type the phone number for the SBS server. Click Next.

4. An icon will appear in the Dial-Up Networking window with the name of the new connection, as shown in Figure 19.04. Double-click on the icon.

5. In the Connect To dialog box (Figure 19.05), type your user name and password (the one you use on the Small Business Server network). Click the Connect button.

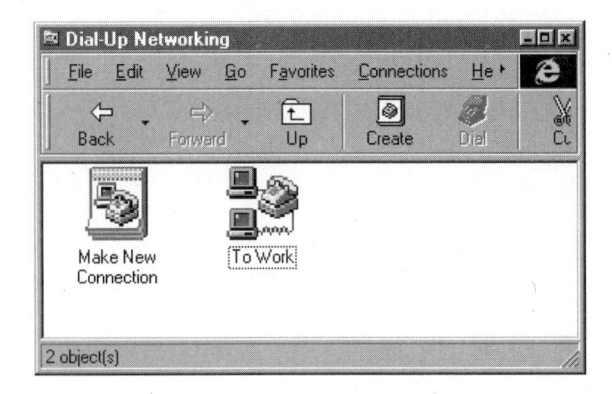

FIGURE 19.04

A Dial-Up Networking icon in Windows 95.

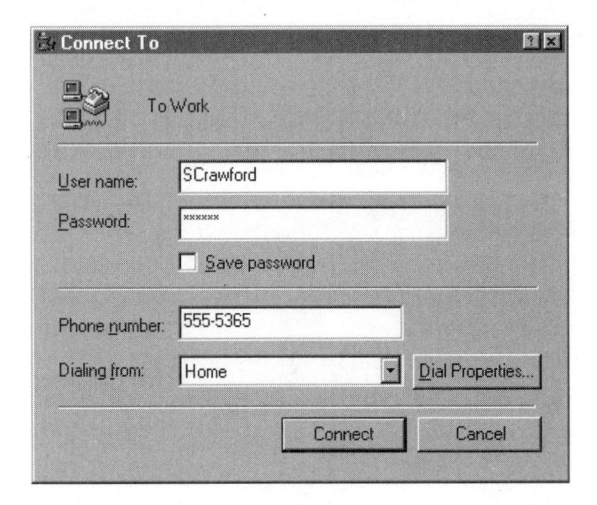

FIGURE 19.05

Provide your user name and password before dialing.

6. The modem will dial the number. When the User Logon dialog box appears, make sure the name of the workgroup matches the name of the Small Business Server domain.

Once the connection is made, you can open Network Neighborhood and access any of the shared folders.

NOTE

If you can connect to the network but can't see any other computers in Network Neighborhood, your computer might be identified incorrectly. In the Control Panel on the client machine, double-click on the Network icon. On the Identification tab, make sure the name in the Workgroup box is the same name as the Small Business Server domain. If it isn't, change the name and then click OK. Note that you'll need to reboot your computer before the change will take effect.

Starting the Outlook Client

One of the main reasons people use remote access is to send and receive e-mail. When the new user on a client machine first logs on, the Exchange Server client isn't configured for use, so the first step is to set it up:

1. On the client computer, choose Settings from the Start menu and then choose Control Panel, and then Mail And Fax. This will open the Mail And Fax dialog box, shown in Figure 19.06. Click the Add button.

FIGURE 19.06

This dialog box will contain no information if the Exchange client hasn't been set up.

360 ORGANIZING COMMUNICATIONS

2. The Microsoft Exchange Setup Wizard will launch. On the first page, select Microsoft Exchange Server as the service you want to use. Click Next.

3. On the next page, provide the name of the server. (It's the same name as the SBS server.) The mail box name should also be the same as your user name. Click Next.

4. On the next page, select Yes when asked whether you travel with this computer. Click Next.

5. Next you'll be asked to approve a default location for your Personal Address Book. Click Next, and then click Finish.

6. Go to the Control Panel again, and double-click on the Mail And Fax icon. Select Microsoft Exchange Server, and click Properties. On the Advanced page, check the location for offline folders.

> **Tip**
>
> *If this client machine has more than one user, specify the user's folder (within the Profiles folder) as the location for the .ost file.*

7. If you haven't configured Dial-Up Networking (as described in the previous section), do so now.

8. Use Dial-Up Networking to connect to the SBS server. Once you are connected, double-click on the Outlook icon on the desktop. Sample items for Outlook will be created automatically, and the Office Assistant might pop in for a visit.

9. From the Tools menu, choose Synchronize and then choose All Folders. This will synchronize the contents of your Outlook folders on the client and the contents of the same folders on the server. (This might take a couple of minutes.)

10. From the Tools menu, choose Synchronize and then choose Download Address Book. This will transfer the contents of the address book on the server to the client.

Now the user can do Outlook chores off line, including reading and writing e-mail. When it's time to send and receive new mail, the user can make the dial-up connection and then open the Outlook shortcut on the desktop. Mail in the Outbox will be sent, and new mail will be deposited automatically in the Inbox.

Using Remote Access Admin

The primary tool for administering remote access is, appropriately, Remote Access Admin. (Yes, that's Admin, not Administrator.) Using this one tool, you can check communication ports, start and stop Remote Access Service (RAS), set dial-in permissions, and send messages to users. To run Remote Access Admin, choose Programs from the Start menu and then choose Programs, Administrative Tools, and finally Remote Access Admin. The window shown in Figure 19.07 will open.

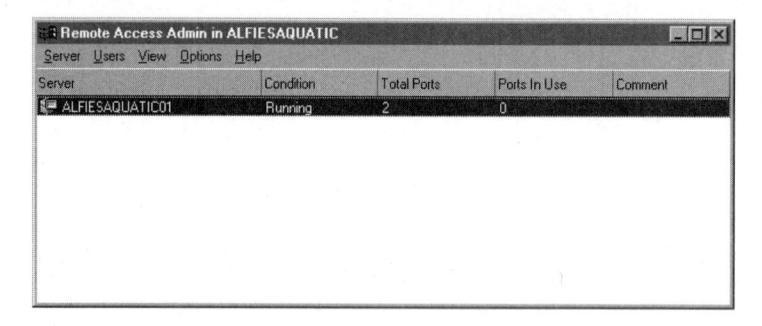

FIGURE 19.07
Managing RAS with Remote Access Admin.

Starting and Stopping RAS

RAS must be running before a dial-up connection can be made. Stopping RAS disconnects connected users and prevents any new connections from being made. You might want to stop RAS during backups.

To start or stop RAS, choose Start or Stop from the Server menu. You can also choose Pause RAS from this menu. A pause will not disconnect connected users but will prevent new calls from coming in.

> **Tip**
>
> *If you want RAS to be always disabled, always started manually, or always running, use Services in the Control Panel.*

Checking Communication Ports

To view the status of a RAS port, choose Communication Ports from the Server menu. Select the port and click the Port Status button. Click the Help button for a detailed explanation of each item.

> **Tip**
>
> *The Reset button does not reset the port; it just zeroes out the counters on the Port Status page.*

Disconnecting RAS Users

To disconnect a user on a particular port, choose Communication Ports from the Server menu. Select the port, and then click the Disconnect User button. In the Disconnect User dialog box (Figure 19.08), click OK if a simple disconnect will do the job. Select the Revoke Remote Access Permissions check box to both disconnect the call and revoke the user's remote access privileges.

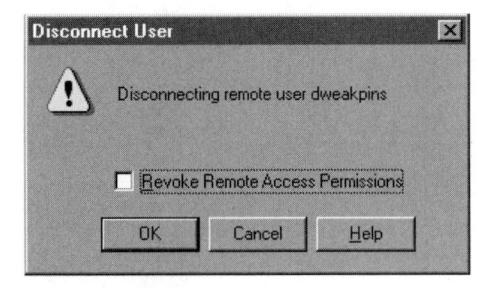

FIGURE 19.08

A user can be disconnected directly from this dialog box.

To disconnect a particular user altogether—you might or might not know what port this user is connected through—choose Active Users from the Users menu. Select the name of the user you want to disconnect, and click the Disconnect User button.

> **Tip**
>
> *You can view Remote Access Permissions by choosing Permissions from the Users menu. In general, though, we recommend that any changes that* can *be made through the Small Business Server console—and that includes RAS Permissions—should be made through the Small Business Server console. Some attempts to bypass the console can lead to unexpected results.*

Sending Messages to Connected Users

To send a message to connected RAS clients, choose Active Users from the Users menu. You can select a particular user or send a message to all users. To send a message to just one connected client, select the user's name and click Send Message. Type the message (as shown in Figure 19.09), and then click OK. To send a message to everyone currently connected, click the Send To All button.

> **Tip**
>
> *The Message text box has automatic word wrap. If you press the Enter key at what appears to be the end of a line, the message will be sent instantly.*

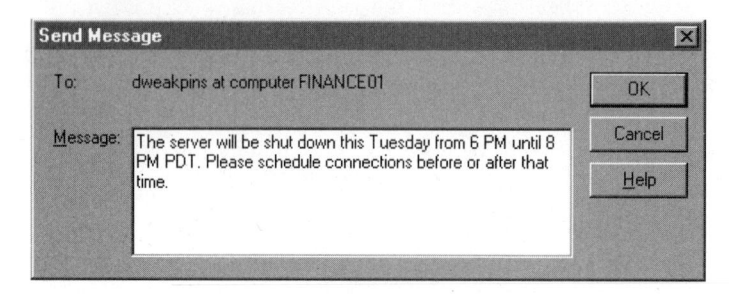

FIGURE 19.09

Sending a message to a remotely connected user.

When you click OK, the message will be delivered to the RAS client's desktop. (See Figure 19.10.)

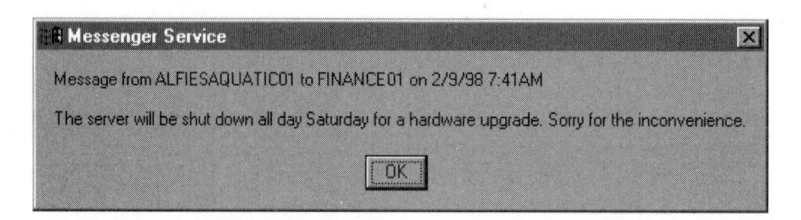

FIGURE 19.10

The remotely connected client receives the message instantly.

Checking User Information

For a quick look at the account information for a connected user, choose Active Users from the Users menu. Select the user, and click the User Account button. The window that appears (Figure 19.11) provides basic facts about the connection.

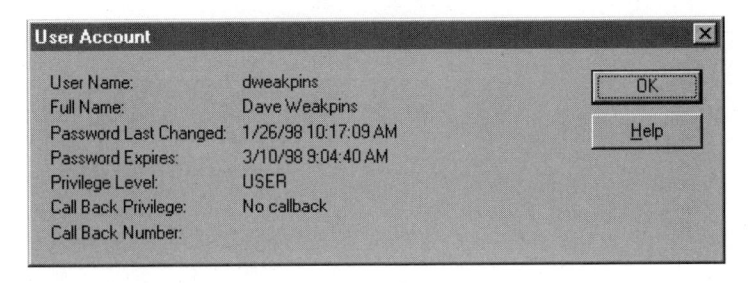

```
User Account                                          [X]
  User Name:              dweakpins              ┌─────────┐
  Full Name:              Dave Weakpins          │   OK    │
  Password Last Changed:  1/26/98 10:17:09 AM    └─────────┘
  Password Expires:       3/10/98 9:04:40 AM     ┌─────────┐
  Privilege Level:        USER                   │  Help   │
  Call Back Privilege:    No callback            └─────────┘
  Call Back Number:
```

FIGURE 19.11

Viewing account information about a connected user.

POINTS TO REMEMBER

- You can easily set up Windows NT Workstation and Windows 95 clients to remotely access Small Business Server.

- Remotely connected computers must have the Exchange client installed in order for the user to remotely send and receive e-mail from the server.

- Remote Access Admin is the tool for controlling remote access on the server.

WHAT'S NEXT

The last six chapters have dealt with the administration of e-mail, fax, and modem communications. In Part Five, we'll move on to communicating through a web site and configuring related server components.

Part Five
Administering Server Components

The chapters in Part Five cover the use of important server components, including Internet Information Server, SQL Server, and Crystal Reports for Small Business Server.

Chapter 20

Creating a Web Site with FrontPage

370	What Is the World Wide Web?
371	Understanding Web Pages
371	Planning a Web Site
372	Organizing a Web Site
372	Installing FrontPage
373	Creating a Web Site
374	How FrontPage Works
374	Using FrontPage Explorer
	Folder View — 374
	Hyperlink View — 375
376	Using FrontPage Editor
	Providing a Logo — 376
	Modifying the Home Page — 377
	Listing Products and Services — 378
	More About Hyperlinks — 380
382	Creating Special Effects with FrontPage
	Including Boilerplate Information — 383
	Adding a Time Stamp — 384
	Adding Scheduled Elements — 385
386	Publishing Your Web Site
386	Creating an Intranet
387	Points to Remember
387	What's Next

Chapter 20
Creating a Web Site with FrontPage

Creating a web site from scratch with complicated elements and links to many pages is far more than we can cover in a single chapter—but we can get a good start using Microsoft FrontPage. You have to give up a certain amount of autonomy when you use FrontPage—the software has its own methods and reasons for doing things in certain ways, and you might not like all of them. The advantage, however, is that FrontPage hides a lot of gruesome code and automates many tedious procedures, which puts the creation of sophisticated sites within reach of less experienced users.

In this chapter, we'll use FrontPage to create a simple web site for Alfie's Aquatic Adventures.

What Is the World Wide Web?

The World Wide Web is part of the Internet—an international network of networks. Only four or five years ago, it was a very small part of the Internet, but today it's the part that everyone knows about and uses. This is partly because the Web is the only part of the Internet with easily accessible pictures, sound, and animation, so it's the most appealing. It's also partly because of web browsers such as Microsoft Internet Explorer and Netscape Navigator, which have made the Web accessible and easy to use.

When you publish a site on the Web, you can potentially reach millions of people. At the very least, you create, for customers and potential customers, a point of contact that's available 24 hours a day and that they can use at their own convenience.

A web site that's available only within a company or an organization is called an *intranet*. It uses the same technology that's used on the Web, but the content is specific to the company and access is limited to authorized users. A basic Microsoft BackOffice Small Business Server intranet becomes available after you install and configure Small Business Server. You can use it as is or use the information in this chapter to modify and expand it.

Understanding Web Pages

Web pages look like documents with graphics, animation, and text, but they are in fact text documents with special HTML formatting codes, or *tags*. The HTML tags tell your browser how to display the text. The tags also indicate which graphics or animation files to include on the page and how to display them. The browser reads the tags and downloads the necessary files from the site to your computer. This is why all-text pages display quickly and why complicated pages display more slowly—text appears first, followed by graphics, animation, and then sound. The delay happens because the browser processes these elements in turn.

A web site is seldom a single page. It's usually a series of pages connected by hyperlinks (highlighted text that, when clicked, moves you to another page) or image maps (graphics that you click on to move to another page).

> **Tip**
>
> *Hyperlinks don't always move you to a page within the same web site; links can also be to other web sites. You can't easily tell when your connection has moved from one server to another.*

Planning a Web Site

Before you start building a web site, you should know what you want to accomplish. Who will the site be for? How will you attract those people? How will you get them to return? What information do you want to share with them? What information do you want to gather from them?

Many web sites are no more than passive billboards. A visitor comes once, looks around, and goes away, never to return. A web site must offer something of interest to the visitor, and that information must be kept current and accurate.

Alfie, of Alfie's Aquatic Adventures, wants to expand the public's knowledge of his retail dive shop and its services. He also wants to advertise the dive trips organized by his company. The target audience for his web site is made up of divers and prospective divers who might visit the shop *and* divers everywhere who are interested in organized dive trips. He'd also like to have a form on the site so that viewers can request more information about specific trips.

Organizing a Web Site

Once you determine the site's purpose and its target audience, you should decide what information you want to include and how to organize it. For example, Alfie's web site will have two separate but related areas—the shopping area and the travel area. He has diagrammed the site as shown in Figure 20.01.

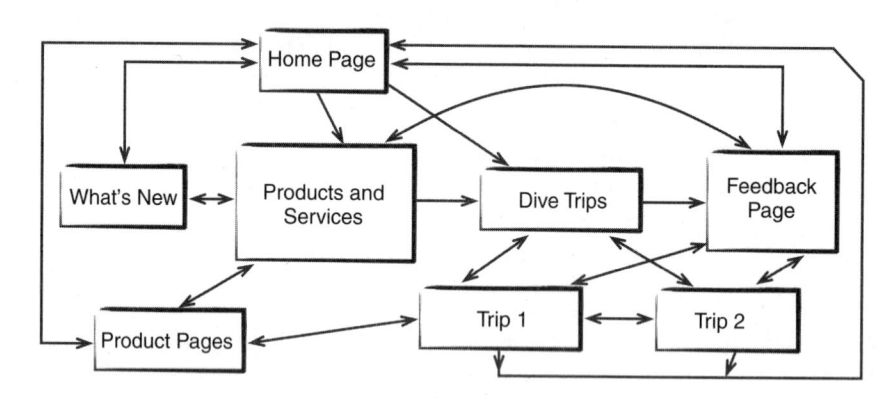

FIGURE 20.01

A simple plan for a web site, including hyperlinks between the various pages.

Installing FrontPage

FrontPage isn't installed automatically when you install Small Business Server. To install it, insert Disk 1 of Small Business Server into your CD-ROM drive. In Microsoft Windows NT Explorer, find the folder named Frontpg and open it. Double-click on Setup.exe, and the installation will begin.

NOTE

The version of FrontPage included with Small Business Server is licensed for installation on one computer only.

The setup program will search for installed components. It will also stop Microsoft Internet Information Server (IIS) if it is running, but it will restart IIS after the installation.

After FrontPage is installed, you'll have the option of opening FrontPage Explorer. Or you can open it later by choosing Programs, and then choosing Microsoft FrontPage from the Start menu.

> **NOTE**
>
> *Although this chapter can give you only an elementary introduction to creating web sites, just playing around with FrontPage can be instructive. If you want to go further— and once you get started, you probably will—you'll need additional help. Everything you need is in* Running Microsoft FrontPage *by Jim Buyens (Microsoft Press).*

Creating a Web Site

To create a new web site (called a *web* in FrontPage), start FrontPage. In the Getting Started dialog box, select From A Wizard Or Template (in the Create A New FrontPage Web section) and then click OK. In the next dialog box, select the type of web site you want; we selected Corporate Presence. Then provide a name for the site. This name will appear in a lot of places, so make it short and descriptive.

FrontPage will launch a wizard that corresponds to the type of site you selected. You'll be asked to specify which types of pages to include. (See Figure 20.02.) No template will fit your needs exactly, but you can easily add and change pages later.

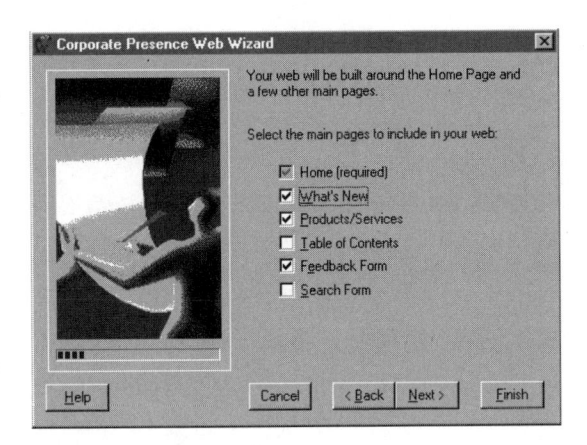

FIGURE 20.02

Answering questions for the wizard.

Keep answering questions and clicking the Next button. After you step through the wizard, you'll see the FrontPage To Do List (which appears in Figure 20.05 on page 376).

How FrontPage Works

FrontPage has two components. The first is FrontPage Explorer, which handles all the tasks associated with FrontPage web sites; you use FrontPage Explorer to create, import, display, or delete a site. FrontPage Editor deals with individual pages; you use it to add and format text, insert images, create hyperlinks, and add other elements that can go into a web page.

Most of the time, you'll first create or open a site in FrontPage Explorer and then use FrontPage Editor to edit individual pages. After you save a changed page, you can use FrontPage Explorer to see how the changes have affected the rest of the site. By switching back and forth in this way, you can see the details of an individual page while keeping the larger perspective in view.

Using FrontPage Explorer

Microsoft obviously loves to call things by the name "Explorer"—FrontPage Explorer is only one of many Explorers in Microsoft software. In this chapter, however, all references to Explorer mean FrontPage Explorer.

FrontPage Explorer does have a family resemblance to Windows NT Explorer. For example, there's a left pane and a right pane, and what you see in each pane is determined by the view you select.

Folder View

When you select Folder View (Figure 20.03), you'll see that the left pane of Explorer contains a hierarchical list of folders inside the current site. The right pane shows a detailed list of folders and files inside the selected folder.

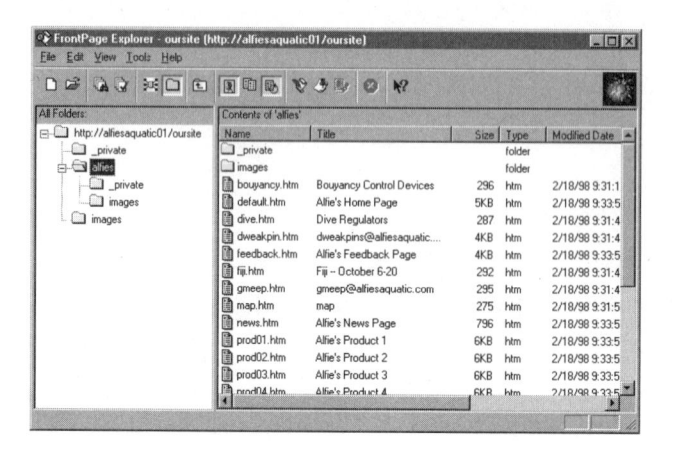

FIGURE 20.03

Looking at a web site in Folder View.

Folder View is useful for renaming files, creating new folders, and dragging files from one folder to another. When you rename a file or a folder or move a file, FrontPage automatically updates the links throughout the site.

Each site is automatically supplied with two standard folders. The *images* folder is, not surprisingly, the recommended place for storing your web site graphics. Keeping web pages and graphic files in separate locations simplifies site management. The *_private* folder stores pages that remain hidden even after the site is published; it's a good place to store pages that are incomplete or files that you don't want to make available to visitors.

NOTE

The _private folder remains private only when the site is published on a server that supports FrontPage extensions.

Hyperlink View

In Hyperlink View (Figure 20.04), the left pane of Explorer shows a sort of site outline. The right pane shows a diagram of the selected page, with incoming hyperlinks on the left and outgoing hyperlinks on the right.

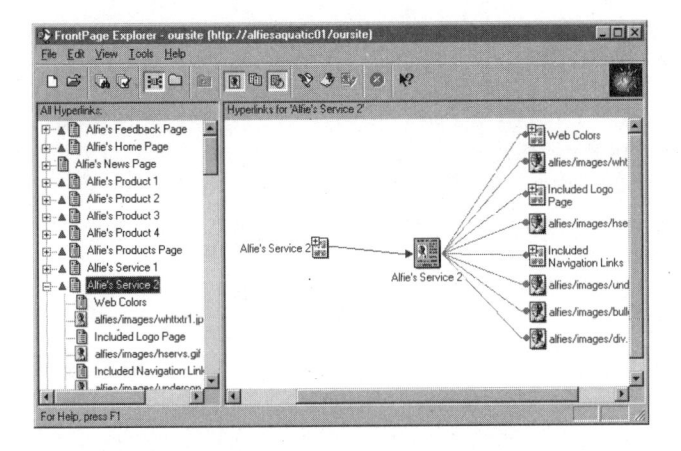

FIGURE 20.04

A page in Hyperlink View.

Click on any page in the left pane, and the pages linked to it will appear below it. Click on the plus sign next to a page, and the diagram will expand from that page. Some pages will show up more than once in the left pane because the outline shows all of the hyperlinks in the site, not just the pages.

Using FrontPage Editor

After the wizard creates the basic structure of your site, you'll see the FrontPage To Do List. (See Figure 20.05.) The To Do List is your lodestar for site development. It's the place where you keep track of the pages that have been added but have not been completed.

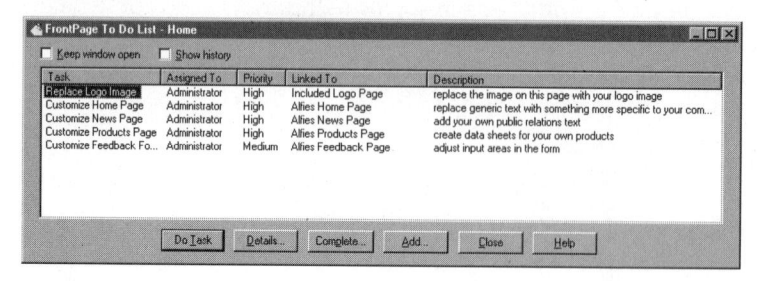

FIGURE 20.05
The list of pages and their current status.

Select the Keep Window Open check box to keep the To Do List open on the desktop as long as FrontPage is open. If you select the Show History check box, a Completed column will be added to the list.

Providing a Logo

The first item on the To Do List is Replace Logo Image. You should complete this task first because the logo will be used on all other pages. Select Replace Logo Image and click the Do Task button. FrontPage Editor will open with a page loaded called Included Logo Page. (See Figure 20.06.) After you create this page, it will be stored in the _private folder and its contents will appear at the top of each page that was created by the wizard.

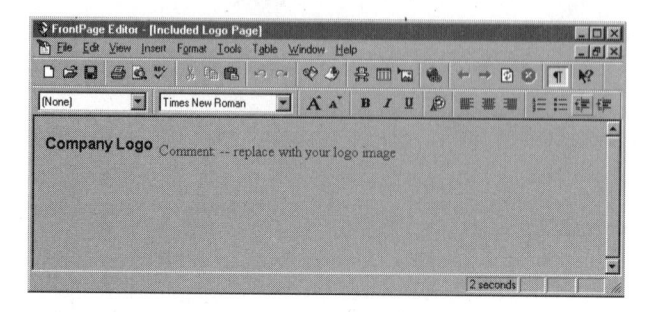

FIGURE 20.06
The page for your company logo.

As it turns out, Alfie's Aquatic Adventures doesn't have a logo that will reproduce well on a web page, so we'll have to create one. Click on Company Logo to cause the image form field to appear. Choose Image from the Insert menu, navigate to the image you want to use, and select it. Then select the text, and change it to something you like better. (See Figure 20.07.) Then save the Included Logo Page.

FIGURE 20.07

The basic logo for Alfie's.

Modifying the Home Page

Next on the To Do List is Customize Home Page. Select it, and click Do Task. The page that opens will include your saved logo plus placeholder text and other elements such as a navigation bar. Select the placeholder text, and replace it with your own. Figure 20.08 shows Alfie's home page with a marquee (see the Insert menu) and hyperlinks to other pages.

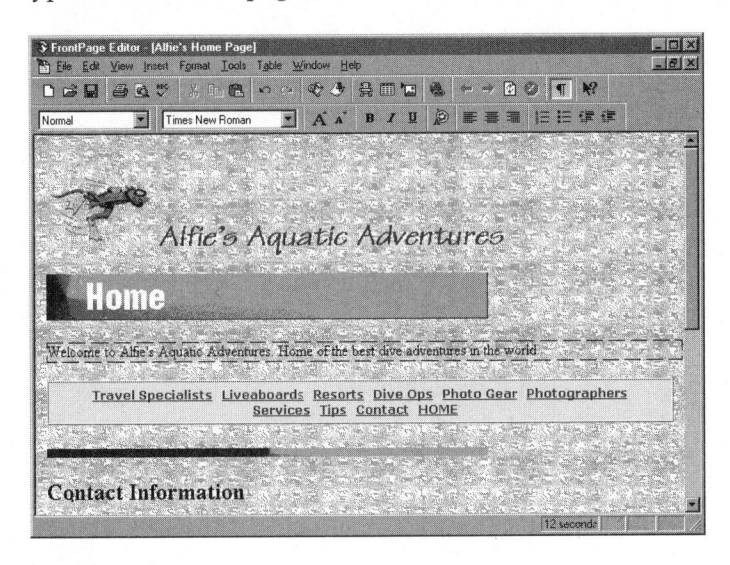

FIGURE 20.08

Alfie's home page after some modifications.

> **Tip**
>
> *As you work on a page, periodically choose Preview In Browser from the Editor's File menu. It can be both encouraging and sobering to see how a page will look to a visitor. Some things will look better than expected and some things…won't. It's best to catch the elements that don't work so well as soon as possible.*

Listing Products and Services

For Alfie's web site, we told the wizard to provide spots for four products and two services. Now we can replace the wizard's placeholder text with real links and information. On the To Do List, select Customize Products Page. In the list of products (and services), select a placeholder such as *Name of product 1* and type the name of an item. Select the text again, and choose Hyperlink from the Insert menu. (See Figure 20.09.)

The Create Hyperlink window will open. Since this is a new site, we clicked on the New Page tab and told FrontPage to add the new page to the To Do List. (See Figure 20.10.)

Converting Documents into Web Pages

You're likely to have a collection of documents that you want to include in your web site. FrontPage Editor can convert several document formats into web pages, which greatly simplifies the process. The Editor can read and convert these file formats:

- Microsoft Word for Windows (version 2 and later)
- Microsoft Word for the Macintosh (version 4 and later)
- Microsoft Works (version 3 and later)
- Microsoft Excel and Lotus 1-2-3
- ASCII text
- RTF
- WordPerfect (version 5 and later)—either directly or through automatic conversion to RTF files

FIGURE 20.09

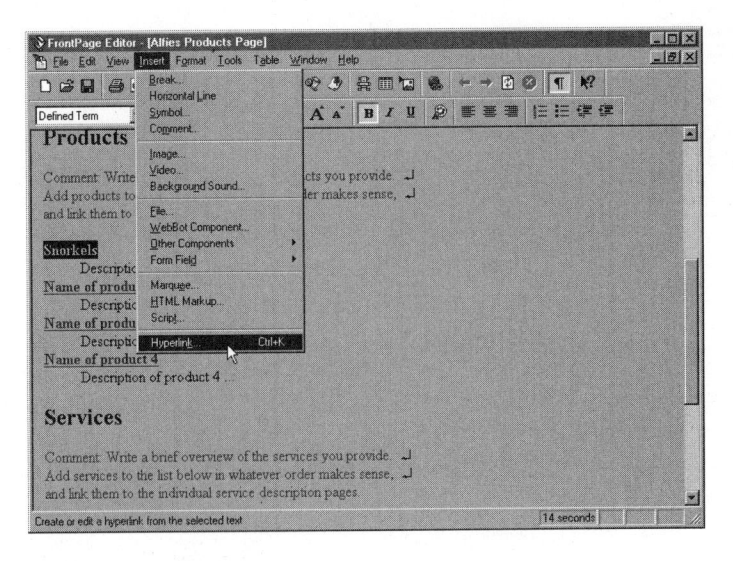

Creating a hyperlink.

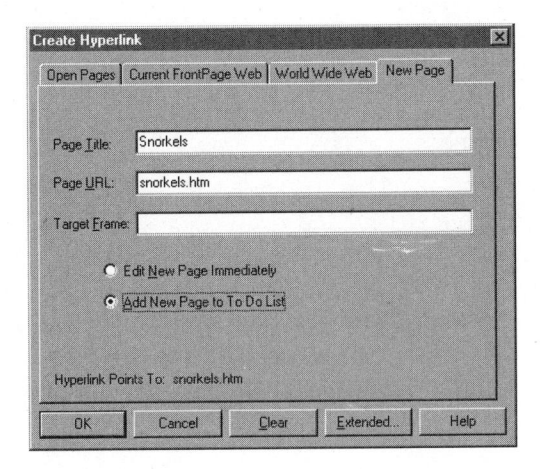

FIGURE 20.10

Linking to a new page.

The resulting list of products and services is made up of links to various pages where users can find more information. In addition, we added a link to a map so that people can easily locate the dive shop. (See Figure 20.11 on the following page.)

CHAPTER 20 *Creating a Web Site with FrontPage* **379**

FIGURE 20.11

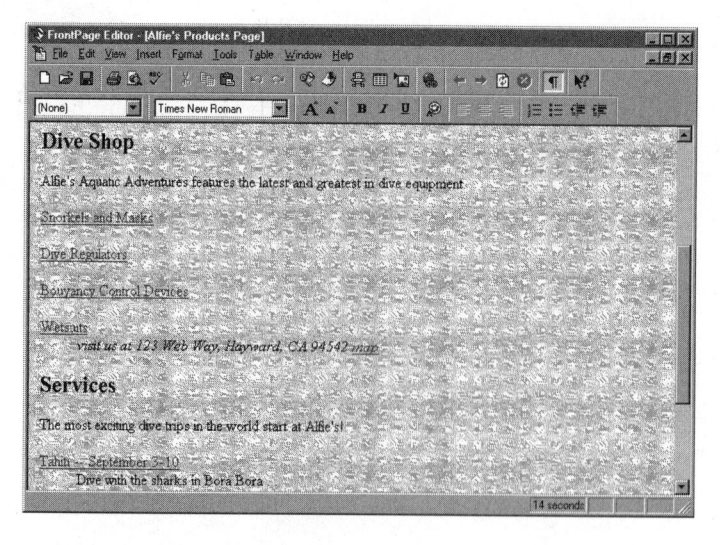

The completed products and services page.

More About Hyperlinks

You can create hyperlinks to web pages that aren't part of the current site by using the World Wide Web tab of the Create Hyperlink dialog box (shown in Figure 20.10 on the previous page). Or you can link to an existing page in the current site by using the Current FrontPage Web tab.

Links are created using either *relative* or *absolute* addresses. A relative address points to a file that resides on the same web server and requires only a partial pathname, which can be as short as a filename (including the extension). Within a single site, it's best to use relative addresses because you can move files around on the server without having to make changes to pages. If you spell out the entire address—for example, *http://www.oursite.com/figs.htm*—you're using an absolute address. An absolute address starts with *http://*, *ftp://*, or another protocol type. Links that point to other servers—including those on the Internet—generally use absolute addresses.

Linking to e-mail addresses

You'll certainly want to provide a way for people to send you e-mail. In fact, you might want to provide several e-mail addresses—including one for the webmaster so that people can send comments about the site. To create a link to an e-mail address, follow these steps:

1. Open the page where you want the e-mail link to appear. Type text that indicates where the link will lead—such as *sales@yourcompany.com*.
2. Select the text you just typed, and choose Hyperlink from the Insert menu.
3. In the Create Hyperlink dialog box, click on the World Wide Web tab. Select Mailto: from the Hyperlink Type drop-down list. Type the e-mail address. (Figure 20.12 shows that the *info@alfiesaquatic.com* link will send mail to the user *gmeep*.)
4. Click OK.

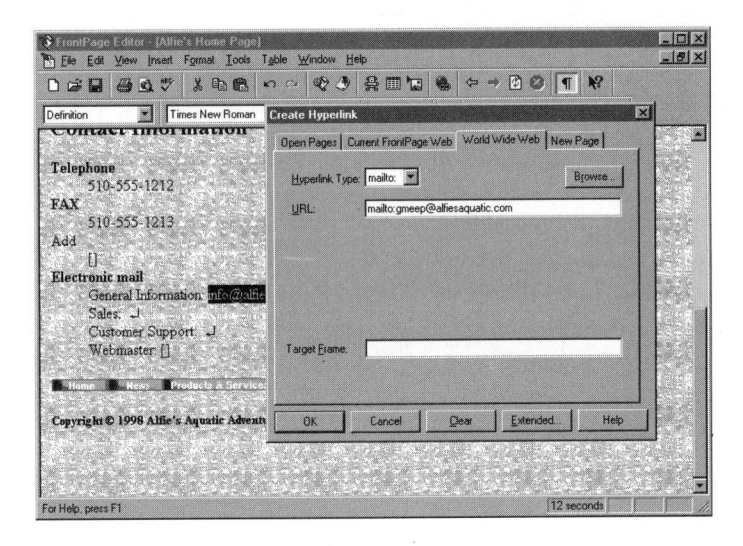

FIGURE 20.12

Creating an e-mail hyperlink.

Linking to a section in the current page

On a longer page, you might want to create internal links so that a click will move the reader to another part of the page. Creating an internal link is a simple two-step process. First you create a bookmark. (Bookmarks are placed at logical points, such as subheads or the beginning of new sections.) Then you create the link.

To create an internal link, take these steps:

1. With the page open in the Editor, click the insertion point at the spot where you want to place the bookmark.
2. Choose Bookmark from the Edit menu.

3. In the Bookmark dialog box, type a name for the bookmark and then click OK. The dialog box will close, and you'll see a flag at the spot where the bookmark was created.

4. Select the text you want to turn into a link. Choose Hyperlink from the Insert menu.

5. In the Create Hyperlink dialog box (Figure 20.13), select the bookmark from the drop-down list.

6. Click OK.

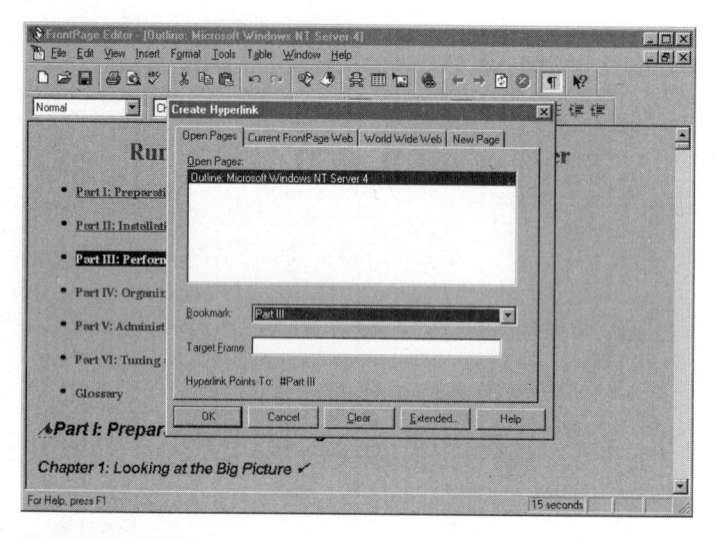

FIGURE 20.13

Linking to a bookmark.

Creating Special Effects with FrontPage

Certain information will appear on many pages in your site—for example, a copyright notice. Typing the same information on every new page can be a chore, but it's not unendurable. However, if the information changes, updating it throughout the site is much too tedious. It's easier to define each repetitive piece of information in a script. If you're a programmer, you can write your own scripts; if you're not, you can use one of the built-in FrontPage scripts.

In FrontPage 97, the scripts are called WebBot components and are represented by this little guy:

In addition to making those pesky changes a lot easier, WebBot components let you add dynamic information to your pages.

Including Boilerplate Information

FrontPage offers the Substitution WebBot component for specifying information that will be included on many pages of your site. This WebBot component uses keywords and values. When FrontPage comes across a certain keyword, it substitutes the value you've assigned to it. For example, in Alfie's web site, virtually every page includes the notice *Copyright 1998 Alfie's Aquatic Adventures*.

Here's how to create a Substitution WebBot component to save you from typing the same boilerplate information on multiple pages:

1. With your site open in Explorer, choose Web Settings from the Tools menu.
2. In the Web Settings dialog box, click on the Parameters tab. Click the Add button.
3. In the Add Name And Value dialog box (Figure 20.14), type a keyword and the corresponding value, and then click OK.

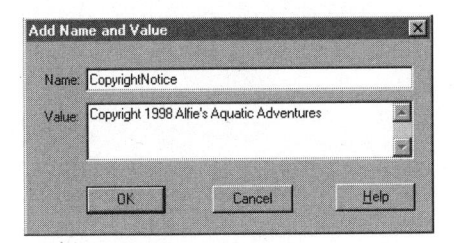

FIGURE 20.14

Specifying a keyword and its value.

4. The Add Name And Value dialog box will close, and the new component will be added to the list on the Parameters page. Click OK again.

To use this new component, open a web page in the Editor and follow these steps:

1. Place the cursor at the point where you want the value inserted.
2. Click on the WebBot icon on the toolbar or choose WebBot Component from the Insert menu.
3. In the Insert WebBot Component dialog box, select Substitution and click OK.

4. In the WebBot Substitution Component Properties dialog box, select the keyword you want from the drop-down list. We've selected CopyrightNotice. (See Figure 20.15.) Click OK.

5. The Editor window will show the value of the keyword inserted in the page.

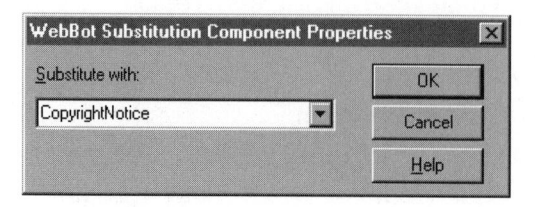

FIGURE 20.15

Specifying a substitution keyword.

Adding a Time Stamp

Nothing discourages repeat visitors to a web site as much as stale, unchanging pages. Since Alfie's Aquatic Adventures plans to have the latest and greatest information available at all times, we're going to add a time stamp. Readers will see that the pages are updated frequently. Here's how to add a time (and date) stamp:

1. With the page open in the Editor, position the cursor where you want the time stamp to appear.

2. Click on the WebBot icon, or choose WebBot Component from the Insert menu.

3. In the Insert WebBot Component dialog box, select Timestamp from the list of components and click OK.

4. Specify whether you want the date to be the "last edited" date or the date the page was automatically updated.

5. Select the date format from the drop-down list.

6. Select the time format from the drop-down list. If you don't want a time to appear with the date, select None.

7. Click OK. The dialog box will close, and the formatted time stamp will appear on the page.

> **NOTE**
>
> Don't use a time stamp if your site won't be updated often. Nothing discourages a visitor more quickly than seeing an old Last Updated date.

Adding Scheduled Elements

It's easy to keep your web pages fresh with the scheduling WebBot components. FrontPage lets you schedule when an image appears and when it disappears. You can also include a page inside another page for a specified amount of time.

To do either type of scheduling, open the page and place the cursor at the point where you want the element to appear. Click on the WebBot icon or choose WebBot Component from the Insert menu, and then choose Scheduled Image or Scheduled Include. The dialog box that opens is virtually identical for both scheduling tasks. The one for an image is shown in Figure 20.16.

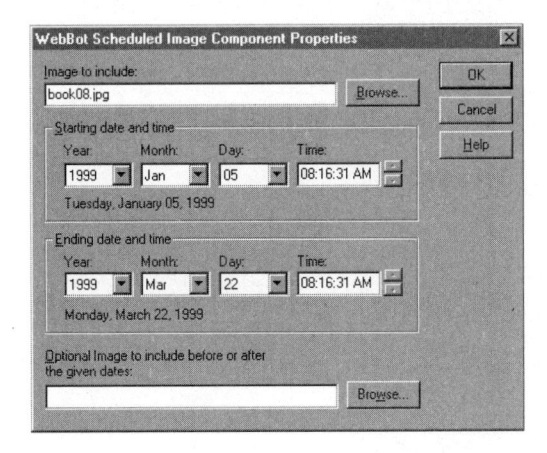

FIGURE 20.16

Scheduling an image to appear on a page.

As you can see, we selected an image and specified starting and stopping dates and times. In a Scheduled Include Component window, you supply the page URL and the starting and stopping dates and times.

Publishing Your Web Site

When you have a completed web site—or at least a site that contains the basic elements—you can publish it. Publishing simply means putting it on a server where others can view it. On an intranet, making the files available publishes a site. To publish on the Internet, you need a web server that's on line all the time—probably one run by an Internet service provider (ISP). When contracting for web services, you should ask the ISP a number of questions:

- Does the ISP's server support FrontPage extensions? (Many advanced FrontPage features won't work without them.)
- How much support does the ISP provide?
- Does the ISP offer a secure server for online transactions?
- How much traffic can the ISP handle?
- How much disk space will the ISP allot to you? How much will additional space cost?
- How reliable is the ISP? Does it have on-site technicians available around the clock, every day?
- How much will this cost?

Once you settle on where you to post your site, the ISP should be able to tell you how to do it. Most ISPs provide a special user name and password for the web site (separate from your dial-up account for e-mail and Internet access). You do the actual publishing by opening the site in FrontPage Explorer and choosing Publish FrontPage Web from the File menu.

Creating an Intranet

Even if you have no interest in a public site on the World Wide Web, using web technology internally on an intranet can be useful. You can make information available to all workstations and update it centrally.

The basics of an intranet are included and ready to go once you install Small Business Server. When a user on a client machine double-clicks Internet Explorer, the window shown in Figure 20.17 opens.

FIGURE 20.17

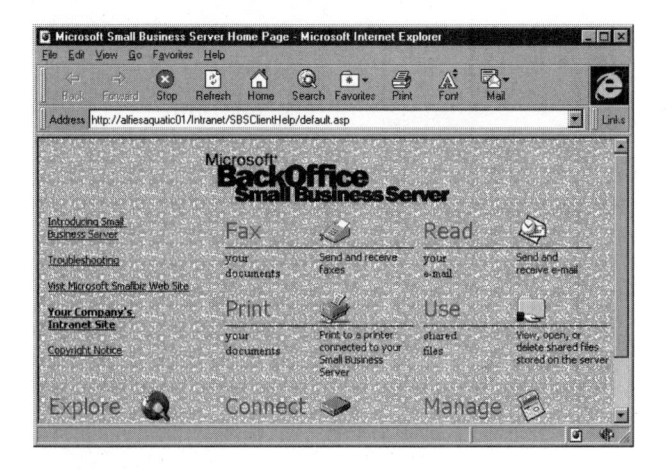

Using the Small Business Server intranet.

All the links on this page will be functional if the individual parts of Small Business Server have been set up and are working. The pages for the intranet are in the *C:\Inetpub\wwwroot\intranet* folder. You can add more pages using FrontPage and link them to existing pages using the methods described earlier in this chapter.

POINTS TO REMEMBER

- Before you create your first web page, think about what you want your web site to do and who you want to attract.

- Consider site organization at the outset. Make a plan, and draw a chart of how pages will be connected.

- Use a template for your first web site to simplify the tasks of organization and of adding necessary elements.

- Keep the information on your site up-to-date, and make other changes frequently. Give your users a reason to return.

WHAT'S NEXT

Now that we've covered the most basic elements of web site construction, we'll move on to Microsoft Internet Information Server (IIS) in the next chapter. We'll explain how to use it in the context of Small Business Server.

Chapter 21

Managing an Intranet Web Server

- 390   **WWW Service**
- 391   **FTP Service**
- 391   **Configuring Services**
  - Service Properties   391
  - Directory Properties   393
  - Logging Properties   394
  - Advanced Properties   394
- 395   **Intranet Resources**
- 396   **Points to Remember**
- 396   **What's Next**

CHAPTER 21

Managing an Intranet Web Server

Microsoft Internet Information Server (IIS) is the mechanism behind the intranet in Microsoft BackOffice Small Business Server. You configure IIS using Microsoft Internet Service Manager (ISM), which is the subject of this chapter. To open ISM, from the Start menu choose Programs, Microsoft Internet Server, and then Internet Service Manager. ISM offers three views; for our purposes, the default Report view (Figure 21.01) is best.

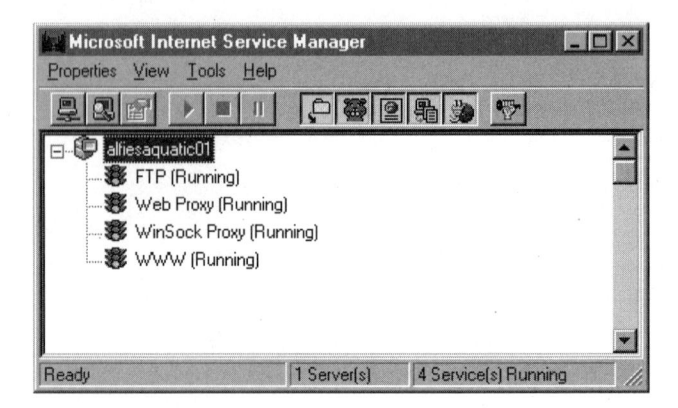

FIGURE 21.01

Report view is the default view for Internet Service Manager.

You can start and stop Internet services from this window. Just right-click on the computer name and choose the command you want. (If the service you select is already running, only Stop and Pause are available.)

WWW Service

The WWW Service handles the publishing of your intranet. It specifies the authentication needed for access, the directories available to users, and a default document that appears if a user doesn't specify a particular file.

FTP Service

The File Transfer Protocol (FTP) was one of the earliest services used on the Internet. As a way of quickly transferring files between computers, it's unrivaled. When you connect to an FTP site outside your network, the browser and the FTP Service on the other server handle the transfer.

So what's the use of FTP in an intranet? Here's an example. Let's say you have a What's New page on the intranet that users see at their initial logon each day. On this page, you can post a link to the newest update for your antivirus software. When the user clicks on the link, the FTP Service delivers the file from your server to the user's computer. Even if you don't use FTP often, it costs very little in terms of processor overhead to keep it running.

Winsock and Web Proxy Services

The Winsock Proxy Service and Web Proxy Service are configured through ISM, but their functions are more closely associated with Microsoft Proxy Server. You'll learn about configuring these two services in the next chapter.

Configuring Services

You can view or change the properties for a service by right-clicking on its name in Internet Service Manager and choosing Service Properties from the pop-up menu.

The properties for the WWW Service and the FTP Service are virtually identical, so we'll describe them together.

Tip

As a rule, you shouldn't change the default settings for any of the services unless you have a good and specific reason for doing so. All the services will work very well without additional tweaking.

Service Properties

On the Service tab of the Service Properties dialog box (Figure 21.02 on the following page), you can control who can use the web server for the intranet and you can specify an account for anonymous users.

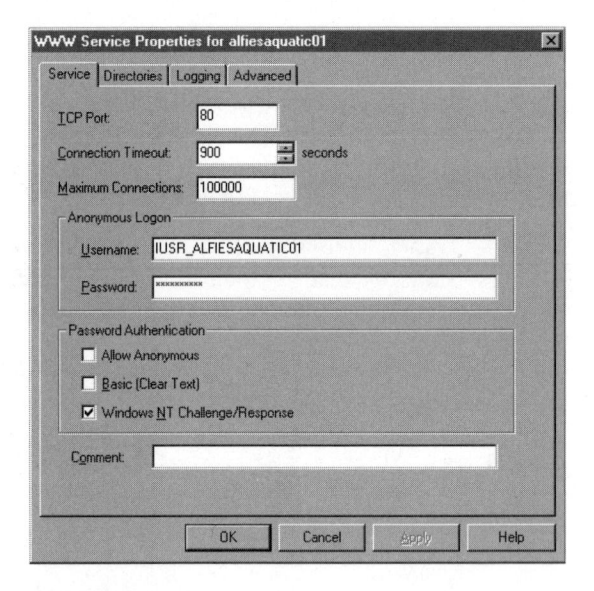

FIGURE 21.02

The Service tab of the Service Properties dialog box.

The following options are available on the Service tab:

- **TCP Port** Sets the port on which the WWW Service and the FTP Service run. The default for the WWW Service is 80. The default for the FTP Service is 21.

- **Connection Timeout** Sets the maximum amount of time before the server automatically disconnects an inactive visitor.

- **Maximum Connections** Specifies the number of simultaneous connections allowed on your server at one time.

- **Anonymous Logon** By default, both the WWW Service and the FTP Service allow anonymous connections. This is not a problem on most intranets because every machine on the network requires network authentication for logging on.

- **Password Authentication** Specifies the types of authentication permitted. Unless you know that you have a clear need for nonsecure access to your server (highly unlikely!), stick with the defaults.

NOTE

The FTP Service Properties dialog box includes a Messages tab on which you can enter a message for all users to read when they log on and when they exit.

Directory Properties

The Directories tab of the Service Properties dialog box (Figure 21.03) lists the directories available to intranet visitors.

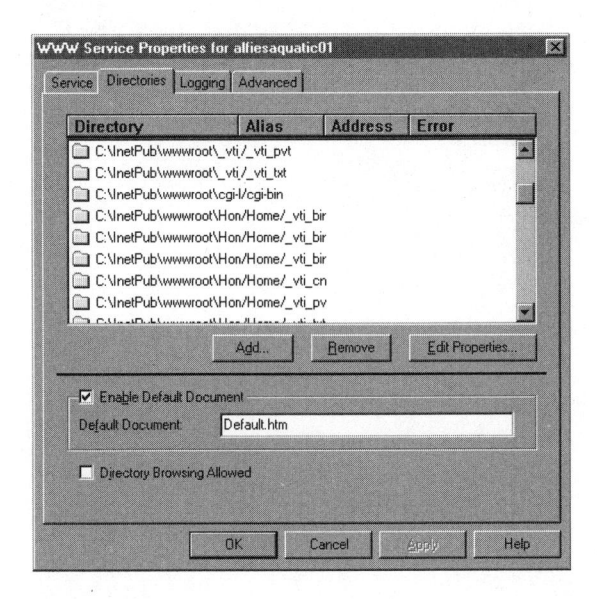

FIGURE 21.03

The Directories tab of the Service Properties dialog box.

Two check boxes are available at the bottom of the Directories tab. If you select the Enable Default Document check box, the file whose name appears in the Default Document text box will be displayed to users who don't request a specific file. If you select the Directory Browsing Allowed check box, users can view a list of the folders and files on the intranet. This is deselected by default, but for an intranet it's reasonable to select it.

At the bottom of the Directories tab of the FTP Services Properties dialog box, you can choose to list your FTP directories in either UNIX or MS-DOS style. UNIX is the default because many browsers expect to see UNIX. However, you can use either view when Microsoft Internet Explorer is the browser.

Logging Properties

The Logging tab of the Service Properties dialog box (Figure 21.04) lets you configure how the service is logged. Daily logging is automatically enabled. This might be overkill on a small network; you might want to change to weekly or even monthly logging. Log To File is the preferred option unless you have a SQL or ODBC database (and application) ready to receive the information.

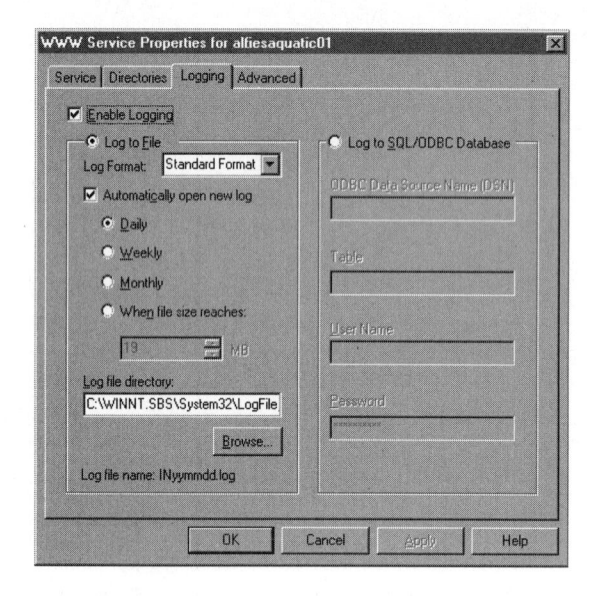

FIGURE 21.04

The Logging tab of the Service Properties dialog box.

Advanced Properties

The Advanced tab of the Service Properties dialog box (Figure 21.05) lets you control which computers can access the intranet web site. If you opted for a standard Small Business Server installation, you cannot use these options because IP addresses are dynamically assigned and are not static. However, on a system with assigned IP addresses, you can enter a computer's IP address to prevent it from browsing the intranet.

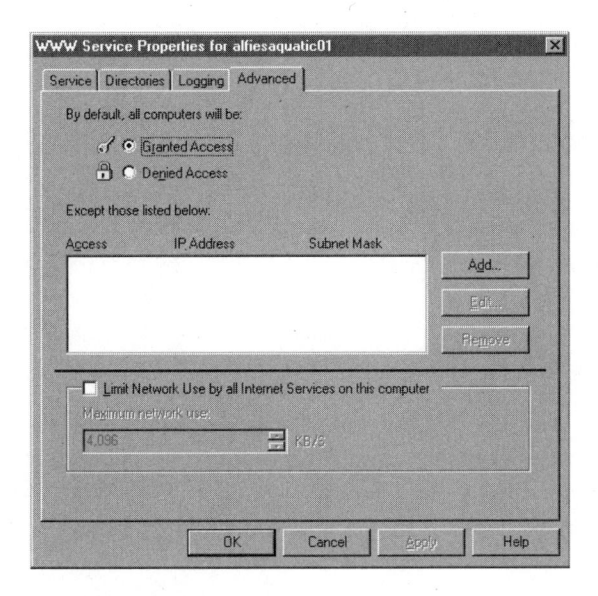

FIGURE 21.05
The Advanced tab of the Service Properties dialog box.

> ◆ **Digging Up Gopher**
>
> Gopher is another older service that is useful for publishing lists of files. It's not installed by default, so if you don't see it in Internet Service Manager, run the IIS setup again. For information on setting up Gopher, consult the IIS Topics on ISM's Help menu.

Intranet Resources

Intranets are hot these days, along with extranets. (An extranet is a portion of an intranet that is accessible to outsiders such as vendors or customers.) An excellent source of information on developing an intranet is Microsoft's Intranet Solutions Center (http://www.microsoft.com/intranet/default.htm). Dozens of free sample applications are available for downloading. Every sample application comes with complete installation information and documentation. Other valuable resources are The Intranet Journal (http://www.intranetjournal.com/) and The Complete Intranet Resource (http://www.intrack.com/intranet/). Both offer technical documentation, sample applications, and intranet discussion lists.

POINTS TO REMEMBER

- You can start and stop Internet Information Server from Internet Service Manager.
- Right-click on a service in ISM to view or change its properties.
- Run the IIS setup program to add services to or remove services from ISM.

WHAT'S NEXT

Even though the Web Proxy Service and the Winsock Proxy Service appear in the Internet Service Manager window, they properly belong to the larger topic of Microsoft Proxy Server, the subject of the next chapter.

Microsoft Proxy Server

CHAPTER 22

398	What Is a Proxy Server?	
398	Installing and Configuring Proxy Server	
	Starting and Stopping Proxy Server	399
	Configuring Web Proxy Service Properties	400
	Configuring Winsock Proxy Service Properties	404
406	Upgrading to Proxy Server 2	
411	Points to Remember	
411	What's Next	

Chapter 22

Microsoft Proxy Server

Underlying your Microsoft BackOffice Small Business Server connection to the Internet, and making it all work in a secure manner, is Microsoft Proxy Server. This proxy server not only controls who has access to the Internet but also handles the address translations and other features of Small Business Server that provide a secure and safe environment for your business, even when it is connected to the Internet.

What Is a Proxy Server?

A proxy server is a way for one or more computers to connect to the Internet indirectly. The proxy server does the actual connecting to the Internet and provides the information to the requester. This shields the computers downstream of the proxy server from the direct connection while making it easy for you to manage the traffic and providing a single point of contact and management.

The proxy server provides a number of services to its downstream clients. It can improve the overall Internet throughput of the network since it caches popular pages on its hard drive. It also allows the entire network to have only a single "public" IP address, by translating all requests for Internet packets so that they appear to come from the proxy server, not the client machine. And it can provide a significant level of security—although it is not, in the strictest sense of the word, a firewall.

The proxy server implemented in Small Business Server also manages who can use the Internet because only users who are on its list of enabled users are permitted to access addresses outside the local network.

Installing and Configuring Proxy Server

If you opted for the default installation of Small Business Server, you already have Microsoft Proxy Server installed and set up. The only task left for you to do is to actually sign up with an Internet service provider (ISP) or connect your Small Business Server network to an existing account.

> **For More Information**
>
> For details on these tasks, see the sections titled "Getting Connected" and "Connecting to an Existing ISP Account" in Chapter 17.

Proxy Server has a number of options you can change, but before you get carried away, we suggest that you ask yourself what you're trying to accomplish. The default configuration for Proxy Server should be appropriate for virtually all situations.

Starting and Stopping Proxy Server

Proxy Server has two components—the Web Proxy Service and the Winsock Proxy Service. The web proxy is the main component in use when you browse the World Wide Web or download a file; the Winsock proxy is used by a wide variety of other applications that need access to the Internet, including Microsoft Exchange. Both can be managed and controlled using Microsoft Internet Service Manager. By default, they start when the server boots and are not normally stopped. However, if you make changes to the configuration of the proxy server, you might have to stop and restart these services for the changes to take effect.

To stop the web proxy or the Winsock proxy, take these steps:

1. Open Internet Service Manager by choosing Programs, Microsoft Proxy Server, and then Internet Service Manager from the Start menu.

2. Select the service you want to stop, as shown in Figure 22.01, and then click the Stop button.

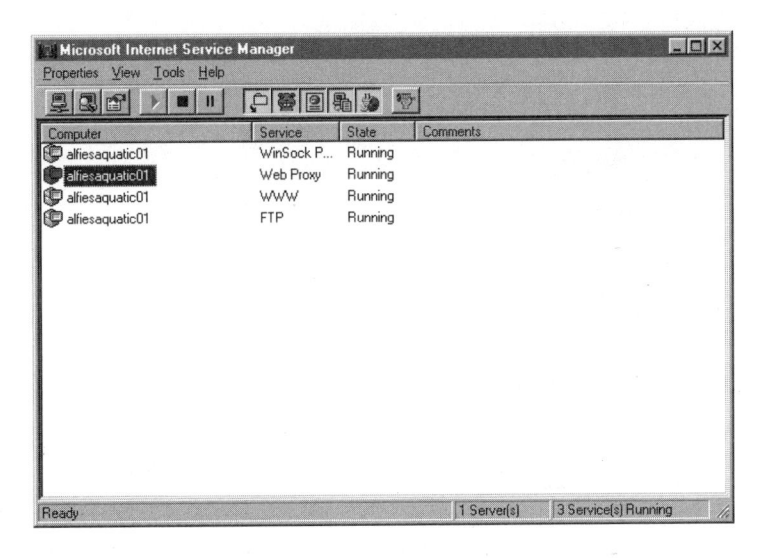

FIGURE 22.01

Internet Service Manager lets you manage and configure the web services on your server.

CHAPTER 22 *Microsoft Proxy Server* **399**

To start the web and Winsock proxies, you follow the same procedure but you use the Start button instead of the Stop button. You can use the same application to start and stop your intranet web and FTP servers.

Configuring Web Proxy Service Properties

The Web Proxy Service has several tuning and security parameters that you can set to ensure that you are getting the most out of Proxy Server. All are reached by double-clicking on the Web Proxy Service in the Internet Service Manager window to open the Web Proxy Service Properties dialog box (Figure 22.02).

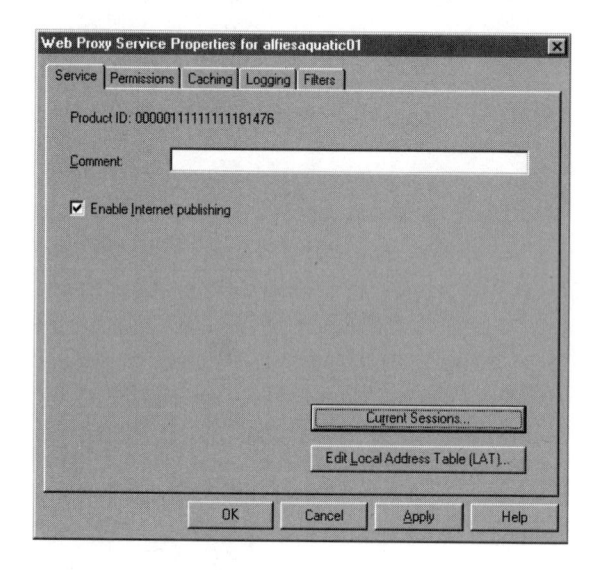

FIGURE 22.02

In the Web Proxy Service Properties dialog box, you can set a number of tuning and security parameters.

This dialog box contains tabs for the service itself, permissions, caching, logging, and filters. The Filters tab is shared between the Web Proxy Service and the Winsock Proxy Service.

On the Service tab, you can click the Current Sessions button to view the users who are currently connected and using the Web. This brings up the Web Proxy Service User Sessions page, as shown in Figure 22.03. Here you can see current statistics on network-to-Internet connections that are using the web proxy.

You can also edit the local address table (LAT) via the Service tab. But do yourself a favor—leave it alone unless you know why you are changing it. The defaults for the LAT should be fine for almost all small business situations. The one situation in which you might need to change it occurs when you are setting up a high-speed Internet account using a dedicated line or an ISDN line. Even then, you should change it only if your ISP gives you a specific setting to change.

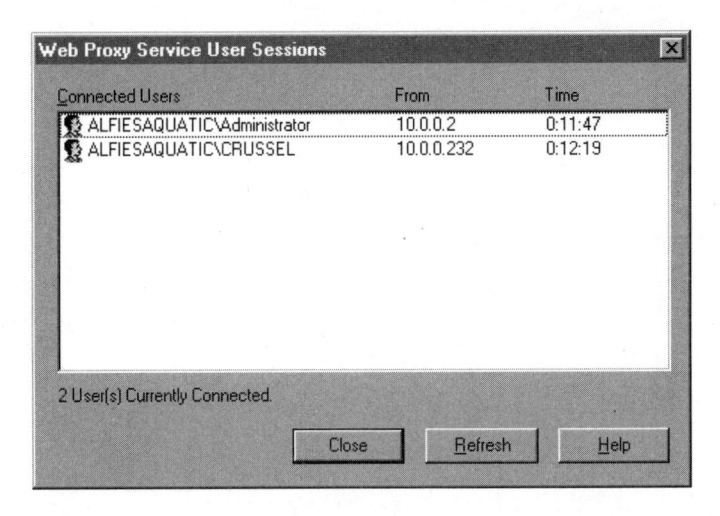

FIGURE 22.03

The Web Proxy Service lets you see who's currently connected to the Web.

On the Permissions tab, shown in Figure 22.04 on the following page, you can change who is permitted to connect to various supported protocols. But we strongly recommend that you stick to using the Small Business Server console to make changes in user permissions. In fact, this is good advice in general with Small Business Server. If you get in the habit of always using the Small Business Server console to create, delete, and modify the objects and properties of Small Business Server, you will encounter far fewer problems in the long run. Microsoft has tied Small Business Server closely to the console, and many features work correctly only through the console.

The Caching tab, shown in Figure 22.05 on the following page, lets you specify the amount of disk space used by the cache, how quickly the cache marks pages as expired, and how aggressively it tries to guess what pages you might need. Frankly, you're better off leaving these settings alone—except, perhaps, for increasing the disk space allowed. The defaults are a pretty good compromise, given that you're connecting via a modem.

FIGURE 22.04

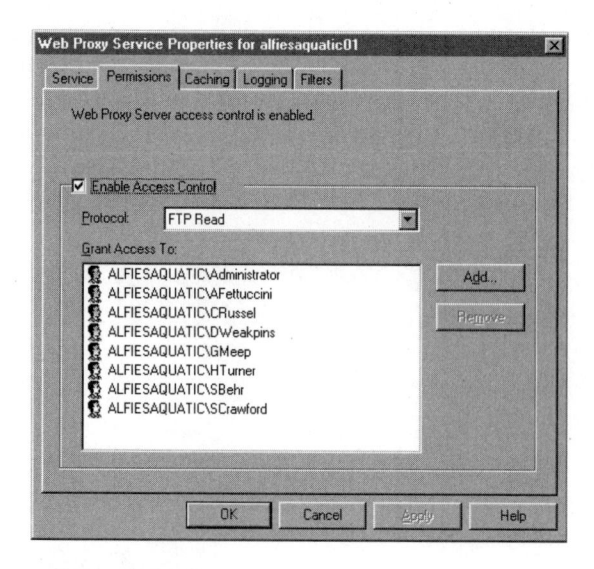

You can use the Permissions tab to change user permissions, but it's safer to make the changes via the Small Business Server console.

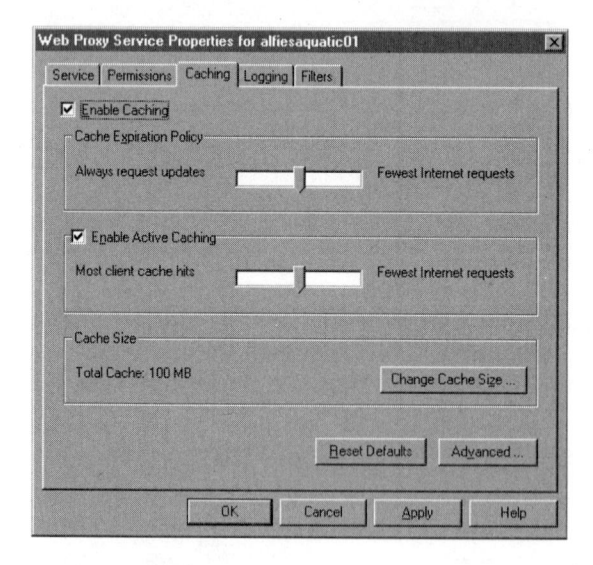

FIGURE 22.05

On the Caching tab, you can adjust the behavior of the Web Proxy Service.

The Logging tab, shown in Figure 22.06, lets you control how often a new log file is created and how much information each file contains. Logging can be useful when you need to track down problems with particular users or pages, but it can quickly eat up large amounts of disk space on the server. Be conservative with logging—you might even want to turn logging off completely after you get past the initial setup and shakedown period. If you decide to leave it on, don't forget to periodically delete the old log files.

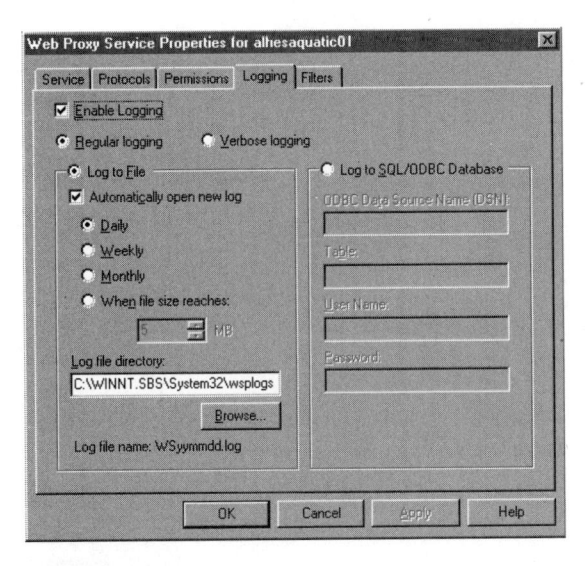

FIGURE 22.06

You can log a great deal of information about which pages have been downloaded and by whom.

The final tab of the Web Proxy Service is the Filters tab, which is shared with the Winsock Proxy Service. This tab lets you specify whether users have access to a particular web site, domain name, or group of IP addresses. This is one of those "features" that might be important in a large corporate environment, but it's not really appropriate in a small business. If you think that any of your employees are abusing their Internet access, the best solution is probably to address the problem directly rather than control access to a particular site or set of sites—especially since there is no way to designate specific sites for specific users.

NOTE

Offensive web sites tend to move around pretty regularly, which makes this type of essentially static filtering less than totally effective. If you have a serious need for filtering in a particular site, you can find commercial add-on products and services that do a much better job of this than Proxy Server by itself. They are regularly updated on the latest places to avoid, based on criteria that you select.

Configuring Winsock Proxy Service Properties

The Winsock Proxy Service has several tuning and security parameters that you can set to ensure that you are getting the most out of Proxy Server. All are reached by double-clicking on the Winsock Proxy Service in Internet Service Manager to open the Winsock Proxy Service Properties dialog box, as shown in Figure 22.07.

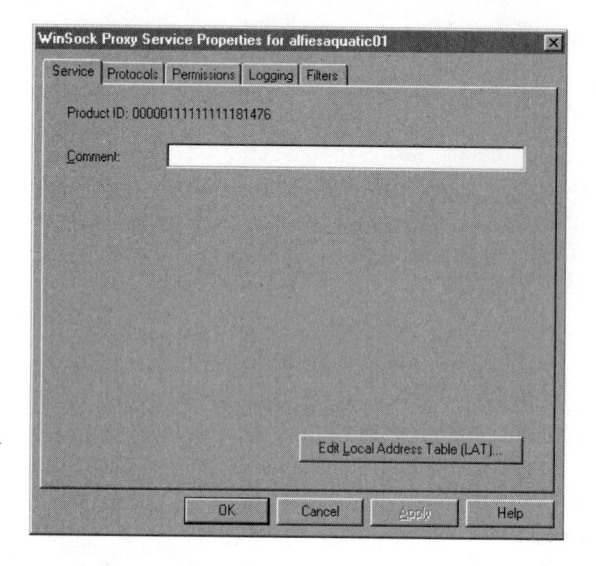

FIGURE 22.07

You can set a number of tuning and security parameters in the Winsock Proxy Service Properties dialog box.

This dialog box contains tabs for the service itself, the protocols it supports, permissions, logging, and filters. (As noted earlier, the Filters tab is shared between the Web Proxy Service and the Winsock Proxy Service.)

On the Service tab, you can edit the local address table (LAT). Just as with the Service tab of the Web Proxy Service Properties dialog box, leave this alone unless you have a specific reason to change it.

The Protocols tab, shown in Figure 22.08, lets you change which protocols are supported through the proxy server and on which ports they are supported. You can add new or special protocols, or you can remove protocols that you don't want to have available to your users. But your best bet is probably to leave the entire thing alone unless you need to change something and you understand what you are changing and why.

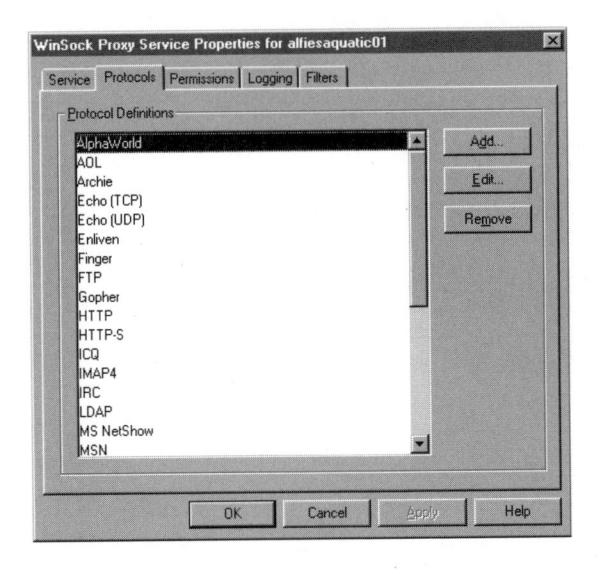

FIGURE 22.08

The Winsock Proxy Service lets you decide which protocols to support and which ports the protocols will use.

The Permissions tab, shown in Figure 22.09 on the following page, lets you control who can connect to various supported protocols. We strongly recommend that you stick to using the Small Business Server console to make changes in user permissions instead of using this tab.

The final two tabs are the Logging tab, which is similar to the Logging tab of the Web Proxy Service Properties dialog box (Figure 22.06), and the Filters tab, which is shared with the Web Proxy Service.

FIGURE 22.09

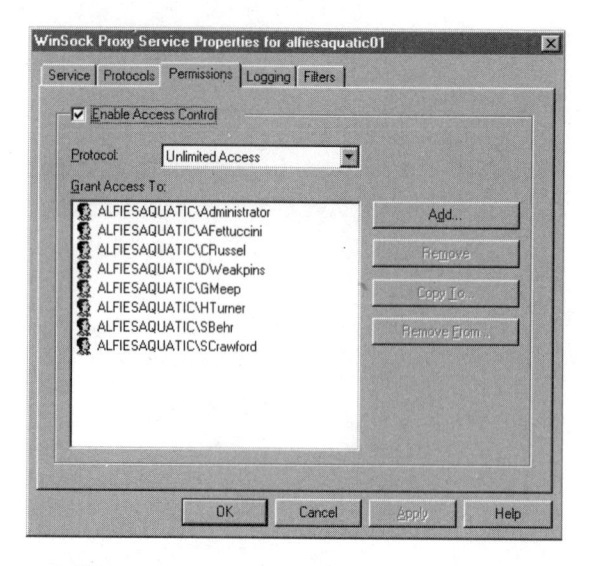

Try to make changes in user permissions via the Small Business Server console instead of on this tab.

Upgrading to Proxy Server 2

After Small Business Server was released, Microsoft released an update to Proxy Server that adds significant new functionality and is also substantially more robust, by all reports. Unfortunately, you have to buy it separately because it isn't (as yet) included in the price of Small Business Server.

Microsoft also offers a wizard that automatically handles the changes necessary in Small Business Server to support Proxy Server 2. You can download this wizard from the Microsoft Small Business web site at *backoffice.microsoft.com/DownTrial/Moreinfo/proxywizard.asp*, as shown in Figure 22.10.

When you're ready for the upgrade, download the wizard and run it. Try to run the wizard and the upgrade when there aren't any users on the system since you'll need to reboot the server a couple of times during the process. Once you start the wizard, you'll see the informational page shown in Figure 22.11. Click Finish, and the wizard will make the necessary changes to your configuration.

FIGURE 22.10

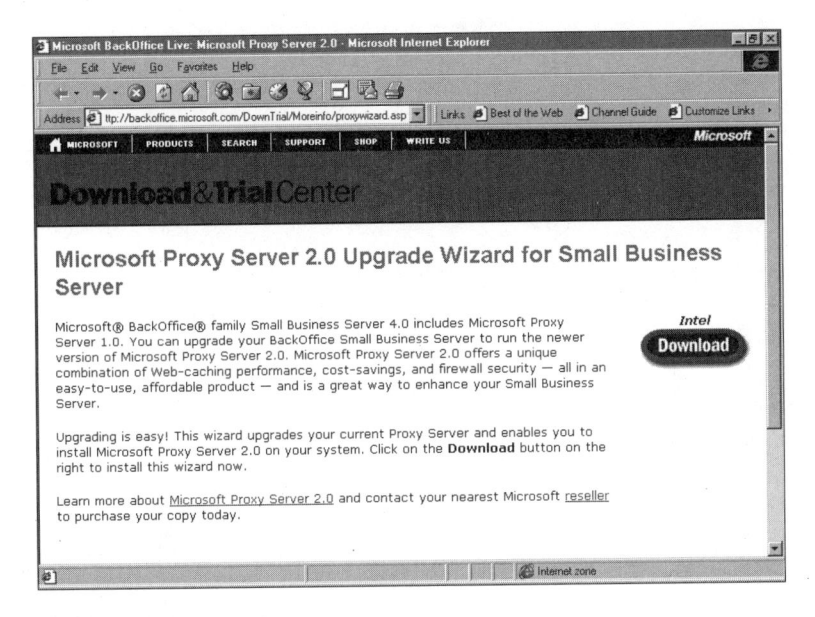

Microsoft offers a wizard that handles the reconfiguration of Small Business Server for Proxy Server 2.

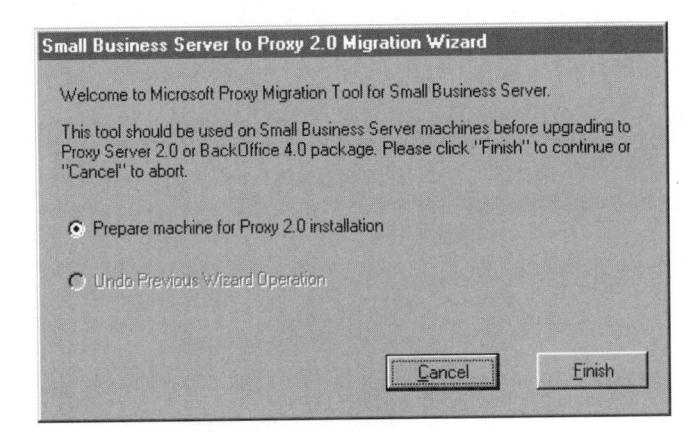

FIGURE 22.11

The wizard will automatically configure Small Business Server for you.

If all goes well, you'll see a confirmation page like that shown in Figure 22.12 on the following page. As indicated, you can find a detailed log file of all the changes in the "Windows" directory—which in most cases is WINNT.SBS.

CHAPTER 22 *Microsoft Proxy Server* **407**

FIGURE 22.12

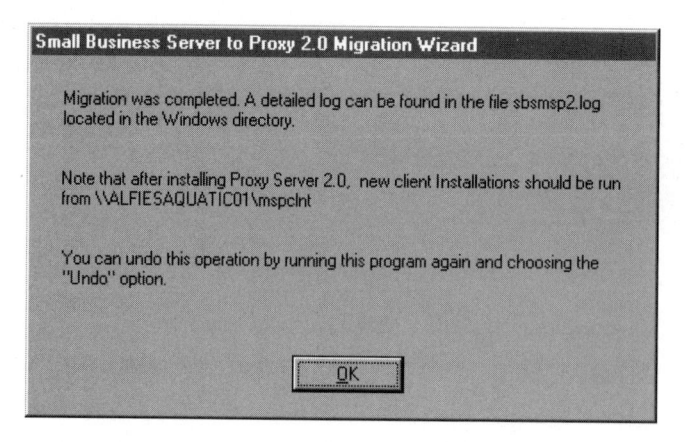

The wizard will confirm that everything went well.

Click OK, and you'll be offered an opportunity to reboot now or later. (In all cases, you have to reboot.) Your best bet is to reboot immediately since the job is only partially done. Once the system reboots, you're ready to do the actual Proxy Server upgrade.

Start the upgrade, accept the license agreement, enter the necessary CD key, and so forth. Eventually, you'll see a warning that an older version of Proxy Server is on your machine, as shown in Figure 22.13. You know that, of course, so accept the default folder and click OK.

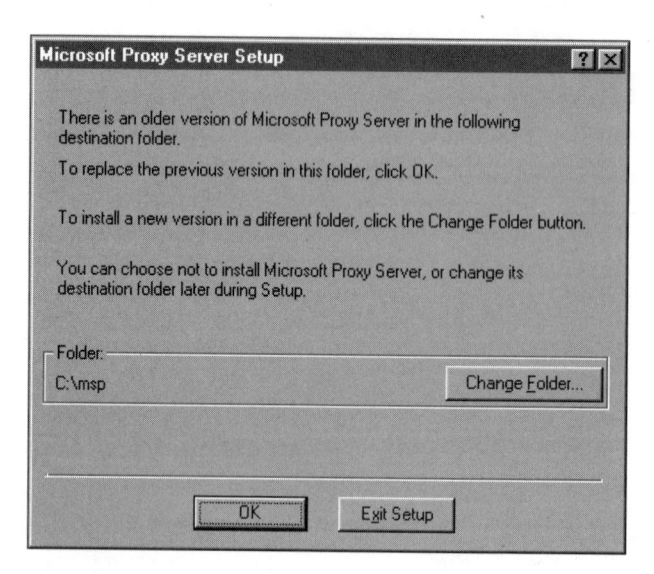

FIGURE 22.13

The Proxy Server upgrade will find your old version of Proxy Server.

Next you'll see the dialog box shown in Figure 22.14. Click the large button, and then click Continue in the next dialog box. Accept the defaults and install everything. The entire installation takes about 10 MB of disk space.

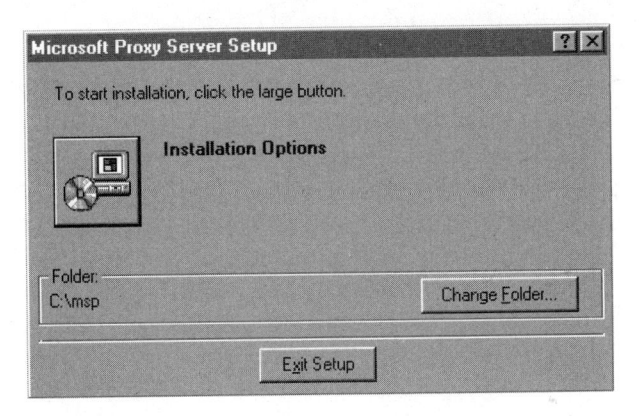

FIGURE 22.14

The Microsoft Proxy Server Setup dialog box.

The upgrade script will stop your current web services. If it detects that you have any of your old caching space on a FAT drive, it will warn you that the new version will not support FAT partitions for a cache, and then it will display the current caching locations, less the FAT partition it didn't like. Make any necessary adjustments, and click OK to move to the Local Address Table Configuration dialog box (Figure 22.15).

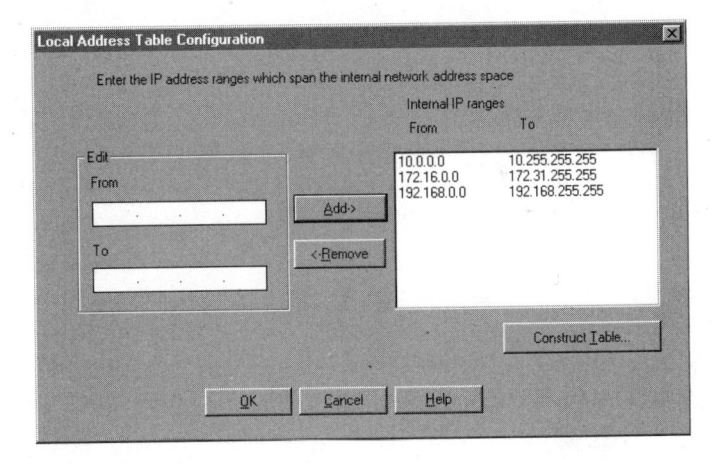

FIGURE 22.15

The default LAT should be fine for almost all Small Business Server installations.

We suggest that you refrain from trying to fine-tune the LAT. The default includes all of the private address ranges and should be fine for Small Business Server. Click OK to bring up the Client Installation/Configuration dialog box (Figure 22.16). Here you set how your clients are configured. The defaults should be fine for almost all installations (although you might want to change the Winsock Proxy Client portion to use the computer name rather than the IP address to connect to Proxy Server).

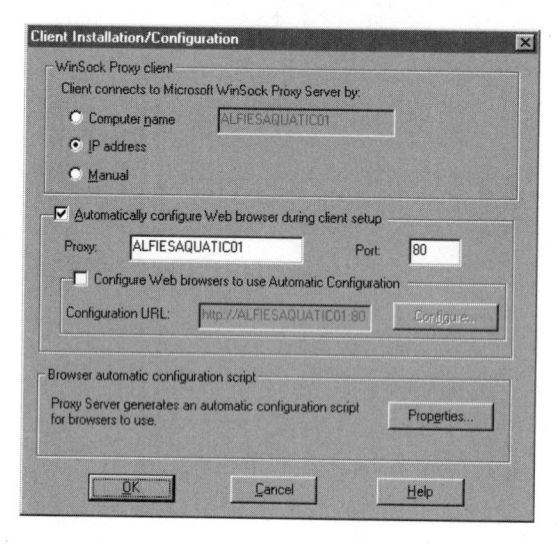

FIGURE 22.16

You configure your client in the Client Installation/Configuration dialog box.

Click OK to move to the Access Control dialog box. The default is to use access control for both the Winsock and web proxy clients. You should leave this as is since it allows Proxy Server to follow your setup preferences for which users should have access to the Internet. Click OK again to finish the installation process. When all is done, you'll see a message confirming that all the steps have worked as expected.

Your final task, after you reboot the server, is to install Proxy Client 2 on the server itself. From the Start menu, choose Programs, Microsoft Proxy Client, and then Setup. You'll see a warning message about an older version that asks for permission to overwrite it. Go ahead and overwrite it, and you'll be finished with your upgrade to Proxy Server 2 on the server. You'll also need to run the Proxy Client installation on each workstation to ensure that it has the correct version.

POINTS TO REMEMBER

- Microsoft Proxy Server translates the private addresses of your Small Business Server network into a single address that the Internet can accept, and it manages the connection to the Internet.

- Proxy Server includes both web clients and a special Winsock proxy client that enables client programs that use Windows sockets to connect through the proxy server successfully.

- You can upgrade to Proxy Server 2, but you must buy a separate license because the upgrade isn't included with Small Business Server.

WHAT'S NEXT

Now that we've covered Proxy Server, your gateway to the Internet, in the next chapter we'll cover the version of Crystal Reports that is included with Small Business Server. Crystal Reports comes with a wide variety of preconfigured reports that will help you monitor the health of your server and your network.

Chapter 23

Using Crystal Reports

- 414 The Sample Reports
- 416 Creating a Report from a Sample
- 418 Distributing Reports
  - Sending a Report to an Exchange Folder — 418
  - Sending a Report by E-Mail — 419
- 420 Points to Remember
- 420 What's Next

Chapter 23

Using Crystal Reports

Around the clock, Microsoft Windows NT Server, Microsoft Fax Server, Microsoft Exchange, and other components of Microsoft BackOffice Small Business Server quietly store away large quantities of information of every type. Some of it will be of interest to you. But even the interesting stuff is of limited value as raw data. What you need is a way to quickly convert the data into a useful form.

Crystal Reports, which comes with Small Business Server and is installed by default, is a sophisticated reporting tool. Because Crystal Reports can sort through great databases in a single bound, it is most suitable for creating the kinds of reports that the head honcho of General Motors needs. (If you need this sort of massive power, check the Help files for information on linking databases and configuring elaborate reports.) But fortunately, the Small Business Server version of Crystal Reports comes with sample reports that are useful in a smaller organization.

The Sample Reports

Table 23.01 describes the sample reports. Not all of them will be useful to everyone, but they're designed to be readable and as comprehensive as you want them to be.

NOTE

> You'll also find several reports based on information from the Microsoft Internet Information Server (IIS) log. In most small businesses, IIS is used only for serving the company's intranet. However, if you have a dedicated line and are using IIS as a server for your Internet web site, these reports can be useful. To see a list of these reports, from the Start menu choose Programs, Crystal Reports, and then Readme. In the Help window, click on Reports Included With Small Business Server, Small Business Server Reports, and then Display.

Table 23.01
Sample Reports

Report Title	Report Filename	Description
Event Detail Report – Application Log	ap010d.rpt	An unsorted list of all the fields in the Application Events Log
Event Detail Report – Security Log	se010d.rpt	An unsorted list of all the fields in the Security Events Log
Event Detail Report – System Log	sy010d.rpt	An unsorted list of all the fields in the System Events Log
Daily Message Tracking	exm03g.rpt	A report on the week's daily message traffic, including both local and non-local traffic
Server Summary	exm06g.rpt	A report on all message traffic on Exchange Server, including total messages, average message size, and maximum message size
Top N Message Receivers	exm09d.rpt	A report on top message receivers for the log days; includes total messages and average message size
Top N Message Senders	exm10d.rpt	A report on top message senders for the log days
Received Faxes Report	receive.rpt	A list of all received faxes, when they were received, their sizes, and the senders and recipients
Sent Faxes Report	sent.rpt	A list of all sent faxes, when they were sent, their sizes, and the senders and recipients
Received Faxes – Top Numbers	toprec.rpt	A list of the top fax receivers, the fax sizes, when they were received, and by whom
Sent Faxes – Top Numbers	topsent.rpt	A list of the top fax senders, the fax sizes, when they were sent, and to whom
Cache to Non-Cache Hits Comparison	cache.rpt	Cache and non-cache hit counts from the Microsoft Proxy Server log
Activity by Hour of the Day	hourly.rpt	A list and graph of Proxy Server hits by hour of the day
Top 10 Sites Hit	topsites.rpt	A list and graph of top 10 web sites, with hit count and percentage of hits for each site
Top 10 Users	topusers.rpt	A list and graph of top 10 users; includes number of hits, percentage of total hits, and total bytes received

Creating a Report from a Sample

Creating a report using actual data is a simple process. Here's how to do it:

1. From the Start menu, choose Programs, Crystal Reports, and then Crystal Reports again. You'll be asked to fill out a registration form. You can click Cancel and bypass the registration, but you'll be prompted to register every time you open Crystal Reports until you comply.

2. Choose Open from the File menu.

3. In the File Open dialog box, double-click on the Reports folder to see a list of sample reports. (See Figure 23.01.) (The Reports folder is in the Crw folder—the main Crystal Reports folder.)

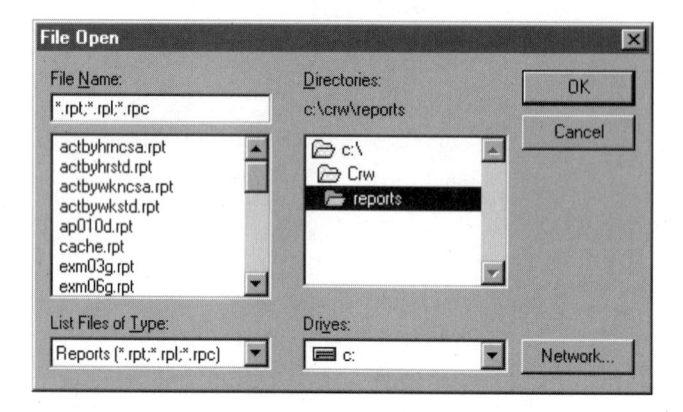

FIGURE 23.01
Double-click on the Reports folder to see a list of sample reports.

4. Select a report from the list. Click OK. The report will open in preview mode, as shown in Figure 23.02. At this point, there will be no actual data in the report.

5. To change elements in the design, click on the Design tab and right-click on any element to open a pop-up menu. You can do a great deal of formatting with this menu. After you make your changes, choose Refresh Report Data from the Report menu.

6. Click Yes in the confirmation dialog box that appears. You'll be asked to select the machine on which the information resides; with Small Business Server, it's always (LOCAL). Click OK.

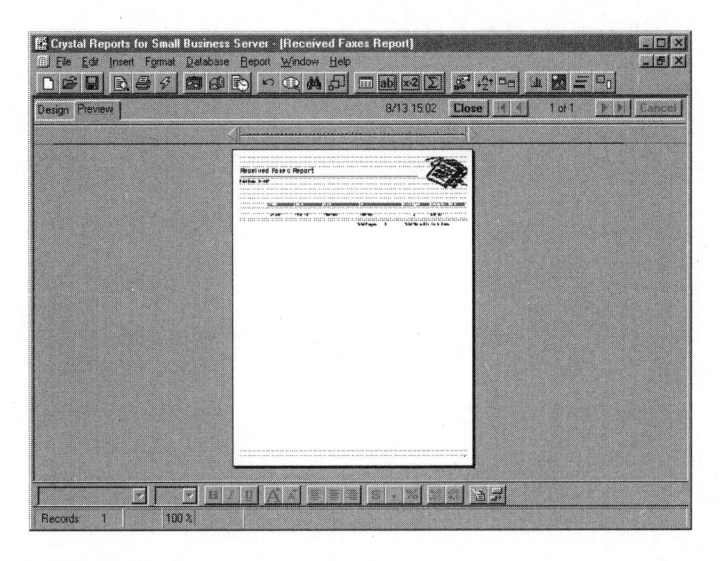

FIGURE 23.02
Previewing a sample report.

7. You'll see a preview of the report with actual data. Choose Zoom from the Report menu for a closer look. (See Figure 23.03.)

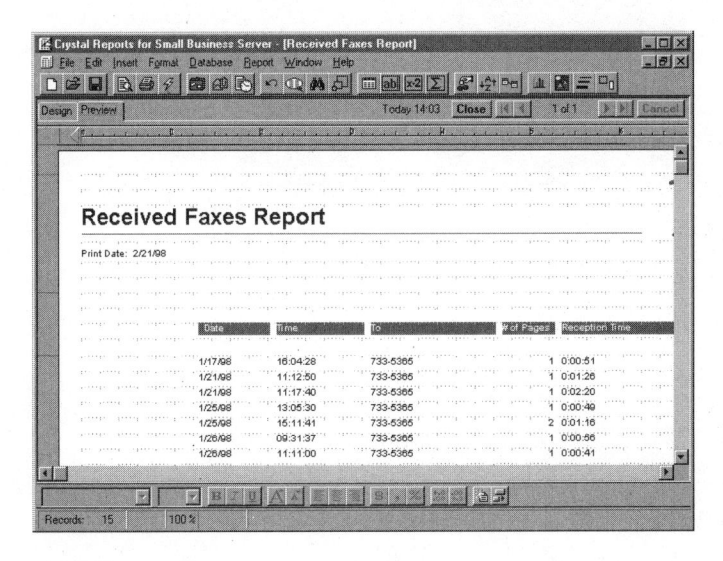

FIGURE 23.03
Choose the Zoom command to see the report in a readable size.

CHAPTER 23 *Using Crystal Reports* **417**

If you redesigned the report and want your changes to show up in future versions of the report, save the report as you would any other file. (Choose Save from the File menu.) The next time you open the report, all you have to do is refresh the data. To keep both the redesigned report and the original report, choose Save As from the File menu and specify a different name for the redesigned report.

Distributing Reports

You can always simply print a report and hand it to the person who needs it. Or, if you're the person who needs it, you can read the report on line and not print it at all. However, Crystal Reports provides other avenues for distribution.

Sending a Report to an Exchange Folder

To send a report to an Exchange folder, open the report in Crystal Reports and follow these steps:

1. From the File menu, choose Print and then Mail. In the Export dialog box (Figure 23.04), select the format you want from the Format drop-down list. (The choices include several varieties of Microsoft Excel, HTML, and plain text.)

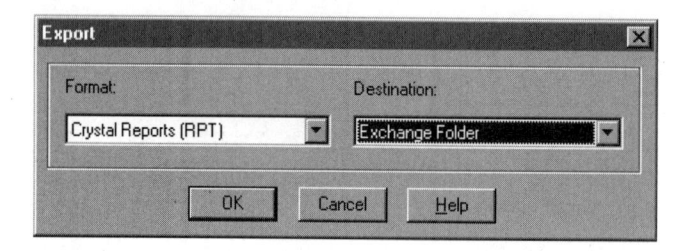

FIGURE 23.04

Selecting the report's format and destination.

2. Select Exchange Folder from the Destination drop-down list. Click OK.

3. Select a profile. (If the person you want to send the report to doesn't have a profile on the server, you can send the report by e-mail; see the next section.)

4. In the Select A Folder dialog box, click on the folder you want as the destination for the report, as shown in Figure 23.05. Click OK.

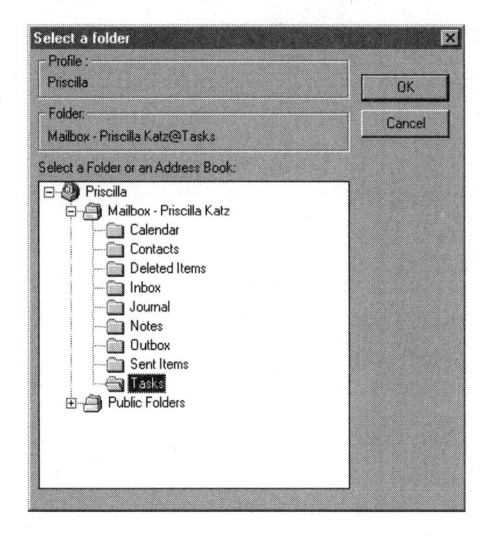

FIGURE 23.05

The report will be delivered to Priscilla Katz's Tasks folder.

Sending a Report by E-Mail

Sending a report by e-mail is much like delivering the report to an Exchange folder. With the report open in Crystal Reports, take these steps:

1. From the File menu, choose Print and then Mail.

2. In the Export dialog box, select the format you want from the Format drop-down list.

3. In the Destination drop-down list, select Microsoft Mail (MAPI). Click OK.

4. In the Send Mail dialog box that appears, type the name of the person you're sending the e-mail to. (If the person is in your Address Book, just type the first few letters and click Check Names, or click Address to see the full list.)

5. Provide a subject, and add a message if you want. (See Figure 23.06 on the following page.) Click Send to send the report and the e-mail message.

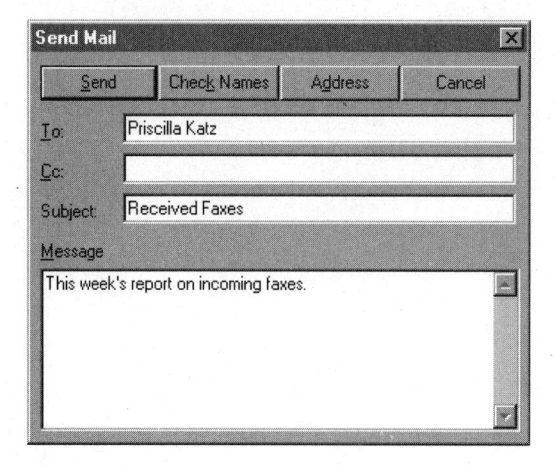

FIGURE 23.06

Attaching an e-mail message to the report.

POINTS TO REMEMBER

- Windows NT Server, Proxy Server, Microsoft Exchange Server, Internet Information Server, and Fax Server provide data for Crystal Reports.
- The sample reports that come with Small Business Server are adequate for most uses; you can modify them if they're not.
- You can print reports or distribute them electronically.

WHAT'S NEXT

In the next chapter, we'll move on to SQL Server, the relational database system that is included in Small Business Server.

Understanding SQL Server

Chapter 24

422	**What Is a Relational Database?**	
423	**Structured Query Language**	
	The SELECT Statement	423
	The UPDATE Statement	425
	The INSERT Statement	426
	The DELETE Statement	426
427	**Rules of Database Design**	
	Defining Primary Keys	427
	Rules of Normalization	428
	Retrieving Data from Multiple Tables	429
430	**Using SQL Server**	
	Creating a Database Device	432
	Creating a Database	434
	Creating a Table	435
	Adding Data to a Table	438
	Stored Procedures	438
	Triggers	440
441	**Administrative Tasks**	
	Managing Logins and Controlling Access	441
	Backups	442
	Scripting	444
445	**Other SQL Server Tools**	
	MS Query	445
	SQL Performance Monitor	446
	SQL Security Manager	446
	SQL Server Web Assistant	446
	SQL Service Manager	446
	SQL Trace	447
448	**User Interface**	
448	**Points to Remember**	
448	**What's Next**	

Chapter 24
Understanding SQL Server

Microsoft SQL Server 6.5, which comes with Microsoft BackOffice Small Business Server, is a relational database system that can handle all your database information storage and retrieval needs. (SQL, which is pronounced "sequel," stands for Structured Query Language.) With SQL Server as a database, you can enter the information once and then access it many times from multiple applications.

You might have heard that databases are hard to understand and use. As you'll see in this chapter, that's something of an exaggeration. Databases, and in particular SQL Server databases, are easy to understand and use. Although SQL Server is a high-powered system, there's no reason why you can't use it in a small business setting. The key to using SQL Server in a smaller enterprise is to keep your use of it as simple as possible. Don't add extra layers of security, and keep your databases *basic*.

What Is a Relational Database?

A *relational database* stores information in tables. Each table is made up of rows and columns, very much like a spreadsheet. Each row represents a *record*, and each column represents an item of data called a *field*. For example, to create a table of names and phone numbers for a phone list, you'd probably want to store each person's first name, last name, and phone number as shown in Table 24.01.

Table 24.01
The Phone_List Table

First_Name	Last_Name	Phone_Number
Sam	Jones	555-1234
Fred	Smith	444-4321
Tom	Peters	222-7654

Each column contains one type of data, such as first name, and each row represents one record in the table.

One important concept to understand from the beginning is that in a relational database, the rows in a table are in no particular order. They are usually in the order that the data was added to the table. When you retrieve information from the table, you do not do so by record number or row number. The order of the rows is of no importance. You retrieve information by asking questions, or querying.

Structured Query Language

If you were Mr. Spock on the starship *Enterprise* and you wanted to retrieve information from the computer, you would ask it a question such as, "Computer, what is Tom's phone number?"

With SQL Server, you use a similar approach. You pose the question using the SQL language. With a table named Phone_List, your question in SQL would be:

```
SELECT Phone_Number FROM Phone_List WHERE First_Name = 'Tom'
```

The answer, or *results set*, from the computer using SQL Server is 222-7654. We'll examine the syntax in detail later in this chapter. The important thing to notice is that the query is easy to read and understand.

You use four basic kinds of SQL statements to work with data in a database: the SELECT, UPDATE, INSERT, and DELETE statements. They belong to the part of the SQL language called the Data Manipulation Language, or DML. Another part of the SQL language, the Data Definition Language (DDL), is used to define and change the structure of the database—for example, to add a table to a database schema or to add a column to a table.

Understanding the syntax of these SQL statements is the key to using a relational database. The syntax is very logical and close to spoken English. You can easily learn to read SQL.

The SELECT Statement

Use the SELECT statement to retrieve data from a database table. The basic SELECT statement syntax is:

```
SELECT ColumnList FROM TableName [WHERE TestCondition] [ORDER BY ColumnName]
```

SELECT tells the database engine (as the database software is called) that information should be retrieved from the database. Next, the columns of information to retrieve are listed in the order in which they should be displayed. This does not have to be the same order in which they are stored in the table. If you want to retrieve all the columns in the table in the order in which they are stored, you can substitute an asterisk (*) or the word ALL for the names of the columns. FROM tells the database engine that what follows is the name of the database table. This is the minimum required for a valid SELECT statement.

For example,

```
SELECT * FROM Phone_List
```

is a legal SELECT statement that returns the entire table in the order in which it is stored; the columns will be retrieved in the order in which they are stored. The results set of this query for the table shown earlier is:

First_Name	Last_Name	Phone_Number
Sam	Jones	555-1234
Fred	Smith	444-4321
Tom	Peters	222-7654

If the columns are named, they will be displayed in the order listed in the SELECT statement. For example, the following statement

```
SELECT Last_Name, Phone_Number, First_Name FROM Phone_List
```

yields this results set:

Last_Name	Phone_Number	First_Name
Jones	555-1234	Sam
Smith	444-4321	Fred
Peters	222-7654	Tom

Adding an ORDER BY clause causes the results set to be sorted. This SELECT statement

```
SELECT Last_Name, Phone_Number, First_Name FROM Phone_List ORDER
BY First_Name
```

produces this results set:

Last_Name	Phone_Number	First_Name
Smith	444-4321	Fred
Jones	555-1234	Sam
Peters	222-7654	Tom

The WHERE clause filters the data to limit the results set. This SQL statement

```
SELECT * FROM Phone_List WHERE Last_Name LIKE 'P%'
```

yields this results set:

First_Name	Last_Name	Phone_Number
Tom	Peters	222-7654

In this example, the test condition uses the logical operator LIKE. The test condition 'P%' uses the wildcard character %. If the test condition is '%P%', any row with the letter *P* anywhere in the Last_Name column is returned.

The UPDATE Statement

An UPDATE statement is used to change the data in an existing record. The syntax is simple and straightforward:

```
UPDATE TableName SET ColumnName1 = Value1, ColumnName2 = Value2
WHERE ColumnName = TestCondition
```

The WHERE clause is very important in the UPDATE statement. Without the WHERE clause to specify the records to be changed, all the records in the table will be changed. For example,

```
UPDATE Phone_List SET First_Name = 'George'
```

changes the first name in all records to George. After this change, the table looks like this:

First_Name	Last_Name	Phone_Number
George	Jones	555-1234
George	Smith	444-4321
George	Peters	222-7654

To change only the record with the last name of Jones, you use this UPDATE statement:

```
UPDATE Phone_List SET First_Name = 'George' WHERE Last_Name = 'Jones'
```

The resulting table is:

First_Name	Last_Name	Phone_Number
George	Jones	555-1234
Fred	Smith	444-4321
Tom	Peters	222-7654

The INSERT Statement

The INSERT statement is used to add a new record to the table. The syntax is:

```
INSERT INTO TableName (ColumnName1, ColumnName2)
VALUES ('Value1', 'Value2')
```

A WHERE clause is never required in an INSERT statement because there is no existing record to be identified, only a new record. For example, to add a new record to the phone list, you use this statement:

```
INSERT INTO Phone_List (First_Name, Last_Name, Phone_Number)
VALUES ('George', 'Washington', '999-8765')
```

Here are the resulting records:

First_Name	Last_Name	Phone_Number
George	Jones	555-1234
Fred	Smith	444-4321
Tom	Peters	222-7654
George	Washington	999-8765

The DELETE Statement

The DELETE statement is very simple and should be used carefully because it can clear all of the data from a table if you don't use it properly. The key point to remember is that a DELETE statement without a WHERE clause deletes all of the records in a table. The syntax is:

```
DELETE TableName WHERE ColumnName = TestCondition
```

The following DELETE statement

```
DELETE Phone_List WHERE First_Name = 'Tom'
```

results in a table with the following records:

First_Name	Last_Name	Phone_Number
George	Jones	555-1234
Fred	Smith	444-4321
George	Washington	999-8765

Rules of Database Design

You must understand certain database design guidelines to use a relational database system such as SQL Server. The following sections provide a brief introduction. The information presented here won't make you an expert in the use of SQL Server, but it should get you started. You can spend many hours learning the ins and outs of using a relational database. Knowledge of SQL will apply to any relational database.

Defining Primary Keys

Each row of a table must be unique so that it can be distinguished by a SQL statement. If an update is to be performed, the record must be identifiable. Because relational database tables don't have "record numbers," you cannot identify a row by number—for example, you cannot specify that you want to update the 10th record. A row must contain some value, or combination of values, that distinguishes it from all other rows. This value is known as the *primary key*.

In a table of personnel records, for example, names don't work as the primary key because names are often duplicated. In a large enough database, just about every last name will be duplicated.

First names pose the same problem because in any sizable group, you're likely to have, for example, at least two Jennifers or two Bobs. Using both first and last names is an improvement, but it still doesn't guarantee uniqueness. One unique property that everyone over the age of two in the United States has in common is a Social Security number (SSN). If the SSN is included in the table, each record is unique because no two people share the same SSN. To update a record, you can use the SSN in the WHERE clause of the UPDATE statement; only one record will be affected. The SSN is thus the primary key for the table.

Table 24.02 shows the Phone_List table with SSNs added.

Table 24.02
The Phone_List Table with an SSN Field Added

SSN	First_Name	Last_Name	Phone_Number
222-32-9876	Sam	Jones	555-1234
321-12-3456	Fred	Smith	444-4321
987-65-4321	Tom	Peters	222-7654

> **Tip**
>
> *You can add columns even after a table is in use by an application because columns are retrieved by column name.*

Rules of Normalization

The rules of normalization are a set of rules based on the work of E. F. Codd, who came up with the idea of relational databases nearly 30 years ago. Using these rules reduces the redundancy of data and ensures that database tables function as you expect them to.

First normal form

The first normal form is the foundation of the relational database system. A table is in the first normal form when the values in each column are *atomic*—which means that each column contains only one value. For example, the Phone_Number column is atomic because it contains one, and only one, phone number per field.

Second normal form

A table is in the second normal form when it does three things: It complies with the first normal form, every column is dependent on the primary key, and each row is unique. The primary key is the column or group of columns that make each row unique. A column depends on the primary key if it describes the subject of the table.

Third normal form

To be in the third normal form, a table must first comply with the first normal form and the second normal form. In addition, the columns must describe the primary key or subject of the table and relate only to the primary key or subject of the table and not to the primary key of any other table.

Retrieving Data from Multiple Tables

If the database contains other tables that relate to the individuals whose phone numbers and names are in the Phone_List table (such as a list of phone calls to or from each individual), the name information need not be in the second table because that information exists in another table. A second table, which we'll call the Call_List table, needs to contain only the date and time of the call and the reason for the call. The table can be designed as shown in Table 24.03. In this table, the Date_Time column is the primary key. The SSN column serves as a *foreign key* because it is the primary key of another table and allows the information to be retrieved from two tables. The SSN column relates the two tables.

Table 24.03
The Call_List Table

Date_Time	SSN	Reason_For_Call
1998-02-04 13:12	222-32-9876	Confirm appointment
1998-02-04 14:23	222-32-9876	Cancel appointment
1998-02-04 15:09	987-65-4321	Invite to dinner

To retrieve information about calls made to Tom Peters, you use a SELECT statement that performs a JOIN:

```
SELECT First_Name, Last_Name, Date_Time, Reason_For_Call
FROM Phone_List, Call_List WHERE SSN.Phone_List = SSN.Call_List
AND First_Name = 'Tom'
```

The results set of this statement is:

First_Name	Last_Name	Date_Time	Reason For Call
Tom	Peters	1998-02-04 15:09	Invite to dinner

Using SQL Server

When SQL Server is installed as part of the Small Business Server, it won't automatically start when the server starts. So the first order of business is to start SQL Server. From the Start menu, choose Programs, Microsoft SQL Server 6.5, and then SQL Enterprise Manager. The SQL Enterprise Manager main window will appear, as shown in Figure 24.01.

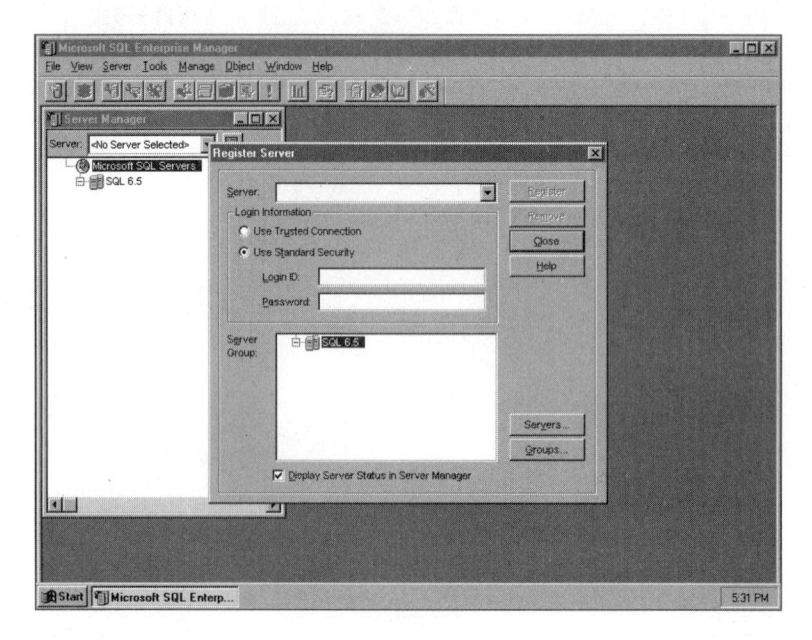

FIGURE 24.01

The server must be registered before it will start.

> **Tip**
>
> SQL Server includes a database named pubs. Its sole purpose is for testing procedures and techniques. (The pubs database is well known among SQL Server users.) Testing is helpful because many actions are irreversible in SQL Server. The world of databases has no Undo button.

In the Register Server dialog box, type the server name in the Server text box. Select the Use Trusted Connection option, and then click the Register button. In the message box that appears, click Yes. Close the Register Server dialog box, and then close the Tip Of The Day dialog box that appears. You'll now see the server name listed in the Server Manager window, as shown in Figure 24.02. The red light on the stoplight icon indicates that SQL Server is not running.

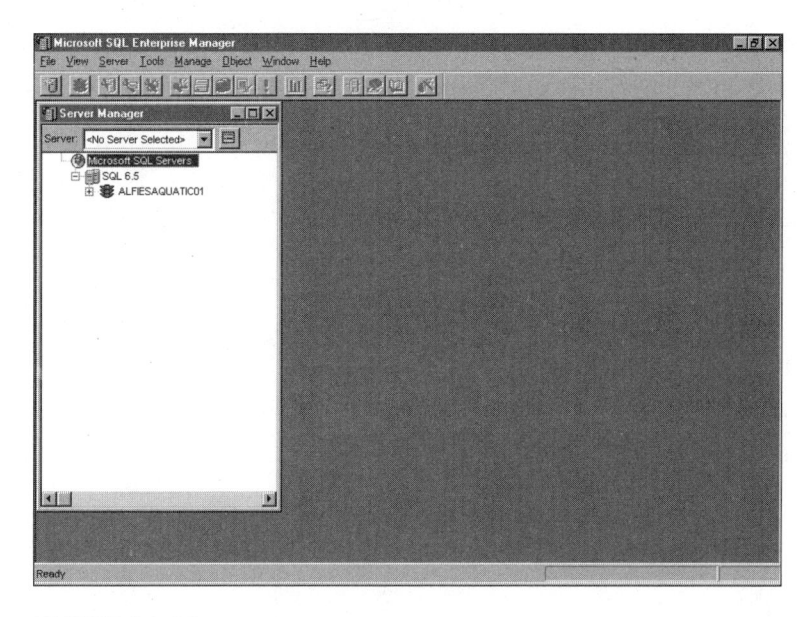

FIGURE 24.02

The stoplight icon indicates whether SQL Server is running.

Right-click on the server name, and choose Start from the pop-up menu. The stoplight icon will show a green light to indicate that SQL Server is running.

Click on the expand symbol, or plus sign (+), to the left of the SQL Server icon to open the following list:

- SQL Mail
- SQL Executive
- Distributed Transaction Coordinator
- Database Devices
- Backup Devices
- Databases
- Logins

SQL Mail, SQL Executive, and Distributed Transaction Coordinator will have red lights on their icons, indicating that those services are not running. Right-click on each item, and choose Start from the pop-up menu for each item.

CHAPTER 24 *Understanding SQL Server* **431**

To set these services to start automatically at bootup, from the Server menu in the SQL Enterprise Manager choose SQL Server and then Configure. In the Server Configuration/Options dialog box (shown in Figure 24.03), select both Auto Start check boxes.

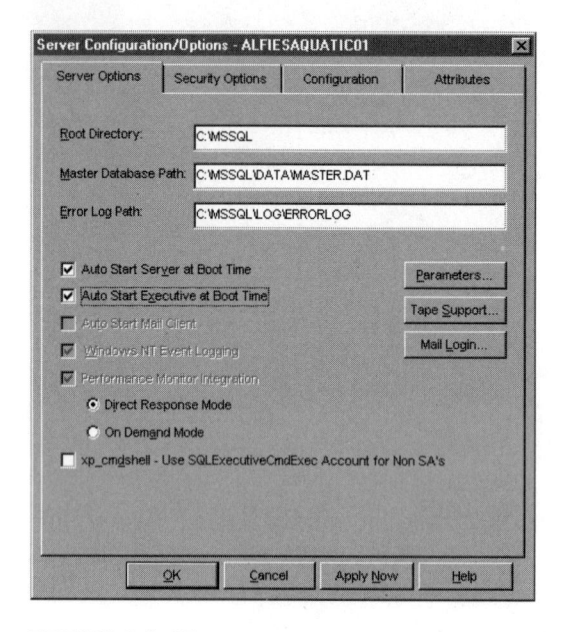

FIGURE 24.03

You can control the startup settings for all services in this dialog box.

Creating a Database Device

SQL Server databases are physically stored in a file called a *database device*. Such files have a .dat extension and are in the C:\Mssql\Data folder. After you install SQL Server, three of these devices will be in the C:\Mssql\Data folder. You can see all three—master.dat, msdb.dat, and msdblog.dat—by clicking the plus sign next to the Database Devices object in the Server Manager window. (See Figure 24.04.)

It's good practice to keep each database in a separate database device. This will give you greater control over the placement of the database for security purposes. To create a database device, right-click on the Database Device object in the SQL Server tree and choose New Device from the pop-up menu. The New Database Device dialog box will open, as shown in Figure 24.05. Type a meaningful name for the database device. The name will be entered automatically in the Location path.

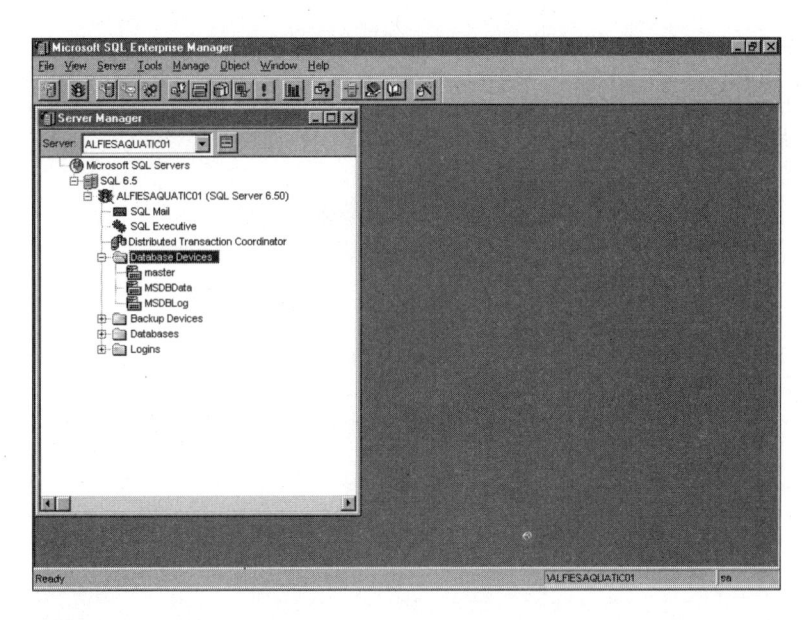

FIGURE 24.04

When you click the plus sign next to Database Devices, the list opens.

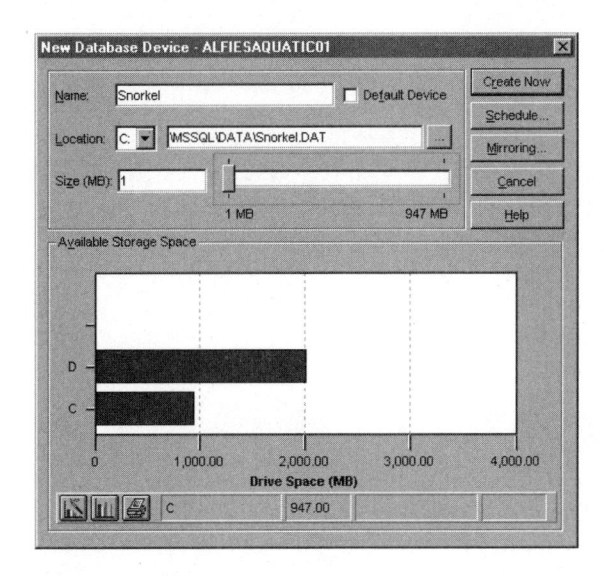

FIGURE 24.05

Creating a new database device.

CHAPTER 24 *Understanding SQL Server* **433**

You must also enter a size, in megabytes, for the database device. As shown in Figure 24.06, you can specify a different location using the Location drop-down list to select another drive. Use the Size slider to set the database device size. The size you specify will be shown graphically in the Available Storage Space section.

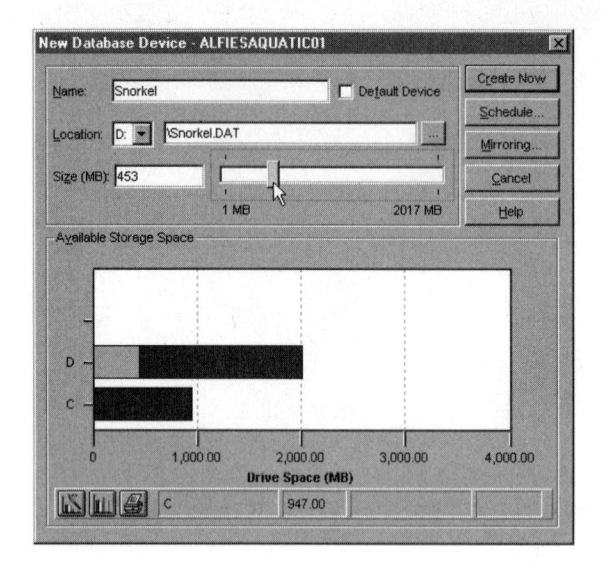

FIGURE 24.06
You can adjust the location and size of the new database device.

After you enter the necessary information, click the Create Now button. A message box will appear stating that the database device was successfully created. Back in the SQL Server tree, the new device will be added to the list, as shown here:

```
Database Devices
    master
    MSDBData
    MSDBLog
    Snorkel
```

Creating a Database

To create a database, right-click on Databases in the tree and choose New Database from the pop-up menu. In the New Database dialog box (shown in Figure 24.07), type a name for the database. From the Data Device drop-down list, select the database device that will house the database.

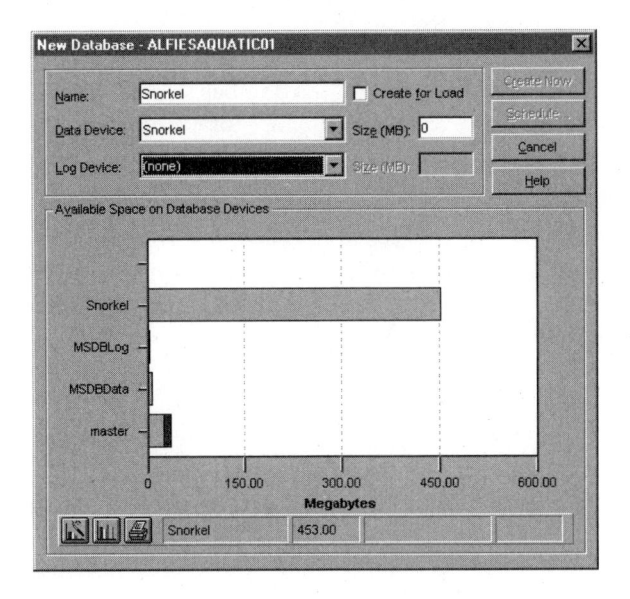

FIGURE 24.07

You must specify a database name and a device to contain the database.

> **Tip**
>
> When you select (None) as the Log Device, the database log will share the database device with the database. It's usually better to separate the two.

Click the Create Now button, and the database will be created. The list of databases will be displayed in the SQL Server tree.

Creating a Table

To create a table, click on the plus sign next to the name of the database in the SQL Server tree. Expand the Objects folder by clicking on the plus sign; then right-click on Table and choose New Table from the pop-up menu, as shown here:

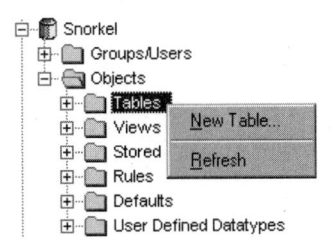

In the Manage Tables window, you can enter seven items of information for each data column in the table, as detailed in the following sections.

Column name

The column name must comply with the SQL Server rules for identifiers. Identifiers can have from 1 to 30 characters. The first character can be an alphabetic character (a-z or A-Z) or the symbols _ (underscore), @ (at), or # (pound). An identifier beginning with @ denotes a variable. An identifier beginning with # denotes a temporary object, either a table or a procedure. After the first character, identifiers can include letters, digits, or the $, #, or _ symbols. It's useful to give a column a descriptive name to make the database understandable to others who will need to work with it.

Datatype

Datatype specifies the category of data—for example, number, characters, or date. The system supplies 20 datatypes. These are divided into several subcategories. SQL Server is strongly typed. So, for example, any attempt to enter characters in an integer field will produce an error.

Datatypes come in five categories:

- **Exact numeric** Includes the decimal and numeric types.
- **Approximate numeric** Includes the float type and the real type.
- **Integer** Consists of the integer, short integer, and tiny integer types.
- **Character data** Includes the char type, which is of fixed length, and varchar, which is of variable length and has a maximum length.
- **Datetime** The date and time, ranging from the year to the second.

Size

The Size column is not used for some datatypes. A char or varchar type requires a length in bytes. The decimal type requires a precision and scale value. The precision is the total number of digits that will be in the number, and the scale is the number of digits to the right of the decimal place. For example, the number 1234.567 has a precision of 7 and a scale of 3.

Nulls

The Nulls column determines whether the column can contain NULLs. A NULL is not a zero-length string or an empty column. It is logically an indeterminate value. NULLs should be allowed but should be used with caution and understanding, and only when blank values are truly required.

Default

In the Default column, you can specify a default value if no value is supplied with an INSERT statement. For example, if you want today's date to be entered in a datetime column when a record is created, you enter the default value of getdate(), which calls a SQL Server function that gets the system date and time. Or you can enter the value 'New York City' as the default city name in an address field.

Key

The Key column is used to show that the column is the primary key for the table. Click the Advanced Features button (the button sporting a green cross), and then select the column for the primary key.

Identity

The value of the Identity column is assigned by the SQL Server database engine. When a new row is added, SQL Server assigns the record the next sequential number. The Identity column can also be set using the advanced functions. There can be only one Identity column in each table. The datatype for an identity must be integer. The numbers assigned are determined by the setting for *seed* and *increment*. Seed is the first or starting number, and increment is the distance between two numbers. A seed of 1 and an increment of 1, which are the defaults, result in records being numbered, 1, 2, 3, and so on. A seed of 10 and an increment of 3 result in numbers of 10, 13, 16, 19, and so on.

After you add all the columns, click the Save button (the one with the floppy disk icon). You will be asked to give the table a name and to save the table. Figure 24.08 on the following page shows a table that is ready to be saved. The last step before saving a table is to name it.

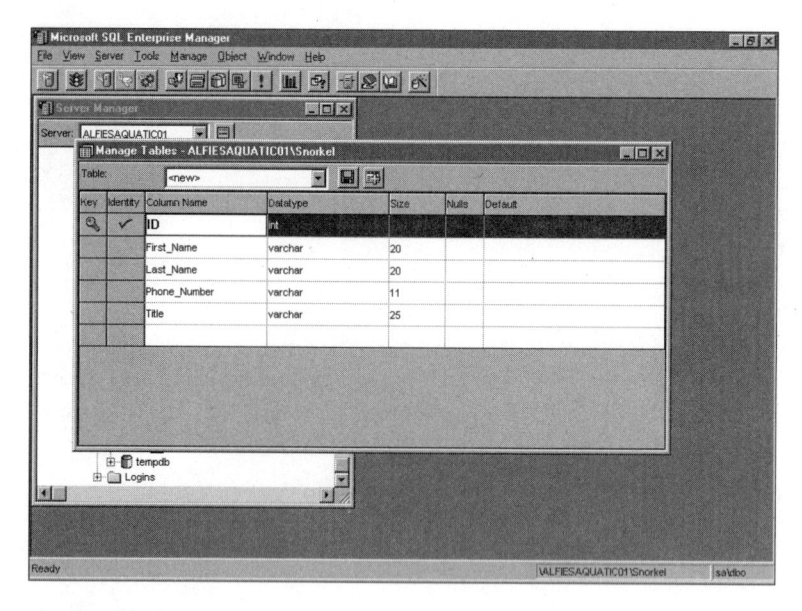

FIGURE 24.08

A table that is ready to be saved.

Adding Data to a Table

You can add data to a table by using the SQL Query Tool. In SQL Enterprise Manager, choose SQL Query Tool from the Tools menu. Figure 24.09 shows the ISQL window with an INSERT statement ready to be executed. The button with the right-pointing green arrow executes the SQL statement.

Stored Procedures

One of the most useful tools that SQL Server provides is the *stored procedure*. A stored procedure is a set of SQL statements that is treated as a code block and given a name. The set can be executed by name at the server. You can also pass parameters to the stored procedure for use during execution. To create a stored procedure, right-click on the Stored Procedures object in the database that will contain the stored procedure and then choose New Stored Procedure from the pop-up menu. The Manage Stored Procedures window will open, as shown in Figure 24.10.

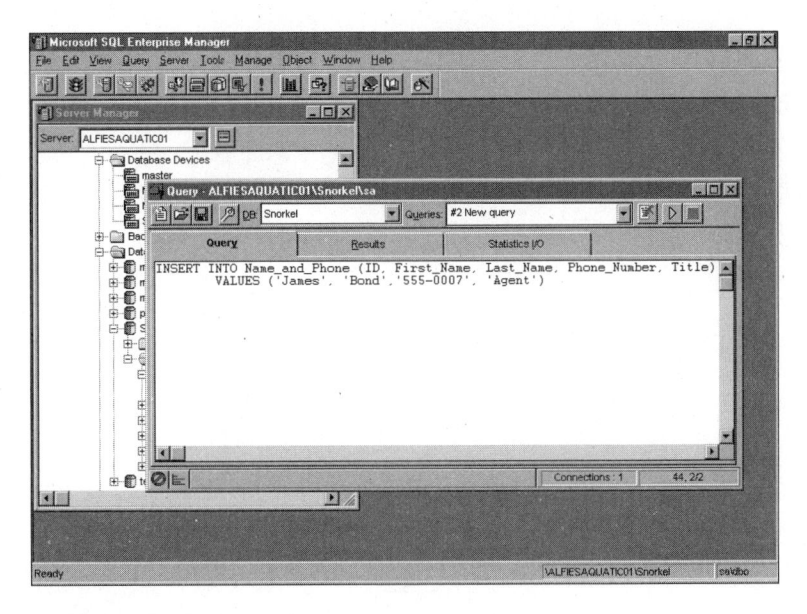

FIGURE 24.09
Adding data with the SQL Query Tool.

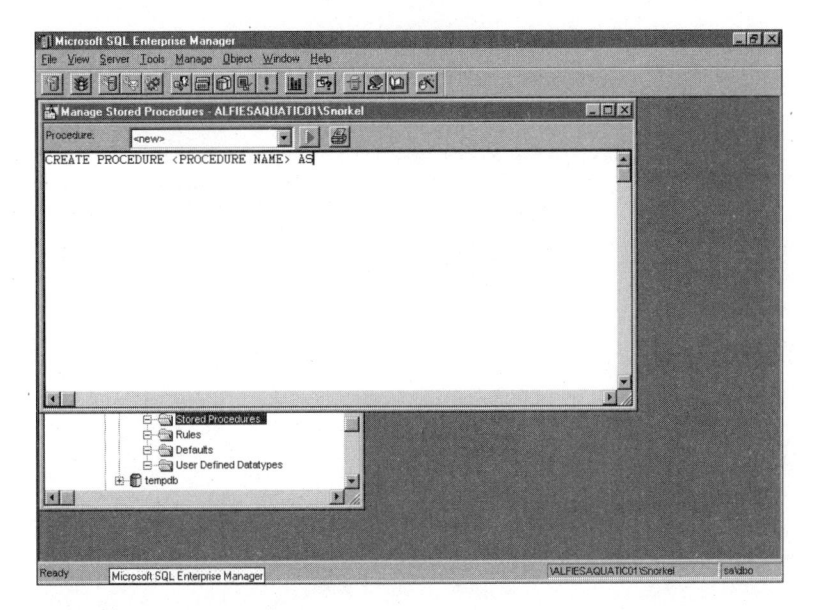

FIGURE 24.10
Creating a stored procedure.

CHAPTER 24 *Understanding SQL Server* **439**

This stored procedure

```
CREATE PROCEDURE MyUpdate (@id int, @fname char(20)) AS

BEGIN
UPDATE Phone_List SET First_Name = @fname WHERE ID = @id
SELECT * FROM Phone_List
END
GO
```

is executed when the SQL statement

```
MyUpdate 3, 'Ralph'
```

is executed through the SQL Query Tool. The results set from the execution of this stored procedure is:

ID	First_Name	Last_Name	Phone_Number	SSN
1	Sam	Jones	555-1234	222-32-9876
2	Fred	Smith	444-4321	321-12-3456
3	Ralph	Peters	222-7654	987-65-4321

(3 row(s) affected)

The first line of the stored procedure names the stored procedure and declares the variables that must be passed when the procedure is executed. Variables in SQL Server have @ as the first character. When a variable name begins with @@, it is a global variable. BEGIN and END mark a code block, which means that everything between BEGIN and END is executed together. The two SQL statements in the code block are standard SQL statements. GO is a command to SQL Server to execute the lines of code that it has just read.

Stored procedures can be very long and involved. They are a powerful tool for enhancing database performance.

Triggers

A *trigger* is a special type of stored procedure that is attached to a table and used to ensure database integrity. An example of an integrity issue: You have a database of all of the employees in a company, and the database contains two tables. The first contains information about employees, and the second contains information about employees' families. If a record is deleted from the Employee table, you will need to delete all records from the Family table that are associated with the employee record. You can set a trigger on the delete action of the Employee table to execute a stored procedure that deletes the associated records from the Family table. To do this, you choose Triggers from the Manage menu in SQL Enterprise Manager.

Administrative Tasks

Administering a database is not difficult, but it does require some planning. The primary goal of the database administrator is to control access to the database and to protect the database against corruption and loss of data. The two keys to effective database administration are to identify the risks and to create a plan to deal with those risks. A recovery plan is also essential for when the database is damaged or lost. The job of the database administrator is to ensure that the plan is followed.

Managing Logins and Controlling Access

You control access to SQL Server databases through the permissions that are granted to users based on their login name and password. To create a new login name, choose Logins from the Manage menu in SQL Enterprise Manager. The Manage Logins dialog box (shown in Figure 24.11) will appear.

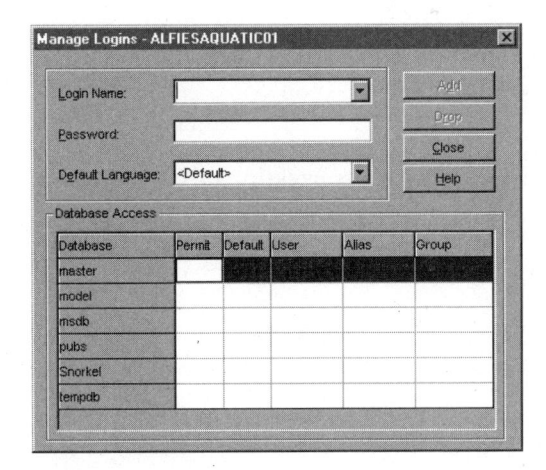

FIGURE 24.11

Creating a new login name.

When you create a login name, you can grant it access to a particular database. You grant specific permissions at the object level, which means a table or a stored procedure. You can grant permission to select, update, insert, or delete records in a table. The default permission for a stored procedure is EXECUTE. To set these permissions, select a database in the SQL Server tree and choose Permissions from the Object menu in SQL Enterprise Manager. In the Object Permissions dialog box (shown in Figure 24.12 on the following page), you can set permissions at the column level as required.

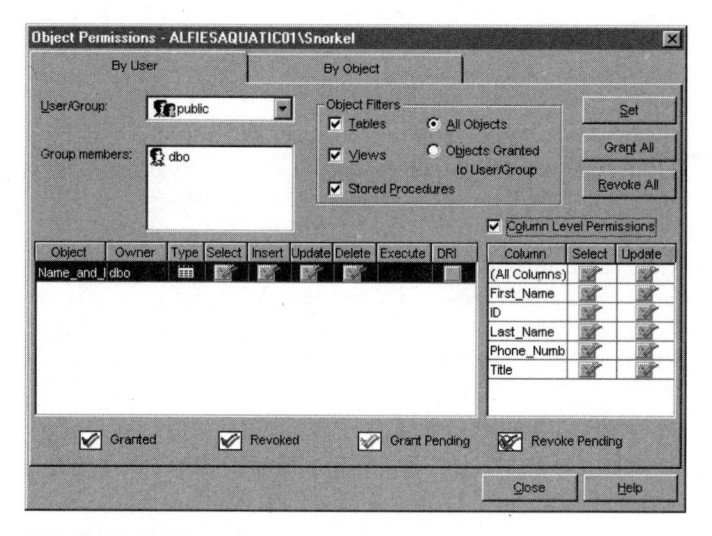

FIGURE 24.12

You can view and manage permissions by user or by object.

Backups

Backups are an important part of managing database security. There are three basic types of backups:

- Full—the entire database is copied to a backup object.
- Differential—all of the changes since that last full backup are copied.
- Incremental—all of the changes since the last full backup or incremental backup are copied.

In SQL Server databases, incremental and differential backups are accomplished through use of the logs. When a change is made to a SQL Server database, the change is captured in a log. A plan to back up a large database might consist of making a full backup each weekend and saving the logs nightly. If the database is damaged, the full backup can be restored and then all the logs since the last full backup can be applied. In the case of nightly backups, if the database is damaged at 10:00 A.M., you have an excellent chance of recovering all of the changes up to a time very near to 10:00 A.M.

A good disaster recovery plan includes storage of backups on a separate system and perhaps even at a different site. Creating a good plan involves a game of "what if" and anticipates possible disasters. Remember that these plans are for *when* a disaster happens, not *if*. There are no computers that *never* go down.

Before you can back up a database, you must first create a backup device. Right-click on Backup Devices in the SQL Server tree, and choose New Backup Device.

Type a name for the backup device in the dialog box that appears, as shown in Figure 24.13.

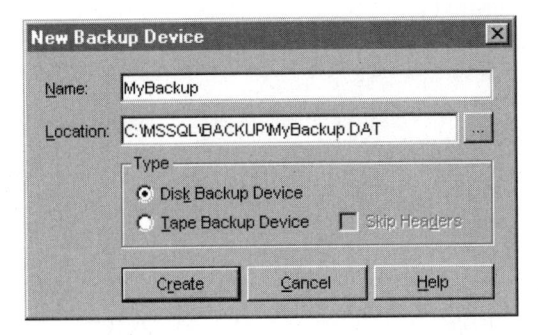

FIGURE 24.13
The default location for the backup device is C:\Mssql\Backup.

To back up the database, from the Tools menu choose Database Backup/Restore. On the Backup tab of the Database Backup/Restore dialog box, select the database and backup device, as shown in Figure 24.14, and click the Backup Now button to perform the backup.

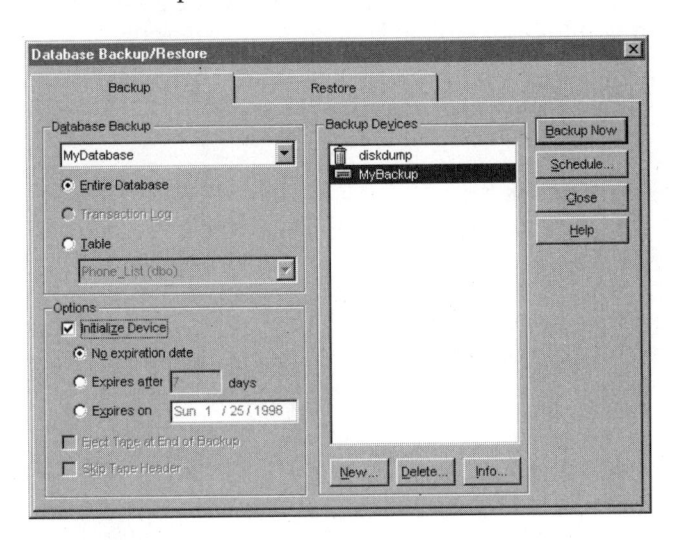

FIGURE 24.14
Backing up a database.

> **Tip**
>
> *Before using a new backup device, you must initialize it.*

CHAPTER 24 *Understanding SQL Server* **443**

To restore a database, from the Tools menu choose Database Backup/Restore. On the Restore tab of the Database Backup/Restore dialog box, you'll see a list of available backups that can be applied.

> **Tip**
>
> *Most database administrators retain several generations of backups. If a table is damaged, it might be necessary to go back to a time when the table was still good to begin the recovery process. Having the most current backup is no guarantee that you can recover everything.*

Scripting

Scripting is the process of creating a test file of SQL statements that, when run, will create all the tables, users, and other objects that constitute a database. The script will capture the complete structure of the database. The script can then be run with the SQL Query tool to rebuild the database structure.

To script a database, select the database in the SQL Server tree and then choose Generate SQL Scripts from the Object menu in SQL Enterprise Manager. In the dialog box that appears, select the options that you want for your script, as shown in Figure 24.15, and then click the Script button. You will be asked for a location in which to save the script file. The file will have a .sql extension.

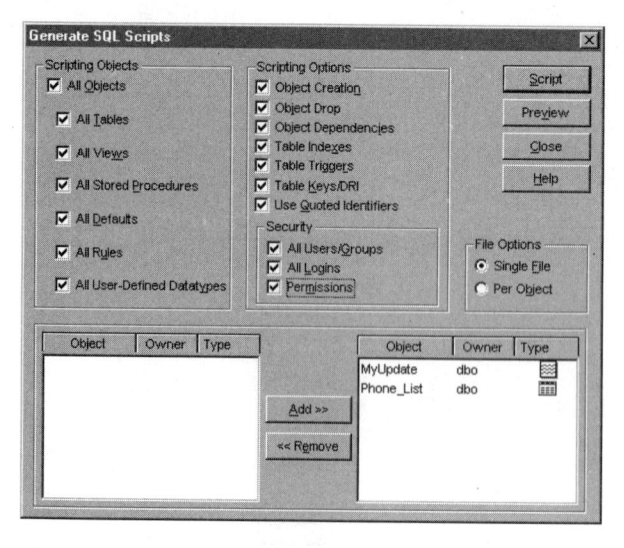

FIGURE 24.15

Setting options for scripting.

Other SQL Server Tools

A whole set of tools is included with SQL Server. In the next sections, we'll briefly describe each.

MS Query

MS Query helps write SQL statements. To open MS Query, from the Start menu choose Programs, Microsoft SQL Server 6.5, and then MS Query. In the MS Query window, choose New Query from the File menu. A dialog box will open with a default of "LocalServer - sa," as shown in Figure 24.16.

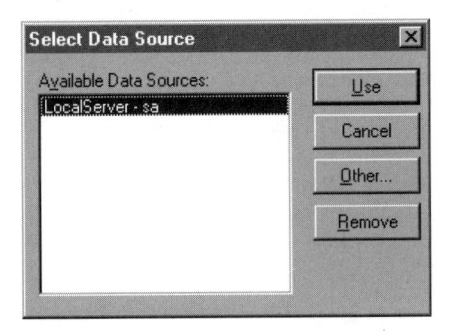

FIGURE 24.16
You can select any SQL Server database on the network.

Click the Use button. Select the database to be used, and click the Add button. You can click the column names to add them to the query being built. When you've built a query that shows the data you want, click the SQL button to see the SQL statement, as shown in Figure 24.17.

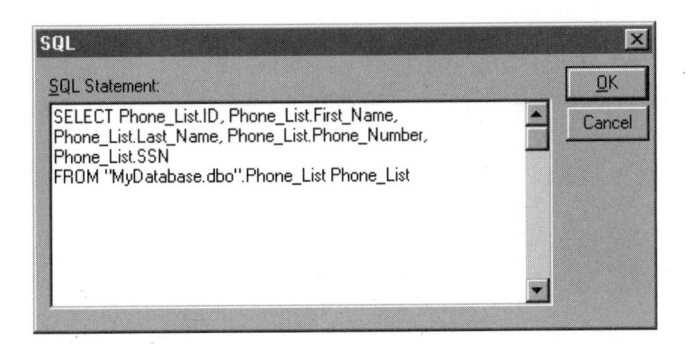

FIGURE 24.17
Viewing the SQL statement.

This SQL statement can be copied and pasted into a stored procedure or any other place that it is needed.

SQL Performance Monitor

SQL Performance Monitor keeps track of many performance measurements, including cache hit ratio, I/O transactions per second, I/O page reads per second, I/O single page writes per second, and user connections. To open SQL Performance Monitor, from the Start menu choose Programs, Microsoft SQL Server 6.5, and then SQL Performance Monitor. The measurements can be recorded and then replayed or compared to readings at different times.

SQL Security Manager

SQL Security Manager provides three types of security for SQL Server:

- Standard—uses the SQL security mechanisms only
- Trusted—relies on the Windows NT security model to control access
- Mixed—uses both types of security

To open SQL Security Manager, from the Start menu choose Programs, Microsoft SQL Server 6.5, and then SQL Security Manager.

SQL Server Web Assistant

SQL Server Web Assistant is a tool for publishing the contents of databases in dynamic web pages. When you open SQL Server Web Assistant, a wizard will guide you through the process of selecting a database to publish. (See Figure 24.18.)

SQL Service Manager

You use SQL Service Manager to start, stop, and pause SQL Server, SQL Executive, and Distributed Transaction Coordinator. It uses a stoplight-type control, as shown in Figure 24.19. Clicking on the red light stops the selected service; clicking on the green light starts the service.

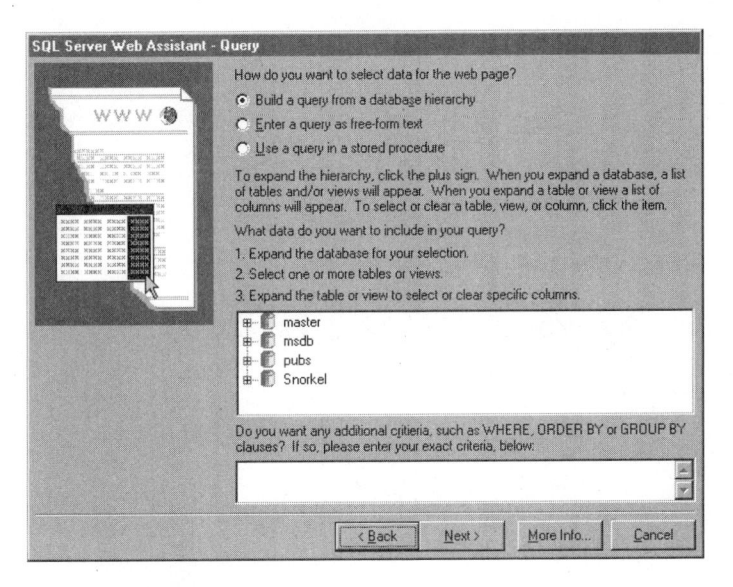

FIGURE 24.18

Using SQL Server Web Assistant.

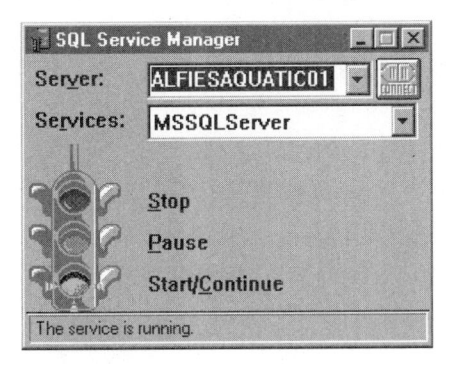

FIGURE 24.19

The color of the stoplight indicates whether the service is running.

SQL Trace

SQL Trace provides a graphical view of information about SQL Server activity. The database administrator can define various filters to monitor specific actions, and these actions can be recorded. When an error occurs, the specific process or connection generating the error can be determined. The information can be displayed as it happens, as shown in Figure 24.20 on the following page.

CHAPTER 24 *Understanding SQL Server* **447**

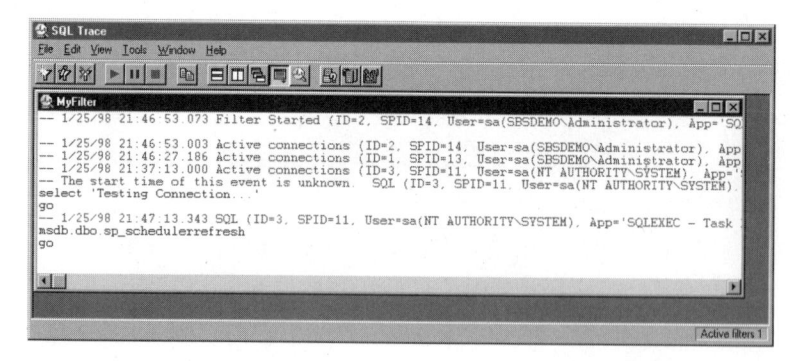

FIGURE 24.20

SQL Trace can show errors as they happen.

User Interface

SQL Server itself doesn't provide an application-style graphical user interface. User interface applications are usually created using Visual Basic, Microsoft Access, or Visual C++. Applications can use Open Database Connectivity and OLE DB to connect to SQL Server databases. Web access to SQL Server databases is accomplished using Active Server Pages with Microsoft Internet Information Server and ADO or ADO/RDS.

POINTS TO REMEMBER

- Microsoft SQL Server is a full-featured relational database that you access using Structured Query Language.
- Use regular Windows NT security for databases instead of adding another layer of logins.
- The standard SQL Server 6.5 package includes a complete set of backup and tuning tools.

WHAT'S NEXT

Now you should have a basic idea of how SQL Server and the other parts of Small Business Server work. In Part Six, we'll show you how to fine-tune the performance of your network as well as how to identify and solve network problems.

Part Six
Fine-Tuning and Troubleshooting

The last part of this book describes how to fine-tune the network and deal with problems that can arise on the server or on client computers. The last chapter explains the critical subject of disaster recovery—how to get your system back in working order in the event of failure.

Chapter 25

Monitoring and Fine-Tuning the Network

452	**Windows NT Diagnostics**	
454	**Performance Monitor**	
	Making a Chart	454
	Setting Up Alerts	456
	Logging Data for Reports	457
458	**Event Viewer**	
	Reading Logs	459
	System Events	459
	Application Events	460
	Security Events	461
462	**Filtering Event Logs**	
463	**Configuring Event Logs**	
464	**Auditing Files, Folders, and Printers**	
	Auditing Files and Folders	464
	Auditing Printers	466
467	**Points to Remember**	
468	**What's Next**	

Chapter 25

Monitoring and Fine-Tuning the Network

A great many events go on in a network operation—much of it invisible to users and administrator alike. This is pleasant and desirable as long as everything is going along smoothly. But with a system as complex as Microsoft BackOffice Small Business Server, problems can crop up in a lot of places. Therefore, it's useful to understand the Microsoft Windows NT tools that allow you to monitor the events and the performance of your server and network.

What distinguishes a Small Business Server network from a large enterprise network is that virtually everything works through a single server. This makes monitoring both easier and more important. Since you are unlikely to have multiple, redundant servers and networking components, you must devote some attention to your server to head off problems.

Windows NT Diagnostics

The Windows NT Diagnostics tool lets you look at information about your server and about server settings that would otherwise be hidden. From the Start menu, choose Programs, Administrative Tools (Common), and then Windows NT Diagnostics to bring up the dialog box shown in Figure 25.01.

Here's what you'll find on the various tabs:

- **Version** The operating system version number, records of service packs installed, and the registered owner.
- **System** ROM BIOS and CPU information.
- **Display** Video information, including the video settings, video card manufacturer, video memory, and video chip type.
- **Drives** All drives connected to this computer, listed by type or by name.

- **Memory** More than you ever wanted to know about memory. Of most interest is the actual physical memory (the amount of RAM installed and available) and the pagefile data. The pagefile space is the swap file—also known as virtual memory.

- **Services** The status of services on this computer. Click the Devices button to see the status of devices. To make changes to either of these lists, use the Services icon or the Devices icon in the Control Panel.

- **Resources** A plethora of arcane information about IRQs, I/O Ports, Direct Memory Access channels, and so forth.

- **Environment** Useful information about the machine you're on—the processor type and the paths and environment variables specific to the current user.

- **Network** Information about the network, including current network statistics.

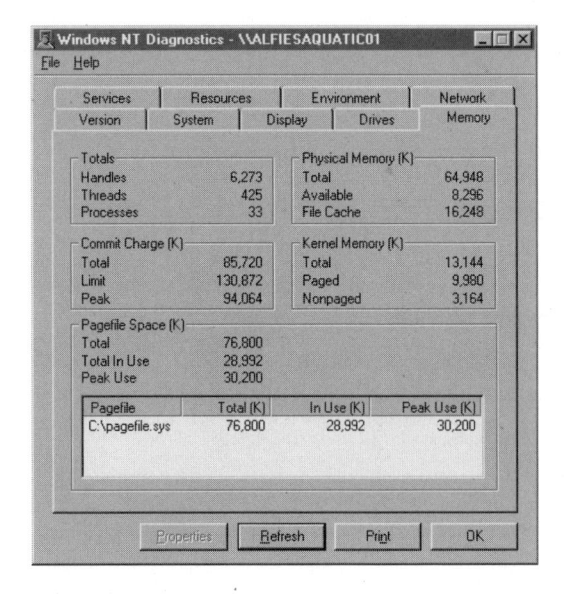

FIGURE 25.01

The Windows NT Diagnostics tool provides information about various aspects of the system.

Performance Monitor

One of the most important tools for serious data collection about your server and network is Performance Monitor. This tool can give you a view of everything happening on your server at the lowest levels—how much RAM each process is using, how many disk writes have occurred, how many disk reads have been met by the cache, and so on.

When you first open Performance Monitor, it is essentially a blank canvas. But when you delve a little deeper, you'll see that it can be overwhelmingly complex. But if you remain calm (and we must all remain calm), you'll realize that you're likely to be interested in only a few settings. Problems in your Small Business Server network will probably be related to either server limitations or network limitations and should show up as processors being overburdened, memory being too scant, disks being overburdened, or network hardware and software not being up to the job. When you begin your exploration, these are the areas you'll want to look at first.

Making a Chart

When you open Performance Monitor, you'll be in Chart View. Choose Add To Chart from the Edit menu. You'll see the Add To Chart dialog box (shown in Figure 25.02).

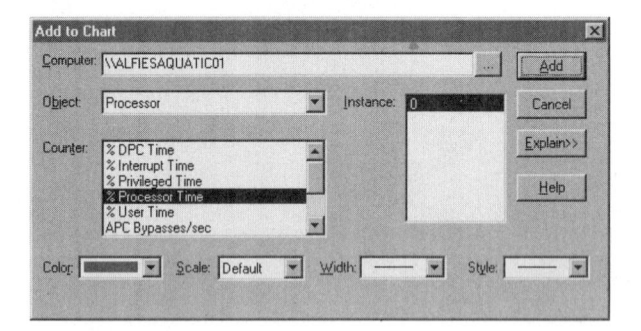

FIGURE 25.02

Adding functions to a chart.

> **Tip**
>
> In the Add To Chart dialog box, select an object and a counter, and then click the Explain button for a description of what the choices mean.

For a good indication of whether a processor is overburdened, you can select % Processor Time in the Counter list box. This will show the percentage of time the processor is busy. To monitor hard drive load, select the counter named Avg. Disk Queue Length (in the LogicalDisk object); it shows how long the line to use the hard drive is. Needless to say, it should be very short indeed if you are concerned about the network's performance. For overall memory usage on the server, start with Pages/Sec from the Memory object to see how often the server is switching information from memory to disk. A high rate means that the server is short of RAM and is using hard drive space to substitute for it. Bad idea—disks are much slower than RAM.

By gathering a variety of statistics on your server's performance, you can see the pattern of how it's being used. (Figure 25.03 shows a chart that tracks the three counters mentioned above.) You can use this information to diagnose problems or simply to get a good picture of where the bottlenecks are in your system and where they're likely to show up next. Then you can decide how to spend your limited resources to improve the performance of the network.

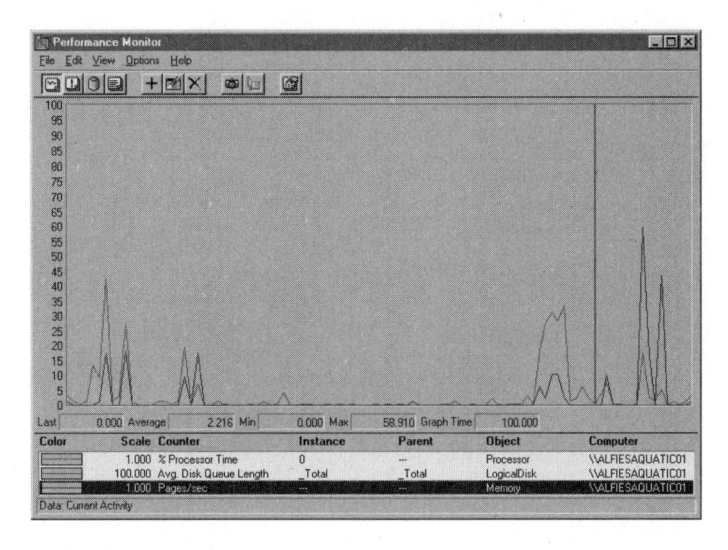

FIGURE 25.03

A Performance Monitor chart.

> **Tip**
>
> *You should periodically log the information in Performance Monitor and save it. When you do this while the network is running well, you are baselining. When something goes sour, you can create new logs and compare them to the old ones to see what the differences are.*

Setting Up Alerts

You can also have Performance Monitor notify you (or anyone else) when a specific event occurs on the network. For example, to specify that an alert should be sent to the administrator whenever the amount of free space on the C drive of ALFIESAQUATIC01 is less than 100 MB (a sure sign that cleanup is required), you can follow these steps:

1. In Performance Monitor, choose Alert from the View menu and then choose Add To Alert from the Edit menu.

2. In the Add To Alert dialog box (shown in Figure 25.04), select an object, a counter, and the conditions for the alert. In this case, we specified an alert if the Free Megabytes counter for the C drive goes under 100. Click OK to activate the new alert.

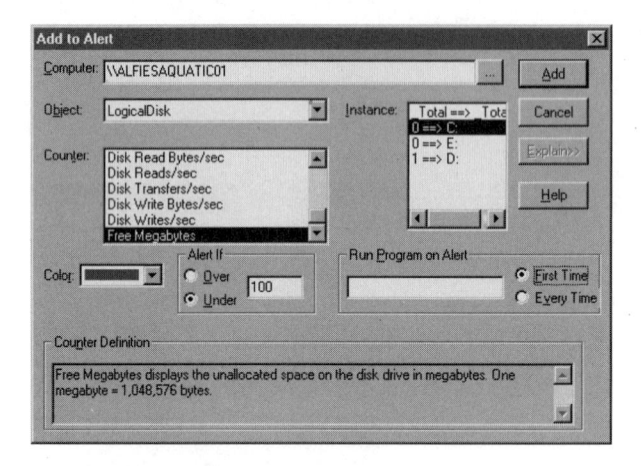

FIGURE 25.04

Adding an alert.

3. Choose Alert from the Options menu, and specify what you want the system to do for the alert. It can open Performance Monitor's Alert View, for example, or simply log the event in the Application log (in Event Viewer). For a network alert, you can select the Send Network Message check box and provide the logon name of the person to be alerted (or the name of the person's computer). You can also specify how often you want the alert updated.

4. Click OK when you're finished.

Whenever the conditions for the alert are met, the alert will go out. Our preference is for the administrator to be notified over the network.

Logging Data for Reports

Performance Monitor can also produce lots and lots of numbers for those mind-numbing reports that management loves. You can log statistical information that can later be exported to a spreadsheet program to be graphed or otherwise displayed. This can be extremely useful for tracking key areas of your system over time and watching for trends that might indicate a potential performance bottleneck.

To log data in Performance Monitor, follow these steps:

1. Choose Log from the View menu, and then choose Add To Log from the Edit menu.

2. In the Add To Log dialog box, you can add objects to the log—but only entire objects, not just individual counters as you can in Chart View. Select the objects you want, clicking Add after each one. Click Done when you're finished.

3. Choose Log from the Options menu. In the Log Options dialog box (shown in Figure 25.05), give your log a name. Set the Update Time you want, and then click Start Log.

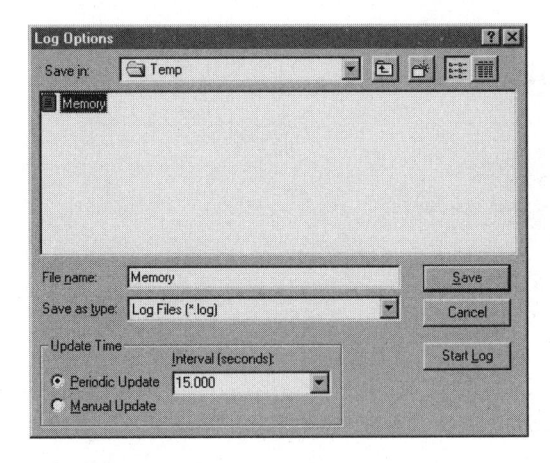

FIGURE 25.05

The Log Options dialog box showing the log file name.

> **WARNING!**
> *Log files can grow very quickly. If you plan to have a log running for an extended period, you should be careful about the update interval so that you don't quickly run out of disk space.*

Event Viewer

From the standpoint of Windows NT Server, and thus from the standpoint of Small Business Server, any event is an incident of potential interest. But most events are, in fact, of little interest; your logs can accumulate long lists of meaningless entries with only a few significant ones scattered in. However, when your system behaves oddly, you'll suddenly find yourself interested in things you never were interested in before.

Event Viewer records three categories of events that are recorded in three different logs. The categories are:

◆ System events, which are generated by the operating system and recorded in the systems log

◆ Application events, which are generated by applications and recorded in the applications log

◆ Security events, which are generated when an activity you select succeeds or fails; a record of these events is kept in the security log

When you open Event Viewer, the default view is that of the system log. To view one of the other logs, select it from the Log menu. Figure 25.06 shows a system log.

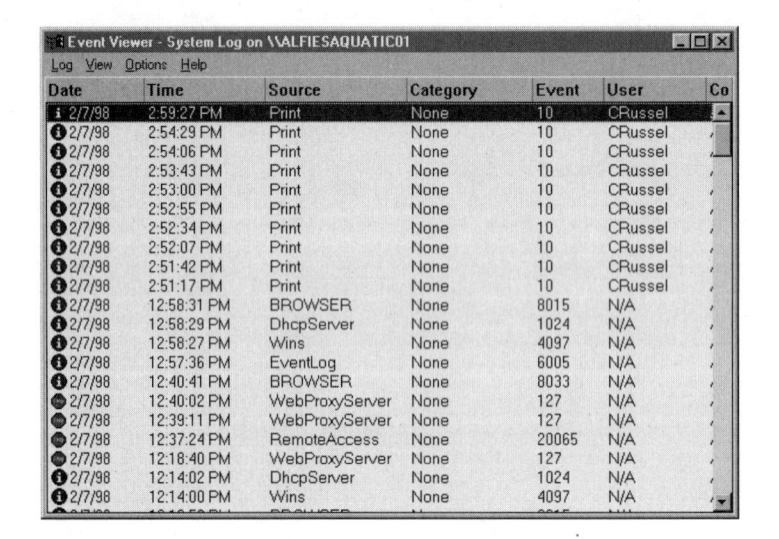

FIGURE 25.06

A system log showing typical events, including alerts about Proxy Server failures.

Reading Logs

Log entries fall into one of five categories. You can tell the category by the icon next to the entry.

Icon	Category
●	System or application error
①	System or application warning
ⓘ	System or application information
🔍	Security success
🔒	Security failure

Each log entry also includes the following data relating to the event:

◆ The date and time of the event

◆ The source of the event, sometimes a component of the system or a driver name

◆ The category of the event—often None, but in the Security log it is identified as Policy Change, Logon/Logoff, Privilege Use, or some other category

◆ The number assigned to the event

System Events

The events recorded in the system log are divided into three categories:

◆ **Errors** System events that represent possible loss of data or network functionality. This can be the failure of a driver or a system component to load during startup.

◆ **Warnings** Events that are less serious than errors but that should be noted nevertheless because some will indicate potential future problems. Warnings can be generated by events such as a nearly full disk or a redirector time-out.

- **Information** All events that don't fall into the first two categories. These can include events such as a synchronization between controllers, the successful loading of a database program, or a successful print job.

To see more information about an event in the system log, double-click on it. Figure 25.07 shows details of a warning that was triggered when the proxy server was unable to connect to the Internet.

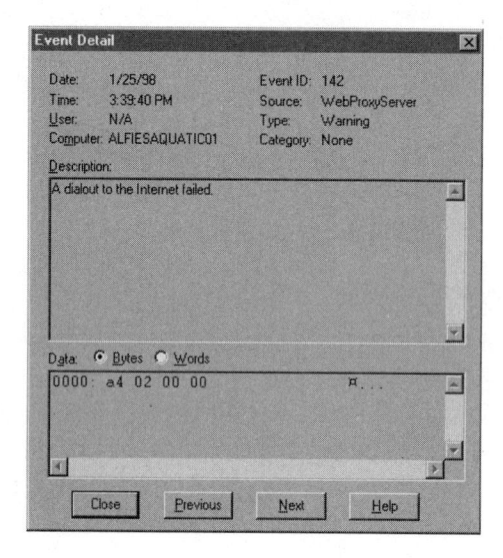

FIGURE 25.07

The Event Detail dialog box showing a noncritical system warning.

Application Events

Application events are usually rarer than the other types. They're logged by applications on the system and will vary widely. Figure 25.08 shows the Event Detail dialog box for an event that was generated by Microsoft Exchange Server when it couldn't connect to the Internet. Exchange Server is quite a "chatty" application and will log all kinds of information to event logs.

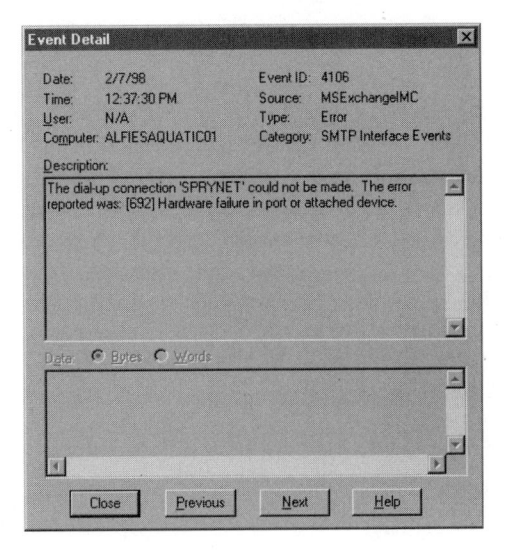

FIGURE 25.08

The details of an application event.

Security Events

Security events and the security log are probably of most interest to an administrator in a large corporate setting and of least interest to small businesses. By default in Small Business Server, these events are not logged at all. But if you want to keep track of security events, you can enable them using User Manager for Domains. To enable security event logging, follow these steps:

1. From the Start menu, choose Programs, Administrative Tools (Common), and then User Manager for Domains.

2. Choose Audit from the Policies menu to open the Audit Policy dialog box, shown in Figure 25.09.

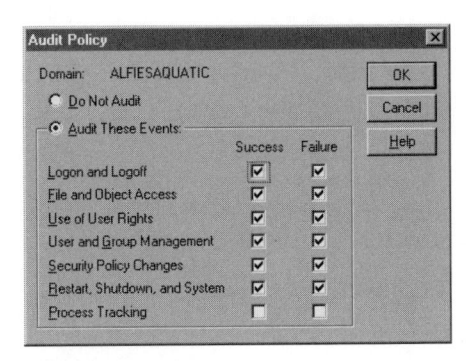

FIGURE 25.09

In User Manager for Domains, you can enable auditing and select events to track.

As you can see, you can have Windows NT Server audit both successes and failures in all categories. Under most circumstances, logging successful logons and file accesses quickly produces a system log of gargantuan proportions. Failures are generally of more interest. However, you can change the items to be audited at any point and for any length of time if it will help you pinpoint a problem.

Filtering Event Logs

It only takes a few minutes to fill up an event log—particularly the system log. So how do you sort through all the junk to find what you need? Simply open the log in Event Viewer, and choose Filter Events from the View menu to open the Filter dialog box, shown in Figure 25.10. You can filter the level of detail that is shown in the event logs so that you see only failures and critical errors.

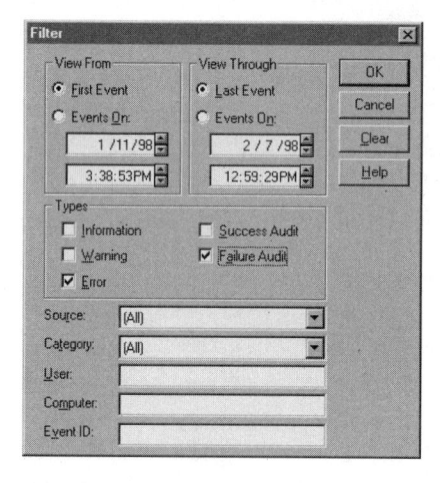

FIGURE 25.10

The Filter dialog box.

Keep in mind that this filter limits only what you see. Events are recorded regardless of the filter settings. And when you change to viewing a different log, the filter options are automatically reset to the defaults.

Here's what you can do in each section of this dialog box to focus your detective work:

- **View From and View Through** Narrow the events by date
- **Types** Select the types of events you want to see

- **Source** Specify events that were logged by a particular source, such as a driver or a system component
- **Category** Specify all events of a particular classification
- **User** Specify all events connected to a particular user
- **Computer** Narrow the events to a particular computer
- **Event ID** Specify events of a particular ID in a category

Through judicious use of these options and perhaps a little Boolean algebra, you can wade through the morass of events in a log to find the points you're looking for—although it might take a few tries before you're used to how the filtering works.

Configuring Event Logs

By default, each event log is limited to 512 KB. You can keep them smaller, or you can let them grow larger if you think you need that much information. To configure the event logs, follow these steps:

1. Open Event Viewer. Choose Log Settings from the Log menu.
2. In the Event Log Settings dialog box (shown in Figure 25.11), select the log you want to change.

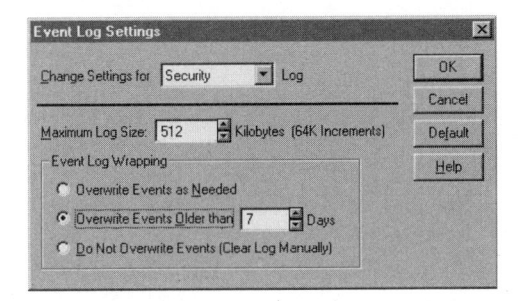

FIGURE 25.11

The Event Log Settings dialog box.

3. Set a maximum log size.

4. In the Event Log Wrapping section, specify how you want a full log to be handled. If you select Overwrite Events As Needed, when the log gets full the newest log entry will push out the oldest. If you select Overwrite Events Older Than X Days, the log will be maintained for the number of days specified. If you select Do Not Overwrite Events, all events will be logged and the log must be cleared manually; it will not clear itself automatically.

5. Click OK when you're done making your selections.

Auditing Files, Folders, and Printers

The basic audit policy for your Small Business Server network is set by using User Manager for Domains. By default, all auditing is turned off. Before you turn on auditing, you should carefully consider what you're trying to accomplish and if this is the way to accomplish it. Auditing not only creates substantial event log files, but it also imposes substantial overhead on network performance. We leave auditing turned off unless we have a particular reason to turn it on, and then we turn it on only for a limited period of time.

You can refine the policy to audit specific files, folders, and printers, but you can't extend the auditing policy beyond what is configured here. To set the auditing ground rules, follow these steps:

1. Open User Manager for Domains. (From the Start menu, choose Programs, Administrative Tools [Common], and then Event Viewer.)

2. Choose Audit from the Policies menu.

3. In the Audit Policy dialog box (shown in Figure 25.09 on page 461), select Audit These Events. Select the successful and unsuccessful events you want to monitor. Click OK.

Auditing Files and Folders

Once you turn on auditing, you can audit who is doing what with a particular folder or even with an individual file. Just follow these steps:

1. In Windows Explorer, right-click on the file or the folder to be audited, and choose Properties from the pop-up menu.

2. On the Security page of the Properties dialog box, click the Auditing button.

3. If you selected a folder, use the two check boxes at the top of the Directory Auditing dialog box (Figure 25.12) to determine the extent of the auditing. To apply auditing to the folder, existing subfolders, and all existing files, select both check boxes. To apply auditing to the folder and its files (ignoring subfolders), select Replace Auditing On Existing Files only. To apply auditing to the folder only (ignoring all files and subfolders), deselect both of the check boxes. To apply auditing to the folder and subfolders (ignoring the files), select Replace Auditing On Subdirectories and deselect Replace Auditing On Existing Files.

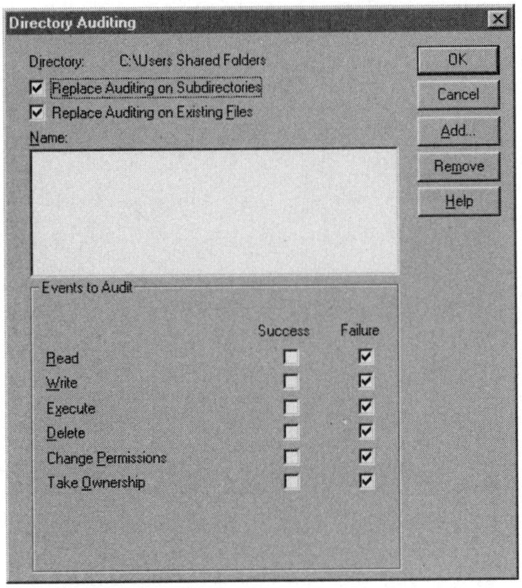

FIGURE 25.12

The Directory Auditing dialog box.

4. To specify whose use of the files or the folders you want to audit, click the Add button.

CHAPTER 25 *Monitoring and Fine-Tuning the Network* **465**

5. In the Add Users And Groups dialog box (shown in Figure 25.13), select the groups or the users whose use of the file or the folder you want to audit. When all the names you want are in the Add Names box, click OK.

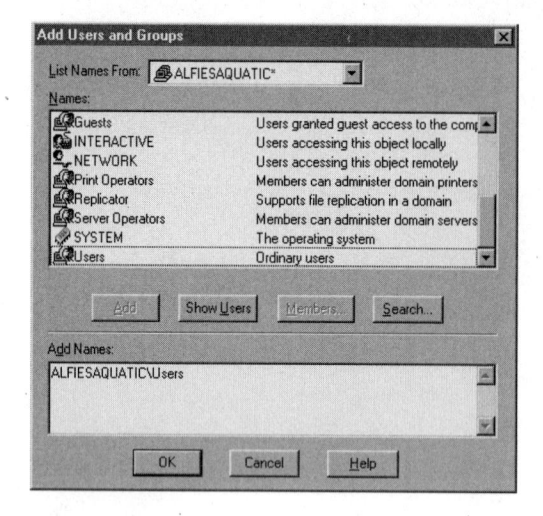

FIGURE 25.13

Selecting the groups and the users to audit.

6. Back in the Directory Auditing dialog box, select the events you want to audit, and then click OK.

Auditing Printers

To configure auditing for a printer, follow these steps:

1. Open the Printers folder. Right-click on the printer you want to audit, and choose Properties from the pop-up menu.

2. In the dialog box that opens, click on the Security tab and then click the Auditing button.

3. In the Printer Auditing dialog box (shown in Figure 25.14), click the Add button.

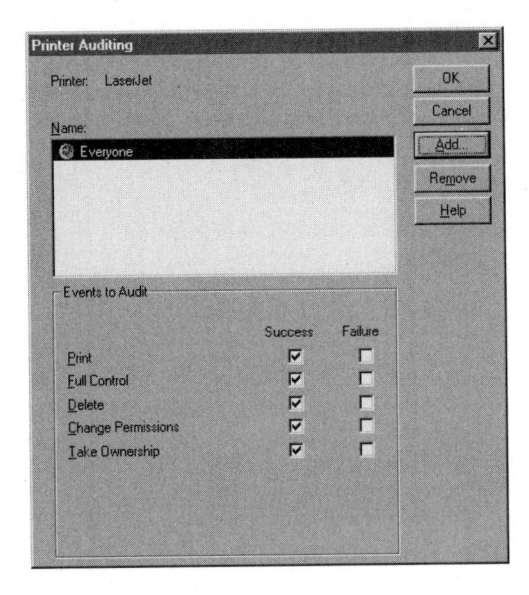

FIGURE 25.14

In the Printer Auditing dialog box, you can audit who is using your printer, and when.

4. In the Add Users And Groups dialog box, select the individuals or the groups whose use of the printer you want to audit, and then click Add. When all the names you want are in the Add Names box, click OK.

5. Back in the Printer Auditing dialog box, select the events you want to audit, and then click OK.

6. The results of the audit will show up in the Security log, which you can read in Event Viewer.

POINTS TO REMEMBER

- The Windows NT Diagnostics tool provides information on both hardware and software resources on your server.

- Performance Monitor lets you look at current information on a wide variety of low-level performance indicators.

- Use Performance Monitor to create alerts and to log data for reports on your system's performance.
- Create a baseline of your server's performance using Performance Monitor so that you'll have a basis of comparison when problems arise.
- Use Event Viewer to find system warnings and failures.
- Even though you can audit a wide variety of security events, you'll quickly fill up your log files if you get carried away.

WHAT'S NEXT

In this chapter, we covered several tools for monitoring the performance of your server and therefore the network. Next we'll look at the Windows NT Registry and how it can affect your system's performance and behavior.

Chapter 26

Introducing the Microsoft Windows NT Registry

- 471 How the Registry Is Structured
- 472 The HKEY_LOCAL_MACHINE Hive
  - HARDWARE Key — 472
  - SAM and SECURITY Keys — 472
  - SOFTWARE Key — 472
  - SYSTEM Key — 472
- 473 The HKEY_USERS Hive
- 475 The HKEY_CLASSES_ROOT Hive
- 475 The HKEY_CURRENT_USER Hive
- 475 The HKEY_CURRENT_CONFIG Hive
- 475 Data Types Used in the Registry
- 477 Files in the Registry
- 479 Backing Up and Restoring the Registry
  - Using regedit.exe — 479
  - Using regedt32.exe — 480
  - Using regback.exe — 481
  - Using regrest.exe to Restore the Registry — 482
- 484 Editing Keys and Values
  - Editing with regedt32.exe — 484
  - Editing with regedit.exe — 489
- 492 Before You Install New Software
- 494 Points to Remember
- 494 What's Next

Chapter 26

Introducing the Microsoft Windows NT Registry

Early versions of Microsoft Windows stored hardware and user information in numerous files—such as autoexec.bat, config.sys, win.ini, and system.ini—that were scattered all over the computer's hard drive. When it came time to design Windows NT, it was clear that all these ASCII files would make it difficult (if not impossible) to manage even a single server. The goal of Windows NT—to manage an environment with multiple servers—required a change in how configuration information was organized and stored.

The Windows NT Registry is a binary, hierarchical database that consolidates and simplifies the task of maintaining and configuring hardware and software information as well as user options. The ability to maintain separate information for each user is a big improvement over the previous "one size fits all" approach.

The Registry eliminates almost all of the configuration files that users previously had to manage. However, Windows NT still supports some of the older configuration files for the sake of backward compatibility with older, 16-bit Windows applications.

◆ Old Files That Aren't Supported

Windows NT does not support the TSR (terminate and stay resident) files that were the mainstay of MS-DOS–based systems. Likewise, it doesn't support drivers in the autoexec.bat, config.sys, and system.ini files. Fortunately, Windows NT provides drivers for most of the hardware in use today. Support in this area is still not on par with MS-DOS, Windows 3.1x, or Windows 95, but it's steadily improving.

The Windows NT Registry and the Windows 95 Registry are similar, but they have some structural differences and are stored differently on disk. Neither can be used on the other operating system, but fortunately they share the same Application Programming Interface (API) that developers use to access them. As more applications migrate to 32-bit, expect to see their configuration files disappear as that information moves to the Registry.

How the Registry Is Structured

The Registry is organized in the hierarchical tree structure familiar to anyone who's dealt with the directory structure in MS-DOS and Windows 3.x, or the folders, subfolders, and files in Windows 95 or Windows NT 4.

At the top level are components called *hives*. Each hive contains numerous keys that divide the configuration information into different areas. The keys are divided into subkeys to further categorize the information. The subkeys can also be divided into lower-level subkeys if required. Under the keys and subkeys are values. Each value is assigned a name and can be set to store a specific piece of configuration information called the value's *data*.

These are the five top-level components you can access:

- HKEY_LOCAL_MACHINE
- HKEY_USERS
- HKEY_CLASSES_ROOT
- HKEY_CURRENT_USER
- HKEY_CURRENT_CONFIG

NOTE

A sixth hive named HKEY_DYN_DATA contains mostly hardware configuration data and can't be accessed directly.

Of these five, only HKEY_LOCAL_MACHINE and HKEY_USERS are really hives. The other three are actually pointers to information in the first two hives. They were created because the information they point to is accessed frequently by many applications. Their sole reason for existence is to make it easier for the developers and the applications to access that information. Since they simply point to keys contained in HKEY_LOCAL_MACHINE and HKEY_USERS, you can change entries in the Registry by directly modifying the entries in HKEY_LOCAL_MACHINE and HKEY_USERS. Or you can use the "pointer hives" for quicker access to the configuration entries. The result is the same; either method will update the entries.

The HKEY_LOCAL_MACHINE Hive

HKEY_LOCAL_MACHINE stores information about the hardware, software, and users of the computer on which the Registry database is located. It has five keys under it—HARDWARE, SAM, SECURITY, SOFTWARE, and SYSTEM.

HARDWARE Key

The HARDWARE key contains information about all of the hardware installed on the computer. It is divided into four subkeys called DESCRIPTION, DEVICEMAP, OWNERMAP, and RESOURCEMAP, which contain all the options and configuration settings for the hardware installed on the computer.

SAM and SECURITY Keys

The SAM and SECURITY keys store information about all the users, local groups, and global groups in the current computer. By default, users (including administrators) can't access this information. To modify information in these keys, you must use the Windows NT administrative tools. User Manager for Domains lets you modify most of this information and is the preferred method for doing so.

SOFTWARE Key

The SOFTWARE key contains the file-type-to-program associations and keys for the application vendors whose software you have installed. When you install application software from a new vendor, the installation program should create a key under SOFTWARE with the vendor's name and, below that, a key for each of the vendor's products that you have installed. Under the product keys are the product settings that are specific to the computer that they are installed on.

SYSTEM Key

The SYSTEM key contains the settings for system software components installed on the computer. This includes information and configuration settings for device drivers, settings and startup information for the services installed, and setup information from the Windows NT installation. This key is divided into six subkeys called ControlSet001, ControlSet002, CurrentControlSet, DISK, Select, and Setup.

ControlSet

The device drivers and services settings are stored under the ControlSet001, ControlSet002, and CurrentControlSet keys. Windows NT generally maintains two copies of this information: the current settings and the last known successful boot settings. This protects the computer from changes that render the system nonoperational. ControlSet001 and ControlSet002 are the current and last known good settings, and CurrentControlSet is a pointer to the control set that was last used to start the computer.

> **Tip**
>
> *The names of the ControlSet001 and ControlSet002 keys can vary depending on how new system software is installed, but there will always be two such keys (unless the settings just used to boot the computer caused a failure) and the last three characters of the key names will be a sequential number. CurrentControlSet will always point to the ControlSet in use, and the other ControlSet will always be the last known good boot settings.*

DISK

The DISK subkey stores the drive letter assignments that deviate from the defaults. The most common value entries you will find under this key are entries for the CD-ROM drive letter and for removable devices.

Select

The Select key stores information about which ControlSet is the CurrentControlSet and which ControlSet is the last known good ControlSet. After a successful boot, ControlSet001 and ControlSet002 should contain the same information. Changes made to the system software during the current boot are added to whichever ControlSet is pointed to by CurrentControlSet. If problems arise after the system is rebooted to put the changes into effect, the user can return to the last known good boot settings, which will revert to the old ControlSet settings.

Setup

After the MS-DOS portion of the installation is complete and the system is rebooted, the Setup key is used by the Windows NT installation and setup process to start the GUI portion of the Windows NT installation.

The HKEY_USERS Hive

The HKEY_USERS hive contains information specific to users that log on to the computer. Under this hive are two keys. The first, .DEFAULT, contains the configuration settings for a default user. When a new user logs onto the computer for the first time, his or her Registry key is populated with the information in the .DEFAULT key. This makes it easy to set up common defaults for new users by modifying the .DEFAULT key's Registry settings.

The second key under HKEY_USERS contains the configuration settings specific to the current user. When a new user account is created, it's assigned a unique security identifier in the security accounts database. This security identifier, or SID, is a unique number that Windows NT uses internally to identify the user. The name of the second key under HKEY_USERS is the SID of the current user.

> ◆ **The Security Accounts Database**
>
> When the Windows NT administrator assigns privileges or permissions to a user account, those privileges and permissions are assigned to the user's SID. Fortunately, all of the Windows NT administrative tools let you reference the user accounts by user name instead of the SID.
>
> Note that deleting a user account and immediately creating a new account with the same name does *not* reestablish the deleted account. Every account is assigned a unique SID; once an account is deleted, there is no easy way to reestablish it.

Under the key for the current user are nine subkeys named AppEvents, Console, Control Panel, Environment, Keyboard Layout, Network, Printers, Software, and UNICODE Program Groups. Following is a description of each:

- The AppEvents subkey contains information about all the system and application events that can have a sound assigned to them and the sound files to play when those events occur.

- The Console subkey contains the settings for the command prompt and the default settings for all console applications.

- The Control Panel subkey contains subkeys for all of the Control Panel applets; under each subkey are the settings for the applets.

- The Environment subkey contains the user-specific environment variable settings. For system-specific environment settings, see the SYSTEM\CurrentControlSet\Control\Session Manager\Environment subkey under HKEY_LOCAL_MACHINE.

- The Keyboard Layout subkey stores the current keyboard layout and information about other keyboard layouts that have drivers installed.

- The Network subkey contains information about the network drives that have been permanently mapped.

- The Printers subkey contains information about the currently installed printers and about network printers that are permanently connected.

- The Software subkey contains separate subkeys for each of the application vendor's software products that you have installed. When you install application software for a new vendor, the vendor's installation program should create a key under Software with its name; under that key, it should create a key for each of the vendor's products that you have installed. Under the product keys are the settings and options for the product that the current user has selected.

- The UNICODE Program Groups subkey stores the settings for the Personal Program Groups that the current user has created in Program Manager. This subkey is for backward compatibility with previous versions of Windows NT that used the Program Manager shell instead of the Windows Explorer shell.

The HKEY_CLASSES_ROOT Hive

As previously noted, the HKEY_CLASSES_ROOT Registry hive is not a true hive; it's a pointer to the Software\Classes key in the HKEY_LOCAL_MACHINE hive. The Software\Classes key stores the file associations that connect a file extension to an application. (The extension .xls is associated with Microsoft Excel, for example.) The primary purpose of this hive is to provide developers and applications with easy access to that information.

The HKEY_CURRENT_USER Hive

Like the HKEY_CLASSES_ROOT hive, HKEY_CURRENT_USER is not a true hive. It's a pointer to the key under HKEY_USERS that represents the current user. As you will recall, the HKEY_USERS hive has two keys under it, .DEFAULT and a key for the current user.

The name of the key for the current user is the SID (security identifier) of that user account. HKEY_CURRENT_USER allows applications to easily store application configuration settings that are specific to the user without having to jump through the hoops required to determine the user's SID. Software applications can simply reference HKEY_CURRENT_USER to set and retrieve the configuration settings for the current user.

The HKEY_CURRENT_CONFIG Hive

Like the previous two hives, HKEY_CURRENT_CONFIG is not a true hive. It's a pointer to the SYSTEM\CurrentControlSet\Hardware Profiles\Current subkey under HKEY_LOCAL_MACHINE. This hive isn't heavily used; it simply sets the stage for Plug and Play support that is planned for the next version of Windows NT and supports the new hardware profiles in Windows NT 4. At this point, only video driver information is maintained there.

Data Types Used in the Registry

Each piece of information stored in the Registry is assigned a name. The name need not be unique to the entire Registry; it must be unique only to the Registry key or subkey under which the value name is created. The data associated with that name is assigned a data type that describes the type of information stored in that Registry entry. The Registry currently supports 12 data types, although only 5 of those are commonly used. Table 27.01 lists all of the data types supported by the Registry and briefly describes each. The most commonly used data types are marked with an asterisk.

Table 27.01
Data Types Used in the Registry

Registry Data Type	Description
REG_NONE	Available when none of the other data types is applicable. Currently, this data type does not appear to be used in the Registry.
REG_SZ *	Used to store a UNICODE null-terminated string. It's commonly used throughout the Registry to store character data.
REG_EXPAND_SZ *	Also used to store a UNICODE null-terminated string, but it allows the string to contain environment variable references. It's commonly used throughout the Registry to store character data that contains environment variables. API functions allow developers to expand the environment variable portion of the strings to their current values.
REG_BINARY *	Used to store binary data in any form. It's commonly used throughout the Registry.
REG_DWORD *	Used to store a 32-bit number. It's commonly used throughout the Registry.
REG_DWORD_LITTLE_ENDIAN	Used to store a 32-bit number in little endian format. It's just another name for the REG_DWORD data type. In little endian format, the most significant byte of a word is the high-order word. This data type is available for RISC-based machines that store DWORD values in both endian formats.
REG_DWORD_BIG_ENDIAN	Used to store a 32-bit number in big endian format. In big endian format, the most significant byte of a word is the low-order word. This data type is available for RISC-based machines.
REG_LINK	Used to store a UNICODE symbolic link. Currently, this data type does not appear to be used in the Registry.
REG_MULTI_SZ *	Used to store an array of null-terminated strings. The array is terminated by an additional null character. This data type is commonly used throughout the Registry when more than one character string needs to be stored in a single Registry entry.

Registry Data Type	Description
REG_RESOURCE_LIST	Used to store a resource list, which is a data structure used to describe the computer's hardware configuration. This data type is used to store many of the entries in the HKEY_LOCAL_MACHINE \HARDWARE\RESOURCEMAP subkey.
REG_FULL_RESOURCE_DESCRIPTOR	Also used to store a resource list. It's used to store many of the entries in the HKEY_LOCAL_MACHINE\HARDWARE \DESCRIPTION subkey.
REG_RESOURCE_REQUIREMENTS_LIST	Used to store the options or requirements for the items in a resource list.

Files in the Registry

In Windows NT versions prior to version 4, the Registry files were stored in the %SystemRoot%\System32\Config folder. SystemRoot is an environment variable set up during Windows NT installation that points to the folder in which Windows NT was installed. The Registry settings specific to each Windows NT user account were stored in a file that used the user account's name as part of the filename.

In Windows NT 4, all files—with the exception of the Registry settings specific to each user account—are still stored in the %SystemRoot%\System32\Config folder. Windows NT 4 adds a new folder to its folder structure called %SystemRoot%\Profiles. This folder has multiple folders under it, one for each Windows NT user account that appears in the Windows NT security accounts database. The folder names are the names of the user accounts. In each folder is a file called NTUSER.DAT. Windows NT 4 stores the Registry information specific to each user in the user's folder in the NTUSER.DAT file. This structure also contains folders under each of the users' folders, such as Application Data, Desktop, Favorites, NetHood, Personal, PrintHood, Recent, SendTo, Start Menu, and Templates.

Table 27.02 on the following page lists all of the files that make up the Windows NT 4 Registry and describes their use.

Table 27.02
Files That Make Up the Windows NT Registry

Registry Filename	Description
default	Contains default settings that are used to create a user profile for a new user who logs onto the computer without a user profile defined.
SAM	Contains the local security information for the user accounts and the group accounts on the computer. For a domain controller, it also contains the domain security information.
SECURITY	Contains the local security information for user rights, password policies, and group membership on the computer.
Software	Contains the local application software configuration database for the software that is installed on the computer.
System	Contains the local system database that controls the system boot process, drivers, services, and general operating system options.
SYSTEM.ALT	A complete copy of the SYSTEM Registry file that is kept in sync with the SYSTEM Registry file and is used as a fallback if a hardware or software error occurs during the update of the SYSTEM Registry file.
default.log	A transaction log that is used to stage changes to the HKEY_USERS\.DEFAULT subkey.
SAM.LOG	A transaction log that is used to stage changes to the HKEY_LOCAL_MACHINE\SAM subkey.
SECURITY.LOG	A transaction log that is used to stage changes to the HKEY_LOCAL_MACHINE\SECURITY subkey.
Software.log	A transaction log that is used to stage changes to the HKEY_LOCAL_MACHINE\SOFTWARE subkey.
system.log	A transaction log that is used to stage changes to the HKEY_LOCAL_MACHINE\SYSTEM subkey.
default.sav	A backup copy of the HKEY_USERS\.DEFAULT subkey that is used during the GUI part of the Windows NT setup.
Software.sav	A backup copy of the HKEY_LOCAL_MACHINE\SOFTWARE subkey that is used during the GUI part of the Windows NT setup.
system.sav	A backup copy of the HKEY_LOCAL_MACHINE\SYSTEM subkey that is used during the GUI part of the Windows NT setup.
Userdiff	Contains settings that must be applied to all users the first time they log on after Windows NT has been upgraded.
ntuser.dat	Contains settings, options, and preferences specific to a user account that define the work environment. Each user account defined has this file in its profile directory. This is the HKEY_CURRENT_USER hive of the Registry.
ntuser.dat.log	A transaction log that is used to stage changes to the HKEY_CURRENT_USER hive. Each user account defined has this file in its profile directory.

Backing Up and Restoring the Registry

Although the Registry structure provides many benefits, it also introduces greater risk because all configuration information is dependent on the Registry. Once you start poking about and making changes in the Registry, it's easy to create problems for yourself. You might even end up with a server that won't boot. So it's prudent (to say the least) to always make a backup copy of the Registry before you start playing Mad Scientist.

Windows NT Server comes with two programs named Registry Editor. The first one, regedit, is a program developed for Windows 95 that is also available in Windows NT; regedt32 is the utility provided with Windows NT after version 1.

Using regedit.exe

The regedit program can easily export a copy of the entire Registry or any particular branch. To back up the Registry, follow these steps:

1. From the Start menu, choose Run.
2. In the Run dialog box, type *regedit* in the Open text box and then click OK.
3. Select My Computer to export the entire Registry, or select a branch.
4. Choose Export Registry File from the Registry menu.
5. In the Export Registry File window, select the folder in which you want to save the Registry. Enter a name for the file.
6. Verify that the Export Range is correct. Click Save.

WARNING!

By default, regedit saves the backup copy of the Registry with a .reg extension. A reasonable person might think that double-clicking on a .reg file will cause regedit.exe to open the file for editing, but that's not the case. Double-clicking on a .reg file causes that file to merge without warning into your existing, active Registry—a probably disastrous result. To preserve your system from such a calamity, rename the .reg file with a different extension immediately after you back it up.

You can restore a backed-up Registry by reversing the process. Open regedit and choose Import Registry File from the Registry menu.

Using `regedt32.exe`

You can back up a hive, a key, or a subkey using regedt32.exe by following these steps:

1. From the Start menu, choose Run.

2. In the Open text box of the Run dialog box, type *regedt32.exe*. Click OK.

3. Select the window that displays the key you want, and then select the section you want to back up. (See Figure 26.01.)

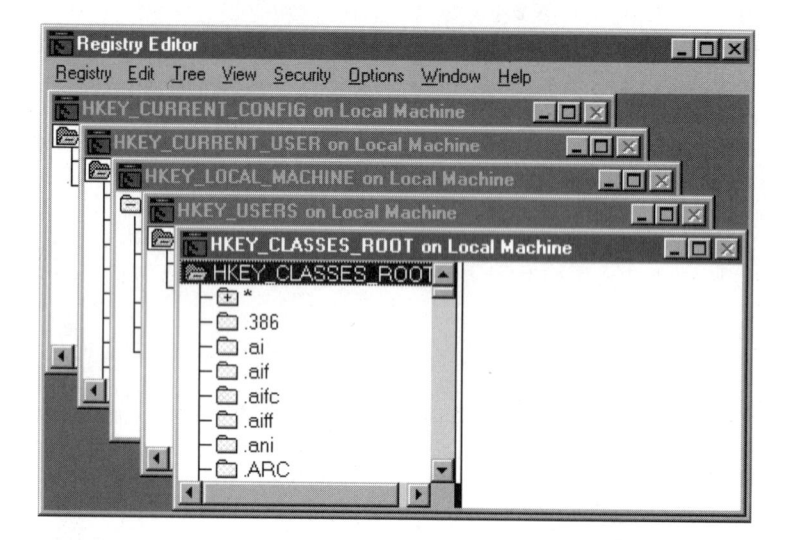

FIGURE 26.01

Selecting a portion of the Registry to save.

4. Choose Save Key from the Registry menu.

5. In the Save Key window, click on the folder in which you want to locate the file and type a name for the saved key.

NOTE

> To save a key as an ASCII file, select it in the Registry Editor window and choose Save Subtree As from the Registry menu.

To restore the saved key, start regedt32 and choose Restore from the Registry menu. You must supply the location for the saved key that you want to restore.

Using regback.exe

The regback program included on the CD in the Windows NT Resource Kit provides an additional method for backing up the Registry. Using regback, you can save a snapshot of the entire Registry while the server is running. This can be very useful if you want to perform a quick backup of the Registry before installing new software.

When running regback, you must specify the location for the backup Registry files. It's a good idea to create a folder to hold the backups. For example, let's create a C:\RegBU folder to hold the folders that we back up. Under the C:\RegBU folder, create a separate folder each time you make a new Registry backup.

Use the following command to back up the Registry information to one of the directories under the C:\RegBu directory:

```
regback c:\regbu\Monday
```

When you execute the above command, you will see messages on the screen indicating the progress of the Registry backup that are similar to the following:

```
saving SECURITY to c:\regbu\monday\SECURITY
saving SOFTWARE to c:\regbu\monday\software
saving SYSTEM to c:\regbu\monday\system
saving .DEFAULT to c:\regbu\monday\default
saving SAM to c:\regbu\monday\SAM

***Hive = \REGISTRY\USER\S-1-5-21-522347448-489971457-886967795-1000

Stored in file \Device\Harddisk1\Partition1\WINNT\Profiles
    \alfie\NTUSER.DAT
Must be backed up manually

regback <filename you choose> users S-1-5-21-522347448-489971457-
    886967795-1000
```

The last four lines of the screen output identify what needs to be done to back up the current user's Registry information. To back up that information, use the command format indicated in the last message on the screen. To easily identify the user account that the Registry information belongs to, you can use a filename that is the same as the user account. For example, to back up the Registry information for the user account indicated above, use the command format shown on the following page. (Be sure to type the command as a single line.)

```
regback c:\regbu\Monday\alfie.dat users S-1-5-21-522347448-489971457-
   886967795-1000
```

After executing the above command, you will see messages on the screen indicating the progress of the Registry backup that are similar to the following:

```
saving S-1-5-21-522347448-489971457-886967795-1000 to
   c:\regbu\Monday\alfie.dat
```

The long number at the end of the above command specifies the SID (security identifier) for the user account whose Registry information you are backing up. This number will appear in the last line of the regback screen output. You can also find it by logging on to the computer using that user account and looking at the second key under the HKEY_USERS hive using the Registry Editor.

> **Tip**
>
> *These regback examples back up all the Registry entries specific to the computer and all the Registry entries for the current user, but they* do not *back up the Registry entries for other users. Backing up the Registry entries for each user would require a separate execution of the regback command for each user account.*

Using regrest.exe to Restore the Registry

The regrest program comes on the CD in the Windows NT Resource Kit. Like the regback program, it requires you to perform an additional step for the Registry information for the current user.

After performing a backup of the local Registry and of the current user's Registry information (as described in the previous section), we have the following files in our c:\regbu\Monday directory:

```
SAM
system
default
SECURITY
software
alfie.dat
```

When the regrest program runs, you must specify the folder that contains the Registry files that you want to restore. You must also specify a folder to save the current Registry files to. For our example, let's create the C:\OldRegBU directory to hold the Registry files that are currently in use.

WARNING!

For the regrest program to successfully restore the Registry, the folder that contains the Registry files you want to restore and *the folder in which you'll store the backups of the current Registry files must be on the same hard drive volume that Windows NT 4 is installed on. The reason has to do with how regrest actually restores the Registry. It does* not *copy the files you are restoring to the correct location; it* renames *them on the volume. If you do not have the Registry files on the same hard drive volume as Windows NT, you must move the Registry backup files to the Windows NT volume.*

To restore the Registry to the previous state that we stored it in the c:\regbu\Monday folder, you use the following command:

```
regrest c:\regbu\Monday c:\oldregbu
```

After executing the above command, you will see messages on the screen indicating the progress of the Registry restore operation that are similar to the following:

```
replacing SECURITY with c:\regbu\monday\SECURITY
replacing SOFTWARE with c:\regbu\monday\SOFTWARE
replacing SYSTEM with c:\regbu\monday\SYSTEM
replacing .DEFAULT with c:\regbu\monday\DEFAULT
replacing SAM with c:\regbu\monday\SAM

***Hive = \REGISTRY\USER\S-1-5-21-522347448-489971457-886967795-1000

Stored in file \Device\Harddisk1\Partition1\WINNT\Profiles
    \alfie\NTUSER.DAT
Must be replaced manually

regrest <newpath> <savepath> users S-1-5-21-522347448-489971457-
    886967795-1000
You must reboot for changes to take effect.
```

The last five lines of the screen output identify what you need to do to restore the previously backed-up Registry user information. To restore the Registry information for that user, use the command format indicated in the last message on the screen. For example, for our previously backed up user information, use the following command format (all one line):

```
regrest c:\regbu\Monday\alfie.dat c:\oldregbu\alfie.dat users
    S-1-5-21-522347448-489971457-886967795-1000
```

After executing the above command, you will see messages on the screen indicating the progress of the Registry restore that are similar to the following:

```
replacing S-1-5-21-522347448-489971457-886967795-1000 with
    c:\regbu\Monday\alfie.dat
You must reboot for changes to take effect.
```

After successfully restoring the Registry files, you should reboot the computer so that Windows NT can use the restored Registry files.

Editing Keys and Values

The regedt32 version of the Registry Editor uses an older user interface than that of regedit; however, it does provide some functionality—such as support for Windows NT extended data types—that regedit doesn't possess.

Editing with `regedt32.exe`

To run regedt32, choose Run from the Start menu. In the Run dialog box, type *regedt32* and click OK. You can also start the utility from a command prompt by typing *regedt32*.

> **Tip**
>
> *If you use regedt32 frequently, you can create a shortcut to it on your desktop or on the Start menu.*

The regedt32 main window contains five windows. Two of the windows are for the two Registry hives (HKEY_LOCAL_MACHINE and HKEY_USERS), and the other three windows are for the three Registry pointer hives (HKEY_CLASSES_ROOT, HKEY_CURRENT_USER, and HKEY_CURRENT_CONFIG).

Each window displays its piece of the Registry in a tree-like structure, much like Windows NT Explorer displays the folders and the files on your hard drive. The windows are divided into two panes; the left pane displays the Registry keys and subkeys, and the right pane displays the Registry values and their contents for the Registry key that is currently selected in the left pane.

Next to each key is a little folder icon that can be blank or can contain a + or – sign. If the folder icon is blank, it means that the key does not have any subkeys under it. If the folder icon is a +, it means that there are subkeys under the key but that they have not been expanded. If the folder icon is a –, it means that there are subkeys under the key and they have already been expanded.

The regedt32 main window has eight menus: Registry, Edit, Tree, View, Security, Options, Window, and Help. The latter two are self-explanatory. The following sections describe the commands on each of the other six menus.

Registry

- **Open Local** Opens the five Registry hive windows for the local computer's Registry. By default, this is performed when you start the regedt32 program.

- **Close** Closes the Registry windows displayed in the current window. If the current window is one of the five Registry windows displayed for the local computer, all five of those windows are closed. If the current window is one of the two Registry windows displayed for a remote computer's Registry, the two windows displaying the remote computer's Registry are closed.

- **Load Hive** Temporarily loads into the Registry hive being displayed a Registry hive that is currently not loaded or open. This command is available only when the current window is displaying the HKEY_LOCAL_MACHINE or HKEY_USERS hives for the local computer or for a remote computer's Registry because the other hives displayed in the Registry Editor are just pointers to entries in those two hives. One use for this command is for modifying the Registry entries for another user. After you load the hive for another user account, the account will appear as another key under the HKEY_USERS hive. You can now view or modify the Registry information for that user. After you finish working with that Registry information, you should unload the hive from the Registry.

- **Unload Hive** Saves modifications made to a previously loaded hive to disk and unloads the hive from memory. You should use this command only for Registry items that you have previously loaded with Load Hive.

- **Restore** Restores a hive that was previously saved to disk as a file. When you restore a hive to another hive, the original hive is overwritten with the restored hive's information. These changes are permanent.

- **Save Key** Saves all the items in a Registry key and its subkeys to a file. The Registry information is saved in a binary format to the filename that you specify. You can later load the file back into the Registry with the Load Hive command or the Restore command.

- **Select Computer** Connects to another computer to display and modify its Registry hives. This command brings up a dialog box that allows you to select the computer from a list or type the computer name. Be sure to prefix the computer name with two backslashes if you type it. Once you specify the computer, two additional windows will open, one to display the HKEY_LOCAL_MACHINE hive and another to display the HKEY_USERS hive for the selected computer.

- **Print Subtree** Prints the currently selected Registry key, all of its subkeys, and all of the values they contain.

- **Printer Setup** Lets you select a particular printer and set options for that printer.

- **Save Subtree As** Saves the currently selected Registry key, all of its subkeys, and all of the values they contain to a text file.

- **Exit** Closes the Registry Editor.

Edit

- **Add Key** Adds a new subkey to the currently selected key. You'll be prompted for the name of the new key and its class name.

- **Add Value** Adds a new value to the currently selected key. You'll be prompted for the name of the key and its data type. The regedt32 Registry Editor doesn't support all the Registry data types previously discussed—only the ones most commonly used. The data types supported by regedt32 are REG_BINARY, REG_DWORD, REG_EXPAND_SZ, REG_MULTI_SZ, and REG_SZ.

- **Delete** Removes the currently selected item. If a key is selected, this command deletes the key, all of its subkeys, and all of the values that they contain. If a value is selected, only that value is deleted.

- **Binary** Displays the binary editor for regedt32 so that you can modify the selected binary value. Double-clicking on the desired binary value has the same effect.

- **String** Opens the string editor for regedt32 so that you can modify the selected string value. Double-clicking on the desired string value has the same effect. This editor is used to modify REG_EXPAND_SZ and REG_SZ values.

- **DWORD** Displays the regedt32 DWORD editor so that you can change the selected DWORD value. Double-clicking on the desired DWORD value does the same thing.

- **Multi String** Opens the multistring editor for regedt32 so that you can modify the selected REG_MULTI_SZ value. Double-clicking on the desired REG_MULTI_SZ value does the same thing.

Tree

- **Expand One Level** Expands the currently selected key to display the next level of subkeys under it.

- **Expand Branch** Shows all the subkeys under the currently selected key.

- **Expand All** Expands all the subkeys for the current Registry window.

- **Collapse Branch** Closes the tree levels for all the subkeys in the currently selected Registry key.

View

- **Tree And Data** Displays both the left pane (tree information) and right pane (values and data) in the current Registry window.

- **Tree Only** Displays only the left pane (tree information).

- **Data Only** Displays only the right pane (values and data).

- **Split** Lets you move the bar separating the left and right panes to adjust the size of the panes.

- **Display Binary Data** Displays the currently selected value in read-only mode.

- **Refresh All** Updates the Registry information displayed for all Registry windows associated with the current Registry window.

- **Refresh Active** Updates the Registry information displayed for the current Registry window to show any changes that have been made to the Registry entries.

- **Find Key** Displays a dialog box that lets you locate a Registry key in the current Registry window.

Security

- **Permissions** Lets you view and modify the level of access to the currently selected Registry key given to the defined user accounts and group accounts. Currently, the access required for specific Registry keys is not well documented, so you should proceed with caution if you modify the security settings of a Registry key.
- **Auditing** Lets you audit additions, changes, and deletions to the currently selected Registry key.
- **Owner** Lets you view or modify the owner of the currently selected Registry key.

Options

- **Font** Lets you specify the font used in Registry windows.
- **Auto Refresh** Displays Registry updates in all Registry windows as they occur. Auto Refresh is turned off when you view another computer's Registry hives.
- **Read Only Mode** Changes all Registry keys and values in all of the displayed Registry windows to read-only so that no changes can be made to any of the Registry keys or values.
- **Confirm On Delete** Displays a confirmation dialog box whenever you delete a Registry key or a value; you must confirm that you really want to delete the selected key or the value.
- **Save Settings On Exit** Saves the window positions, window sizes, and font selection currently in use so that they are used the next time you run the regedt32 program.

Some advantages

The regedt32 program provides several features that are not readily available anywhere else unless you develop your own application using the Software Development Kit (SDK) from Microsoft. These features include:

- The ability to view and modify the security permissions on Registry keys
- The ability to audit access to Registry keys and audit additions, changes, and deletions
- The ability to take ownership of a Registry key if the appropriate security permissions have been set

- The ability to connect to, view, and modify the Registry settings of another computer on the network if the appropriate security permissions have been set

- The ability to load and modify a Registry hive that has been saved to disk and that is not currently loaded in the Registry

- Display of the data type of each value, along with the value's data contents

The user performing these functions must have administrative rights on the computer whose Registry is being accessed or modified.

And disadvantages

The most significant weakness of regedt32 is its poor search capability. You're limited to searching the Registry for a specific Registry key. (Choose Find Key from the View menu.) This is a significant limitation because you'll often want to search for a specific value's name or a specific piece of information in a value's data.

Also, regedt32 still has the old Windows 3.1 interface. Although this isn't a major disadvantage, it does mean that context menus and right mouse button support aren't available.

Editing with regedit.exe

When Windows 95 was released, it came with a new and much improved Registry Editor, regedit.exe. Most of the core improvements introduced in the Windows 95 version are also in the Windows NT 4 version.

The obvious place to look for regedit would be under Administrative Tools (Common), but as with regedt32, there's no Registry Editor icon on the Start Menu. This is probably because of the dangers involved if improper changes are made to the Registry. We cannot overstate the importance of having a reliable backup process in place and making sure that you have recent backups of the Registry before you attempt to make any changes.

To run regedit, choose Run from the Start menu. In the Run dialog box, type *regedit*, and then click the OK button. You can also run regedit from a command prompt by typing *regedit*. If you find yourself using this utility frequently, you can create a shortcut to it on your desktop or on the Start menu.

When you run regedit, it will display its main program window, as shown in Figure 26.02 on the following page. The window has two panes. The left pane displays the computer names you are connected to, with their Registry hives listed under them. When a Registry key is selected in the left pane, the right pane displays the Registry values and their contents.

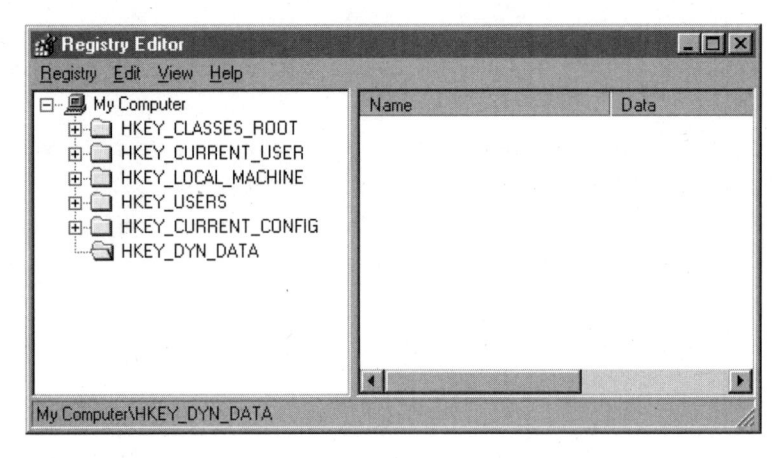

FIGURE 26.02

The regedit main window.

The Registry, Edit, and View menus provide access to the program's functions. The commands on these menus are described in the following sections:

Registry

- **Import Registry File** Imports a text file formatted in the regedit4 format into the Registry.
- **Export Registry File** Exports all or a selected part of the Registry to a regedit4-formatted text file. This file can be easily edited with any text editor and reimported back into the Registry.
- **Connect Network Registry** Lets you connect to another computer's Registry to view and modify the Registry entries. Unfortunately, this command is currently not functional. To edit another computer's Registry, use regedt32.
- **Disconnect Network Registry** Disconnects the previously made connection to another computer's Registry.
- **Print** Lets you print the entire Registry or print the selected key, all of its subkeys, and all of the values they contain.
- **Exit** Closes the Registry Editor.

Edit

- **Modify** Lets you edit the value currently selected in the right pane of the window.

- **New** Creates a new subkey of the currently selected key and allows you to create a new string, binary, or DWORD value for the key.
- **Delete** Deletes the currently selected item. If a key is selected, this deletes the key, all of its subkeys, and all of the values that they contain. If a value is selected, only that value is deleted.
- **Rename** Lets you change the name of the currently selected key, subkey, or value.
- **Copy Key Name** Copies the fully qualified name of the selected key or subkey to the Clipboard.
- **Find** Lets you search the entire Registry for a specified character string. Key names, subkey names, value names, and their data can all be searched for the specified character string.
- **Find Next** Lets you find the next occurrence of the previously specified character string.

View

- **Status Bar** Toggles the display of the status bar at the bottom of the regedit window. The status bar shows a description of the currently selected menu command and displays the path to the currently selected Registry key.
- **Split** Lets you move the splitter bar that separates the left and right panes so that you can adjust the size of the panes.
- **Refresh** Updates the Registry display to reflect any changes that might have been made to the Registry by another program.

Some advantages

The most significant advantages of regedit over the older regedt32 include:

- A greatly improved Find feature that can search the key names, value names, and value data for the specified search criteria.
- The ability to limit the areas that the find feature will search. Key names, value names, and value data can be included or excluded from the search.
- The ability to import a text file formatted with the regedit4 format into the Registry.

- The ability to export the entire Registry, a specific Registry hive, or a specific Registry branch and all the entries it contains to a text file in regedit4 format.
- A much improved interface that provides all of the nice features of the Windows NT 4 user interface such as context menus and right mouse button support.

And disadvantages

Despite the significant advantages of regedit, several areas need improvement, including the following:

- Even though the Registry menu contains the Connect Network Registry and Disconnect Network Registry commands, you cannot use regedit to connect to the Registry of another computer.
- The Import and Export features provide methods for saving and restoring Registry information to and from a text file in regedit4 format (a very useful and powerful feature), but there is no method to load the Registry information of a currently unloaded Registry hive (such as the Registry hive of a user who is not currently logged on).
- The data type of each value is not displayed along with the value's data contents. You must invoke the editor for the data value to see the data type displayed.

Before You Install New Software

You should always back up the Registry before installing new software. This provides you with a recovery option if something goes wrong and the Registry information becomes corrupt or if the changes made to the Registry produce undesirable results.

The following batch file performs a complete Registry backup for the local computer and also backs up the Registry information for *all* the user accounts on the local computer using the NTBackup program that comes with Windows NT. After the backup is complete, Notepad is launched to display the log file that NTBackup created during the backup.

```
@Echo Off
REM
REM Back up the local computer's Registry information and the
REM Registry information for all user accounts on the local
REM computer using NTBACKUP.
REM
```

```
ntbackup backup c:\winnt\system32\config c:\winnt\profiles /a /v
   /d "Registry BU" /b /t normal /l "c:\bu.log" /e notepad c:\bu.log
```

Note that the line that begins with the *ntbackup* command and the line immediately below it must be typed as a single line in the batch file.

The following batch file performs a complete Registry backup for the local computer and also backs up the Registry information for a single user account (that you specify) on the local computer using the regback program in the Windows NT Resource Kit.

Note that you *must* modify this batch file to specify the SID (security identifier) for the user account that you want to backup. The SID must be for the current user account. To determine the SID for the current user, run the regedit program and expand the HKEY_USERS hive. There will be two subkeys under HKEY_USERS—the .DEFAULT subkey and the SID for the current user. Modify the batch file where noted to specify this number for the user account to back up. Also note that this batch file assumes that the Windows NT Resource Kit has been installed and has been added to the path so that the regback program can be located.

```
@Echo Off
REM
REM Back up the local computer's Registry information and the
REM Registry information for the specified user account on
REM the local computer using the regback program from the
REM Windows NT Resource Kit.
REM
if .%1==. goto NoDir

REM Ensure that the specified directory exists
if NOT exist %1\nul goto NotExist

REM Back up the local computer's Registry information
regback %1
if ErrorLevel 2 goto RegFail

REM Back up the Registry information for the specified user
REM account on the local computer
REM
REM The NEXT line MUST be modified to specify the user accounts
REM SID that you wish to backup.
regback %1\NTUSER.DAT users s-1-1-12-123456789-1234567890-1234567890-1234
if ErrorLevel 1 goto URegFail
```

(continued)

```
    goto End

:NoDir
Echo No directory specified to back up the Registry to.
goto End

:NotExist
Echo The directory specified does NOT exist.
goto End

:RegFail
Echo Error backing up the local computer Registry information.
goto End

:URegFail
Echo Error backing up the specified user's Registry information.
goto End

:End
```

POINTS TO REMEMBER

- The Registry in Windows NT is a database that stores file type associations and maintains information used by other applications.

- Each piece of information stored in the Registry is assigned a name. The name need not be unique to the entire Registry; it must be unique only to the Registry key or subkey under which the value name is created.

- Data associated with a name is assigned a data type, which describes the type of information stored in that Registry entry.

- Two programs are included with Windows NT Server, the older regedt32 and the newer regedit. The regedt32 program has superior editing tools, whereas regedit has better search capabilities.

- Always back up the Registry before you install new software.

WHAT'S NEXT

In the next chapter, we'll discuss both general and specific ways of troubleshooting common problems on servers.

Chapter 27

Troubleshooting

- 496 Standard Operating Procedures
- 497 Printers and Printing
- 499 E-Mail
- 499 Managing Users
- 500 Backups
- 500 Files and Folders
- 501 Internet Access
- 501 Modems
- 502 Remote Access Service
- 503 Faxes
- 503 Security
- 504 Setting Up Computers
- 504 Disks
- 505 Tips and Tricks from the Experts
- 508 Points to Remember
- 508 What's Next

Chapter 27
Troubleshooting

Sooner or later, any computer network will have a problem. And it's usually sooner. Most problems are pretty straightforward and simple to fix, although others take a bit more work and thought. Microsoft BackOffice Small Business Server provides some useful troubleshooting wizards and help files to guide you through even the most difficult problems. In this chapter, we'll set up a framework for using these excellent wizards and help files. At the end of the chapter, you'll find a selection of the best tips and fixes.

In a highly server-centric computing environment such as Small Business Server, most of the problems originate on the server even though they're more likely to be reported on the client end. When someone reports a problem, your first instinct will probably be to start poking around and changing things on the client machine. Resist this instinct. Your first task when troubleshooting any problem is to decide where the problem is *really* located. Only then can you start to narrow it down further and actually fix it. Take the time to locate the problem before you start changing anything; you'll save yourself untold amounts of grief in the long run.

In any network environment, there are four basic locations for any problem—the server, the client, the peripherals hanging off various machines, and the physical network itself. Small Business Server offers one advantage over a typical peer-to-peer network—virtually all the peripherals are either physically connected to the server or at least controlled by it.

Standard Operating Procedures

Most of the problems that you're likely to encounter on Small Business Server will be due to improper performance of some administrative task. All the proper procedures are covered somewhere in the documentation. But expecting someone to read all the documentation before adding a user isn't realistic. One useful solution is to create a set of standard operating procedures (SOPs) for the most common administrative tasks. This is particularly helpful if you have several people carrying out these tasks at different times. But even if you have only one administrator, SOPs can be useful for ensuring that no steps are forgotten and that they are always done in the same way.

One caution about SOPs, however. They tend to get out of date. Be sure to update them when you make a change in your procedures. And keep a hard copy of your SOPs in a handy binder right by the server.

Printers and Printing

It's no accident that we're discussing printing problems first in this chapter. They account for a huge percentage of network problems. Printing problems can also be among the most annoying to track down because they can be located at any one of the four problem locations. The complaint will almost always be some variant of "I tried to print my document but nothing happened," which tells you almost nothing about the actual cause.

Your first task, as always, is to identify where the problem is located. For printing problems, we like to start at the end of the chain—the printer itself. Look for the usual things: Is the printer on? More to the point, is it on line? Is it connected to the server (or to the network if it's a network printer)? Is there paper? Are there any error messages on the display? Assuming that all of these things look normal, try turning the printer off and then back on. If a job is "stuck" in the printer, this might clear it and let other jobs through.

The next place to look is the server. Check to see if any jobs are waiting to print by opening the printer's folder. To do so, you must log onto the server and choose Settings and then Printers from the Start menu. Double-click on the icon of the printer that is having problems to open its folder, as shown in Figure 27.01.

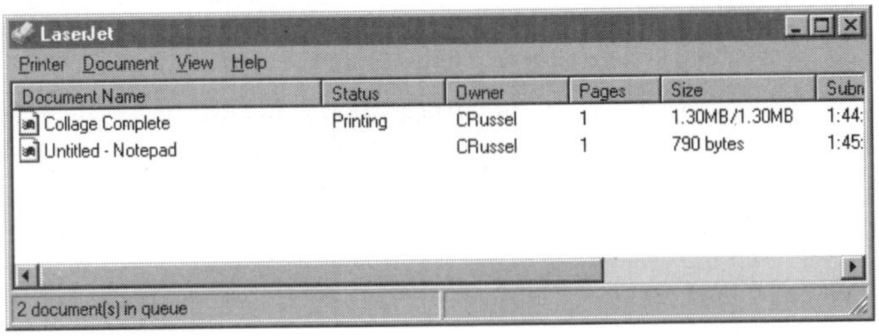

FIGURE 27.01

If a job is stuck in the printer queue, the jobs behind it will be stuck as well.

If the problem is in the connection between the server and the printer, you might see an error message on the server itself. Of course, that error message might bear little relation to the actual cause of the problem. A loose parallel printer cable, for example, will yield an out-of-paper message like that shown in Figure 27.02 on the following page.

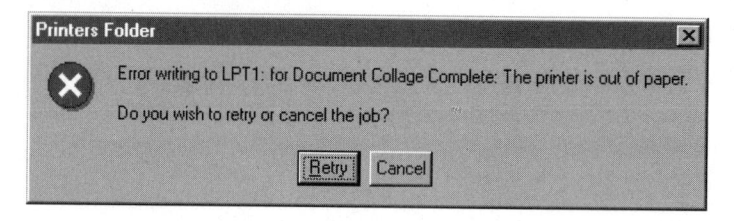

FIGURE 27.02

Windows NT error messages don't always tell you the real problem.

A bad network connection to a network printer will usually result in an empty printer queue, not a backed-up one. If no jobs are showing in the printer's folder but users report that they can't print, try printing a simple test job from the server using Windows Notepad. This is the most basic printing test and should work even if there are problems with more complicated jobs or applications.

> **Tip**
>
> *Always use Notepad for printing tests. If you can print a test from Notepad, you know that all is well with the printing subsystem and that the problem is with an application or a printer driver.*

If you can get jobs to print from the server but all the clients are still having problems, check the printer share on the server and make sure that no one has accidentally changed or deleted a printer share name.

If only some clients are having problems, the most likely explanation is a problem with the network or with individual settings on the clients that are having problems. Start by doing a test from Notepad on the machines that are having problems. If you can print from Notepad but not from an application, check the application settings.

If you have problems from only certain machines or one specific machine and you can't print from Notepad, try printing as a different user from the same machine. If you can print successfully, the problem probably has to do with the user permissions on the printer. If you still can't print successfully, try reinstalling the printer and the printer drivers.

E-Mail

One area that will cause your users a lot of grief is e-mail. E-mail is one of those things that we can no longer live without. Disrupt the users' e-mail and the screaming will start almost immediately.

Problems with e-mail tend to be located in three areas:

- The connection to your Internet Service Provider
- The server
- The connection between the client workstation and the server

We covered the troubleshooting of your e-mail connection in detail in Chapter 14, so we won't repeat ourselves here. But we'll reiterate the advice that you should treat e-mail problems extremely seriously. Once e-mail is part of your business, the business will depend on it. And e-mail problems do seem to cause the most emotional response from users, so handle the problems promptly.

Managing Users

The most common problems with users and user accounts have to do with passwords. For reasons known only to Microsoft, by default Small Business Server user passwords expire in 41 days. This is totally annoying, and we suggest that you change this setting. Open User Manager for Domains (by choosing Programs, Administrative Tools [Common], and then User Manager For Domains from the Start menu), and choose Account from the Policies menu to bring up the dialog box shown in Figure 27.03 on the following page. Select the Password Never Expires option in the Maximum Password Age section. Your users will stop getting those annoying messages about changing their passwords.

Another thing that happens more often than one would reasonably expect is that users forget their passwords. Small Business Server does a reasonable job of not requiring a hopelessly arcane password, but users will still manage to forget their passwords. When this happens, simply run the Change Password Wizard from the Manage Users page of the Small Business Server console. When you use this wizard as an administrator, you can issue a user a new password without knowing the old one. You can also let Small Business Server generate a new password, but the ones that Small Business Server generates can be hopelessly difficult to remember, so you should probably let the user choose his or her own password. There's at least a chance that the user will remember it that way.

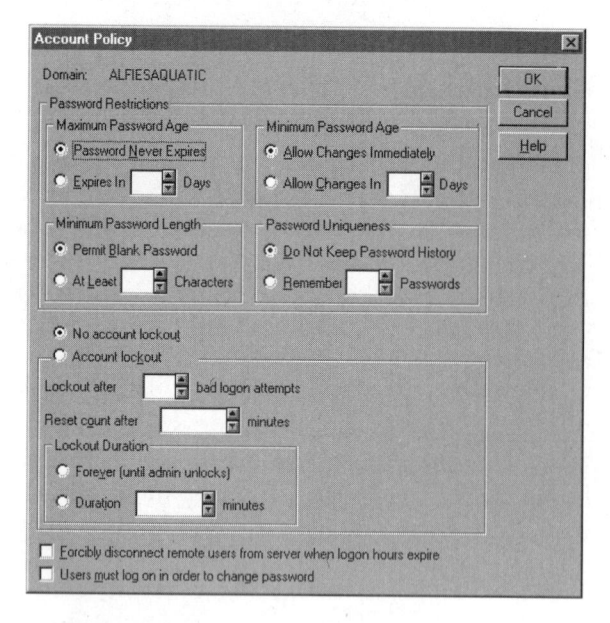

FIGURE 27.03

Turning off password aging makes for happier users.

Backups

Backups are one of those things that no one pays any attention to until it's too late. As we pointed out in Chapter 13, the Microsoft Backup utility included with Small Business Server has some serious shortcomings—not the least of which is that it provides no way to automatically back up files on client computers. Getting your users to do backups manually might take some training—most people think that information stored on their local workstations is "safer" and more secure. This is untrue, of course. So try to get everyone in the habit of keeping important documents on the server (in their own private directories if the documents are sensitive).

If you really need to back up the client workstations on your Small Business Server network, you can do so with the Backup program, but we think you'll find it less than satisfactory. You might as well spring for a full-featured backup program.

Files and Folders

If you have problems accessing certain files or folders, the problem is almost certainly with permissions or file sharing, so you'll have to fix the problem at the server. Use the Troubleshooting page of the Small Business Server console to investigate the possible problems and their fixes.

The other possible source of such a problem is a general network failure or the failure of networking on a specific client machine. If only one client has problems, check that the network is functioning correctly on that client and that all the physical connections to it are solid. You might find a network cable that's inserted *almost* all the way into the socket. Check basic network connectivity before you start looking at other possible failures.

Internet Access

The entire Internet access portion of Small Business Server depends on the correct functioning of Microsoft Proxy Server and of your modems. This means it can be pretty fragile—especially the modem portion. If your modems are all from the short list of supported modems and you haven't tried to "fix" something, chances are that they'll work fine.

But if you do have trouble accessing the Internet, you should first identify the source of the problem. Start by trying to dial your Internet Service Provider (ISP) directly using Dial-Up Networking. If the modem connects to the ISP, the problem is probably in the Proxy Server setup or the Proxy Client setup. If some workstations can access the Internet but others can't, the problem is in the Proxy Client setup. Reinstalling the Proxy Client on the problem computers will likely solve the problem. If you can't connect to the Internet from the server but others on the network can, the Proxy Client for the server is munged. (That's the highly technical computer science term for "it won't ever work right again.") Again, reinstalling will likely solve the problem.

If no computers on the network can connect to the Internet but you can manually dial and connect, you have a problem with the setup for Proxy Server itself. See Chapter 22 for details on Proxy Server. You might also consider upgrading to Proxy Server 2.0. It is substantially more robust than version 1.0 and has significant performance enhancements as well.

Modems

Modems are probably *the* most fragile area of Small Business Server. Therefore, we strongly urge you to leave them alone if possible. If they have worked in the past but have stopped working, you can try to correct the problem. But be prepared for pain and suffering.

The first requirement for modem sharing is that the modems be identical—not similar, and not just the same model. They must be the same make, model, *and* firmware revision. If you have a failed modem and need to replace it, keep this in mind.

Remote Access Service

To use Remote Access Service (RAS), users must have permission to access the server over a modem. Use the Manage User Permissions icon on the Manage Users page of the Small Business Server console to start the User Resource Wizard. On the next-to-last page of the wizard, you can specify whether a user is allowed to access the server over a modem. (See Figure 27.04.) This will let the user dial up and connect to the server (but not to the entire network) from a remote location.

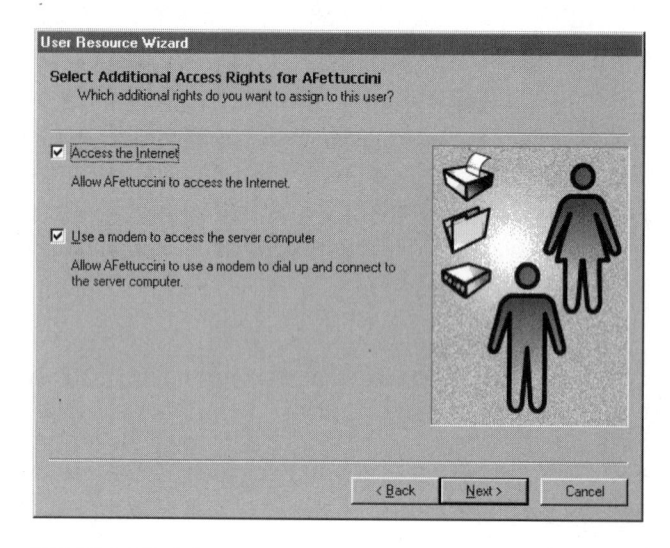

FIGURE 27.04

Users must have permission to use RAS to dial up and connect to the server.

If you want a user to be able to see other computers on the network, you must change a setting for RAS itself. In the Control Panel, double-click on the Network icon. In the Network dialog box, click on the Services tab, select Remote Access Service, and click Properties. In the Remote Access Setup dialog box, click Network. In the Network Configuration dialog box, click the Configure button to the right of the TCP/IP check box. In the RAS Server TCP/IP Configuration dialog box, make sure that the Entire Network option is selected. Now click OK, OK again, Continue, and OK once more to close all those dialog boxes.

Faxes

If for any reason you need to modify your modem configuration, you must uninstall and reinstall the Fax Server. Another common problem with the Fax Server is that occasionally modems are inexplicably set for no hardware flow control. This means they won't work. To fix this, go to the Control Panel and double-click on the Modems icon. Select the modem in question, and click Properties. In the modem's Properties dialog box, click on the Connection tab and then click the Advanced button. In the Advanced Connection Settings dialog box, select the Use Flow Control check box and then select the Hardware (RTS/CTS) option. Click OK, OK again, and then Close to "dig" your way out.

Security

Security issues generally don't show up as separate problems. Often, one or more users will be unable to access particular files or folders or to use one of the shared resources such as the Fax Server.

If you stick to the Small Business Server console for adding or removing shares, you're unlikely to have incorrectly set permissions. But if you use Windows Explorer to create shares manually or to change the underlying security permissions of the files or the folders, you'll probably have problems later. By default, Small Business Server sets wide-open permissions for a new share and then uses folder permissions to limit access to only users who are supposed to be able to access the files or the folders. This is the best way to handle permissions—if you make the mistake of trying to fine-tune permissions by adjusting the permissions of the share itself, you'll have nothing but problems trying to figure out where it's actually being controlled. Stick to a single point of control.

If you have any file systems that are FAT formatted (as opposed to NTFS formatted), you'll run into permissions problems on those systems. Because of the way that Small Business Server manages security, it must be able to control access at the directory or file level, not at the share point. Unfortunately, the FAT file system won't support proper security, so you should carefully consider whether you want *any* sharing of FAT file systems—and, in fact, whether you want or need any FAT file systems at all. By default, you won't get any, and we think that's probably best. The one possible exception is for removable media such as Jaz or Zip drives. But these are unlikely to be storage points for sensitive information unless you use them as a form of backup.

Setting Up Computers

Small Business Server makes certain assumptions about the computers that will be on the network and how they should be set up. While these assumptions are a necessary part of the Small Business Server process, they can create problems in the real world, especially if you're not starting from scratch.

If you are installing Small Business Server on an existing network, you'll probably experience some difficulties as you set up the client machines. Some of these obstacles are intentional—for example, Small Business Server deliberately doesn't overwrite existing e-mail setups. You can use the Troubleshooting Wizard to walk through that one. Other snags are not intentional but might require you to make a manual change, such as selecting the setting that allows a client computer to use a local modem.

Disks

One of the most common problems with Small Business Server and disks occurs during the initial setup. In most cases, you must install Small Business Server onto a formatted disk. If you start with a blank, unpartitioned drive, you'll end up with the "blue screen of death," in which case you should start over with an MS-DOS boot disk and partition and format the drive. Boot from the floppy, run FDISK, and create a single, primary MS-DOS partition of the maximum available size. Reboot using the MS-DOS floppy again, and format the partition by running FORMAT/S from the floppy.

Your initial partition will be limited to 2 GB (due to the nature of MS-DOS), but don't worry about that at this point. Your goal is to get enough of an operating system on the drive so that Small Business Server can handle the installation. Simply leave the rest of the drive unpartitioned, and you can use the Disk Administrator (from the Start menu, choose Programs, Administrative Tools [Common], and then Disk Administrator) after you get Small Business Server up and running to create another partition for the rest of your hard drive.

One exception to this process is when you are installing onto a RAID controller or another unlisted controller and disk configuration. When you are performing an installation onto a RAID controller or if you need to manually intervene in the installation process, press the F6 key while the computer is booting from the first installation disk when the screen says it is detecting hardware. This will cause the computer to stop during the boot process at the end of disk 2 and let you add drivers for your unlisted card.

Tips and Tricks from the Experts

This section offers troubleshooting tips and tricks that we culled from the Small Business Server newsgroup, *microsoft.public.backoffice.smallbiz*, which is on the *msnews.microsoft.com server*. Many users and administrators regularly contribute to this group, and it is a wonderful resource for anyone implementing Small Business Server. Many thanks to Grey Lancaster, Paul Fitzgerald, Doug Swallow, Birk Binnard, Andy Dunda, Larry Buchanan, John Nelson, and Reynald Valliere, who contributed to this list, and to all the others who've assisted us. If you have a tip of your own that you'd like to see in a future edition of this book, send it to us at *SBSBook@scribes.com*.

- If the Administrative shares have been lost or deleted on the server, the Small Business Server console will fail to correctly create new users or to update folder permissions on an existing user. Re-create the administrative shares to correct the problem. Table 27.01 shows the administrative shares and their default locations.

Table 27.01
Default Administrative Shares for Small Business Server

Administrative Share	Default Location
ADMIN$	C:\WINNT.SBS
C$	C:\
Connect$	C:\exchsrvr\CONNECT
FaxStore	C:\WINNT.SBS\FaxStore
Print$	C:\WINNT.SBS\system32\spool\drivers

- If you decide to set up your Internet connection manually because you already have an ISP and don't want to change, you must set up each of the necessary services (Dial-Up Networking, Proxy Server, and Exchange Server) manually. When setting up Exchange, remember to set the Internet Mail Service address space to route everything via SMTP. Open the Exchange Administrator. Under the sitename in the left-hand pane, open the Configuration container and then click on the Connections container. In the right-hand pane, double-click on Internet Mail Connector. In the Internet Mail Connector Properties dialog box, click on the Address Space tab and make sure that there is an entry for SMTP with an address of * and a cost of 1. This tells Exchange how to route Internet mail.

- Never attempt to install the client software on a Microsoft Windows 95 or Microsoft Windows NT Workstation machine that loads Norton Utilities during startup.

> **Tip**
>
> *When you install Norton Utilities—or any other new program—always disable any automatic programs that run on startup, such as antivirus utilities and system utilities. This will significantly reduce installation problems.*

- The default user permissions for Small Business Server allow everyone to read everyone else's shared files on the server. If file security is an issue in your organization, change the default permissions when you set up a new user.

- If your system hangs during initial installation, particularly if it's because you have unlisted hardware that is otherwise supported by Windows NT, you should install a base Windows NT system first. Make sure that all hardware is properly recognized and configured, and then run SBSSETUP.EXE from the Small Business Server CD #1. If you know that you have specialized hardware, especially unlisted modems, try this right from the beginning to avoid the problem.

- If server security isn't an issue in your organization, you can install TweakUI (available from the Microsoft web site), which allows you to set up the Administrator account to automatically log on and start up your monitoring tools.

- The default for Microsoft SQL Server and SQL Executive services is for manual startup. You can change to automatic startup using the Services applet in the Control Panel so that they are always available.

- The default temporary database size for SQL Server is 2 MB. This is woefully inadequate for many installations. Change it to a minimum of 25 or 30 MB to reduce problems.

- Always install Small Business Server with a fax modem during initial installation. If the modem is detected as a Standard Modem, manually change it to the correct type. This will save you a lot of grief later.

- The template.bat file contains the sample logon script that is used to define all new user logon scripts. Modify it by adding a call to another batch file where you can set up default drive mappings that are different for each user.

- Modify the installed MSPCLNT.INI file (usually in \proxy\clients or \msp\clients) to support third-party mail and newsgroup clients by modifying the following lines in it:

```
[Explorer]
Disable=0
[MAPISP32]
Disable=0
```

  On the client machines, run the WSP Client update from the Control Panel, and then reboot.

- Never move users' shared folders. This will cause the Add A Computer Wizard to not see any users.

- Copy the file WINNT.SIF from the \I386 directory of CD #1 onto floppy boot disk #2. This will give you more control over the initial installation partitions and settings. (But you will have to interact with the installation more than if you didn't do this.)

- If the Internet Mail Service refuses to start, make sure that the default mail box for the service points to the Administrator mail box. (Use Exchange Administrator to see this.) If it points somewhere else, change it back to the Administrator. If that fails, delete the service and re-create it. If you are prompted to run the Exchange optimization, you should probably do so.

- You can use a batch file to more quickly shut down several services before shutting down the server. This can speed up the process by several minutes. Here's a SHUTDOWN.CMD file that we've used successfully:

```
@echo "Starting Shutdown"
net stop "Microsoft Exchange Internet Mail Service" /y
net stop "Microsoft Exchange Message Transfer Agent" /y
net stop "Microsoft Exchange Information Store" /y
net stop "Microsoft Exchange Directory" /y
net stop "Microsoft Exchange System Attendant" /y
net stop "Modem Sharing Service" /y
net stop "Microsoft WinSock Proxy Service" /y
net stop "Microsoft Proxy Server Administration" /y
net stop "Microsoft Fax Service" /y
net stop "Microsoft DHCP Server" /y
net stop "Computer Browser" /y
net stop "Net Logon" /y
net stop "Alerter" /y
net stop "Messenger" /y
net stop "Server" /y
net stop "Workstation" /y
```

We keep this file in our \WINNT.SBS\System32 directory, with a shortcut to it on the desktop of the Administrator account. When you need to shut down the server because of a configuration change, it can easily save you five minutes.

POINTS TO REMEMBER

- Take the time to identify the location and the source of any problem before you start changing things.
- Always use listed hardware if possible.
- For modem sharing to work, your modems must be of the same model, hardware, and firmware revision. Buy listed modems with downloadable firmware for the best results.
- Cut down on your users' grief by specifying that passwords never expire.
- For installation on unlisted SCSI or RAID controllers, use the F6 key during the hardware detection phase so that you can add the necessary drivers.

WHAT'S NEXT

In this chapter, we covered some common problems and ways to troubleshoot and correct them. In the next chapter, we'll deal with the ultimate problem—a disaster that causes a major failure or a total failure—and how to recover from it.

Chapter 28

Disaster Recovery: When All Else Fails

510	**Creating a Recovery Plan**
511	**The Server Won't Boot—Now What?**
512	**The Last Known Good Configuration Menu**
	Creating a Copy of Your Current Hardware Profile — 512
513	**Emergency Repair Disks**
	Creating an ERD — 514
516	**The Emergency Boot Disk**
	Creating a Windows NT Boot Disk—*x86* Version — 516
	Creating a Windows NT Boot Disk—Digital Alpha Version — 517
518	**Mirrored Boot Partitions**
519	**Restoring a Failed Server**
	Creating and Using a Recovery Drive — 520
	Replacing a Server — 520
521	**Points to Remember**

Chapter 28

Disaster Recovery: When All Else Fails

Bicycle riders wear helmets even if they ride carefully and hope to never, ever need that helmet to stay in one piece. But as the saying goes, "There are only two kinds of riders—those who've crashed and those who haven't…yet."

Similarly, we all hope to never need verified backups and Emergency Repair Disks, but we keep them because there are only two types of networks—those that have experienced disaster and those that haven't…yet.

In this chapter, we'll cover emergency preparedness as well as the recovery process itself. Keep in mind that large, enterprise networks are not the only networks that need a disaster recovery plan. Where would your business be if your entire network were to fail or if a major civil disaster such as a flood or an earthquake were to occur? Could you easily recover and rebuild your network and the business it supports? If so, great—you're doing your job. But if not, this chapter will help you prepare for the unthinkable.

We'll discuss how to create a disaster recovery plan, and we'll show you how to create a Windows NT Emergency Repair Disk (ERD). We'll also explain what changes you should make to your recovery procedures if you're using mirrored root disks and how to replace a server if the worst happens.

Creating a Recovery Plan

It is a fact of life that emergencies bring out both the best *and* worst in people. To be truly prepared for a system disaster, you must plan ahead and prepare for as many possibilities as you can. Even the most level-headed person can get flustered when a system crashes, because customers will be screaming, the boss will be asking every five minutes when the system will go back up, and the server won't boot.

One important thing to do is to write up a set of standardized recovery procedures. For starters, you should figure out as many different breakdown scenarios as you can and then practice what to do if they happen, writing down all the steps to follow. This is similar to a fire drill, and you should do it for the same reasons.

Get as many people as possible involved in the process. The more people you involve in brainstorming about potential disaster scenarios, the more ideas you'll get and the more procedures you can develop and practice. Once you have a list, assemble the same people to create and practice the recovery procedures.

Start by outlining the steps, without really filling in the details yet. When you have the outlines finished, get the same group back together again. Go over the each of the procedures you've outlined and smooth over the rough edges, refining the outlines, and *listening* to make sure you didn't miss anything critical. Then, when you feel confident that you've actually captured the essence of the procedures, it's time to test them out and document them completely.

Be sure to write down every detail. What might seem obvious to you now will not seem at all obvious six months or a year from now when you suddenly need to use the recovery plan. Keep the current version of your plan in several places so that you can get at it no matter what the source of the emergency is or where you are when the pager goes off. Then keep the plan up to date! This seems obvious, but it's not that easy to do, and it is the second most common failing of an emergency plan. (The first, by a long margin, is the absence of one at all!) Systems change over time, and recovery procedures need to change accordingly. Make sure the plan is updated in all locations.

The Server Won't Boot—Now What?

If your Microsoft Windows NT Server won't boot, that pretty much defines an emergency for most people. At that point, you should haul out your recovery plan and follow the procedures step by step.

Oh, we get it—you're reading this section now for the first time because you're actually in the middle of a disaster, and you don't *have* a disaster recovery plan. Well, don't panic…yet. You can still survive.

In the following sections, we'll discuss recovery measures from the least drastic to the most drastic. Which one works for you will depend on how thoroughly munged up your system is and how much preparatory work you've done.

The important thing to keep in mind is that in any recovery procedure, you should take a *minimalist* approach. Always try the least invasive and least drastic steps first. If they succeed, you'll have made the least impact on the network and on your business. Which is the point, of course.

The Last Known Good Configuration Menu

If you make a change to your system, you might inadvertently create a configuration that prevents you from being able to boot. The easiest and usually the best recovery tool will be right there as you're booting. You'll see a message that says:

```
Press spacebar NOW to invoke Hardware Profile/
Last Known Good Configuration
```

Press the spacebar to bring up a menu of possible logon choices that will, in many cases, let you simply bypass that last ill-advised change. But be forewarned: This approach might eliminate all changes that you've made to your system since the last saved configuration. You might not actually have a good fallback position.

If you've made a change that *is* captured by the system, you might still have problems. If you successfully log onto a system after a configuration change, Windows NT will assume that the configuration is good—even if it isn't. The Last Known Good Configuration menu is effective only for a problem that has prevented you from logging on, since any logon will clear the fallback position.

The Last Known Good Configuration menu can also be helpful if your server has multiple hardware configurations. Most servers don't, but the Last Known Good Configuration menu can create a safe fallback position before you make a major hardware change. If you're going to make a change to your hardware, it's a good idea to create a new hardware profile that's a copy of your current hardware profile before you start. Reboot your server using that new profile, and then make your changes. This will allow you to return to your previous configuration if something doesn't work as you'd hoped.

Creating a Copy of Your Current Hardware Profile

To create a copy of your current hardware profile and make that the preferred boot option:

1. Right-click on the My Computer icon in the upper left corner of the desktop, and choose Properties from the pop-up menu.

2. In the System Properties dialog box, click on the Hardware Profiles tab (shown in Figure 28.01).

3. Select the current profile, and click the Copy button. Type a name for the new configuration, and click OK.

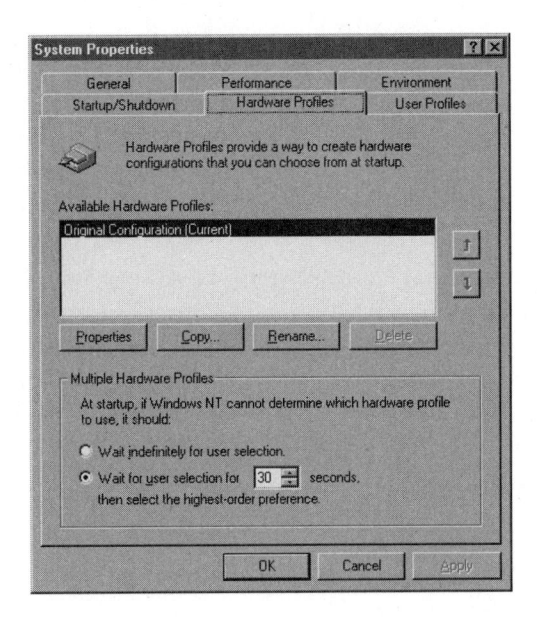

FIGURE 28.01

You should create a copy of your hardware configuration as a fallback position before you make major hardware changes.

4. If you want to make this the preferred boot option, select the new profile you just created and then click the up arrow button next to the list box to move your new hardware profile to the top of the list.

5. In the Multiple Hardware Profiles section, specify whether you want Windows NT to select the new hardware profile automatically (after a delay) when you boot up or if you want the boot process to wait indefinitely until you select the option you want.

6. Click OK, and the new configuration will be saved and your startup options set.

Emergency Repair Disks

When you first installed Windows NT Server, the installation program prompted you to create an Emergency Repair Disk (ERD). We hope that you followed our advice and agreed to let the installation program create that disk. But the ERD is useful only if you keep it current. Most systems are subject to constant evolution, and your ERD can bail you out of a mess only if it contains information about your current setup.

So, what exactly is on the ERD? The ERD contains the various hives of the registry, along with copies of the MS-DOS subsystem initialization files (AUTOEXEC.NT and CONFIG.NT) and the Security Accounts Manager database. Whenever you make a major change to your system, it's a good idea to make a fresh copy of the ERD before *and* after you make the change. This gives you a fallback position if something goes wrong; you can easily restore the previous configuration if you need to.

So what's a major change to the system? A major change might be adding, removing, or otherwise modifying the hard drives or their partitions, formats, and configurations, for example. Any time you make a change to the hard drive configuration, you should create a fresh ERD just before you make the change and just after. Another example of a major change is when you add a new component to the server. You should also create a fresh ERD before and after you make changes from the Control Panel.

Creating an ERD

To create an ERD, you need a freshly formatted floppy disk. Also keep in mind that it's good to have a backup of your ERD; always keep at least one generation back. We also keep the original ERD created during the installation process as a kind of ultimate fallback position.

To create an ERD, take the following steps:

1. Insert a fresh, 3.5-inch, 1.44 MB floppy disk in drive A.
2. Choose Run from the Start menu.
3. Type *rdisk,* and then click OK to bring up the dialog box shown in Figure 28.02.

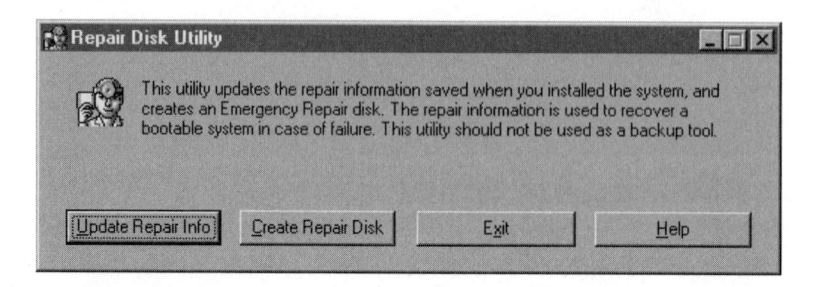

FIGURE 28.02

The Repair Disk utility saves information to help you recover from a disaster.

4. Click the Update Repair Info button to bring up the confirmation dialog box shown in Figure 28.03. You might want to discontinue the process (click No) here when you're doing an update after a major change until you're sure the change is stable and desirable.

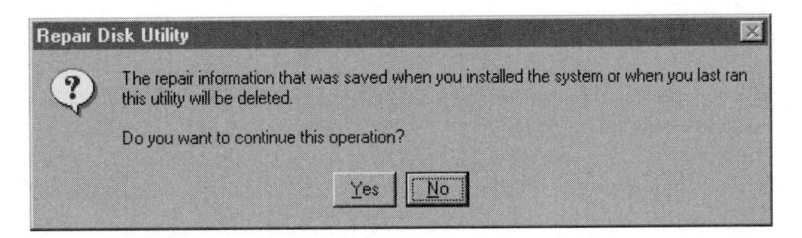

FIGURE 28.03
Updating the repair information overwrites the previously saved information.

5. Once the repair information has been updated, you'll be prompted to create an ERD, as shown in Figure 28.04. Click Yes to create the disk.
6. Store the disk in a safe and secure place.

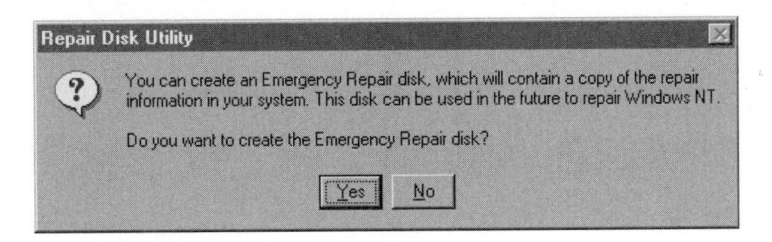

FIGURE 28.04
Creating the ERD.

> **Tip**
>
> *Since all of your user account and security information is on the server, you should make sure that you've backed it up by running* rdisk /s *instead of* rdisk *alone. This will bypass the initial screen (shown in Figure 28.02 on the previous page) and its confirmation step and take you directly to the updating of the repair directory information. Once your current configuration is saved, you'll be prompted to create the ERD, as shown in Figure 28.04. Click Yes, and then click OK after you put a fresh floppy disk in drive A. The information will be saved to the floppy disk.*

The Emergency Boot Disk

The ERD is useful and necessary, but it's *not* a bootable disk. Nor is there room on it for both the boot files and the repair information. So if your system won't boot, you have to use the initial installation disks to reboot or use an Emergency Boot Disk. The latter will get you up and running much more quickly in many situations.

> ◆ **Why MS-DOS Boot Disks Won't Help**
>
> More than one Windows NT novice has accidentally deleted or corrupted a key file required to boot Windows NT and has tried to recover by digging out an old MS-DOS boot floppy. This doesn't work too well, unfortunately, especially since your system is using NTFS with Microsoft BackOffice Small Business Server and the files you need to get your hard drive back to booting on its own aren't on an MS-DOS floppy disk. When you install Windows NT, it modifies the system's boot sector to look for and run a file called NTLDR. When you format a floppy disk under MS-DOS, even when you make it a system disk, this file isn't created because MS-DOS doesn't know anything about Windows NT.

The boot disk we'll create is *not* generic for every Windows NT machine. It is essentially specific to the machine on which it is created. So you should create one for each Windows NT workstation on your Small Business Server network in addition to the server. However, if your Windows NT workstations are all identical, which they are likely to be if you bought them at the same time, you can create a single boot disk for all of them.

Creating a Windows NT Boot Disk—x86 Version

Insert a floppy disk into drive A and, from the command line or from Microsoft Windows Explorer, format the disk. (This disk must be formatted under Windows NT.) Then copy the following files to it from the root directory of the system partition:

- ◆ NTLDR
- ◆ NTDETECT.COM
- ◆ NTBOOTDD.SYS (if present)
- ◆ BOOT.INI

The file NTBOOTDD.SYS will be present only if you're using a SCSI controller that doesn't use its BIOS to control the boot process. If it's not there, you won't need it.

You can use the boot disk you've just created to boot from and get directly into your existing Windows NT partition, even if one of the critical files in your system partition has been accidentally deleted or corrupted.

Creating a Windows NT Boot Disk—Digital Alpha Version

To create a Windows NT boot disk for a Digital Alpha–based machine, follow the procedure in the previous section, but copy the following files instead:

- OSLOADER.EXE
- HAL.DLL

On RISC-based systems, like those based on Digital's Alpha chip, the information equivalent to that stored in BOOT.INI on an $x86$ computer is stored in nonvolatile RAM. So you must modify the boot selection menu to add an option that will point to the floppy disk. The ARC name to use for the SYSTEMPARTITION on the floppy disk is:

```
scsi(0)disk(0)fdisk(0)
```

Set the necessary values for the following:

- OSLOADER—This should point to the disk you just created.
- OSLOADPARTITION—This should be your primary partition (unless you're running mirrored root partitions, in which case you should point to the secondary mirror partition).
- OSLOADFILENAME—This should be the path to the \systemroot directory.

◆ ARC Naming Conventions

Unfortunately, it's tricky to understand how the hard drives and partitions are named on your system. To provide a uniform naming convention across multiple platforms, Microsoft uses a fairly arcane designation for all the disks and partitions on your computer, called ARC (short for Advanced RISC Computing). ARC is a generic naming convention that can be used in the same way for both Intel *x*86 and RISC-based computers.

ARC describes the adapter type and number, the disk number, the rdisk number, and finally the partition number. The format takes this form:

adaptertype(*x*)disk(*y*)rdisk(*z*)partition(*n*)

where *adaptertype* can be either *scsi* or *multi*. Use *multi* for all non-SCSI adapters and for SCSI adapters that use a BIOS—as most adapters used with *x*86 processors do. The value of *x* is the adapter number, starting at 0.

The value for *y* is the SCSI ID of the disk for SCSI adapters. For *multi* this is always 0. The number for *z* is 0 for SCSI; it is the ordinal number of the disk for *multi*, starting with 0. Finally, the partition number *n* is the number of the partition on the target disk. Here the partitions start at 1, with 0 reserved for unused space.

Mirrored Boot Partitions

If you're using mirrored boot partitions and your primary boot drive fails, you'll need a boot disk to get into the system. We all know that hard drives have become much more dependable in recent years; the general rule is that if they last the first couple of months, they should last at least as long as the computer does. The problem, of course, is that as soon as you become totally dependent on a system, Murphy comes along and smiles on you. And the whole point of running a mirrored boot drive, of course, is that you really, really don't want to have trouble—and if you do have problems, you want to get back on line quickly.

So if your boot disk crashes, you must quickly switch to running off the mirror while you get a replacement for the boot disk. To do this, you have to create a boot disk using the procedure outlined previously, but with one additional step. For an Intel *x*86 processor, you must edit the BOOT.INI file on the floppy disk to change the ARC name of the boot partition to point to the secondary mirror drive rather than to the primary mirror drive. For example, if you have a pair of Adaptec 2940 adapters, have duplexed your boot drives, and are using the SCSI BIOS to boot from the primary partition on the first hard disk, you might have a line like this in your BOOT.INI:

```
multi(0)disk(0)rdisk(0)partition(1)\WINNT.SBS="BackOffice
    Small Business Server"
```

But if you need to boot off the secondary mirror pair, you have to change that to:

```
multi(1)disk(0)rdisk(0)partition(1)\WINNT.SBS="BackOffice
    Small Business Server"
```

Notice the change? Since you are now trying to boot off of the *second* SCSI controller, you must point your system to that controller by changing *multi(0)* to *multi(1)*. The rest of the line remains the same (except for the configuration name), since the mirror is on an identical partition. If you were mirroring onto a separate drive but using the same controller, you would have to change the value for *rdisk* to the appropriate number.

Restoring a Failed Server

So the worst has happened. Your server has totally crashed. You've replaced the failed hard drive, and you've got a backup tape to restore with, but first you have to get back to the point where you can at least boot so that you can restore the tape.

The first step is reinstalling Windows NT Server on the new hard drive. Once you have the minimal system installed, you can restore the registry and partition information from the ERD or from the tape, whichever is most current. Restart the server from the boot disk, and select the Repair option if you'll be using the ERD to repair your downed server. This will allow you to restore your partition information and much of the registry.

Once the ERD has done its best, restart the server and restore the rest of your lost data from your most recent normal backup. The tape drive must be locally attached, not networked, and you must select the Restore Local Registry option to recover the rest of your registry information. Restart the server, and you're ready to go.

This whole process will take a long time. In an environment in which your Small Business Server network *must* be available, you might not be able to afford the time that this process takes. In that case, the most efficient solution is to mirror, or better yet duplex, the system disk. This will get you up and running in the minimum amount of time—basically the time it takes to edit the BOOT.INI on your boot disk and then reboot your system.

The catch, of course, is that having a full, duplexed boot drive is not a cheap option, and few small businesses can afford this level of redundancy. But since the cost of hardware, and especially hard drives, has fallen so much, we won't rule out this choice. To get back up quickly but at a more reasonable cost, you can create and use a special recovery drive.

Creating and Using a Recovery Drive

A somewhat cheaper alternative to mirroring the drive is keeping a smallish, external recovery drive. This drive must have a minimum of only 100 MB. You can easily use an old, small drive that's not good for much else. The drive can even be an external drive that you simply plug into the back of the SCSI controller.

To create the recovery drive, you must install Windows NT Server on the drive and configure your swap file to be on that drive. Note that you won't install the full Small Business Server suite, just the Windows NT portion (and only a minimal version of that). Make sure that the installation includes the tape driver that you will be using. Create a bootable Windows NT ERD by following the procedure outlined earlier in the chapter, and edit the BOOT.INI file on it to point to the SCSI address of the recovery drive.

> **Tip**
>
> *You can create a special set of installation floppy disks that will install only Windows NT Server, not the full Small Business Server suite. Insert Disk 1 of Small Business Server in your CD-ROM drive and then type D:\i386\winnt32 /ox (where D is the drive letter of your CD-ROM drive) from the command line or from the Run command on the Start Menu. You will need three fresh, formatted floppies, however, so be prepared.*

When a system failure occurs, simply cable the recovery drive to the server and boot from the boot disk—the one you created—that points to the recovery drive. If the recovery drive has enough user accounts and software to keep your system running, you can simply run off the recovery drive until you can schedule a full-scale repair or replacement of the failed drive. However, with Small Business Server, this is unlikely to be the case. But at least you'll have saved yourself the time of the initial Windows NT Server installation to begin the recovery process—a savings of an hour at least. If you do have a failure, simply replace the failed drive, boot to the recovery hard drive using the boot disk, and restore your latest backup tape.

Replacing a Server

In the case of a total server failure or the kind of civil disaster that requires you to relocate your business and re-create your network, you'll need that offsite backup tape that we suggested back in Chapter 13. If you've also kept a version of the recovery drive off site, you'll save yourself a bit more time getting back up and running. However, time is likely to be less important in this situation than simply the certainty that you can, in fact, get your business running again.

Here again, you should first do a minimal, temporary Windows NT installation so that you can run the restoration portion of the Windows Backup program and restore your full backup set. Not fun, but it will work. Some of the third-party backup products, such as BEI's UltraBac, provide special emergency recovery options that can completely re-create your failed server without requiring you to do a temporary Windows NT installation first.

POINTS TO REMEMBER

- Plan ahead for disaster. Under extreme stress, people make mistakes and forget important steps, so create detailed recovery procedures and keep them up to date.
- Always use the least invasive repair procedure first. There are better ways to ring a doorbell than with a bazooka.
- Always create a fresh Emergency Repair Disk before making any major change to your system or installing a new software package.
- Create a boot floppy disk that will let you bypass corrupted boot information.

Appendix

Appendix

Keyboard Shortcuts

Even though Microsoft BackOffice Small Business Server relies heavily on the mouse, you still can do practically everything from the keyboard. Of course, you probably can't be bothered memorizing all of the keyboard combinations, but you might want to consider retaining a few of them in your memory bank (the one in your head), particularly if there are actions that you perform repeatedly and if you find the mouse too clumsy to use for them. The following list includes the most useful (and, in many cases, undocumented) keyboard shortcuts.

KEY	ACTION
F1	Opens Help.
F2	Allows renaming of the selected file or folder.
F3	Opens the Find program.
F4	Opens the drop-down list in the toolbar. Press F4 a second time, and the drop-down list will close.
F5	Refreshes (or updates) the view in the active window.
Tab or F6	Moves the focus from the drop-down window in the toolbar to the left pane, to the right pane (in Windows NT Explorer), and back again.
F10 or Alt	Puts the focus on the menu bar. To move between menus, use the Left (←) and Right (→) arrow keys. The Down arrow (↓) key will open the menu.
Backspace	Moves up one level in the folder hierarchy.
Right arrow (→)	Expands the highlighted folder. In Explorer, if the folder is already expanded, it will move to the first subfolder.
Left arrow (←)	Collapses the highlighted folder. In Explorer, if the folder is already collapsed, it will move up one level in the folder hierarchy.
Alt-Esc	Moves the focus between open applications. Hold down the Alt key and press Esc. Each press of Esc moves the focus to another application. Applications on the taskbar, once they are highlighted, are activated by pressing Enter.

Alt-Tab	Opens a window in the middle of the screen; icons in the window represent all open files and folders. (See the illustration at the end of this list.) Hold down the Alt key and press Tab to move the cursor from item to item. Release Alt to switch to the corresponding file or folder.

[illustration: window showing icons with caption "Microsoft Word - Document1"]

Alt-Shift-Tab	Moves the cursor through the open items in the opposite direction from Alt-Tab.
Ctrl-Esc	Opens the Start menu.
Alt-F4	Closes the current application. If no application is open, this will activate the Shut Down window.
Alt-Spacebar	Opens the Control Menu of the active window. (It functions the same as clicking the icon at the extreme upper left corner of the application or folder window.)
Spacebar	Toggles the choice when the selection cursor in a dialog box is selected.
Tab	Moves the selection cursor to the next choice in a folder or dialog box.
Shift-Tab	Moves the selection cursor in the opposite direction from Tab.
Shift-Print Screen	Copies the current screen to the Clipboard, from which the screen contents can be pasted into Paint or another graphics application.
Alt-Print Screen	Copies the active window to the Clipboard.

APPENDIX *Keyboard Shortcuts* **525**

Glossary

Glossary

Absolute URL A URL that includes a complete specification for protocol, machine name, and pathname on the network for the resource it locates.

Address Code by which the Internet identifies a specific user. The format is *username@hostname*, where *username* is the user name, logon name, or account number and *hostname* is the name of the computer or Internet service provider (ISP) being used. A host name can consist of a few words separated by periods.

Address resolution protocol A TCP/IP protocol that provides IP-address–to–MAC-address resolution for IP packets.

Alias An alternative name for a person, a group, or a file. For example, the alias *Vendors* could be used to send an e-mail message to all of a company's vendors.

Anonymous FTP A program for using FTP to log onto another computer to copy files when you don't have an account on that computer. When you log on, enter *anonymous* as the user name and your address as the password. This gives you access to publicly available files. (*See also* File Transfer Protocol [FTP].)

Associate To logically connect files having a particular extension to a specific program. When you double-click a file with this extension, the associated program opens and the file you clicked also opens.

Audit policy A network system policy that defines the types of security events to be logged. It can be defined for a server or for an individual computer.

Authentication Verification of the identity of a user or a computer process. In Microsoft Windows NT, this involves comparing the user's security identifier (SID) and password to a list of authorized users on a primary domain controller or backup domain controller.

Backbone A high-speed line or a series of connections that forms a major pathway within a network. The term is relative because a backbone in a small network is likely to be much smaller than many nonbackbone lines in a large network.

Binding A software connection between a network card and a network transport protocol (such as TCP/IP).

Cache   An area on a disk or in RAM in which copies of files are temporarily stored for quick access.

Conversation   A two-way connection between two applications that alternately transmit and receive data.

Daemon   A background program that runs unattended, gathering information or performing other tasks.

DNS name servers   Servers that contain information about part of the Domain Name System database. These servers make computer names available to queries for name resolution across the Internet.

Domain   In Windows NT, a group of computers that share a security policy and a user account database. (The SBS server and clients make up a single domain.) On the Internet, a TCP/IP network domain. (*See also* Domain name.)

Domain controller   A server in a domain that accepts user names and passwords from users logging onto the system and initiates their authentication.

Domain name   The unique name that identifies an Internet site. A computer can have more than one domain name, but a given domain name can point to only one computer. It's also possible for a domain name to exist but not to be associated with an actual machine. This is often the case when a group or a business wants to have an Internet e-mail address without having to establish a real Internet site; an ISP's computer handles the mail on behalf of the listed domain name.

Domain Name System (DNS)   A distributed database that provides a hierarchical naming system for identifying hosts on the Internet. DNS differs from WINS in that DNS is a static configuration; WINS is a fully dynamic configuration. (*See also* Windows Internet Name Service [WINS].)

Dynamic Data Exchange (DDE)   Communication between processes. When programs that support DDE run at the same time, they can exchange data by means of conversations.

Dynamic link library (DLL)   A program module that contains executable code and data that can be used by various programs. A program uses the DLL only when the program is active. The DLL is unloaded when the last program using it exits.

Enterprise   An entire business operation, including all remote offices and branches.

Environment variable   A small storage area that contains a string of environment information, such as a drive, a path, or a filename associated with a symbolic name. You can use the System option in the Control Panel or the Set command from the Windows NT command prompt to define environment variables.

Extranet   A portion of an intranet that is available to users on other networks via the Internet; these users are typically external business partners with no direct access to the LAN.

File allocation table (FAT)   A file system used by MS-DOS and Microsoft Windows 95 consisting of a table that keeps track of the file size and location on a hard drive.

File Transfer Protocol (FTP)   A tool for transferring one or more files from one computer to another over a network or a telephone line.

Finger   A program that displays information about someone on the Internet. On most UNIX systems, it tells you who is currently logged on. On most Internet hosts, Finger tells you the person's name and the last time that the person logged on (and possibly other information based on the person's Internet address).

Firewall   A protective filter for messages and logons. Organizations that connect directly to the Internet use firewalls to prevent unauthorized access to their networks.

Frame   In HTML, a pane on a web page that can display its own content and can be scrolled independently from the rest of the browser window.

Fully qualified domain name (FQDN)   An Internet domain name that includes the names of all network domains leading back to the root. For example, the following is the fully qualified domain name for a computer at the University of California at Berkeley:

german.modlangs.ucberk.edu

A commercial enterprise can have a fully qualified domain name such as this:

accts.finance.dataflointl.com

Gateway   A device used to connect networks that are using different protocols so that information can be passed from one network to another.

Gopher   A menu-driven tool that allows a user to find information on remote computers. Telnet is usually used to connect with a Gopher server, where menus are available for browsing.

Graphic Interchange Format (GIF)   A popular file format used to store graphics images.

Helper application   Launched or employed by a web browser, a program that processes a file that the browser can't handle. A helper application that handles video, animation, or graphics is called a viewer. A helper application that plays sound files is called a player.

Hive   One of six sections of the registry on your hard disk. Each hive is a discrete body of keys, subkeys, and values that records configuration information for the computer. Each hive is a file and can be moved from one system to another, but it can be edited only using the Registry Editor.

Home domain   A domain in which a user account or a group account resides.

Host   Any device on a network that uses TCP/IP. Also, a computer on the Internet that you can log onto. You can use FTP to retrieve files from a host computer on the Internet. Other programs (such as Telnet) allow you to connect to and use an Internet host computer.

Hot spot   An area, usually in a graphic, that constitutes a hyperlink.

Hyperlink   An element in an electronic document that connects to another place in the same document or to an entirely different document. Clicking on the hyperlink takes you to a new location. Hyperlinks are the essential ingredient of all hypertext systems, including the World Wide Web and intranets.

Hypertext   A system of writing and displaying text that makes it possible for the text to be linked in many ways. Hypertext documents can contain links to related documents, such as documents referred to in footnotes. Hypermedia also can contain pictures, sounds, and video.

Hypertext Markup Language (HTML)   A system for writing web pages. HTML allows text to include codes that define fonts, layout, embedded graphics, and hypertext links.

Hypertext Transfer Protocol (HTTP)   The method by which pages are transferred over the Web.

Internet   The worldwide collection of interconnected networks that uses TCP/IP and that evolved from the ARPANET of the late 1960s and early 1970s. The Internet connects roughly 70,000 independent networks into a vast global network. An internet (lowercase) is any large network made up of a number of smaller networks.

Internet Control Message Protocol (ICMP)   A protocol for reporting problems with the delivery of data, such as an unreachable host or an unavailable port. ICMP is also used to send a request packet to determine whether a host is available; if the receiving host is alive and functioning, it sends back a packet. (*See also* Ping.)

Internet Explorer   Microsoft's Windows-based, WinSock-compliant program for browsing the World Wide Web that ships with Small Business Server.

Internet Protocol (IP)   The transport layer protocol that is a basis of the Internet. IP makes it possible for data to be divided into discrete packets of information for routing from one network to another and then to be reassembled from these packets at the destination.

Internet Relay Chat (IRC)   A system that enables Internet users to communicate with each other in real time over the Internet.

Internet service provider (ISP)   A company that provides individuals and organizations with access to the Internet by way of a dial-up or dedicated connection. Each ISP has a number of servers and a high-speed connection to the Internet backbone. (*See also* Backbone.)

Intranet   A network of interconnected computers within an organization.

IP address   A unique, four-part number separated by periods (for example, *165.113.245.2*) that identifies a machine on the Internet. Every machine on the Internet has a unique IP address; if a machine does not have an IP address, it is not really on the Internet. Most machines also have one or more domain names that are easier to remember.

IPX/SPX   Transport protocols used in Novell NetWare networks.

ISAPI (Internet Services Application Programming Interface)   A new version of CGI that uses DLLs rather than external applications. ISAPI was invented by Purveyor and Microsoft to extend the performance of Windows-based HTTP servers.

ISDN (Integrated Services Digital Network)   Essentially a digital phone line. Provides higher bandwidth (56 Kbps to 128 Kbps) and better signal quality than analog lines.

Java   A programming language similar to C and C++ that is used to design applets in web pages.

JavaScript   A scripting language that's less powerful than Java but much easier to use. JavaScript is used to design simple web programs.

JPEG (Joint Photographic Experts Group) A graphics file format commonly used on the Internet. JPEG (pronounced *jay-peg*) reduces graphics files to about 5 percent of their original size, although some detail is lost.

Kbps (kilobits per second) A data transfer rate measurement; one kilobit equals 1,024 bits.

Kernel The part of the Windows NT executive that manages the processor. The kernel performs thread scheduling and dispatching, interrupt and exception handling, and multiprocessor synchronization.

Leased line A telephone line that is rented for exclusive 24-hour access between two locations.

Listserv A family of programs that manages Internet mailing lists by distributing the messages posted to the list and by adding and deleting members automatically when a user sends an e-mail message to subscribe to or be removed from the list.

Local area network (LAN) A group of computers connected by a communications link and usually located close together (for example, in the same building or on the same floor of a building) so that data can be shared among them.

Log on To identify oneself to the authenticating computer, usually by providing an account name and a password. Also *log in*.

Logon name The account name used to gain access to a computer system. Unlike a password, a logon name is not usually secret. Also *login name*.

Logon script Typically a batch file that executes when a user logs on. It's used to configure a user's initial environment. A logon script can be assigned to multiple users.

MAC address A unique, 48-bit number assigned to network interface cards by the manufacturer. MAC addresses are used for mapping in TCP/IP network communication.

Mirror Two partitions on separate hard drives that are configured to contain identical data. If one drive fails, the partition on the other drive will still contain valid data, and processing can continue. A mirror can also be an FTP server that "mirrors" another FTP server—it provides copies of the same files as the other FTP server. Some FTP servers are used so often that other servers are set up to mirror them and spread the FTP load to more than one site.

Modem Short for modulator/demodulator. A device that enables a computer to transmit data over a telephone line to another computer. Modems convert the computer's digital signals into analog waves that can be transmitted over standard voice telephone lines. Modem speeds are measured in bits per second (bps) or kilobits per second (Kbps). For example, 28.8 Kbps and 28,800 bps are essentially the same thing.

Multitasking A mode of operation that makes a computer appear to run more than one program at the same time. Each program is allowed to run for a brief amount of time before the next program is loaded into the processor. Programs are switched in and out of the processor so quickly that it appears the computer is using them simultaneously. The stability of a multitasking system depends on how well the various programs are isolated from one another.

Multithreading The simultaneous running of several processes (also known as threads) within a program. Because several threads can be processed in parallel, one thread does not have to finish before another one can start. (*See also* Thread.)

Named pipe An interprocess communication that allows one process to send data to another process either remotely or locally.

Name resolution The process of mapping a name to its corresponding address.

NetBIOS Extended User Interface (NetBEUI) A small and fast network protocol that requires little memory but can't be routed. Remote locations linked by routers can't use NetBEUI to communicate.

Netlogon service A service that accepts logon requests from any client and provides authentication from the Security Account Manager accounts database.

Network Two or more computers connected by a communications link in order to share resources.

Network News Transfer Protocol (NNTP) A protocol for the distribution, inquiry, retrieval, and posting of news articles on the Internet.

Newsgroup On the Internet, a distributed bulletin board system covering a particular topic. Usenet News (also known as Netnews) is a system that distributes thousands of newsgroups to all parts of the Internet.

Node A computer on the Internet, also called a host. Computers that provide a service, such as FTP sites or places that run Gopher, are also called servers.

NTFS The native file system for Microsoft Windows NT. It supports long filenames, a variety of permissions for sharing files, and a transaction log that allows Windows NT to finish incomplete file-related tasks if the operating system is interrupted.

Packet   A chunk of information sent over a network. Each packet contains the destination address, the sender's address, error-control information, and data.

Page   A document or a collection of information that is available via the Web. A page can contain text, graphics, video, and sound files. A page can also be a portion of memory that the virtual memory manager can swap to and from a hard disk.

Paging   A virtual memory operation in which pages are transferred from memory to disk when memory becomes full. When a thread accesses a page that's not in memory, a page fault occurs; the memory manager then uses page tables to find the page on disk and load it into memory.

Peer-to-peer network   A type of network in which two or more computers can communicate with each other without the need for any intermediary device. On a peer-to-peer network, a computer can be both a client and a server.

Permission   Authorization to perform certain actions such as reading or changing files. Only an administrator can set certain permissions; individual users can set others.

Ping   A network management tool that checks to see whether another computer is alive and functioning. It sends a short message to which the other computer responds automatically. If the other computer does not respond, you usually cannot establish communications with it.

Plug-in   An add-in program module that enhances the capabilities of another application, such as a web browser.

Point of Presence (POP)   A physical site at which a network access provider, such as MCI, has equipment to which users connect. The local telephone company's central office in a particular area is also sometimes referred to as its POP for that area.

Point-to-Point Protocol (PPP)   A protocol that provides router-to-router and host-to-network connections over a telephone line (or over a network link that acts like a telephone line). Similar to SLIP.

Post Office Protocol (POP)   A system by which a mail server on the Internet lets you download e-mail to your PC or Macintosh. Most people refer to this protocol with its version number (POP2, POP3, and so on) to avoid confusing it with Point of Presence.

Primary domain controller (PDC)   A Windows NT domain server that authenticates users logging onto the domain and maintains the security policy and the master database for a domain. The server in an SBS domain can be set up only as a primary domain controller.

Proxy server A network service that manages Internet connectivity by acting as the go-between when users attempt to access Internet resources. Proxy server software filters all outgoing connections to appear as if they come from only one machine. This prevents external hackers from learning the structure of your network.

RAID (Redundant Array of Inexpensive Disks) A range of disk management and striping techniques for implementing fault tolerance.

Remote Access Service (RAS) A service that allows users to dial in from remote locations and gain access to their networks for file and printer sharing, e-mail, and scheduling, and to access SQL databases.

Replication A service that allows the contents of a directory (designated as an export directory) to be copied to other directories (called import directories) on network computers.

Request for Comment (RFC) A document that allows Internet users to communicate and agree on the architecture and functionality of the Internet. Some RFCs are official documents of the Internet Engineering Task Force (IETF), which defines the standards of TCP/IP and the Internet; others are proposals for new standards or documents that fall somewhere in between—some are tutorial in nature, others are quite technical.

Router A special-purpose computer (or software package) that handles the connection between two or more networks. Routers look at the destination addresses of the packets passing through them and decide which route to use to send the packets.

SCSI (Small Computer Systems Interface) A commonly used computer peripheral interface for scanners, disk drives, and other external devices. Because of its speed, reliability, and ability to support as many as 7 (or 14 on some models) devices on a single controller, SCSI (pronounced *scuzzy*) is the interface of choice for network servers and high-end workstations.

Security Accounts Manager (SAM) The manager of all security rules and information in Windows NT Server and Windows NT Workstation.

Security ID (SID) A unique number assigned to every computer and user account on a Windows NT network. A SID is never reused.

Serial Line Internet Protocol (SLIP) A protocol for running IP over serial lines or telephone lines using modems. This protocol is rapidly being replaced by the Point-to-Point Protocol (PPP).

Server A computer that provides a service to other computers on a network. A file server, for example, provides files to client computers.

Simple Mail Transfer Protocol (SMTP) A protocol used to transfer e-mail messages between computers.

Socket An endpoint to a connection. Two sockets form a complete path for a bidirectional pipe for incoming and outgoing data between networked computers. The Windows Sockets API is a networking API for programmers writing for the Windows family of products. (API stands for application programming interface.)

Synchronize To replicate the domain database on the primary domain controller to one or all of the backup domain controllers in a domain. The system performs this automatically, but the administrator can also do this using Server Manager.

T1 A data communications link that has a capacity of 1.544 megabits per second. It can handle 24 voice channels or data channels at 64 Kbps each.

T3 A data communications link that is the equivalent of 28 T1 lines—45 megabits per second. It is usually found only in the Internet backbone or in large institutions.

Telnet The program used to log on from one Internet site to another. Telnet gets you to the logon prompt of another host.

Terminal A device that lets you send commands to another computer. At a minimum, this usually means a keyboard, a display screen, and some simple circuitry. Usually you use terminal software in a personal computer; the software emulates a physical terminal and lets you type commands to another computer.

Thread An executable entity that belongs to one (and only one) process. In a multitasking environment, a single program can contain several threads, all running at the same time.

Transmission Control Protocol/Internet Protocol (TCP/IP) The protocol combination that networks use to communicate with each other on the Internet.

Trust relationship A relationship in which a workstation or a server trusts a domain controller to authenticate a user logon on its behalf. Also, a relationship in which a domain controller in one domain trusts a domain controller from another domain to authenticate users who are logging on to the domain from the other domain. Small Business Server *cannot* be part of a trust relationship—that aspect of Windows NT Server is disabled in Small Business Server.

Uniform Resource Locator (URL) The standard format for specifying addresses of resources on the Internet that are part of the World Wide Web. The following is an example of a URL:

`http://www.capecod.net/~fcollege/index.htm`

The most common way to use a URL is in a web browser program such as Microsoft Internet Explorer or Netscape Navigator.

UNIX A computer operating system designed for use by many users at the same time (in a "multiuser" system) with TCP/IP built in. It is the most common operating system for servers on the Internet.

User account A user's access to a Windows NT machine. Each user account has a unique user name and security ID.

User profile Information about and the access restrictions for a user account.

Viewer A program used by Gopher, WAIS, or web client programs to display files that contain graphics or video files or to play files that contain sounds.

Virtual Reality Markup Language (VRML) A language for writing web pages. With VRML, a web page can include codes that define animations and 3-D graphics.

WebBot component A dynamic object on a web page that is interpreted and executed when the author saves the page to the server or a user links to the page.

Webmaster An individual, often an administrator, who is in charge of the management and usually the design of a company's web site, either internal or external.

Wide area network (WAN) Any Internet or intranet network that covers an area larger than a single building or campus. (*See also* Internet, Local area network, Network.)

Windows Internet Name Service (WINS) A name resolution service that converts computer names to IP addresses in a routed environment.

Windows Socket (WinSock) A standard interface for Windows-based programs working with TCP/IP. You can use WinSock if you use SLIP to connect to the Internet.

World Wide Web A hypermedia-based system for gaining access to information on the Internet.

Workstation In the context of Windows NT, a computer that is running the Windows NT Workstation operating system. In a wider context, a workstation is any powerful computer optimized for graphics, computer-aided design (CAD), or any of a number of other functions requiring high performance.

Index

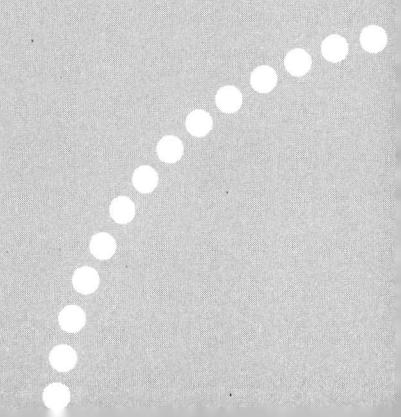

Index

Note: Page numbers in italics refer to figures or graphics.

A

absolute addresses, 380
absolute limitations, 9–10
access control, 19. *See also* permissions; users
   NTFS format and, 40
Access Control dialog box, 410
accessibility options, 196
Accessibility Options icon, 196
Accessibility Properties dialog box, 196, *197*
access security, 39
Access Through Share Permissions dialog box, *176*
account lockout, 127
Account Name field, 68
Account Policy dialog box, *126, 500*
Add dialog box, *224*
Add Fax Printer dialog box, *293*
Add Fonts dialog box, *208*
Add Key command, 486
Add Port dialog box, *144*
Add Printer Wizard, 65–67, *65*
   adding server-controlled printers with, 142–47
Add RAS Device dialog box, *290*
Add/Remove feature, 192–93
Add/Remove Programs icon, 198
Add/Remove Programs Properties dialog box, *190, 193*
addresses
   absolute, 380
   e-mail, hyperlinks to, 380–81
   fax, sending e-mail to, 283
   IP, 337–40
      class A networks, 338
      class B networks, 338

addresses, IP, *continued*
      class C networks, 338–39
      class D and E, 339–40
      Domain Name System (DNS) and, 343
      resolving domain names into, 345–46
      user access to, 403
   relative, 380
Address Resolution Protocol (ARP), 342
Add To Alert dialog box, *456*
Add To Chart dialog box, 454
Add User Licenses icon, 81
Add Users And Groups dialog box, 155, *156, 178, 186, 466*
Add Value command, 486
administrative privileges
   accessing Manage Printers page and, 140
   configuring tape backup devices and, 84
   Dial-Up Networking options for, 357
   granting, 74
   installing software and, 193
   managing computers and, 182
   managing e-mail distribution lists with, 267–68
   printer ownership, 157
   user rights and, *129–30*
administrative shares, default, *505*
administrative tasks, 9
   creating standard operating procedures for, 496–97
Administrator account, 59. *See also* administrator passwords
administrator passwords, 51, 58–59
Advanced RISC Computing (ARC), 518
AppEvents subkey, 474
application events, 458, 460, *461*
applications. *See also* software
   adding and removing on server, 191–93
   foreground, 232

applications, *continued*
    subkeys for installed, 474
    supporting international symbols, 226
    user interface for SQL Server, 448
applications server, 7
ARC. *See* Advanced RISC Computing (ARC)
ARP. *See* Address Resolution Protocol (ARP)
ASCII files, saving keys as, 480
at command, 256
    running batch files with, 260
audio. *See* sound schemes
audio settings, 223
auditing
    files and folders, 464–66
    printers, 466–67
Auditing command, 487
Audit Policy dialog box, *461*
Auto Refresh command, 487

B

backing up. *See also* restoring
    alternative software for, 261
    clients, 260–61
    closing open files before, 188
    cold, 250
    data, 246–51
    databases, 442–44
    differential, 240, 242–43, 442
    extended volume sets and, 106
    full, 240, 442
    hardware for, 241
    hot, 250–52
    importance of, 240–41
    incremental, 240, 242–43, 442
    Microsoft Exchange Server, 249–52
    Registry, 479–82, 492–94
    scheduling, 256–60
    strategies for, 241–42
    troubleshooting, 500
    verifying, 256

Backup application, *247*, 248–49
    restoring information with, 252–56
backup command files. *See* batch files
backup devices, 29–30, 240, 241. *See also* tape devices
    configuring, 243–45
    Microsoft SQL Server, 442–43
    removing, 245
Backup dialog box, *248*
backup domain controller (BDC), 7, 20–21
backup media, 240
    overwrite warnings, 248, *249*
    storing, 241–42
batch files, 258–60
    backing up Registry with, 492–94
    modifying to specify security identifier (SID), 493
    shutting down services with, 507
BDC. *See* backup domain controller (BDC)
Binary command, 486
bookmarks, 381
boot partitions. *See* partitions

C

cables
    connecting, 50
    selecting, 28
Cancel A Print Job icon, 159
CD key, 53
Change Password Wizard, 121–22
Change Printer Settings icon, 148
checklists, preinstallation, 48–51
Client Installation/Configuration dialog box, *410*
clients
    adding components to, 190–91
    adding computer to network at, 184
    adding software to, 78–79
    adding users to, 77–78
    backing up, 260–61

clients, *continued*
   configuring e-mail, 283
   configuring to use modem pools, 307, *308*
   defined, 15
   enabling and disabling proxy, 236–37
   faxing options for, 300
   hardware for, 31–32
   logging on locally, 186–87
   managing e-mail distribution lists from, 285
   multiple messages received by, 285
   naming, 76
      reconnecting to network and, 187–88
   newsgroup, 507
   Outlook, 360–61
   vs. servers, 16–17
   setting up, 75–79
      for remote access, 354–61
   system requirements, 42–43
   trouble connecting to mail server, 280–81
   types for Small Business Server, 8
   workstation operating systems and, 17
client-server networks, 16
Close command, 485
color, adjusting, 200–201
commands
   at, 256
      running batch files with, 260
   Add Key, 486
   Add Value, 486
   Auditing, 487
   Auto Refresh, 487
   Binary, 486
   Close, 485
   Confirm On Delete, 487
   Connect Network Registry, 490
   Copy Key Name, 491
   Create Volume Set, 104
   Delete, 486, 491
   Disconnect Network Registry, 490
   Exit, 486, 490
   Export Registry File, 490
   Extend Volume Set, 104

commands, *continued*
   Find, 491
   Find Next, 491
   Font, 487
   Format, 101
   history of, 199
   Import Registry File, 490
   List Fonts By Similarity, 206–7
   Load Hive, 485
   Modify, 490
   New, 491
   ntbackup, 256, 258–60
   Open Local, 485
   Owner, 487
   Permissions, 487
   Preview In Browser, 378
   Print, 490
   Printer Setup, 486
   Print Subtree, 486
   Read Only Mode, 487
   Refresh, 491
   Rename, 491
   Restore, 485
   Save Key, 486
   Save Settings On Exit, 487
   Save Subtree As, 486
   Select Computer, 486
   Split, 491
   Status Bar, 491
   String, 486
   Unload Hive, 485
   Zoom, *417*
Company folder, 170
   company information
      entering in Small Business Server Setup Wizard, 56–57
      entering on Company Information page, 70
      gathering, 50
components
   adding to client, 190–91
   adding to server, 189–90
   adding Windows NT Server, 193–94

components, *continued*
- domain, 20–21
- network, 15
- removing Windows NT Server, 193–94
- Small Business Server, 6

Compress A Folder icon, 173
computers. *See also* clients; servers
- adding to network, 183–84
- adding users to, 185–86
- creating new policy for, 133–35
- as default distributed transaction coordinator, 222
- managing, 182–83
- naming, 40–41
- problems setting up, 504
- reconnecting to network, 187–88
- removing from network, 187
- viewing information about, 453

Configure Port Usage dialog box, *290, 306*
Confirm On Delete command, 487
Connect Network Registry command, 490
Connect To Server dialog box, *272, 319*
Console icon, 198–99
Console subkey, 474
Console window, 198–99
Console Windows Properties dialog box, *198*
- Colors tab, 200–201
- Font tab, 199
- Layout tab, 200
- Options tab, 199

Control Panel subkey, 474
ControlSet keys, 472–73
Control User Access To Printers icon, 141
Copy Key Name command, 491
cover pages. *See* faxes
Create An Emergency Repair Disk icon, 81
Create Volume Set command, 104
Crystal Reports
- creating reports from samples, 416–18
- overview, 414

Crystal Reports, *continued*
- sample reports in, *415*
- sending reports by e-mail, 419, *420*
- sending reports to Microsoft Exchange folders, 418
- version 4.5, *6*

cursor
- blink rate, 211
- size of, 199

D

Daily Message Traffic report, 279, *415*
data
- adding to tables, 438
- backing up, 246–51
- changing in existing database records, 425–26
- collecting network, 454–57
- collecting server, 454–57
- controlling access to, 441–42
- logging for reports, 457
- restoring, 252–56
- types used in Registry, 475, *476–77*

Database Backup/Restore dialog box, *443*
database devices, 432–34
database logs, 435
databases. *See also* Microsoft SQL Server
- adding new records to, 426
- backing up, 442–44
- changing data in existing records, 425–26
- controlling access to, 441–42
- creating, 434–35
- defining primary keys for, 427–28
- deleting records from, 426–27
- directory, 7
- ensuring integrity of, 440–41
- first normal form, 428
- managing logins/controlling access to, 441–42
- pubs, 430
- rebuilding structure of, 444
- relational, 422

INDEX 543

databases, *continued*
    retrieving information from, 423–25
        multiple tables, 429
    rules of designing, 427–29
    second normal form, 428
    SQL Server 6.5 and, *6*
    stored procedures and, 438–40
    third normal form, 429
    using Structured Query Language with, 423–27
Data Definition Language (DDL), 423
Data Manipulation Language (DML), 423
Date/Time icon, 201
Date/Time Properties dialog box, 54–55, *55*, 201, *202*
DDL. *See* Data Definition Language (DDL)
DEC Alpha processor, 26
dedicated printer servers. *See* printer servers
.DEFAULT subkey, 473, *478*
Delete command, 486, 491
deleting
    e-mail distribution lists, 270
    printer ports, 151–52
    records from databases, 426–27
    volume sets, 107
Description field, 69
desktop, as part of user profile, 130
devices. *See also* keyboards; mouse; printers
    backup, 29–30, 240, 241
        configuring, 84, 243–45
        Microsoft SQL Server, 442–43
        removing, 245
    database, 432–34
    inventory of, 202–3
    MIDI, 223
    multimedia
        adding, 223–24
        changing properties of, 224
        removing, 224
        viewing properties of, 224
    ODBC, 225

devices, *continued*
    tape, *245*
        backing up and, 241–42
        configuring, 84
        setting up, 243–44
        viewing properties of, 234
Devices dialog box, *203*
Devices icon, 202–3
DHCP. *See* Dynamic Host Configuration Protocol (DHCP)
DHCP Manager, 349–51
Diagnostics tool. *See* Microsoft Windows NT Diagnostics
Dialing Properties dialog box, 217, *218*, 234–35, *235*
dial-up access, 74. *See also* remote access
    security and, 127
dial-up accounts. *See* Internet service providers (ISPs), dial-up accounts
Dial-Up Monitor icon, 203
Dial-Up Networking, 89–90
    configuring connection, 356–57
    modem sharing services and, 355
    window, *356*
Dial-Up Networking icon, *359*
Dial-Up Networking Monitor, 357
differential backup. *See* backing up, differential
Directory Auditing dialog box, *465*
disaster protection. *See also* Disk Administrator; Emergency Repair Disk (ERD)
    creating new system policy and, 133
disaster recovery, 510
    emergency boot disks and, 516–18
    Emergency Repair Disks and, 81, 513–15
    Last Known Good Configuration menu and, 512–13
    mirrored boot partitions and, 518–19
    plan for, 510–11
    restoring failed servers, 519–21
Disconnect Network Registry command, 490
discretionary access control, 19

Disk Administrator, 94
  assigning drive letters, 100
  breaking mirror sets, 109–12
  Confirm dialog box, 105
  Create Primary Partitions dialog box, *100*
  creating logical drives, 103
  creating mirror sets, 108–9
  creating partitions, 99–103
    extended, 102–3
    primary, 99–102
  creating volume sets, 104–5
  extending volume sets, 105–6
  Formatting dialog box, *102*
  overview, 97–98
  screen, *98*
disk duplexing, 96. *See also* mirror sets
  failed servers and, 519–20
DISK key, 473
disks. *See also* emergency boot disk; Emergency Repair Disk (ERD); hard drives
  creating setup, 77
  formatting floppies, 51
  managing, 96–97. (*see also* Disk Administrator)
  troubleshooting, 504
Display icon, 204
display options, 199
Display Properties dialog box, *204*
DML. *See* Data Manipulation Language (DML)
DNS. *See* Domain Name System (DNS)
documents
  changing properties of, 162
  managing on print queues, 161–62
  stacking in print queue, 151
  viewing properties of, 162
domain name space, 343–44
Domain Name System (DNS), 343–46
Domain Registration Wizard, 325–30
domains
  components, 20–21
  configuring for second-level name, 321–24
  defined, 18–19

domains, *continued*
  Microsoft networking vs. TCP/IP, 19
  names
    acquiring, 50, 53, 315, 324–30, 344–45
    registering, 88–89
    resolving into IP addresses, 345–46
    user access to, 403
  registration password, 329
  root, 344
  security, 7
  Set Up An Internet Domain Name Wizard, 80
  vs. workgroups, 17–21
drivers
  ODBC, 225
  printer, changing and adding, 150–51
  tape device, 243–45
  telephony, 235
drives. *See also* hard drives
  listing, 452
  listing contents of, 167
  mapped network, 474
  recovery, 520
duplexing. *See* disk duplexing; mirror sets
Dynamic Host Configuration Protocol (DHCP), 346

E

editing
  e-mail distribution lists, 270
  fax cover pages, 298–99
  keys, 484–92
  with regedit.exe, 489–92
  registry for dial-up account use, 318
  values, 484–92
electronic mail. *See* e-mail
e-mail, 5
  addresses, hyperlinks to, 380–81
  configuring clients, 283

e-mail, *continued*
    Daily Message Traffic report, 279, *415*
    determining outgoing status, 282
    dial-up interval, 272–73
        changing, 281
    downloading, 282
    managing mail box size, 271–72, 283
    message tracking, 274–76
    Microsoft Exchange Server 5 and, *6*
    overview, 266–67
    remaining in Outbox, 281
    reports, 274
    send and receive cycle, 273
    sending reports by, 419, *420*
    sending to fax address, 283
    Server Summary report, 277, *415*
    third-party, 507
    Top N Message Receivers report, 277–78, *278*, *415*
    Top N Message Senders report, 278, *279*, *415*
    troubleshooting, 280–83, 499
e-mail distribution lists, 267
    adding users to, 71
    creating, 268–69
        of contacts, 284–85
    deleting, 270
    editing, 270
    managing, 267–68
    owner of, 285
    troubleshooting, 284–85
E-mail Distribution List Wizard, *269*, *270*
    creating e-mail distribution lists with, 268
    deleting e-mail distribution lists with, 270
    editing e-mail distribution lists with, 270
emergencies. *See* disaster protection; disaster recovery; emergency boot disk; Emergency Repair Disk (ERD)
emergency boot disk
    creating Windows NT, DEC Alpha version, 517
    creating Windows NT, *x*86 version, 516–17
    overview, 516

Emergency Repair Disk (ERD)
    creating, 51, 81, 112, 514–15
    overview, 513–14
    updating, 101
        after mirroring, 109
Environment subkey, 474
ERD. *See* Emergency Repair Disk (ERD)
error messages, troubleshooting, 123
errors, 459
    filtering event logs to see, 462–63
    in server log files, 281
    STOP, 233
Event Detail dialog box
    showing application event, *461*
    showing system event, *460*
event logs
    configuring, 463–64
    filtering, 462–63
    recording events in, 458–62
Event Log Settings dialog box, *463*, *464*
events, recording, 458–62
Event Viewer, 458–62
    system log, *458*
Exit command, 486, 490
Export dialog box, *418*
Export Registry File command, 490
extended partitions, 99
    creating, 102–3
    defined, 95
Extend Volume Set command, 104
extranets, 395

F

FAT format, 39, 40
    installing Small Business Server on FAT partition, 52
    permissions problems and, 503
    selecting file systems and, 49–50
    share permissions and, 174
    sharing folders and, 170, 176
    upgrading to Microsoft Proxy Server 2 and, 409

Fax Client icon, 205
faxes. *See also* Microsoft Fax Server
    addresses, sending e-mail to, 283
    canceling jobs, 297
    changing receive options, 295–97
    client options, 300
    "confidential" cover sheet, *298*
    configuring settings for, 290–92
    creating cover pages for, 299
    editing cover pages for, 298–99
    managing job activity, 297
    Microsoft Fax Server 1 and, *6*
    overview, 288
    receiving, 291
    reports, 297–98, *415*
    saving on server, 292
    sending, 291
        to Exchange Mailbox, 292
        through servers, 5
    troubleshooting, 299–300, 503
fax modems. *See also* modem pools; modems
    access to shared, 73–74
    hardware compatibility and, 24
    installation recommendations, 506
    installing, 289–90
    overview, 288
    planning for, 48–49
    refusing to answer calls, 295
fax numbers, 57
fax printers. *See also* fax modems
    adding, 292–93
    controlling user access to, 294–95
    removing, 294
Fax Server icon, 205
Fax Server Properties dialog box, *296*
fields, 422
File Allocation Table format. *See* FAT format
file extensions
    .dat, 432
    file associations connecting, 475
    .reg, 479

File Open dialog box, *416*
file permissions, 174–75. *See also* permissions
    assigning, 177–79
File Permissions dialog box, *178*
files
    auditing, 464–66
    backing up, 246–51
    backing up open, 250–52
    batch, 258–60
        backing up Registry with, 492–94
        modifying to specify security identifier (SID), 493
        shutting down services with, 507
    closing, 188
    database devices, 432–34
    disaster protection, 94
    ensuring security of, 94
    errors in server log, 281
    log, 403, 457
    not supported by Microsoft Windows NT, 470
    problems accessing, 500–501
    in Registry, 477, *478*
    saving keys as ASCII, 480
    sharing, 5
    sound, 474
    swap, 453
    verifying individual backed-up, 256
file security, 38
file systems, selecting, 39–40, 49–50
file transfer protocol (FTP), 391
Filter dialog box, *462*
filtering, event logs, 462–63
Find command, 491
Find Next command, 491
folder permissions, 174–75. *See also* permissions
    viewing, 177
folders
    auditing, 464–66
    Company, 170
    compressing, 173

folders, *continued*
   managing size of, 172–74
   Media, 231
   Microsoft Exchange, sending reports to, 418
   Microsoft FrontPage and, 375
   moving unshared, 174
   Printer, 149
   problems accessing, 500–501
   Reports, 416
   saving faxes in, 292
   selecting users to share, 179
   shared, 167–70
      access to, 73, 122–23, 171
      on FAT and NTFS drives, 170
      moving, 173–74, 507
   storing Registry files in, 483
   uncompressing, 173
   unsharing, 171
   Users, 170
   Users Shared Folders, 170
Font command, 487
fonts
   Console window, 199
   installing, 208–9
   non-TrueType, 207, *208*
   selecting, 206–8
Fonts icon, 206
Format command, 101
formatting
   floppy disks, 51
   volume sets, 105
fragmentation, NTFS format and, 40
FTP. *See* file transfer protocol (FTP)
FTP Service, 391
   configuring, 391–95
FTP Service Properties dialog box, 393
full backup. *See* backing up, full
Full Name field, 68

G

gateways, 341
Generate SQL Scripts dialog box, *444*

H

hard drives. *See also* logical drives; mirror sets; partitions
   assigning letters, 100
   dividing into partitions, 99–103
   extended partitions to other, 103, 104, 105–6
   monitoring load of, 455
   naming conventions for, 518
   selecting client, 32
   space
      adding, 31
      Microsoft Exchange Server services errors and, 282
      required for Small Business Server, 77
      used by cache, 401
      volume sets and, 103
   system requirements for, 27–29
hardware. *See also specific items*
   for backing up, 241
   client, 31–32
   compatibility list, 24–25
   configuring additional, 82–87
   connecting, 50
   displaying available profiles, 232
   failures. (*see also* backing up; restoring)
      breaking mirror sets and, 109–12
      replacing with mirror sets, 110–11
   server, 25–31
   setup detecting, 54
   system requirements
      for clients, 42–43
      for server, 41–42
   verifying compatibility, 48–49
HARDWARE key, 472
hardware profile, copying current, 512–13

HCL. *See* hardware, compatibility list
hives
    HKEY_CLASSES_ROOT, 475
    HKEY_CURRENT_CONFIG, 475
    HKEY_CURRENT_USER, 475
    HKEY_LOCAL_MACHINE, 471, 472–73
    HKEY_USERS, 471, 473–75
    overview, 471
hot fixes, 40
HTML tags, 371
hyperlinks, 371
    creating, *379*
    to e-mail addresses, 380–81
    Microsoft FrontPage Hyperlink View and, 375
    overview, 380
    to web page sections, 381–82

I

icons
    accessibility options, 196
    Add/Remove Programs, 198
    Add User Licenses, 81
    Cancel A Print Job, 159
    Change Printer Settings, 148
    Compress A Folder, 173
    Console, 198–99
    Control User Access To Printers, 141
    Create An Emergency Repair Disk, 81
    Date/Time, 201
    Devices, 202–3
    Dial-Up Monitor, 203
    Dial-Up Networking, *359*
    Display, 204
    Fax Client, 205
    Fax Server, 205
    Fonts, 206
    Internet, 209
    Keyboard, 210
    Licensing, 212–13

icons, *continued*
    Mail, 213
    Modem, 214
    Modem Sharing, 213
    Mouse, 218
    Move A Folder, 173–74
    MS DTC, 222
    Multimedia, 223
    Network, 225
    non-TrueType fonts, 207
    ODBC, 225
    Pause A Print Job, 159
    PC Card (PCMCIA), 225
    Ports, 226
    Printers, 226
    Regional Settings, 226
    SCSI Adapters, 227
    Server, 227
    Services, 229
    Share A Folder, 167
    Sign Up With An Internet Service Provider, 79
    Sounds, 229
    Speaker, 230
    System, 231
    Tape Devices, 234
    Telephony, 234
    Troubleshoot A User's Problem, 123
    Uncompress A Folder, 173
    UPS, 235
    WSP Client, 236
IDE hard drives, 27–28
IIS. *See* Microsoft Internet Information Server (IIS)
Import Registry File command, 490
incremental backup. *See* backing up, incremental
Information Store Site Configuration Properties dialog box, *275*
Insert mode, 199
installation
    complete vs. custom, 58

installation, *continued*
  customizing, 64–81
  preinstallation checklist, 48–51
  remote, 52
  steps for, 51–52
  time necessary for, 60
  To Do List, 64–81, *64*
Install New Modem dialog box, 54
Install New Modem Wizard, 214–16, 289–90, *304, 305*
  adding modems to pools with, 304–7
Install Program From Floppy Disk Or CD-ROM Wizard, 192–93
Intel *x*86 processor, 26
international symbols, applications supporting, 226
Internet. *See also* World Wide Web
  access to, 74
  configuring connection to, 209
  connecting to, 5, 88–89, 310–17
  controlling user access to, 330–31
  high-speed connections to, 322
  ISDN routers, 322
  Microsoft Proxy Server 1 and, *6*
  problems accessing, 501
  setting up connection manually, 505
  "surfing," 316
Internet Connection Wizard, 79–80, *79, 311*
  signing up with an ISP, 311–13
Internet dialog box, 209
Internet icon, 209
Internet Mail Service, failure to start, 507
Internet Mail Service Properties dialog box, *276*
Internet Mail Wizard, 319, *320*
Internet Network Information Center. *See* InterNIC (Internet Network Information Center)
Internet Protocol (IP), 335–36. *See also* IPng; Transmission Control Protocol/ Internet Protocol (TCP/IP)
Internet service providers (ISPs)
  configuring for second-level domain name, 321–24

Internet service providers (ISPs), *continued*
  connecting to existing account, 317–24
  dial-up accounts, 317, 318–21
  dial-up connection to, 272–73
  failure to connect to, 281
  finding, 311–13
  full-time connection to, 318, 321
  multilinking and, 307
  need for, 88
  Properties dialog box, *273*
  signing up with, 79–80, 310–16
InterNIC (Internet Network Information Center), 337–38
  and domain names, 344–45
intranets
  advanced properties, 394, *395*
  configuring services on, 391–95
  creating, 386–87
  defined, 370
  directory properties, 393–94
  file transfer protocol (FTP) service and, 391
  logging properties, 394
  managing web server for, 390–96
  resources, 395
  service properties, 391–93
  WWW Service and, 390
IP. *See* Internet Protocol (IP)
IP addresses, 337–40
  class A networks, 338
  class B networks, 338
  class C networks, 338–39
  class D and E, 339–40
  Domain Name System (DNS) and, 343
  resolving domain names into, 345–46
  user access to, 403
IPng, 346–47
IPv6. *See* IPng
ISDN routers, 322
ISM. *See* Microsoft Internet Service Manager (ISM)
ISPs. *See* Internet service providers (ISPs)

K

Keyboard icon, 210
Keyboard Layout subkey, 474
Keyboard Properties dialog box, *210*, 211–12, *212*
keyboards
    changing, 211
    language support, 211–12
    layout, 474
    settings for, 210
    speed settings, 211
keyboard shortcuts, 524–25
keys
    editing, 484–92
    HKEY_LOCAL_MACHINE, 472–73
    overview, 471
    saving as ASCII files, 480

L

languages. *See also* Data Definition Language (DDL); Data Manipulation Language (DML); Structured Query Language (SQL)
    keyboard support for multiple, 211
Last Known Good Configuration menu, 512–13
LAT. *See* local address table (LAT)
License Agreement page, 53
licenses, 8–9, 212–13
    adding user, 81
    Microsoft FrontPage, 372
    Microsoft Proxy Server 2, 408
    reviewing user, 88
Licensing icon, 212–13
links. *See* hyperlinks
Load Hive command, 485
local address table (LAT), 401, 404
    upgrading to Microsoft Proxy Server 2 and, 409–10
Local Address Table Configuration dialog box, *409*

Local Group Properties dialog box, *185*
log files, 403, 457
logging on locally, 186–87
logical drives
    creating, 103
    defined, 95
logical printers
    managing, 161–62
    vs. printers, 138
logins, managing database, 441–42
login scripts, 506
logon hours, restricting, 124–25
Log Options dialog box, *457*
logos, web site, 376–77
logs
    database, 435
    event
        configuring, 463–64
        filtering, 462–63
        recording events in, 458–62

M

Mail And Fax dialog box, *360*
Mail icon, 213
Manage Computers page, *182*
Manage Disks page, *96*, *97*
Manage E-mail Distribution Lists page, *268*
Manage Folder Size page, *172*
Manage Internet Access page, *330*
management consoles, 9, *9*
Manage Printers page, *141*
    accessing, 140
Manage Shared Folders page, 166, *167*
Media folder, sound schemes stored in, 231
member servers, 7
memory. *See also* virtual memory
    adding, 31
    client, 32

INDEX 551

memory, *continued*
  Microsoft Exchange Server services errors and, 282
  system requirements for, 26–27
  viewing hidden information about, 453
microprocessors. *See* processors
Microsoft Active Server Pages 1, *6*
Microsoft BackOffice Small Business Server HCL, 24–25
Microsoft Exchange
  Administrator
    configuring for dial-up ISP accounts, 319
    enabling message tracking with, 274–76
  checking services function, 281
  configuring for second-level domain name, 323–24
  folders, sending reports to, 418
  Internet Mail Service, 276
  Outlook client, 360–61
  sending faxes to Mailbox, 292
  Server
    backing up and, 249–52
    and e-mail, 266
    starting services error, 282–83
    using with dial-up ISP accounts, 319
    version 5, *6*
  setting up Internet connection manually and, 505
Microsoft Exchange Setup Wizard, 361
Microsoft Fax Server, *6*, 90
Microsoft FrontPage
  creating special effects with, 382–85
  creating web sites with, 373
  Editor, 376–82
    Preview In Browser command, 378
  Explorer, 374–75
    Folder View, *374*
    Hyperlink View, *375*
  installing, 372
  overview, 374
  To Do List, 376
Microsoft Index Server 1.1, *6*

Microsoft Internet Explorer, setting options for, 209
Microsoft Internet Information Server (IIS), *6*, 390
  log, reports in, 414
Microsoft Internet Referral Service, 80, 310, *312*, *313*, *314*, *315*
  signing up with an ISP, 313–16
Microsoft Internet Service Manager (ISM), 390, *399*
  configuring Web Proxy Service, 400–403
  configuring Winsock Proxy Service, 404–6
  controlling Microsoft Proxy Server, 399–400
Microsoft Loopback adapter, 54
Microsoft Modem Sharing Server 1, *6*
Microsoft networking domains vs. TCP/IP domains, 19
Microsoft Proxy Server, *6*. *See also* proxy servers
  configuring, 398–99
    with ISPs, 320–21
  installing, 398–99
  starting, 399–400
  stopping, 399–400
  upgrading, 406–10
Microsoft Proxy Server Setup dialog box, *408*, *409*
Microsoft Small Business Server Setup Wizard, 56–60, *56*
  Company Information page, *57*
Microsoft SQL Enterprise Manager, 430
Microsoft SQL Server. *See also* databases
  adding data to tables, 438
  automatic startup, 506
  backing up in, 442–44
  creating database devices, 432–34
  creating databases, 434–35
  creating tables, 435–37
  MS Query, 445–46
  overview, 422
  pubs database, 430
  scripting, 444
  SQL Performance Monitor, 446
  SQL Security Manager, 446
  SQL Server Web Assistant, 446, *447*

Microsoft SQL Server, *continued*
   SQL Service Manager, 446, *447*
   SQL Trace, 447, *448*
   starting, 430–32
   stored procedures, 438–40
   temporary database size, 506
   triggers, 440–41
   user interface applications for, 448
   version 6.5, *6*
   viewing SQL statement, *445*
Microsoft Windows 95
   clients using, 8
   connecting remotely using, 358–60
   installing on new computer, 184
   Registry, 470
   setting up computers to use Small Business Server, 76–77
Microsoft Windows NT
   Diagnostics tool, 452–53, *453*
   emergency boot disk, DEC Alpha version, 517
   emergency boot disk, *x*86 version, 516–17
   Event Viewer tool, 458–62
      system log, *458*
   Performance Monitor tool, 454–57
      chart, *455*
   Registry, 470
      backing up, 479–82, 492–94
      connecting to remotely, 136
      data types used in, 475, *476–77*
      editing, 484–92
      editing for dial-up account use, 318
      files in, 477, *478*
      restoring, 482–84
      structure of, 471
   Server
      adding components, 193–94
      applications server and, 7
      backup domain controller and, 7
      failure to boot, 511
      features of, 17
      hardware compatibility and, 48

Microsoft Windows NT, Server, *continued*
   HCL, 24–25
   removing components, 193–94
   vs. Small Business Server, 18
   tape devices and, *245*
   user rights, 128–30
   using DHCP Manager for TCP/IP, 350–51
   using WINS Manager for TCP/IP, 347–49
   version 4, *6*
   services, 229
   setting up computers to use Small Business Server, 76–77
   types of share permissions, *175*
   upgrading user settings for, *478*
   Workstation
      clients, setting up for remote access, 355–56
      clients using, 8
      connecting remotely using, 358
      installing on new computer, 184
Microsoft Windows NT Diagnostics, 452–53, *453*
Microsoft Windows NT Hardware Compatibility List (HCL), 48
Microsoft Windows Sockets, 336
Microsoft WinSock Proxy Client dialog box, 236–37, *237*
MIDI devices, 223
mirroring. *See* mirror sets
mirror sets, 107. *See also* partitions
   of boot partition, 112
   breaking, 109–12
   broken, *111*
   creating, 108–9
   defined, 96
   failed servers and, 519–20
   overview, 107
   primary boot drive failure, 518–19
   setting up, *97*
Modem icon, 214
modem pools, 5
   adding modems to, 304–7

modem pools, *continued*
   checking status of, 308
   configuring clients to use, 307, *308*
   creating, 303–4
   fax modems, 288
   overview, 302
Modem Properties dialog box, 214–18
modems. *See also* fax modems; modem pools
   adding, 302
   adding to modem pools, 304–7
   changing properties of, 216–17
   creating a modem pool and, 303
   dialing properties, 217–18, 234–35
   dial-up access via, 74
   installing new, 214–16
   Microsoft Modem Sharing Server 1 and, *6*
   Properties dialog box for individual, *216*
   removing, 216
   setup identifying, 54
   sharing, Dial-Up Networking and, 355
   Small Business Server recommended, 24–25
   troubleshooting, 501
   typical settings for "approved," *217*
   viewing properties of, 216–17
Modem Sharing Admin dialog box, *303*
Modem Sharing icon, 213
Modify command, 490
mouse
   changing type of, 221–22
   pointers for, 219–21
   swapping buttons on, 219
Mouse icon, 218
Mouse Properties dialog box, 218–22, *219*
Move A Folder icon, 173–74
Move Folder Wizard, 173–74
MS-DOS boot disks, 516
MS DTC Client Configuration dialog box, 222
MS DTC icon, 222
MS Query, 445–46
multilinking, 307

multimedia devices
   adding, 223–24
   changing properties of, 224
   removing, 224
   viewing properties of, 224
Multimedia icon, 223
Multimedia Properties dialog box, 223–24
multiport serial boards, 303
   hardware compatibility and, 24

N

Name And Organization dialog box, 53
names. *See also* Domain Name System (DNS)
   client, 40–41, 76
   column, 436
   database, *435*
   domain, 50, 53, 315
      acquiring, 324–30, 344–45
      configuring for second-level, 321–24
      registering, 88–89
      resolving into IP addresses, 345–46
      user access to, 403
   login, 441–42
   printer, 66, 145
      for sharing, 67
   printer port, 145
   server, 40, 50, 53
   user, policy for, 69
network adapter cards
   configuring additional, 84–85
   hardware compatibility and, 24
network adapters, installation process and, 54
network administrators, accounts for, 39
Network Configuration dialog box, *306*
Network icon, 225
network interface cards, using with printers, 139–40
network media, 15
Network Neighborhood, failure to see other computers in, 360

network operating system (NOS)
    client requirements, 41–42
    default, 233
    hanging, 506
    listed at system startup, 56
    Microsoft NT Server 4 with Service Pack 3 as, *6*
    overview, 16
    RISC-based, 517
    server requirements, 41–42
    servers and, 16
    specifying for setup, 76
networks
    adding computers to, 183–84
    alerts, 456
    class A, 338
    class B, 338
    class C, 338–39
    client-server, 16
    collecting data about, 454–57
    components, 15
    configuring hardware and software for, 225
    controlling fax printer traffic on, 294–95
    disconnecting users from, 188
    monitoring, 452
    overview, 14–15
    performance indicators, 455
    reconnecting computers to, 187–88
    removing computers from, 187
    security domain, 7
    selecting default distributed transaction coordinator for, 222
    small businesses and, 4
    TCP/IP domains vs. Microsoft networking domains on, 19
    viewing information about, 453
Network subkey, 474
New Account Wizard, 118–19
    Manage Users page, *119*
New Backup Device dialog box, *443*
New command, 491
non-TrueType fonts icon, 207

Norton Utilities, 506
NOS. *See* network operating system (NOS)
Notepad
    creating backup command file with, 258–60
    printing tests and, 498
ntbackup command, 256, 258–60
NT File System format. *See* NTFS format
NTFS format, 39–40
    installing Small Business Server on NTFS partition, 52
    selecting file systems and, 49–50
    sharing folders and, 170

O

ODBC devices/drivers, 225
ODBC icon, 225
Open Local command, 485
operating systems. *See* network operating system (NOS)
Outbox, e-mail remaining in, 281
Owner command, 487
Owner dialog box, *158*

P

PARP. *See* Proxy Address Resolution Protocol (PARP)
partitions. *See also* extended partitions; mirror sets; primary partitions
    creating, 99–103
    defined, 95
    locked, 102
    naming conventions for, 518
    reviewing for installation, 49
passwords
    access security and, 39
    account lockout and, 127
    changing user, 121–22
    creating, 69–70

passwords, *continued*
    domain, 329
    guidelines for, 37–38
    Internet account, 315
    network access and, 18
    Password Information page, 70
    restrictions, 126
    selecting administrator, 51, 58–59
    setting rules for, 125–28
    troubleshooting problems with, 499
Pause A Print Job icon, 159
PC Card (PCMCIA), 225–26
PC Card (PCMCIA) Devices dialog box, 225–26
PC Card (PCMCIA) icon, 225
PCMCIA. *See* PC Card (PCMCIA)
PDC. *See* primary domain controller (PDC)
peer-to-peer networks, 18. *See also* workgroups
Pentium processors, 26
Performance Monitor, 454–57
    chart, 455
permissions, 128. *See also* file permissions; folder permissions; share permissions
    connecting to supported protocols, 401, 405
    database, 441–42
    default user, 506
    defined, 166
    granting, 169
    managing, 442
    printer, 141, 155–56
    Remote Access, 363
    for shared folders, 167–72
    vs. shares, 174–75
    troubleshooting, 503
    viewing, 442
Permissions command, 487
phone book. *See* Remote Access Service (RAS), phone book, changing settings in
Phonebook Entry Wizard, 355–56
physical drive, 95
physical security, 37
pointers
    changing, 220–21

pointers, *continued*
    functions of Small Business Server, 221
    setting speed of, 221
pointing devices. *See* mouse
Policy Template Options dialog box, 132
pop-up menus, 98
    changing volume set drive letters, 106
    opening in Disk Administrator, 98
pop-up windows, changing colors in, 200
ports
    displaying, 226
    modem pools and, 303
    printer, 142
        adding, 144, 151–52
        configuring, 151–52
        deleting, 151–52
        naming, 145
        selecting, 66
    Remote Access Service (RAS), 362–63
    selecting modem, 215
    setting for WWW Service and FTP Service, 392
    supported by protocols, 401, 404
Ports dialog box, 226
Ports icon, 226
preinstallation checklist, 48–51
primary domain controller (PDC), 7, 20
primary keys, 427–28
primary partitions
    creating, 99–102
    defined, 95
Print command, 490
print devices. *See* logical printers; printers
Printer Access Wizard, 141, *142*, 294–95
Printer Auditing dialog box, 156, 157–58, *157*, *467*
Printer Permissions dialog box, *155*
printer pooling, 139, 142
Printer Ports dialog box, *144*
Printer Properties dialog box, *150*, *151*, *153*, *154*, *159*
printers. *See also* logical printers; printer servers
    access to shared, 73

printers, *continued*
- adding, 65–67, 142
  - server-controlled, 142–48
- adding drivers, 150–51
- adding ports, 151–52
- adding separator page, 151
- auditing, 156–58, 466–67
- bad network connections to, 498
- canceling print jobs, 159
- changing, 150
- changing drivers, 150–51
- changing properties, *149*
- changing settings, 148–59
- comment or location information, 150
- configuring additional, 86–87
- configuring for security, 154–58
- configuring ports, 151–52
- controlling from server, 139
- controlling user access to, 141
- deleting ports, 151–52
- device settings, 158–59
- fax
  - adding, 292–93
  - controlling user access to, 294–95
  - removing, 294
- folders, 149
- vs. logical printers, 138
- managing, 140–62
- managing jobs on, 159–60
- naming, 66, 145
  - for sharing, 67
- ownership of, 157, 158
- pausing print jobs, 159
- removing, 161
- resuming print jobs, 160
- setting availability, 152
- setup, 147
- sharing, 5, 67, 146, 153–54
- specifying manufacturer and model of, 66, 145
- troubleshooting, 146–47, 160, 497–98
- using network, 30–31
- using network interface card with, 139–40

printer servers, 30–31, 140
- controlling printers, 147–48

Printer Setup command, 486
Printers icon, 226
Printers Properties page, 148
Printers subkey, 474
printing
- test page, 146
- tests, 498
- troubleshooting, 497–98

print queues. *See also* printers
- backed up, 497–98
- changing auditing on, 157–58
- documents stacking in, 151
- managing documents on, 161–62
- viewing auditing on, 157–58

Print Subtree command, 486
Private Information Store Properties dialog box, *271, 272*
processors
- adding, 31
- displaying use time of, 455
- selecting
  - client, 32
  - server, 26

Properties dialog box, *162*
protocols. *See* Address Resolution Protocol (ARP); Dynamic Host Configuration Protocol (DHCP); file transfer protocol (FTP); Internet Protocol (IP); Proxy Address Resolution Protocol (PARP); Reverse Address Resolution Protocol (RARP); routing protocols; Transmission Control Protocol (TCP); Transmission Control Protocol/Internet Protocol (TCP/IP)

Proxy Address Resolution Protocol (PARP), 342
proxy servers. *See also* Microsoft Proxy Server
- changing protocols supported by, 404
- configuring with ISPs, 320–21
- overview, 398

Q

queues. *See* print queues
QuickEdit mode, 199

R

RAID (Redundant Array of Inexpensive Drives)
    defined, 95
    system requirements and, 28–29
RAID 1. *See* mirror sets
RAM. *See* memory
RARP. *See* Reverse Address Resolution Protocol (RARP)
RAS. *See* Remote Access Service (RAS)
read-edit-delete privileges, 73
Read Only Mode command, 487
read-only privileges, 73
rebooting
    to add components to server, 189
    adding modems and, 302
    breaking mirror sets and, 110–11
    closing open files before, 188
    creating volume sets and, 105
    extending volume sets and, 106
    installing fax modems and, 289
    installing modems and, 305
    while upgrading Microsoft Proxy Server, 408
records, 422. *See also* logs
    changing data in existing, 425–26
recovery. *See* disaster recovery
recovery drives, 520
Redundant Array of Inexpensive Drives. *See* RAID (Redundant Array of Inexpensive Drives)
Refresh command, 491
regback.exe, backing up Registry with, 48
regedit.exe
    backing up Registry with, 479
    editing with, 489–92
    main window, *490*

regedt32.exe
    backing up Registry with, 480
    editing with, 484–89
Regional Settings icon, 226
registration
    domain, 325–30
    information needed for, 50
Registry. *See* Microsoft Windows NT, Registry
regrest.exe, restoring Registry with, 482–84
relational databases. *See* databases
relative addresses, 380
relative limitations, 9–10
remote access
    configuring modems for, 306
    connecting remotely
        using Microsoft Windows 95, 358–60
        using Microsoft Windows NT Workstation, 358
    overview, 354
    security and, 39
    setting up clients for, 354–61
    setting users up for, 354
Remote Access Admin, 362–65
Remote Access Permissions, 363
Remote Access Service (RAS), 89–90
    checking user information, 364, *365*
    phone book, changing settings in, 86
    port status, 362–63
    starting, 362
    stopping, 362
    troubleshooting, 501
Remote Access Setup dialog box, *290*
    adding modems to a pool and, 305
remote installation, 52
Rename command, 491
Repair Disk Utility, *514*, 515
Repair Disk Utility dialog box, *514*
reports
    creating from samples, 416–18
    e-mail, 274, 278–79, *415*
    fax, 297–98, *415*

reports, *continued*
   generating with Crystal Reports 4.5, *6*
   logging data for, 457
   in Microsoft Internet Information Server
      (IIS) log, 414
   previewing sample, *417*
   sample, *415*
   sending by e-mail, 419, *420*
   sending to Exchange folders, 418
Reports folder, 416
Restore command, 485
restoring. *See also* backing up
   data, 252–56
   differential vs. incremental backups, 242–43
   failed servers, 519–20
   Registry, 482–84
Reverse Address Resolution Protocol (RARP), 342
RFCs, 336–37
   sample of, *337*
rights. *See* users, rights policy
root domains. *See* domains, root
routers, 341–42
routing protocols, 342

S

SAM subkey, 472, *478*
Save Key command, 486
Save Settings On Exit command, 487
Save Subtree As command, 486
SBS. *See* Small Business Server (SBS)
Scheduled Image WebBot component, 385–86
Scheduled Include WebBot component, 385–86
scheduling
   Microsoft Exchange Server 5 and, *6*
   through networks, 5
Screen Buffer Size setting, 200
screens
   display settings, 204–5
   startup, *189*

screen savers, setting for, 204
scripting, 444
SCSI adapters, 227
SCSI Adapters icon, 227
SCSI hard drives, 28
search engines, Microsoft Index Server 1.1, *6*
security. *See also* access control; disaster
      protection; passwords
   access, 39
   configuring printers for, 154–58
   dial-up access and, 127
   file, 38
   Internet settings for, 209
   Microsoft Proxy Server 1 and, *6*
   monitoring printer use, 156–58
   network operating systems and, 16
   physical, 37
   planning for, 36–39
   printer permissions, 155–56
   Registry files and, *478*
   setting granularity of, 19
   shared folders and, 122–23
   SQL Security Manager and, 446
   troubleshooting, 503
   user, 37–38
security domains, 7
security events, 458, 461–62
security identifier (SID), 473–74, 475
   modifying batch file to specify, 493
SECURITY subkey, 472, *478*
Select Computer command, 486
Select Data Source dialog box, *445*
SELECT key, 473
Server Configuration/Options dialog box, *432*
Server dialog box, 227–28
Server icon, 227
servers
   acting as workstations, 37
   adding computer to network at, 183–84
   adding applications to, 191–93

servers, *continued*
- adding Small Business Server components to, 189–90
- vs. clients, 16–17
- collecting data about, 454–57
- controlling printers, 139
- defined, 15
- designing system for, 25–26
- detecting patterns of use, 455
- failure to boot, 511
- hardware for, 25–31
- mail, client difficulty connecting to, 280–81
- managing intranet web, 390–96
- monitoring, 452
- naming, 40, 50, 53
- network operating systems and, 16
- PDC/BDC, 7
- print, 30–31, 140
  - controlling printers, 147–48
- properties, 227–28
- removing applications from, 191–93
- replacing, 520–21
- restoring failed, 519–20
- saving faxes on, 292
- selecting for printer management, 65
- system requirements, 41–42
- troubleshooting and, 496
- troubleshooting printer problems and, 497
- viewing hidden information about, 452–53
- WINS, 347

Server Summary report, 277
Service Pack 3, *6*
Service Properties dialog box, 391–93, *392, 393, 395*
Services dialog box, 229
Services icon, 229
setup
- starting, 51–52
- steps for, 53–60

Set Up An Internet Domain Name Wizard, 80, 88–89

Set Up Computer Wizard, 75–79, *75*, 183–84, 190–91
setup disk, creating, 77
Setup key, 473
Share A Folder icon, 167
Share A Folder Wizard, 167–70
Shared Resources dialog box, *228*
share names. *See* names
share permissions, 174–75. *See also* permissions
- assigning, 175–76
- types in Windows NT 4, *175*
shares. *See also* folders
- defined, 166
- vs. permissions, 174–75
sharing. *See also* modem pools
- files, 5
- folders, 167–70, 176
  - listing users for, 169
- modems, Dial-Up Networking and, 355
- printers, 5, 67, 146, 153–54
shortcuts, keyboard, 524–25
shutdown options, 233
SID. *See* security identifier (SID)
Sign Up With An Internet Service Provider icon, 79
Site Addressing Properties dialog box, *323*
SLED (Single Large Expensive Disk), defined, 96
small businesses
- gathering company information for, 50
- ideal characteristics for Small Business Server use, 10
- network availability for, 4
- Small Business Server definition of, 8
Small Business Server (SBS)
- intended users, 9–10
- overview, 4–6
- vs. Windows NT Server 4, 18
Small Business Server Hardware Compatibility List Supplement, 48
Small Business Server Online Guide
- configuring additional network cards, 84–85
- configuring additional printers, 86–87

Small Business Server Online Guide, *continued*
    configuring sound cards, 82–84
    configuring tape backup devices, 84
Small Business Server To Proxy 2 Migration Wizard, *407*
SMTP Properties dialog box, *324*
software. *See also* applications
    adding client, 78–79
    installing client, 76–77
        when adding users, 78
    installing new, 492–94
SOFTWARE subkey, 474, *478*
SOPs. *See* standard operating procedures (SOPs)
sound cards, configuring, 82–84
sound schemes, 230
Sounds icon, 229
Sounds Properties dialog box, *229*, 230
Speaker icon, 230
Split command, 491
Sprynet, 315
SQL. *See* Structured Query Language (SQL)
standard operating procedures (SOPs), 496–97
startup options, 233
startup screen, *189*
Status Bar command, 491
STOP error, 233
stored procedures, 438–40
String command, 486
stripe set, defined, 95
Structured Query Language (SQL), 423
    DELETE statement, 426–27
    INSERT statement, 426
    SELECT statement, 423–25
    UPDATE statement, 425–26
subnets, 340–41
Substitution WebBot component, 383–84
swap files, 453
system events, 458
system failure. *See also* disaster recovery; restoring NTFS format and, 40

System icon, 231
SYSTEM key, 472–73
system policy
    creating new default, 133–36
    managing user environments with, 130
System Policy Editor, *131*
    connecting to Registry remotely, 136
    creating new system policy and, 133–36
    opening, 131
    templates in, 131–33
System Properties dialog box, *231*, *513*
system requirements
    clients, 42–43
    hard drives, 27–29
    hardware
        for clients, 42–43
        for server, 41–42
    memory, 26–27
    and RAID (Redundant Array of Inexpensive Drives), 28–29
    reviewing for installation, 49
    servers, 41–42
    tape drives, 29–30
system resources. *See also specific resources*
    access to shared, 122–23
    setting user access to, 72–74
    viewing information about, 453
systems log, *458*, 459–60
SYSTEM subkey, *478*
system variables, 231–32

T

tables, *438*. *See also* databases
    adding data to, 438
    columns, 422
        entering information for, 436–37
    creating, 435–37
    rows, 422
    triggers and, 440–41

tape devices. *See also* backup devices
    backing up and, 241–42
    configuring, 84
    setting up, 243–44
    system requirements and, 29–30
    viewing properties of, 234
Tape Devices dialog box, 234, 243
Tape Devices icon, 234
tapes. *See* backup media
TCP. *See* Transmission Control Protocol (TCP)
TCP/IP. *See* Transmission Control Protocol/ Internet Protocol (TCP/IP)
telephony drivers, 235
Telephony icon, 234
templates, System Policy Editor, 131–33
time, setting properties for, 54–55, 201–2
Timestamp WebBot component, 383–84
time zones, selecting, 54–55, 202
To Do List, 64–81, *64*
    adding printers, 65–67
    adding users, 67–72
    opening, 65
ToggleKeys option, 197
Top N Message Receivers report, 277–78, *278*
Top N Message Senders report, 278, *279*
Transmission Control Protocol (TCP), 335
Transmission Control Protocol/Internet Protocol (TCP/IP)
    gateways, 341
    Internet Protocol (IP), 335–36
    IP addresses, 337–40
    Microsoft Windows Sockets, 336
    overview, 334
    RFCs, 336–37
    routers, 341–42
    routing protocols, 342
    subnets, 340–41
    Transmission Control Protocol (TCP), 335
    User Data Program (UDP), 335
    using DHCP Manager for, 349–51
    using WINS Manager for, 347–49
triggers, 440–41

Troubleshoot A User's Problem icon, 123
troubleshooting. *See also* Microsoft Windows NT Diagnostics; Microsoft Windows NT Performance Monitor
    backups, 500
    e-mail, 280–83, 499
    e-mail distribution lists, 284–85
    faxes, 299–300, 503
    file and folder access problems, 500–501
    Internet access problems, 501
    modems, 501
    overview, 496
    printers, 147, 160
    printing, 497–98
    Remote Access Service (RAS), 501
    security, 503
    standard operating procedures and, 496–97
    tips, 505–8
    user access problems, 123
Troubleshooting Printers utility, 160
TrueType fonts. *See* fonts
TweakUI, 506

U

UDP. *See* User Data Program (UDP)
Uncompress A Folder icon, 173
UNICODE Program Groups subkey, 475
uninterruptible power supply (UPS), 235–36
Unload Hive command, 485
UPS. *See* uninterruptible power supply (UPS)
UPS dialog box, *236*
UPS icon, 235
user accounts, 67–72
    defining work environment, *478*
    on local computers, 186–87, 194
    local security information for, *478*
    SIDs and, 474
    troubleshooting problems with, 499
User Account Wizard, 67–72, *68*, 120–21
    Delete User Account page, *120*
    User Account Information page, *121*

User Data Program (UDP), 335
User Manager for Domains, 124
    audit policy and, 464–67
    setting logon hours, 124–25
    setting password rules, 125–28
    tracking security events with, 461
user profiles
    default settings, *478*
    managing, 130
    switching between types of, 234
User Properties dialog box, *124*
User Resource Wizard, 72–74, *73*, 123, 502
User Rights Policy dialog box, *128*
users
    access to domain names, 403
    access to IP addresses, 403
    access to printers, 141
    access to protocols, 401, 405
    access to web sites, 403
    adding, 19, 67–72
    adding information about, 70–71
    adding licenses for, 81
    adding new, 118–19
    adding to client computers, 77–78, 185–86
    adding to e-mail distribution lists, 71
    changing information on, 120–21
    changing passwords for, 121–22
    checking Remote Access Service (RAS) information, 364, *365*
    controlling access of, 19
    controlling access to databases, 441–42
    controlling access to fax printers, 294–95
    controlling access to Internet, 330–31
    controlling access to shared folders, 171
    creating new policy for, 135
    denying access to shared folders, 169, 171–72
    disconnecting, 188
        Remote Access Service (RAS), 363
    establishing remote access, 89–90
    listing for folder sharing, 169
    logging on to clients locally, 186–87

users, *continued*
    managing access by, 122–23
    managing e-mail use, 271–72
    managing Remote Access Service (RAS), 363
    name policy, 69
    personal fax cover pages and, 299
    removing, 119–20
    restricting logon hours for, 124–25
    reviewing information on, 120–21
    rights policy, 128–30
        advanced, 130
        regular, *129–30*
    selecting to audit, 466, 467
    selecting to share folders, 179
    sending messages to Remote Access Service (RAS), 363–64
    setting system resource access for, 72–74
    setting up for remote access, 354
    sharing folders with, 167–70
    troubleshooting problems with, 499
    variables, 231–32
user security, 37–38
Users folder, 170
Users Shared Folders, 170

V

versions. *See also specific software*
    displaying, 452
video, settings for, 223
View menu, *206*
virtual memory, 233, 453. *See also* memory
volume sets
    backing up, 106
    creating, 104–5
    defined, 95
    deleting, 107
    extending, 105–6
    formatting, 105
    hard drive space and, 103
    overview, 103

W

wallpaper, settings for, 204
warnings, 459, *460*
    Disk Administrator, 99
WebBot components, *382*
    Scheduled Image, 385–86
    Scheduled Include, 385–86
    Substitution, 383–84
    Timestamp, 383–84
web pages. *See* web sites, pages in
Web Post Wizard, dial-up accounts and, 318
web proxy, 399–400
Web Proxy Service, configuring, 400–403
Web Proxy Service Properties dialog box, *400, 402, 403*
web sites. *See also* hyperlinks; Microsoft FrontPage
    adding scheduled elements to, 385–86
    adding time stamp to, 384–85
    boilerplate information on, 383–84
    bookmarks, 381
    creating, 373
    folders in, 374–75
    home page, 377–78
    hyperlinks in, 375
    listing products and services on, 378–79, *380*
    offensive, 403
    organizing, 372
    pages in
        database contents on, 446
        linking to sections on, 381–82
        overview, 371
        settings for, 209
    planning, 371, *372*
    publishing, 386
    reports, *415*
    restricting access to certain, 331
    user access to, 403
    using dial-up accounts and, 318
Window Position setting, 200
Windows 95. *See* Microsoft Windows 95
Windows Internet Name Service (WINS), 346
Window Size setting, 200
Windows NT. *See* Microsoft Windows NT
WINS. *See* Windows Internet Name Service (WINS)
WINS Manager, 347–49
Winsock Proxy Service, 399–400
Winsock Proxy Service Properties dialog box, *404*
wizards
    Add Printer, 65–67, *65*
        adding server-controlled printers with, 142–47
    Change Password, 121–22
    creating web sites with, 373
    Domain Registration, 325–30
    E-mail Distribution List, *269, 270*
        creating e-mail distribution lists with, 268
        deleting e-mail distribution lists with, 270
        editing e-mail distribution lists with, 270
    Install New Modem, 214–16, 289–90, *304*
        adding modems to pools with, 304–7
    Install Program From Floppy Disk Or CD-ROM, 192–93
    Internet Connection, 79–80, *79*
    Internet Mail, 319, *320*
    listing products and services on web site with, 378–79
    Microsoft Exchange Setup, 361
    Microsoft Small Business Server Setup, 56–60, *56*
    Move Folder, 173–74
    New Account, 118–19
    Phonebook Entry, 355–56
    Printer Access, 141, *142*, 294–95
    Set Up An Internet Domain Name, 80, 88–89
    Set Up Computer, 75–79, *75*, 183–84, 190–91
    Share A Folder, 167–70
    Small Business Server To Proxy 2 Migration, *407*
    upgrading Microsoft Proxy Server with, 406–10

wizards, *continued*
    User Account, 67–72, *68*, 120–21
    User Resource, 72–74, *73*, 123, 502
    Web Post, dial-up accounts and, 318
workgroups
    vs. domains, 17–21
    overview, 17–18
    selecting to audit, 466, 467
workstation operating systems, 17
workstations, 21
    configuring, 317
    restricting web site access on, 331
    servers acting as, 37
World Wide Web. *See also* Internet
    overview, 370
WSP Client icon, 236
WWW Service, 390
    configuring, 391–95

Z

Zoom command, *417*

Charlie Russel and Sharon Crawford

Charlie Russel and Sharon Crawford are coauthors of numerous books on operating systems, including *Running Microsoft Windows NT Server 4, UNIX and Linux Answers, NT and UNIX Intranet Secrets,* and *Upgrading to Windows 98.*

Charlie has years of system administration experience with a specialty in combined Windows NT and UNIX networks. He is the author of *ABCs of Windows NT Workstation 4.0* and *SCO OpenServer and Windows Networking.*

Sharon is a former editor who writes books and magazine articles full-time. In addition to the books she has coauthored with Charlie, she has written *Windows 98: No Experience Required, ABCs of Windows 95,* and *Your First Modem.* She is also co-author of *NT for Dummies* (with Andy Rathbone).

Sharon and Charlie live in northern California with six cats and a dog named Dave.

The manuscript for this book was prepared and submitted to Microsoft Press in electronic form. Text files were prepared using Microsoft Word 7.0 for Windows 95. Pages were composed by Microsoft Press using Adobe PageMaker 6.52 for Windows 95, with text in Palatino and display type in Emigre BaseNine. Composed pages were delivered to the printer as electronic prepress files.

Cover Designer
Tim Girvin Design

Interior Graphic Designer
Pam Hidaka

Electronic Artist
Travis Beaven

Desktop Publishers
Elizabeth Hansford, principal
Paula Gorelick

Principal Proofreader/Copy Editor
Patricia Masserman

Indexer
Leslie Leland Frank

Register Today!

Return this
*Running Microsoft® BackOffice®
Small Business Server*
registration card for
a Microsoft Press® catalog

U.S. and Canada addresses only. Fill in information below and mail postage-free. Please mail only the bottom half of this page.

1-57231-688-8 **RUNNING MICROSOFT® BACKOFFICE® SMALL BUSINESS SERVER** *Owner Registration Card*

_____
NAME

_____
INSTITUTION OR COMPANY NAME

_____
ADDRESS

_____
CITY   STATE   ZIP

Microsoft Press
Quality Computer Books

For a free catalog of
Microsoft Press products, call
1-800-MSPRESS

BUSINESS REPLY MAIL
FIRST-CLASS MAIL   PERMIT NO. 53   BOTHELL, WA

POSTAGE WILL BE PAID BY ADDRESSEE

NO POSTAGE
NECESSARY
IF MAILED
IN THE
UNITED STATES

MICROSOFT PRESS REGISTRATION
RUNNING MICROSOFT® BACKOFFICE®
SMALL BUSINESS SERVER
PO BOX 3019
BOTHELL WA   98041-9946